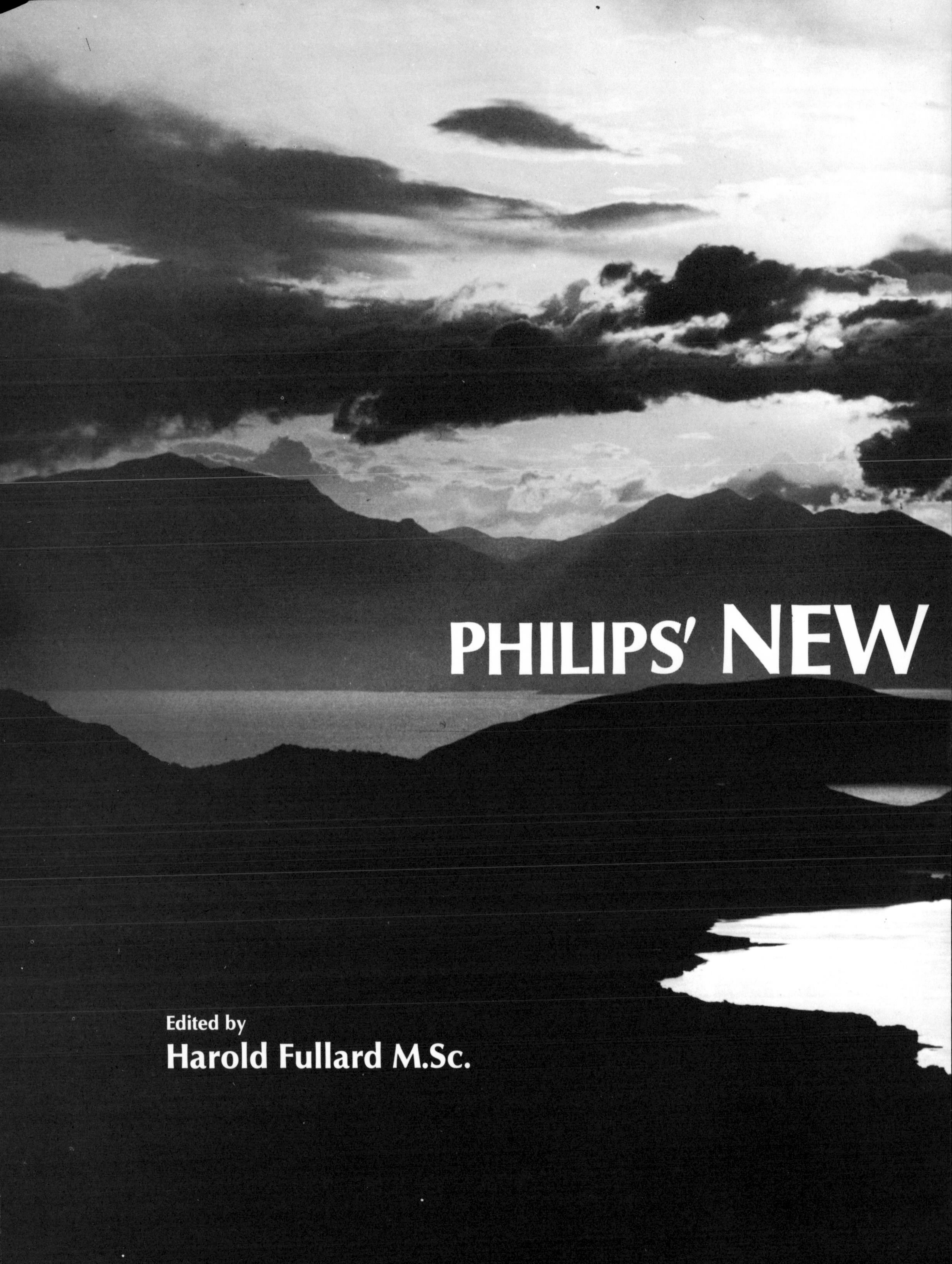

PHILIPS' NEW

Edited by
Harold Fullard M.Sc.

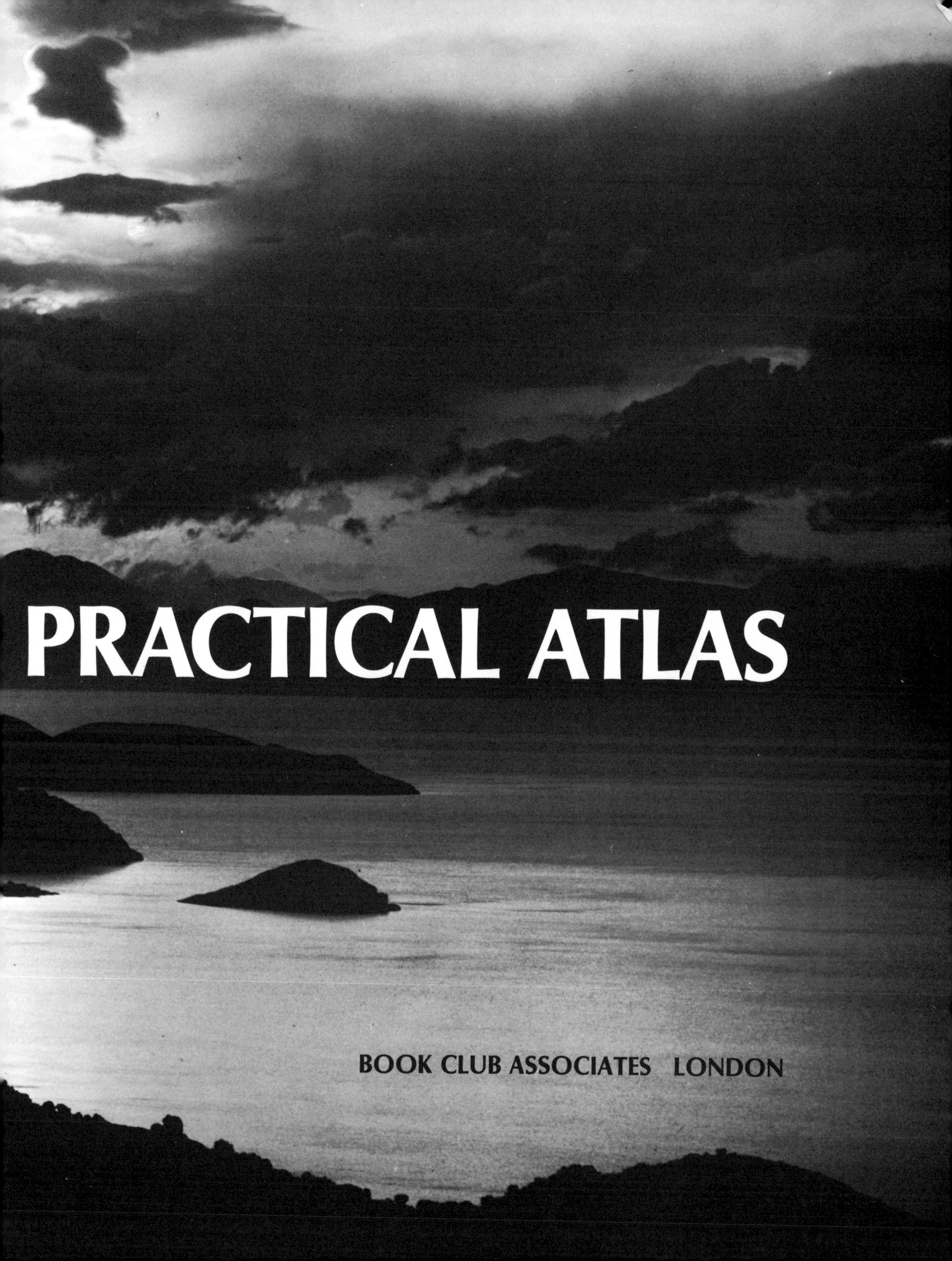

PRACTICAL ATLAS

BOOK CLUB ASSOCIATES   LONDON

This edition published in 1979 by
Book Club Associates
by arrangement with
George Philip & Son Limited

First Edition © December, 1960
Second Edition © January, 1965
Third Edition © January, 1967
Fourth Edition © September, 1969
New Impression © January, 1971
Revised Impression © May, 1972
Fifth Edition © February 1974
Sixth Edition © May 1975
Seventh Edition © February 1978
New Impression © February 1979

Printed in Great Britain

Preface

PHILIPS' PRACTICAL ATLAS has been specially planned to meet the need for an atlas of convenient size and of modest proportions but which, so far as the contents are concerned, nevertheless provides enough exact information for normal reference purposes. This is essentially an atlas that a practical person needs when dealing with correspondence and business matters, or reading, with little time to spare, the principal news in the daily papers. The atlas is concise, light in weight, and of a size to stand conveniently on a bookshelf, and not to occupy much space when lying opened on a desk or table.

The page size is not overlarge yet is big enough to depict a continent, a region, or a country on a scale sufficiently large to display all the more important places and features to which the user is likely to refer. The maps, indeed, carry a wealth of topographical and geographical information, the inclusion of which has been possible only as a result of fine draughtsmanship and the use of lettering chosen carefully for its legibility in limited spaces.

Included in the atlas is a reference index of more than 22,000 names indexed to the appropriate page and giving the latitude and longitude by which it may be located.

Throughout the atlas political boundaries between states have been drawn in accordance with those accepted by the states concerned; but where no such international agreement exists, the *de facto* position has been shown.

H. FULLARD

Contents

GENERAL REFERENCE

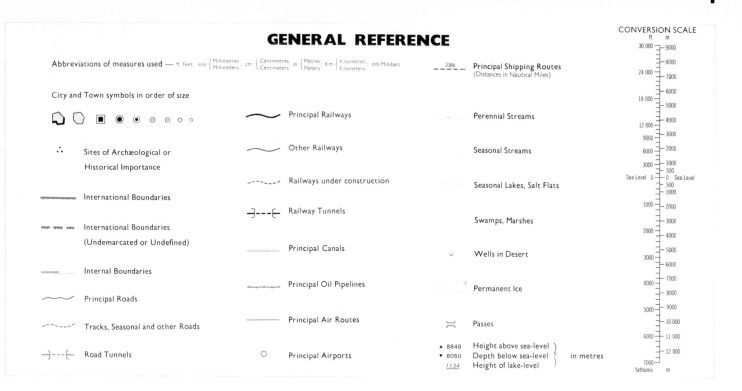

Abbreviations of measures used — ft Feet, mm {Millimetres / Millimeters} cm {Centimetres / Centimeters} m {Metres / Meters} Km {Kilometres / Kilometers} mb Millibars

City and Town symbols in order of size

⬡ ⬡ ■ ◉ ● ◎ ○ ○ ○

∴ Sites of Archæological or Historical Importance

International Boundaries

International Boundaries (Undemarcated or Undefined)

Internal Boundaries

Principal Roads

Tracks, Seasonal and other Roads

Road Tunnels

Principal Railways

Other Railways

Railways under construction

Railway Tunnels

Principal Canals

Principal Oil Pipelines

Principal Air Routes

☼ Principal Airports

3386 Principal Shipping Routes (Distances in Nautical Miles)

Perennial Streams

Seasonal Streams

Seasonal Lakes, Salt Flats

Swamps, Marshes

⌄ Wells in Desert

Permanent Ice

⌣ Passes

▲ 8848 Height above sea-level ⎫
▼ 8050 Depth below sea-level ⎬ in metres
1134 Height of lake-level ⎭

CONVERSION SCALE

ft	m
30 000	9000
24 000	8000
	7000
18 000	6000
	5000
12 000	4000
9000	3000
6000	2000
3000	1000
	500
Sea-Level 0	0 Sea-Level
	500
	1000
1000	2000
	3000
2000	4000
	5000
3000	6000
	7000
4000	8000
	9000
5000	10 000
	11 000
6000	12 000
7000	
fathoms	m

THE WORLD
Physical
1:150 000 000

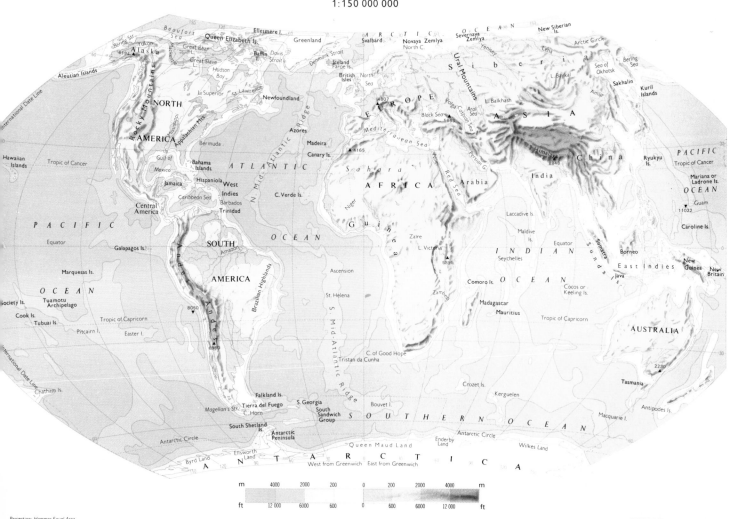

| m | 4000 | 2000 | 200 | 0 | 200 | 2000 | 4000 | m |
| ft | 12 000 | 6000 | 600 | 0 | 600 | 6000 | 12 000 | ft |

Projection: Hammer Equal Area

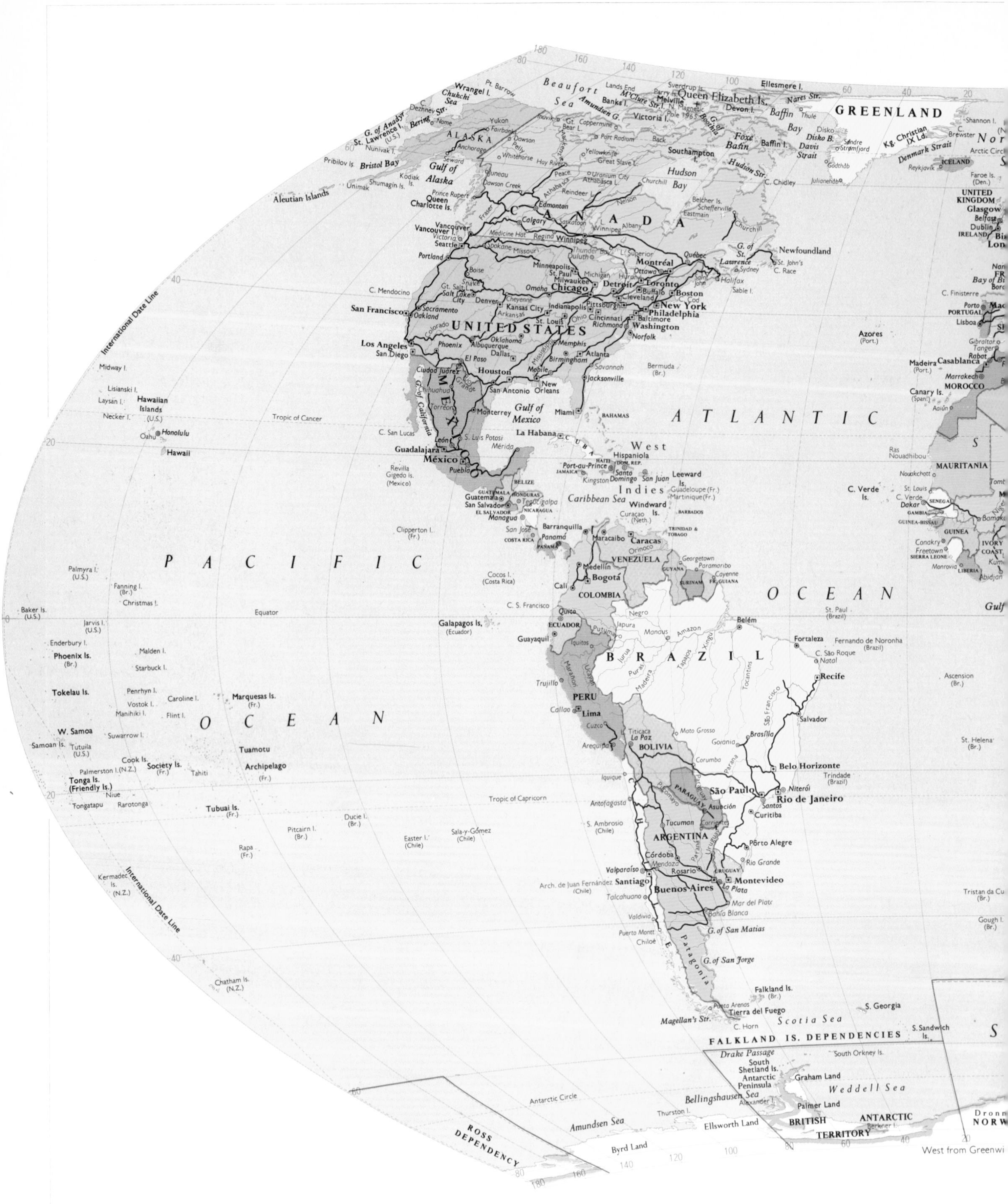

Projection : Hammer Equal Area

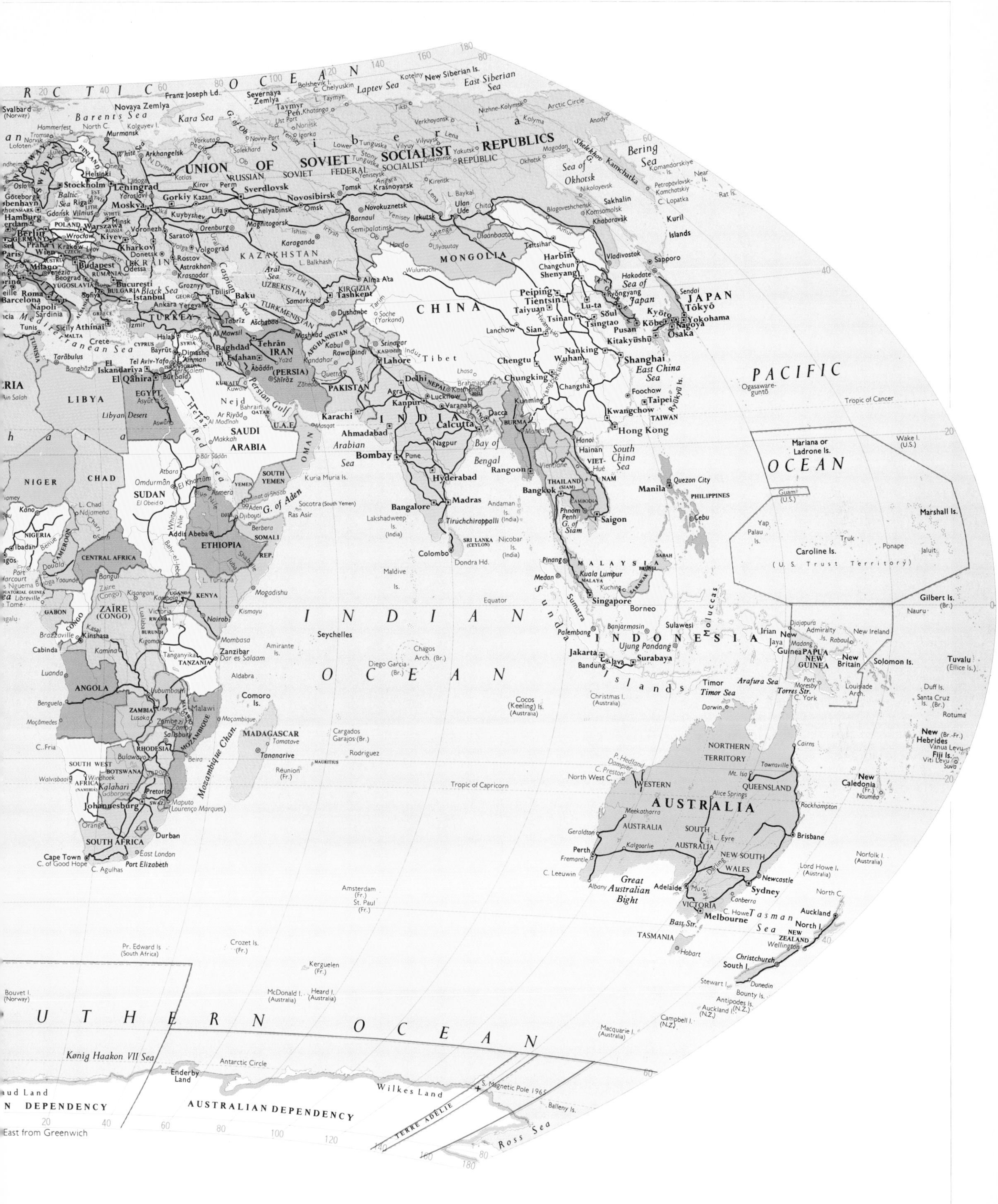

UNION OF SOVIET SOCIALIST REPUBLICS
RUSSIAN SOVIET FEDERAL SOCIALIST REPUBLIC
Siberia
ARCTIC OCEAN
Barents Sea
Kara Sea
Laptev Sea
East Siberian Sea
Bering Sea
Sea of Okhotsk
Arctic Circle
Moskva
Leningrad
Sverdlovsk
Novosibirsk
Omsk
Kiyev
Kharkov
Gorkiy
Kuybyshev
Volgograd
Baku
Tashkent
KAZAKHSTAN
UZBEKISTAN
TURKMENISTAN
KIRGIZIA
MONGOLIA
CHINA
Peiping
Tientsin
Shanghai
Nanking
Wuhan
Chungking
Chengtu
Sian
Kunming
Canton
Hong Kong
TAIWAN
Taipei
JAPAN
Tōkyō
Yokohama
Ōsaka
Nagoya
Kōbe
Kyōto
Sapporo
Sea of Japan
Sŏul
Pusan
Harbin
Vladivostok
East China Sea
South China Sea
PACIFIC OCEAN
Tropic of Cancer
Mariana or Ladrone Is.
Wake I. (U.S.)
Marshall Is.
Caroline Is.
(U. S. Trust Territory)
Gilbert Is.
PHILIPPINES
Manila
Quezon City
Cebu
VIET-NAM
Hanoi
Saigon
THAILAND (SIAM)
Bangkok
CAMBODIA
BURMA
Rangoon
MALAYSIA
Kuala Lumpur
Singapore
Borneo
Sulawesi
Moluccas
INDONESIA
Jakarta
Surabaya
Sumatra
Sunda Islands
PAPUA NEW GUINEA
Arafura Sea
Timor Sea
INDIA
Delhi
Bombay
Calcutta
Madras
Bangalore
Hyderabad
Kanpur
Nagpur
Ahmadabad
Bay of Bengal
Arabian Sea
SRI LANKA (CEYLON)
Colombo
PAKISTAN
Karachi
Lahore
AFGHANISTAN
Kabul
IRAN (PERSIA)
Tehrān
IRAQ
Baghdad
Persian Gulf
SAUDI ARABIA
Red Sea
G. of Aden
SOUTH YEMEN
OMAN
U.A.E.
TURKEY
Ankara
Istanbul
Black Sea
Caspian Sea
Mediterranean Sea
EGYPT
El Qāhira
LIBYA
SUDAN
Khartūm
ETHIOPIA
Addis Abeba
SOMALI REP.
Mogadishu
KENYA
Nairobi
TANZANIA
Dar es Salaam
ZAÏRE (CONGO)
Kinshasa
ANGOLA
ZAMBIA
RHODESIA
Salisbury
MOZAMBIQUE
Mozambique Chan.
MADAGASCAR
Tananarive
BOTSWANA
SOUTH WEST AFRICA (NAMIBIA)
SOUTH AFRICA
Johannesburg
Pretoria
Durban
Cape Town
C. of Good Hope
CHAD
NIGER
NIGERIA
CENTRAL AFRICA
INDIAN OCEAN
Equator
Tropic of Capricorn
Seychelles
AUSTRALIA
WESTERN AUSTRALIA
NORTHERN TERRITORY
QUEENSLAND
SOUTH AUSTRALIA
NEW SOUTH WALES
VICTORIA
TASMANIA
Perth
Adelaide
Melbourne
Sydney
Brisbane
Canberra
Great Australian Bight
Tasman Sea
NEW ZEALAND
Auckland
Wellington
Christchurch
North I.
South I.
New Caledonia
New Hebrides
Fiji Is.
SOUTHERN OCEAN
Antarctic Circle
Kønig Haakon VII Sea
Enderby Land
Wilkes Land
AUSTRALIAN DEPENDENCY
TERRE ADÉLIE
Ross Sea
East from Greenwich

1:20 000 000

100 0 100 200 300 400 500 miles

100 0 200 400 600 800 km

COPYRIGHT GEORGE PHILIP & SON LTD.

Ob

Ural

CASPIAN SEA
28

Obshchi Syrt

Kama

Ural Mountains

1617

Narodnaya
1894

Pechora

Volga

Kura

Caucasus
5633

Elbrus 5165

Ararat

Terek

Rion

L. Urmia
L. Van

Kurdistan

Armenia

Taurus
3770

Kanin Peninsula

Mezen

N. Dvina

Onega

L. Onega

Tundra

Kola Peninsula

White Sea

Volga Uplands

Central Russian Uplands

Don

Volga

Oka

Rybinsk Res.

L. Ladoga

Chudskoye

Neva

S. Dvina

Dnepr (Dnieper)

Bug

Pripet (Pripyat)

Pripyat Marshes

Dnstr (Dniester)

Prut

Sea of Azov

Str. of Kerch

Crimea

Manych

Tsimlyansk Res.

BLACK SEA

Bosporus

Sakarya
2211

Anatolia

Kizil Irmak

Cyprus 1951

Nordkinn

North Cape

Lapland

Tornio

Muonio
Kemijoki
2123

Finland

Plain

Niemen

Wista (Vistula)

Pripet

Balkan Peninsula

Wallachia

Danube

Tisza

Morava

Plain of Hungary

Transylvanian Alps

Carpathians

Tatra
2655

Balkans

Rhodope

Pindus

Aegean Sea

Ida 1766

Sea of Marmara

Morea

Crete

L'Onega

G. of Finland

G. of Riga

Gotland

BALTIC SEA

G. of Bothnia

Ume

Indals

Mälaren

Vänern

Vättern

Öland

Odra (Oder)

North

Elbe

Sudetes

Erz Geb.

Bohemian For.

Moravian Heights

Böhmerwald

Danube

Drava

Sava

Dinaric Alps

ADRIATIC SEA

Gran Sasso 2914

Apennines

Str. of Otranto

Ionian Is.

Ionian Sea

C. Matapan

5121

Scandinavia

Vesterålen

Lofoten

Glittertind 2469

Skagerrak

Kattegat

Jutland

Lindesnes

Helgoland

GERMAN BIGHT

Weser

Wester wald

Harz 1142

Thüringer wald

Taunus

Rhine

Eifel

Ardennes

Netherlands

Moselle

Vosges

Jura

Black For.

Alps

Mt. Blanc 4807

Po

Ligurian Sea

Corsica

Str. of Bonifacio

Sardinia

Tyrrhenian Sea

Calabria

Str. of Messina

Etna 3263

Sicily

Malta

MEDITERRANEAN SEA

NORWEGIAN SEA

3734

FISHER

VIKING

FORTIES

DOGGER
Dogger Bank

NORTH SEA

HUMBER

THAMES

DOVER

Seine

Rhône

Cévennes

Central Massif
Mt. Dore 1886

Garonne

Gironde

Loire

Bay of Biscay

Pyrenees
Pico de Aneto 3404

Cantabrian Mts.
Picos de Europa

Old Castile

New Castile

Iberian Peninsula

Sierra Morena

Sierra Nevada 3478

Andalusia

Guadalquivir

Guadiana

Tagus

Douro

Ebro

Maritime Atlas

Plateau of the Shotts

Arctic Circle

Vatnajökull

Hekla 1447

Iceland

2119

1491

SOUTH EAST ICELAND

Faroe Is.

FAEROES

Fisher Bank

BAILEY

ROCKALL

Rockall

ROCKALL Sea area named in weather forecasts

Shetland Is.

Fair Isle

Orkney Is.

FAIR ISLE

CROMARTY

FORTH

TYNE

HEBRIDES

Hebrides

Ben Nevis 1343

Great Britain

British Isles

Ireland

Irish Sea

IRISH SEA

LUNDY

Snowdon 1085

English Channel

PORTLAND

WIGHT

Channel

Brittany

FINISTERRE

C. Finisterre

C. St. Vincent

Str. of Gibraltar

C. Trafalgar

C. Spartel

PLYMOUTH

Land's End

FASTNET

SHANNON

Valentia

C. Clear

SOLE

FINISTERRE

BISCAY

ATLANTIC OCEAN

Projection: Bonne   West from Greenwich 0 East from Greenwich

m ft

4000 12 000

2000 6000

1000 3000

600 1200

200 600

0   0

200-600

2000 6000

4000 12 000

ft   m

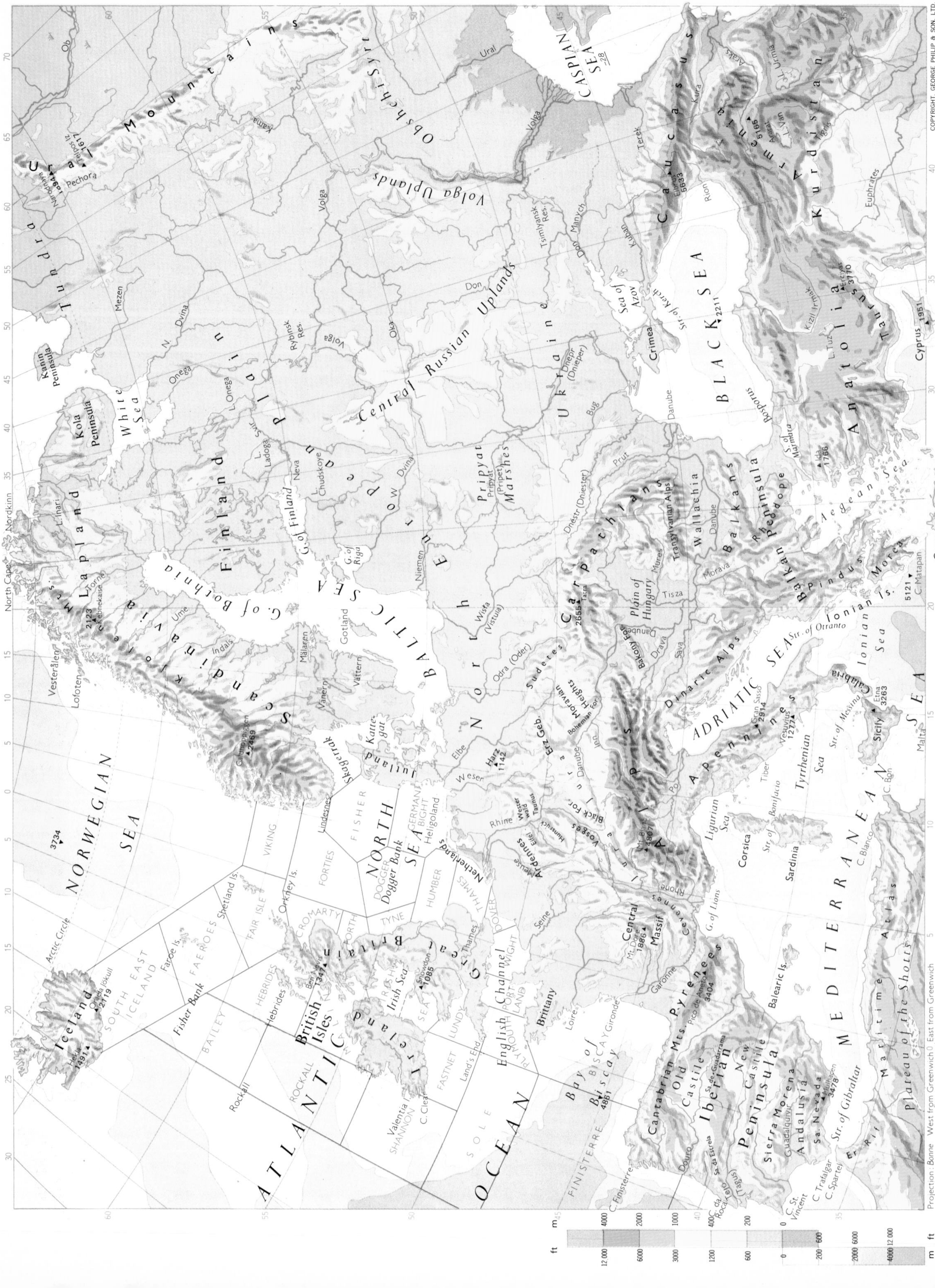

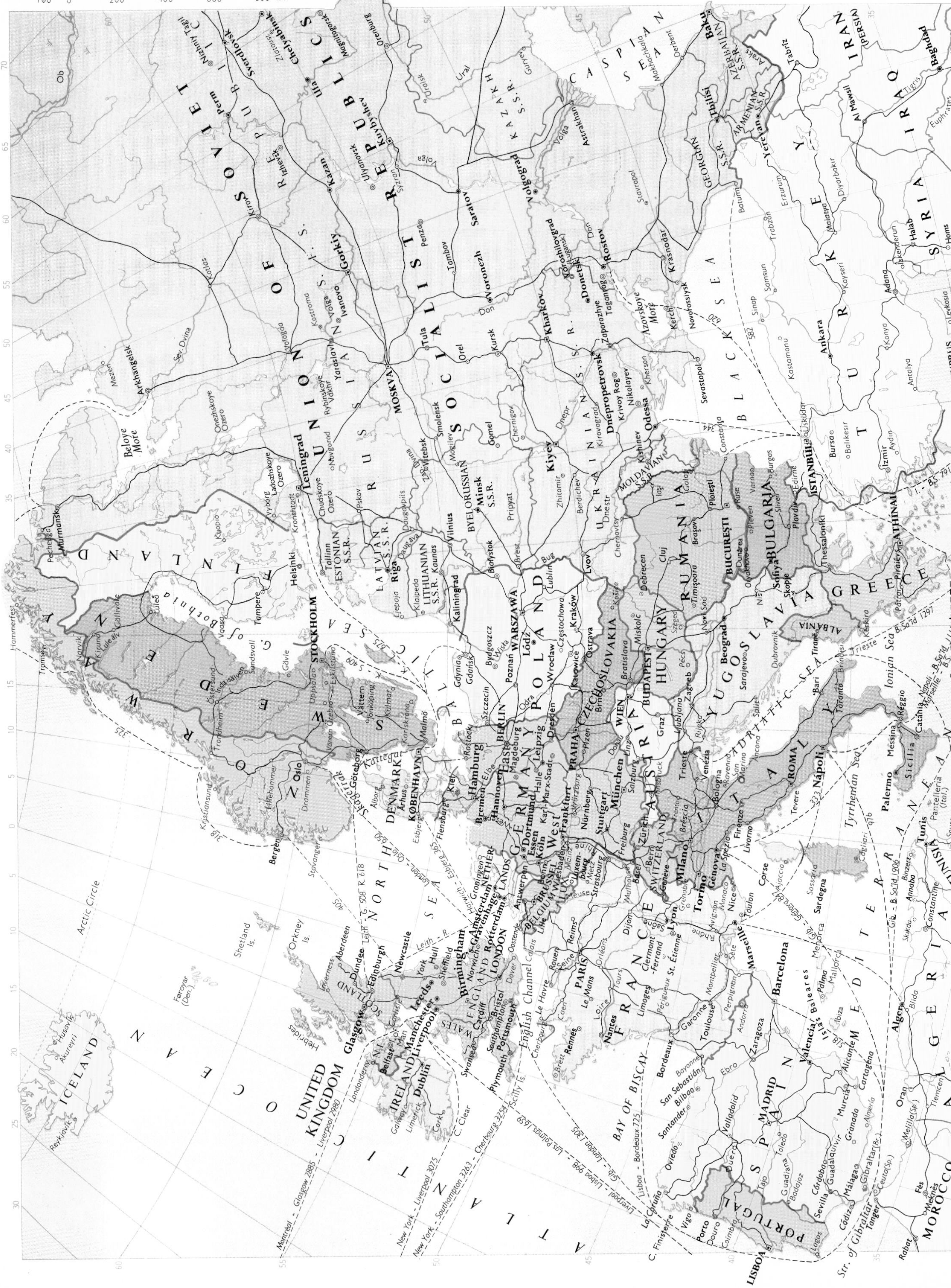

1:20 000 000

Projection : Bonne   West from Greenwich 0 East from Greenwich

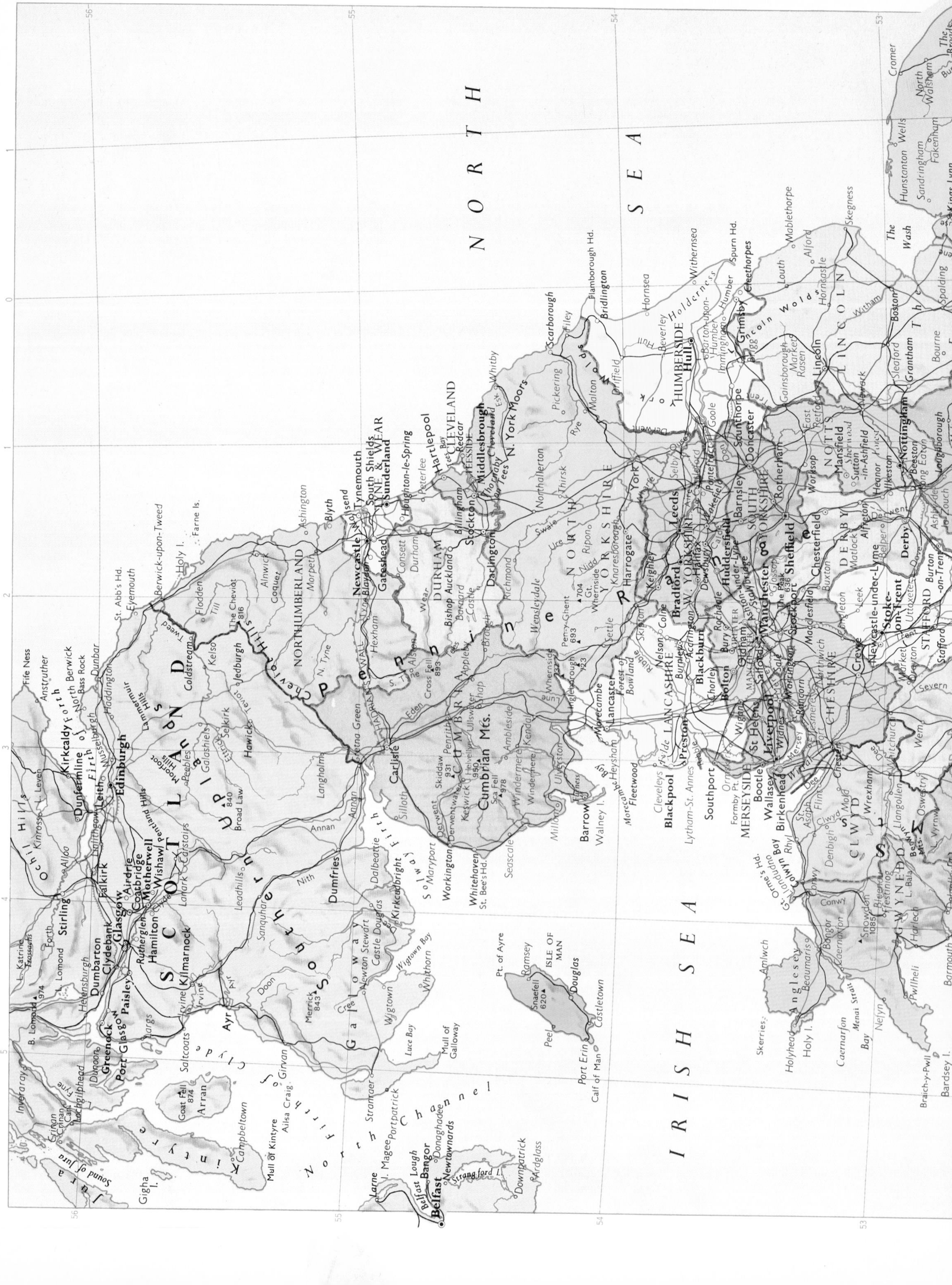
NORTH SEA
IRISH SEA
North Channel
Firth of Clyde
Firth of Forth
Solway Firth
SCOTLAND
SOUTHERN UPLANDS
Pennines
Cheviot Hills
Cumbrian Mts.
NORTHUMBERLAND
TYNE & WEAR
DURHAM
CLEVELAND
CUMBRIA
NORTH YORKSHIRE
W. YORKSHIRE
SOUTH YORKSHIRE
HUMBERSIDE
LANCASHIRE
MERSEYSIDE
CHESHIRE
DERBY
NOTTS
STAFFORD
LINCOLN
CLWYD
GWYNEDD
ISLE OF MAN
Edinburgh
Glasgow
Newcastle
Sunderland
Middlesbrough
Carlisle
Leeds
Bradford
Hull
Sheffield
Manchester
Liverpool
Nottingham
Derby
Lincoln
Stoke-on-Trent
Blackpool
Preston
York
Scarborough
Douglas
Belfast
Anglesey
Snowdon 1085

1:2 000 000

10   0   10   20   30   40   50 miles
10 0 10 20 30 40 50 60 70 80 km

East from Greenwich COPYRIGHT GEORGE PHILIP & SON LTD.

West from Greenwich

Projection: Conical with two standard parallels.

SCILLY ISLES
On same Scale

St. Ives
Penzance
Land's End
Isles of Scilly
St. Mary's

ENGLISH CHANNEL

Bristol Channel

SUFFOLK
CAMBRIDGE
ESSEX
BEDFORD
NORTHAMPTON
BUCKS
OXFORD
BERKS
HERTFORD
HANTS
SURREY
KENT
EAST SUSSEX
WEST SUSSEX
ISLE OF WIGHT
WILTS
DORSET
SOMERSET
DEVON
CORNWALL
AVON
GLOUCESTER
WORCESTER
WARWICK
WEST MIDLANDS
HEREFORD & WORCESTER
SALOP
POWYS
DYFED
GWENT
MID GLAMORGAN
WEST GLAMORGAN
SOUTH GLAMORGAN

London
Birmingham
Bristol
Cardiff
Southampton
Portsmouth
Plymouth
Exeter
Brighton
Reading
Oxford
Gloucester
Cheltenham
Swindon
Bath
Salisbury
Bournemouth
Poole
Weymouth
Dorchester
Torquay
Paignton
Newport
Swansea
Cambridge
Colchester
Ipswich
Bedford
Northampton
Luton
Watford
Dover
Folkestone
Canterbury
Maidstone
Chatham
Gravesend
Hastings
Eastbourne
Worthing
Guildford
Winchester
Southend
Channel Islands
Guernsey
Jersey
Alderney
Sark
St. Peter Port
St. Helier

France
Rouen
Dieppe
Le Havre
Cherbourg
Bayeux
Caen
Lisieux

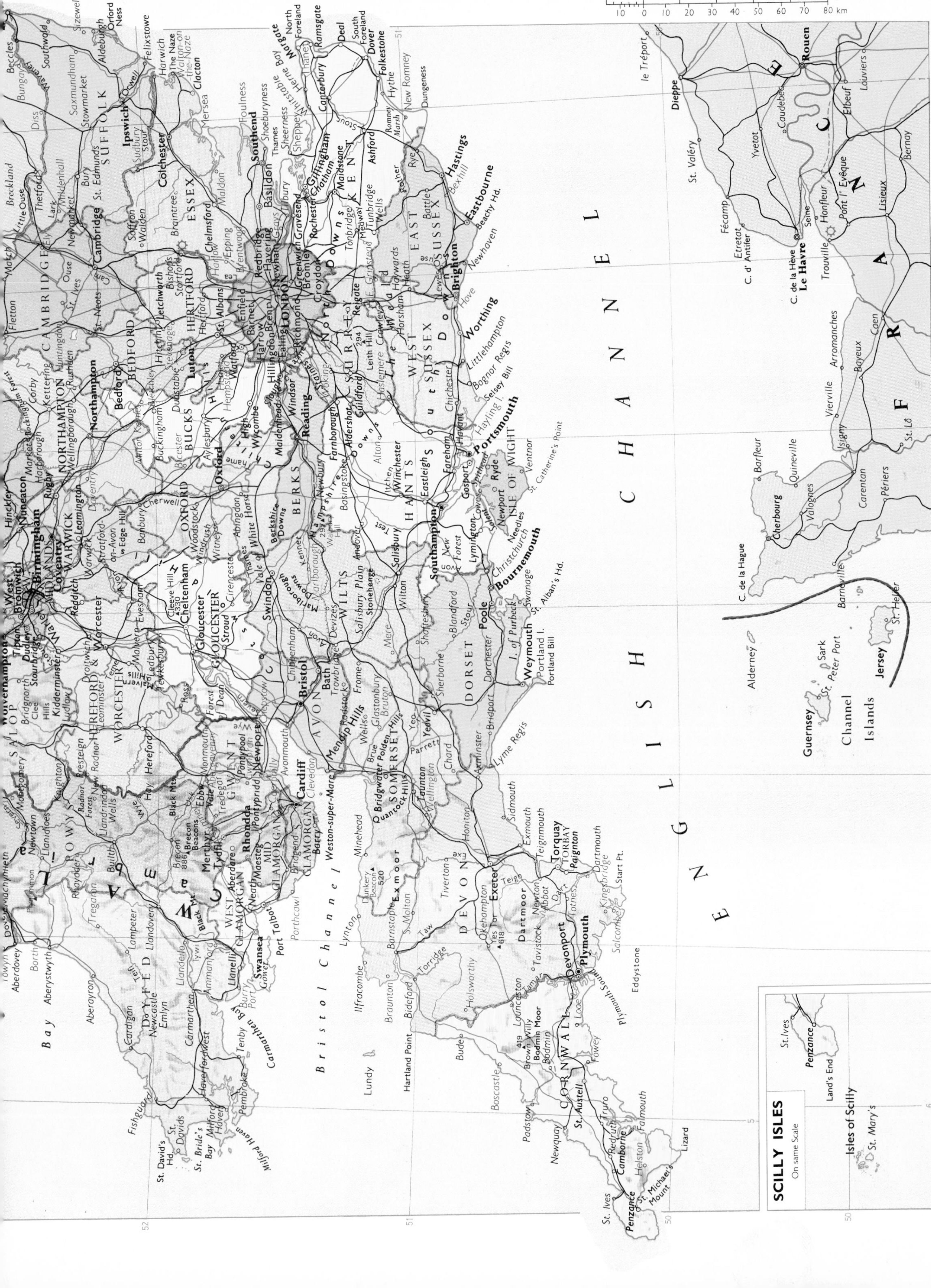

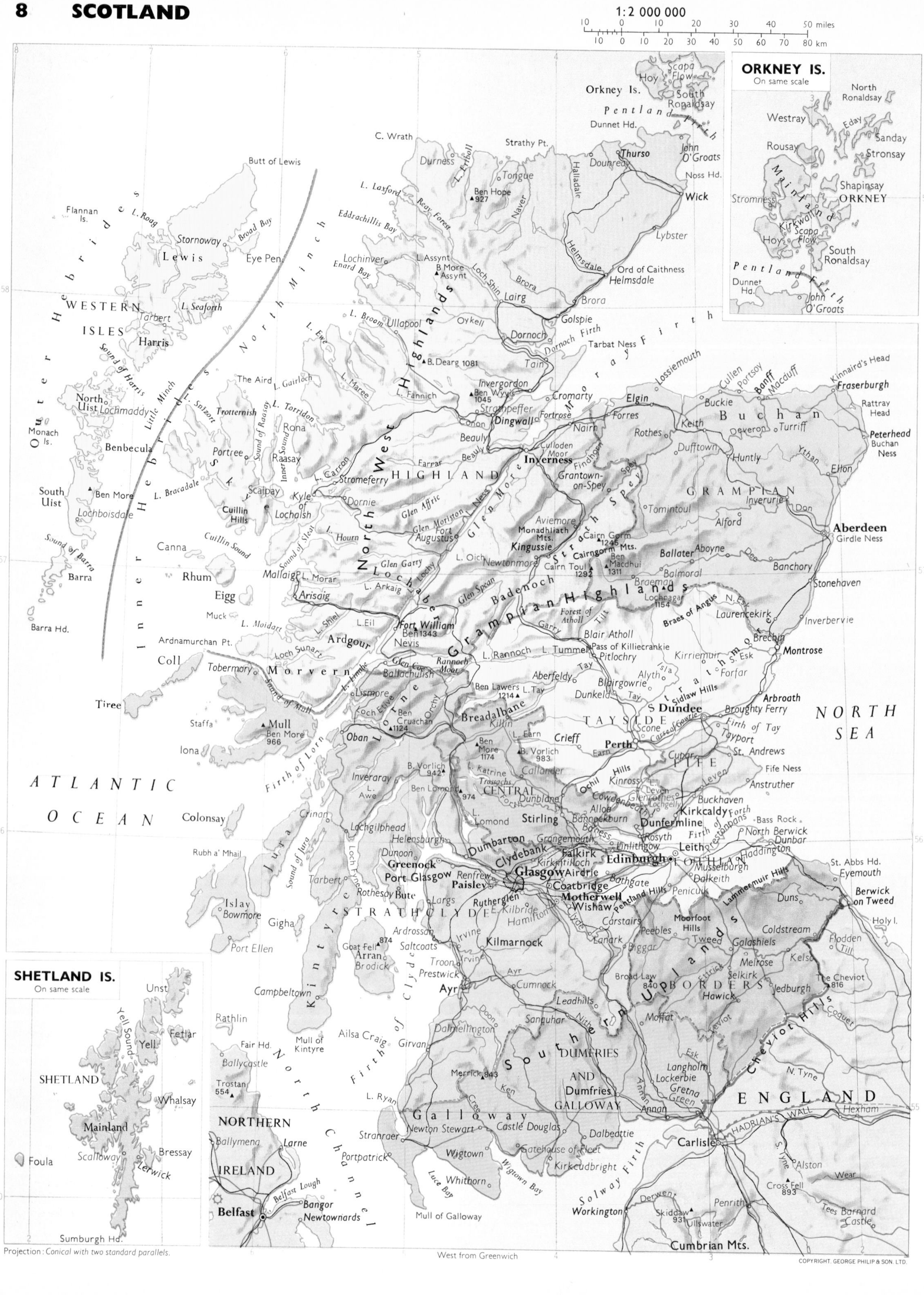

1:2 000 000

ORKNEY IS.
On same scale

SHETLAND IS.
On same scale

Projection: Conical with two standard parallels.

West from Greenwich

COPYRIGHT. GEORGE PHILIP & SON. LTD.

1:2 000 000

10 0 10 20 30 40 50 miles
10 0 10 20 30 40 50 60 70 80 km

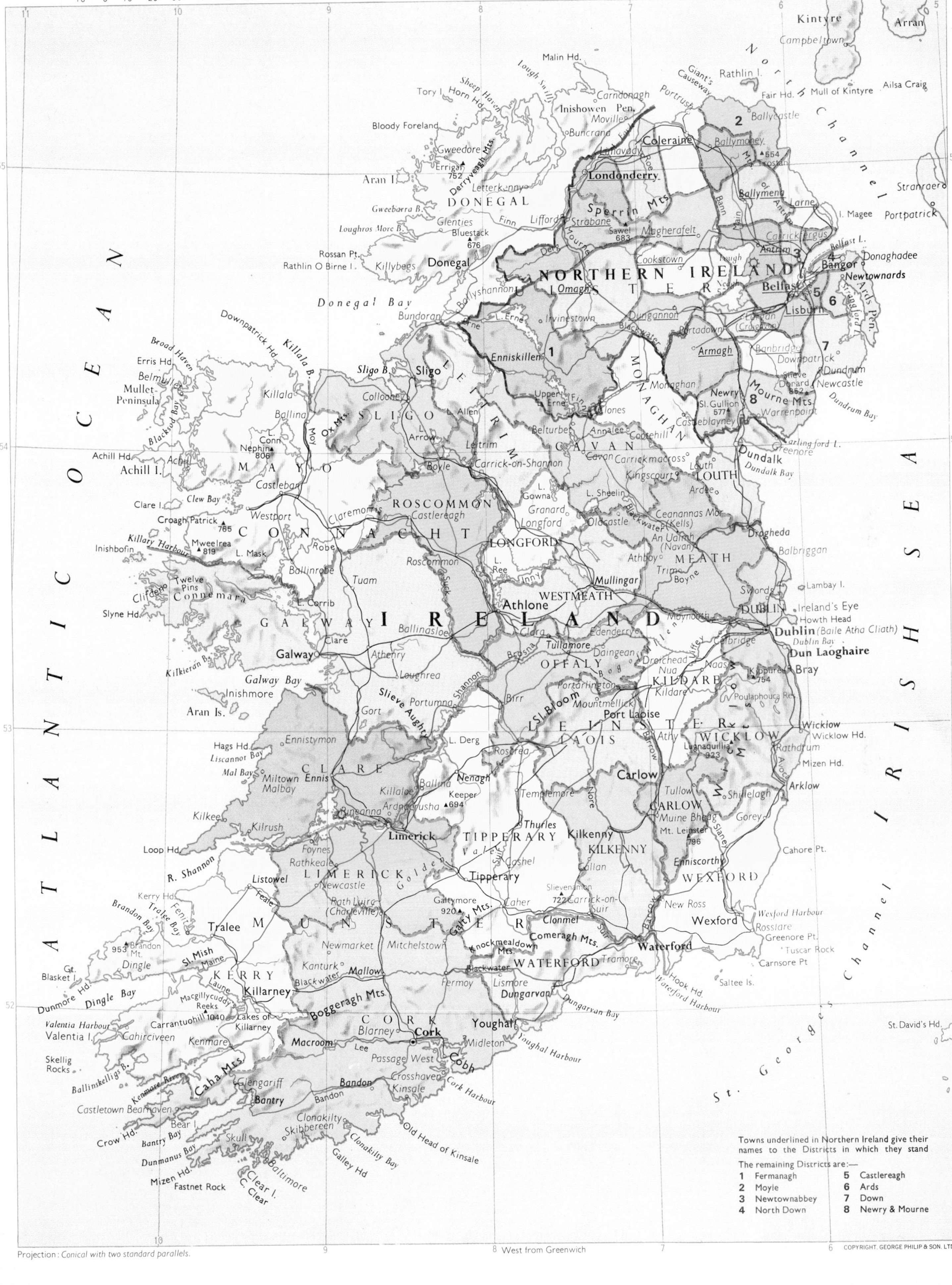

NORTH CHANNEL

Kintyre
Campbeltown
Arran
Mull of Kintyre
Ailsa Craig
Stranraer
Portpatrick
I. Magee
Donaghadee
Bangor
Newtownards
Ards Pen.

Malin Hd.
Tory I. Horn Hd.
Sheep Haven
Lough Swilly
Carndonagh
Inishowen Pen.
Moville
Buncrana
Giant's Causeway
Rathlin I.
Fair Hd.
Ballycastle
Portrush
Coleraine
Ballymoney
554
▲ Trostan
Larne
Belfast L.

Bloody Foreland
Gweedore
Errigal 752
Derryveagh Mts.
Letterkenny
Lifford
Strabane
Sperrin Mts.
Sawel 683
Magherafelt
Antrim
Ballymena
Carrickfergus
Belfast
Lisburn

DONEGAL
Glenties
Bluestack 676
Rossan Pt.
Killybegs
Rathlin O Birne I.
Donegal

Finn
NORTHERN IRELAND ULSTER
Omagh
Cookstown
Dungannon
Portadown
Armagh
Banbridge
Downpatrick
Slieve Donard 852
Newcastle
Dundrum
Dundrum Bay

Loughros More B.

ATLANTIC OCEAN

Downpatrick Hd.
Killala B.
Sligo B.
Sligo
LEITRIM
Enniskillen
Irvinestown
Blackwater
Newry
St. Gullion 577
Mourne Mts.
Warrenpoint
Carlingford L.
Greenore

Donegal Bay
Bundoran
Ballyshannon
L. Erne
Erne
Belturbet
Annalee
Clones
Upper L. Erne
MONAGHAN
Monaghan
Castleblayney
Cootehill
Dundalk

Broad Haven
Erris Hd.
Belmullet
Mullet Peninsula
Blacksod Bay
Killala
Ballina
Colloney
Arrow
L. Allen
Leitrim
CAVAN
Cavan
Carrickmacross
Kingscourt
LOUTH
Dundalk Bay
Ardee
Louth
Drogheda
Balbriggan

Achill Hd.
Achill
Achill I.
Clare I.
Clew Bay
Nephin 806
Castlebar
MAYO
Boyle
Carrick-on-Shannon
L. Gowna
L. Sheelin
Ceanannas Mor (Kells)
Oldcastle
Blackwater

Croagh Patrick 765
Westport
Claremorris
ROSCOMMON
Castlereagh
Granard
Longford
LONGFORD
An Uaimh (Navan)
MEATH
Trim
Boyne
Lambay I.

Inishbofin
Killary Harbour
Mweelrea ▲ 819
L. Mask
Ballinrobe
Robe
Roscommon
L. Ree
Athlone
Mullingar
WESTMEATH
Swords
Clifden
Twelve Pins
Connemara
Slyne Hd.
L. Corrib
Tuam
IRELAND
Ballinasloe
Clara
Maynooth
DUBLIN
Ireland's Eye
Howth Head
Dublin (Baile Atha Cliath)
Dublin Bay
Dun Laoghaire

GALWAY
Galway
Clare
Athenry
Loughrea
Tullamore
OFFALY
Daingean
Edenderry
Droichead Nua
Naas
Celbridge
Bray

Kilkieran B.
Galway Bay
Inishmore
Aran Is.
Gort
Slieve Aughty
Portumna
Shannon
Birr
Sl. Bloom
Portarlington
Mountmellick
Port Laoise
KILDARE
Kildare
Athy
Kippure ▲ 754
Poulaphouca Res.

Hags Hd.
Ennistymon
L. Derg
Roscrea
LEINSTER
LAOIS
WICKLOW
Wicklow
Wicklow Hd.

Liscannor Bay
Mal Bay
Miltown Malbay
Ennis
CLARE
Killaloe
Ballina
Nenagh
Templemore
Nore
Carlow
Tullow
Luanaquilla 923
Rathdrum
Mizen Hd.

Kilkee
Loop Hd.
Ardnacrusha
Keeper ▲ 694
Thurles
CARLOW
Muine Bheag
Mt. Leinster 796
Shillelagh
Gorey
Arklow

R. Shannon
Foynes
Rathkeale
Limerick
TIPPERARY
Cashel
Kilkenny
KILKENNY
Enniscorthy
Cahore Pt.

Kerry Hd.
Tralee Bay
Fenit
Listowel
LIMERICK
Newcastle
Rath Luirc (Charleville)
Gortmore 920
Galty Mts.
Caher
Slievenamon 722
Carrick-on-Suir
Clonmel
WEXFORD
New Ross
Wexford
Rosslare
Wexford Harbour
Greenore Pt.
Tuscar Rock
Carnsore Pt.

Brandon Bay
Brandon Mt. 953
Dingle
St. Mish
Maine
MUNSTER
Newmarket
Mitchelstown
Knockmealdown Mts.
Comeragh Mts.
Waterford
Tramore
Hook Hd.
Saltee Is.

Gt. Blasket I.
Dingle Bay
Macgillycuddy Reeks
Tralee
KERRY
Killarney
Mallow
Fermoy
WATERFORD
Lismore
Dungarvan
Dungarvan Bay
Waterford Harbour

Valentia Harbour
Carrantuohill 1040
Lakes of Killarney
Blackwater
Boggeragh Mts.
Youghal
St. David's Hd.

Valentia I.
Cahirciveen
Kenmare
Macroom
Blarney
Cork
Midleton
Youghal Harbour

Skellig Rocks
Ballinskelligs B.
Caha Mts.
Glengarriff
Bantry
Lee
Passage West
Cobh
Crosshaven
Cork Harbour

Castletown Bearhaven
Bear I.
Bantry Bay
Bandon
Clonakilty
Kinsale
Dunmanus Hd.
Skull
Baltimore
Clonakilty Bay
Galley Hd.
Old Head of Kinsale

Mizen Hd.
Fastnet Rock
Crow Hd.
Clear I.
C. Clear

IRISH SEA

St. George's Channel

Towns underlined in Northern Ireland give their
names to the Districts in which they stand

The remaining Districts are:—

1	Fermanagh	5	Castlereagh
2	Moyle	6	Ards
3	Newtownabbey	7	Down
4	North Down	8	Newry & Mourne

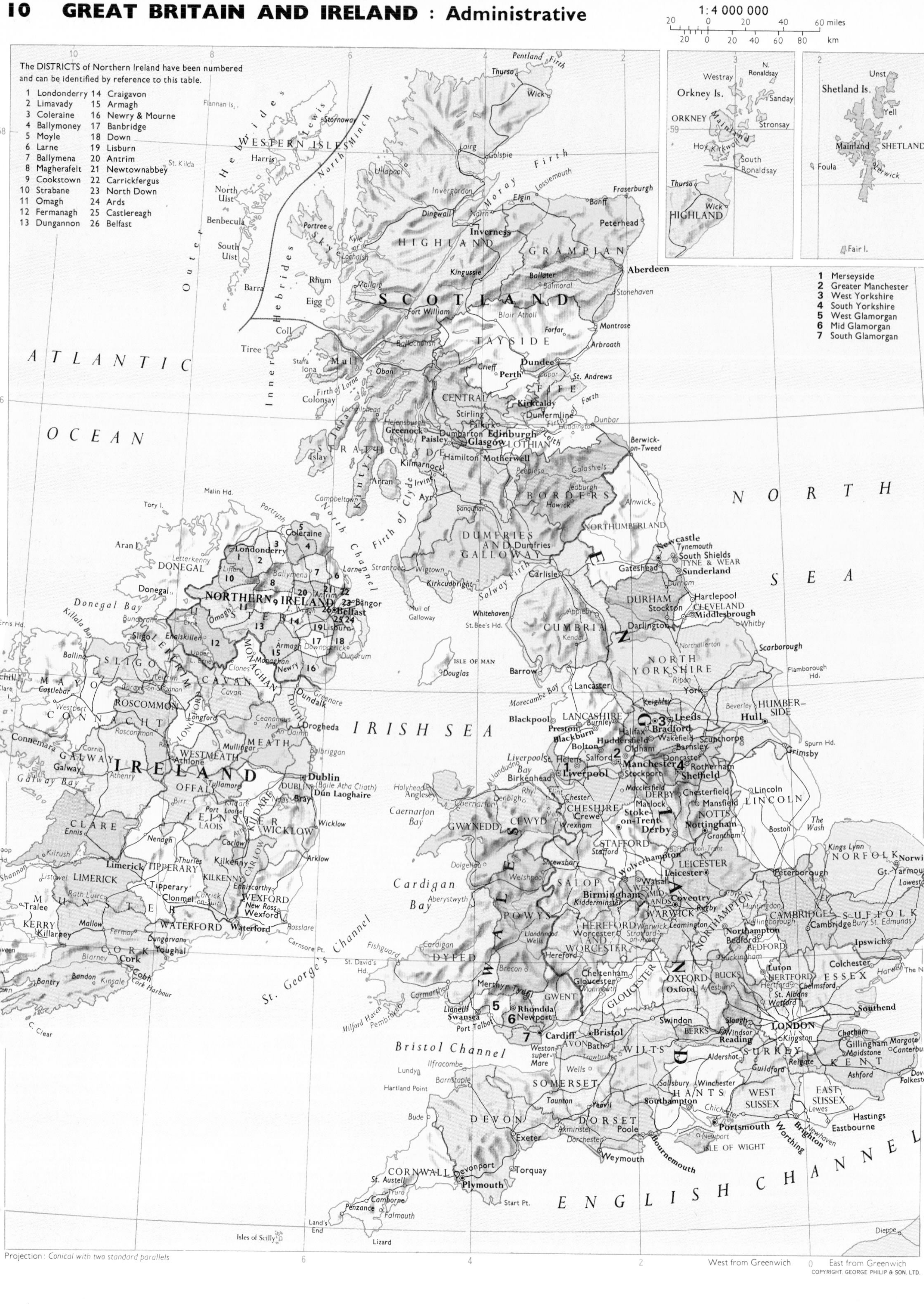

10 GREAT BRITAIN AND IRELAND : Administrative

1 : 4 000 000

The DISTRICTS of Northern Ireland have been numbered and can be identified by reference to this table.

1 Londonderry 14 Craigavon
2 Limavady 15 Armagh
3 Coleraine 16 Newry & Mourne
4 Ballymoney 17 Banbridge
5 Moyle 18 Down
6 Larne 19 Lisburn
7 Ballymena 20 Antrim
8 Magherafelt 21 Newtownabbey
9 Cookstown 22 Carrickfergus
10 Strabane 23 North Down
11 Omagh 24 Ards
12 Fermanagh 25 Castlereagh
13 Dungannon 26 Belfast

1 Merseyside
2 Greater Manchester
3 West Yorkshire
4 South Yorkshire
5 West Glamorgan
6 Mid Glamorgan
7 South Glamorgan

Orkney Is.
Shetland Is.

ATLANTIC OCEAN
SCOTLAND
HIGHLAND
GRAMPIAN
TAYSIDE
CENTRAL
STRATHCLYDE
BORDERS
DUMFRIES AND GALLOWAY
NORTHUMBERLAND
NORTH SEA
IRISH SEA
IRELAND
NORTHERN IRELAND
CONNACHT
MUNSTER
LEINSTER
WALES
ENGLAND
ENGLISH CHANNEL

Projection: Conical with two standard parallels
West from Greenwich   East from Greenwich
COPYRIGHT. GEORGE PHILIP & SON. LTD.

1:2 500 000

10 0 10 20 30 40 50 miles
10 0 10 20 30 40 50 60 70 80 km

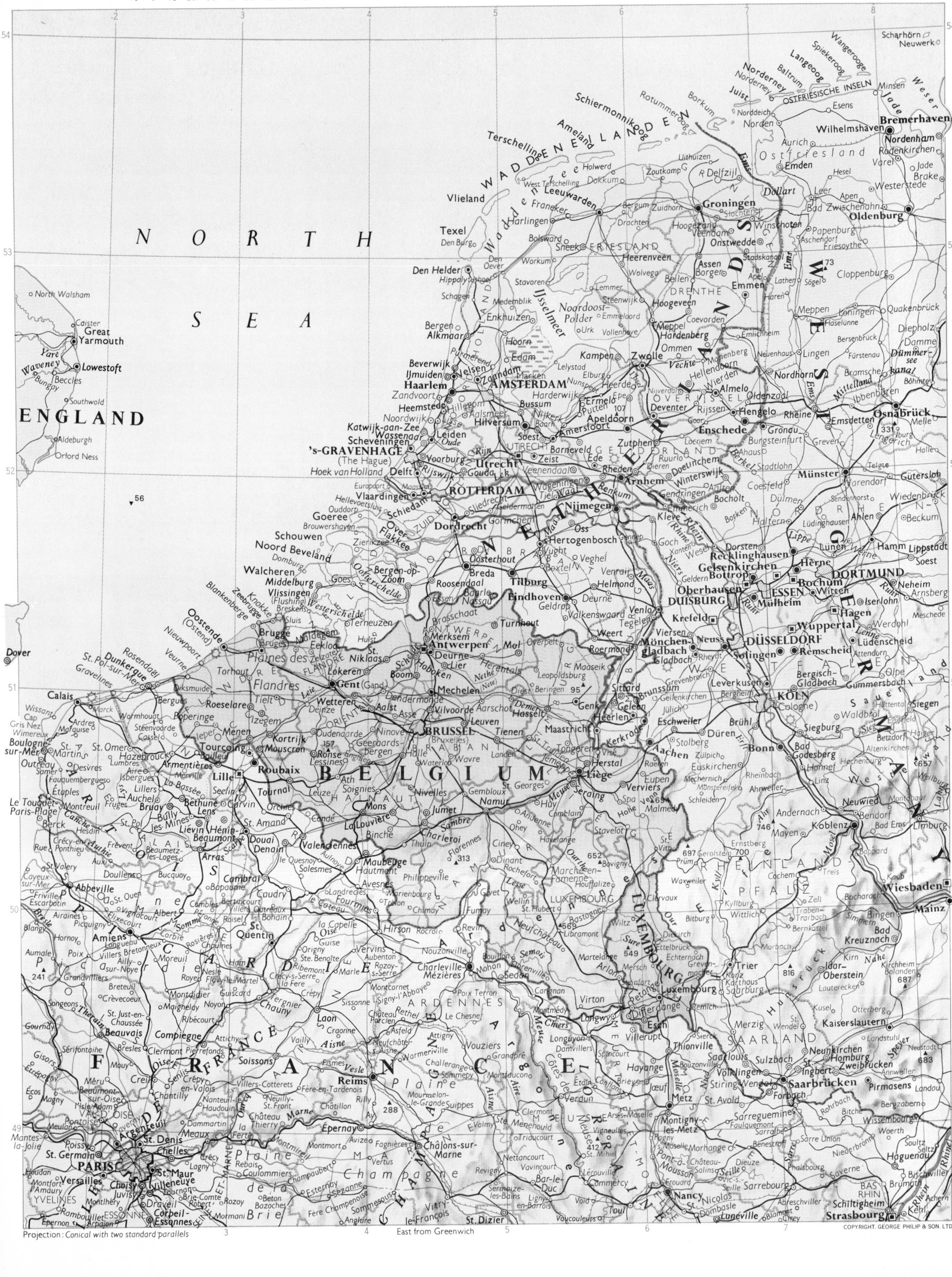

Projection: Conical with two standard parallels

East from Greenwich

1:5 000 000

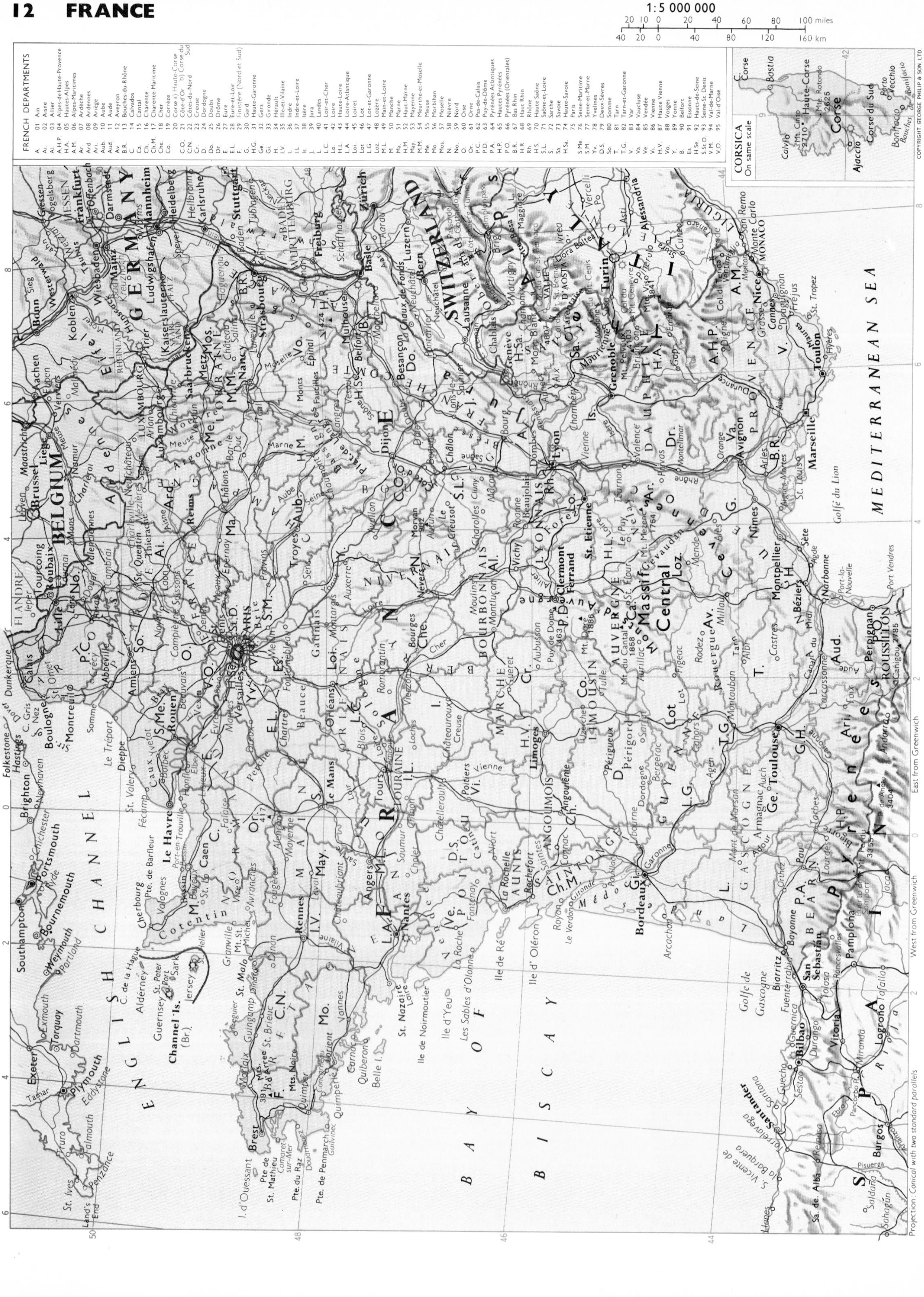

Scale:
```
20 10 0        20    40      60    80    100 miles
40   20    0    20    40    80    120    160 km
```

CORSICA On same scale

Corse — Calvi — Bastia — Mt. Cinto 2710 — Haute-Corse — Mt. Rotondo 2625 — Porto — Corse du Sud — Vecchio — Ajaccio — Bonifacio

GERMANY — BELGIUM — SWITZERLAND — ITALY — LIGURIA — MONACO — LORRAINE — FRANCHE COMTÉ — BOURGOGNE — NIVERNAIS — BOURBONNAIS — AUVERGNE — Massif Central — LIMOUSIN — MARCHE — POITOU — ANJOU — TOURAINE — MAINE — NORMANDIE — BRETAGNE — VENDÉE — AUNIS — SAINTONGE — ANGOUMOIS — PÉRIGORD — GUYENNE — GASCOGNE — BÉARN — ROUSSILLON — PROVENCE — DAUPHINÉ — SAVOY — LYONNAIS — BEAUJOLAIS — BEAUCE — FLANDRE — ARTOIS — PICARDIE — CHAMPAGNE — ALSACE

Paris — Versailles — Reims — Rouen — Le Havre — Caen — Cherbourg — Rennes — Brest — Nantes — St. Nazaire — Angers — Le Mans — Tours — Orléans — Bourges — Poitiers — La Rochelle — Limoges — Clermont-Ferrand — Vichy — St. Étienne — Lyon — Grenoble — Turin — Nice — Monte Carlo — Cannes — Toulon — Marseille — Montpellier — Béziers — Narbonne — Perpignan — Carcassonne — Toulouse — Auch — Pau — Bayonne — Biarritz — San Sebastián — Pamplona — Bordeaux — Angoulême — Périgueux — Bergerac — Agen — Montauban — Rodez — Mende — Nîmes — Avignon — Arles — Valence — Montélimar — Dijon — Besançon — Belfort — Mulhouse — Strasbourg — Nancy — Metz — Épinal — Chaumont — Troyes — Auxerre — Sens — Chartres — Évreux — Amiens — Abbeville — Calais — Boulogne — Dunkerque — Lille — Roubaix — Tourcoing — Arras — St. Quentin — Laon — Charleville-Mézières — Verdun — Bar-le-Duc — Châlons — Épernay

MEDITERRANEAN SEA — ENGLISH CHANNEL — BAY OF BISCAY

Southampton — Portsmouth — Brighton — Hastings — Folkestone — Dover — Exeter — Plymouth — Torquay — Bournemouth — Weymouth — Land's End

Mont Blanc 4810 — Mt. Pelvoux 4103

Projection: Conical with two standard parallels

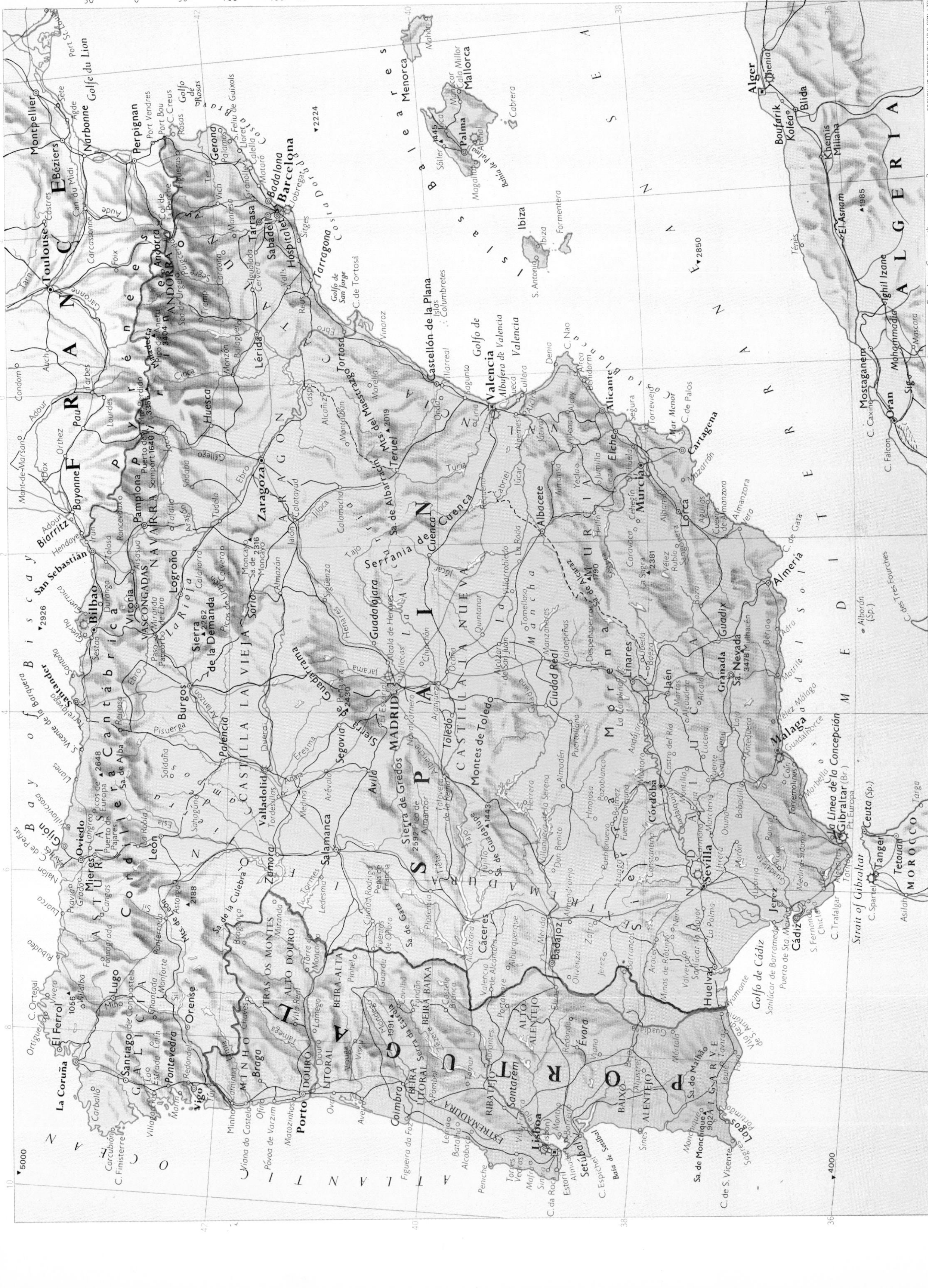

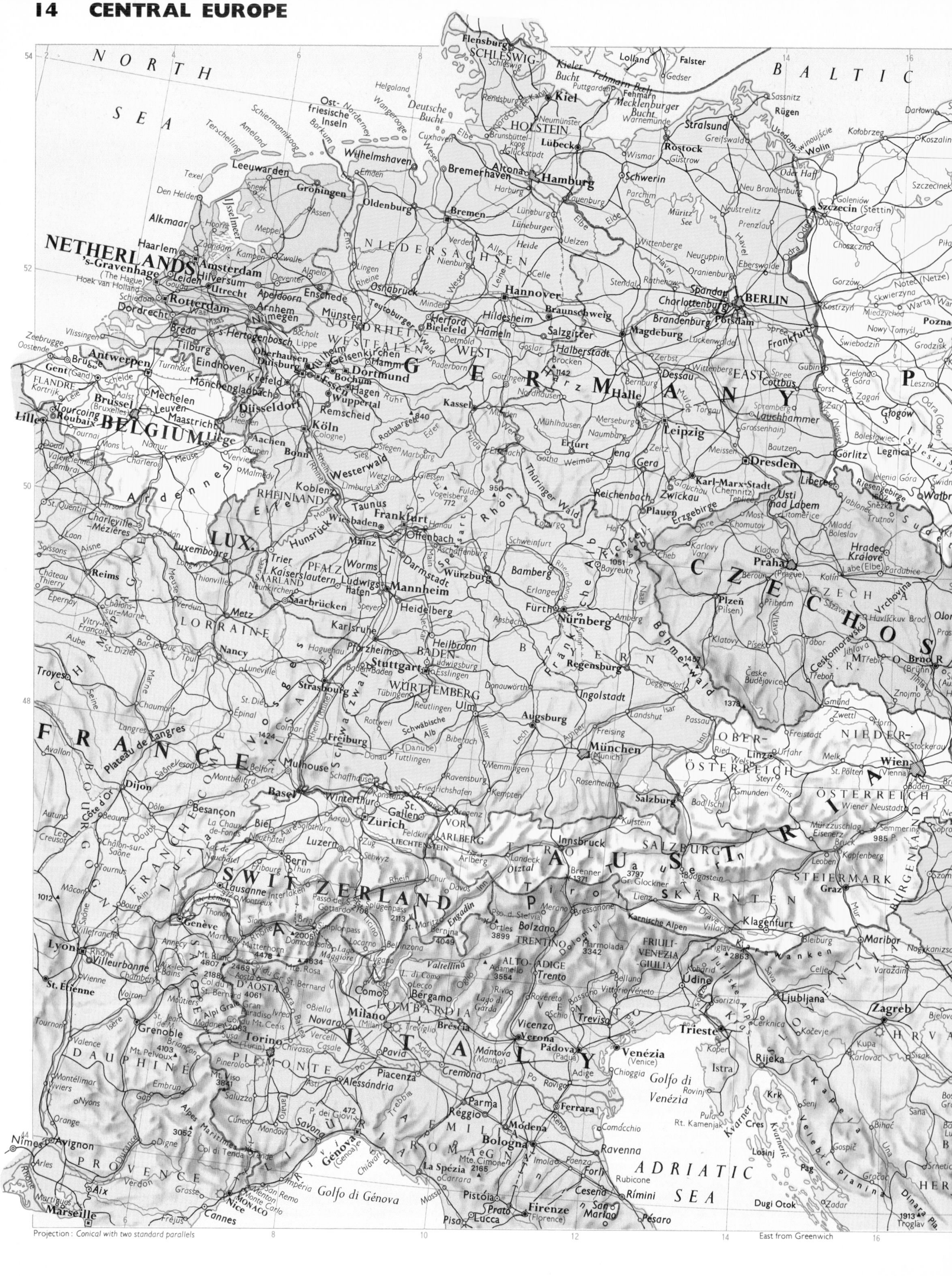

NORTH SEA

BALTIC

Flensburg
SCHLESWIG-
Kieler Bucht
Fehmarn Belt
Lolland
Falster
Gedser

Helgoland
Deutsche Bucht
Ost-Norderney
friesische Inseln
Schiermonnikoog
Wangerooge
Borkum
Ameland
Terschelling
Den Helder
Texel

Rendsburg
Neumünster
HOLSTEIN
Brunsbüttel-koog
Glückstadt
Altona
Hamburg
Harburg
Elbe

Kiel
Puttgarden
Mecklenburger Bucht
Warnemünde
Wismar
Schwerin
Lauenburg
Lüneburg
Lüneburger Heide

Sassnitz
Rügen
Stralsund
Greifswald
Rostock
Güstrow
Neu Brandenburg
Müritz See
Parchim
Elde

Kolberg
Usedom
Swinoujście
Wolin
Szczecin (Stettin)
Dobie
Stargard
Koszalin
Szczecinek

Wilhelmshaven
Emden
Cuxhaven
Bremerhaven
Oldenburg
Bremen
Verden
Weser
Nienburg
Celle
Stendal
Rathenow
Havel
Neuruppin
Oranienburg
Eberswalde
Prenzlau
Neustrelitz
Wittenberge
Oder Haff

Leeuwarden
Groningen
Sneek
Assen
Meppel
Almelo
NIEDERSACHSEN
Aller
Leine
Hannover

Alkmaar
Hoorn
Zwolle
Kampen
Deventer
Osnabrück
Minden
Bielefeld
Herford
Hildesheim
Braunschweig
Salzgitter
Magdeburg
Brandenburg
Potsdam
Spandau
BERLIN
Charlottenburg
Spree
Frankfurt
Gubin

NETHERLANDS
's-Gravenhage (The Hague)
Amsterdam
Hilversum
Haarlem
Leiden
Utrecht
Apeldoorn
Enschede
Arnhem
Nijmegen
Münster
NORDRHEIN-
WESTFALEN
Teutoburger Wald
Detmold
Paderborn
WEST
Göttingen
Nordhausen
Halberstadt
Brocken
Wittenberg
Dessau
Bernburg
Luckenwalde
Cottbus
Forst

Zeebrugge
Oostende
Brugge
Gent (Gand)
Antwerpen
Turnhout
Eindhoven
Venlo
Krefeld
Essen
Duisburg
Oberhausen
Mülheim
Gelsenkirchen
Bochum
Dortmund
Hamm
GERMANY
Ruhr
Lippe
Hagen
Wuppertal
Remscheid
Kassel
Eisenach
Eder
Göttingen
Halle
Leipzig
Merseburg
Naumburg
Zerbst
Torgau
Grossenhain
Riesa
Meissen
Bautzen
Görlitz
Legnica
Głogów
Zielona Góra
Poznań
Gorzów
Notec (Netze)
Schwerin
Piła
Choszczno
Nowy Tomyśl
Miedzychod
Skwierzyna
Warta (Warthe)
Grodzisk
Leszno
Gostyń
Zary
Zagań

FLANDRE
Kortrijk
Lille
Roubaix
Tourcoing
BELGIUM
Brussel (Bruxelles)
Leuven
Mechelen
Aalst
Liège
Maastricht
Aachen
Heerlen
Düsseldorf
Mönchengladbach
Köln (Cologne)
Bonn
Siegen
Marburg
Giessen
Fulda
Eisenach
Gotha
Erfurt
Weimar
Jena
Gera
Zeitz
Karl-Marx-Stadt (Chemnitz)
Zwickau
Plauen
Reichenbach
Dresden
Liberec
Usti nad Labem
Litomerice
Mladá Boleslav
Jablonec
Trutnov
Hradec Králové
Walbrz
Świdni
Jelenia Góra
Boleslawiec
Riesengebirge
Snezka
Sud

LUX
Luxembourg
Trier
Koblenz
Bonn
Westerwald
Wetzlar
Limburg
Lahn
TAUNUS
Frankfurt
Wiesbaden
Mainz
Offenbach
Hanau
Aschaffenburg
Schweinfurt
Bamberg
Bayreuth
Hof
Cheb (Eger)
Karlovy Vary
Kladno
Plzen (Pilsen)
PRAHA (Prague)
Beroun
Kolín
Pardubice
Pribram
CZECH
Jihlava

RHEINLAND
Eifel
HUNSRÜCK
Mosel
Worms
Darmstadt
Würzburg
PFALZ
Kaiserslautern
Ludwigshafen
Mannheim
Heidelberg
Speyer
Karlsruhe
Heilbronn
Ansbach
Erlangen
Fürth
Nürnberg
Amberg
Regensburg
Deggendorf
Böhmerwald
Ceske Budejovice
Trebon
Znojmo

METZ
LORRAINE
Saarbrücken
SAARLAND
Neunkirchen
Pforzheim
BADEN
Stuttgart
Ludwigsburg
Esslingen
Tübingen
WÜRTTEMBERG
Ulm
Donauwörth
Ingolstadt
BAYERN
Landshut
Passau
OBER-
Linz
Urfahr
NIEDER-

Reims
Verdun
Nancy
Lunéville
Épinal
Strasbourg
Colmar
Freiburg
Schwäbische Alb
Donau
Augsburg
Freising
München (Munich)
Ried
Salzburg
Bad Ischl
ÖSTERREICH
Wels
Steyr
Gmunden
Melk
St. Pölten
Wien (Vienna)
Wiener Neustadt

FRANCE
Plateau de Langres
Besançon
Belfort
Mulhouse
Basel
Schaffhausen
Konstanz
Friedrichshafen
Ravensburg
Kempten
Memmingen
Rosenheim
Kufstein
Innsbruck
SALZBURG
Bad Gastein
STEIERMARK
Graz
Semmering
Sopron
BURGENLAND

Dijon
Dôle
SWITZERLAND
Winterthur
Zürich
St. Gallen
Bregenz
VOR-
ARLBERG
Feldkirch
LIECHTENSTEIN
Arlberg
Landeck
Ötztal
TIROL
Brenner
Gr. Glockner
KÄRNTEN
Klagenfurt
Villach
Bleiburg
Maribor
Nagykanizsa

Besançon
Biel
Solothurn
Aarau
Luzern
Zug
Schwyz
Chur
Davos
St. Moritz
Engadin
Ortles
Merano
Bolzano
Bressanone
Karnische Alpen
Drava
Lienz
Leoben
Kapfenberg

Bern
Fribourg
Neuchâtel
Interlaken
Passo del Gottardo
Splügenpass
Bernina
ALTO-ADIGE
Trento
TRENTINO
Dolomiti
Marmolada
FRIULI-VENEZIA GIULIA
Udine
Gorizia
Ljubljana
Zagreb
HRVA

Lausanne
Montreux
Thonon
Matterhorn
Mt. Blanc
Mte. Rosa
Simplonpass
Domodossola
Locarno
Bellinzona
Lugano
L. Maggiore
L. di Como
Valtellina
Adamello
Rovereto
Belluno
Vittorio Veneto
VENETO
Treviso
Trieste
Koper
Rijeka

Lyon
Villeurbanne
St. Étienne
Annecy
Aix-les-Bains
Chambéry
Grenoble
Gran Paradiso
Gran S. Bernardo
D'AOSTA
Biella
Novara
Milano (Milan)
LOMBARDIA
Brescia
Bergamo
Verona
Vicenza
Padova (Padua)
Venezia (Venice)
Golfo di Venezia

DAUPHINÉ
Briançon
Mt. Pelvoux
PIEMONTE
Torino (Turin)
Asti
Alessandria
Pavia
Cremona
Mantova (Mantua)
Rovigo
Chioggia
Adige

Montélimar
Mt. Viso
Cuneo
Mondovì
Savona
Piacenza
Parma
Reggio
Modena
Ferrara
EMILIA
Bologna
Ravenna
Comácchio

Nîmes
Avignon
Arles
Alpes Maritimes
Col di Tenda
Imperia
San Remo
Génova (Genoa)
Golfo di Génova
La Spézia
Carrara
Massa
Pistóia
Lucca
Firenze (Florence)
Pisa
Forlì
Cesena
Rímini
Pésaro
ADRIATIC SEA

Marseille
Aix
Cannes
Nice
MONACO
Monte Carlo
Fréjus

PROVENCE

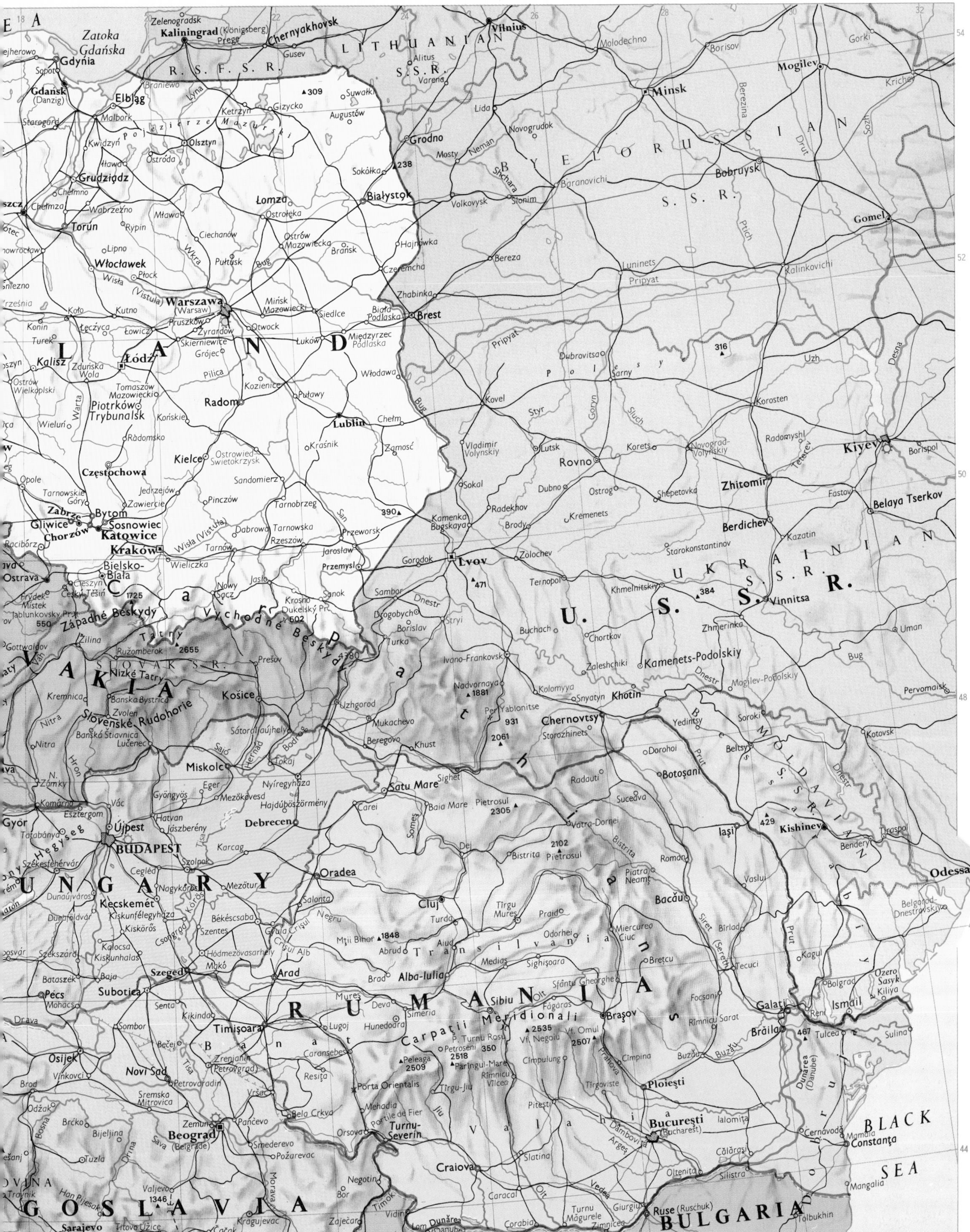

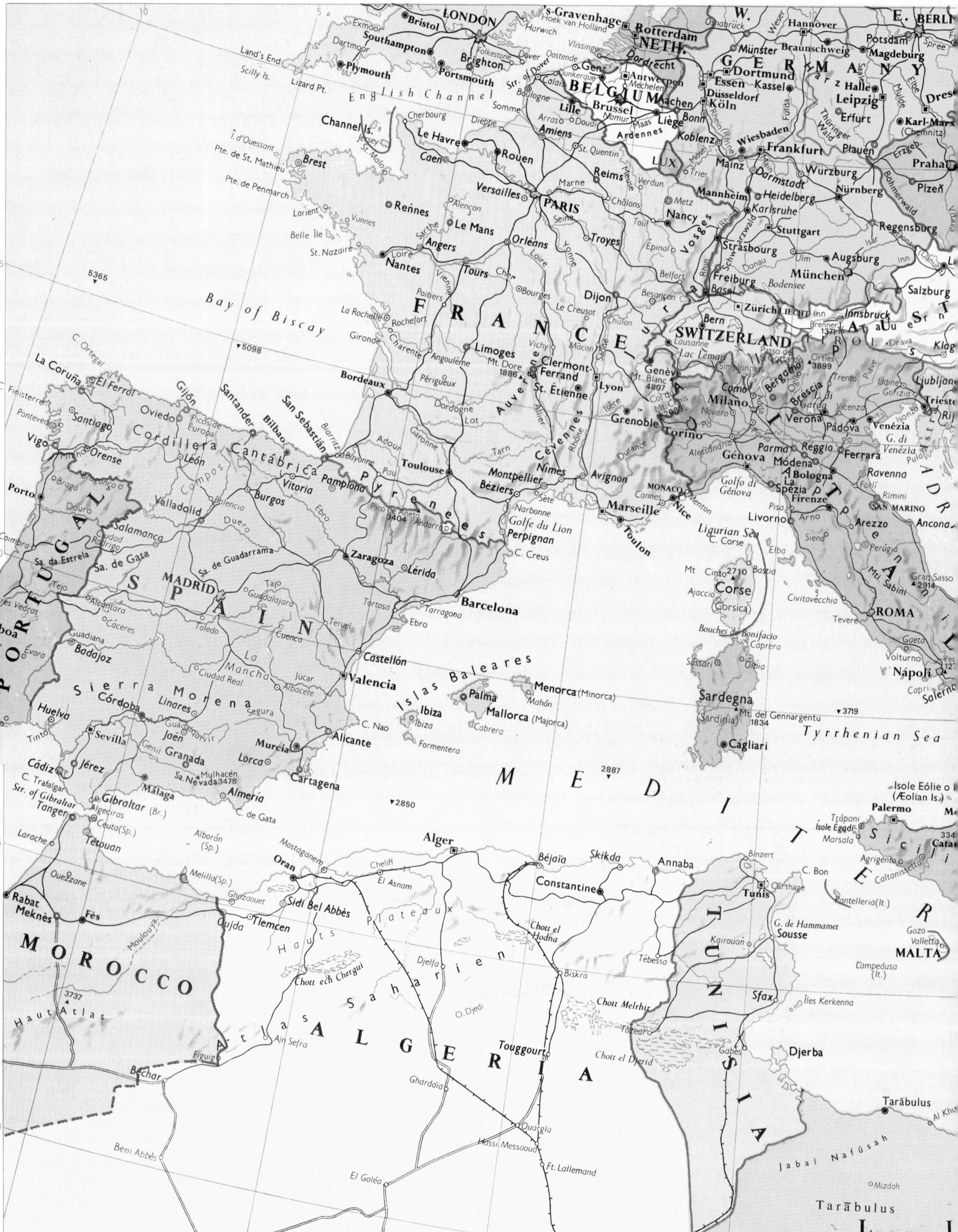

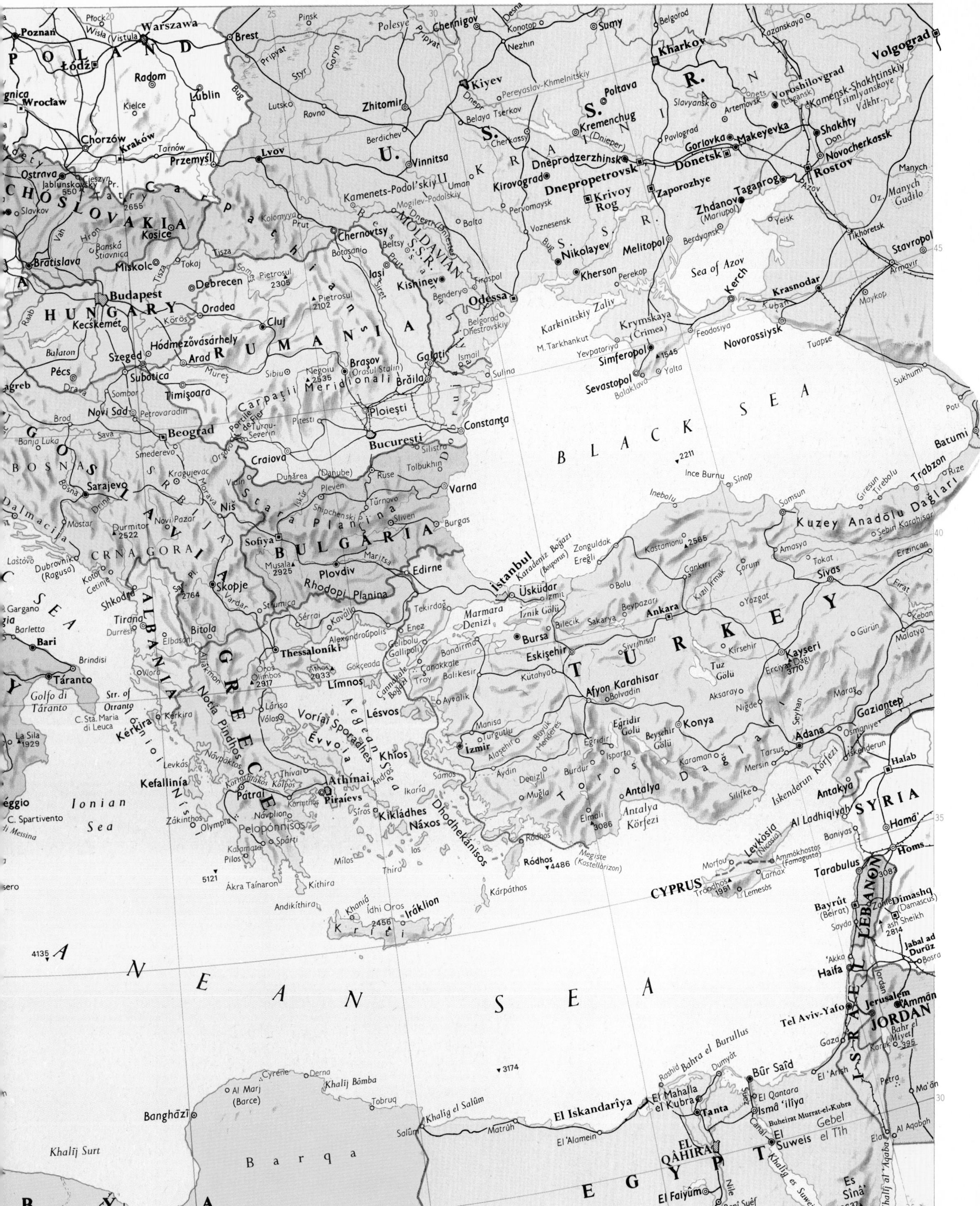

1:10 000 000

50   0   50   100   150   200 miles
50   0   100   200   300   km

POLAND
Poznań
Płock
Warszawa
Łódź
Wrocław
Brest
Pinsk
Polesye
Chernigov
Konotop
Sumy
Belgorod
Kharkov
Volgograd
Radom
Wisła (Vistula)
Lublin
Pripyat
Kielce
Kiyev
Poltava
Voroshilovgrad (Lugansk)
Kamensk-Shakhtinskiy
Tsimlyanskoye
Vdkhr.
Chorzów
Kraków
Tarnów
Przemyśl
Lvov
Vinnitsa
U. S. S. R.
Kremenchug
Slavyansk
Artemovsk
Donets
Ostrava
Żylina
Jablunkovský Pr.
CHOSLOVAKIA
Tatry
2655
Carpathians
Kolomyya
Chernovtsy
MOLDAVIAN
Kishinev
Nikolayev
Kherson
Melitopol
Mariupol
Zhdanov
Shakhty
Novocherkassk
Rostov
Azov
Manych
Oz. Manych
Gudilo
Slavkov
Bánská
Štiavnica
Miskolc
Košice
Tisza
Tokaj
Debrecen
Iași
Belgorod Dnestrovskiy
Odessa
Perekop
Sea of Azov
Kerch
Tikhoretsk
Stavropol
Bratislava
Budapest
HUNGARY
Kecskemét
Oradea
Cluj
Sibiu
Brașov (Orașul Stalin)
Galați
Ismail
Sulina
Karkinitskiy Zaliv
Krymskaya (Crimea)
Simferopol
Feodosiya
Novorossiysk
Tuapse
Maykop
Szeged
Hódmezővásárhely
Arad
RUMANIA
Negoiu
2535
Pitești
Ploiești
Bucuresti
Constanța
M. Tarkhankut
Yevpatoriya
Sevastopol
Balaklava
Yalta
BLACK SEA
Sukhumi
Pécs
Subotica
Timișoara
Mureș
Carpații Meridionali
Craiova
Dunărea (Danube)
Ruse
Silistra
Tolbukhin
Varna
Sinop
Ince Burnu
Poti
Batumi
Rize
Trabzon
Kuzey Anadolu Dağları
BOSNA
Sarajevo
Beograd
Smederevo
Kragujevac
Niš
Morava
Pleven
Stara Planina
Turnovo
Sofiya
BULGARIA
Plovdiv
Burgas
Giresun
Tirebolu
Samsun
Amasya
Zonguldak
Ereğli
Inebolu
Kastamonu
2565
Çorum
Tokat
Sivas
Dubrovnik (Ragusa)
Kotor
Cetinje
CRNA GORA
2522
Musala
2925
Rhodopi Planina
Edirne
İstanbul
Karadeniz Boğazı (Bosporus)
Üsküdar
İzmit
Bolu
Çankırı
Kızıl Irmak
Yozgat
Ankara
TURKEY
Kayseri
Erciyas Dağı
3770
Sivrihisar
Bari
Taranto
Golfo di Táranto
Brindisi
ALBANIA
Tirana
Durrës
Elbasani
Shkodra
2764
Skopje
Vardar
Štrumica
Thessaloníki
Sérrai
Kavalla
Alexandroúpolis
Tekirdağ
Marmara Denizi
İznik Gölü
Bilecik
Sakarya
Beypazarı
Eskişehir
Tuz Gölü
Afyon Karahisar
Bolvadin
Aksaray
Niğde
Maraş
Gaziantep
La Sila
1929
Str. of Otranto
C. Sta. Maria di Leuca
Vorai Pindhos
2917
Áthos
2033
Límnos
Gelibolu (Gallipoli)
Çanakkale Boğazı
Troy
Bandırma
Balıkesir
Kütahya
Büyük Menderes
Konya
Adana
Toros Dağları
Osmaniye
İskenderun
Halab
GREECE
Nótia Pindhos
Lárisa
Vólos
Évvoia
Khíos
Lésvos
Gökçeada
Ayvalık
İzmir
Urgutlu
Alaşehir
Eğridir
Isparta
Beyşehir
Egridir Gölü
Beyşehir Gölü
Karaman
Mersin
Tarsus
Silifke
İskenderun Körfezi
Antakya
SYRIA
Hamā
Homs
Kérkira
Levkás
Návpaktos
Thívai
Athínai
Piraiévs
Sýros
Ándros
Ikaría
Sámos
Manisa
Aydın
Denizli
Muğla
Burdur
Elmalı
3086
Antalya
Antalya Körfezi
Al Ladhiqiyah
Baniyas
Kefallinía
Pátrai
Kórinthos
Kikládhes
Náxos
Íos
Dhodhekánisos
Ródhos
4486
Megiste (Kastellórizon)
CYPRUS
Troödhos
1951
Levkosía (Nicosia)
Ammókhostos (Famagusta)
Larnax
Lemesós
Tarabulus
Bayrût (Beirut)
Sayda
Dimashq (Damascus)
Iónian Sea
Zákinthos
Olympía
Pelopónnisos
Návplion
Spárti
Kalamáta
Pílos
5121
Ákra Taínaron
Kíthira
Khaniá
Ídhi Oros
2456
Iráklion
Krití
Jabal ash Sheikh
2814
Jabal ad Durūz
Bosra
Haifa
'Akka
Jordan
Tel Aviv-Yafo
Jerusalem
Amman
JORDAN
Gaza
ISRAEL
LEBANON
3083
Reggio
C. Spartivento
di Messina
Andikíthira
4135
MEDITERRANEAN SEA
3174
Petra
Ma'ān
El 'Arish
Bahr el Miyet
Karak
395
Cyrene
Derna
Al Marj (Barce)
Khalīj Bômba
Tobruq
Khalīg el Salûm
Rashid
Bahra el Burullus
Damyāt
Bûr Saîd
El Qantara
Ismâ'îlîya
Buheirat Murrat el-Kubra
El 'Aqaba
Banghāzī
El Iskandarîya
El Mahalla el Kubra
Tanta
El Suweis
Gebel el Tih
Khalīj Surt
Barqa
Matrûh
El 'Alamein
Salûm
EGYPT
EL QÂHIRA
El Faiyûm
Benî Suêf
Khalīg es Suweis
Es Sinâ
2637
Khalīj al 'Aqaba
LIBYA

- - - - - Division between Greeks
and Turks in Cyprus;
Turks to the north.

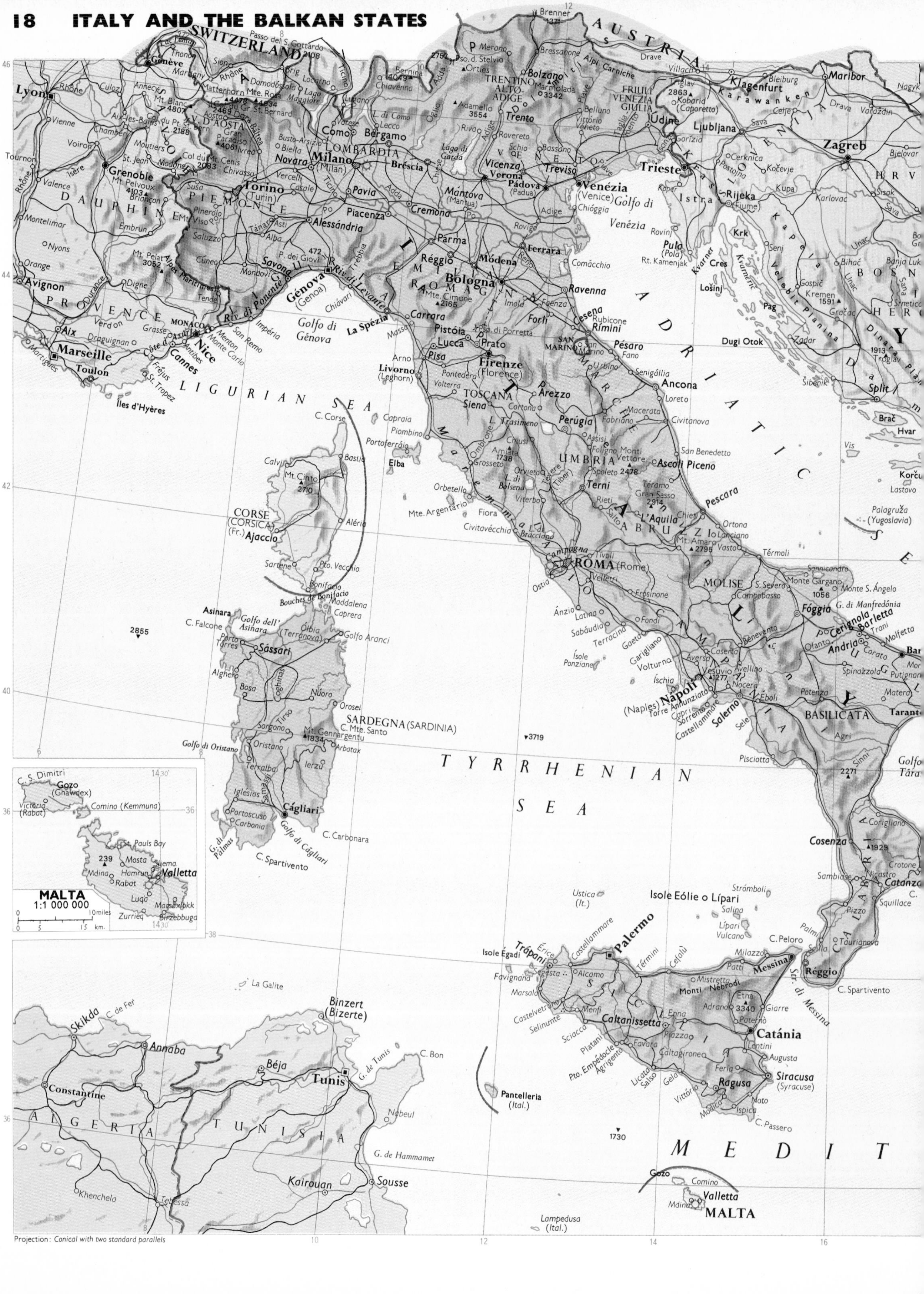

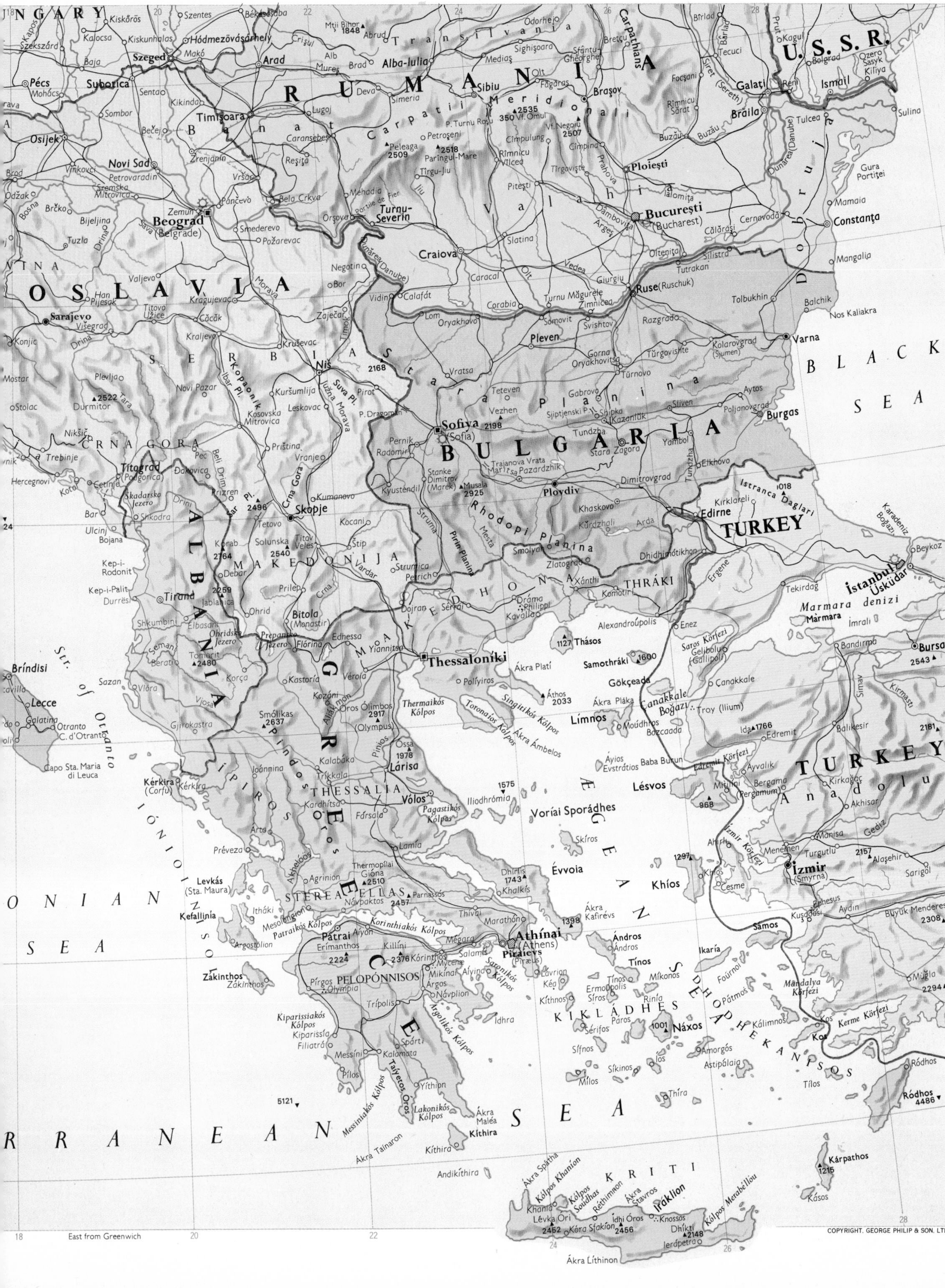

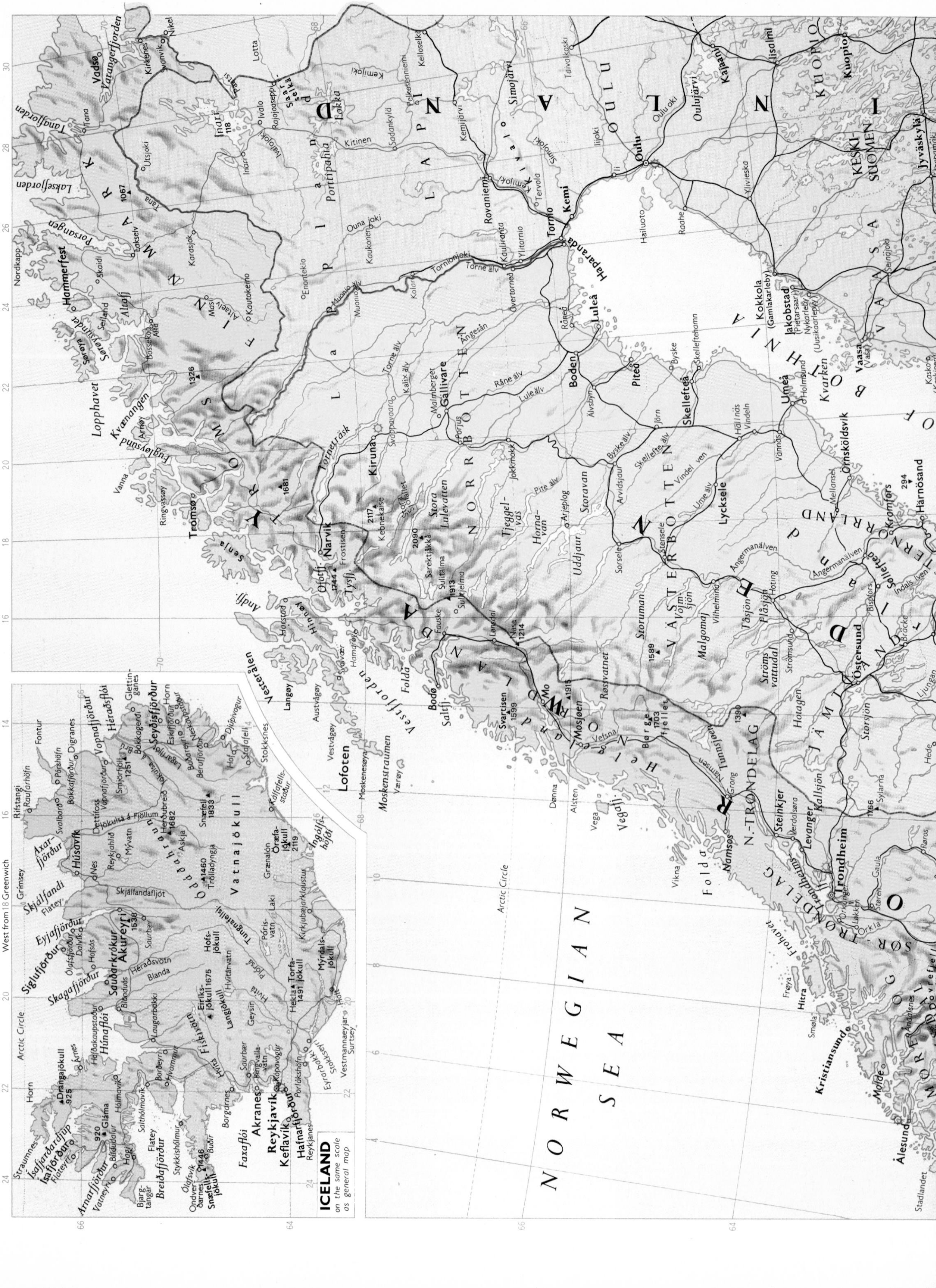
ICELAND
on the same scale as general map
NORWEGIAN SEA
Vestfjorden
Lofoten
Vesterålen
Arctic Circle
FINNMARK
TROMS
NORDLAND
NORRBOTTEN
VÄSTERBOTTEN
JÄMTLAND
VÄSTERNORRLAND
N.-TRØNDELAG
SØR-TRØNDELAG
LAPPI
OULU
KESKI-SUOMEN
KUOPIO
VAASA
GULF OF BOTHNIA
Kvarken
Hammerfest
Vadsø
Kirkenes
Tromsø
Narvik
Kiruna
Gällivare
Boden
Luleå
Piteå
Skellefteå
Umeå
Haparanda
Tornio
Kemi
Rovaniemi
Oulu
Kajaani
Kokkola
Jakobstad
Vaasa
Jyväskylä
Kuopio
Örnsköldsvik
Härnösand
Östersund
Lycksele
Bodø
Mo
Mosjøen
Namsos
Steinkjer
Levanger
Trondheim
Kristiansund
Molde
Ålesund
Reykjavík
Keflavík
Akranes
Akureyri
Ísafjörður
Húsavík
Vatnajökull
Hofsjökull
Langjökull
Mýrdalsjökull
Faxaflói
Breiðafjörður
Húnaflói
Skagafjörður
Eyjafjörður
Vopnafjörður
Seyðisfjörður

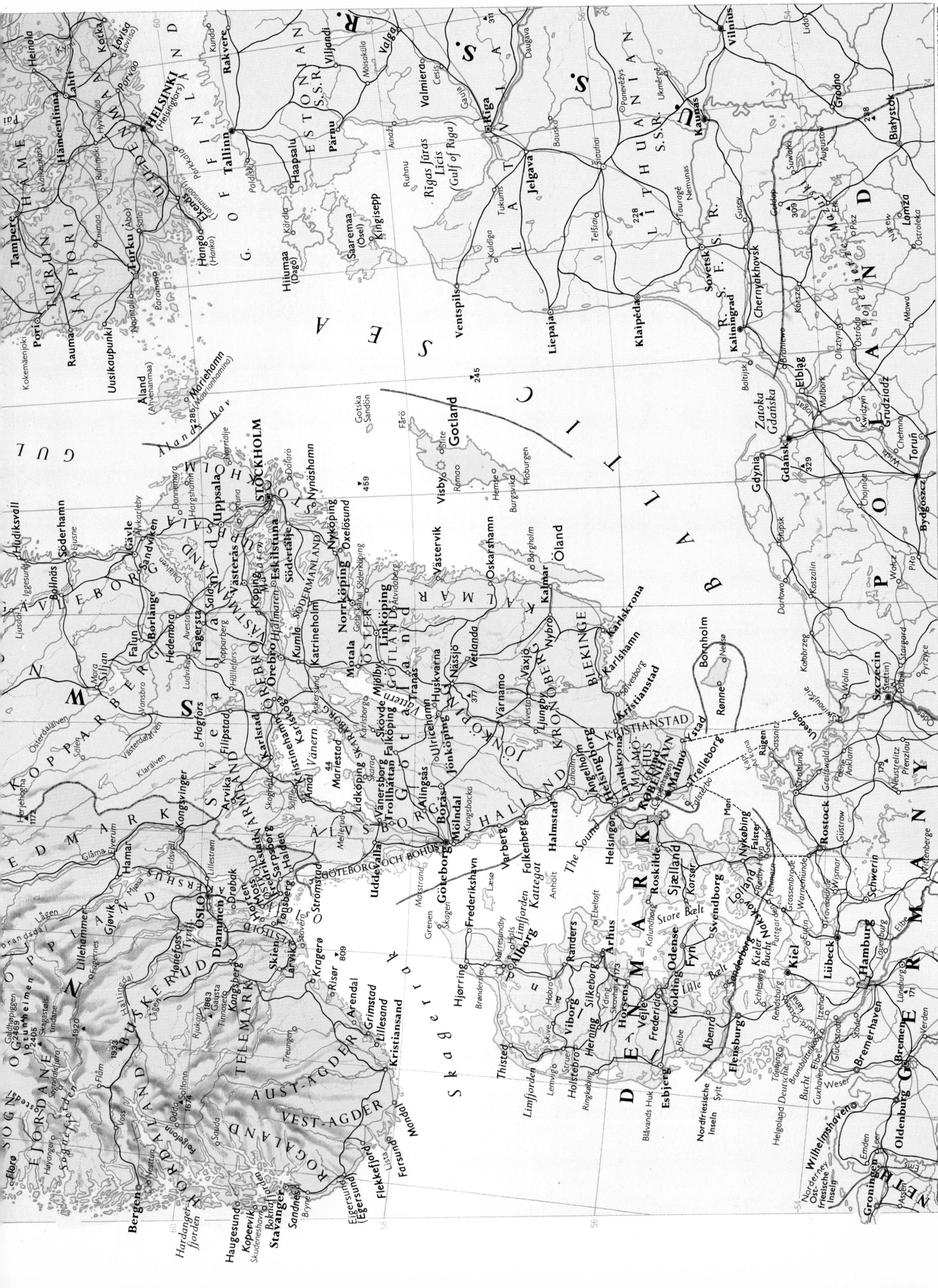

1:5 000 000

20 10 0 20 40 80 100 miles
40 20 0 40 120 160 km

Heinola
Kotka
Lovisa
(Loviisa)
Lahti
Tampere
TURUN
JA PORIN
Pori
Rauma
Uusikaupunki
HELSINKI
(Helsingfors)
FINLAND
HÄME
HÄMEenlinna
Turku (Åbo)
Ekenäs
(Tammisaari)
Hangö
(Hanko)
G. of FINLAND
Rakvere
Tallinn
ESTONIAN S.S.R.
Haapsalu
Hiiumaa
(Dagö)
Saaremaa
(Ösel)
Kingisepp
Pärnu
Viljandi
Valga
Valmiera
Riga
LATVIA
Rigas Juras Licis
(Gulf of Riga)
Ventspils
Kuldiga
Liepaja
Klaipėda
LITHUANIAN S.S.R.
Jelgava
Bauska
Šiauliai
Telšiai
Panevėžys
Ukmergė
Vilnius
Kaunas
Kaliningrad
Sovetsk
Chernyakhovsk
R.S.F.S.R.
Gusev
Grodno
Białystok
Augustów
Łomża
Ostrołęka
POLAND
Suwałki
Ełk
Olsztyn
Ostróda
Grudziądz
Elbląg
Malbork
Gdańsk
Gdynia
Toruń
Bydgoszcz
Słupsk
Koszalin
Kołobrzeg
Szczecin (Stettin)

BALTIC SEA

Åland
(Ahvenanmaa)
Mariehamn
(Maarianhamina)
STOCKHOLM
Uppsala
Västerås
Eskilstuna
Södertälje
Nyköping
Norrköping
Linköping
Motala
Katrineholm
Örebro
Gotland
Visby
Fårö
ÖSTER
GÖTLAND
Vättern
Jönköping
Vänern
Vänersborg
Trollhättan
GÖTEBORG
OCH BOHUS
Uddevalla
Borås
Mölndal
Halmstad
HALLAND
Varberg
Falkenberg
Helsingborg
Landskrona
Malmö
KØBENHAVN
Kristianstad
KRISTIANSTAD
Karlshamn
Karlskrona
BLEKINGE
KRONOBERG
Växjö
Nässjö
Vetlanda
Oskarshamn
Kalmar
KALMAR
Öland
Borgholm
Västervik
Bornholm
Rønne
Ystad
Trelleborg
Rügen
Rostock
Stralsund
GERMANY
Schwerin
Lübeck
Hamburg
Bremen
Bremerhaven
Wilhelmshaven
Oldenburg
Groningen
NETHERLANDS
Emden

DENMARK
Ålborg
Randers
Århus
Silkeborg
Viborg
Herning
Esbjerg
Kolding
Vejle
Fredericia
Odense
Svendborg
Roskilde
Sjælland
Korsør
Fyn
Kiel
Flensburg
Helsingør
The Sound
Skagerrak
Kattegat
Frederikshavn
Hjørring
Thisted
Limfjorden

NORWAY
OSLO
Drammen
Tønsberg
Skien
Larvik
Kristiansand
Arendal
Grimstad
Lillesand
Stavanger
Haugesund
Bergen
TELEMARK
AUST-AGDER
VEST-AGDER
ROGALAND
Lillehammer
Hamar
Gjøvik
Kongsvinger
Kongsberg
Hønefoss
OPPLAND
BUSKERUD
HEDMARK
SOGN OG FJORDANE
HORDALAND
Galdhøpiggen
2468
Jotunheimen

SWEDEN
VÄRMLAND
Karlstad
Arvika
Kristinehamn
Filipstad
Hagfors
Falun
Borlänge
Gävle
Sandviken
Söderhamn
Hudiksvall
GÄVLEBORG
DALARNA
KOPPARBERG
Mora
Siljan
ÖREBRO
Lidköping
Mariestad
Skövde
Falköping
Ulricehamn
Alingsås
VÄSTMANLAND
Sala
Köping
Arboga
Hällefors
Ludvika
Avesta
Hedemora
Fagersta
SÖDERMANLAND

East from Greenwich
Projection: Conical with two standard parallels

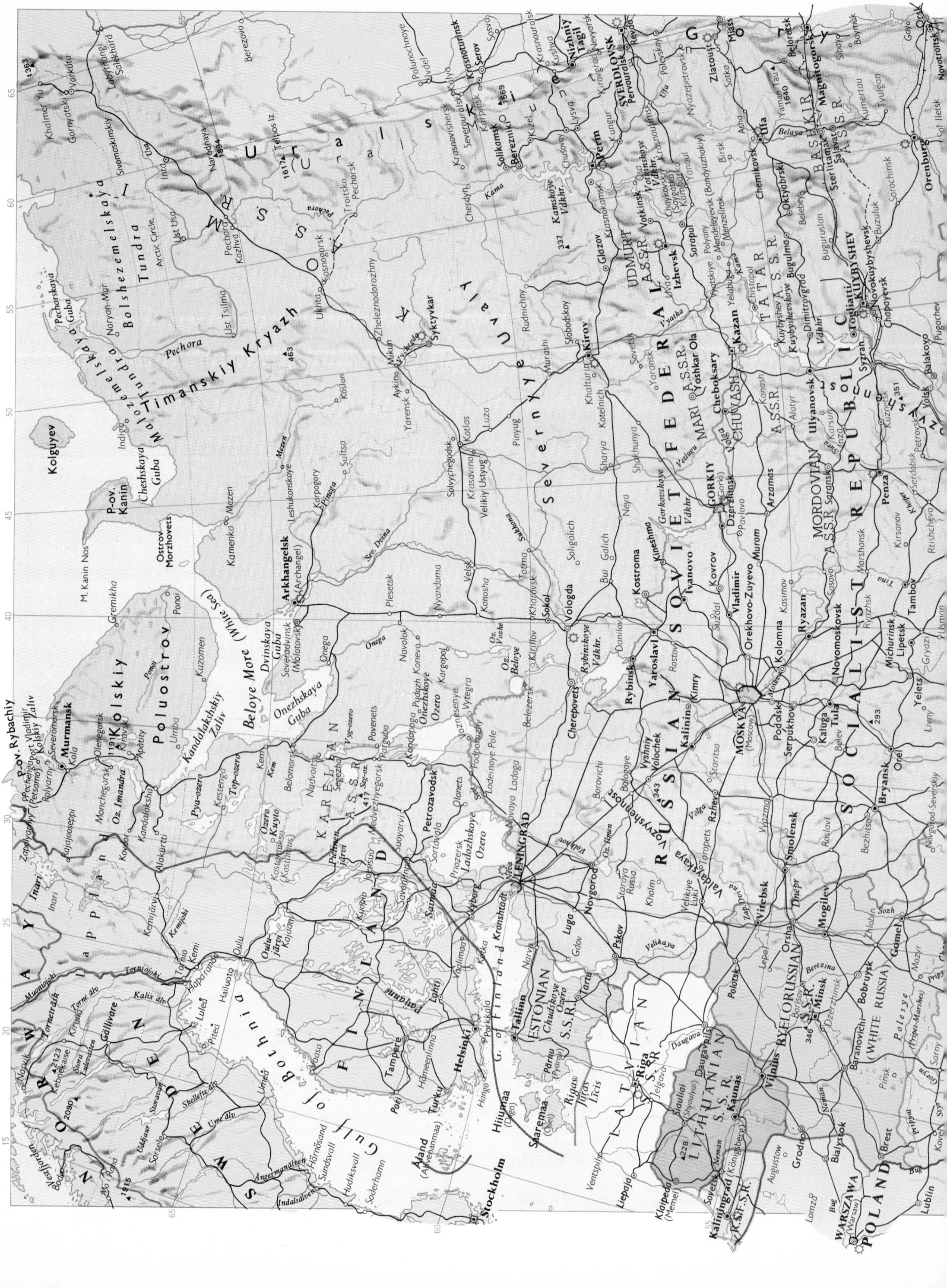

Kolguyev
P-ov. Kanin
Cheshskaya Guba
Timanskiy Kryazh
Malozemelskaya Tundra
Bolshezemelskaya Tundra
Pechorskaya Guba
Pechora
Arctic Circle
Ural Mts.
Severnyye Uvaly
Beloye More (White Sea)
Dvinskaya Guba
Onezhskaya Guba
Kandalakshskiy Zaliv
Kolskiy Poluostrov
P-ov. Rybachiy
Murmansk
Arkhangelsk (Archangel)
Ostrov Morzhovets
Kamenka
Mezen
Kotlas
Syktyvkar
Kirov
Perm
SVERDLOVSK
Nizhniy Tagil
Zlatoust
Magnitogorsk
Orenburg
Ufa
Kazan
GORKIY
Vologda
Yaroslavl
Ivanovo
Kostroma
Vladimir
MOSKVA (Moscow)
Kalinin
Tula
Ryazan
Kaluga
Bryansk
Orel
Smolensk
Vitebsk
Mogilev
Minsk
Gomel
Vilnius
Kaunas
Riga
Tallinn
Pskov
Novgorod
LENINGRAD
Petrozavodsk
Ladozhskoye Ozero
Onezhskoye Ozero
Rybinskoye Vdkhr.
Penza
Ulyanovsk
KUYBYSHEV
Syzran
Tambov
Lipetsk
Helsinki
Tampere
Turku
Oulu
Stockholm
WARSZAWA (Warsaw)
Kaliningrad (Königsberg)
Gulf of Bothnia
G. of Finland
FINLAND
SWEDEN
NORWAY
LAPPLAND
POLAND
KARELIAN A.S.S.R.
ESTONIAN S.S.R.
LATVIAN S.S.R.
LITHUANIAN S.S.R.
BYELORUSSIAN S.S.R. (WHITE RUSSIA)
RUSSIAN SOVIET FEDERAL SOCIALIST REPUBLIC
UDMURT A.S.S.R.
TATAR A.S.S.R.
CHUVASH A.S.S.R.
MARI A.S.S.R.
MORDOVIAN A.S.S.R.
BASHKIR A.S.S.R.
Polesye (Pripet Marshes)

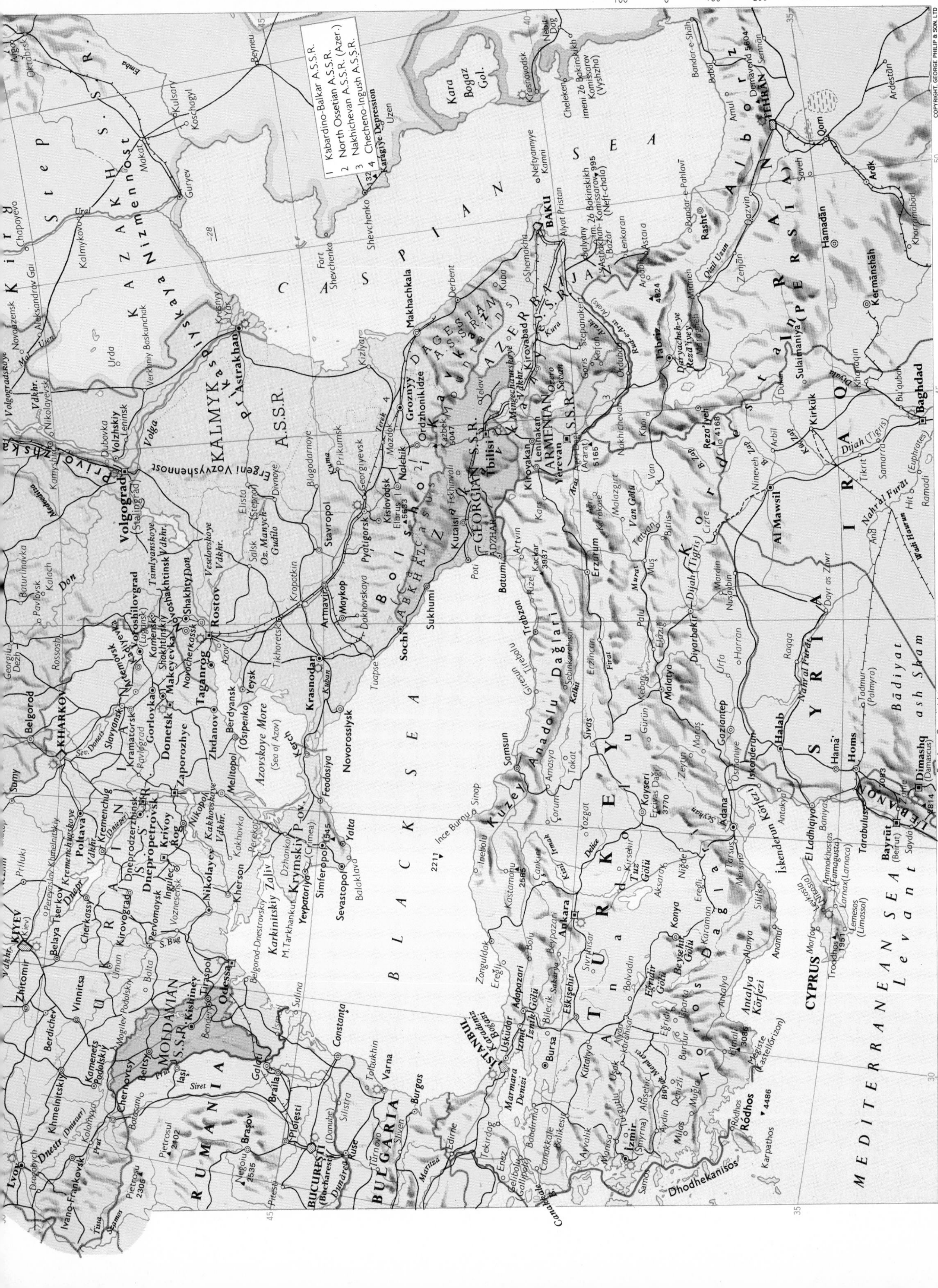

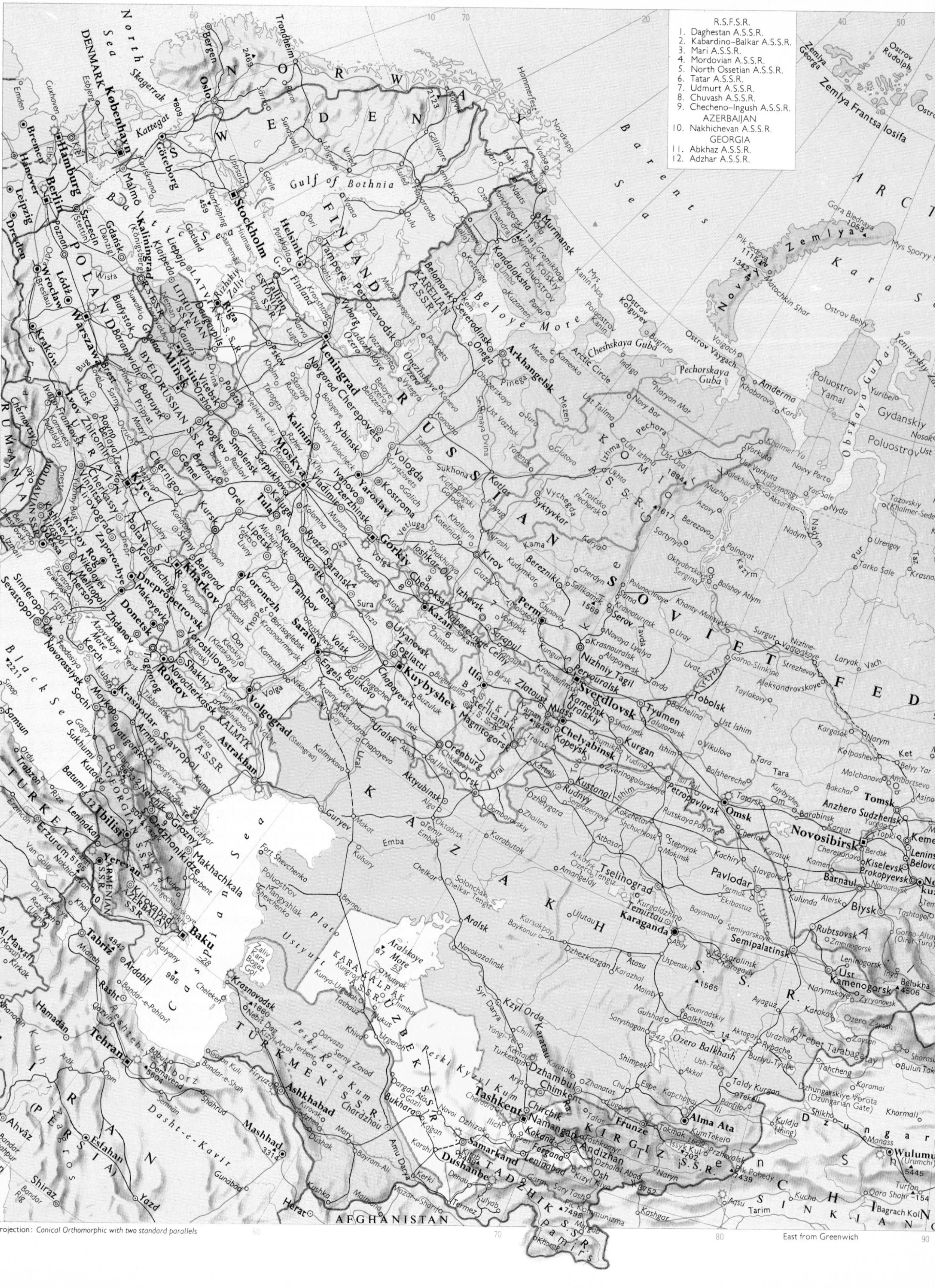

R.S.F.S.R.
1. Daghestan A.S.S.R.
2. Kabardino–Balkar A.S.S.R.
3. Mari A.S.S.R.
4. Mordovian A.S.S.R.
5. North Ossetian A.S.S.R.
6. Tatar A.S.S.R.
7. Udmurt A.S.S.R.
8. Chuvash A.S.S.R.
9. Checheno–Ingush A.S.S.R.
AZERBAIJAN
10. Nakhichevan A.S.S.R.
GEORGIA
11. Abkhaz A.S.S.R.
12. Adzhar A.S.S.R.

Projection: *Conical Orthomorphic with two standard parallels*   East from Greenwich

1:20 000 000

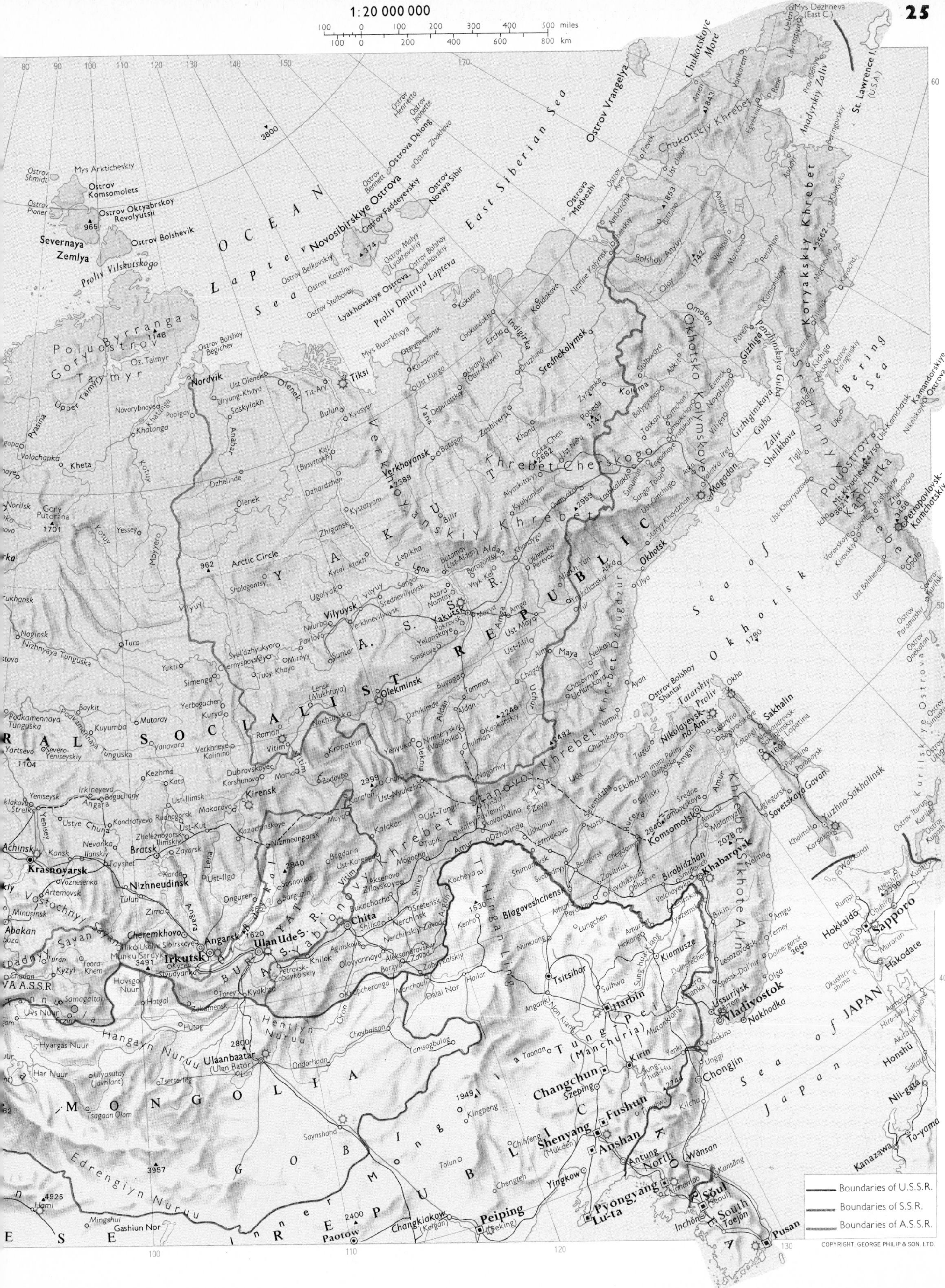

100 0 100 200 300 400 500 miles
100 0 200 400 600 800 km
Boundaries of U.S.S.R.
Boundaries of S.S.R.
Boundaries of A.S.S.R.
OCEAN
Laptev Sea
East Siberian Sea
Bering Sea
Sea of Okhotsk
Sea of Japan
Severnaya Zemlya
Novosibirskiye Ostrova
Ostrov Vrangelya
Chukotskoye More
Chukotskiy Khrebet
Koryakskiy Khrebet
Poluostrov Kamchatka
Poluostrov Taymyr
Verkhoyanskiy Khrebet
Khrebet Cherskogo
Khrebet Dzhugdzur
Stanovoy Khrebet
Yablonovyy Khrebet
Sikhote Alin
Sakhalin
Kurilskiye Ostrova
Hokkaido
Honshū
YAKUTSK A.S.S.R.
BURYAT A.S.S.R.
MONGOLIA
INNER MONGOLIA
NORTH KOREA
SOUTH KOREA
Tung Pei (Manchuria)
Arctic Circle
Yakutsk
Verkhoyansk
Magadan
Okhotsk
Petropavlovsk-Kamchatskiy
Khabarovsk
Komsomolsk
Blagoveshchensk
Vladivostok
Nakhodka
Irkutsk
Angarsk
Ulan Ude
Chita
Krasnoyarsk
Bratsk
Ulaanbaatar (Ulan Bator)
Harbin
Changchun
Kirin
Shenyang (Mukden)
Fushun
Anshan
Peiping (Peking)
Changkiakow (Kalgan)
Paotow
Lu-ta
Pyongyang
Sŏul (Seoul)
Pusan
Sapporo
Hakodate
Yuzhno-Sakhalinsk
Tiksi
Nordvik
COPYRIGHT. GEORGE PHILIP & SON. LTD.

1:50 000 000

250   0   250   500   750   1000 miles
250   0   500   1000   1500 km

PACIFIC OCEAN

ARCTIC OCEAN

INDIAN OCEAN

Aleutian Is.
7822
Bering Sea
Bering Str.
C. Dezhnev
Kamchatka Peninsula
Andreanof Vol. 4750
Sredinny Ra.
Sea of Okhotsk
Kurili Is.
10 542
Hokkaido
Sakhalin
Honshu
Japan
Sea of Japan
Kyushu
Shikoku
Ryukyu Is.
East China Sea
Tsugaru Str.
Koreo Str.
Yellow Sea
Korea
Formosa
Bonin Is.
Volcano Is.
Guam
Caroline Is.
Pelew Is.
Philippine Is.
Luzon
Cape Johnson Deep 10 497
Mindanao
Halmahera
Moluccas
Celebes
Ceram
Banda Sea
Celebes Sea
Sulu Sea
Palawan
Kinabalu 4100
Borneo
Makasar Strait
Flores
Timor
Arafura Sea
Java Sea
Eastern
Java
Bali
Sunda Str.
Sumatra
Sunda Is.
Malay Peninsula
Str. of Malacca
G. of Siam
Menam
Mekong
Tonkin
G. of Tonkin
Si-kiang
Hainan
Hwang
South China Sea
Great Plain of China
Chin
Kunlun Shan
Plateau of Tibet
Tsangpo
Everest 8840
Kunlun Shan
Koko Nor
Tsaidam
Altai
Plateau of Mongolia
Gobi
Manchurian Plain
Great Khingan Mts.
Amur
Stanovoy Ra.
Yablonovy Ra.
Aldan
Lena
Lop Nor
Takla Makan
Tarim Basin
Tarim
Turfan Basin
Tien Shan
Pamirs
Communism Pk. 7495
Hindu Kush
Karakoram Ra. K2 8611
Himalaya
Brahmaputra
Ganges
Yamuna
Suldej
India
Thar Desert
Salween
Irrawaddy
Bay of Bengal
Andaman Is.
Nicobar Is.
Ceylon
Polk Strait
C. Comorin
Maldive Is.
Laccadive Is.
Chagos Arch.
Godavari
Krishna
Western Ghats
Eastern Ghats
Deccan
Narmada
Gulf of Kutch
Arabian Sea
Thar
Salaiman Ra.
Helmand
Plateau of Iran
Amu Darya
Syr Darya
Aral Sea
Turanian Plain
Lake Balkhash
Ili
Chu
Belukha 4506
Sayan Mts.
Selenga
Angara
Lower Tunguska
Central Siberian Plateau
Yenisei
Ob
Irtysh
West Siberian Plain
Tobol
Irtysh
Naradnaya 1894
Ural Mountains
1640
Ural
Volga
Steppe
Caspian Sea
Elburz Mts.
Demavend 5604
Great Salt Desert
Ararat 5165
Tigris
Euphrates
Mesopotamia
Persian Gulf
G. of Oman
Ar Rub'al Khali
Arabia
Syrian Desert
Red Sea
Dead Sea
Sinai Pen.
Suez Canal
Nile
G. of Aden
Socotra
Ras Asir (C. Guardafui)
Somali Peninsula
Seychelles
Amirantes
Lake Victoria
Libyan Desert
Mediterranean Sea
Cyprus
Anatolia
Taurus Mts.
Bosporus
Black Sea
Caucasus
Elbrus 5633
Dnieper
Don
Adriatic Sea
Danube
Carpathians
Elbe
Oder
Vistula
Rhine
North Sea
British Isles
Iceland
Greenland
Arctic Circle
Scandinavia
Finland
Baltic Sea
North European Plain
Central Russian Uplands
White Sea
N. Dvina
Kola Pen.
North Cape
Kolguyev
Barents Sea
Novaya Zemlya
Kara Sea
Severnaya Zemlya
Chelyuskin
Taimyr Peninsula
Kotuy
Olenek
Khatanga
Laptev Sea
New Siberian Is.
Indigirka
Kolyma
Gydan Ra. (Kolyma)
Verkhoyansk Range
Wrangel I.
Svalbard
Tropic of Cancer
Equator
East from Greenwich
Australia
New Guinea

Projection: Bonne

m: 6000 4000 2000 1000 400 200 0
ft: 18 000 12 000 6000 3000 1200 600 0

0 200 2000/6000 6000/18 000 6000/24 000
0 -200 -2000 -6000 m
ft

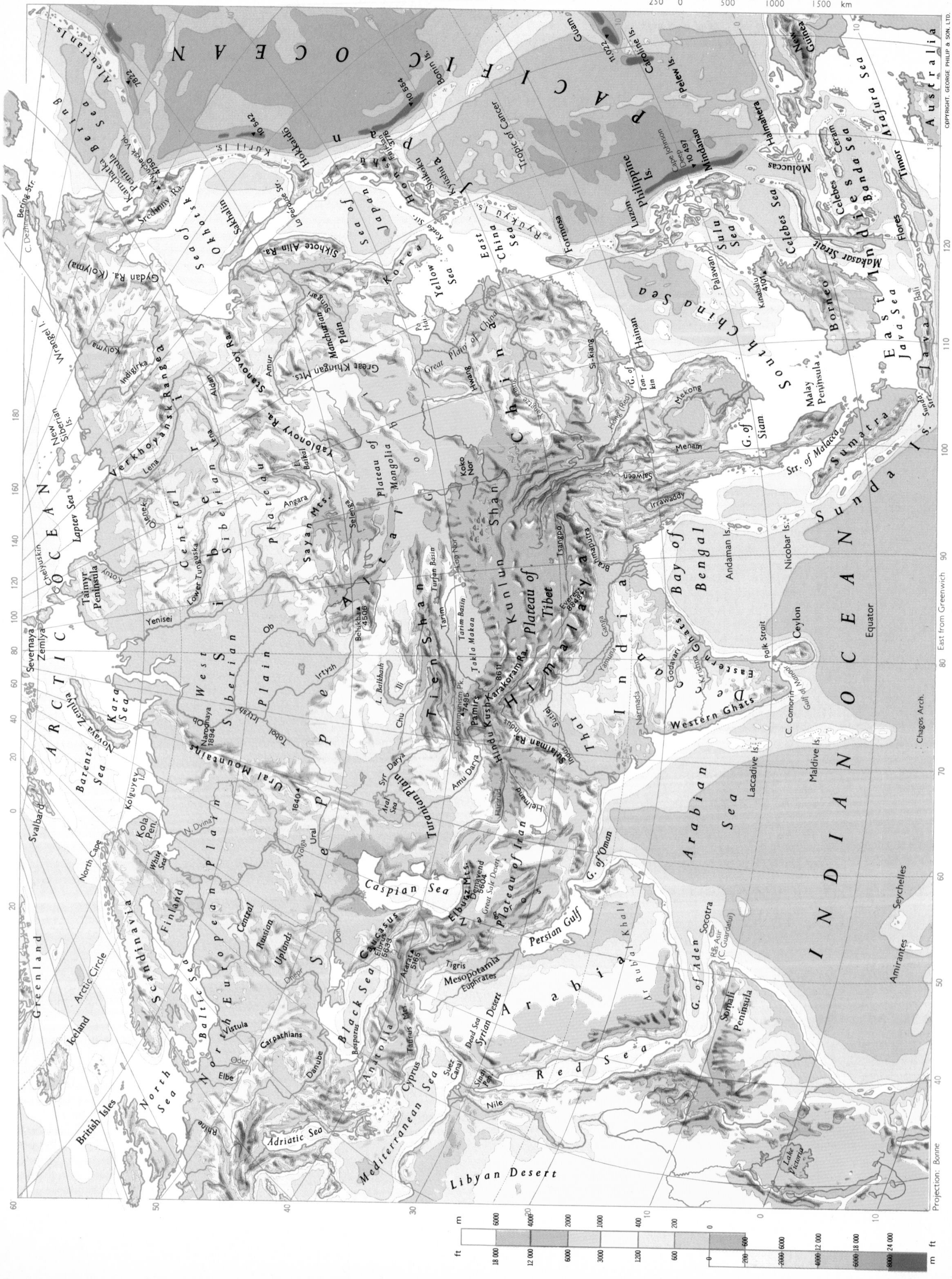

1:50 000 000

250   0   250   500   750   1000 miles
250   0   500   1000   1500 km

PACIFIC OCEAN

ARCTIC OCEAN

INDIAN OCEAN

S. S. R.

Bering Sea
Aleutian Is.
Sea of Okhotsk
Kamchatskiy
Sakhalin
Kuril Is.
Hokkaido
Tokyo
Yokohama
Kyoto
Osaka
JAPAN
Sea of Japan
Vladivostok
Khabarovsk
Manchuria
Harbin
Changchun
Shenyang
Peking
Tientsin
KOREA
Pusan
Nagasaki
Shanghai
Nanking
Wuhan
Yellow Sea
East China Sea
Ryukyu
Tropic of Cancer

MONGOLIA
INNER MONGOLIA
Ulaanbaatar (Ulan Bator)
Chita
Irkutsk
Lake Baykal
Wulumuchi (Urumchi)
SINKIANG UIGUR
CHINESE REPUBLIC
CHINA
TIBET
Lhasa
Chengtu
Chungking
Lanchow
Sian
Canton
Hong Kong
Macau
Hainan
Foochow
Amoy
Tsingtao

U. S. S. R.
Lena
Yakutsk
Tunguska
Krasnoyarsk
Novosibirsk
Omsk
Tomsk
Barnaul
Semipalatinsk
Yenisey
Ob
Sverdlovsk
Chelyabinsk
Magnitogorsk
Orenburg
Tobolsk
Alma Ata
Tashkent
Samarkand
Bukhara
Ashkhabad
Khiva
Syr Darya
U R A L S
Kara Sea
Barents Sea
Novaya Zemlya
Severnaya Zemlya
Svalbard
Murmansk
Arkhangelsk
Leningrad
Moskva
Volga
Astrakhan
Rostov
Caspian Sea
Baku
Tbilisi
Yerevan
Tabriz
Tehran
IRAN (PERSIA)
Esfahan
Shiraz
Bandar e Bushehr
AFGHANISTAN
Kabul
Herat
Kandahar
Quetta
Mashhad
Zahedan

PAKISTAN
Peshawar
Lahore
Karachi
KASHMIR
Delhi
Agra
Kanpur
Lucknow
Allahabad
Varanasi
INDIA
NEPAL
BANGLADESH
Calcutta
Hyderabad
Bombay
Ahmadabad
Madras
Pondicherry
Bangalore
Calicut
Goa
SRI LANKA (CEYLON)
Colombo
Bay of Bengal
Arabian Sea
Andaman Is. (India)
Nicobar Is. (India)
Laccadive Is.
Maldive Is.

BURMA
Rangoon
Mandalay
Irrawaddy
Mytkyina
THAILAND (SIAM)
Bangkok
LAOS
VIETNAM
Hanoi
CAMBODIA
Saigon
G. of Tong king
G. of Siam
Chungking
Yunnan
Kunming
PHILIPPINES
Manila
Luzon
Mindanao
Davao
Zamboanga
South China Sea
Sulu Sea
Celebes Sea
MALAYA
MALAYSIA
Kuala Lumpur
Kuching
Singapore
BRUNEI
SARAWAK
SABAH
Borneo
Sumatera
Jakarta
Jawa
INDONESIA
Sulawesi
Maluku (Moluccas)
Halmahera
Ceram
Banda Sea
Flores
Timor
New Guinea
Irian
Caroline Is.
Palau Is.

AUSTRALIA
Darwin
Thursday I.

SAUDI ARABIA
Al Madinah
Makkah (Mecca)
Riyadh
Al Basrah
Baghdad
IRAQ
Euphrates
Tigris
KUWAIT
BAHRAIN
QATAR
UNITED ARAB EMIRATES
OMAN
Muscat
G. of Oman
Persian Gulf
YEMEN
SOUTH YEMEN (South Yemen)
Aden
G. of Aden
Socotra
SYRIA
Halab
Dimashq
JORDAN
ISRAEL
LEBANON
Bayrut
Jerusalem
TURKEY
Ankara
Istanbul
Izmir
Erzurum
Black Sea
Red Sea

EUROPE
London
Paris
Berlin
Wien
Warszawa
Roma
Beograd
Thessaloniki
Athinai
Odesa
Danube
Rhine
Mediterranean Sea
North Sea
Baltic Sea
UNITED KINGDOM
ICELAND

AFRICA
EGYPT
LIBYA
SUDAN
El Khartum
El Obeid
ETHIOPIA
Addis Abeba
SOMALI REP.
Mogadishu
KENYA
Nairobi
Mombasa
UGANDA
TANZANIA
Dar es Salaam
ZAIRE
ZAMBIA
MALAWI
SEYCHELLES
Amirantes
Equator

East from Greenwich

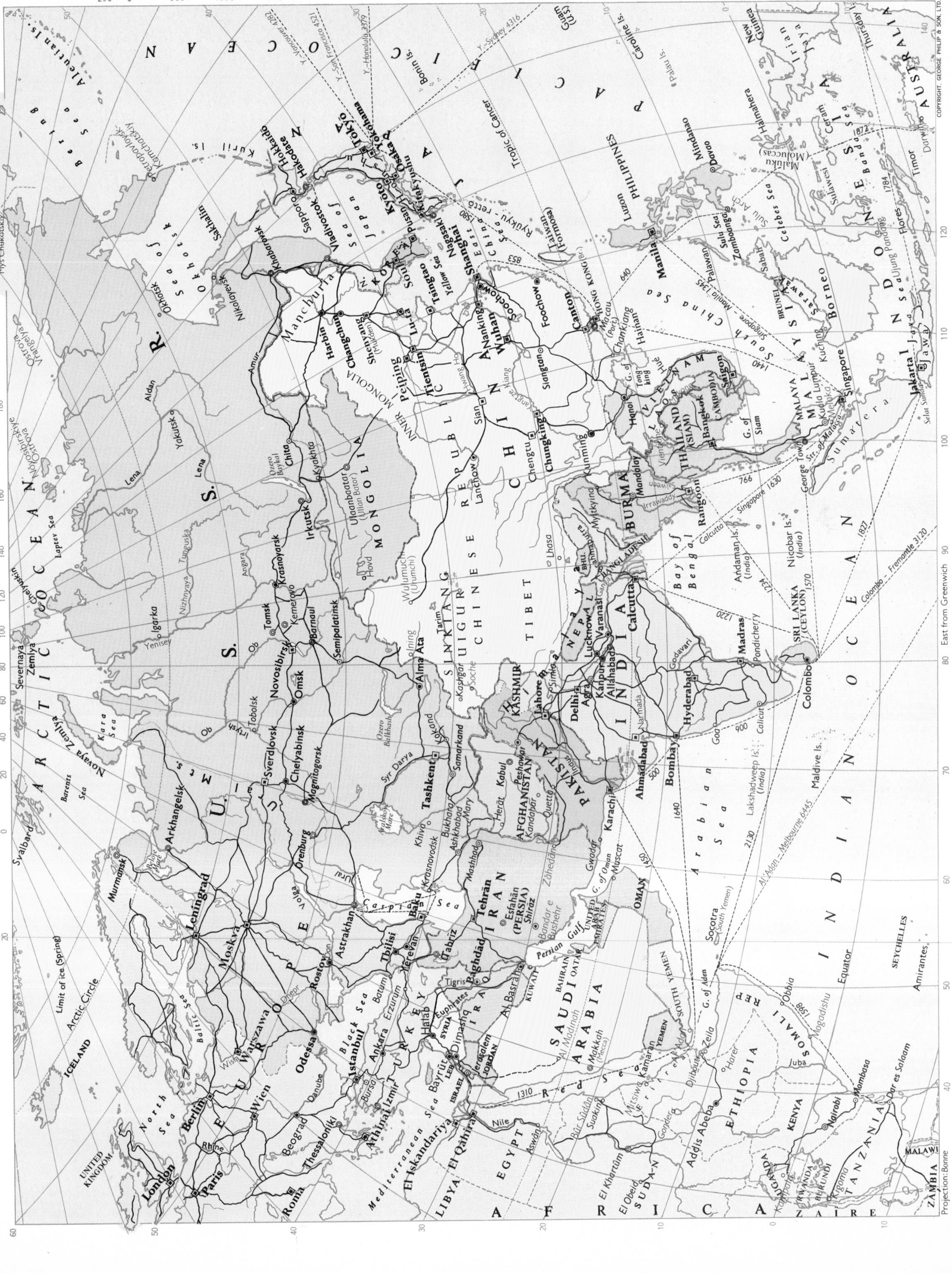

1 : 1 000 000

10   0   10   20 miles
10   0   10   20   30 km

1949–1967 Armistice lines between
Israel and the Arab States.

LEBANON

SYRIA

MEDITERRANEAN SEA

HAIFA

Hagalil
(Galilee)

KEFAR NAHUM
(CAPERNAUM)

Yam Kinneret
(Sea of
Galilee)
−209

Nazareth

Tiberias

MEGIDDO

'Afula

Shomron
(Samaria)

Nabulus
SHECHEM
JACOB'S WELL

Netanya

Tūlkarm

SAMARIA

Under   Israeli   JORDAN

TEL AVIV
YAFO (Jaffa)

Ramat
Gan

Petah Tiqwa

Bat Yam
Holon

Occupation

Rishon Le Zion

Ramla
Rehovot

'AMMĀN

Ashdod

Rām Allāh

Al Barah

El Arīhā

As Salt

Az-Zarqā'

JERUSALEM
(Yerūshalayim, Al Quds)

Bayt Lahm (Bethlehem)

BURAK SULAYMAN
(SOLOMON'S POOLS)

Ashqelon

Qiryat Gat

BET GUVRIN
TEL
LAKHISH

Hebron

Gaza

Gaza
Strip

Khān
Yūnis

Be'er Sheva'

MESADA

EGYPT

ISRAEL

Gaza

Khān
Yūnis

Gaza
Strip

Hebron

Be'er Sheva'

Dimona

ISRAEL

Ha Negev

SHIVTA

Makhtesh Ramon

EGYPT

JORDAN

PETRA

1727

Continuation
Southwards
1 : 2 500 000
0   10   20 miles
0   10   20   30 km

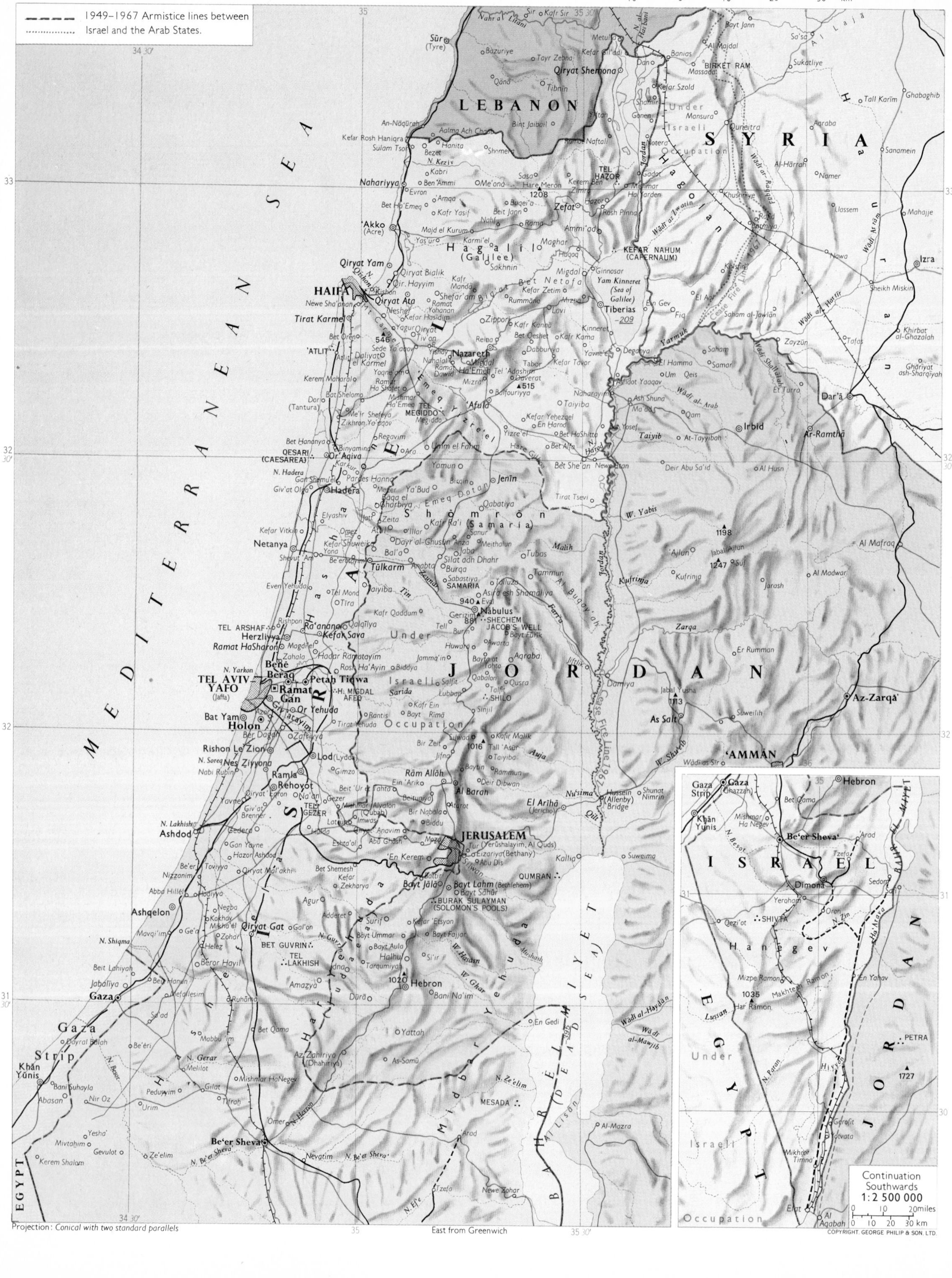

Projection: Conical with two standard parallels

East from Greenwich

COPYRIGHT GEORGE PHILIP & SON. LTD.

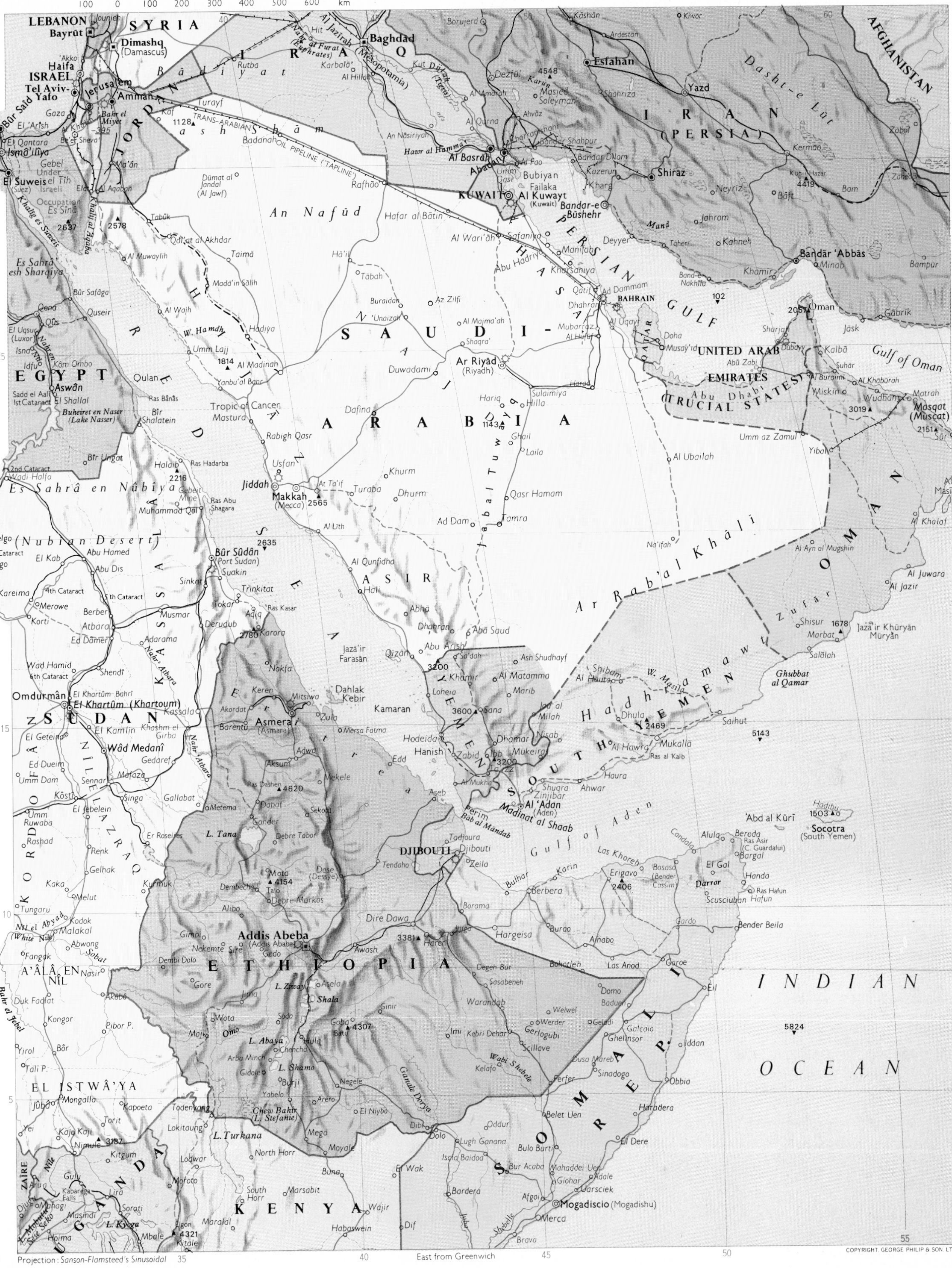

1:15 000 000

SYRIA
LEBANON
Bayrūt
Jounieh
Dimashq
(Damascus)
Haifa
ISRAEL
Tel Aviv-
Yafo
Jerusalem
Amman
Gaza
Bahr el
Miyet
El 'Arīsh
Bûr Said
El Qantara
Ismā'ilīya
El Suweis
(Suez)
Gebel
Under
Es Sīnâ
El Aqaba
Khalig es Suweis
Israeli
Occupation
Tîh

SYRIA
IRAQ
Hit
Al Jazīra
Ar
(Mesopotamia)
Baghdād
al Furāt
(Euphrates)
Rutba
Kut Dûra
Karbalā'
Al Hillah
Turayf
TRANS-ARABIAN
OIL PIPELINE (TAPLINE)
Badanah
Rafhāo
An Nāsiriyah
Al Qurna
Al 'Amāra
Hawr al Hamma
Al Basrah
At Fao
Umm
Qasr
Bubiyan
Failaka
KUWAIT
Al Kuwayt
(Kuwait)
Hafar al Bātin
Safānīya
Al Warī'āh
Abu Hadrīy
Al Hasā

AFGHANISTAN
Borūjerd
Kāshān
Khvor
Ardestan
Esfahān
Dezfūl
Karūn
Masjed-e
Soleymān
Shahrezā
Yazd
IRAN
(PERSIA)
Dasht-e Lūt
Kermān
Zābol
Ahvāz
Bākhtarān
Bandar Shāhpur
Ābādān
Bandar Dīom
Bandar-e
Būshehr
Kharg
Kāzerūn
Shīrāz
Neyrīz
Bam
Bandar 'Abbās
Minab
Kahneh
Mand
Deyyer
Tāheri
Khāmir
Gābrik
Bampūr

EGYPT
El Uqsur
(Luxor)
Qena
Qūs
Ras Bānās
Bīr
Shalatein
Būr Safāga
Quseir
Aswān
Tropic of Cancer
Buheiret en Nâser
(Lake Nasser)
2nd Cataract
Wādi Halfa
Abri
Delgo
(Nubian Desert)
3rd Cataract
Argo
El Kab
Kareima
Korti
Merowe
4th Cataract

An Nafūd
2637
2578
Tabūk
Qal'at al Akhdar
Al Muwaylih
Taimā
Madā'in Sālih
Hā'il
Tābah
Buraidan
Az Zilfi
N 'Unaizah
Al Majma'ah
Shaqra'
1814
Al Madinah
Duwadami
Ar Riyād
(Riyadh)
Harīq
Hilla
Sulaimiya
Hared
Al Wajh
Umm Lajj
Yanbu' al Bahr
Rabigh
Qasr
Dafina
Khurm
Ghail
Laila
Al Ubailah
SAUDI-ARABIA
JABAL TUWAIQ
1143
Qasr Hamam
Hadiya
Mastura
Usfan
Jiddah
Makkah
(Mecca)
At Tā'if
Turaba
Dhurm
Tamra
2565
Ad Dam
Al Līth
Na'ifah
Ar Rab' al Khālī

BAHRAIN
Dhahrān
Al Dammam
102
QATAR
Al 'Uqayr
Mubarraz
Al Hufūf
Doha
Musay'id
UNITED ARAB
EMIRATES
(TRUCIAL STATES)
Abū Zabi
Abu Dhabi
Dubay
Sharjah
Kalbā
2057
Oman
Umm az Zamul
Yibal
Al Buraimi
Miskin
Suhār
Al Khābūrah
3019
OMAN
2151
Masqat
(Muscat)
Matrah
Sūr
Al Māsīrah
Al Khalaf
Al Ayn al Mugshin
Shisur
1678
Jazā'ir Khūryān
Mūryān
Marbat
Salālah
Ghubbat al Qamar
Zufār
Gulf of Oman
Jāsk
Khāmir
Bandar 'Abbās

RED SEA
Es Sahrā esh Sharqīya
W. Hamdh
Halaib
2216
Ras Hadarba
2635
Bûr Sûdân
(Port Sudan)
Suakin
Sinkat
Tokar
Trinkitat
Ras Kasar
Muhammad Qol
Ras Abu Shagara
Bīr
ASIR
Al Qunfidha
Hali
Abha
2780
Karora
Jazā'ir Farasān
Qizān
Jīzān
3200
Al Khamir
Abu Arīsh
Sa'dah
Ash Shudhayf
Marib
Al Matamma
Loheia
Al Milah
Kamaran
Sana
3600
YEMEN
3200
Zabid
Ibb
Hodeida
Mukeiras
Dhamar
Nisab
SOUTH
Al Hawra
Mukalla
Dhula
2469
Saihut
5143
Shibam
Al Hauta
W. Masīla
HADHRAMAUT
W. Hadramaut

SUDAN
Es Sahrā en Nūbīya
Abu Hamed
Abu Dis
Atbara
Berber
Muḥar
Ed Dāmer
Wad Hamid
5th Cataract
Nahr-el-Atbara
Shendi
Adarama
Derudeb
Aqiq
Omdurmân
El Khartûm Bahri
El Khartûm (Khartoum)
Kassala
Keren
Mitsiwa
Dahlak Kebir
Asmera (Asmara)
Akordat
Khashm el
Girba
Gedaref
Barentu
Zula
Adwa
Mersa Fatma
ERITREA
Aksum
Edd
Hanish
Adigrat
Mekele
Massawa
Bab el Mandeb
Perim
Madinat al Shaab
Al 'Adan
Aden
(South Yemen)
SOUTH YEMEN
Shuqra
Zinjibar
Ahwar
Ras al Kalb
Gulf of Aden
'Abd al Kūrī
1503
Socotra
(South Yemen)
Hadibu
Candala
Bereda
Ras Asir
(C. Guardafui)
Bargal
Alula
Bosaso
(Bender Cassim)
El Gal
Darror
Handa
Scuscīubān
Ras Hafun

Wād Medanî
Sennar
Singa
Gedaref
Mafaza
ZILELAZRAQ
Er Roseires
Gallabat
Metema
Gonder
L. Tana
4620
Ras Dashen
Dabat
Sekota
Debre Tabor
Debre Markos
Dembecha
Talo
4154
Mota
Dase (Dessye)
Tendaho
DJIBOUTI
Djibouti
Tadjoura
Zeila
Bulhar
Borama
Berbera
2406
Erigavo
Las Khoreh
Karin
Bosaso
SOMALI
Burao
Hargeisa
Las Anod
Eil
Garoe
INDIAN
OCEAN

KORDOFAN
El Jebelein
Kôsti
Ed Dueim
Umm Dam
Rashad
Renk
Gelhak
Kaka
Melut
Nahr
Nil el Abyad
(White Nile)
Kodok
Malakal
Fangak
Abwong
Sobat
A'ÂLÂ EN NÎL
Nasir
Zeraf
Bahr el Jebel
Duk Fadiat
Kongor
Bor
Pibor P.
Yirol
Tali P.
EL ISTWÂ'YA
Jūba
Mongalla
Kapoeta
Torit
Kaja Kaji
Nimule
3187
Kitgum
Gulu
ZAÏRE
UGANDA
L. Kyoga
Masindi
Hoima
4321
Mbale
L. Kyoga

ETHIOPIA
Nekemte
Gimbi
Dembi Dolo
Sire
Gedo
Addis Abeba
(Addis Ababa)
Awash
Harer
3381
Dire Dawa
Jima
Gore
L. Zway
Asela
Welk
Sodo
L. Shala
Ginir
Degeh Bur
Sasabeneh
Warandab
Gobā
4307
Batu
Chenchia
Gidole
L. Abaya
L. Shamo
Burji
Negele
Arero
Ganāle Darya
Wabi Shebele
Kebri Dehar
Imi
Gerlogubi
Welwel
Gelladi
Galcaio
Ghelinsor
5824
Domo
Baduen
Warder
Werder
Kelafo
Perfer
Dusa Mareb
Obbia
SOMALI P.

Chew Bahir
(L. Stefanie)
Arba Minch
Yabelo
El Niybo
Dila
Mega
Moyale
El Wak
Lugh Ganana
Bulo Burti
Dolo
Dinsor
Bulo
Baidoa
Bur Acaba
Afgoi
Giohar
Adale
Warsciek
Mogadiscio (Mogadishu)
Merca
Brava
Bardera
KENYA
North Horr
Marsabit
Wajir
Habaswein
Dif
Isha Baidoa
El Dere
Haradera
Belet Uen
Mahaddei Uen
Bur
Sinadogo

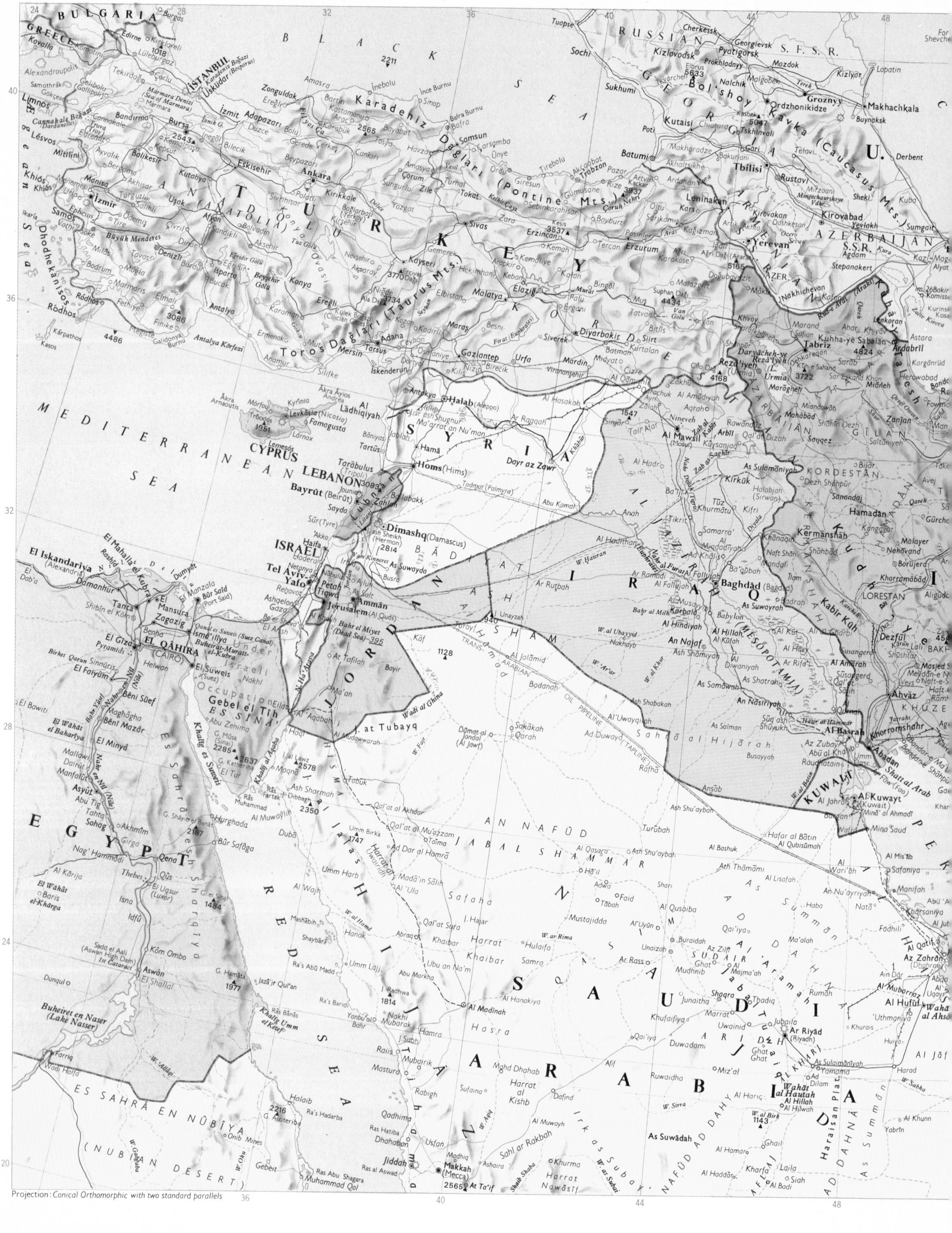

Projection: Conical Orthomorphic with two standard parallels

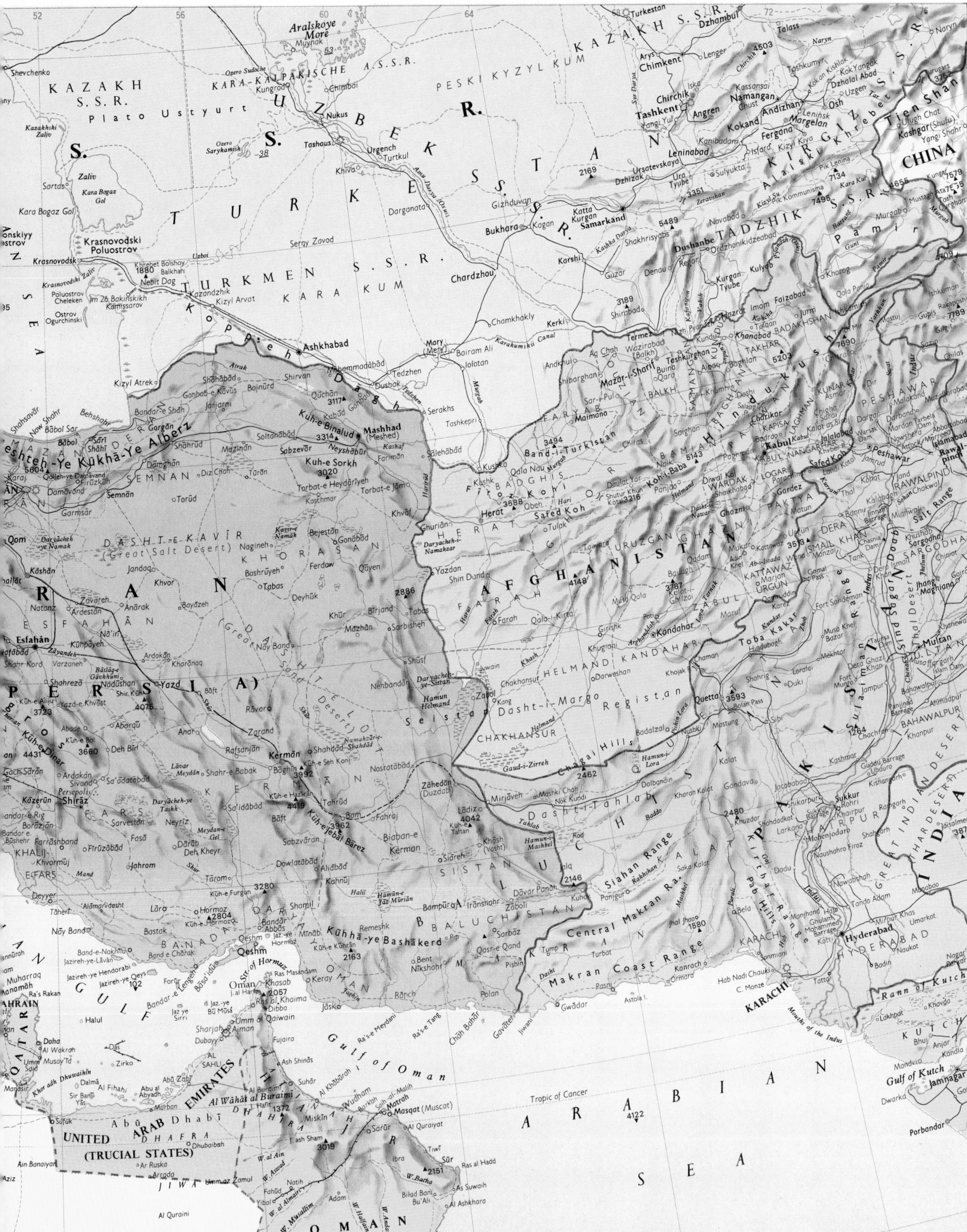

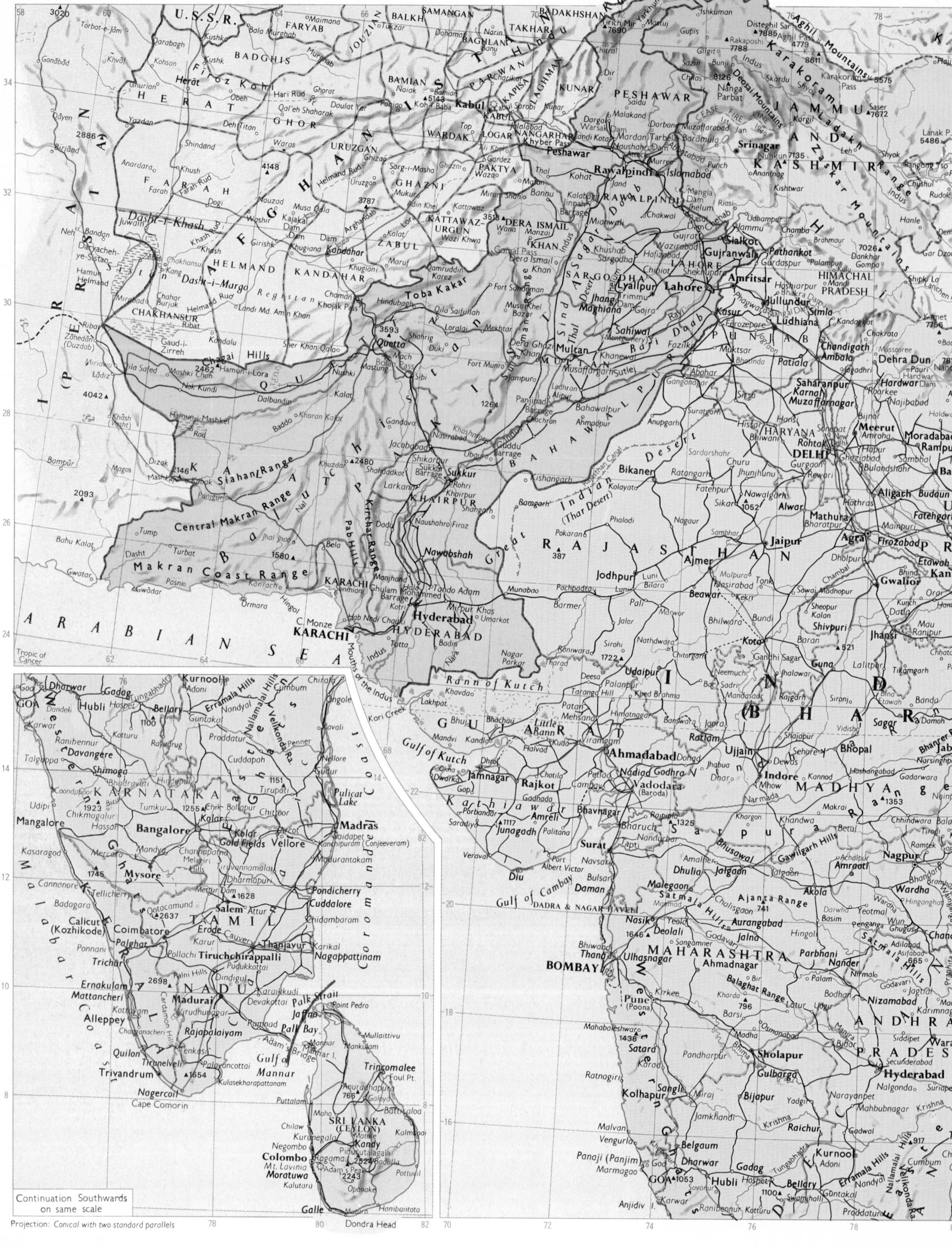

U.S.S.R.

BALKH SAMANGAN BADAKHSHAN

FARYAB JOUZJAN TAKHAR KUNDUZ

BADGHIS BAGHLAN PARWAN KAPISA LAGHMAN KUNAR

HERAT GHOR BAMIAN WARDAK KABUL NANGARHAR PESHAWAR

A F G H A N I S T A N

URUZGAN GHAZNI LOGAR PAKTYA

FARAH KANDAHAR ZABUL KATTAWAZ-URGUN KHAN DERA ISMAIL

HELMAND CHAKHANSUR

I R A N (P E R S I A)

CHAGAI Hills QUETTA

Siahan Range Central Makran Range Makran Coast Range

A R A B I A N S E A

B A L U C H I S T A N Kirthar Range Pab Hills

KARACHI HYDERABAD KHAIRPUR

JAMMU and KASHMIR Karakoram Range Ladakh Range

Srinagar PESHAWAR Rawalpindi Islamabad

HIMACHAL PRADESH

Lahore Amritsar Jullundur Simla Ludhiana

SARGODHA P U N J A B Chandigarh Ambala Dehra Dun

Multan BAHAWALPUR Patiala Saharanpur Hardwar

Sind Thar (Indian) Desert Great Thar Desert

Bikaner Meerut DELHI Moradabad Rampur

R A J A S T H A N HARYANA

Jaipur Agra Gwalior Jhansi

Jodhpur Ajmer Alwar Mathura

Rann of Kutch G U J A R A T Udaipur I N D I A (B H A R A T)

Gulf of Kutch Ahmadabad Ujjain Indore Bhopal M A D H Y A

Jamnagar Rajkot Vadodara (Baroda) MADHYA PRADESH

Kathiawar Junagadh Bhavnagar Surat Nagpur

Gulf of Cambay DADRA & NAGAR HAVELI Nasik Aurangabad Amraoti

Diu Daman M A H A R A S H T R A Wardha

BOMBAY Thana Ulhasnagar Ahmadnagar

Pune (Poona) Satara Sholapur A N D H R A P R A D E S H

Kolhapur Sangli Bijapur Gulbarga Hyderabad

Belgaum Panaji (Panjim) GOA Hubli Bellary Kurnool

Inset (Continuation Southwards on same scale)

GOA Dharwar Gadag Kurnool Adoni

Hubli Bellary Erramala Hills Cumbum

Davangere Shimoga K A R N A T A K A Cuddapah Nellore

Mangalore Chikmagalur Bangalore Kolar Gold Fields Vellore Madras

Mysore Salem Pondicherry Cuddalore

Calicut (Kozhikode) Coimbatore Erode T A M I L N A D U Chidambaram

Trichur Tiruchirappalli Thanjavur Nagappattinam

Ernakulam Mattancheri Madurai Karaikkudi Palk Strait

Alleppey Rajapalaiyam Jaffna Mullaittivu

Quilon Tirunelveli Gulf of Mannar Trincomalee

Trivandrum Nagercoil Cape Comorin Adam's Bridge

S R I L A N K A (C E Y L O N) Anuradhapura Batticaloa

Colombo Kandy Moratuwa Mt. Lavinia Adam's Peak 2243 Galle

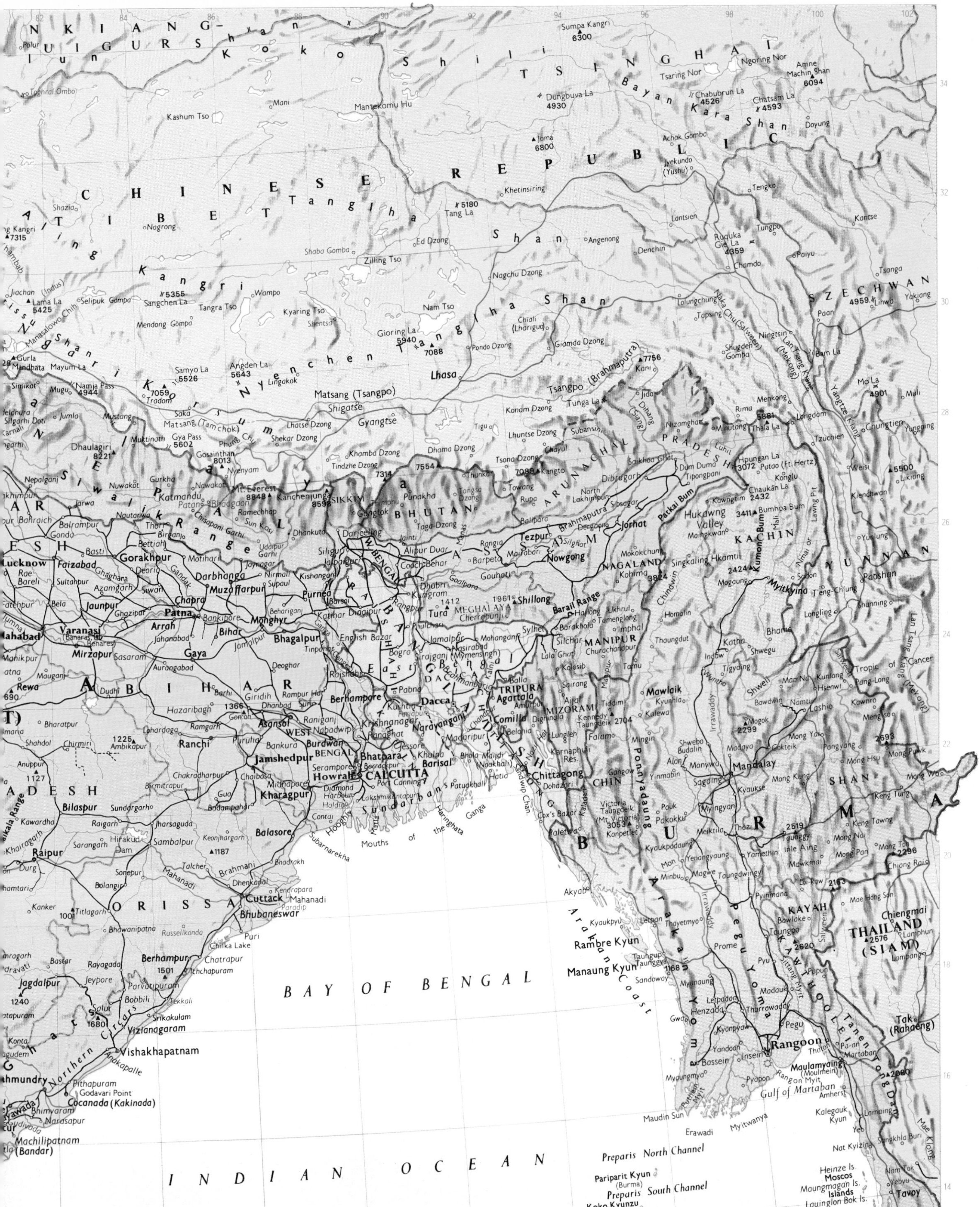

1:10 000 000

50   0   50   100   150   200 miles
50   0   50   100 150 200 250 300 km

N K I A N G-
I u i n G U R S Shan
Polur   Koko Shili   Sumpa Kangri
            Mantekomu Hu   6300
Toghral Ombo   Ngoring Nor
                                    T S I N G H A I   Amne
Kashum Tso   Mani   Dungbuva La   Machin Shan 6094
                                         4930   Tsaring Nor   Chatsam La
                        C H I N E S E   R E P U B L I C   Chabubrun La 4593
                                                          4526 Kara Shan Doyung
                                    Khetinsiring   Achok Gomba
                    T I B E T   T a n g l h a   Shan   Tengko   Kantse
Shazidi   5180   Lantsien
            Tang La   Ed Dzong Tang La   Angenong   Ruguka Tungbo
Kangri   Nagrong   Denchin   Gie La Paiyu
7315   Zilling Tso   Nagchu Dzong   Tapsing Chu(Salween) 4359
            Mendong Gompa   Nam Tso   Shugden Gomba Tsonga
Lama La Selipuk Gompa Sangchen La   Kyaring Tso N yenchen Tanglha Shan Chamdo 4959 Yaklang
5425   5355   Shientso   Nagchu   S Z E C H W A N
Tradom 5526 Samyo La Gioring La 7088 Tsangpo(Brahmaputra)   Paan Mo La Chungtien
Gurla Mayum La   5940 5643   Lhasa   Tsangpo Kani 7756 4901 Muli Yungning
Mandhata   Lingkok   Matsang(Tsangpo)   Nizamghat 5881
Simikot Mugu Namia Pass Lhatse Dzong Matsang(Tam chok) Konda Dzong Tunga Jido Rima Longdam
4944 7059 Tradom Gyangtse Shigatse Gyangtse Giamda Dzong   Minutong 5881 Tzuchien
Jumla   Muktinath Gya Pass Phuntse Ch. Shekar Dzong Tsona Dzong Chayul Subansiri Sadikhoa Ghat Hpungan La 3072 Putao(Ft.Hertz) Weisi 5500
Dhaulagiri Gosainthan Tindzhe Dzong Dhama Dzong Thunki 7089 Kangto North Dibrugarh Tipongpani Konglu Likiang
8221 8013 Kanchenjunga 7314 7554   Rupa Lakhimpur Dum Duma 3411 Bhamo Kienchwan
Nepalganj Nyenyam 8593 SIKKIM Punakha Tongso Towang A R U N A C H A L P R A D E S H Hukawng Bumhpa Bum YUNNAN
Siwalik Gurkha Darjeeling Gangtok BHUTAN Balipara Brahmaputra Jorhat Valley 2432 Myitkyina Teng-Chung
Katmandu Bhadgaon Kanchenjunga Taga-Dzong Rangia A S S A M Dergaon Patkai Bum Maingkwan 2424 Shunning
Thori Birganj Siliguri Jalpaiguri W.BENGAL Cooch Behar Barpeta Gauhati NAGALAND Singkaling Hkamti Longling
Balrampur Nautanwa Uddari Garhi Dhankuta Alipur Duar Dhabri Kurigram Goalpara Kohima Mokokchung Mogaung Teng-Chung
Gorakhpur Motihari Darbhanga Jaynagar Purnea Rangpur 1412 Shillong 3824 Chinowin Bhamo Shwegu
Faizabad Deoria Nirmali Supaul Katihar Dinajpur MEGHALAYA Barail Range Haflong Tamenglong Katha Lashio
Lucknow Bela Muzaffarpur Purnea 1961 Cherrapunji Shillong Ukhrul Imphal Homalin
Rae Bareli Sultanpur Azamgarh Siwan Chapra Bankipore Patna Kishanganj Bogra Jamalpur Mohanganj Sylhet Silchar MANIPUR Thaungdut Indaw
Jaunpur Ghazipur Arrah Bihar Monghyr Bhagalpur English Bazar Tinpara Mymensingh Barakhola Churachandpur Tamu
Varanasi Mirzapur Gaya Jamalpur Rajshahi Pabna BANGLA Sirajganj Balla TRIPURA Aijal MIZORAM Mawlaik Kyaungle
Allahabad Sasaram Auroagabad Barhi Deoghar Rampur Hat Berhampore DESH Dacca Narayanganj Agartala Comilla Diqinada Kennedy 2704 Kalewa
Rewa Dudhi B I H A R Giridih Dhanbad Nabadwip Kushtia Pabna Naraganj Madaripur Bela Falam Mingin
Bharatpur Chirmiri Hazaribagh Asansol Ranaganj WEST Jessore Khulna Barisal Bhola CHIN Gangaw Alon Pakokku
1225 Lohardaga Ramgarh Purulia Bankura BENGAL Burdwan Bhatpara Bonakbackrel Patuakhali Victoria Sagaing Mandalay
Ambikapur Ranchi Chakradharpur Jamshedpur Serampore Howrah CALCUTTA Diamond Barisal Dohazari 3053 Kyaukse Mong Yai
Bilaspur 1127 Gua Midnapore Kharagpur Harbour Haldia Canning Patuakhali Cox's Bazar Kaladan Pauk Myingyan Meiktila
Kawardha Birmitrapur Chaibasa Balasore Contai Sundarbans Ganga Mouths Akyab Mt.Victoria Kanpetlet Kyaukpadaung SHAN
Raipur Raigarh Hirakud Keonjhargarh Bhadrakh Brahmani of the Myohaung Minbu Magwe Taungdwingyi Keng Tung
Durg Sambalpur Talcher Dhenkanal Kendrapara Ganga Ramree Kyun Prome Yenangyaung Yamethin Keng Tawng
Bolangir Sonepur Mahanadi Cuttack Paradip Rambre Kyun Kyaukpyu Letpan Thayetmyo Pyawbwe Lai-Hka
Bhawanipatna Russellkonda Bhubaneswar ORISSA Manaung Kyun Taungup Minhla Madauk Meiktila Mong Pan
Kanker Titlagarh Puri Chatrapur Chilka Lake Sandoway Arakan 1168 BURMA Henzada KAYAH 2296
Jagdalpur Rayagada Berhampur Bastar Akyab Coast Gwa Pyu Tharrawaddy Bawlake Chiengmai Lamphun
Bobbili Jeypore 1501 Itchapuram Bay of Bengal Kyonpyaw Pegu Tungoo Papun Lampang
Salur Tekkali Srikakulam Myanaung Madauk Taungoo 2576 THAILAND(SIAM)
1240 Parvatipuram Vizianagaram Yandoon Thonze Prome 2620
Konta Salur 1680 Vishakhapatnam Bassein Insein Rangoon Mae-Hong Son
Rajahmundry Anakapalle Pithapuram Myaungmya Rangon Myit Maulmyaing(Moulmein) Taka(Rahaeng)
Cocanada(Kakinada) Godavari Point Pyapon Thaton Amherst 2090
Narasapur Bhimavaram Myitwanya Erawadi Gulf of Martaban Pa-an
Machilipatnam(Bandar) INDIAN OCEAN Preparis North Channel Maudin Sun Kalegauk Kyun Lanbe
                                                    Kyun
                        Pariparit Kyun(Burma) Preparis South Channel Heinze Is. Nat Kyizing Lauinglon Bok Is.
                        Koko Kyunzu(Burma) Islands Moscos Tavoy Mae Klong
                                                          Maungmagan Is. Nam Tok
                                                          Yeby Yebyu

B A Y   O F   B E N G A L

Tropic of Cancer

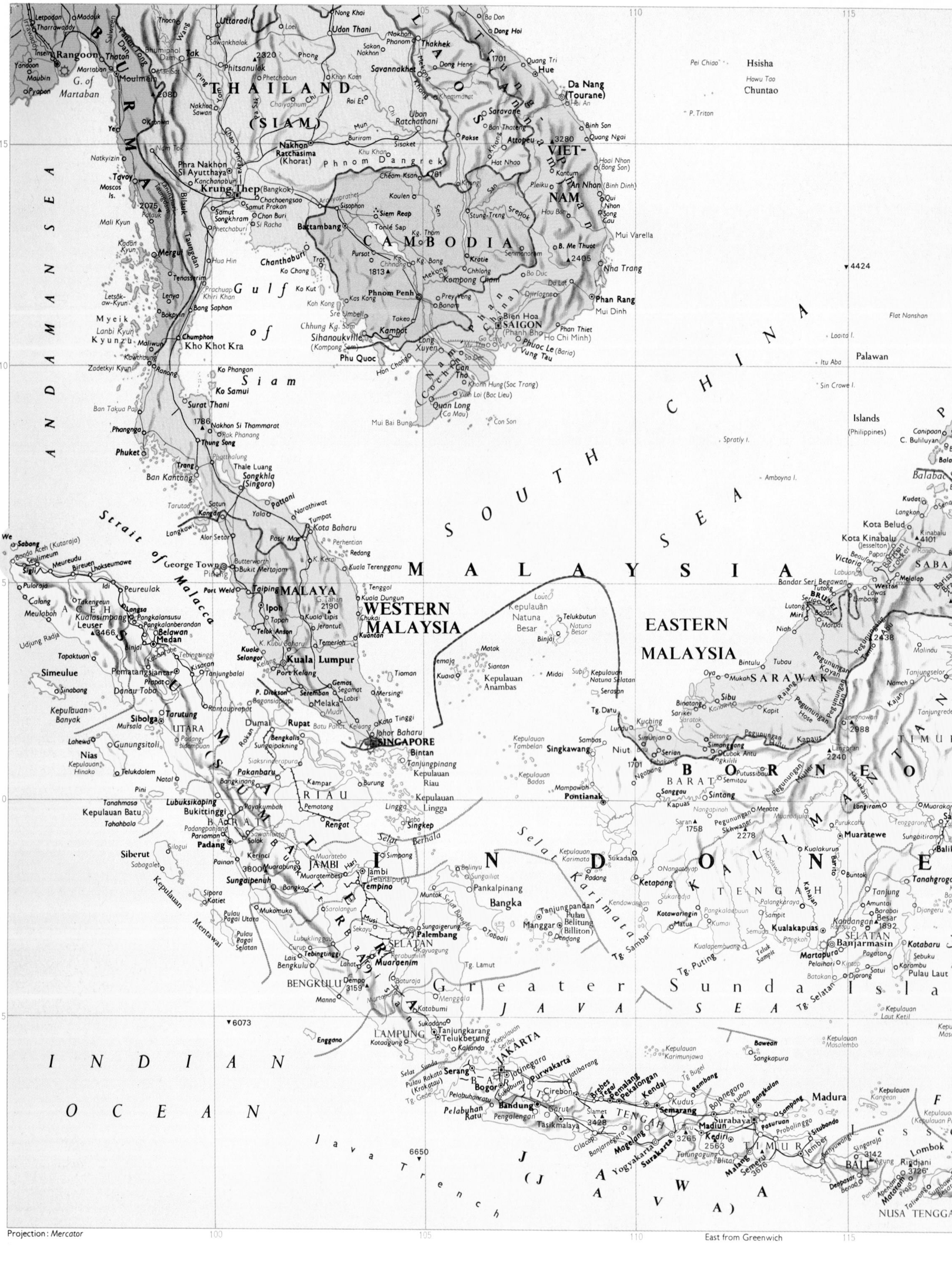
BURMA
THAILAND (SIAM)
LAOS
VIET-NAM
CAMBODIA
MALAYSIA
WESTERN MALAYSIA
EASTERN MALAYSIA
MALAYA
SARAWAK
SABAH
BRUNEI
INDONESIA
SUMATERA (SUMATRA)
BORNEO
KALIMANTAN
JAWA (JAVA)
ANDAMAN SEA
SOUTH CHINA SEA
INDIAN OCEAN
JAVA SEA
Gulf of Siam
Strait of Malacca
G. of Martaban
Java Trench
Greater Sunda Islands
Selat Karimata
Rangoon
Moulmein
Krung Thep (Bangkok)
Phnom Penh
SAIGON
Da Nang (Tourane)
Hue
Kuala Lumpur
SINGAPORE
George Town
Medan
Padang
Palembang
Jambi
Pontianak
Banjarmasin
JAKARTA
Bandung
Semarang
Surabaya
Kota Kinabalu (Jesselton)
Kinabalu 4101
Hsisha
Chuntao
Palawan
Islands (Philippines)
Madura
Bangka
Billiton
Nias
Siberut
Simeulue
Lombok
BALI
Phnom Dangrek
Projection: Mercator
East from Greenwich
100
105
110
115
15
10
5
0

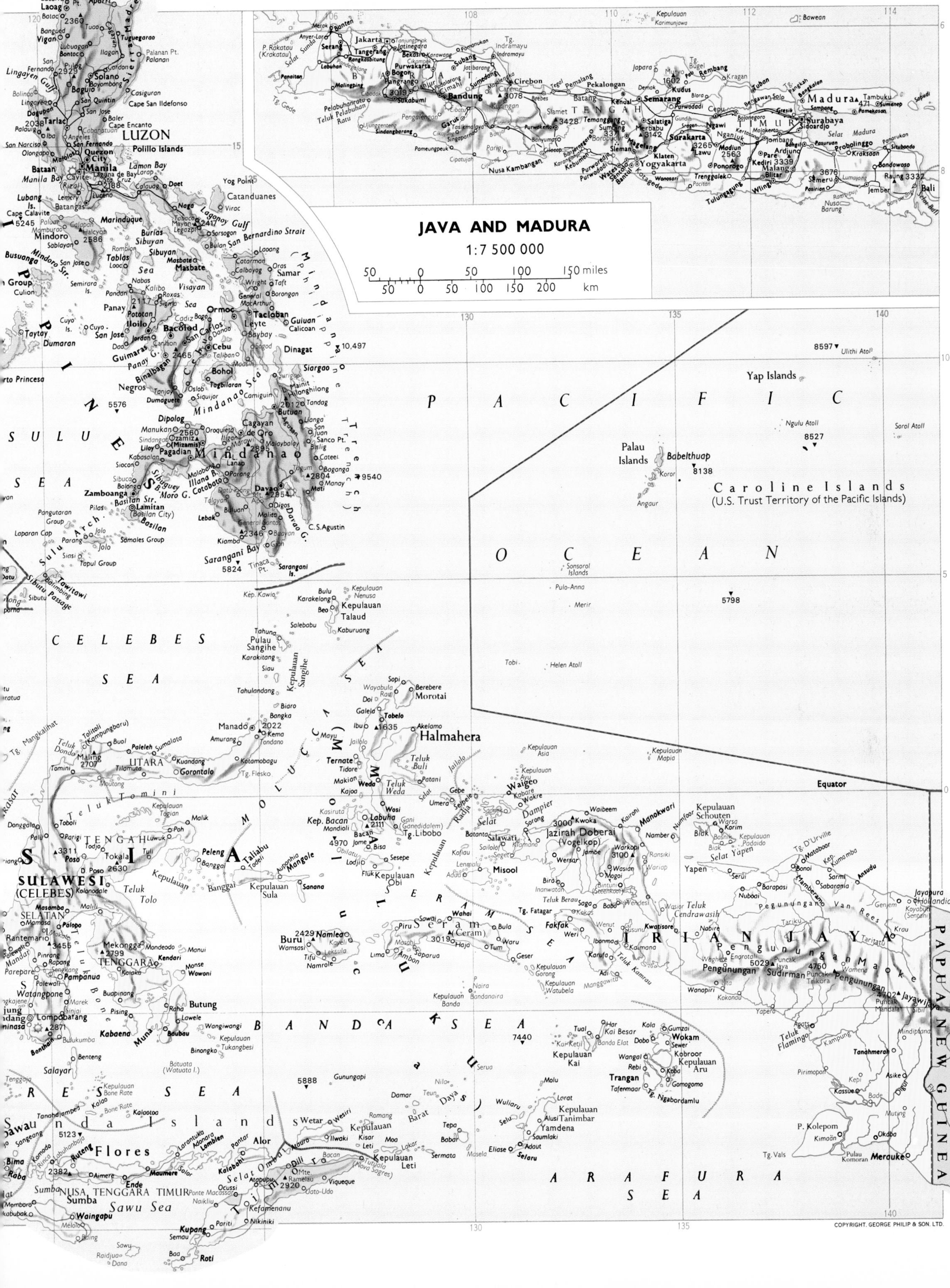

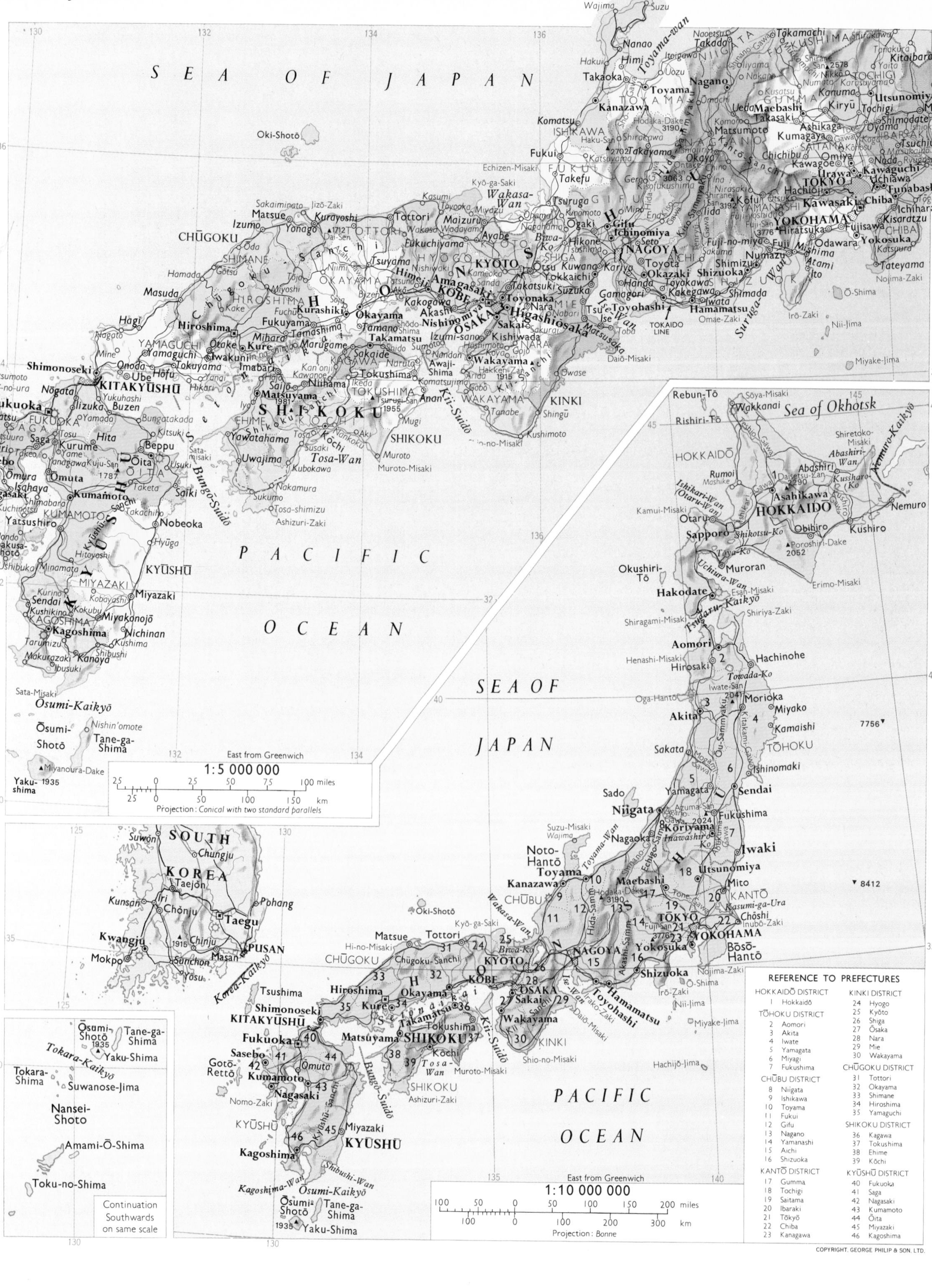

SEA OF JAPAN

PACIFIC OCEAN

SEA OF JAPAN

PACIFIC OCEAN

Sea of Okhotsk

HOKKAIDŌ

SOUTH KOREA

Pusan
Taegu
Taejon
Kwangju
Mokpo

Tokara-Shima
Nansei-Shoto
Amami-Ō-Shima
Toku-no-Shima

Ōsumi-Shotō
Tane-ga-Shima
Yaku-Shima
Suwanose-Jima

Continuation Southwards on same scale

1:5 000 000
East from Greenwich
Projection: Conical with two standard parallels

1:10 000 000
East from Greenwich
Projection: Bonne

REFERENCE TO PREFECTURES

HOKKAIDŌ DISTRICT	KINKI DISTRICT
1 Hokkaidō	24 Hyogo
TŌHOKU DISTRICT	25 Kyōto
2 Aomori	26 Shiga
3 Akita	27 Ōsaka
4 Iwate	28 Nara
5 Yamagata	29 Mie
6 Miyagi	30 Wakayama
7 Fukushima	CHŪGOKU DISTRICT
CHŪBU DISTRICT	31 Tottori
8 Niigata	32 Okayama
9 Ishikawa	33 Shimane
10 Toyama	34 Hiroshima
11 Fukui	35 Yamaguchi
12 Gifu	SHIKOKU DISTRICT
13 Nagano	36 Kagawa
14 Yamanashi	37 Tokushima
15 Aichi	38 Ehime
16 Shizuoka	39 Kōchi
KANTŌ DISTRICT	KYŪSHŪ DISTRICT
17 Gumma	40 Fukuoka
18 Tochigi	41 Saga
19 Saitama	42 Nagasaki
20 Ibaraki	43 Kumamoto
21 Tōkyō	44 Ōita
22 Chiba	45 Miyazaki
23 Kanagawa	46 Kagoshima

COPYRIGHT. GEORGE PHILIP & SON, LTD.

1:20 000 000

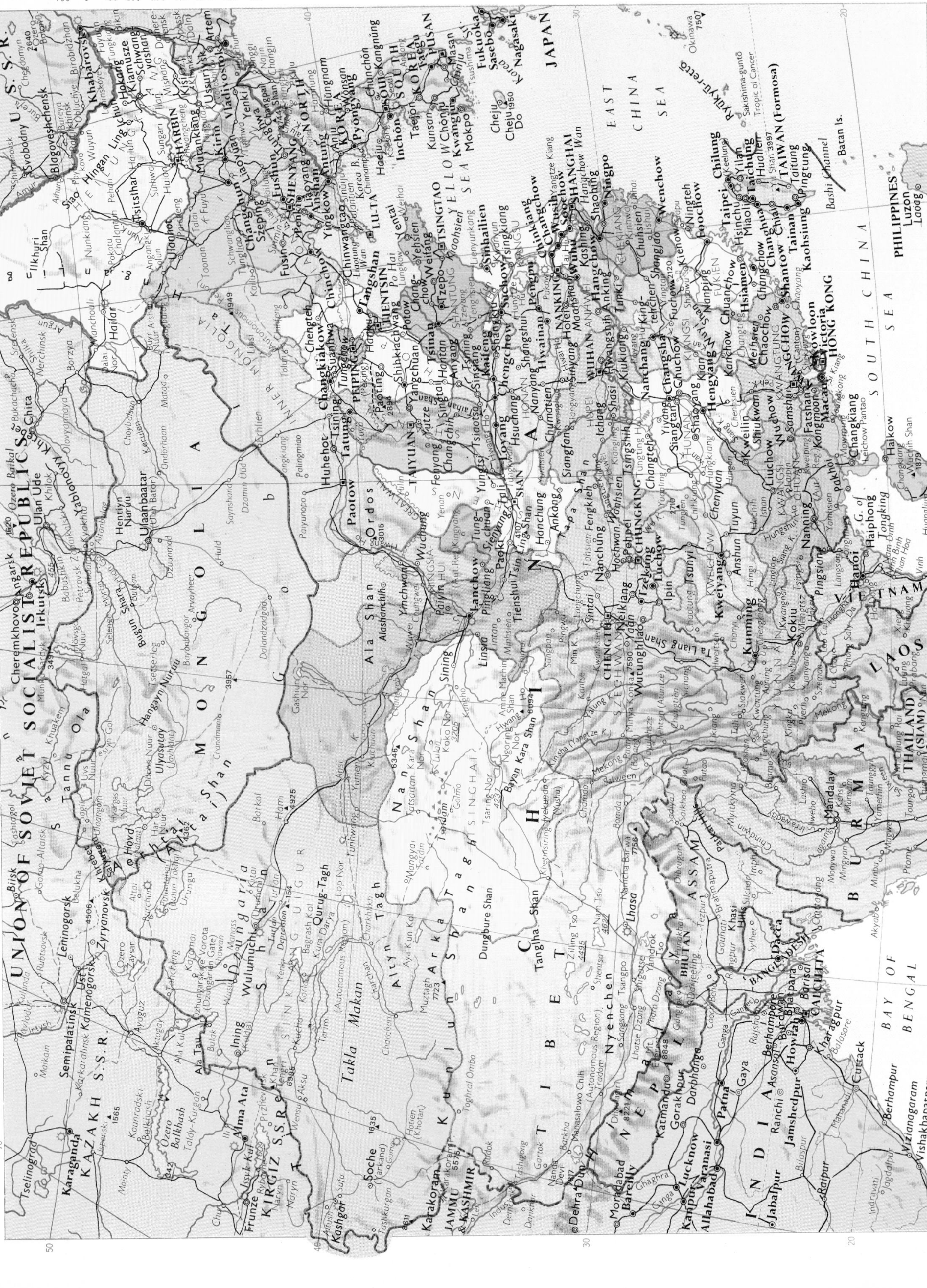
UNION OF SOVIET SOCIALIST REPUBLICS
MONGOLIA
CHINA
TIBET
JAPAN
NORTH KOREA
SOUTH KOREA
INDIA
BURMA
NEPAL
LAOS
VIETNAM
THAILAND (SIAM)
PHILIPPINES
TAIWAN (Formosa)
EAST CHINA SEA
SOUTH CHINA SEA
BAY OF BENGAL
YELLOW SEA
PEIPING
SHANGHAI
NANKING
HONG KONG
CHUNGKING
Projection: Bonne
East from Greenwich
COPYRIGHT GEORGE PHILIP & SON, LTD

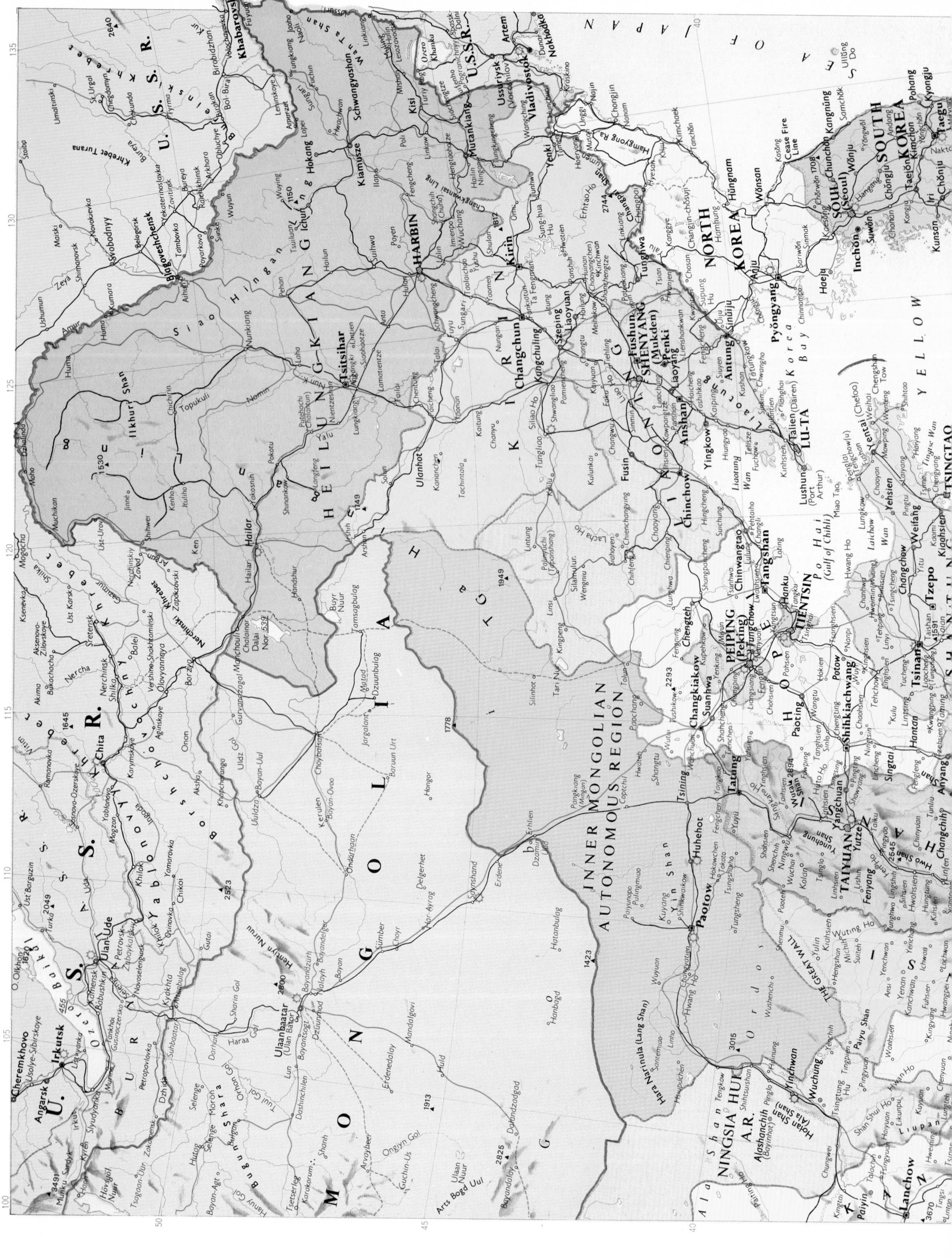
U. S. S. R.
MONGOLIA
INNER MONGOLIAN AUTONOMOUS REGION
HEILUNGKIANG
KIRIN
LIAONING
HOPEH
NORTH KOREA
SOUTH KOREA
SEA OF JAPAN
YELLOW
Korea Bay
Po Hai (Gulf of Chihli)
NINGSIA HUI A.R.
THE GREAT WALL
Khabarovsk
Vladivostok
Artem
Nakhodka
Ussuriysk
Blagoveshchensk
Svobodnyy
Chita
Ulan Ude
Irkutsk
Angarsk
Cheremkhovo
Ulaanbaatar (Ulan Bator)
Choybalsan
HARBIN
Tsitsihar
Kiamusze
Mutankiang
Kirin
Changchun
Szeping
Fushun
SHENYANG (Mukden)
Anshan
Penki
Liaoyang
Antung
Talien (Dairen)
LU-TA
Lushun (Port Arthur)
Yingkow
Chinchow
Fusin
Ulanhot
Hailar
Manchouli
Chinwangtao
Tangshan
TIENTSIN
PEIPING (Peking)
Changkiakow
Tatung
Huhehot
Paotow
Yinchwan
Wuchung
TAIYUAN
Yutze
Shihkiachwang
Paoting
Tsinan
Tzepo
Tsingtao
Yentai (Chefoo)
Weifang
Lanchow
Pyongyang
Hungnam
Wonsan
SOUL (Seoul)
Inchon
Taejon
Taegu
Chongjin
Ulan Bator
Lake Baikal
Amur
Sungari
Hwang Ho
Cease Fire Line
Siao Hingan Ling
Ilkhuri Shan
Yin Shan
Ordos
Hentiyn Nuruu
Yablonovyy Khrebet
Khrebet Turana
Buyr Nuur
Dalai Nor
Ala Shan
Holan Shan (Ala Shan)
100
105
110
115
120
125
130
135
140
40
45
50

1:10 000 000

50   0   50   100   150   200   250 miles
50 0 50 100 150 200 250 300 350 400 km

JAPAN

KITAKYUSHU
Fukuoka
Kurume
Sasebo
Omuta
Nagasaki
Amakusa
Minamata
Makurazaki
Kagoshima
Sendai
Iki
Tsushima
Goto-retto
Koshiki-shima
Uji-gunto
Kusagaki-jima

Cheju Do
(Quelpart)

Tokara-gunto
Nansei-shoto
Amami-o-shima
Amami-gunto
Tokuno-shima
Oku
Okino erabu-shima

Okinawa-gunto
Okinawa
Naha
Kume
Iheya

Miyako-retto
Sekibi-sho
Senkaku-gunto
Iriomote
Yaeyama-retto
Ishigaki-shima
Sakishima-gunto

EAST CHINA SEA

PACIFIC OCEAN

Tropic of Cancer

TAIWAN (FORMOSA)
Chilung (Keelung)
Taipei
Taoyuan
Hsinchu
Miaoli
Taichung
Nantou
Hualien
Yilan
Chiai
Tainan
Kaohsiung
Pingtung
Taitung
Lu Tao
Lan Yu
Pescadores
Penghu

PHILIPPINES
Batan Is.
Babuyan Is.
Luzon
Laoag
Aparri
Tuguegarao
Vigan
C. Bojeador
C. Engaño
Balintang Channel
Bashi Channel
Babuyan Channel

SHANGHAI
NANKING
CHEKIANG
Hangchow
Ningpo
Shaohing
Wenchow
Wusih
Soochow
Changchow
Chinkiang
Nantung
Taichow
Hwainan
Yangchow
Pengpu
Suchow
Kaifeng

KIANGSU
ANHWEI
HONAN
Loyang
Chengchow
HUPEH
WUHAN
Hankow
Wuchang
Hanyang

FUKIEN
Foochow (Minhow)
Nanping
Amoy (Hsiamen)
Changchow

KIANGSI
NANCHANG
Kiukiang

HUNAN
Changsha
Hengyang
Shaoyang

KWEICHOW
Kweiyang

SZECHWAN
CHUNGKING
Luchow
Neikiang

SIAN
SHENSI

KWANGTUNG
KWANGCHOW (Canton)
Kowloon
Victoria
HONGKONG (Br.)
Macau (Port.)
Shantow (Swatow)
Shekki

KWANGSI-CHUANG A.D.
NANNING
Kweilin
Liuchow

HAINAN
Haikow
Kiungchow

SOUTH CHINA SEA

Gulf of Tongking

VIETNAM
HANOI
Haiphong
Nam Dinh

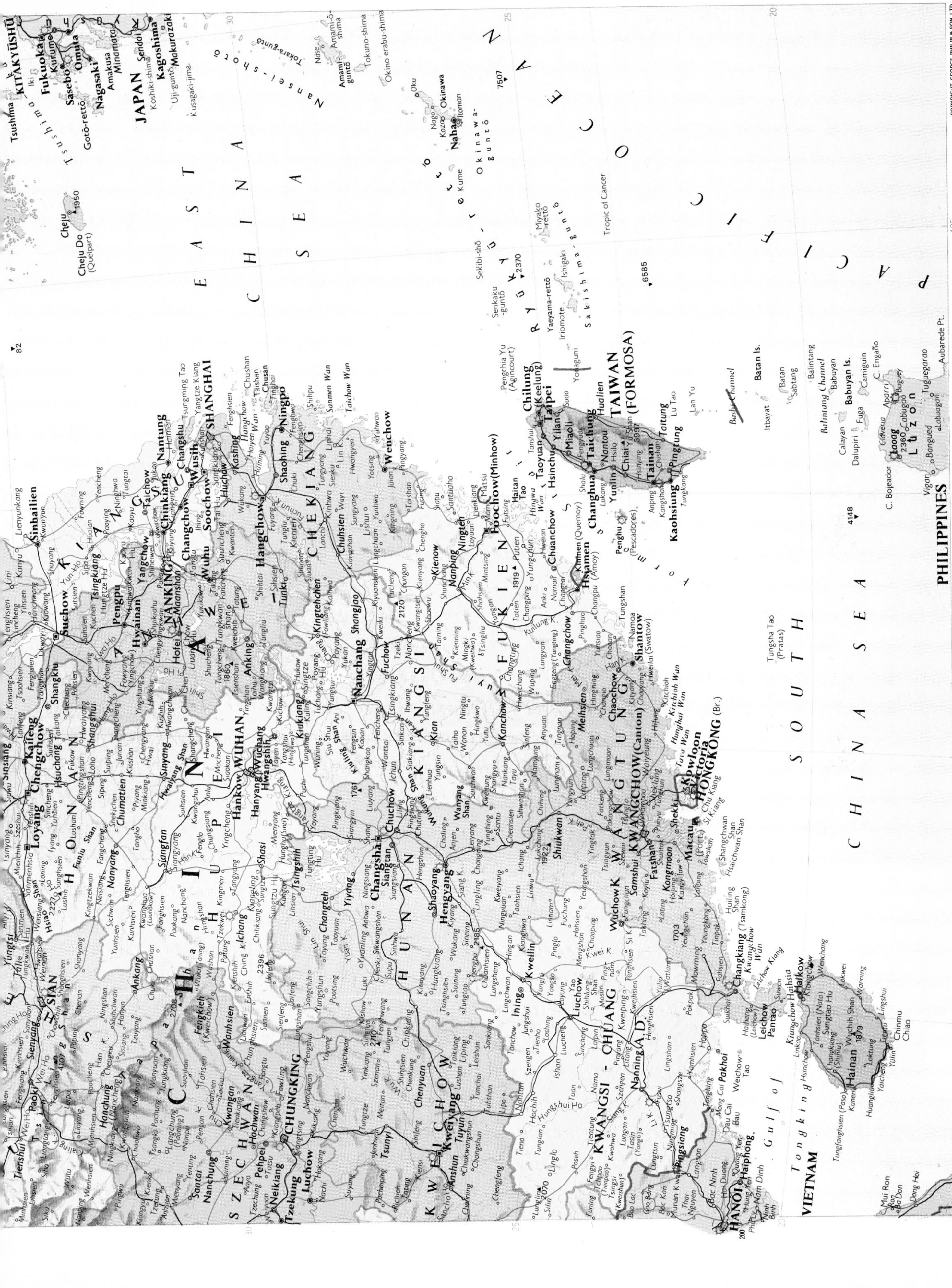

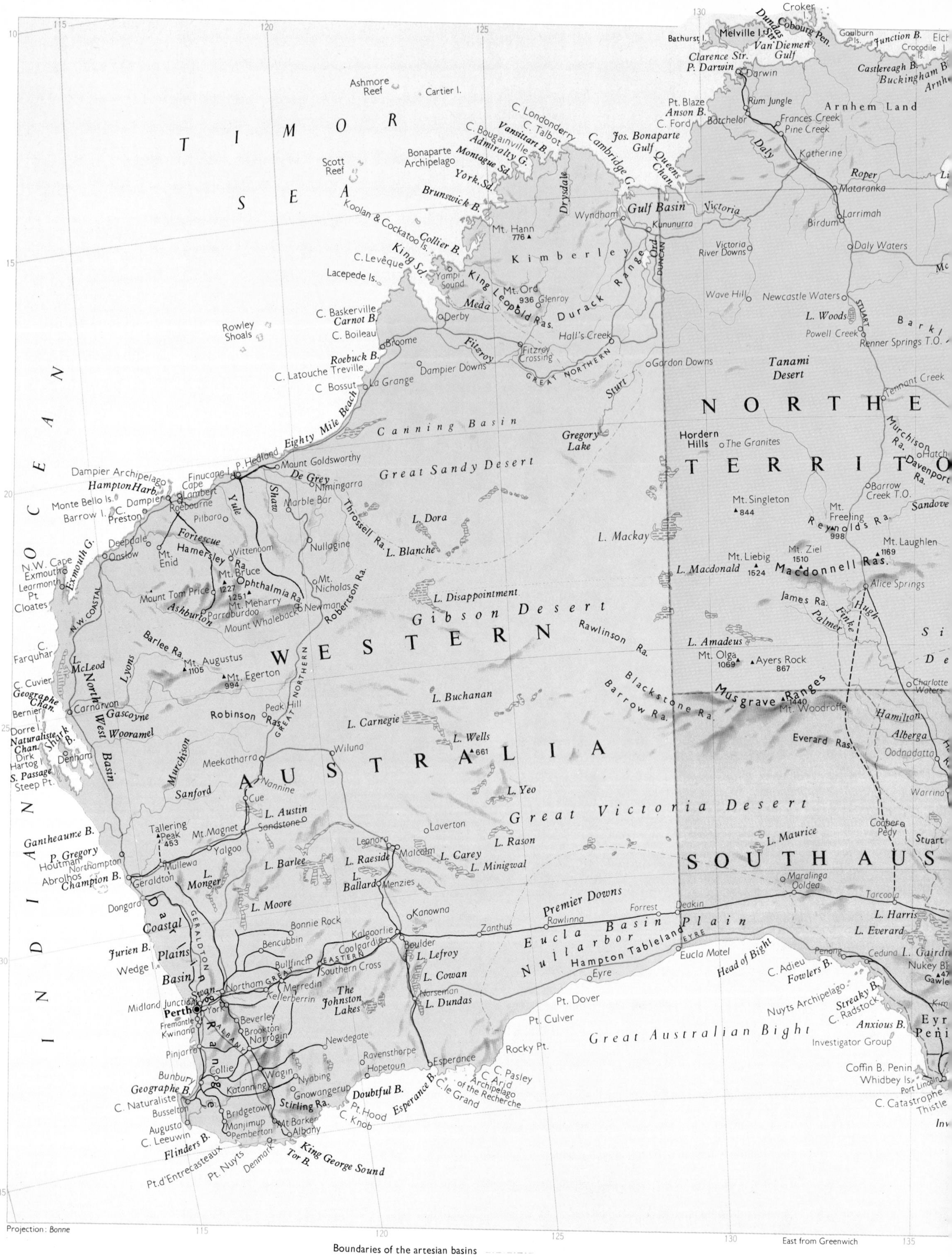

Projection: Bonne

Boundaries of the artesian basins

East from Greenwich

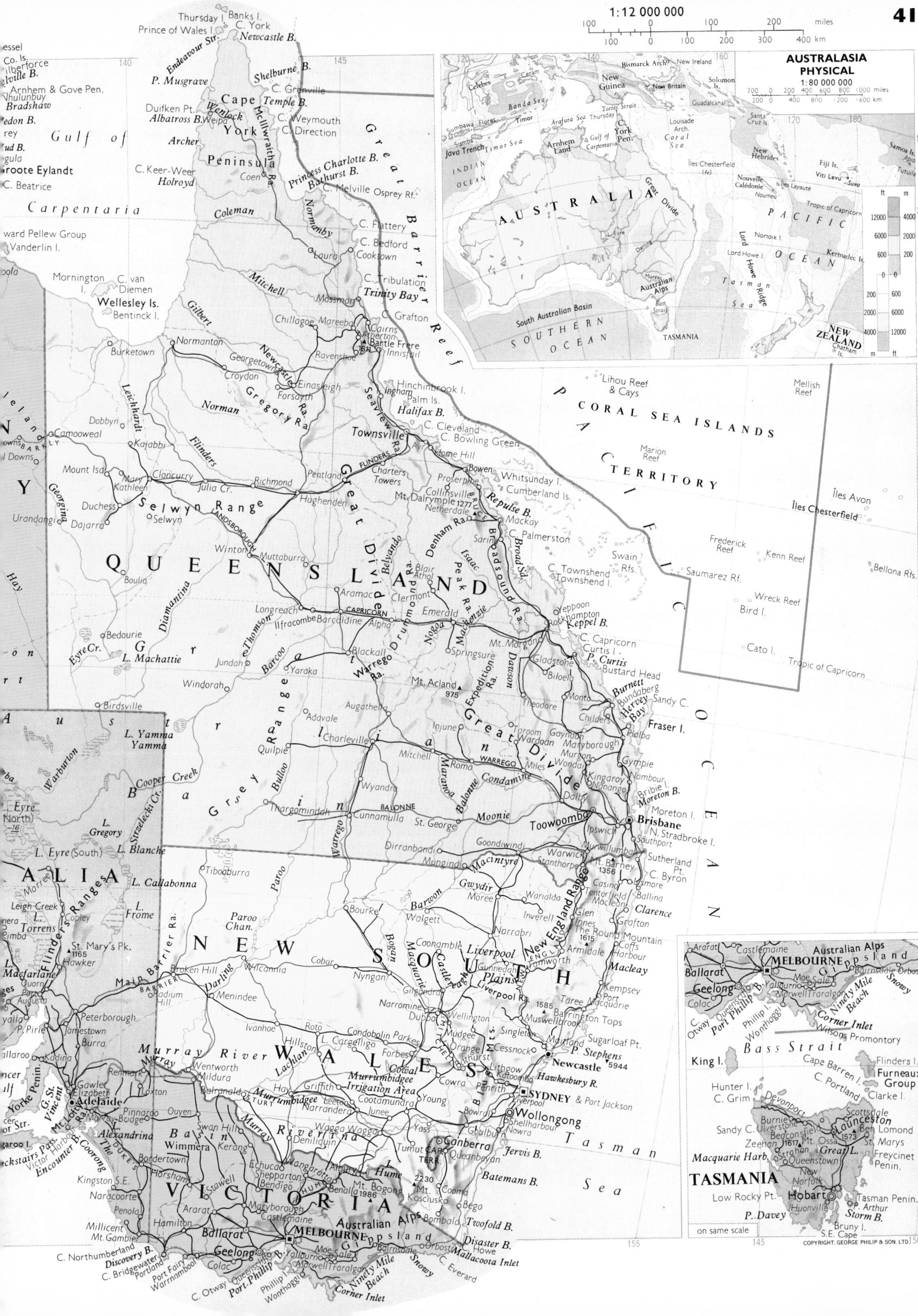
1:12 000 000
miles
km
AUSTRALASIA PHYSICAL
1:80 000 000
New Guinea
Bismarck Arch.
New Ireland
New Britain
Solomon Is.
Guadalcanal
Celebes
Ceram
Banda Sea
Timor
Arafura Sea
Torres Strait
Java Trench
Timor Sea
Arnhem Land
Gulf of Carpentaria
C. York Pen.
Louisiade Arch.
Coral Sea
Santa Cruz Is.
New Hebrides
Fiji Is.
Viti Levu
Suva
Samoa Is.
Tutuila
INDIAN OCEAN
AUSTRALIA
Great Divide
Îles Chesterfield
Nouvelle Calédonie
Noumea
Îles Layauté
Tropic of Capricorn
PACIFIC OCEAN
Norfolk I.
Lord Howe I.
Lord Howe Rise
Kermadec Is.
Eyre
Darling
Murray
Australian Alps
Tasman Sea
Bass Strait
South Australian Basin
SOUTHERN OCEAN
TASMANIA
NEW ZEALAND
Chatham Is.
Thursday I.
Banks I.
Prince of Wales I.
C. York
Newcastle B.
Endeavour Str.
P. Musgrave
Shelburne B.
C. Grenville
Cape York Peninsula
Temple B.
Weipa
C. Weymouth
C. Direction
Gulf of Carpentaria
Groote Eylandt
C. Beatrice
Wellesley Is.
Mornington I.
Bentinck I.
Princess Charlotte B.
Bathurst B.
C. Melville
Osprey Rf.
C. Flattery
C. Bedford
Cooktown
C. Tribulation
Trinity Bay
Great Barrier Reef
Cairns
Atherton
Innisfail
Normanton
Burketown
Croydon
Georgetown
Hinchinbrook I.
Palm Is.
Halifax B.
Townsville
C. Cleveland
C. Bowling Green
Home Hill
Camooweal
Mount Isa
Cloncurry
Julia Cr.
Richmond
Hughenden
Charters Towers
Bowen
Whitsunday I.
Cumberland Is.
Proserpine
Collinsville
Mt. Dalrymple 1277
Mackay
C. Palmerston
Selwyn Range
QUEENSLAND
CORAL SEA ISLANDS TERRITORY
Lihou Reef & Cays
Mellish Reef
Marion Reef
Îles Avon
Îles Chesterfield
Frederick Reef
Kenn Reef
Bellona Rfs.
Saumarez Rf.
Wreck Reef
Bird I.
Cato I.
Tropic of Capricorn
PACIFIC OCEAN
Winton
Muttaburra
Longreach
Barcaldine
Emerald
Rockhampton
Yeppoon
Keppel B.
Gladstone
C. Capricorn
Curtis I.
P. Curtis
Bustard Head
Bundaberg
Hervey Bay
Sandy C.
Fraser I.
Maryborough
Gympie
Nambour
Bribie I.
Moreton B.
Moreton I.
Brisbane
N. Stradbroke I.
Southport
Toowoomba
Ipswich
Dalby
Roma
Charleville
Cunnamulla
St. George
Goondiwindi
Warwick
Great Dividing Range
Birdsville
Windorah
Quilpie
Thargomindah
Great Artesian Basin
L. Eyre (North)
L. Eyre (South)
Cooper Creek
L. Blanche
L. Callabona
L. Frome
L. Torrens
Flinders Ranges
St. Mary's Pk. 1165
Tibooburra
Bourke
Walgett
Moree
Inverell
Glen Innes
Armidale
Tamworth
Grafton
Lismore
C. Byron
Coffs Harbour
Kempsey
Port Macquarie
NEW SOUTH WALES
Broken Hill
Wilcannia
Menindee
Cobar
Nyngan
Dubbo
Orange
Bathurst
Lithgow
Newcastle
Maitland
P. Stephens
Hawkesbury R.
SYDNEY
Wollongong
Canberra
A.C.T.
Queanbeyan
Goulburn
Jervis B.
Batemans B.
Mt. Kosciusko 2230
Twofold B.
Eden
Disaster B.
Mallacoota Inlet
C. Howe
C. Everard
Tasman Sea
Murray River
Mildura
Wagga Wagga
Albury
Riverina
Murrumbidgee Irrigation Area
Adelaide
Port Pirie
Yorke Penin.
Kangaroo I.
Encounter B.
Coorong
VICTORIA
Bendigo
Ballarat
Geelong
MELBOURNE
Port Phillip B.
Australian Alps
Gippsland
Corner Inlet
Ninety Mile Beach
Wilsons Promontory
C. Otway
Portland
Discovery B.
C. Northumberland
Mt. Gambier
Bass Strait
King I.
Flinders I.
Furneaux Group
Cape Barren I.
C. Portland
Clarke I.
Hunter I.
C. Grim
Devonport
Burnie
Launceston
Ben Lomond 1573
Mt. Ossa 1617
Queenstown
Macquarie Harb.
Great L.
Freycinet Penin.
TASMANIA
Hobart
Tasman Penin.
P. Arthur
Storm B.
Bruny I.
S.E. Cape
P. Davey
Low Rocky Pt.
on same scale
COPYRIGHT. GEORGE PHILIP & SON. LTD.

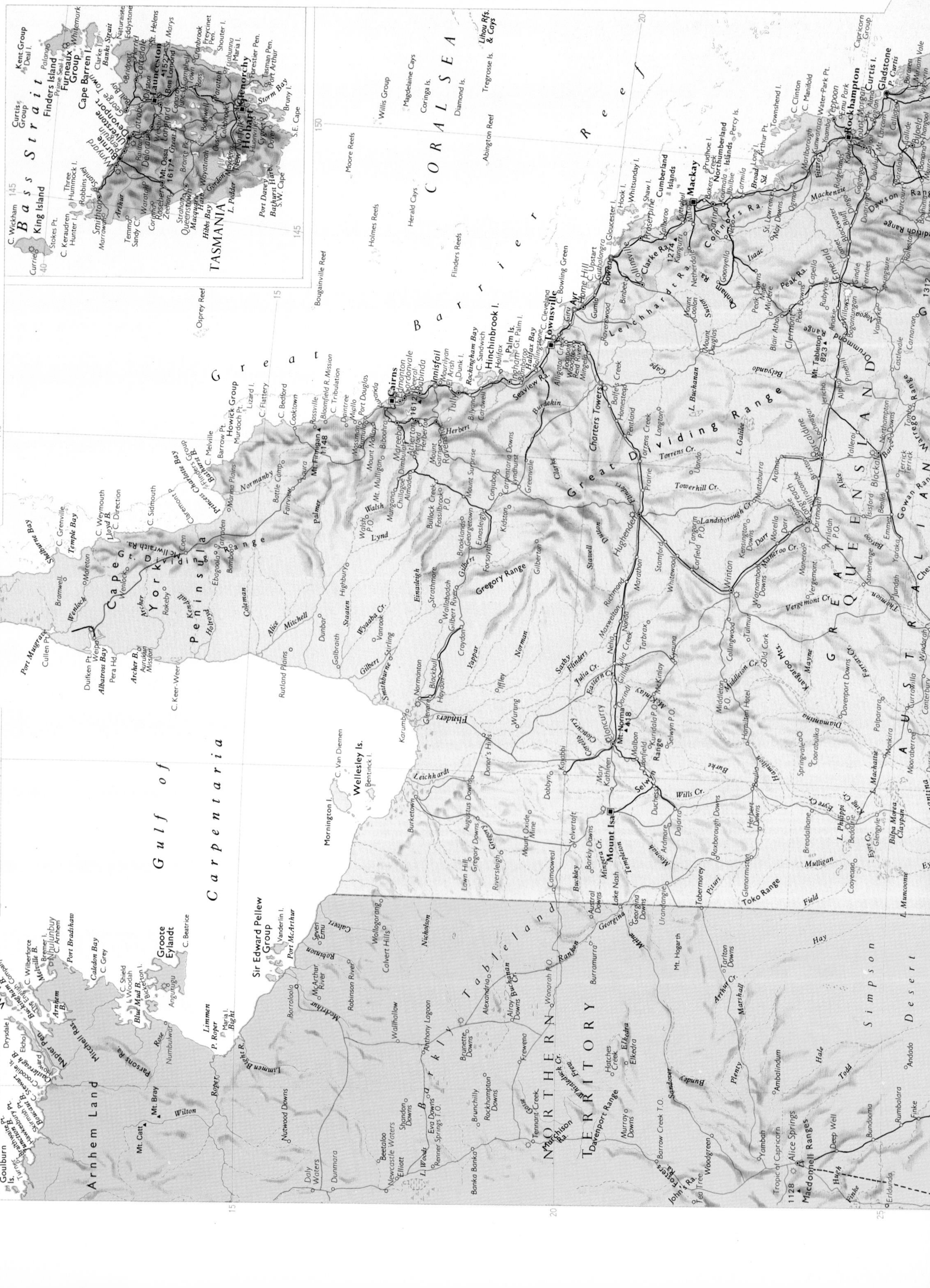

TASMANIA
Bass Strait
King Island
Flinders Island
Furneaux Group
Cape Barren I.
Launceston
Devonport
Burnie
Hobart
Glenorchy
Storm Bay
Great Barrier Reef
CORAL SEA
Gulf of Carpentaria
Cape York Peninsula
Great Dividing Range
QUEENSLAND
GREAT AUSTRALIAN
NORTHERN TERRITORY
Arnhem Land
Barkly Tableland
Simpson Desert
Groote Eylandt
Wellesley Is.
Mornington I.
Sir Edward Pellew Group
Cairns
Townsville
Mackay
Rockhampton
Gladstone
Mount Isa
Cloncurry
Charters Towers
Hughenden
Winton
Longreach
Alice Springs
Macdonnell Ranges
Tennant Creek
Tropic of Capricorn
Hinchinbrook I.
Whitsunday I.
Cumberland Islands
Northumberland Islands
Curtis I.
Gregory Range
Selwyn Range
Toko Range
Davenport Range
Murchison Ra.
Mt. Bartle Frere 1612
Mt. Norma 418
Mt. Tabletop 823
Mt. Ossa 1617
Dawson Range
Leichhardt Ra.
Clarke Ra.
Connors Ra.
Peak Ra.
Drummond Range
Kangaroo Mts.

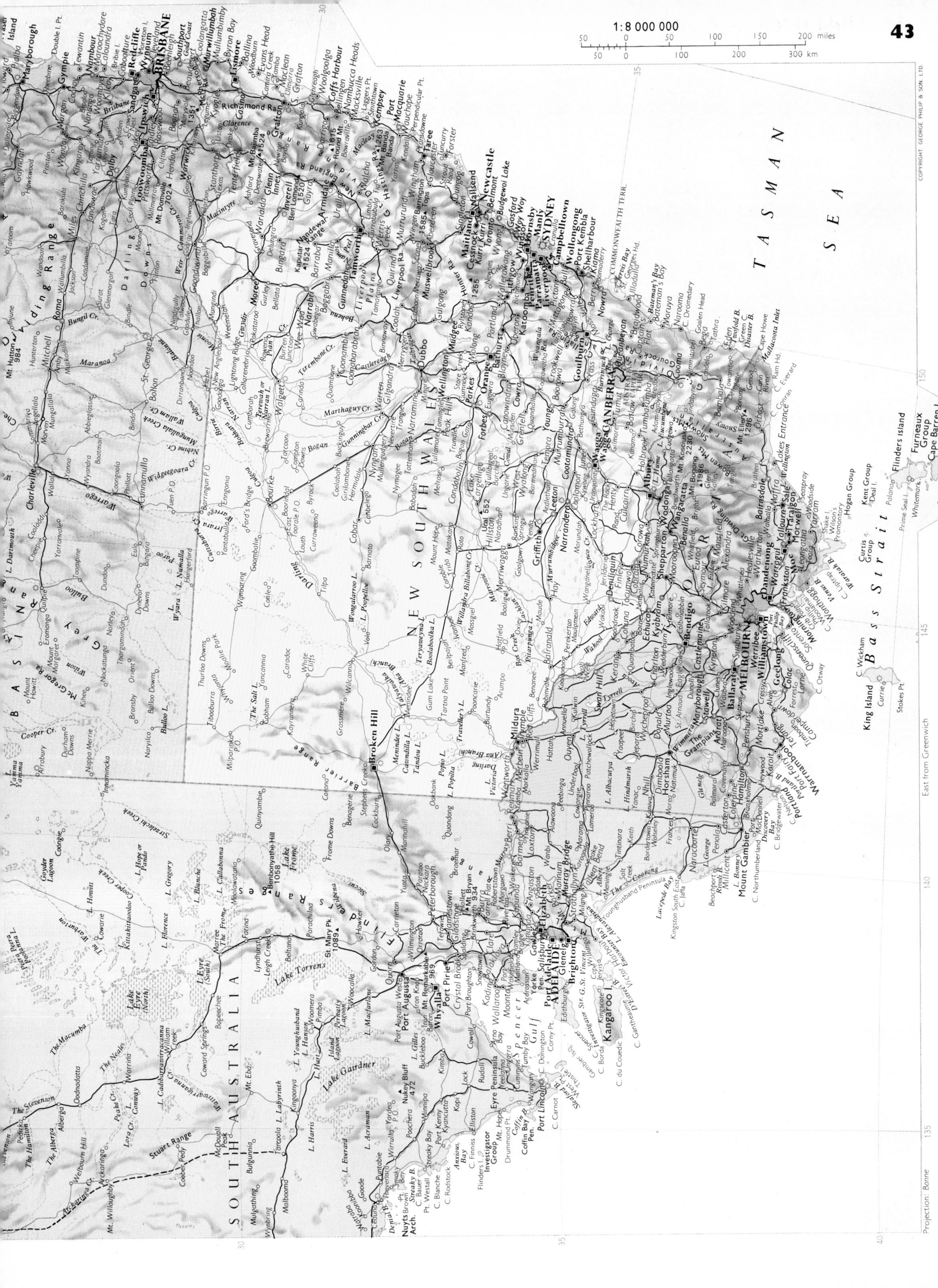
1:8 000 000
50 0 50 100 150 200 miles
50 0 100 200 300 km
TASMAN SEA
Bass Strait
NEW SOUTH WALES
SOUTH AUSTRALIA
SYDNEY
BRISBANE
MELBOURNE
ADELAIDE
CANBERRA
Newcastle
Wollongong
Broken Hill
Toowoomba
Bendigo
Ballarat
Geelong
Albury
Wagga Wagga
Dubbo
Tamworth
Mildura
Port Augusta
Port Pirie
Whyalla
Port Lincoln
Mount Gambier
Warrnambool
Kangaroo I.
King Island
Flinders Island
Furneaux Group
Cape Barren I.
Lake Eyre (North)
Lake Eyre (South)
Lake Torrens
Lake Gairdner
Lake Frome
Spencer Gulf
Flinders Ranges
Grey Range
Darling
Murray
COMMONWEALTH TERR.
East from Greenwich
Projection: Bonne
COPYRIGHT GEORGE PHILIP & SON, LTD.

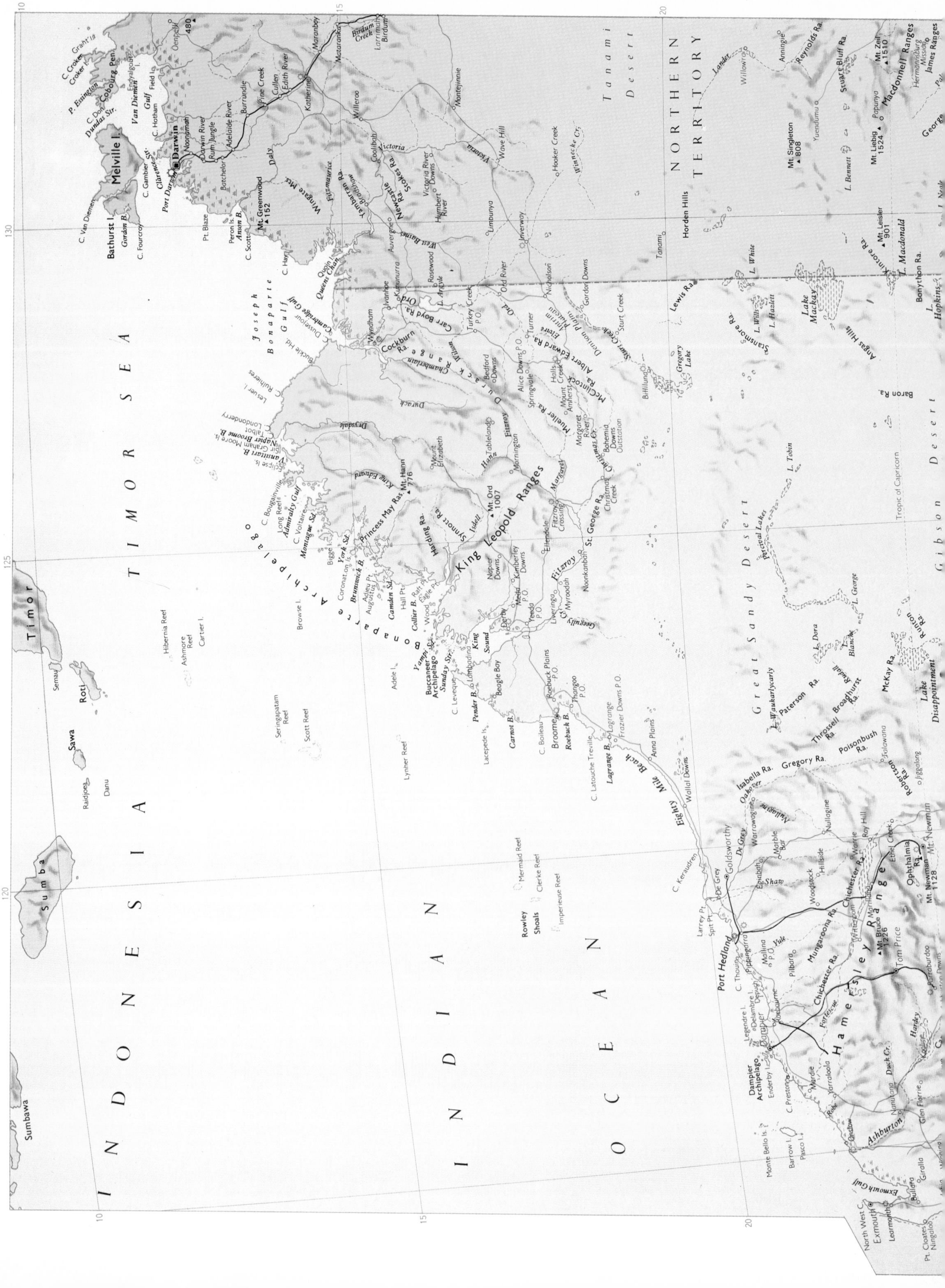

INDONESIA
TIMOR SEA
INDIAN OCEAN
Timor
Sumba
Sumbawa
Sawa
Roti
Semau
Raidjoea
Danu
NORTHERN TERRITORY
Tanami Desert
Great Sandy Desert
Gibson Desert
Melville I.
Bathurst I.
Darwin
Port Darwin
Clarence Str.
Van Diemen Gulf
Cobourg Pen.
Dundas Str.
C. Croker
Croker I.
Goulburn Is.
P. Essington
C. Don
C. Hotham
Field I.
Oenpelli
480
C. Van Diemen
C. Fourcroy
Gordon B.
C. Gambier
Pt. Blaze
Peron Is.
Anson B.
C. Scott
Mt. Greenwood
152
Noonamah
Darwin River
Rum Jungle
Adelaide River
Batchelor
Burrundie
Pine Creek
Cullen
Edith River
Katherine
Mataranka
Maranboy
Birdum Creek
Birdum
Larrimah
Daly
Fitzmaurice
Wingate Mts.
Willeroo
Montejinnie
Victoria
Victoria River Downs
Coolibah
Newcastle Ra.
Stokes Ra.
Humbert River
Wave Hill
Limbunya
Inverway
Hooker Creek
Winnecke Cr.
Auvergne
West Baines
Rosewood
Kununurra
L. Argyle
Ivanhoe
Wyndham
Cambridge Gulf
Joseph Bonaparte Gulf
C. Dussejour
Queens Chan.
Quoin I.
C. Hay
Buckle Hd.
Cockburn Ra.
Carr Boyd Ra.
Ord
Turkey Creek P.O.
Old River
Nicholson
Gordon Downs
Sturt Creek
Denison Plains
Turner
Elvire
Albert Edward Ra.
Bedford Downs
Alice Downs P.O.
Springvale
Halls Creek
Mount Amherst
McClintock Ra.
Mueller Ra.
Durack Ra.
Durack
Chamberlain
C. Rulhieres
Lesueur I.
C. Londonderry
Drysdale
C. Talbot
Napier Broome B.
Sir Graham Moore Is.
Vansittart B.
Eclipse Is.
King Edward
Mount Elizabeth
Tableland
Hann
Mornington
Fitzroy
Margaret River
Margaret
Bohemia Downs Outstation
Christmas Cr.
Christmas Creek
Mt. Ord 1007
Mt. Hann 776
King Leopold Ranges
Synnott Ra.
Isdell
Harding Ra.
Princess May Ras.
Bonaparte Archipelago
C. Bougainville
Long Reef
Admiralty Gulf
C. Voltaire
Montague Sd.
Bigge I.
York Sd.
Coronation Is.
Brunswick B.
Adieu Pt.
Augustus I.
Camden Sd.
Hall Pt.
Collier B.
Raft Pt.
Wood
Yampi Sd.
Buccaneer Archipelago
Sunday Str.
King Sound
Derby
Meda
Yeeda P.O.
Napier Downs
Kimberley Downs
Ellendale
Fitzroy Crossing
St. George Ra.
Noonkanbah
Liveringa
Myroodah
Geegully Cr.
Browse I.
Hibernia Reef
Ashmore Reef
Cartier I.
Adele I.
Seringapatam Reef
Scott Reef
Lynher Reef
C. Leveque
Lombadina
Beagle Bay
Pender B.
Lacepede Is.
Carnot B.
Roebuck Plains P.O.
Thangoo P.O.
C. Boileau
Broome
Roebuck B.
C. Latouche Treville
Lagrange B.
Lagrange
Frazier Downs P.O.
Anna Plains
Eighty Mile Beach
Wallal Downs
Mermaid Reef
Clerke Reef
Imperieuse Reef
Rowley Shoals
C. Keraudren
De Grey
Goldsworthy
Larrey Pt.
Spit Pt.
Port Hedland
C. Thouin
Depuch I.
Legendre I.
Delambre I.
Dampier
Dampier Archipelago
Enderby I.
Roebourne
Monte Bello Is.
Barrow I.
Pascoe I.
C. Preston
Mardie
Yarraloola
Onslow
Ashburton
Exmouth Gulf
Exmouth
Learmonth
North West C.
Pt. Cloates
Ningaloo
Giralia
Bullara
Glen Florrie
Nanutarra
Duck Cr.
Hamersley Range
Mt. Bruce 1226
Tom Price
Wittenoom
Mt. Newman 1128
Ophthalmia Ra.
Chichester Ra.
Fortescue
Mungaroona Ra.
Pilbara
Yule
Mallina
Woodstock
Hillside
Marble Bar
Shaw
Warrawagine
Nullagine
Oakover
Isabella Ra.
Gregory Ra.
Roy Hill
Ethel Creek
Robertson Ra.
Jigalong
Poisonbush Ra.
Throssell Ra.
Broadhurst Ra.
Paterson Ra.
L. Waukarlycarly
Rudall
McKay Ra.
Lake Disappointment
Runton Ra.
L. Dora
L. Blanche
L. George
Percival Lakes
L. Tobin
Tropic of Capricorn
Baron Ra.
Angas Hills
Stansmore Ra.
L. Wills
L. Hazlett
Lake Mackay
L. White
Lewis Ra.
Gregory Lake
Billiluna
Tanami
Horden Hills
Lander
Willowra
Anningie
Reynolds Ra.
Stuart Bluff Ra.
Mt. Zeil 1510
Hermannsburg Mission
James Ranges
Macdonnell Ranges
Papunya
Mt. Liebig 1524
Yuendumu
Mt. Singleton 808
L. Bennett
Mt. Leisler 901
Kintore Ra.
L. Macdonald
Bonython Ra.
L. Hopkins

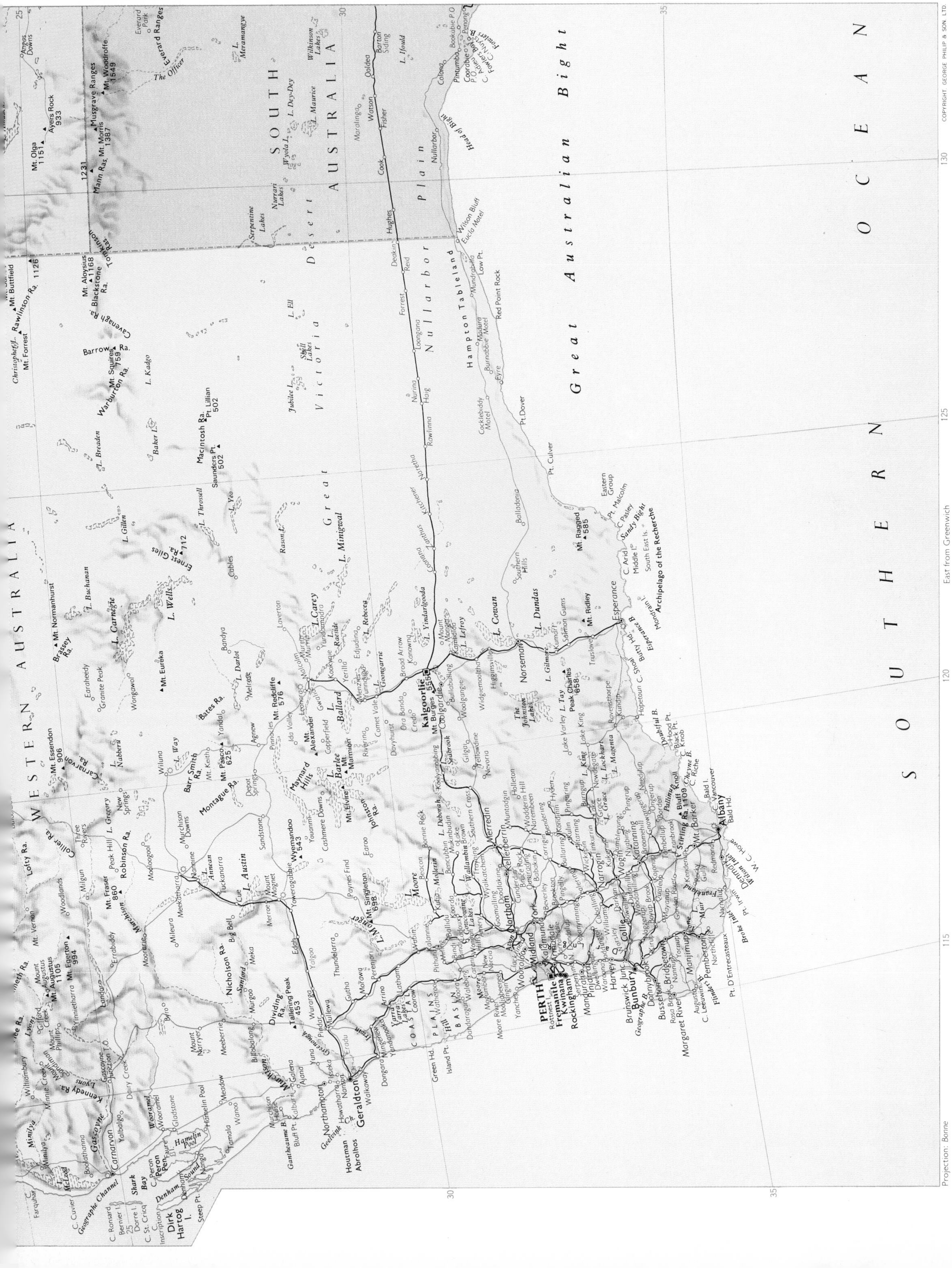

1:8 000 000

50   0   50   100   150   200 miles

50   0   100   200   300 km

O C E A N

COPYRIGHT GEORGE PHILIP & SON LTD.

S O U T H E R N

East from Greenwich

Projection: Bonne

S   O   U   T   H

A U S T R A L I A

WESTERN AUSTRALIA

Great Australian Bight

Great Victoria Desert

Nullarbor Plain

Hampton Tableland

Mt. Woodroffe 1435

Ayers Rock 933

Mt. Olga 1151

Mt. Morris 1387

Musgrave Ranges

The Officer

Everard Ranges

L. Meramangye

Wilkinson Lakes

Serpentine Lakes

Narrari Lakes

Mt. Aloysius 1168

Blackstone Ra.

Cavenagh Ra.

Rawlinson Ra.

Mt. Forrest

Mt. Buttfield 1126

Warburton Ra.

Mt. Squires 759

Barrow Ra.

L. Breaden

L. Baker

L. Kadjo

Macintosh Ra.

Saunders Pt. 502

Pt. Lillian 502

Jubilee L.

Shell Lakes

L. Throssell

L. Yeo

L. Gillen

L. Buchanan

Ernest Giles Ra. 712

L. Wells

Cobbies

Rason L.

L. Minigwal

L. Rebecca

L. Carey

L. Carnegie

Mt. Eureka

Granite Peak

Brassey Ra.

Mt. Normanhurst 906

Bates Ra.

Mt. Keith

Agnew

Yundamindra

Kookynie

Mt. Leonard

Leonora

Laverton

Broad Arrow

Kalgoorlie 5656

Mt. Burges

Coolgardie

Menzies

Kookynie

Comet Vale

Ora Banda

Bulla Bulling

Boulder

Widgiemooltha

Norseman

The Johnston Lakes

L. Cowan

L. Dundas

Mt. Ridley 585

Mt. Raggled 585

Esperance

Archipelago of the Recherche

Cape Arid

Pt. Malcolm

Eastern Group

Middle I.

South East Is.

Sandy Bight

L. Lefroy

L. Gilmore

Salmon Gums

Grass Patch

L. King

L. Magenta

Ravensthorpe

Hopetoun

Pt. Culver

Pt. Dover

Eucla Motel

Wilson Bluff

Low Pt.

Mundrabilla Motel

Madura Motel

Red Point Rock

Eyre

Cocklebiddy Motel

Burnabbie Motel

Deakin

Reid

Forrest

Hughes

Cook

Fisher

Watson

Ooldea

Barton

Nullarbor

Maralinga

Koonibba P.O.

Penong

Denman

Fowlers B.

Coorabie

Nundroo

Colona

L. Ifould

L. Dey-Dey

L. Maurice

Pt. Sinclair

WESTERN AUSTRALIA

Carnarvon Ra.

Mt. Essendon 906

Robinson Ra.

Collier Ra.

Lofty Ra.

Mt. Vernon 906

Mt. Augustus 1105

Mt. Fraser 860

Nicholson Ra.

Montague Ra.

Barr Smith Ra.

Mt. Fisher 625

L. Way

L. Darlot

L. Nabberu

Wiluna

Mt. Redcliffe 576

Maynard Hills

Mt. Burtle

Mt. Marmion

Mt. Elvire

Johnston Ra.

Mt. Singleton 688

L. Austin

L. Barlee

L. Moore

Cue

Mt. Magnet

Sandstone

Youanmi

Paynes Find

Mt. Kenneth

Lyons

Mt. Egerton 994

Gascoyne

Carnarvon

Shark Bay

Denham

Hamelin Pool

Dirk Hartog

Steep Pt.

Geographe Channel

Edel Land

Useless Inlet

Dorre I.

Bernier I.

Murchison

Geraldton

Northampton

Houtman Abrolhos

Green Hd.

Island Pt.

Dongara

Mingenew

Three Springs

Morawa

Perenjori

Wubin

Dalwallinu

Moora

COASTAL PLAINS

Gingin

Bindoon

Toodyay

Northam

York

Beverley

Brookton

Corrigin

Narrogin

Wagin

Katanning

Kojonup

Broome Hill

Tambellup

Cranbrook

Mt. Barker

Stirling Ra. 1109

Albany

King George Sound

Two Peoples Bay

Gnowangerup

Ongerup

Jerramungup

Ravensthorpe

Bremer Bay

Pt. Henry

Pallinup

Hood Pt.

Bald Hd.

W. C. HOWE

PERTH

Fremantle

Kwinana

Rockingham

Midland

Armadale

Mandurah

Pinjarra

Harvey

Brunswick Jun.

Bunbury

Collie

Donnybrook

Busselton

Geographe B.

Cape Naturaliste

C. Leeuwin

Margaret River

Nannup

Bridgetown

Manjimup

Pemberton

Northcliffe

Augusta

Flinders Bay

C. D'Entrecasteaux

Broke Inlet

Walpole

Denmark

Mt. Singleton

1 : 4 500 000

```
20    0        20    40    60    80   100 miles
20  0      40      80     120    160 km
```

T A S M A N   S E A

N E W   S O U T H   W A L E S

V I C T O R I A

S O U T H   A U S T R A L I A

A U S T R A L I A N   C A P I T A L   T E R R I T O R Y

SYDNEY
Newcastle
Wollongong
MELBOURNE
Canberra
Ballarat
Bendigo
Geelong
Albury
Wagga Wagga
Dubbo
Bathurst
Orange
Parramatta
Liverpool
Manly
Maitland
Cessnock
Lithgow
Katoomba
Penrith
Goulburn
Queanbeyan
Griffith
Narrandera
Leeton
Junee
Temora
Young
Cowra
Forbes
Parkes
Cootamundra
Gundagai
Tumut
Broken Hill
Mildura
Swan Hill
Echuca
Shepparton
Wangaratta
Benalla
Traralgon
Morwell
Warrnambool
Hamilton
Ararat
Horsham
Maryborough
Castlemaine
Taree

C E N T R A L   T A B L E L A N D

S O U T H E R N   T A B L E L A N D

W E S T E R N   S L O P E

S O U T H   W E S T E R N   S L O P E

R I V E R I N A

W I M M E R A

M A L L E E

HUNTER AND MANNING

NEW ENGLAND

Liverpool Range

Great Dividing Range

Blue Mts.

Snowy Mts.

Murray River

Murrumbidgee River

Darling River

Lachlan River

Wilson's Promontory

Port Phillip

5030

1 : 4 500 000

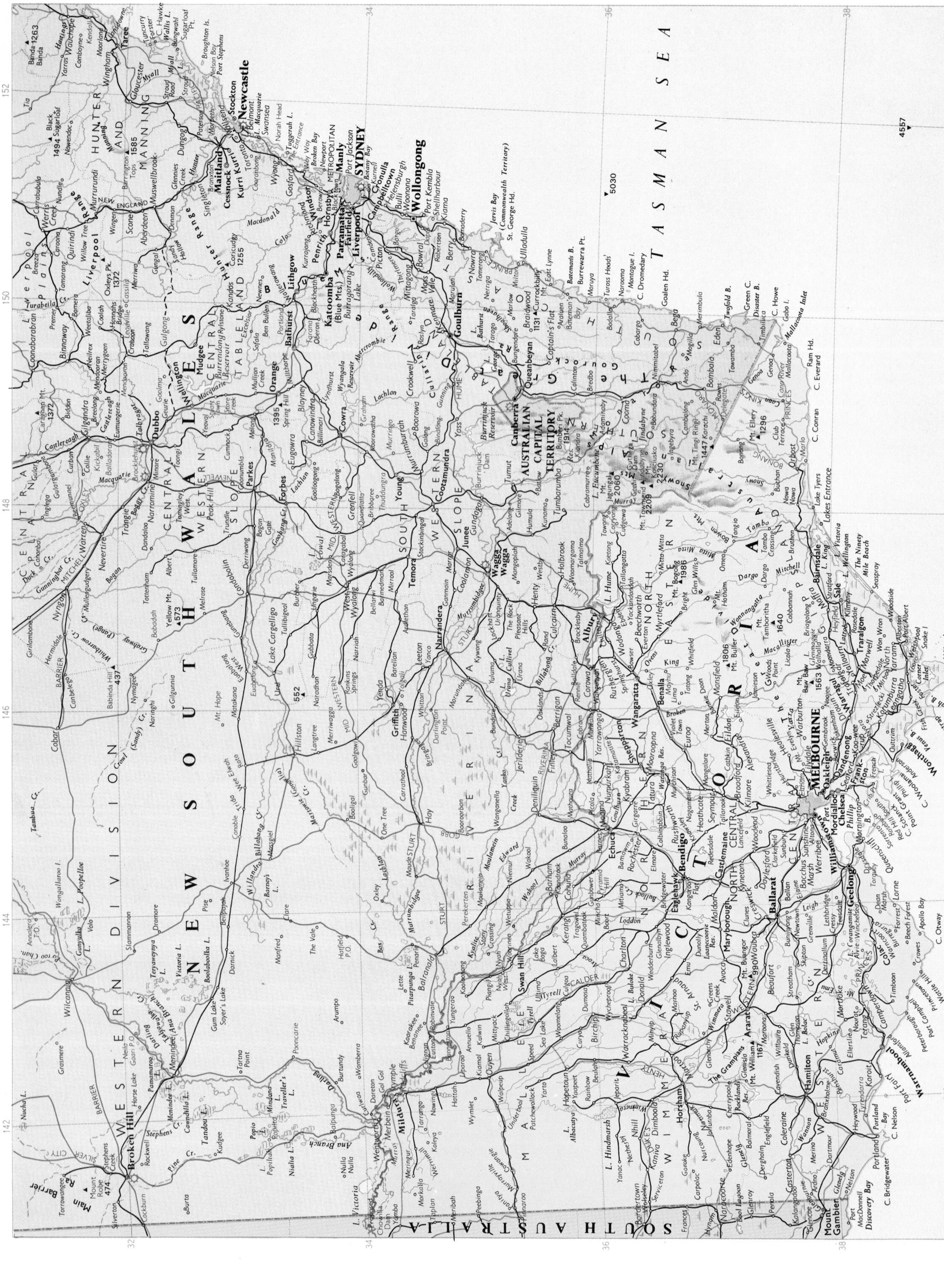

Projection: Albers' Equal Area with two standard parallels

East from Greenwich

152. COPYRIGHT GEORGE PHILIP & SON, LTD.

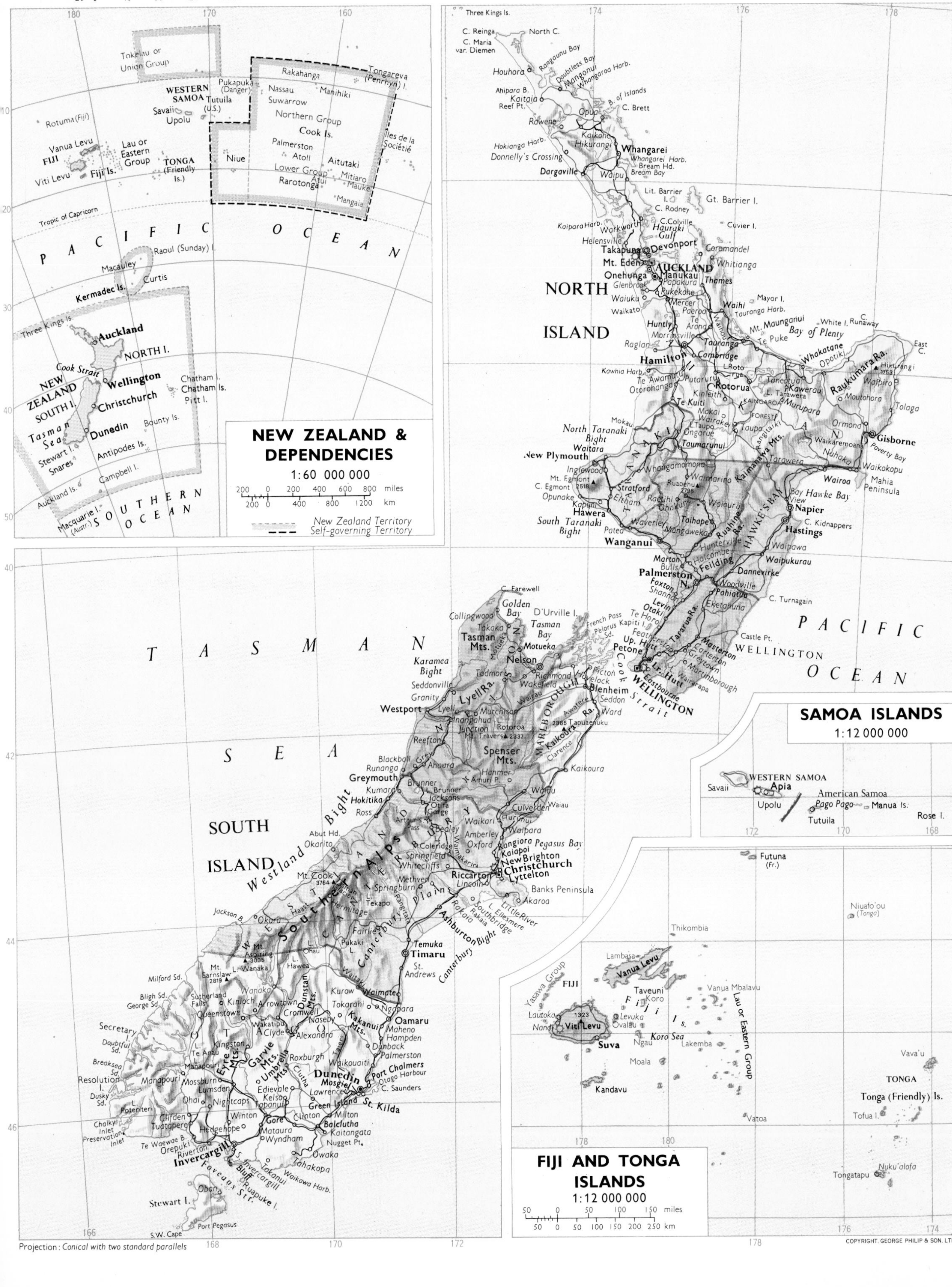

1:6 000 000
20 0 20 40 60 80 100 miles
20 0 40 80 120 160 km

NEW ZEALAND & DEPENDENCIES
1:60 000 000
200 0 200 400 600 800 miles
200 0 400 800 1200 km

New Zealand Territory
Self-governing Territory

SAMOA ISLANDS
1:12 000 000

WESTERN SAMOA
Savaii   Apia
Upolu   American Samoa
         Pago Pago Manua Is.
         Tutuila   Rose I.

FIJI AND TONGA ISLANDS
1:12 000 000
50 0 50 100 150 miles
50 0 50 100 150 200 250 km

Projection: Conical with two standard parallels

COPYRIGHT. GEORGE PHILIP & SON. LTD.

1:40 000 000

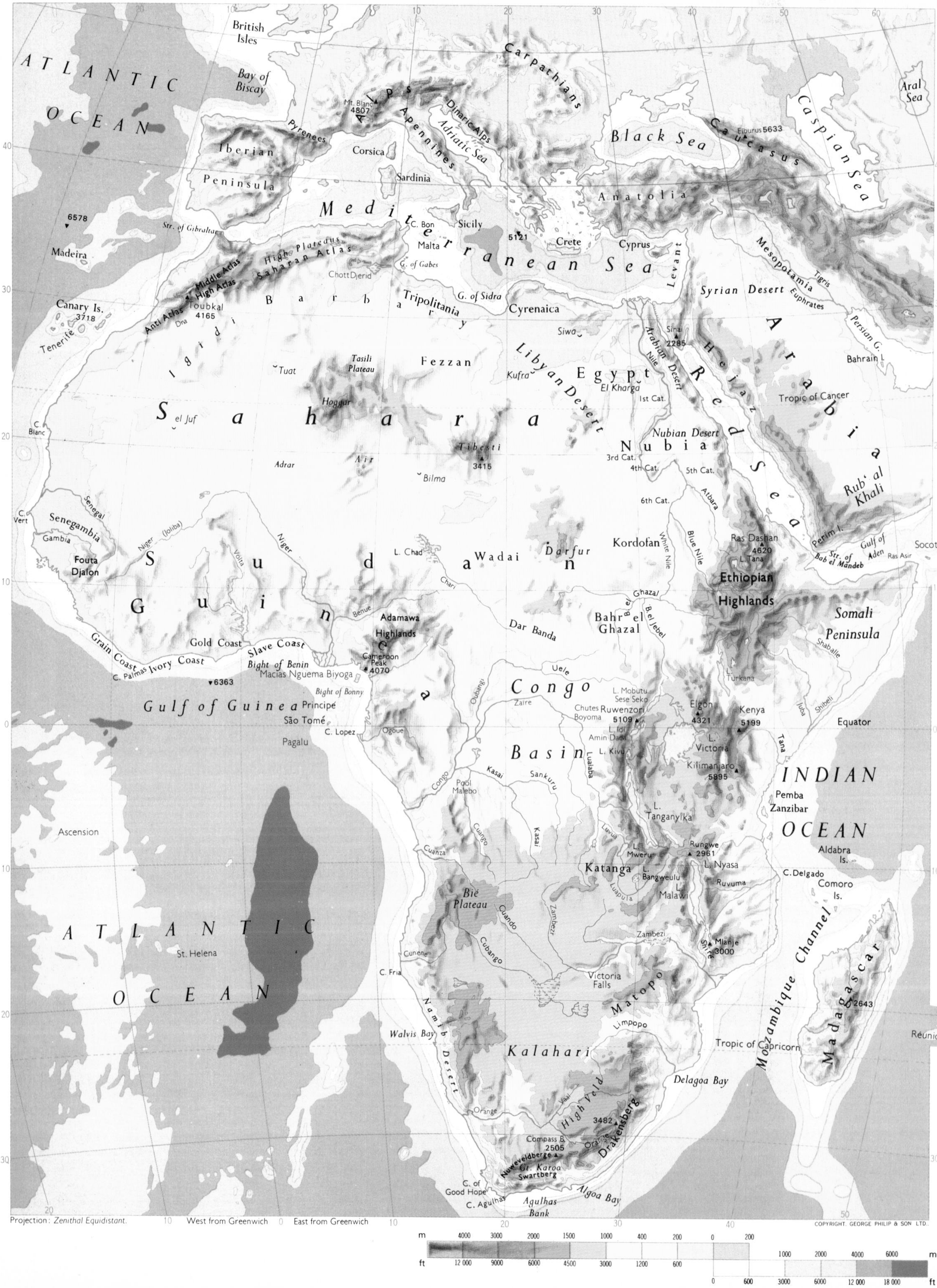

200 0 200 400 600 800 1000 miles
200 0 200 400 600 800 1000 1200 1400 1600 km

ATLANTIC OCEAN

British Isles
Bay of Biscay
Iberian Peninsula
Pyrenees
Mt. Blanc 4807
Alps
Apennines
Corsica
Sardinia
Dinaric Alps
Adriatic Sea
Carpathians
Black Sea
Caucasus
Elburus 5633
Anatolia
Caspian Sea
Aral Sea

Madeira 6578
Str. of Gibraltar
High Plateaus
Saharan Atlas
Middle Atlas
High Atlas
Toubkal 4165
Dra
Anti Atlas
Canary Is. 3718
Tenerife
C. Blanc

Mediterranean Sea
C. Bon
Sicily
Malta 5121
Crete
Cyprus
Levant
Mesopotamia
Tigris
Euphrates
Syrian Desert
Persian G.
Bahrain I.

Barbary
G. of Gabes
Chott Djerid
Tripolitania
G. of Sidra
Cyrenaica

Igidi
Sahara
S. el Juf
Tuat
Adrar
Air
Bilma
Tasili Plateau
Fezzan
Hoggar
Tibesti 3415

Siwa
Egypt
Libyan Desert
Kufra
El Kharga
1st Cat.
Arabian Desert
Nile
Sinai 2285
Hejaz
Red Sea
Arabia
Tropic of Cancer
Rub' al Khali

Nubian Desert
3rd Cat.
Nubia
4th Cat.
5th Cat.
6th Cat.
White Nile
Blue Nile
Atbara
Ras Dashan 4620
L. Tana
Perim I.
Str. of Bab el Mandeb
Gulf of Aden
Ras Asir
Socotra

C. Vert
Senegambia
Senegal
Gambia
Fouta Djalon
Sudan
Niger (Joliba)
Volta
Niger
Guinea
L. Chad
Chari
Wadai
Darfur
Kordofan
Bahr el Ghazal
Bel Ghazal
Bel Jebel
Ethiopian Highlands
Somali Peninsula
Shabelle

Grain Coast
Gold Coast
Ivory Coast
Slave Coast
C. Palmas
Bight of Benin
Adamawa Highlands
Benue
Cameroon Peak 4070
Macias Nguema Biyoga
6363
Dar Banda
Uele
Ubangi
Congo
Zaire
Kasai

Gulf of Guinea
Principe
São Tomé
C. Lopez
Pagalu
Bight of Bonny
Ogooué

L. Mobutu Sese Seko
Chutes Boyoma
Ruwenzori 5109
L. Idi Amin Dada
L. Kivu
Elgon 4321
Kenya 5199
L. Victoria
Kilimanjaro 5895
Turkana
Juba
Tana
Shibeli
Equator

INDIAN OCEAN
Pemba
Zanzibar
Aldabra Is.
C. Delgado
Comoro Is.

Ascension
Congo Basin
Congo
Kasai
Sankuru
Lualaba
L. Tanganyika
Katanga
Lavui
L. Mweru
L. Bangweulu
Luapula
Rungwe 2961
L. Nyasa
Malawi
Ruvuma
Mozambique Channel
Madagascar 2643
Réunion

ATLANTIC OCEAN
St. Helena

Bié Plateau
Cuanza
Cubango
Cuando
Cunene
C. Fria
Namib Desert
Walvis Bay
Zambezi
Victoria Falls
Mlanje 3000
Shire
Zambezi
Matopo
Tropic of Capricorn

Kalahari
Limpopo
Delagoa Bay
Orange
Vaal
High Veld 3482
Drakensberg
Compass B. 2505
Nieuveldberge
Gt. Karoo
Swartberg
C. of Good Hope
C. Agulhas
Agulhas Bank
Algoa Bay

COPYRIGHT. GEORGE PHILIP & SON LTD.

m 4000 3000 2000 1500 1000 400 200 0 200
ft 12 000 9000 6000 4500 3000 1200 600
1000 2000 4000 6000 m
0 600 3000 6000 12 000 18 000 ft

1:40 000 000

200 0 200 400 600 800 1000 miles
200 0 200 400 600 800 1000 1200 1400 1600 km

LES.   Lesotho
O.-V. Oranje-Vrystaat
SWAZ. Swaziland

Projection: Zenithal Equidistant.

West from Greenwich   East from Greenwich

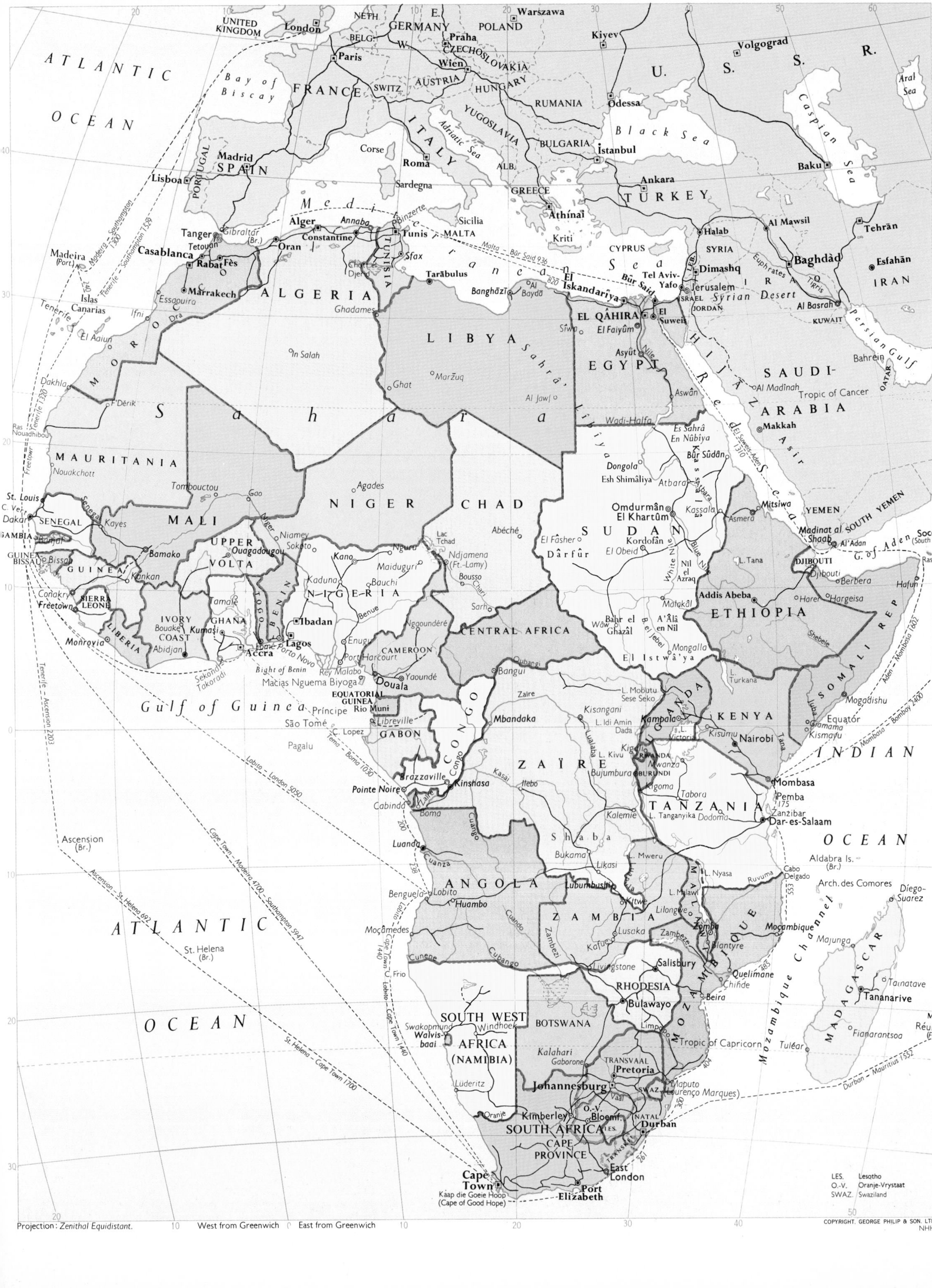

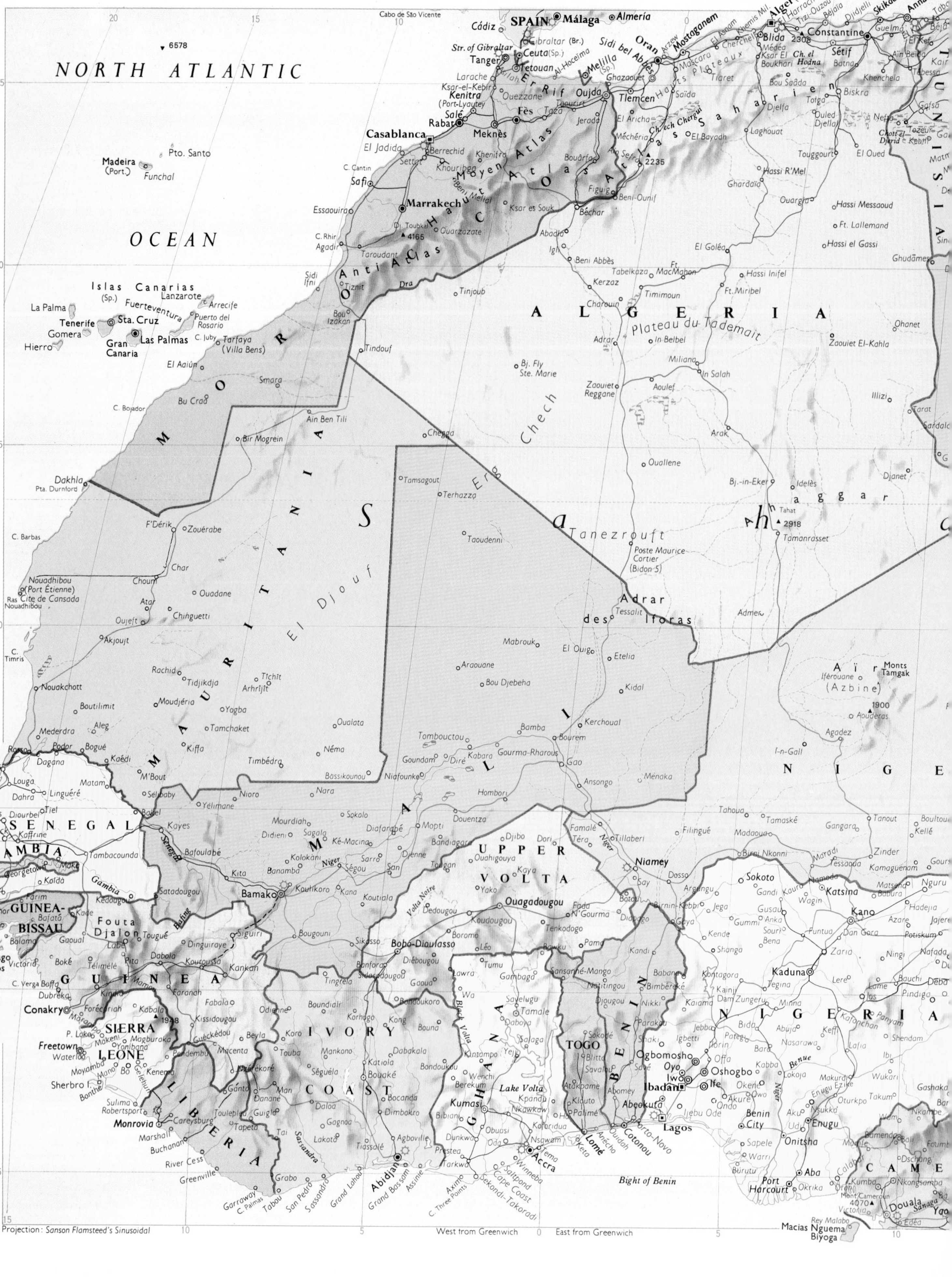
NORTH ATLANTIC
OCEAN
SPAIN
Málaga
Almería
Cádiz
Gibraltar (Br.)
Str. of Gibraltar
Ceuta (Sp.)
Tanger
Tetouan
Al-Hoceima
Melilla (Sp.)
Oran
Mostaganem
Alger (Algiers)
Blida
Médéa
Skikda
Annaba
Constantine
Sétif
Biskra
Larache
Ksar-el-Kebir
Kenitra (Port-Lyautey)
Salé
Rabat
Fès
Meknès
Taza
Oujda
Tlemcen
Sidi bel Abbès
Casablanca
El Jadida
Berrechid
Settat
Khouribga
Safi
C. Cantin
Essaouira
Marrakech
Dj. Toubkal
4165
Ouarzazate
Agadir
C. Rhir
Taroudant
Tiznit
Sidi Ifni
Ksar es Souk
Figuig
Beni-Ounif
Béchar
Abadla
Beni Abbès
Moyen Atlas
Haut Atlas
Anti Atlas
Rif
Hauts Plateaux
Atlas Saharien
Chott el Hodna
Chott ech Chergui
El Aricha
Méchéria
Aïn Sefra
2235
2308
El Bayadh
Laghouat
Djelfa
Ghardaïa
Hassi R'Mel
Ouargla
Touggourt
El Oued
Hassi Messaoud
Ft. Lallemand
Hassi el Gassi
El Goléa
Ghudāmes
Madeira (Port.)
Funchal
Pto. Santo
6578
Islas Canarias (Sp.)
Lanzarote
Arrecife
Fuerteventura
Puerto del Rosario
La Palma
Tenerife
Sta. Cruz
Gomera
Hierro
Gran Canaria
Las Palmas
C. Juby
Tarfaya (Villa Bens)
Bou Izakan
Dra
Tinjoub
Tindouf
El Aaiún
Smara
Bu Craa
C. Bojador
MOROCCO
ALGERIA
Plateau du Tademait
Tabelkoza
Ft. MacMahon
Kerzaz
Timimoun
Charouin
Adrar
In Belbel
Hassi Inifel
Ft. Miribel
Ohanet
Zaouiet El-Kahla
Bj. Fly Ste. Marie
Miliana
In Salah
Zaouiet Reggane
Aoulef
Illizi
Tarat
Arak
Chegga
Chech
Erg
Ain Ben Tili
Bir Mogrein
Ouallene
Bj.-in-Eker
Idelès
Djanet
Ahaggar
Tahat
2918
Tamanrasset
Tanezrouft
Poste Maurice Cortier (Bidon 5)
Sahara
Dakhla
Pta. Durnford
C. Barbas
F'Dérik
Zouérabe
Tamsagout
Terhazza
Taoudenni
Char
Choum
Nouadhibou (Port Étienne)
Ras Nouadhibou
Cite de Cansada
Atar
Ouadane
Chinguetti
Oujeft
Akjoujt
C. Timris
El Djouf
MAURITANIA
Adrar des Iforas
Tessalit
Admer
Aïr (Azbine)
Monts Tamgak
Iférouane
1900
Aouderas
Agadez
I-n-Gall
Rachid
Tidjikdja
Tichit
Arhrijit
Mabrouk
El Ouig
Etelia
Araouane
Bou Djebeha
Kidal
Nouakchott
Boutilimit
Moudjéria
Yogba
Aleg
Tamchaket
Oualata
Mederdra
Kiffa
Néma
Bamba
Kerchoual
Bourem
Tombouctou
Kabara
Gourma-Rharous
Rosso
Podor
Bogué
Kaédi
Dagana
St. Louis
Timbédra
Goundam
Diré
Gao
Ansongo
Ménaka
Bassikounou
Niafounké
MALI
NIGER
Louga
Matam
M'Bout
Dahra
Linguère
Selibaby
Hombori
Nioro
Nara
Yélimané
Tivaoune
Rufisque
Thiès
Diourbel
Tiel
Vert
Dakar
Kaolack
Mbour
Koffrine
SENEGAL
Bakel
Kayes
Mourdiah
Sokolo
Douentza
Diafarabé
Mopti
Didieni
Sagala
Ké-Macina
Bandiagara
Djibo
Dori
Famalé
Téra
Tillaberi
Filingué
Madaoua
Tahoua
Tamaské
Gangara
Tanout
Zinder
Maradi
Tessaoua
Birni Nkonni
Kamaguenam
Matsena
Babura
Nguru
GAMBIA
Banjul (Bathurst)
Georgetown
Tambacounda
Bafoulabé
Kolokani
Banamba
Sarro
Djenné
San
Tougan
Ouahigouya
Kaya
UPPER VOLTA
Niamey
Say
Dosso
Argungu
Sokoto
Gandi
Kaura Namoda
Katsina
Kano
Wagin
Sedhiou
Kolda
Gambia
Kita
Koulikoro
Ségou
Niger
Bamako
Kana
Koutiala
Yako
Ouagadougou
Fada N'Gourma
Diapaga
Botou
Birnin-Kebbi
Gaya
Jega
Gusau
Anka
Gummi
Sokoto
Kende
Souri
Bena
Funtua
Dan Gora
Azare
Hadejia
Potiskum
Ziguinchor
Farim
GUINEA-BISSAU
Bafatá
Bissau
Bolama
Arquipélago dos Bijagós
Kadé
Fouta Djalon
Gaoual
Tougué
Dinguiraye
Kédougou
Satadougou
Bafing
Siguiri
Bougouni
Sikasso
Volta Noire
Dédougou
Koudougou
Boromo
Tenkodogo
Pama
Kandi
Shanga
Zaria
Ningi
Nafada
Boké
Télimélé
Labé
Pita
Dabola
Kouroussa
Kankan
Bobo-Dioulasso
Léo
Banfora
Sidéradougou
Diébougou
Tumu
Bawku
Sansanné-Mango
Natitingou
Babana
Bimberéké
Kontagora
Kainji
Kaduna
Tegina
Lere
Lame
Bauchi
Pindiga
Victoria
C. Verga
Boffa
Dubréka
GUINEA
Mamou
Kindia
Faranah
Tingréla
Gaoua
Lawra
Gambaga
Wa
Djougou
Nikki
Kaiama
Dam
Zungeru
Minna
Conakry
Forécariah
Kabala
1948
Fabala
Kissidougou
Odienné
Boundiali
Bondoukoro
Korhogo
Kong
Bouna
Black Volta
Savelugu
Tamale
Daboya
Salaga
Yeji
Parakou
Shaki
Jebba
Ilorin
Bida
Pategi
Abuja
Nasarawa
Keffi
Katonchan
Panyam
Shendam
Lafia
P. Loko
Marampa
Magburaka
Yonibana
SIERRA LEONE
Freetown
Waterloo
Moyamba
Mano
Bo
Pendembu
Kenema
Guéckédou
Macenta
Beyla
Koro
Touba
IVORY COAST
Mankono
Dabakala
Katiola
Bouaké
Kintampo
Wenchi
Berekum
Bondoukou
GHANA
Lake Volta
Kpandu
TOGO
Sokodé
Blitta
Savalou
BENIN
Ogbomosho
Oyo
Iwo
Oshogbo
Ife
Ibadan
Igbetti
Offa
Kabba
Okene
Lokoja
Benue
Makurdi
Wukari
Ibi
Takum
Gashaka
NIGERIA
Sherbro I.
Bonthe
Sulima
Robertsport
Monrovia
Careysburg
Marshall
Buchanan
River Cess
Greenville
LIBERIA
Gánto
Nzérékoré
Man
Danané
Toulepleu
Guiglo
Tapeta
Daloa
Séguéla
Bocanda
Dimbokro
Gagnoa
Lakota
Agboville
Tiassalé
Abidjan
Grand Bassam
Assinie
Grand Lahou
Sassandra
San Pedro
Tabou
Grabo
Garraway
C. Palmas
Tai
Kumasi
Bibiani
Obuasi
Dunkwa
Oda
Prestea
Tarkwa
Axim
C. Three Points
Sekondi-Takoradi
Cape Coast
Saltpond
Winneba
Accra
Tema
Nsawam
Koforidua
Nkawkaw
Atakpamé
Klouto
Palimé
Keta
Lomé
Anécho
Ouidah
Cotonou
Porto-Novo
Abomey
Abeokuta
Ijebu Ode
Lagos
Akure
Ondo
Owo
Benin City
Sapele
Warri
Burutu
Onitsha
Enugu
Nsukka
Oturkpo
Udi
Aku
Port Harcourt
Okrika
Aba
Calabar
Mamfe
Bamenda
Kumba
Nkongsamba
Mont Cameroun
4070
Victoria
Douala
Sanaga
Edéa
Bight of Benin
Rey Malabo
Macias Nguema Biyoga
CAMEROON
TUNISIA
Tabarka
Béja
Kairouan
Tebessa
Khenchela
Gafsa
Tozeur
Nefta
Chott el Djerid
Kebili
Djelfa
Saïda
Tiaret
Mascara
Relizane
Tizi-Ouzou
Bejaïa
Djidjelli
Guelma
Aïn Beïda
El Kef
Batna
Bou Saâda
Tolga
Ouled Djellal
Ghazaouet
Jerada
Taourirt
Bouârfa
Khenifra
Ouezzane
Chechaouen
Boukhari
Ksar El Boukhari
Khemis Mil.
El Harrach
El Asnam
Cherchell
Arzew
Cabo de São Vicente
West from Greenwich
East from Greenwich
Projection: Sanson Flamsteed's Sinusoidal

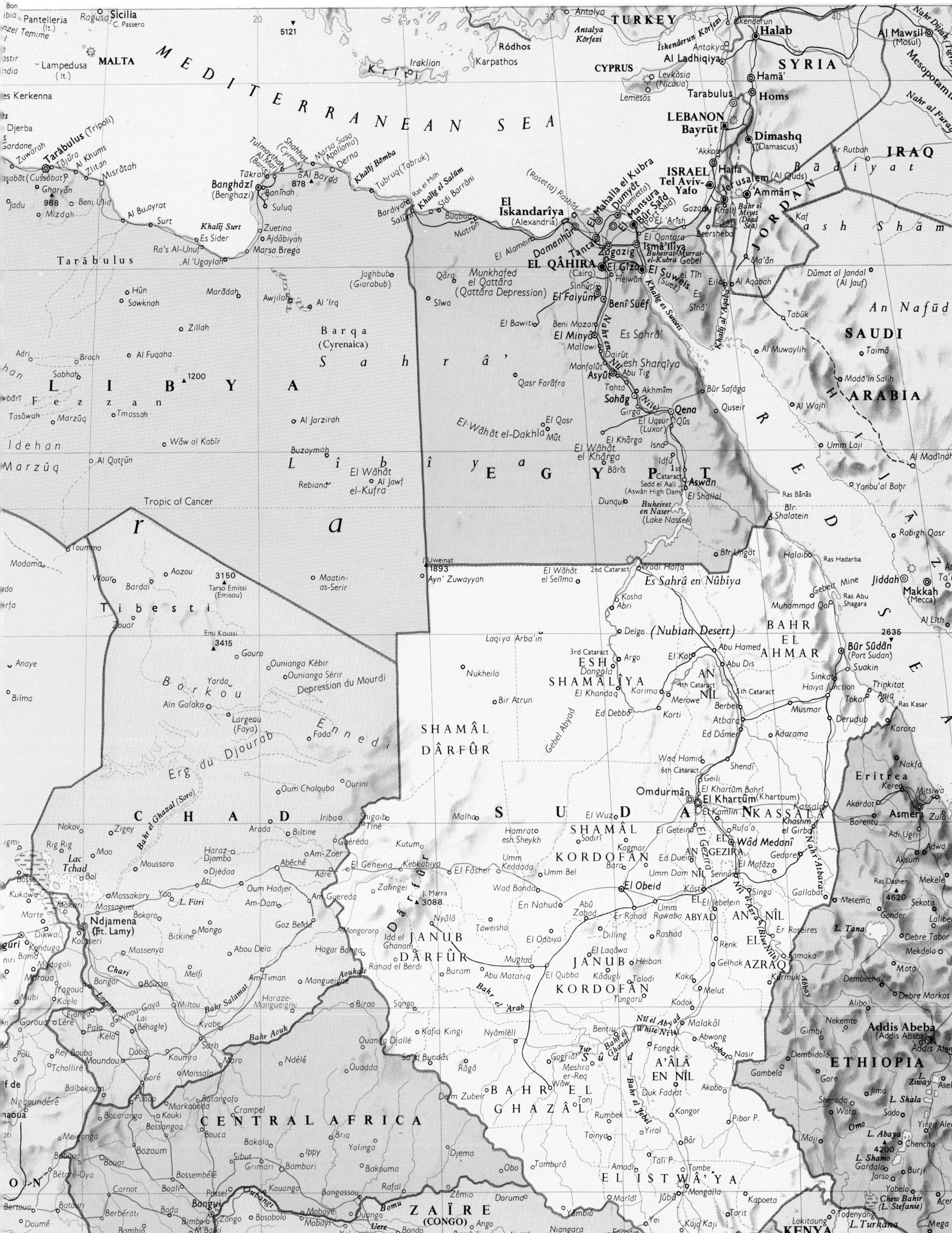

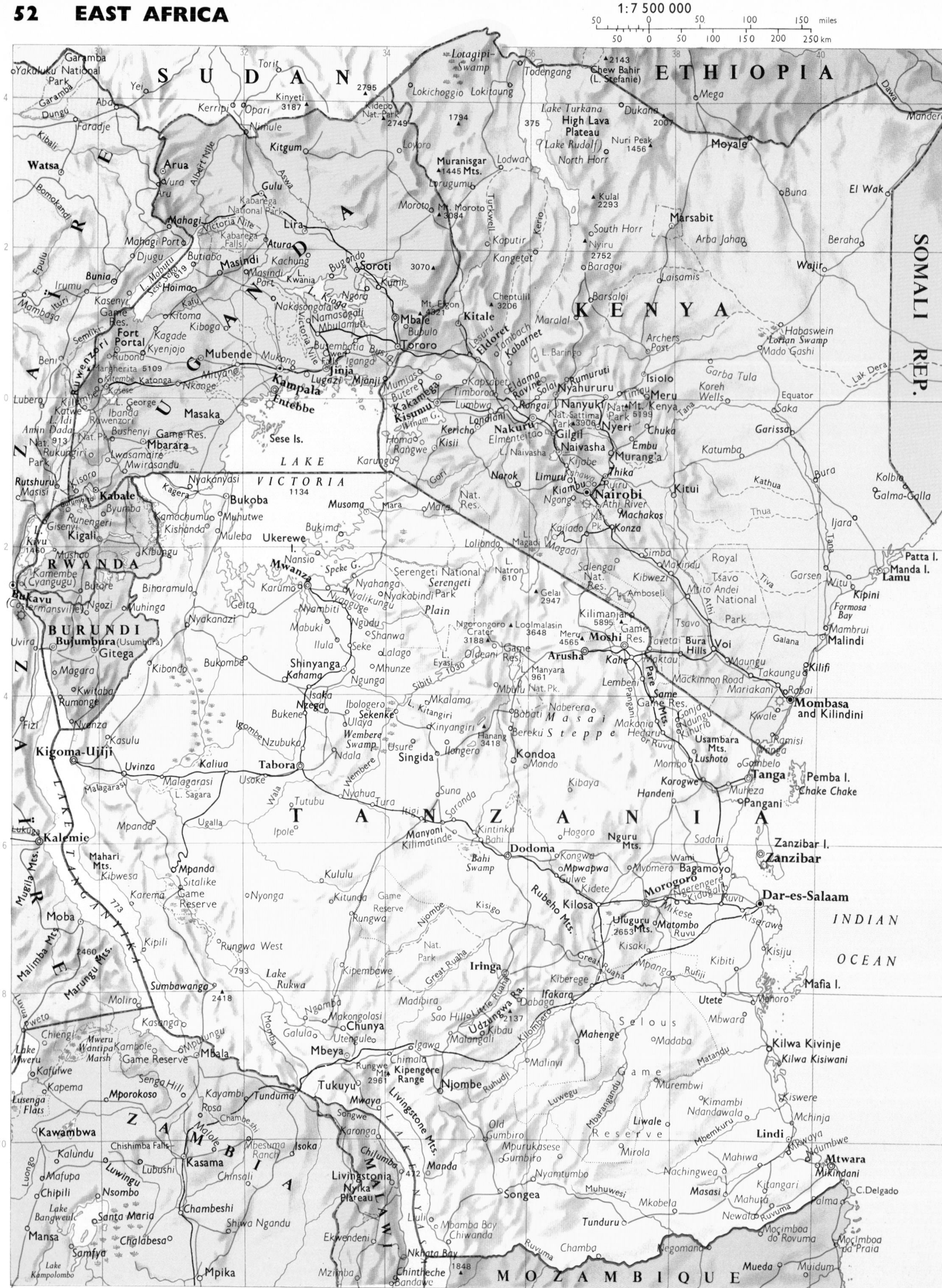

1 : 7 500 000

50 0 50 100 150 miles
50 0 50 100 150 200 250 km

SUDAN

ETHIOPIA

UGANDA

KENYA

SOMALI REP.

ZAÏRE

RWANDA

BURUNDI

TANZANIA

LAKE VICTORIA

LAKE TANGANYIKA

LAKE NYASA

ZAMBIA

MALAWI

MOZAMBIQUE

INDIAN OCEAN

Watsa · Arua · Gulu · Kitgum · Lira · Soroti · Kitale · Eldoret · Moyale · Marsabit · Wajir

Kampala · Entebbe · Jinja · Kisumu · Kakamega · Nakuru · Nyeri · Nairobi · Machakos

Fort Portal · Masindi · Hoima · Mubende · Masaka · Mbarara · Kabale · Kigali · Bukoba

Bujumbura (Usumbura) · Gitega · Kigoma-Ujiji · Mwanza · Musoma · Arusha · Moshi · Voi · Mombasa and Kilindini · Malindi · Lamu

Tabora · Singida · Dodoma · Morogoro · Dar-es-Salaam · Zanzibar · Tanga · Pemba I. · Zanzibar I. · Mafia I.

Kalemie · Mpanda · Sumbawanga · Mbeya · Iringa · Njombe · Songea · Kilwa Kivinje · Lindi · Mtwara · Mikindani

Lake Turkana (Lake Rudolf) · Lake Victoria 1134 · Lake Tanganyika · Lake Nyasa · Lake Rukwa

Serengeti National Park · Ngorongoro Crater · Kilimanjaro 5895 · Meru 4565 · Tsavo National Park · Selous Game Reserve

Mt. Kenya 5199 · Mt. Elgon 4321 · Margherita 5109

East from Greenwich

1:8 000 000

50   0   50   100   150   200 miles
50   0   50 100 150 200 250 300 km

COPYRIGHT. GEORGE PHILIP & SON LTD.

CHAD

NIGER

MALI

UPPER VOLTA

NIGERIA

GHANA

IVORY COAST

DAHOMEY

TOGO

NIGER

CAMEROUN

EQUATORIAL GUINEA

MACIAS NGUEMA BIYOGA

GULF OF GUINEA

Gold Coast

Slave Coast

Bight of Benin

Niger Delta

Kano
Kaduna
Zaria
Maiduguri
IBADAN
LAGOS
Benin City
Port Harcourt
Enugu
Ogbomosho
Oyo
Abeokuta
Ilorin
Makurdi
Calabar
Aba
DOUALA
Yaoundé

ACCRA
Kumasi
Tema
Sekondi Takoradi
Cape Coast

LOMÉ
Cotonou
Porto-Novo
Ouidah
Abomey

Niamey
Ouagadougou
Koudougou
Tamale

Sokoto
Katsina
Gusau
Zinder
Maradi
Gashua

Timbuktu (Tombouctou)

East from Greenwich

Projection: Lambert's Equivalent Azimuthal

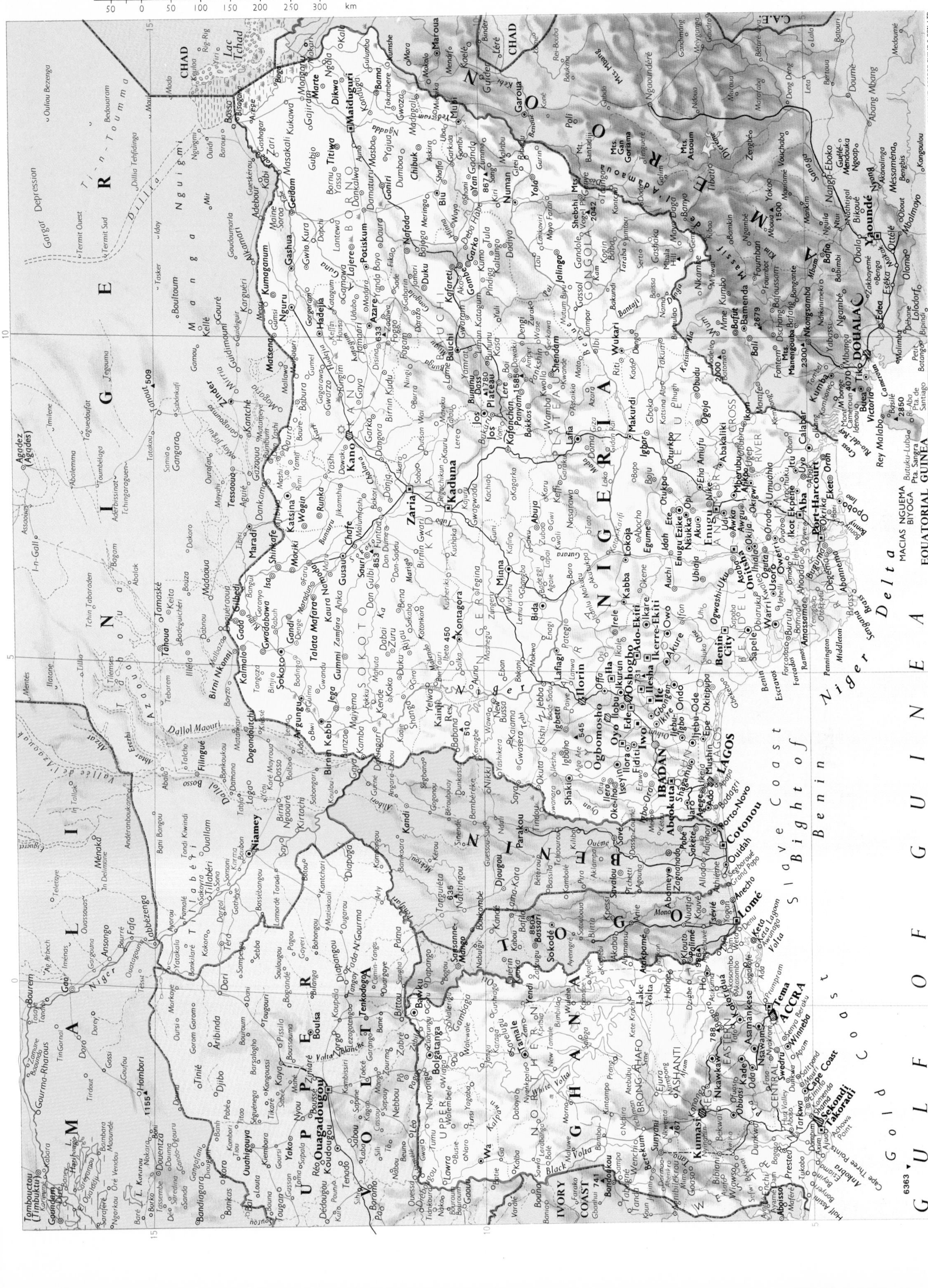

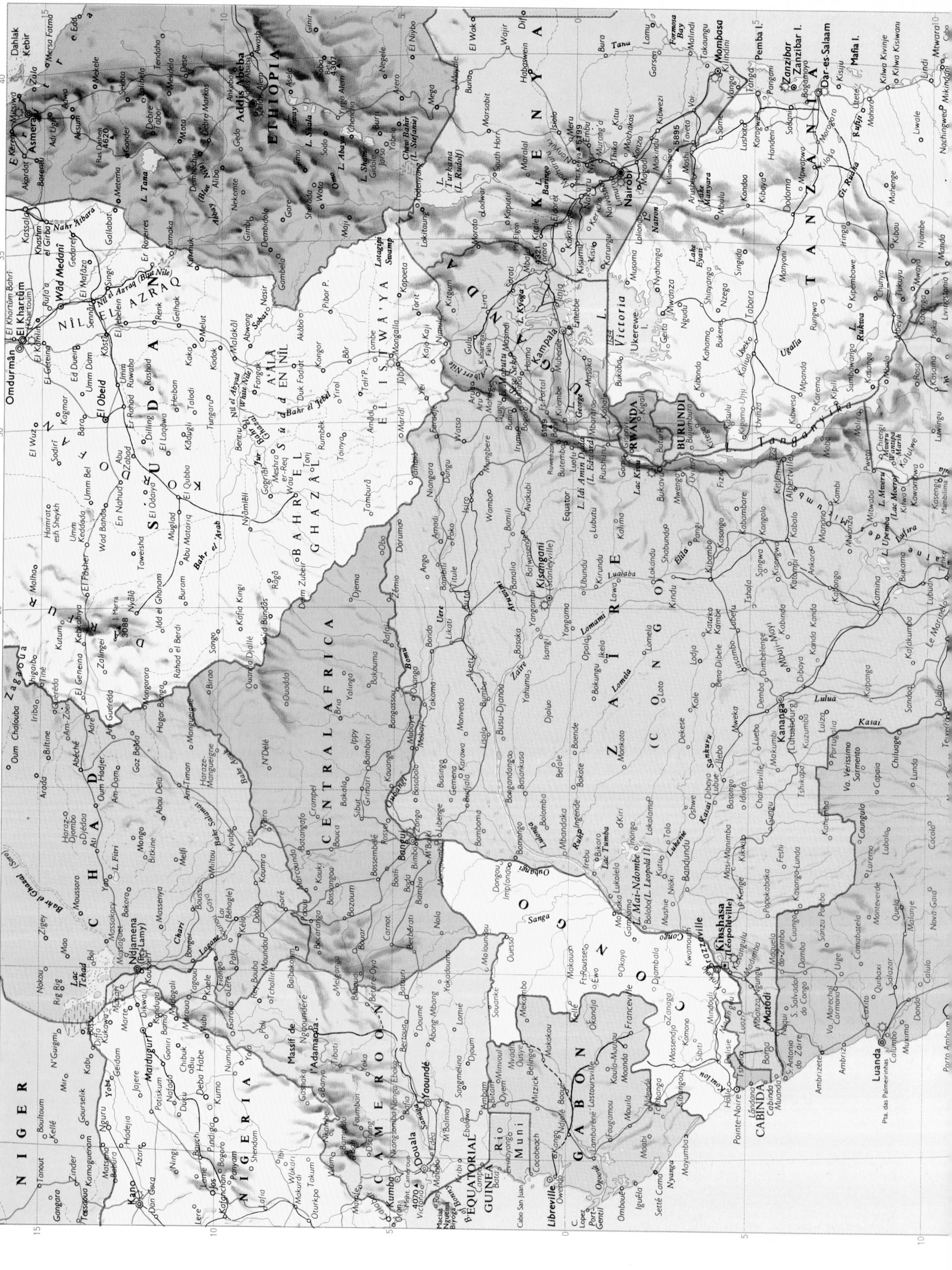

NIGER
CHAD
NIGERIA
CAMEROON
CENTRAL AFRICA
SUDAN
ETHIOPIA
KENYA
UGANDA
TANZANIA
RWANDA
BURUNDI
ZAIRE
CONGO
GABON
EQUATORIAL GUINEA
Rio Muni
CABINDA
Omdurmân
El Khartûm
Addis Ababa
Asmera
Nairobi
Mombasa
Dar-es-Salaam
Zanzibar
Kampala
Kinshasa (Léopoldville)
Brazzaville
Libreville
Yaoundé
Douala
Ndjamena (Ft-Lamy)
Bangui
Kisangani (Stanleyville)
Luanda
Kano
Maiduguri
Lac Tchad
L. Victoria
L. Turkana (L. Rudolf)
L. Tana
Tanganyika
Bahr el Ghazal
Nîl el Azraq (Blue Nile)
Nîl el Abyad (White Nile)

1:15 000 000

100 0 100 200 300 400 miles

100 0 100 200 300 400 500 600 km

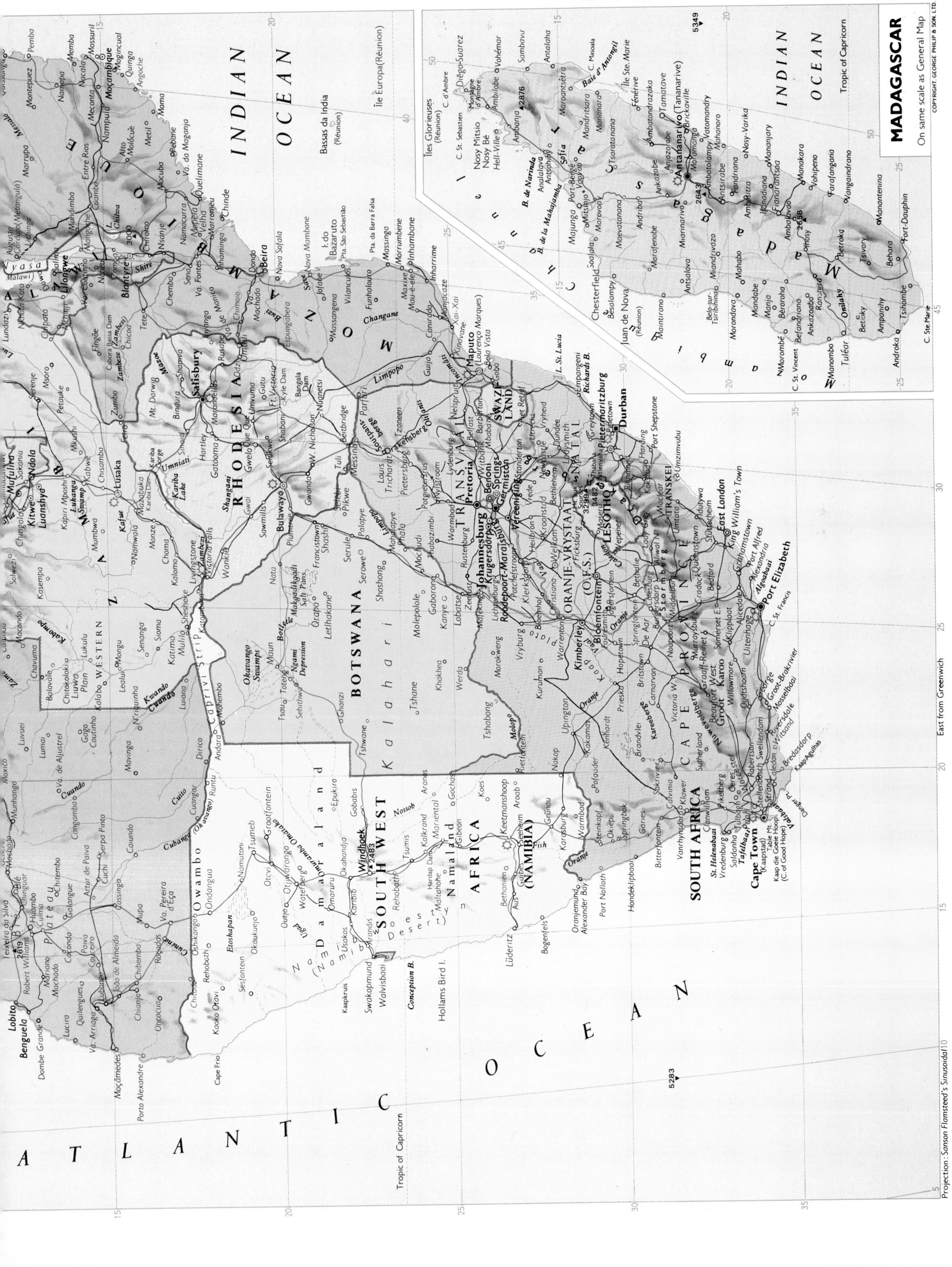

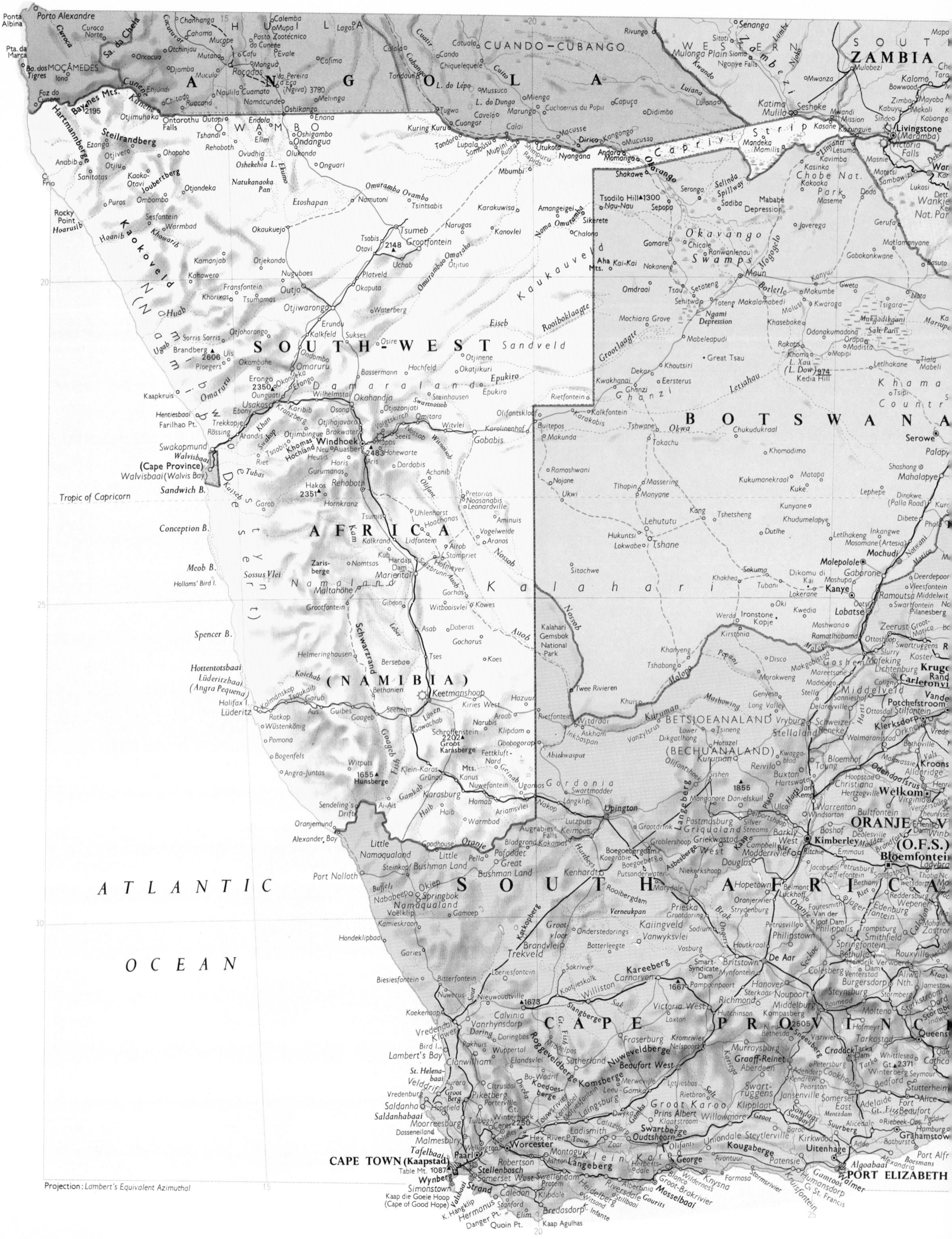

Projection: Lambert's Equivalent Azimuthal

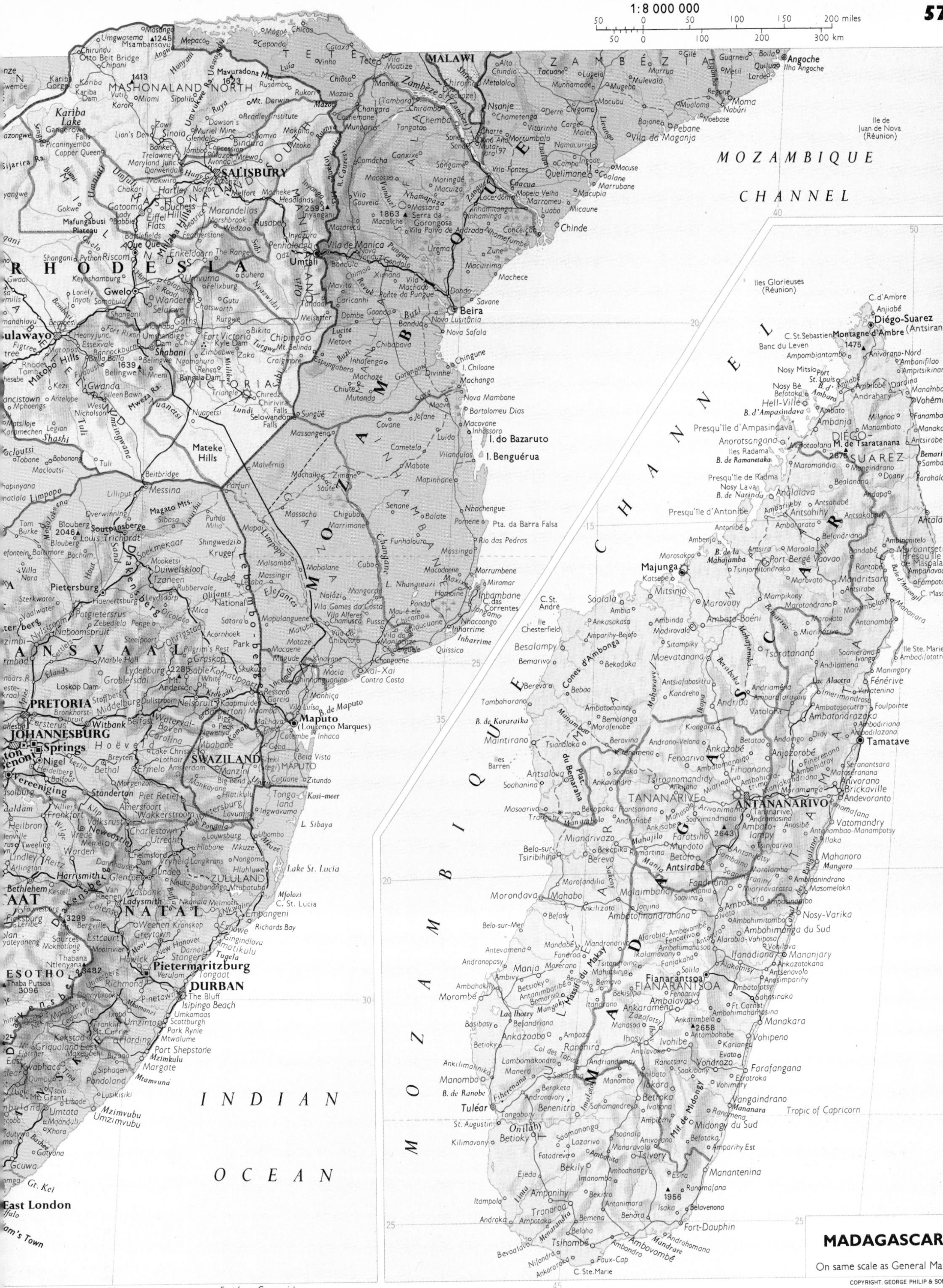

1:8 000 000

50   0   50   100   150   200 miles
50   0   50   100   200   300 km

MOZAMBIQUE

CHANNEL

MADAGASCAR

On same scale as General Map

COPYRIGHT GEORGE PHILIP & SON LTD.

East from Greenwich

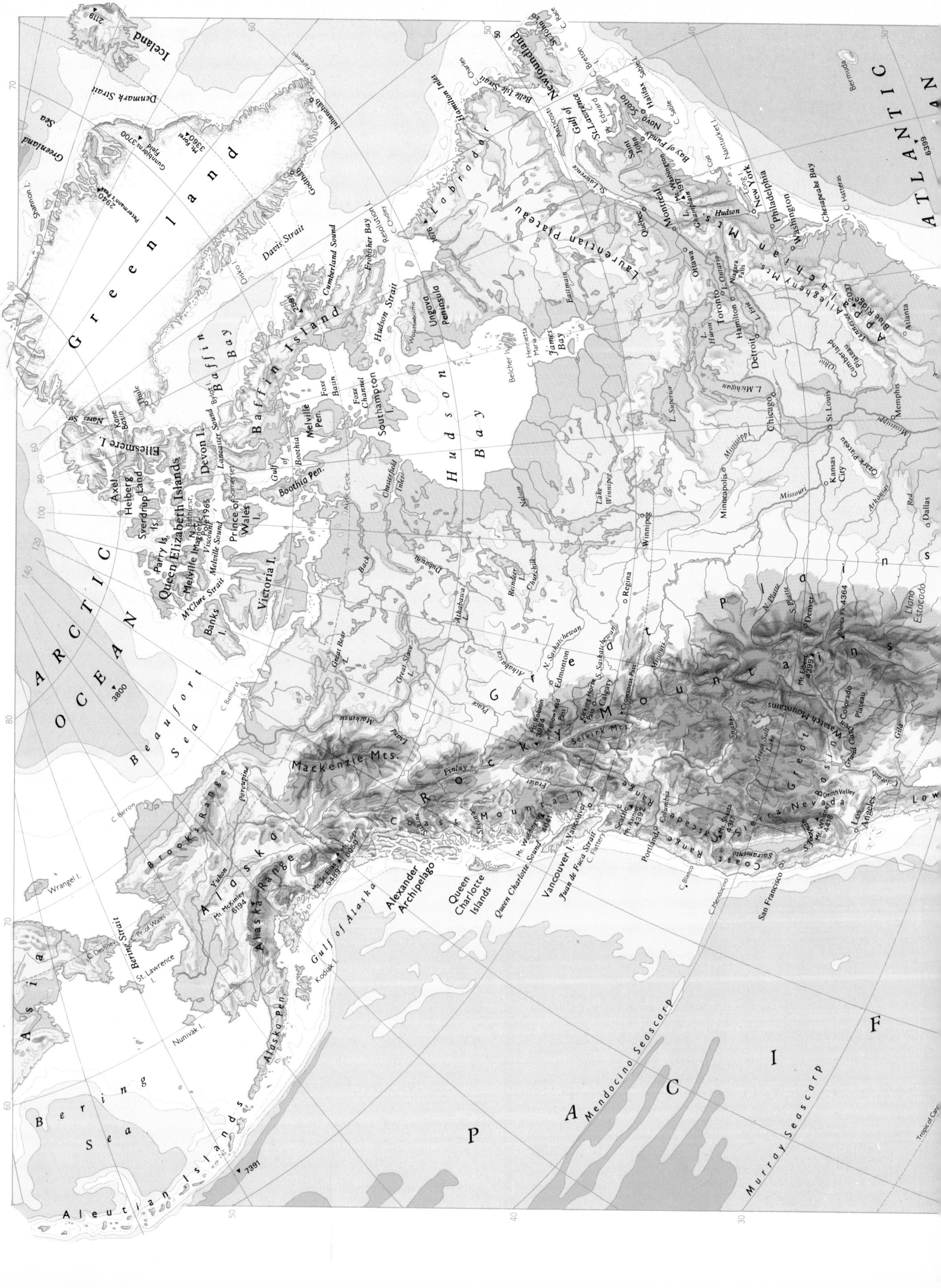
Iceland
Denmark Strait
Greenland Sea
Greenland
Davis Strait
Cumberland Sound
Frobisher Bay
Baffin Bay
Baffin Island
Labrador
Hudson Strait
Ungava Peninsula
Hudson Bay
James Bay
Belcher Is.
Laurentian Plateau
Newfoundland
Gulf of St. Lawrence
Belle Isle Strait
Hamilton Inlet
Nova Scotia
Bay of Fundy
Halifax
Sable I.
Cape Breton I.
Nantucket I.
Long I.
New York
Philadelphia
Washington
Chesapeake Bay
C. Hatteras
Bermuda
ATLANTIC
Hudson
Montreal
Quebec
Ottawa
L. Ontario
Toronto
Niagara Falls
Hamilton
L. Erie
Detroit
L. Huron
L. Michigan
L. Superior
Chicago
St. Louis
Kansas City
Memphis
Atlanta
Dallas
Appalachian Mts
Allegheny Mts
Blue Ridge
Cumberland Plateau
Ohio
Mississippi
Missouri
Arkansas
Red
Ozark Plateau
Minneapolis
Winnipeg
Lake Winnipeg
Regina
Edmonton
Calgary
N. Saskatchewan
S. Saskatchewan
Reindeer L.
Churchill
Nelson
Athabasca L.
Great Slave L.
Great Bear L.
Peace
Mackenzie
Liard
Dubawnt
Back
Chesterfield Inlet
Southampton I.
Foxe Basin
Foxe Channel
Melville Pen.
Gulf of Boothia
Boothia Pen.
Arctic Circle
Ellesmere I.
Kane Basin
Nares Str.
Thule
Axel Heiberg
Sverdrup Land
Queen Elizabeth Islands
Parry Is.
Melville I.
Devon I.
Lancaster Sound
Prince of Wales I.
Victoria I.
Banks I.
M'Clure Strait
Melville Sound
ARCTIC OCEAN
Beaufort Sea
C. Bathurst
C. Barrow
Wrangel I.
Brooks Range
Porcupine
Yukon
Alaska
Alaska Range
Mt. McKinley 6194
Mt. St. Elias 5489
Mt. Logan 6050
Mackenzie Mts.
Great Plains
Rocky Mountains
Selkirk Mts.
Mt. Robson 3954
Coast Mountains
Coast Range
Cascade Range
Sierra Nevada
Great Basin
Wasatch Mountains
Colorado Plateau
Grand Canyon
Mt. Elbert 4399
Blanca Pk. 4364
Denver
Llano Estacado
N. Platte
S. Platte
Gila
Colorado
Death Valley
Mt. Whitney 4418
Los Angeles
San Francisco
Sacramento
Mt. Shasta 4317
Mt. Rainier 4392
Portland
Seattle
Columbia
Snake
Great Salt Lake
Fraser
Finlay
Vancouver
Vancouver I.
Juan de Fuca Strait
C. Flattery
Queen Charlotte Sound
Queen Charlotte Islands
Alexander Archipelago
Gulf of Alaska
Kodiak I.
Alaska Pen.
Bering Strait
C. Prince of Wales
C. Dezhnev
St. Lawrence I.
Nunivak I.
Asia
Bering Sea
Aleutian Islands
7391
3800
C. Blanco
C. Mendocino
Mendocino Seascarp
Murray Seascarp
PACIFIC
Tropic of Cancer

59

1:30 000 000

100   0   100   200   300   400   500   600   700 miles
100   0   200   400   600   800   1000 km

Tropic of Cancer

Bahama
Islands

Hispaniola
Puerto Rico
Milwaukee 9700

Sierra de Mérita
Venezuelan
Basin
G. of Venezuela
Maracaibo

Bolivian Plateau
La Paz
Trench

Cuba
La Habana
Jamaica
Greater
Antilles
Sea
Colombian
Basin
Port-au-Prince
Caribbean
Trench
1680
Trough Cayman

Florida Strait
C. Sable

Cordillera Occidental
Cordillera Central
Bogotá
Cordillera Oriental
A
n
d
e
s

Quito Cotopaxi 5897
Chimborazo 6267
Peru

Orinoco
Negro
Juruá
Purus
Ucayali

Lima

Chile
Chincha Is.
Illampu 6650

Yucatán
Strait
G. of Mexico
C.Catoche
Yucatán
Basin
Yucatán
Peninsula

C. de San Francisco
G. de Guayaquil
Pta Pariñas
Lobos Is.

Gulf of Honduras
G. of Darién
G. of Panamá
Panama Canal
Gracias a Dios

Guatemala
Coco
L. Nicaragua
3337

Mississippi
Delta

Gulf of
Mexico

Gulf of Campeche
Isthmus of Tehuantepec
Orizaba 5700
Puebla
Popocatepetl 5452

G. of Tehuantepec
Guatemala Trench
6662

Galapagos

N

Rio Grande del Norte
Monterrey
Eastern Sierra Madre
México
Guadalajara Santiago
Balsas

Mexican Plateau
Western Sierra Madre

C. Corrientes

E

O
C
E
A
N

Gulf of California
C. San Lucas
California

Revilla Gigedo Is.

Clarion Fracture Zone

POLITICAL
1:70 000 000

Projection: Bonne

GREENLAND
(Denmark)

ICELAND
Denmark Str.
Davis Strait
Baffin Island
Hudson Strait

ARCTIC OCEAN
C. Barrow
Beaufort Sea
Banks I.
Victoria I.
M Clure Str.
Pr. Patrick I.
Queen Elizabeth Is.
Ellesmere I.
Parry Islands
Lancaster Sd.
Upernavik

ALASKA (U.S.)
Anchorage
Yukon
Arctic Circle
Dawson
Mackenzie
Gt. Bear L.
Gt. Slave L.
Athabasca L.
Edmonton
Reindeer L.
Churchill
Nelson

CANADA
Winnipeg
L. Winnipeg
Regina
Medicine Hat
Calgary
Lethbridge
Saskatoon

Bering Str.
Bering Sea
Aleutian Is. (U.S.)
Queen Charlotte Is.
Pr. Rupert
Skagway
Victoria
Vancouver
Fraser
Seattle
Spokane
Portland

San Francisco
Oakland
Los Angeles

UNITED STATES
Gt. Salt Lake
Salt Lake City
Denver
Kansas City
St Louis
Omaha
Minneapolis
St Paul
Milwaukee
Chicago
Cincinnati
Pittsburgh
Detroit
Buffalo
Toronto
Ottawa
Montreal
Québec
Boston
New York
Philadelphia
Baltimore
Washington
Memphis
Atlanta
New Orleans
Dallas
Houston
Galveston
El Paso
Red
Missouri
Mississippi

Labrador
Newfoundland
C. Breton I.
Nova Scotia
Bermuda (Br.)
C. Hatteras
ATLANTIC OCEAN

Tropic of Cancer
Florida
Miami
BAHAMAS
CUBA
La Habana
Yucatán Strait
Gulf of Mexico
Tampico
Veracruz
Mérida
Monterrey
MEXICO
México
Guadalajara
Acapulco
Revilla Gigedo (Mex.)

HAITI
DOM. REP.
JAMAICA
Kingston
PUERTO RICO (U.S.)
Caribbean Sea
GUADELOUPE
MARTINIQUE
TRINIDAD & TOBAGO
Caracas
VENEZUELA
Maracaibo
COLOMBIA
SOUTH AMERICA
CENTRAL AMERICA
BELIZE
GUATEMALA
HONDURAS
EL SALVADOR
NICARAGUA
COSTA RICA
PANAMA
Cartagena

PACIFIC OCEAN
Valparaíso
Guadalajara

West from 90 Greenwich

m 4000 3000 2000 1500 1000 600 400 200 0 200 600
ft 12 000 9000 6000 4500 3000 1200 0 2000 6000 12 000 18 000 24 000
ft   m

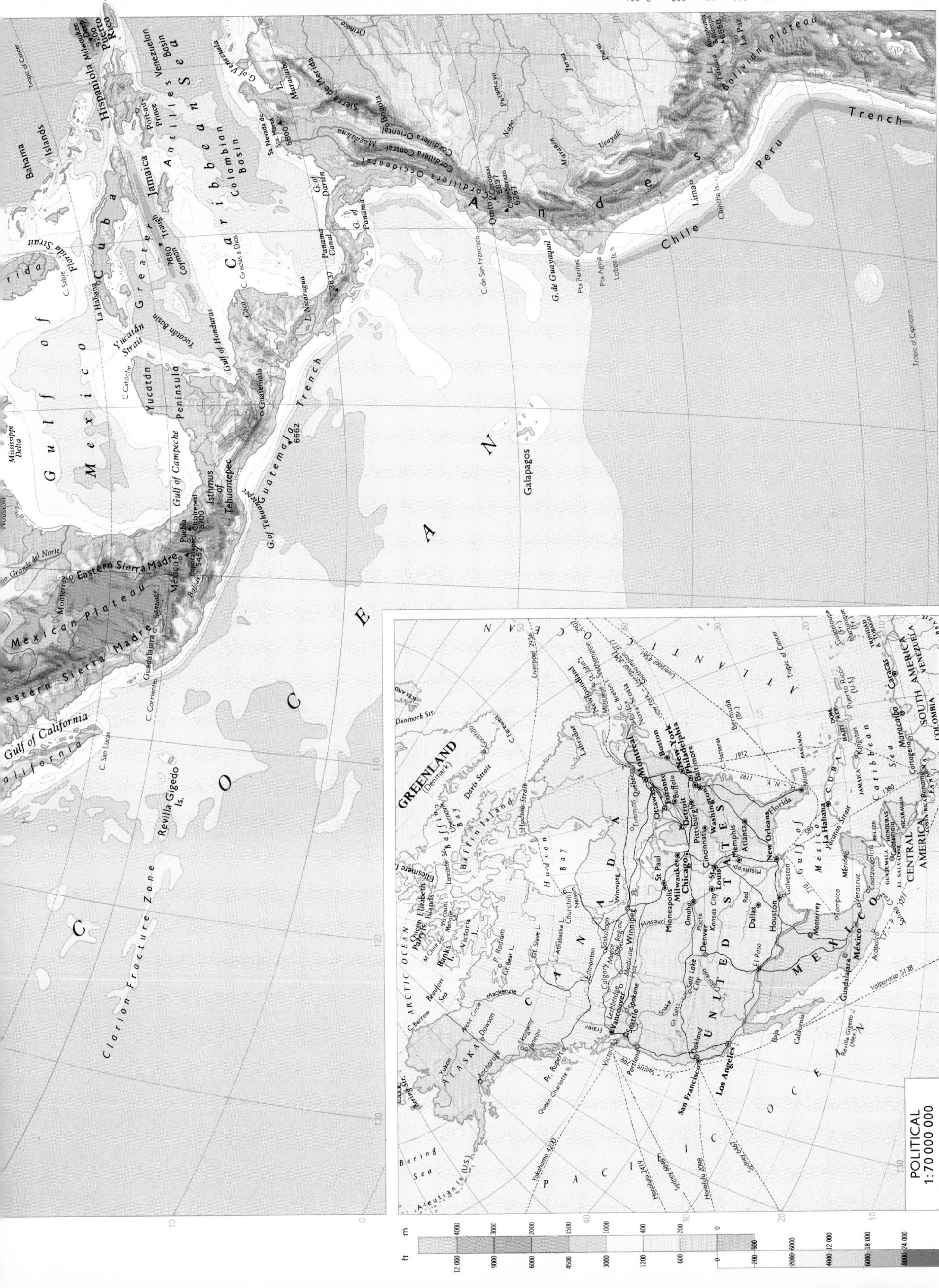

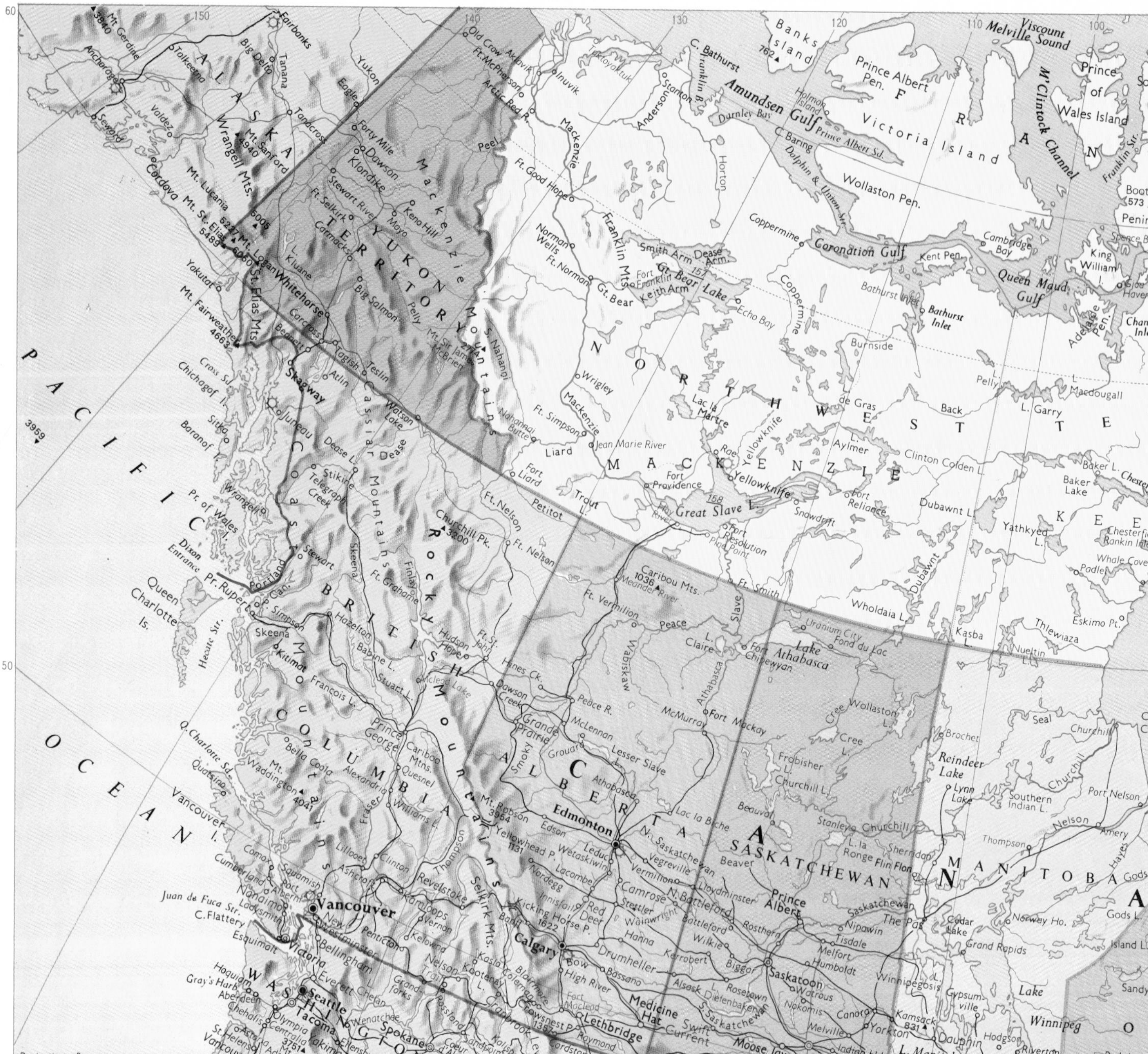

ALASKA
YUKON TERRITORY
NORTHWEST TERRITORIES
MACKENZIE
KEEWATIN
FRANKLIN
BRITISH COLUMBIA
ALBERTA
SASKATCHEWAN
MANITOBA
UNITED STATES
WASHINGTON
MONTANA
NORTH DAKOTA
SOUTH DAKOTA
NEBRASKA
MINNESOTA
WYOMING
PACIFIC OCEAN
Banks Island
Victoria Island
Prince of Wales Island
Amundsen Gulf
Coronation Gulf
Queen Maud Gulf
M'Clintock Channel
Viscount Melville Sound
Great Bear Lake
Great Slave L.
Lake Athabasca
Mackenzie Mountains
Rocky Mountains
Coast Mountains
Cassiar Mountains
Queen Charlotte Is.
Vancouver I.
Whitehorse
Dawson
Skagway
Juneau
Yellowknife
Edmonton
Calgary
Vancouver
Victoria
Seattle
Tacoma
Spokane
Lethbridge
Medicine Hat
Saskatoon
Regina
Moose Jaw
Prince Albert
Winnipeg
St. Boniface
Brandon
Minneapolis
St. Paul
Omaha
Des Moines
Projection: Bonne

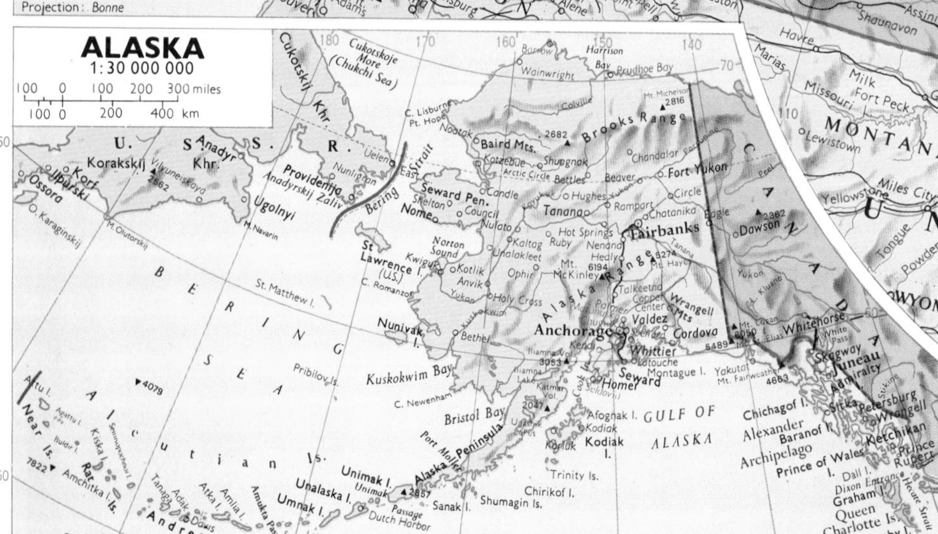

ALASKA
1:30 000 000
100 0 100 200 300 miles
100 0 200 400 km
Brooks Range
Fairbanks
Anchorage
Nome
Mt. McKinley 6194
Alaska Range
Seward Pen.
Bering Strait
BERING SEA
Aleutian Is.
Alaska Peninsula
Kodiak I.
GULF OF ALASKA
Bristol Bay
Kuskokwim Bay
Alexander Archipelago
Queen Charlotte Is.
CANADA
U.S.S.R.
PACIFIC OCEAN
West from Greenwich

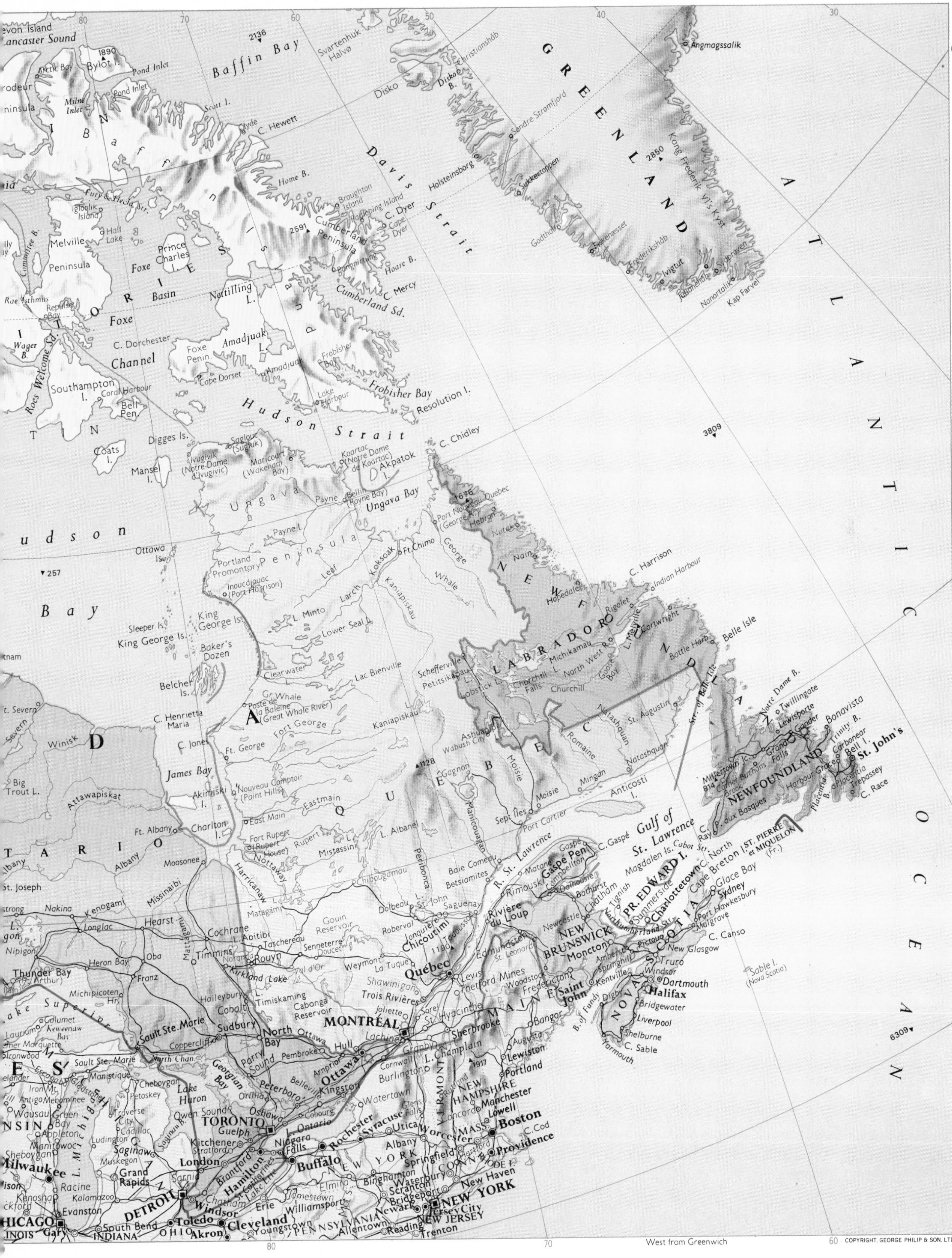

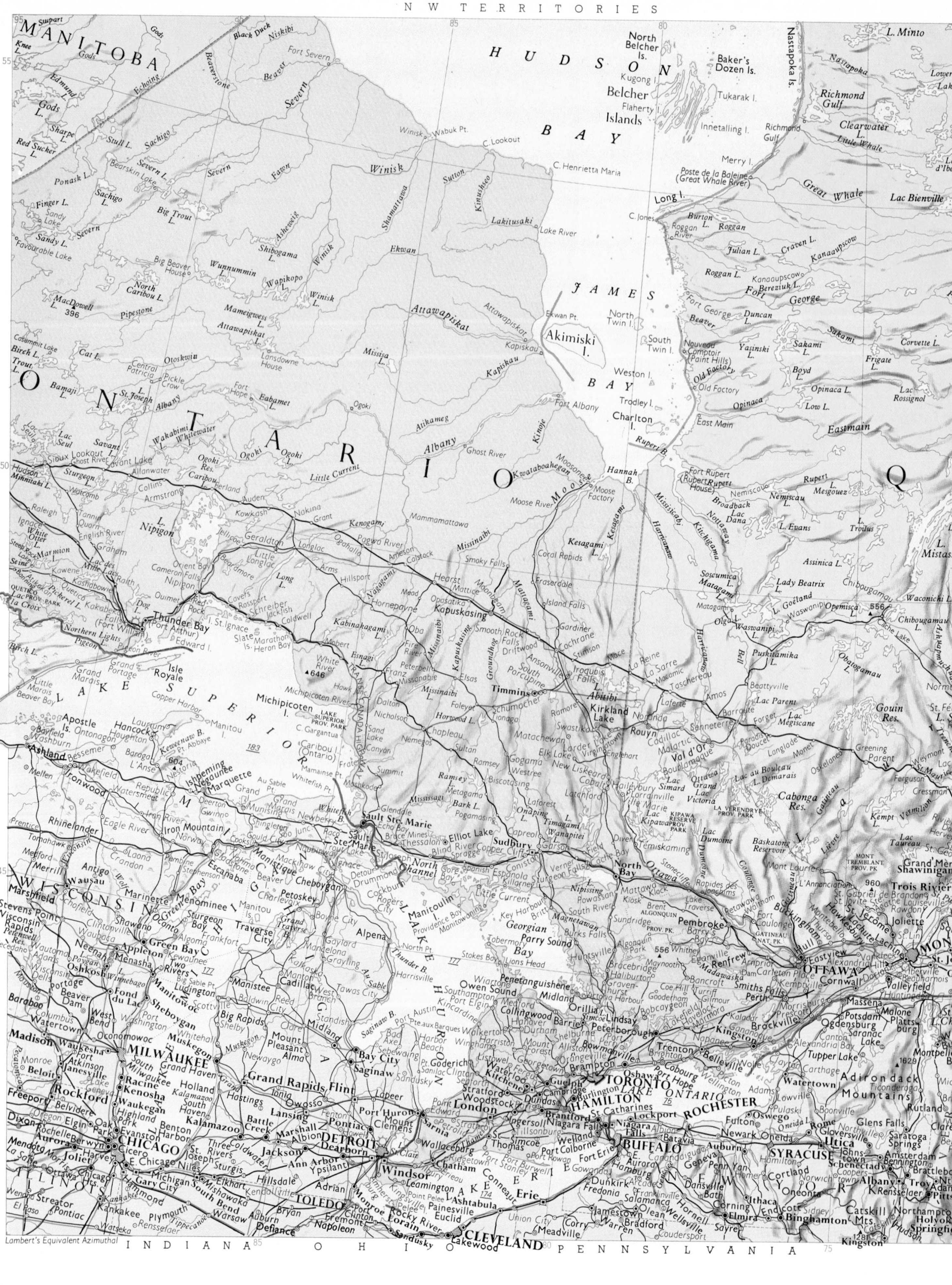
N W TERRITORIES
MANITOBA
HUDSON BAY
JAMES BAY
ONTARIO
Q
Belcher Islands
Akimiski I.
LAKE SUPERIOR
LAKE MICHIGAN
LAKE HURON
LAKE ONTARIO
LAKE ERIE
WISCONSIN
MICHIGAN
ILLINOIS
NEW YORK
Thunder Bay
Sault Ste. Marie
Sudbury
Timmins
Kapuskasing
North Bay
OTTAWA
TORONTO
HAMILTON
London
Windsor
DETROIT
CHICAGO
MILWAUKEE
TOLEDO
CLEVELAND
BUFFALO
ROCHESTER
SYRACUSE
Kingston
Grand Rapids
Flint
Adirondack Mountains
Georgian Bay
Manitoulin I.
Isle Royale
Lambert's Equivalent Azimuthal
INDIANA
OHIO
PENNSYLVANIA

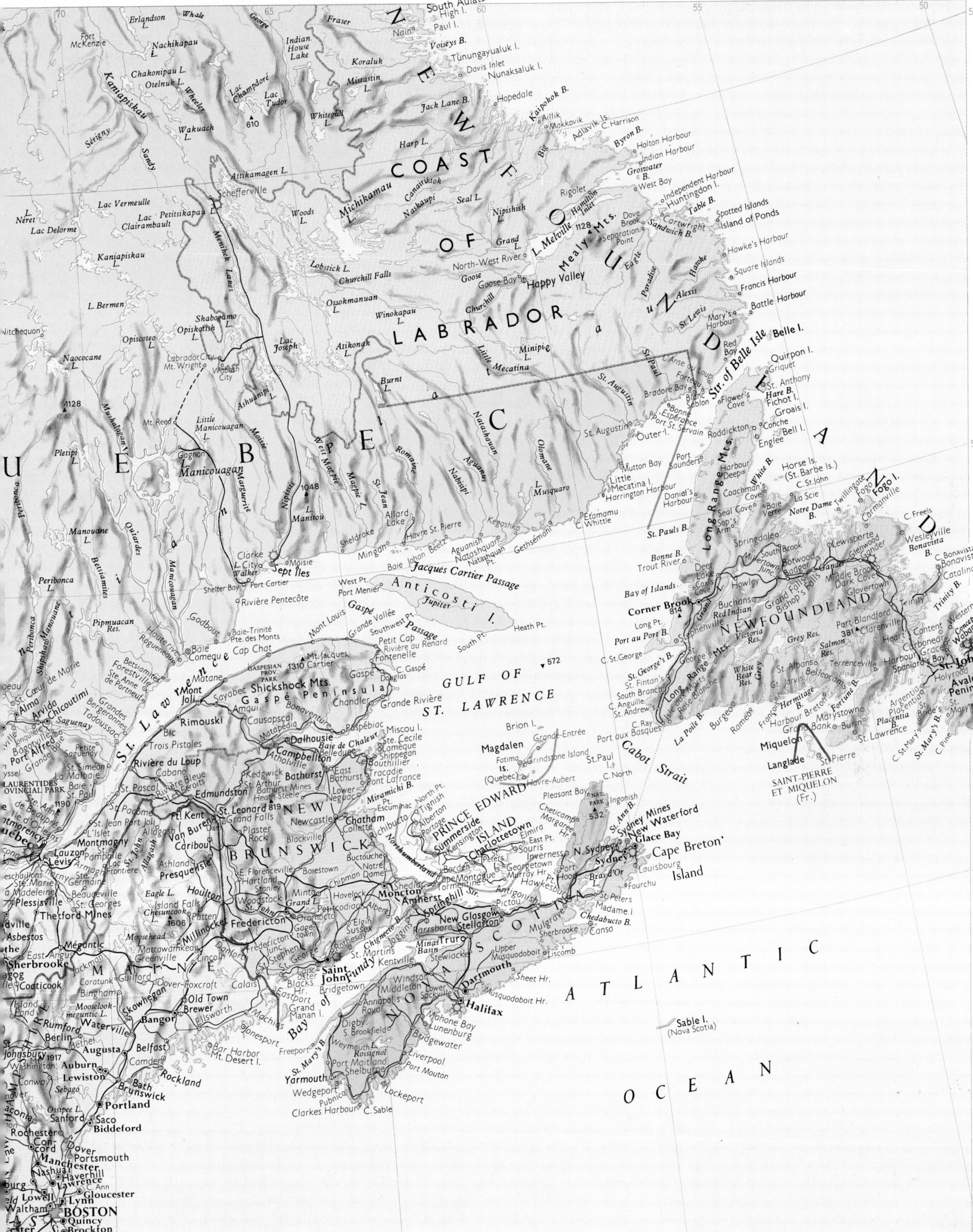

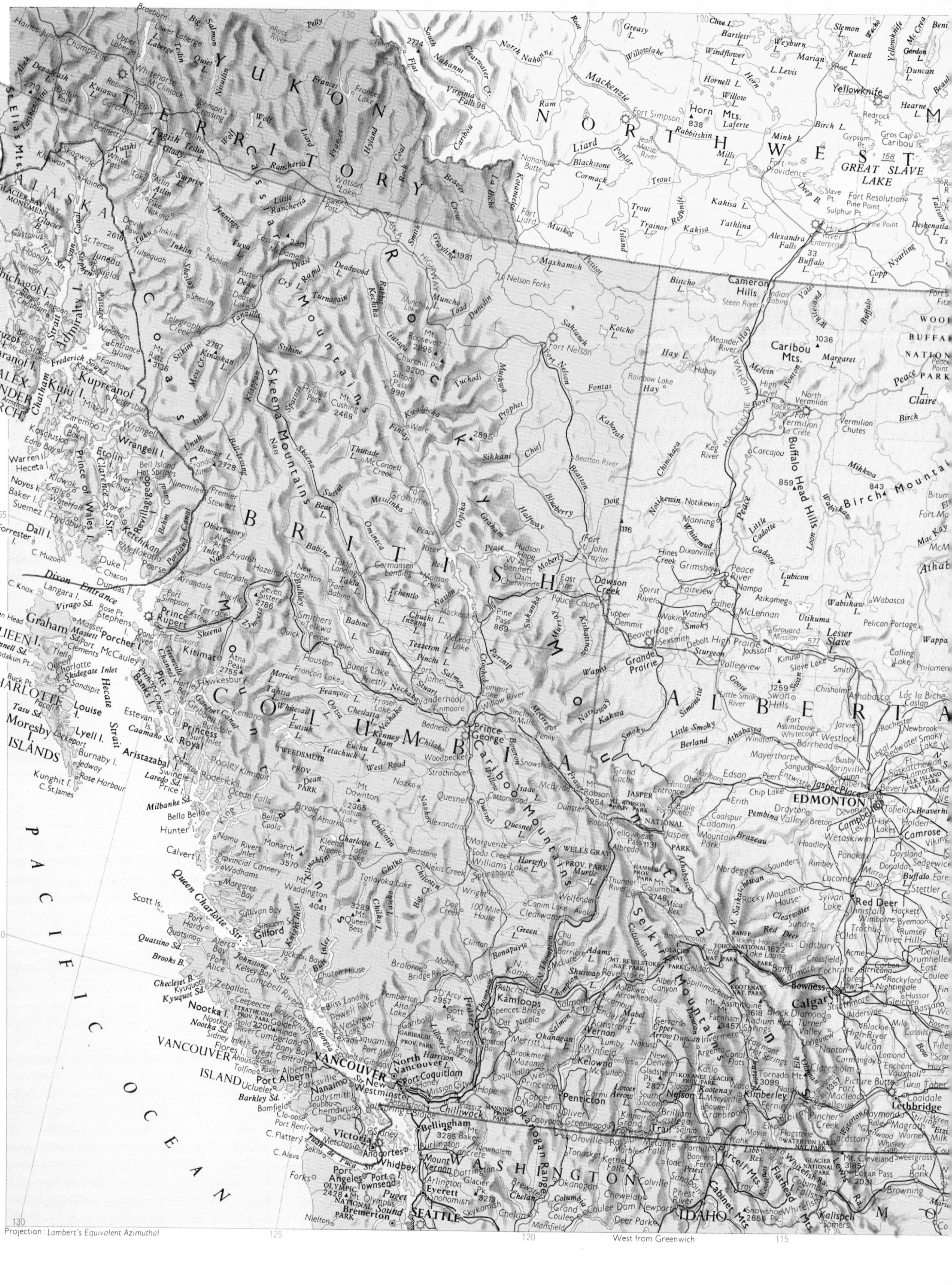

YUKON TERRITORY
NORTHWEST TERRITORIES
BRITISH COLUMBIA
ALBERTA
ALASKA
WASHINGTON
IDAHO
PACIFIC OCEAN
ROCKY MOUNTAINS
Cassiar Mts.
Coast Mountains
Skeena Mountains
Cariboo Mountains
Selkirk Mountains
Purcell Mts.
Cabinet Mts.
Caribou Mts.
Birch Mountains
Horn Mts.
Cameron Hills
Buffalo Head Hills
St. Elias Mts.
QUEEN CHARLOTTE ISLANDS
Graham I.
Moresby I.
VANCOUVER ISLAND
ALEXANDER ARCH.
Chichagof I.
Admiralty I.
Baranof I.
Kupreanof I.
Prince of Wales I.
Revillagigedo I.
Dixon Entrance
Hecate Strait
Queen Charlotte Str.
Str. of Georgia
Juan de Fuca Str.
GREAT SLAVE LAKE
Lesser Slave L.
Whitehorse
Juneau
Yellowknife
Fort Simpson
Hay River
Fort Nelson
Fort St. John
Dawson Creek
Grande Prairie
Peace River
Prince Rupert
Prince George
Kamloops
Vernon
Kelowna
Penticton
Nelson
Kimberley
VANCOUVER
New Westminster
Nanaimo
Port Alberni
Victoria
Bellingham
Everett
SEATTLE
Bremerton
EDMONTON
Red Deer
Calgary
Lethbridge
Jasper
Banff
Mt. Robson 3954
TWEEDSMUIR PROV. PARK
WELLS GRAY PROV. PARK
JASPER NATIONAL PARK
Mackenzie
Liard
Peace
Athabasca
Fraser
Skeena
Stikine
Columbia
Okanagan
Pend Oreille
Projection: Lambert's Equivalent Azimuthal
West from Greenwich
130
125
120
115
55
50

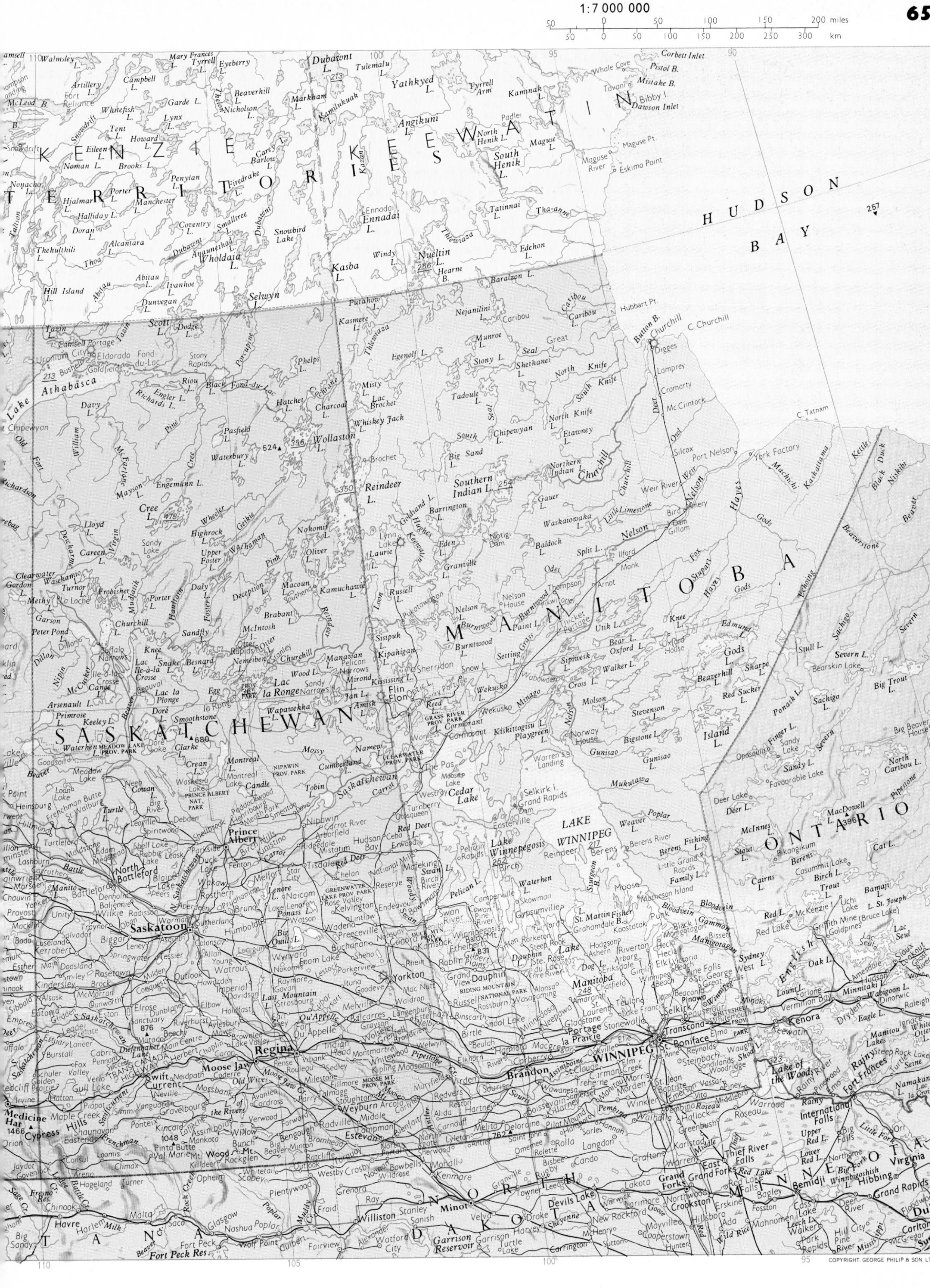

1:7 000 000

HUDSON
BAY

KENZIE
TERRITORIES KEEWATIN

SASKATCHEWAN

MANITOBA

ONTARIO

LAKE
WINNIPEG

Prince
Albert

Saskatoon

Regina

Moose Jaw
Swift
Current

Medicine
Hat

Brandon

WINNIPEG
St. Boniface

Portage
la Prairie

MINNESOTA

NORTH DAKOTA

Duluth

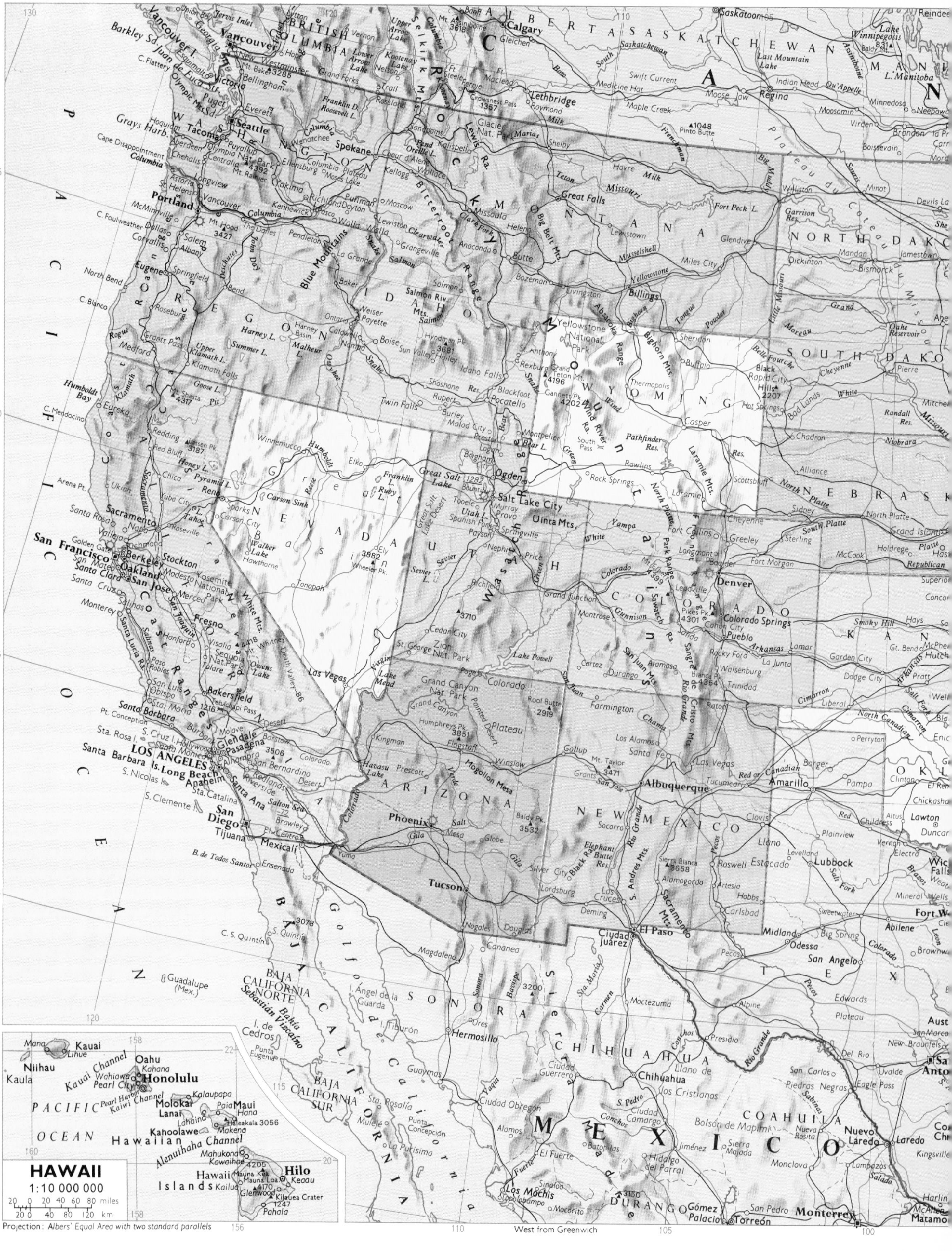

HAWAII 1:10 000 000

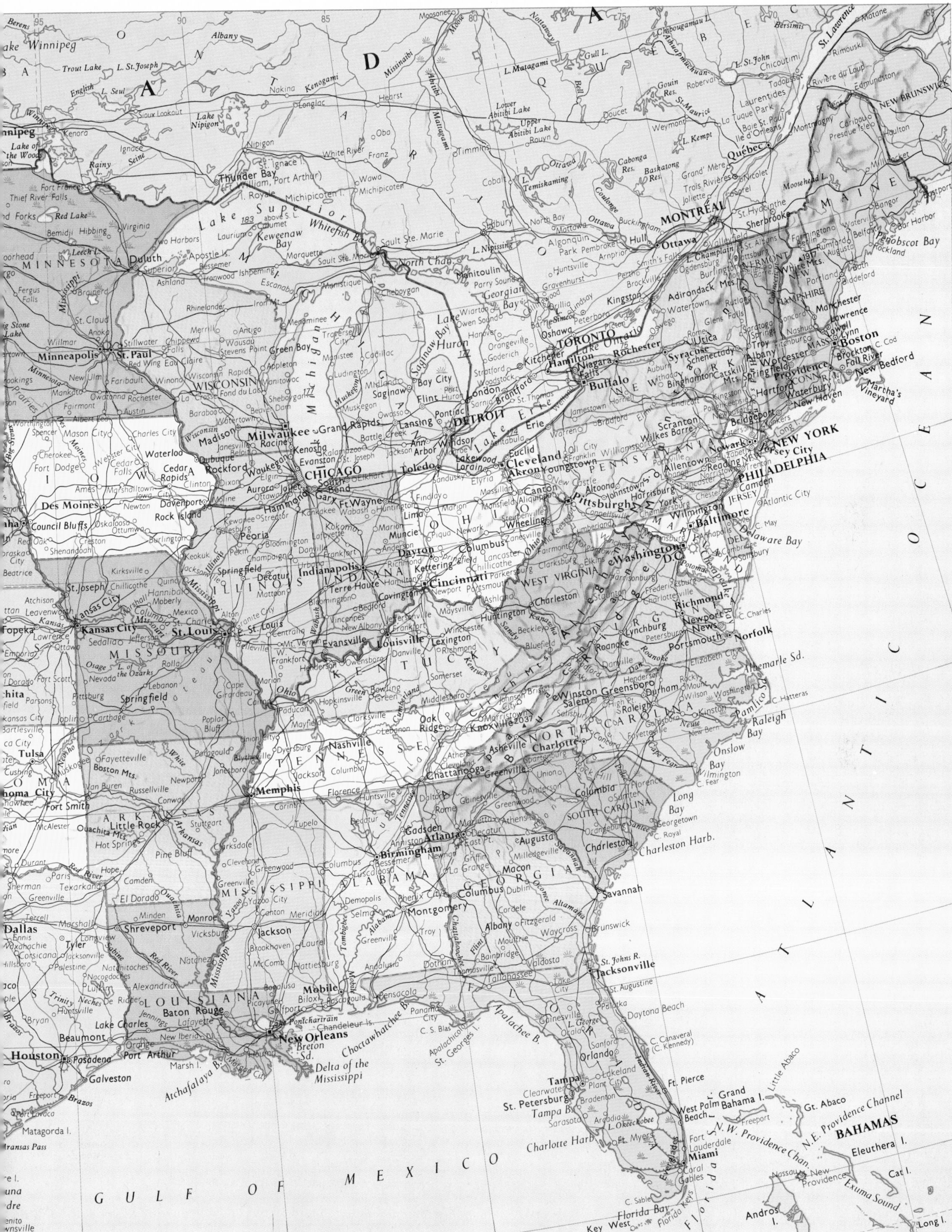

1:12 000 000

50   0   50   100   150   200   250   300 miles
50   0   50   100   150 200 250 300 350 400 450 km

COPYRIGHT GEORGE PHILIP & SON LTD

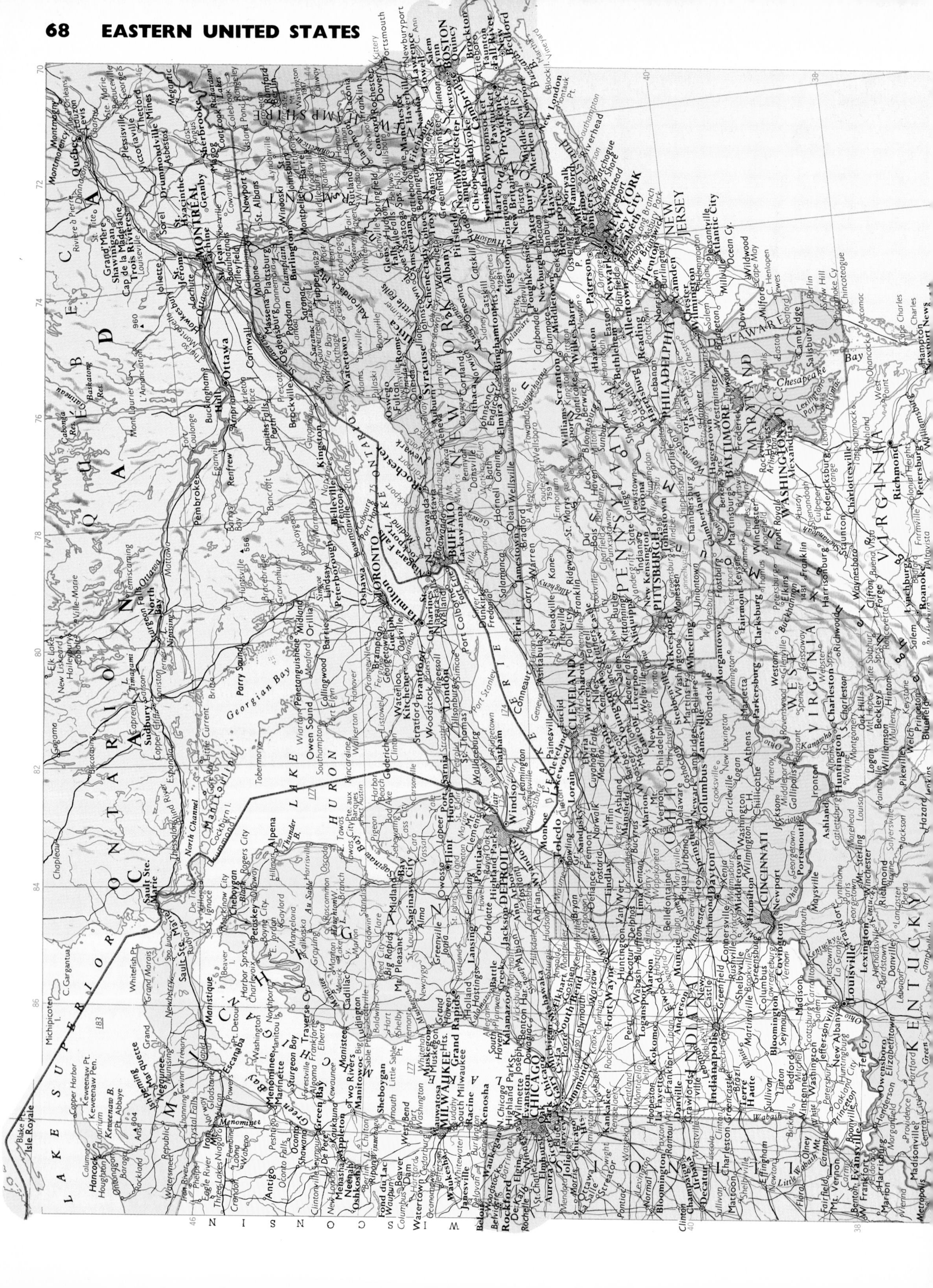
QUEBEC
ONTARIO
LAKE SUPERIOR
LAKE HURON
LAKE ONTARIO
LAKE ERIE
Georgian Bay
MICHIGAN
WISCONSIN
ILLINOIS
INDIANA
OHIO
PENNSYLVANIA
NEW YORK
NEW JERSEY
DELAWARE
MARYLAND
WEST VIRGINIA
VIRGINIA
KENTUCKY
VERMONT
NEW HAMPSHIRE
MASS.
CONN.
Chesapeake Bay
Quebec
Montreal
Ottawa
Toronto
Hamilton
Buffalo
Rochester
Syracuse
Albany
Boston
Providence
Hartford
New Haven
New York
Newark
Philadelphia
Baltimore
Washington
Richmond
Pittsburgh
Cleveland
Toledo
Detroit
Windsor
Columbus
Cincinnati
Dayton
Indianapolis
Louisville
Chicago
Milwaukee
Grand Rapids
Lansing
Flint
Saginaw
Sault Ste. Marie
Sudbury
Kingston
London
Erie
Scranton
Harrisburg
Wheeling
Charleston
Lexington
Evansville
Fort Wayne
South Bend
Green Bay
Madison
Rockford
Peoria

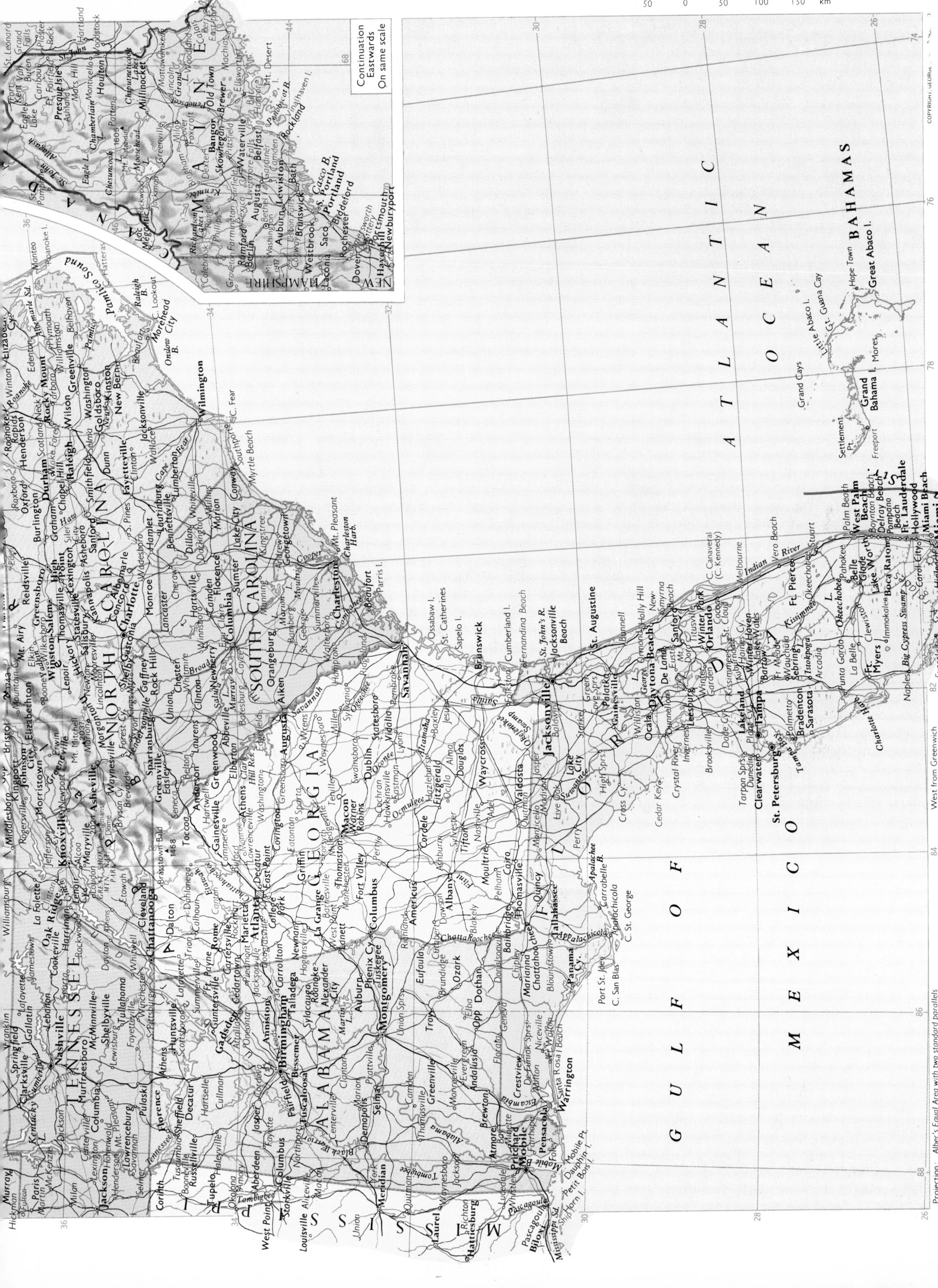

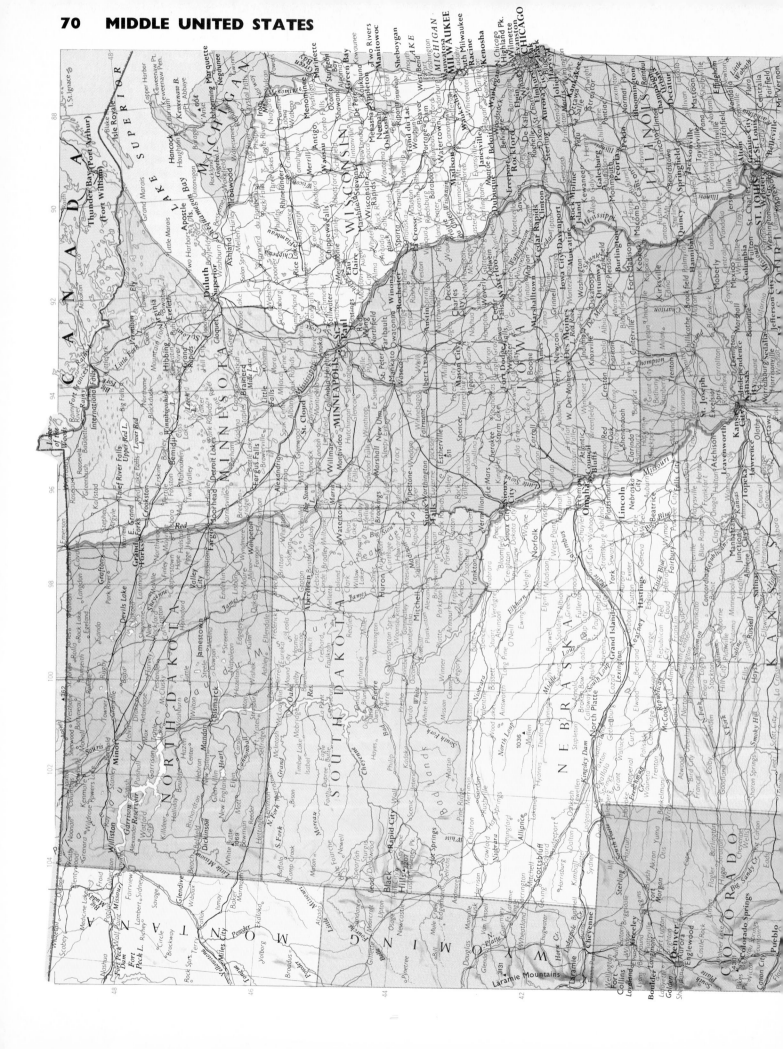
C A N A D A
LAKE SUPERIOR
LAKE MICHIGAN
NORTH DAKOTA
SOUTH DAKOTA
MINNESOTA
WISCONSIN
MICHIGAN
IOWA
ILLINOIS
NEBRASKA
KANSAS
MONTANA
WYOMING
COLORADO
MILWAUKEE
CHICAGO
MINNEAPOLIS
St. Paul
Duluth
Des Moines
Omaha
Lincoln
Bismarck
Pierre
Madison
Springfield
Topeka
Denver
Cheyenne
Kansas City
St. Joseph
Sioux City
Sioux Falls
Fargo
Grand Forks
Rapid City
Green Bay
Thunder Bay (Port Arthur) (Fort William)
Laramie Mountains
Colorado Springs

1:6 000 000

50   0   50   100 miles
50 0 50 100 150 km

States and Regions

TENNESSEE

MISSISSIPPI

ARKANSAS

LOUISIANA

OKLAHOMA

TEXAS

NEW MEXICO

MEXICO

COAHUILA

CHIHUAHUA

GULF OF MEXICO

Major Cities

Memphis, Little Rock, Hot Springs, Pine Bluff, El Dorado, Texarkana, Shreveport, Monroe, Alexandria, Baton Rouge, NEW ORLEANS, Natchez, Vicksburg, Jackson, Meridian, Tupelo, Biloxi, Pascagoula, Mobile

Wichita, Tulsa, Oklahoma City, Norman, Enid, Lawton, Muskogee, Ardmore

Dallas, Fort Worth, Waco, Austin, San Antonio, HOUSTON, Galveston, Beaumont, Port Arthur, Orange, Corpus Christi, Laredo, Del Rio, Brownsville, Abilene, Amarillo, Lubbock, Midland, Odessa, Big Spring, San Angelo

Roswell, Carlsbad, Clovis, Hobbs, Santa Fe, Las Vegas

Nuevo Laredo, Piedras Negras, Ciudad Acuña, Nueva Rosita

Inset

Laguna Madre, Kingsville, Harlingen, Brownsville, Edinburg, McAllen, Reynosa, Matamoros

Continuation Southwards on same scale

West from Greenwich

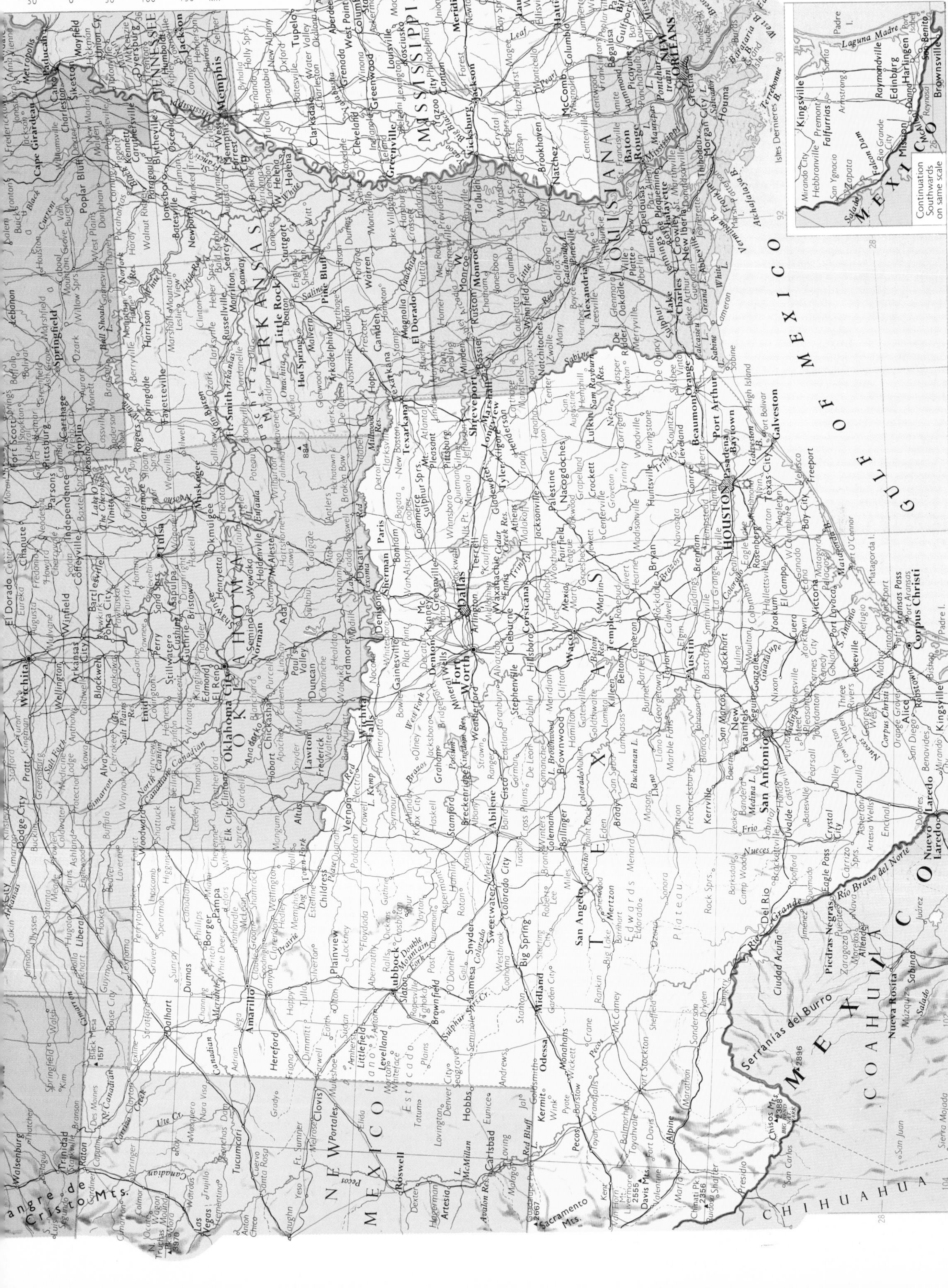

Projection: Albers' Equal Area with two standard parallels

COPYRIGHT GEORGE PHILIP & SON LTD

1 : 6 000 000

50 0 50 100 miles

50 0 50 100 150 km

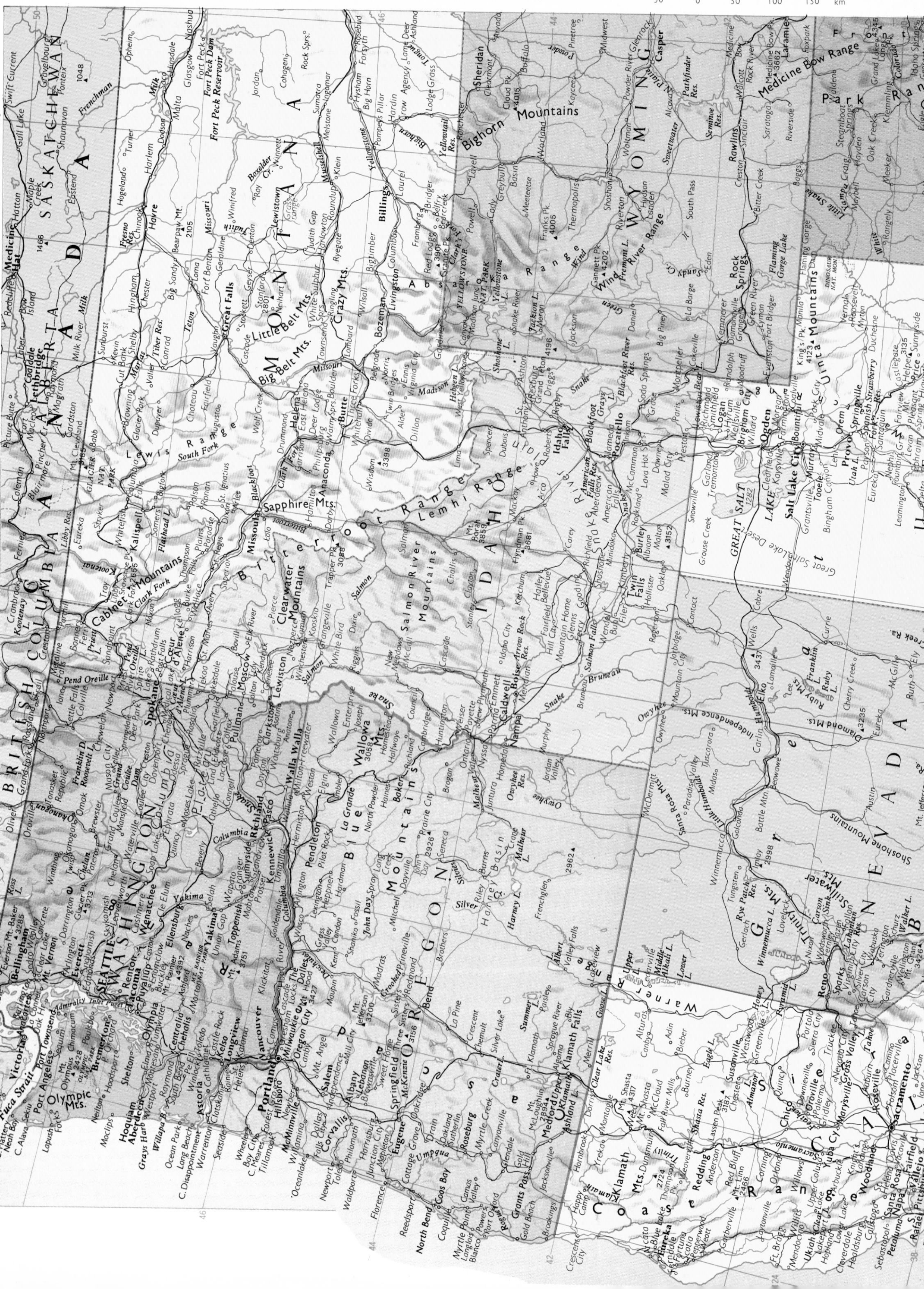

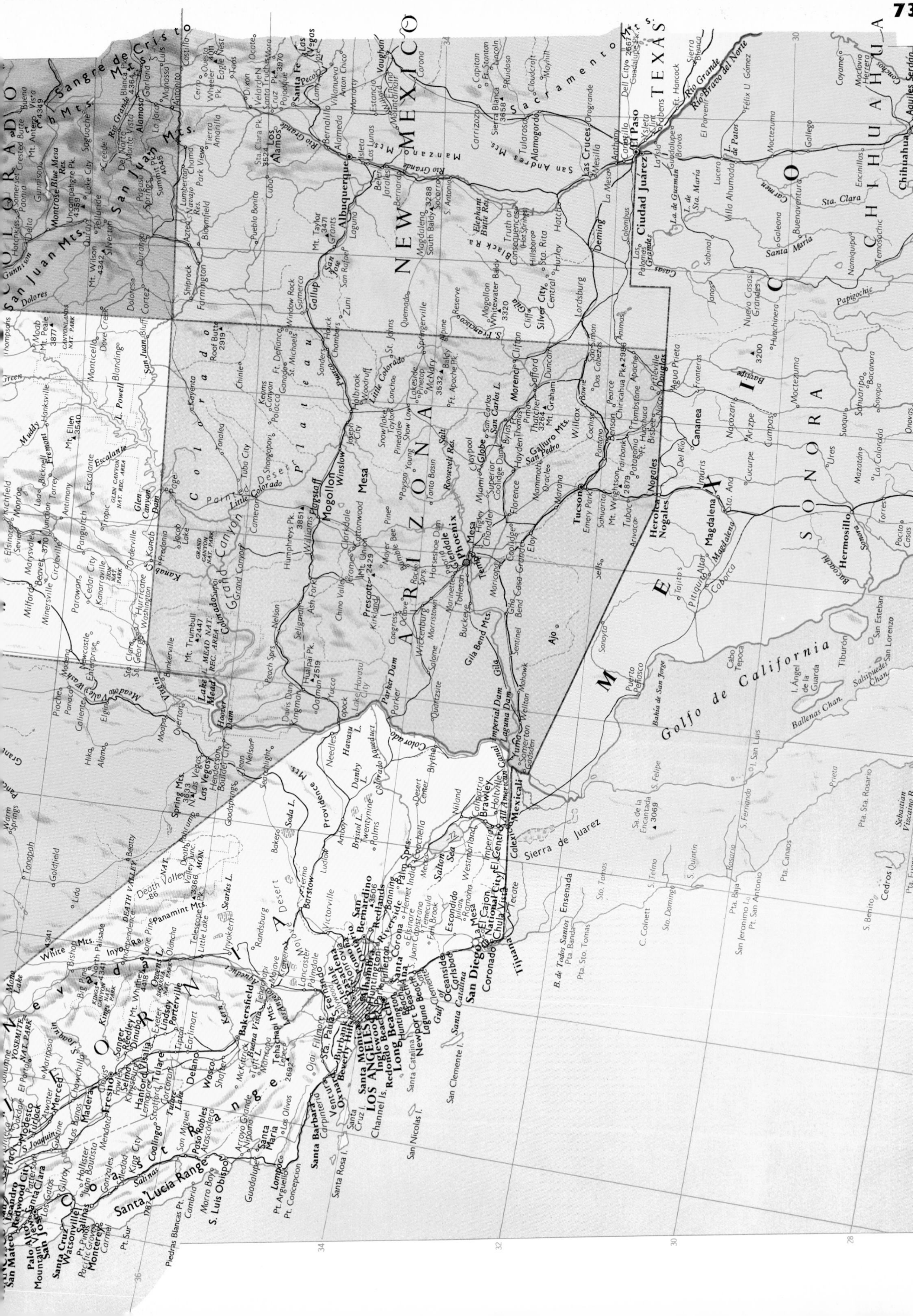
COLORADO
NEW MEXICO
ARIZONA
TEXAS
CHIHUAHUA
SONORA
MEXICO
NEVADA
CALIFORNIA
Colorado Plateau
Grand Canyon
Golfo de California
Sangre de Cristo Mts.
San Juan Mts.
Sacramento Mts.
Santa Fe
Albuquerque
Los Alamos
Gallup
Farmington
Las Cruces
El Paso
Ciudad Juárez
Deming
Silver City
Lordsburg
Alamogordo
Phoenix
Tucson
Flagstaff
Prescott
Yuma
Nogales
Douglas
Bisbee
Globe
Mesa
Tempe
Chihuahua
Hermosillo
Cananea
Magdalena
Mexicali
Tijuana
Ensenada
San Diego
Los Angeles
Long Beach
Santa Barbara
Bakersfield
Fresno
Las Vegas
Hoover Dam
Lake Mead
Death Valley
Salton Sea
Parker Dam
Imperial Dam
Laguna Dam
Sierra de Juarez
Santa Lucia Range
Monterey
Salinas
San Jose
West from Greenwich
COPYRIGHT, GEORGE PHILIP & SON, LTD.

1:12 000 000

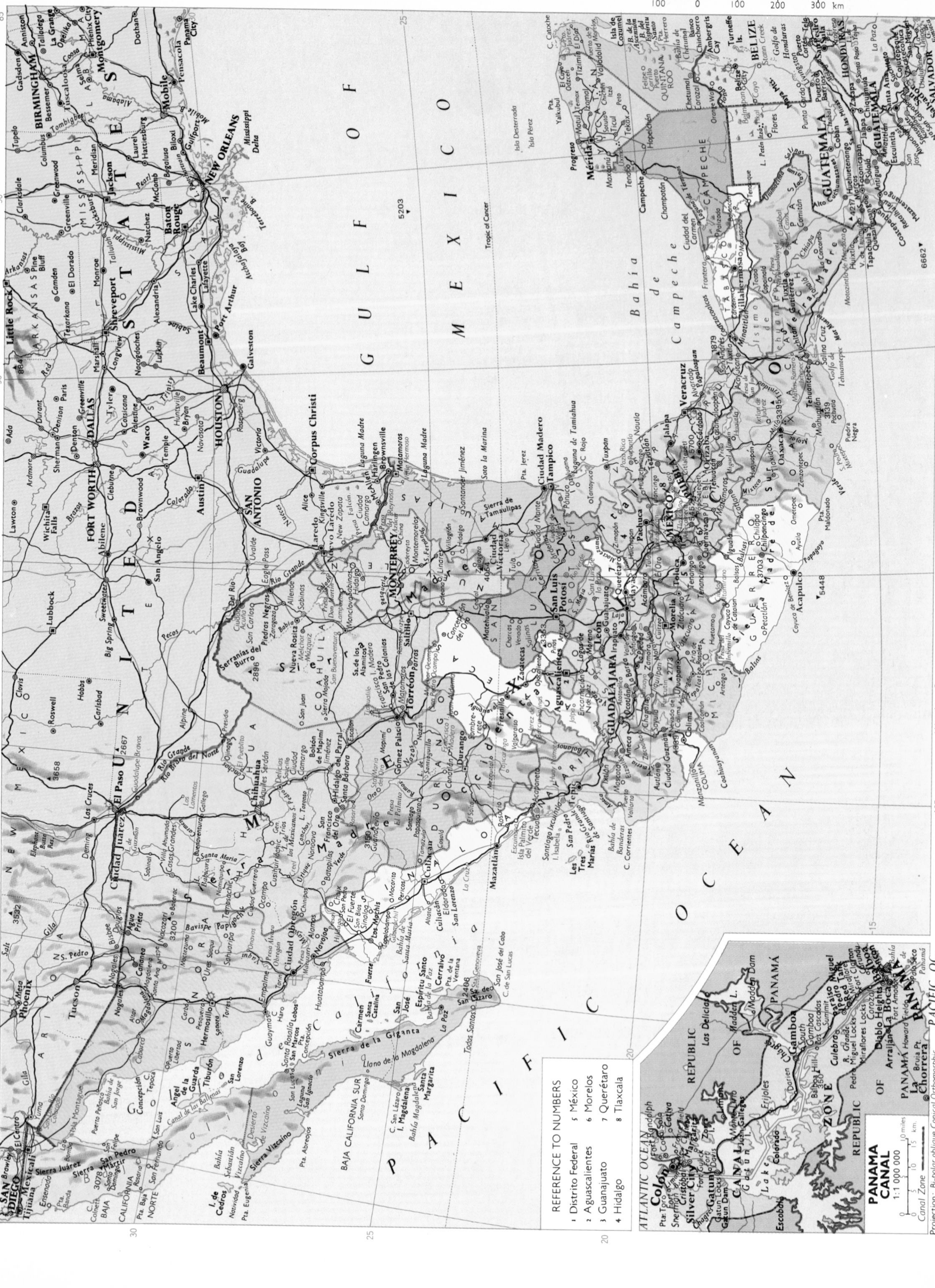

100 0 100 200 miles
100 0 100 200 300 km

REFERENCE TO NUMBERS

1 Distrito Federal
2 Aguascalientes
3 Guanajuato
4 Querétaro
5 México
6 Morelos
7 Querétaro
8 Tlaxcala

GULF OF MEXICO

PACIFIC OCEAN

UNITED STATES

Tropic of Cancer

West from Greenwich

GUATEMALA

BELIZE

HONDURAS

EL SALVADOR

PANAMA CANAL
1:1 000 000

ATLANTIC OCEAN

PACIFIC OC.

PANAMÁ

CANAL ZONE

REPUBLIC OF PANAMA

Colón

Projection: Bi-polar oblique Conical Orthomorphic

COPYRIGHT GEORGE PHILIP & SON LTD.

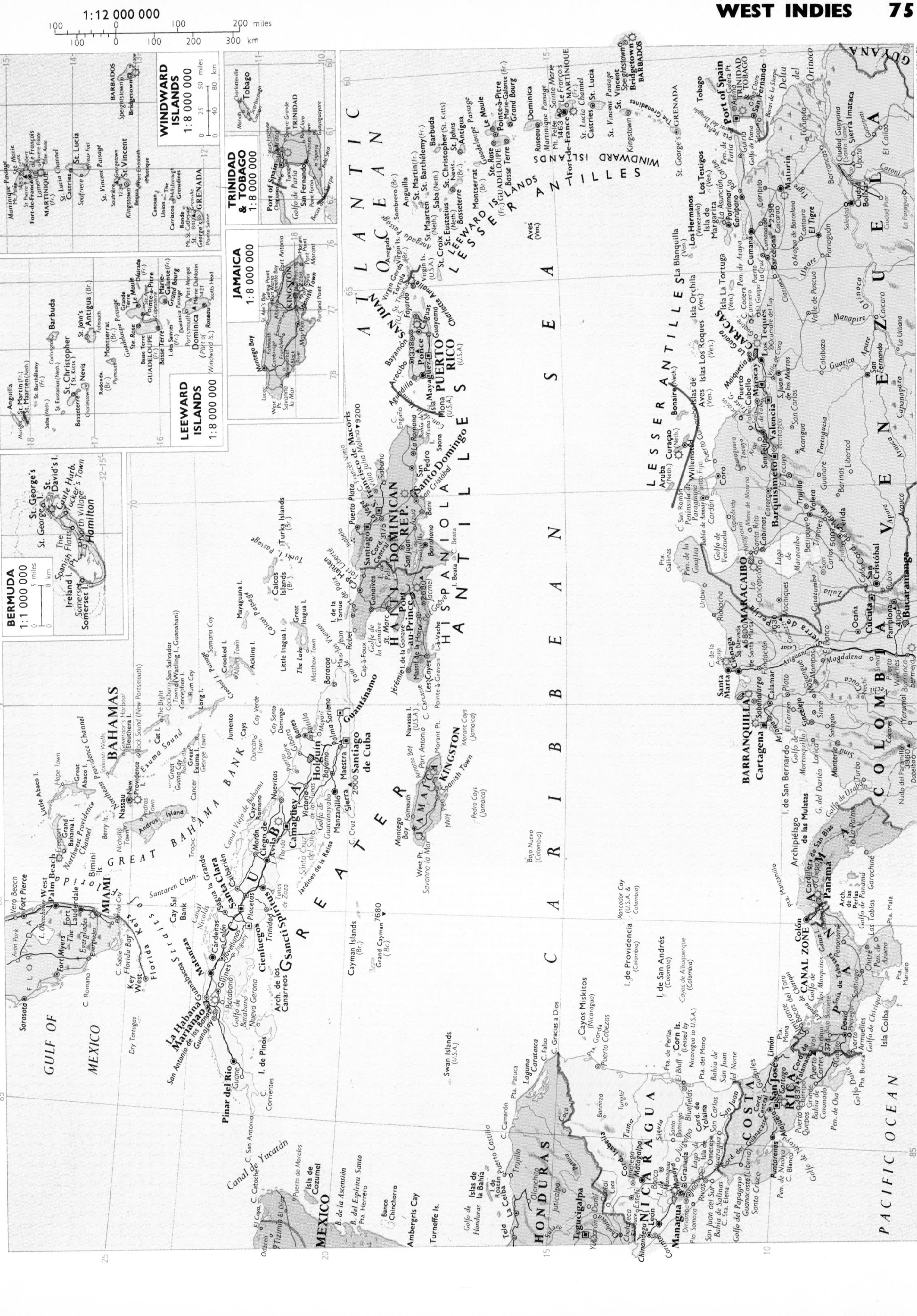

1:12 000 000

100   0   100   200 miles
100   0   100   200   300 km

WINDWARD ISLANDS
1:8 000 000

TRINIDAD & TOBAGO
1:8 000 000

JAMAICA
1:8 000 000

LEEWARD ISLANDS
1:8 000 000

BERMUDA
1:1 000 000

ATLANTIC OCEAN

CARIBBEAN SEA

GULF OF MEXICO

PACIFIC OCEAN

GREATER ANTILLES

LESSER ANTILLES

WINDWARD ISLANDS

LEEWARD ISLANDS

BAHAMAS

CUBA

JAMAICA

HAITI — Port-au-Prince

DOMINICAN REP. — Santo Domingo

HISPANIOLA

PUERTO RICO (U.S.A.)

CARDENAS

La Habana   Matanzas

Pinar del Río

Santiago de Cuba

Camagüey

Cienfuegos

Sancti Spíritus

Holguín

KINGSTON

Montego Bay

GRENADA

BARBADOS

TRINIDAD & TOBAGO — Port of Spain

MARTINIQUE   St. Lucia   St. Vincent

GUADELOUPE   Dominica   Antigua

MIAMI

Fort Lauderdale

FLORIDA

MEXICO

HONDURAS — Tegucigalpa

NICARAGUA — Managua

COSTA RICA — San José

PANAMA — Panamá   CANAL ZONE   Colón

COLOMBIA

Barranquilla   Cartagena

VENEZUELA

CARACAS   Maracaibo   Valencia   Barquisimeto

GUIANA

Projection: Bi-polar oblique Conical Orthomorphic

West from Greenwich

1:30 000 000

100 0   100 200 300 400 500 miles
100 0   200   400   600   800 km

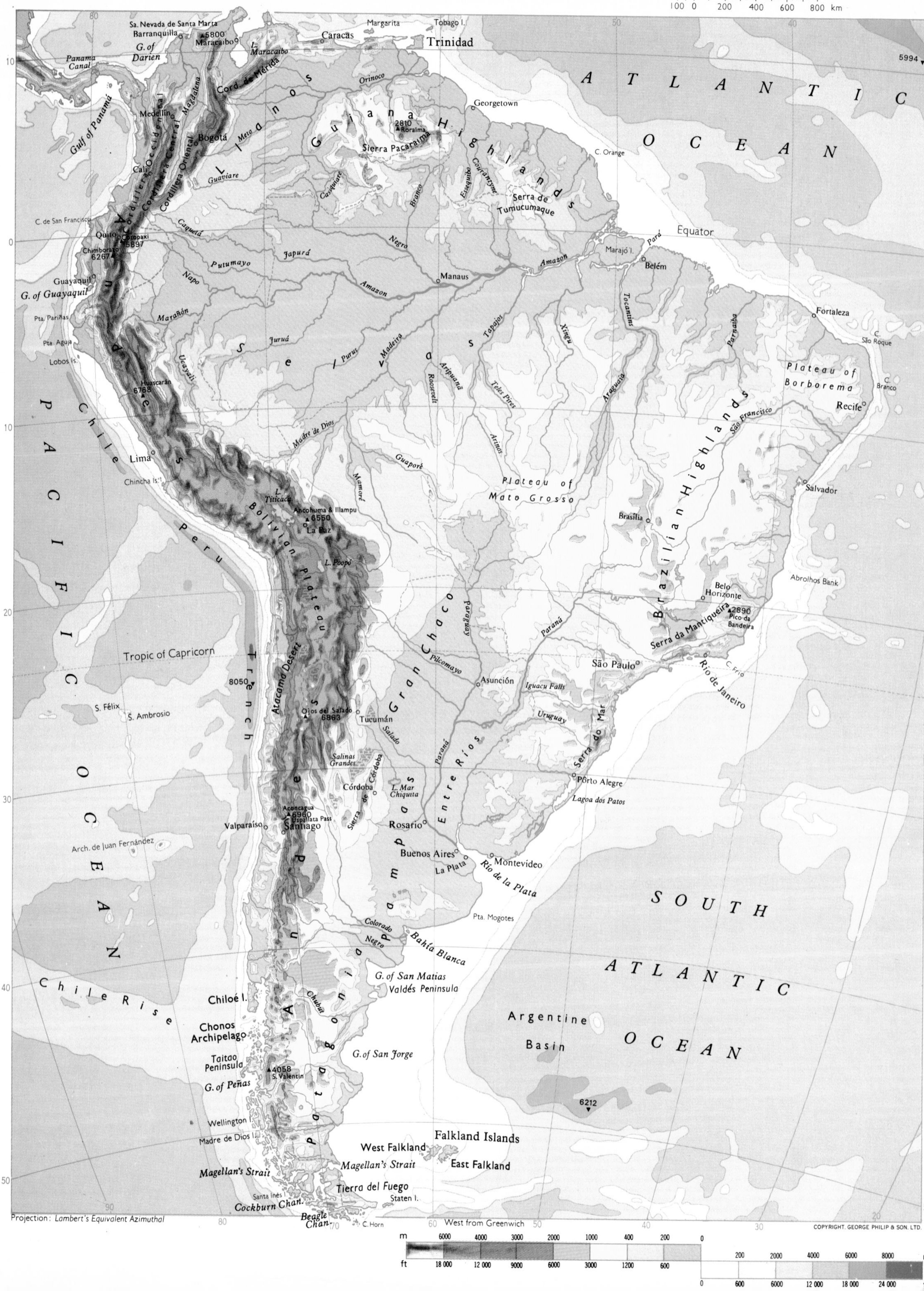

Sa. Nevada de Santa Marta
Barranquilla
△5800
■Maracaibo
Panama Canal
G. of Darien
L. Maracaibo
Cord. de Mérida
Caracas
Margarita
Tobago I.
Trinidad
5994

ATLANTIC OCEAN

Medellín
Bogotá
Cali
Llanos
Orinoco
Meta
Guaviare
Guiana Highlands
Georgetown
C. Orange

Cordillera Occidental
Cordillera Central
Cordillera Oriental
Magdalena
Sierra Pacaraima
Roraima △2810
Serra de Tumucumaque

C. de San Francisco
Quito
Cotopaxi △5897
Chimborazo 6267
Guaviare
Caquetá
Casiquiare
Caroní
Branco
Negro
Amazon
Pará
Marajó I.
Equator
5994

Guayaquil
G. of Guayaquil
Napo
Putumayo
Japurá
Manaus
Belém
Fortaleza
C. São Roque

Pta. Pariñas
Pta. Aguja
Lobos Is.
Marañón
Ucayali
Juruá
Purus
Selvas
Madeira
Amazon
Tapajós
Xingu
Tocantins
Plateau of Borborema
Recife
C. Branco

Huascarán △6768
Madre de Dios
Aripuanã
Roosevelt
Teles Pires
Araguaia
São Francisco

Lima
Chincha Is.
L. Titicaca
Bolivian Plateau
Ancohuma & Illampu △6550
La Paz
L. Poopó
Guaporé
Mamoré
Plateau of Mato Grosso
Brasília
Brazilian Highlands
Belo Horizonte
Salvador
Abrolhos Bank

Peru
Chile
Tropic of Capricorn
Atacama Desert
8050
Ojos del Salado 6863
Gran Chaco
Paraguay
Paraná
Pilcomayo
Asunción
São Paulo
Serra da Mantiqueira
Pico da Bandeira △2890
Rio de Janeiro
C. Frio

S. Félix
S. Ambrosio
Salinas Grandes
Tucumán
Salado
Córdoba
Sierra de Córdoba
L. Mar Chiquita
Entre Ríos
Iguaçu Falls
Uruguay
Pôrto Alegre
Lagoa dos Patos
Serra do Mar

PACIFIC OCEAN
French Trench

Aconcagua △6960
Espallata Pass
Santiago
Valparaíso
Rosario
Paraná
Buenos Aires
La Plata
Montevideo
Rio de la Plata

Arch. de Juan Fernández
Chile Rise
Chiloé I.
Chonos Archipelago
Taitao Peninsula
G. of Peñas
Wellington
Madre de Dios I.
Colorado
Negro
Bahía Blanca
Pta. Mogotes
G. of San Matías
Valdés Peninsula
Pampas
Patagonia
G. of San Jorge
S. Valentín △4058

SOUTH ATLANTIC OCEAN
Argentine Basin
6212 ▽

Magellan's Strait
Santa Inés I.
Cockburn Chan.
Beagle Chan.
C. Horn
Tierra del Fuego
Staten I.
Falkland Islands
West Falkland
East Falkland
Magellan's Strait

Projection: Lambert's Equivalent Azimuthal
West from Greenwich
COPYRIGHT. GEORGE PHILIP & SON. LTD

m 6000 4000 3000 2000 1000 400 200 0
ft 18 000 12 000 9000 6000 3000 1200 600

200 2000 4000 6000 8000 m
600 6000 12 000 18 000 24 000 ft

1:30 000 000

100   0   100   200   300   400   500 miles
100   0   200   400   600   800 km

NORTH ATLANTIC OCEAN

COSTA RICA
CANAL ZONE (U.S.)
San José
David
PANAMA
Golfo de Panamá
S.F. 3277
Honolulu 4683

Punta Fijo
Barranquilla
Cartagena
Ciénaga
Maracaibo
Cabimas
Golfo de Darién
Montería
Cúcuta
San Cristóbal
Barquisimeto
Cumaná
Port of Spain
Trinidad
TRINIDAD AND TOBAGO
Isla de Margarita
Tobago
Valencia
Caracas
Maturín
Medellín
Manizales
Pereira
Ibagué
Bucaramanga
Bogotá
San Fernando
Orinoco
Ciudad Guayana
Ciudad Bolívar
Georgetown
New Amsterdam
Paramaribo
Cayenne
C. Orange

VENEZUELA
Pto. Ayacucho
Meta
GUYANA
SURINAM
FRENCH GUIANA

Cali
Buenaventura
Popayán
Pasto
COLOMBIA
Caquetá
Branco
Essequibo
Courantyne

C. de San Francisco
Quito
Riobamba
ECUADOR
Guayaquil
Cuenca
Honolulu 4834
G. de Guayaquil
Pta. Aguja

Napo
Putumayo
Iapurá
Macapá
Ilha de Marajó
Belém (Pará)
Equator

Marañón
Iquitos
Benjamim Constant
Tefé
Amazonas (Amazon)
Santarém
Manaus
São Luis
Bacabal
Teresina
Fortaleza (Ceara)
C. de São Roque
Natal

Chiclayo
Trujillo
Pucallpa
Juruá
Purus
Madeira
Manicoré
Aripuanã
Xingu
Tapajós
Araguaia
Juazeiro do Norte
João Pessoa (Paraíba)
Recife (Pernambuco)
Maceió

PERU
Callao
Lima
Huancayo
Ayacucho
Cuzco
Islas de Chincha
Cruzeiro do Sul
Rio Branca
Pôrto Velho
Guajará-Mirim
Guaporé
B R A Z I L
Tocantins
São Francisco
Aracaju
Salvador (Bahia)

Madre de Dios
Mamoré
Arros

Juliaca
Titicaca
Arequipa
La Paz
Cochabamba
Santa Cruz
Mollendo
Oruro
Cuiabá
Brasília
Goiânia
Jataí
Montes Claros
Gov. Valadares
Tacna
Sucre
BOLIVIA
Corumbá
Uberaba
Belo Horizonte
Vitória
Arica
Uyuni
Tarija
Campo Grande
Paraná
Ribeirão Prêto
Juiz de Fora
Campos
Iquique
Pedra Juan Caballero
PARAGUAY
Bauru
Pres. Prudente
Londrina
Campinas
Niterói
RIO DE JANEIRO
Antofagasta
Salta
Asunción
Ponta Grossa
Santos
SÃO PAULO

San Miguel de Tucumán
Resistencia
Corrientes
Uruguay
Curitiba
Florianópolis
Santiago del Estero
Uruguaiana
Santa Maria
Pôrto Alegre
Lagoa dos Patos
Pelotas

Coquimbo
Salado
ARGENTINA
Córdoba
Santa Fe
Paraná
Rosario
URUGUAY
Mendoza
Valparaíso
Arch. de Juan Fernández (Chile)
Santiago
San Rafael
Mercedes
BUENOS AIRES
Montevideo
Río de la Plata
La Plata

Talca
Concepción
Santa Rosa
Tandil
Mar del Plata
Bahía Blanca
Valdivia
Zapala
Colorado
Negro
Viedma

Puerto Montt
Isla de Chiloé
San Carlos de Bariloche
Trelew
Chubut
Península Valdés

Archipiélago de los Chonos
Golfo Comodoro Rivadavia
San Jorge
G. de Penas
I. Wellington
Santa Cruz
Río Gallegos
FALKLAND ISLANDS (ISLAS MALVINAS) (U.K.)
Stanley
West Falkland
East Falkland
Estrecho de Magallanes
Strait of Magellan
Punta Arenas
Isla Grande de Tierra del Fuego
Cabo de Hornos (Cape Horn)

C H I L E
P A C I F I C   O C E A N
Tropic of Capricorn
Isla San Félix (Chile)
Isla San Ambrosio (Chile)

SOUTH ATLANTIC OCEAN

Projection: Lambert's Equivalent Azimuthal
West from Greenwich

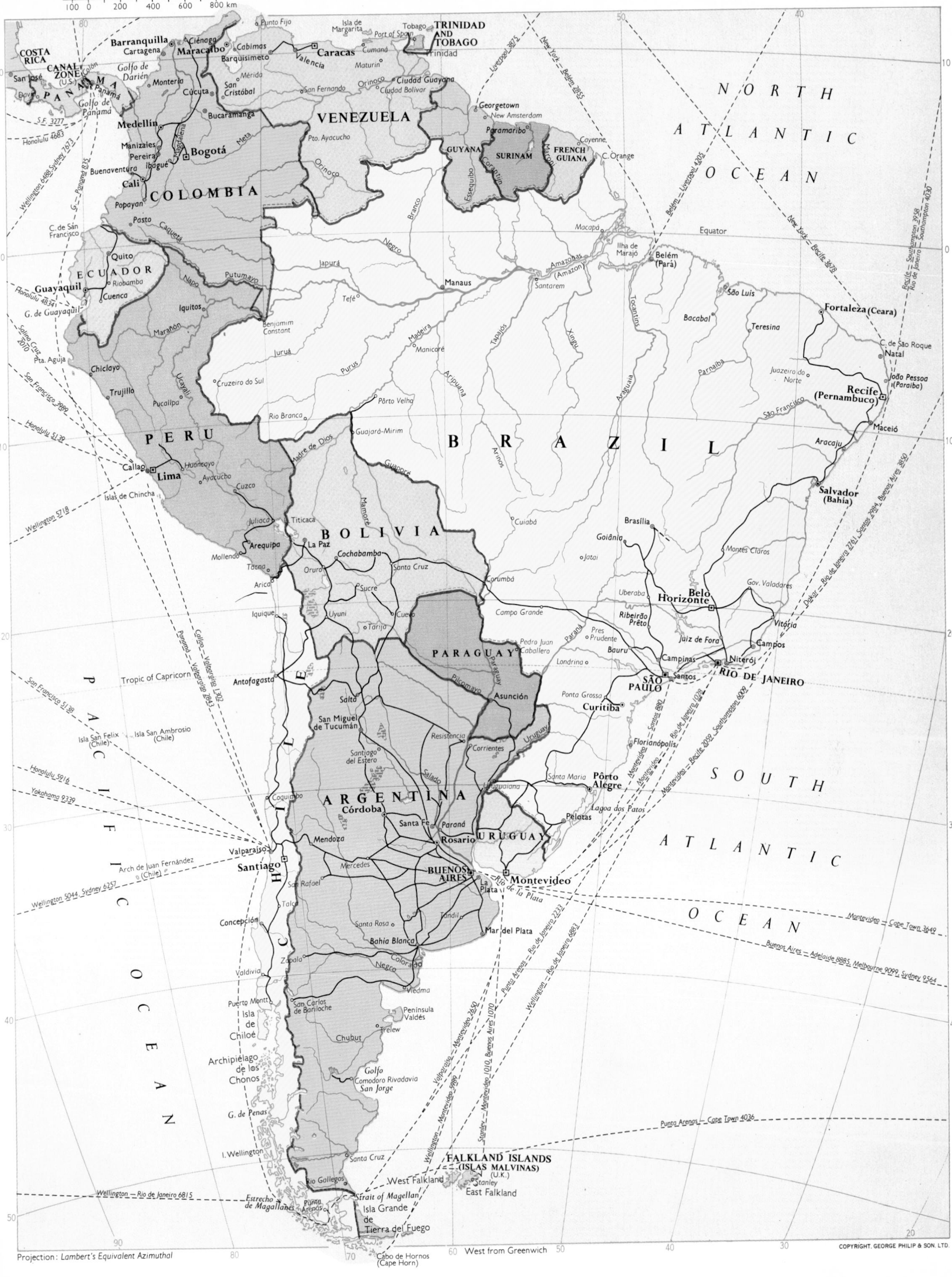

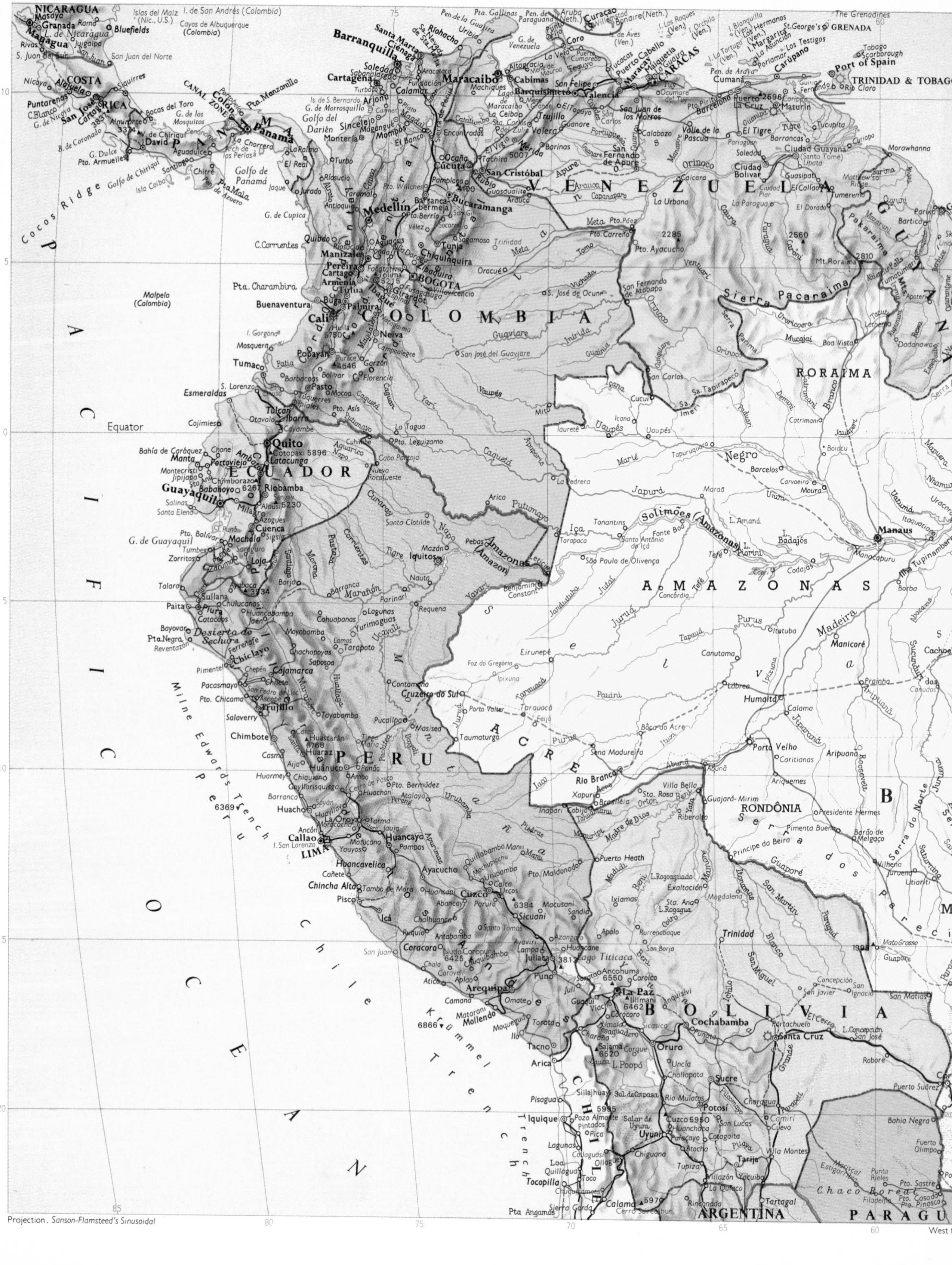

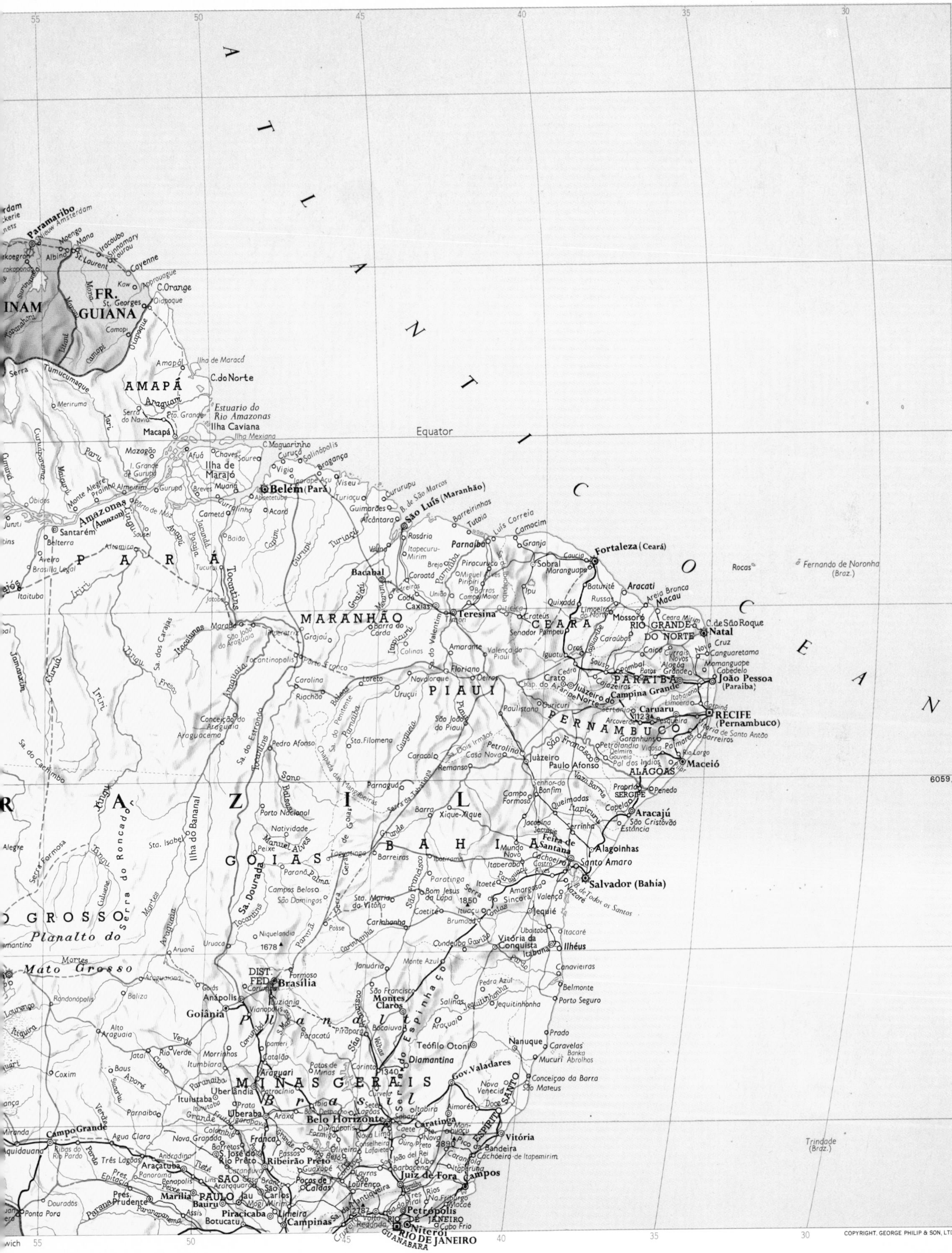

1:16 000 000

100   0   100   200   300   400   500 miles
100   0   100   200   300   400   500   600   700   800 km

A T L A N T I C   O C E A N

Paramaribo
Nieuw Amsterdam
Moengo   Mana   Iracoubo   Sinnamary
Albina   St. Laurent   Kourou
Cayenne
Kaw
C. Orange
Approuague
C. Diapoque

FR.
GUIANA
SURINAM
INAM

Serra
Tumucumaque
Amapá
Ilha de Maracá
C. do Norte
Merinna
Serra
do Navio
AMAPÁ
Araguari
Estuario do
Rio Amazonas
Macapá
Ilha Caviana
Ilha Mexiana
C. Maguarinho

Equator

Chaves
Afuá
Souré
Curuçá
Salinópolis
Mazagão
I. Grande
de Gurupá
Ilha de
Marajó
Muaná
Breves
Vigia
Bragança
Igarapé-Açu
Viseu

Monte Alegre
Prainha   Almeirim
Gurupá
Belém (Pará)
Acará
Curupurú
Bacia   de São Marcos
São Luís (Maranhão)
Guimarães
Barreirinhas
Tutoia

Santarém
Óbidos
Alenquer
Curuá   de Moz
Cametá
Capim
Turiaçu
Afcântara
Rosário
Parnaíba
Luís Correia
Camocim
Granja

Belterra
Aveiro
Altamira
Baião
Turiú
Brejo
Vigia   Barreirinhas
Caucóia
Fortaleza (Ceará)

Brasília Legal
Itaituba
Portel
Souzel
Capin
Bacabal
Piracuruca
Maranguape
Sobral

PARÁ
Tucuruí
Jacundá
Coroatá
Miguel
Piripiri
Barras
Ipu
Baturité
Aracati

Amazonas
(Amazon)
Itacaiúnas   Marabá
Grajaú
Caxias
Codó
União
Quixadá
Mossoró
Areia Branca
Macau

Tocantinópolis
MARANHÃO
Barra do
Corda
Teresina
CEARÁ
Crateús
Limoeiro
do Norte
RIO GRANDE
DO NORTE
Ceará Mirim
Natal
C. de São Roque

Sa. dos Carajás
São João
do Araguaia
Porto Franco
Colinas
Amarante
Oeiras
Floriano
Iguatú
Oros
Caraúbas
Caicó
Nova
Cruz
Canguaretama

Conceição do
Araguaia
Carolina
Loreto
Uruçuí
Navioreve
Valença
do Piauí
Senador
Pompeu
Sousa
Patos
Alagóa
Grande
Momanguape
Cabedelo
João Pessoa
(Paraíba)

Araguacema
Pedro Afonso
Riachão
São João
do Piauí
Serra do Araripe Norte
PARAÍBA
Campina Grande

Sta. Filomena
PIAUÍ
Crato
Juàzeiro do Norte
Pesqueira
Caruaru
RECIFE
(Pernambuco)

BRAZIL
Peixe
Porto Nacional
Balsas
Chapada do Araripe
Caracol
Casa Nova
Petrolina
Juàzeiro
São Francisco
FERNAMBUCO
Garanhuns
Palmares
Barreiros
Rio Largo

Manuel Alves
Natividade
Barra
Remanso
Paulo Afonso
Petrolândia
Maceió

Sta. Isabel
Ilha do Bananal
Xique-Xique
Senhor do
Bonfim
Queimadas
Vaza Barris
Propriá
SERGIPE
Penedo
ALAGOAS

GOIÁS
Campos Belos
Campo
Formoso
Itapicuru
Capela
Aracajú
Santo Amaro

Planalto do
Mato Grosso
Aruana
1678
BAHIA
Feira de
Santana
Alagoinhas
São Cristóvão
Estância

MATO GROSSO
Niquelândia
Barreiras
Santo Amaro
Salvador (Bahia)

DIST.
FED.
Brasília
Formoso
Jacobina
Serrinha

Goiás
Anápolis
Bom Jesus
da Lapa
1850
Valença
Baía de Todos os Santos

Goiânia
Luziânia
São Francisco
Montes
Claros
Carinhanha
Posse
Vitória da
Conquista
Ilhéus
Itabuna

Planalto
Formoso
Salinas
Pedra Azul
Canavieiras

Januária
Monte Azul
Jequitinhonha
Belmonte
Porto Seguro

Teófilo Otoni
Nanuque
Prado
Caravelas
Abrolhos

MINAS GERAIS
Diamantina
Gov. Valadares
Nova
Venécia
Conceição da Barra
São Mateus

Uberlândia
Belo Horizonte
Caratinga
Vitória
ESPÍRITO
SANTO

SÃO PAULO
Ribeirão Preto
Juiz de Fora
Campos
Petrópolis
Niterói
RIO DE JANEIRO
GUANABARA

Campo Grande
Marília
Bauru
Piracicaba
Campinas

Fernando de Noronha
(Braz.)
Rocas

Trindade
(Braz.)

6059

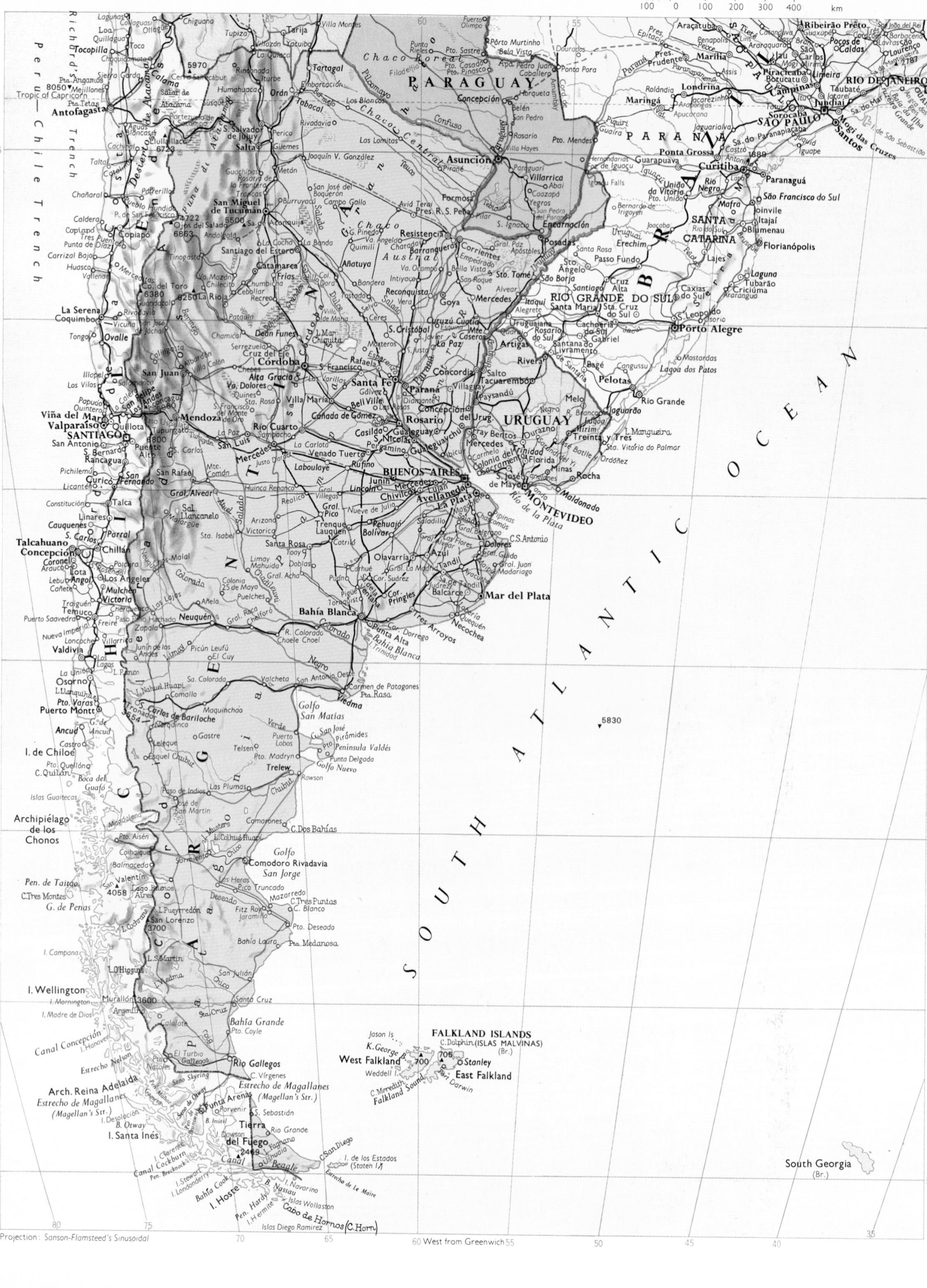

1:16 000 000

100 50 0   100   200   300 miles
100   0   100   200   300   400 km

Projection: Sanson-Flamsteed's Sinusoidal   60 West from Greenwich 55

INDEX

Introduction

The number in bold type which precedes each name in the index refers to the number of the page where that feature or place will be found.

The geographical co-ordinates which follow the place name are sometimes only approximate but are close enough for the place name to be located.

An open square □ signifies that the name refers to an administrative division of a country while a solid square ■ follows the name of a country.

Rivers have been indexed to their mouth or to their confluence.

The alphabetical order of names composed of two or more words is governed primarily by the first word and then by the second. This is an example of the rule:

> West Wyalong
> West Yorkshire
> Westbrook
> Westbury
> Western Australia

Names composed of a proper name (Gibraltar) and a description (Strait of) are positioned alphabetically by the proper name. All river names are followed by R. If the same word occurs in the name of a town and a geographical feature, the town name is listed first followed by the name or names of the geographical features.

Names beginning with M', Mc are all indexed as if they were spelled Mac.

If the same place name occurs two or more times in the index and all are in the same country, each is followed by the name of the administrative subdivision in which it is located. The names are placed in the alphabetical order of the subdivisions. For example:

> Stour, R., Dorset
> Stour, R., Hereford and Worcester
> Stour, R., Kent
> Stour, R., Suffolk

If the same place name occurs twice or more in the index and the places are in different countries they will be followed by the country names and the latter in alphabetical order.

> Sydney, Australia
> Sydney, Canada

If there is a mixture of these situations, the primary order is fixed by the alphabetical sequence of the countries and the secondary order by that of the country subdivisions. In the latter case the country names are omitted.

> Rochester, U.K.
> Rochester, Minn.   (U.S.A.) are omitted from
> Rochester, N.H.   (U.S.A.) the index
> Rochester, N.Y.   (U.S.A.)

The following is a list of abbreviations used in the index

A.S.S.R. – *Autonomous Soviet Socialist Republic*
Ala. – *Alabama*
Alas. – *Alaska*
Ang. – *Angola*
Arch. – *Archipelago*
Arg. – *Argentina*
Ariz. – *Arizona*
Ark. – *Arkansas*
B. – *Baie, Bahía, Bay, Boca, Bucht, Bugt*
B.C. – *British Columbia*
Br. – *British*
C. – *Cabo, Cap, Cape*
C.A.E. – *Central African Empire*
C. Prov. – *Cape Province*
Calif. – *California*
Chan. – *Channel*
Col. – *Colombia*
Colo. – *Colorado*
Conn. – *Connecticut*
Cord. – *Cordillera*
D.C. – *District of Columbia*
Del. – *Delaware*
Dep. – *Dependency*
Des. – *Desert*
Dist. – *District*
Dom. Rep. – *Dominican Republic*
E. – *East*
Eng. – *England*

Fd. – *Fjord*
Fed. – *Federal, Federation*
Fla. – *Florida*
Fr. – *France, French*
G. – *Golfe, Golfo, Gulf, Guba*
Ga. – *Georgia*
Gt. – *Great*
Hants. – *Hampshire*
Hd. – *Head*
Hts. – *Heights*
I.(s) – *Ile, Ilha, Insel, Isla, Island (s)*
Id. – *Idaho*
Ill. – *Illinois*
Ind. – *Indiana*
J. – *Jezero (L.)*
K. – *Kap, Kapp*
Kans. – *Kansas*
Kep. – *Kepulauan (I.)*
Kól. – *Kólpos (B.)*
Ky. – *Kentucky*
L. – *Lac, Lacul, Lago, Lagoa, Lake, Limni, Loch, Lough*
La. – *Louisana*
Ld. – *Land*
Mad. P. – *Madhya Pradesh*
Man. – *Manitoba*
Mass. – *Massachusetts*
Md. – *Maryland*
Me. – *Maine*
Mich. – *Michigan*
Minn. – *Minnesota*

Miss. – *Mississippi*
Mo. – *Missouri*
Mont. – *Montana*
Mt.(s) – *Mont, Monte, Monti, Muntii, Montaña, Mountain (s)*
Mys. – *Mysore*
N. – *North, Northern*
N.B. – *New Brunswick*
N.C. – *North Carolina*
N.D. – *North Dakota*
N.H. – *New Hampshire*
N. Ire. – *Northern Ireland*
N.J. – *New Jersey*
N. Mex. – *New Mexico*
N.S.W. – *New South Wales*
N.Y. – *New York*
N.Z. – *New Zealand*
Nat. Park – *National Park*
Nebr. – *Nebraska*
Neth. – *Netherlands*
Nev. – *Nevada*
Newf. – *Newfoundland*
Nic. – *Nicaragua*
Nig. – *Nigeria*
O.F.S. – *Orange Free State*
Okla. – *Oklahoma*
Ont. – *Ontario*
Oreg. – *Oregon*
Os. – *Ostrov (I.)*
Oz – *Ozero (L.)*
P. – *Pass, Passo, Pasul*

P.N.G. – *Papua New Guinea*
Pa. – *Pennsylvania*
Pak. – *Pakistan*
Pass. – *Passage*
Pen. – *Peninsula*
Pk. – *Peak*
Plat. – *Plateau*
Pol. – *Poluostrov*
Port. – *Portugal, Portuguese*
Prov. – *Province, Provincial*
Pt. – *Point*
Pta. – *Ponta, Punta*
Pte. – *Pointe*
Que. – *Quebec*
Queens. – *Queensland*
R. – *Rio, River*
R.S.F.S.R. – *Russian Soviet Federal Socialist Republic*
Ra.(s) – *Range(s)*
Reg. – *Region*
Rep. – *Republic*
Res. – *Reserve, Reservoir*
S. – *South*
S. Africa – *South Africa*
S.C. – *S. Carolina*
S.D. – *South Dakota*
S. Leone – *Sierra Leone*
S.S.R. – *Soviet Socialist Republic*
Sa. – *Serra, Sierra*
Sask. – *Saskatchewan*
Scot. – *Scotland*

Sd. – *Sound*
Sp. – *Spain, Spanish*
St. – *Saint*
Str. – *Strait, Stretto*
Switz. – *Switzerland*
Tanz. – *Tanzania*
Tas. – *Tasmania*
Tenn. – *Tennessee*
Terr. – *Territory*
Tex. – *Texas*
U.K. – *United Kingdom*
U.S.A. – *United States of America*
U.S.S.R. – *Union of Soviet Socialist Republics*
Ut. P. – *Uttar Pradesh*
Va. – *Virginia*
Vdkhr. – *Vodokhranilishche (Res.)*
Ven. – *Venezuela*
Vic. – *Victoria*
Vt. – *Vermont*
W. – *West*
W. Va. – *West Virginia*
Wis. – *Wisconsin*
Wyo. – *Wyoming*
Yorks. – *Yorkshire*
Yug. – *Yugoslavia*

In the index each placename is followed by its geographical co-ordinates which allow the reader to find the place on the map. These co-ordinates give the latitude and longitude of a particular place.

The latitude (or parallel) is the distance of a point north or south of the Equator measured as an angle with the centre of the earth. The Equator is latitude 0°, the North Pole is 90°N and the South Pole 90°S. On a globe the lines could be drawn as concentric circles parallel to the Equator, decreasing in diameter from the Equator until they become a point at the Poles. On the maps these lines of latitude are usually represented as lines running across the map from East to West in smooth curves. They are numbered on the sides of the map; north of the Equator the numbers increase northwards, to the south they increase southwards. The degree interval between them depends on the scale of the map. On a large scale map (for example, 1:2 000 000) the interval is one degree, but on a small scale (for example 1:50 000 000) it will be ten degrees.

Lines of longitude (or meridians) cut the latitude lines at right angles on the globe and intersect with one another at the Poles. Longitude is measured by the angle at the centre of the earth between it and the meridian of origin which runs through Greenwich (0°). It may be a measurement East or West of this line and from 0° to 180° in each direction. The longitude line of 180° runs North – South through the Pacific Ocean. On a particular map the interval between the lines of longitude is always the same as that between the lines of latitude and normally they are drawn vertically. They are numbered in the top and bottom margins and a note states East or West from Greenwich.

The unit of measurement for latitude and longitude is the degree and it is subdivided into 60 minutes. An index entry states the position of a place in degrees and minutes, a space being left between the degrees and minutes. The latitude is followed by N(orth) or S(outh) and the longitude by E(ast) or W(est).

The diagrams below illustrate how the reader has to estimate the required distance from the nearest line of latitude or longitude. In the case of the first diagram there is one degree, or 60 minutes between the lines and so to find the position of Calais an estimate has to be made, 57 parts of 60 north of the 50 degree latitude line and 50 parts of 60, or 50 minutes east of the one degree longitude line. In the case of the second diagram it is a little more difficult to estimate since there are 10 degrees between the lines. In the example of Anchorage the reader has to estimate 1 degree 10 minutes north of 60° and 9° 50 minutes west of 140°.

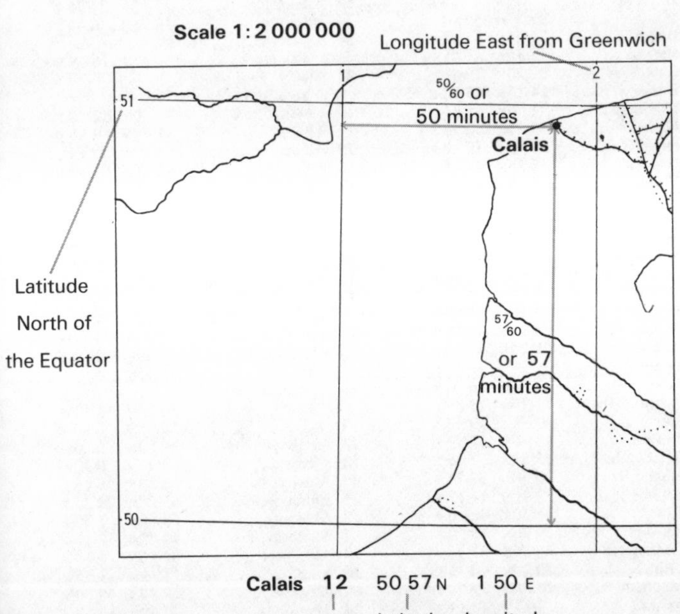

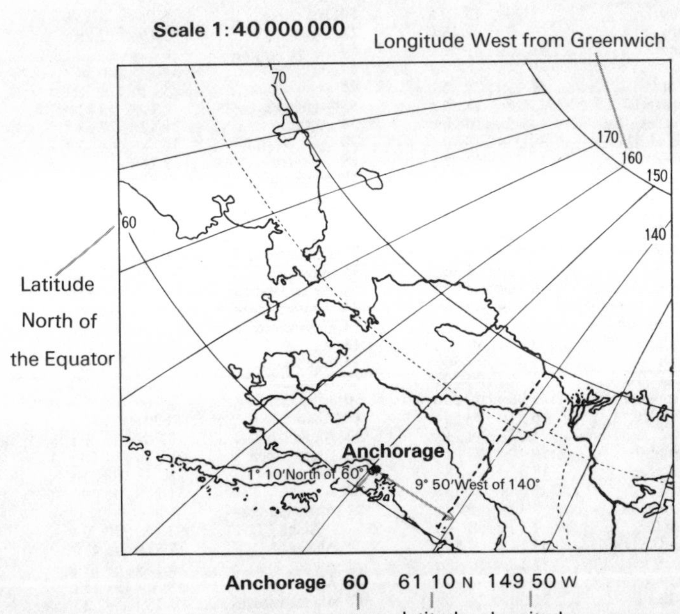

Aachen Aleksandrovskiy Zavod

A

14 Aachen 50 47N 6 4E
51 A'Âlâ en Nîl □ 8 50N 29 55E
11 Aalsmeer 52 17N 4 43E
11 Aalst 50 56N 4 2E
11 Aalten 51 56N 6 35E
14 Aarau 47 23N 8 4E
14 Aare, R. 47 37N 8 13E
11 Aarschot 50 59N 4 49E
53 Aba 5 10N 7 19E
29 Abā Saud 17 15N 43 55E
30 Abadan 30 22N 48 20E
80 Abai 25 58S 55 54W
53 Abakaliki 6 22N 8 2E
25 Abakan 53 40N 91 10E
31 Abarqu 31 10N 53 20E
28 Abasan 31 19N 34 21E
36 Abashiri 44 0N 144 15E
36 Abashiri-Wan, G. 44 0N 144 30E
24 Abay 49 38N 72 53E
54 Abaya, L. 6 30N 37 50E
24 Abaza 52 39N 90 6E
28 Abba Hillēl 31 42N 34 38E
12 Abbeville, Fr. 50 6N 1 49E
69 Abbeville, U.S.A. 30 0N 92 7W
32 Abbottabad 34 10N 73 15E
51 Abéché 13 50N 20 35E
21 Åbenrå 55 3N 9 25E
53 Abeokuta 7 3N 3 19E
7 Aberayron 52 15N 4 16W
7 Aberdare 51 43N 3 27W
46 Aberdeen, Australia 32 9S 150 56E
56 Aberdeen, S. Africa 32 28S 24 2E
8 Aberdeen, U.K. 57 9N 2 6W
72 Aberdeen, Id. 42 57N 112 50W
69 Aberdeen, Miss. 33 49N 88 13W
70 Aberdeen, S.D. 45 28N 98 29W
72 Aberdeen, Wash. 46 59N 123 50W
7 Aberdovey 52 33N 4 3W
8 Aberfeldy 56 37N 3 50W
7 Abergavenny 51 49N 3 1W
7 Aberystwyth 52 25N 4 6W
29 Abhā 18 0N 42 34E
50 Abidjan 5 26N 3 58W
70 Abilene, Kans. 39 0N 97 16W
71 Abilene, Tex. 32 22N 99 40W
7 Abingdon 51 40N 1 17W
23 Abkhaz A.S.S.R. 43 0N 41 0E
25 Abkit 64 10N 157 10E
53 Abocho 7 35N 6 56E
32 Abohar 30 10N 74 10E
53 Aboisso 5 30N 3 5W
53 Abomey 7 10N 2 5E
54 Abong Mbang 4 0N 13 8E
53 Abonnema 4 41N 6 49W
53 Aboso 5 23N 1 57W
51 Abou Deïa 11 20N 19 20E
8 Aboyne 57 4N 2 48W
30 Abqaiq 26 0N 49 45E
13 Abrantes 39 24N 8 7W
15 Abrud 46 19N 23 5E
18 Abruzzi □ 42 15N 14 0E
72 Absaroka Ra. 44 40N 110 0W
30 Abū al Khasib 30 25N 48 0E
29 Abu Arish 16 53N 42 48E
51 Abu Dis 19 12N 33 38E
28 Abū Ghōsh 31 48N 35 6E
51 Abu Hamed 19 32N 33 13E
51 Abu Tig 27 4N 31 15E
51 Abû Zabad 12 25N 29 10E
31 Abū Zabī 24 28N 54 36E
53 Abuja 9 16N 7 2E
51 Abyad, Gebel, Reg. 17 30N 28 0E
29 Abyssinia ■ = Ethiopia ■ 8 0N 40 0E
74 Acajutla 13 36N 89 50W
74 Acámbaro 20 0N 100 40W
74 Acaponeta 22 30N 105 20W
74 Acapulco 16 51N 99 56W
79 Acará 1 57S 48 11W
74 Acatlan 18 10N 98 3W
74 Acayucan 17 59N 94 58W
53 Accra 5 35N 0 6W
6 Accrington 53 46N 2 22W
34 Aceh □ 4 50N 96 0E
9 Achill 53 56N 9 55W
9 Achill, I. 53 58N 10 5W
25 Achinsk 56 20N 90 20E
75 Acklins I. 22 30N 74 0W
64 Acme 51 33N 113 30W
80 Aconcagua, Mt. 32 39S 70 0W
28 Acre=Akko 32 55N 35 4E
78 Acre □ 9 1S 71 0W
29 Ad Dam 20 33N 44 45E
30 Ad Dammam 26 20N 50 5E
30 Ad Khālis 33 40N 44 55E
53 Ada, Ghana 5 44N 0 40E
71 Ada, U.S.A. 34 50N 96 45W
29 Adale 2 58N 46 27E
53 Adamaoua, Massif de l' 7 20N 12 20E
18 Adamello, Mt. 46 10N 10 34E
68 Adams, N.Y. 43 50N 76 3W
70 Adams, Wis. 43 59N 89 50W
72 Adams, Mt. 46 10N 121 28W
32 Adam's Bridge 9 15N 79 40E
32 Adam's Pk. 6 55N 80 45E
30 Adana 37 0N 35 16E
35 Adaut 8 8S 131 7E
18 Adda, R. 45 8N 9 53E
51 Addis Ababa= Addis Abeba 9 2N 38 42E
51 Addis Abeba 9 2N 38 42E
53 Adebour 13 17N 11 50E
43 Adelaide, Australia 34 52S 138 30E
56 Adelaide, S. Afr. 32 42S 26 20E
60 Adelaide Pen. 67 40N 98 0W
44 Adelaide River 13 15S 131 7E
29 Aden= Al 'Adan 12 50N 45 0E
29 Aden, G. of 13 0N 50 0E
18 Adige, R. 45 10N 12 20E
68 Adirondack Mts. 44 0N 74 15W
53 Adjohon 6 41N 2 32E
44 Admiralty, G. 14 20S 125 55E
72 Admiralty Inlet 48 0N 122 40W
64 Admiralty I. 57 50N 134 30W
3 Admiralty Is. 2 0S 147 0E
53 Ado 6 36N 2 56E
53 Ado-Ekiti 7 38N 5 12E
32 Adoni 15 33N 77 18E
12 Adour, R. 43 32N 1 32W
13 Adra 36 43N 3 3W
18 Adrano 37 40N 14 19E
50 Adrar des Iforas, Mts. 19 40N 1 40E
68 Adrian 41 55N 84 0W
18 Adriatic Sea 43 0N 16 0E
23 Adzhar A.S.S.R. 42 0N 42 0E
19 Ægean Sea 37 0N 25 0E
18 Æolian Is.= Eólie o Lípari, I. 38 30N 14 50E
37 Aerhtai Shan, Mts. 48 0N 90 0E
31 Afghanistan ■ 33 0N 65 0E
29 Afgoi 2 7N 44 59E
53 Afikpo 5 53N 7 54E
1 Africa 5 0N 20 0E
79 Afuá 0 15S 50 10W
28 Afula 32 37N 35 17E
30 Afyon 38 20N 30 15E
53 Agadez 16 58N 7 59E
50 Agadir 30 28N 9 25W
25 Agapa 71 27N 89 15E
33 Agartala 23 50N 91 23E
35 Agats 5 34S 138 5E
50 Agboville 5 55N 4 15W
12 Agde 43 19N 3 28E
53 Agege 6 37N 3 20E
12 Agen 44 12N 0 38E
45 Agnew 28 1S 120 30E
53 Agnibilekrou 7 10N 3 11W
32 Agra 27 17N 77 58E
30 Ağri Daği, Mt. 39 50N 44 15E
18 Agrigento 37 19N 13 33E
19 Agrinion 38 37N 21 27E
79 Agua Clara 20 25S 52 45W
74 Agua Prieta 31 20N 109 32W
78 Aguadas 5 40N 75 38W
75 Aguadilla 18 27N 67 10W
63 Aguanish 50 14N 62 2W
80 Aguas Blancas 24 15S 69 55W
74 Aguascalientes 22 0N 102 12W
74 Aguascalientes □ 22 0N 102 20W
13 Aguilas 37 23N 1 35W
56 Agulhas, K. 34 52S 20 0E
28 Agur 31 42N 34 55E
50 Ahaggar, Reg. 23 0N 6 30E
47 Ahaura 42 20S 171 32E
32 Ahmadabad 23 0N 72 40E
32 Ahmadnagar 19 7N 74 46E
74 Ahuachapán 13 54N 89 52W
30 Ahvāz 31 20N 48 40E
21 Ahvenanmaa= Åland, I. 60 15N 20 0E
29 Ahwar 13 31N 46 42E
31 Aibaq 36 15N 68 5E
36 Aichi □ 35 0N 137 15E
12 Aigues-Mortes 43 35N 4 2E
38 Aihun 49 55N 127 30E
33 Aijal 23 40N 92 44E
69 Aiken 33 44N 81 50W
8 Ailsa Craig, I. 55 15N 5 7W
25 Aim 59 0N 133 55E
79 Aimorés 19 30S 41 4W
12 Ain □ 46 5N 5 20E
50 Aïn Beida 35 50N 7 35E
30 Ain Dār 25 55N 49 10E
29 Ainabo 9 0N 46 25E
50 Aïr 18 0N 8 0E
8 Airdrie 55 53N 3 57W
6 Aire, R. 53 44N 0 44W
12 Aisne, R. 49 26N 2 50E
12 Aisne □ 49 42N 3 40E
37 Aitush 39 54N 75 40E
15 Aiud 46 19N 23 44E
12 Aix-en-Provence 43 32N 5 27E
12 Aix-les-Bains 45 41N 5 53E
12 Ajaccio 41 55N 8 40E
45 Ajana 27 56S 114 35E
32 Ajanta Ra. 20 28N 75 50E
51 Ajdābiyah 30 54N 20 4E
28 'Ajlun 32 18N 35 47E
31 Ajman 25 25N 55 30E
32 Ajmer 26 28N 74 37E
73 Ajo 32 18N 112 54W
53 Ajua 4 50N 1 55W
53 Akaba 8 10N 1 2E
47 Akaroa 43 49S 172 59E
36 Akashi 34 45N 135 0E
21 Akershus □ 60 10N 11 15E
54 Aketi 2 38N 23 47E
19 Akhelóös, R. 38 36N 21 14E
30 Akhisar 38 56N 27 48E
51 Akhmîm 26 31N 31 47E
62 Akimiski I. 52 50N 81 30W
36 Akita 39 45N 140 0E
36 Akita □ 39 40N 140 30E
50 Akjoujt 19 45N 14 15W
28 Akko 32 55N 35 4E
24 Akkol 43 36N 70 45E
60 Aklavik 68 25N 135 0W
36 Akō, Japan 34 45N 134 24E
53 Ako, Nigeria 10 19N 10 48E
32 Akola 20 42N 77 2E
51 Akordat 15 30N 37 40E
53 Akosombo Dam 6 20N 0 5E
61 Akpatok I. 60 30N 68 0W
20 Akranes 64 19N 22 6W
68 Akron 41 7N 81 31W
24 Aksarka 66 31N 67 50E
30 Aksehir 38 18N 31 30E
25 Aksenovo Zilovskoye 53 20N 117 40E
37 Aksu 41 4N 80 5E
51 Aksum 14 5N 38 40E
24 Aktogay 44 25N 76 44E
24 Aktyubinsk 50 10N 57 3E
53 Aku 6 40N 7 18E
53 Akure 7 15N 5 5E
20 Akureyri 65 40N 18 5W
33 Akyab 20 15N 92 45E
29 Al 'Adan 12 50N 45 0E
30 Al Amārah 31 55N 47 15E
30 Al 'Aqabah 29 37N 35 0E
28 Al Barah 31 55N 35 12E
30 Al Basrah 30 30N 47 55E
51 Al Baydā 32 30N 21 40E
31 Al Buraimi 24 15N 55 53E
30 Al Hadithan 34 0N 41 13E
30 Al Hadr 35 35N 42 44E
30 Al Hasa, Reg. 25 40N 50 0E
30 Al Hasakah 36 35N 40 45E
29 Al Hauta 16 5N 48 20E
29 Al Hawra 13 49N 47 37E
30 Al Hillah, Iraq 32 30N 44 25E
30 Al Hillah, Saudi Arabia 23 35N 46 50E
15 Al Hilwah 23 24N 46 48E
30 Al Hindiyah 32 30N 44 10E
50 Al-Hoceïma 35 15N 3 58W
30 Al Hufūf 25 25N 49 45E
30 Al Jahrah 29 25N 47 40E
30 Al Jalāmid 31 20N 39 45E
29 Al Jazir 18 30N 56 31N
30 Al Jazirah, Reg. 26 10N 21 20E
30 Al Jubail 27 0N 49 50E
29 Al Juwara 19 0N 57 13E
31 Al Khābūrah 23 57N 57 5E
30 Al Khalaf 20 30N 57 56E
51 Al Khums 32 40N 14 17E
30 Al Kūt 32 30N 46 0E
30 Al Kuwayt 29 20N 48 0E
30 Al Lādhiqiyah 35 30N 35 45E
29 Al Līth 20 9N 40 15E
30 Al Madīnah 24 35N 39 52E
28 Al Mafraq 32 17N 36 14E
31 Al Manamah 26 10N 50 30E
51 Al Marj 32 25N 20 30E
29 Al Masırah 20 25N 58 50E
29 Al Matamma 16 43N 33 22E
30 Al Mawsil 36 15N 43 5E
28 Al Mazra' 31 18N 35 32E
30 Al Miqdadıyah 34 0N 45 0E
30 Al Mubarraz 25 30N 49 40E
31 Al Muharraq 26 15N 50 40E
29 Al Mukha 13 18N 43 15E
30 Al Qamishli 37 10N 41 10E
30 Al Qatif 26 35N 50 0E
51 Al-Qatrūn 24 56N 15 3E
29 Al Qunfidha 19 3N 41 4E
29 Al Ubailah 21 59N 50 57E
51 Al 'Ugaylah 30 12N 19 10E
31 Al Wakrah 25 10N 51 40E
30 Al Wari 'ah 27 50N 47 30E
38 Ala Shan, Reg. 40 0N 104 0E
69 Alabama, R. 31 8N 87 57W
69 Alabama □ 31 0N 87 0W
79 Alagôa Grande 7 3S 35 35W
79 Alagôas □ 9 0S 36 0W
79 Alagoinhas 12 0S 38 20W
75 Alajuela 10 2N 84 8W
22 Alakurtti 67 0N 30 30E
73 Alameda 35 10N 106 43W
73 Alamogordo 32 59N 106 0W
73 Alamosa 37 30N 106 0W
21 Åland, I. 60 15N 20 0E
21 Ålands hav 60 0N 19 20E
24 Alapayevsk 57 52N 61 42E
38 Alashanchih 38 58N 105 14E
60 Alaska □ 65 0N 150 0W
60 Alaska, G. of 58 0N 145 0W
60 Alaska Pen. 56 0N 160 0W
60 Alaska Ra. 62 50N 151 0W
22 Alatyr 54 45N 46 35E
78 Alausi 2 0S 78 50W
43 Alawoona 34 45S 140 30E
18 Alba 44 41N 8 1E
15 Alba-Iulia 46 4N 23 35E
13 Albacete 39 0N 1 50W
19 Albania ■ 41 0N 20 0E
45 Albany, Australia 35 1S 117 58E
69 Albany, Ga. 31 40N 84 10W
68 Albany, N.Y. 42 40N 73 47W
72 Albany, Oreg. 44 41N 123 0W
62 Albany, R. 52 17N 81 31W
80 Albardón 31 20S 68 30W
13 Albarracin 40 25N 1 26W
13 Albarracin, Sa. de 40 30N 1 30W
69 Albemarle 35 27N 80 15W
13 Alberche, R. 39 58N 4 46W
64 Alberni 49 20N 124 50W
63 Albert 45 51N 64 38W
54 Albert, L.= Mobutu Sese Seko, L. 1 30N 31 0E
70 Albert Lea 43 32N 93 20W
54 Albert Nile, R. 3 36N 32 2E
75 Albert Town 18 17N 77 33W
64 Alberta □ 54 40N 115 0W
56 Albertinia 34 11S 21 34E
46 Alberton 38 35S 146 40E
54 Albertville= Kalemie 5 55S 29 9E
31 Alberz, Reshteh-Ye-Kūkhā-Ye, Mts. 36 0N 52 0E
12 Albi 43 56N 2 9E
79 Albina, 5 37N 54 15W
68 Albion 42 15N 84 45W
13 Alboran, I. 35 57N 3 0W
21 Ålbôrg 57 2N 9 54E
73 Albuquerque 35 5N 106 47W
46 Albury 36 3S 146 56E
13 Alcalá de Henares 40 28N 3 22W
13 Alcalá la Real 37 27N 3 57W
13 Alcaníz 41 2N 0 8W
79 Alcántara, Brazil 2 20S 44 30W
13 Alcântara, Sp. 39 41N 6 57W
13 Alcaraz, Sa. de 38 40N 2 20W
13 Alcaudete 37 35N 4 5W
13 Alcazar de San Juan 39 24N 3 12W
13 Alcira 39 9N 0 30W
13 Alcobaça 39 32N 9 0W
13 Alcoy 38 43N 0 30W
49 Aldabra Is. 9 22S 46 28E
25 Aldan, R. 63 28N 129 35E
7 Aldeburgh 52 9N 1 35E
7 Alderney, I. 49 42N 2 12W
7 Aldershot 51 15N 0 43W
50 Aleg 17 3N 13 55W
80 Alegrete 29 40S 56 0W
24 Aleisk 52 40N 83 0E
23 Aleksandrov Gai 50 15N 48 35E
25 Aleksandrovsk-Sakhalinskiy 50 50N 142 20E
25 Aleksandrovskiy Zavod 50 40N 117 50E

Aleksandrovskoye Anupgarh

24	Aleksandrovskoye	60 35N	77 50E
12	Alençon	48 27N	0 4E
66	Alenuihaha Chan.	20 25N	156 0W
30	Aleppo=Ḩalab	36 10N	37 15E
64	Alert Bay	50 30N	127 35W
12	Alès	44 9N	4 5E
18	Alessandria	44 54N	8 37E
20	Ålesund	62 28N	6 12E
2	Aleutian Is.	52 0N	175 0W
64	Alexander Arch.	57 0N	135 0W
55	Alexander Bay	28 36S	16 33E
69	Alexander City	32 56N	85 57W
2	Alexander I.	69 0S	70 0W
47	Alexandra	45 14S	169 25E
51	Alexandria=El Iskandarîya	31 0N	30 0E
62	Alexandria, Canada	45 19N	74 38W
56	Alexandria, S. Africa	33 38S	26 28E
71	Alexandria, La.	31 20N	92 30W
70	Alexandria, Minn.	45 50N	95 20W
68	Alexandria, Va.	38 47N	77 1W
68	Alexandria Bay	44 20N	75 52W
19	Alexandroúpolis	40 50N	25 24E
8	Alford	53 16N	0 10E
6	Alfreton	53 6N	1 22W
24	Alga	49 46N	57 20E
13	Algarve, Reg.	37 15N	8 10W
13	Algeciras	36 9N	5 28W
13	Algemesí	39 11N	0 27W
50	Alger	36 42N	3 8E
50	Algeria ■	35 10N	3 0E
18	Alghero	40 34N	8 20E
50	Algiers=Alger	36 42N	3 8E
56	Algoabaai	33 50S	25 45E
62	Algonquin Prov. Park	45 35N	78 35W
13	Alhama de Murcia	37 51N	1 25W
73	Alhambra	34 0N	118 10W
19	Aliákmon, R.	40 30N	22 36E
13	Alicante	38 23N	0 30W
13	Alicante □	38 30N	0 37W
71	Alice	27 47N	98 1W
64	Alice Arm	55 29N	129 23W
44	Alice Downs	17 45S	127 56E
42	Alice Springs	23 40S	135 50E
55	Alicedale	33 15S	26 4E
32	Aligarh	27 55N	78 10E
30	Aligudarz	33 25N	49 45E
21	Alingsås	57 56N	12 31E
32	Alipur	29 25N	70 55E
33	Alipur Duar	26 30N	89 35E
68	Aliquippa	40 38N	80 18W
56	Aliwal Nord	30 45S	26 45E
13	Aljustrel	37 55N	8 10W
53	Alkamari	13 27N	11 10E
11	Alkmaar	52 37N	4 45E
73	All American Canal	32 45N	115 0W
53	Allada	6 41N	2 9E
33	Allahabad	25 25N	81 58E
65	Allan	51 53N	106 4W
56	Allanridge	27 45S	26 40E
63	Allard Lake	50 40N	63 10W
58	Allegheny Mts.	38 0N	80 0W
68	Allegheny, R.	40 27N	80 0W
74	Allende	28 20N	100 50W
68	Allentown	40 36N	75 30W
32	Alleppey	9 30N	76 28E
14	Aller, R.	52 57N	9 11E
70	Alliance, Nebr.	42 10N	102 50W
68	Alliance, Ohio	40 53N	81 7W
12	Allier, R.	46 58N	3 4E
12	Allier □	46 25N	3 0E
42	Alligator Creek	19 23S	146 58E
62	Alliston	44 15N	79 55W
8	Alloa	56 7N	3 49W
62	Alma, Canada	48 35N	71 40W
63	Alma, U.S.A.	43 25N	84 40W
24	Alma Ata	43 15N	76 57E
13	Almada	38 40N	9 9W
42	Almaden	17 22S	144 40E
13	Almadén	38 49N	4 52W
13	Almansa	38 51N	1 5W
13	Almanzor, P. de	40 15N	5 18W
13	Almazán	41 30N	2 30W
79	Almeirim, Brazil	1 30S	52 0W
11	Almelo	52 22N	6 42E
13	Almendralejo	38 41N	6 26W
13	Almería	36 52N	2 32W
75	Almirante	9 10N	82 30W
6	Alnwick	55 25N	1 42W
33	Alon	22 12N	95 5E
65	Alonsa	50 50N	99 0W
35	Alor, I.	8 15S	124 30E
34	Alor Setar	6 7N	100 22E
45	Aloysius, Mt.	26 0S	128 38E
68	Alpena	45 6N	83 24W
12	Alpes-Maritimes □	43 55N	7 10E
12	Alpes-de-Haute-Provence □	44 8N	6 10E
42	Alpha	24 8S	146 39E
18	Alpi Carniche, Mts.	46 36N	13 0E
71	Alpine	30 35N	103 35W
4	Alps, Mts.	47 0N	8 0E
42	Alroy Downs	19 20S	136 5E
12	Alsace, Reg.	48 15N	7 25E
13	Alsasua	42 54N	2 10W
6	Alston	54 48N	2 26W
20	Alta	69 55N	23 12E
80	Alta Gracia	31 40S	64 30W
64	Alta Lake	50 10N	123 0W
20	Altaelv, R.	69 57N	23 17E
78	Altagracia	10 45N	71 30W
26	Altai, Mts.	48 0N	90 0E
37	Altai, Mts.= Aerhtai Shan, Mts.	48 0N	90 0E
79	Altamira	3 0S	52 10W
38	Altanbulag	50 19N	106 30E
13	Altea	38 38N	0 2W
13	Alto-Alentejo, Reg.	38 50N	7 40W
79	Alto Araguaia	17 15S	53 20W
7	Alton, U.K.	51 8N	0 59W
70	Alton, U.S.A.	38 55N	90 5W
14	Altona	53 32N	9 56E
68	Altoona	40 32N	78 24W
71	Altus	34 30N	99 25W
37	Altyn Tagh, Mts.	39 0N	89 0E
29	Alula	11 50N	50 45E
35	Alusi	7 35S	131 40E
71	Alva	36 50N	98 50W
74	Alvarado	18 40N	95 50W
80	Alvear	29 5S	57 40W
21	Alvesta	56 54N	14 35E
46	Alvie	38 15S	143 30E
21	Älvkarleby	60 34N	17 35E
21	Alvsborgs □	58 30N	12 30E
20	Älvsbyn	65 39N	20 59E
32	Alwar	27 38N	76 34E
23	Alyat Pristan	39 59N	49 28E
8	Alyth	56 38N	3 15W
51	Am-Timan	11 0N	20 10E
61	Amadjuak	64 0N	72 50W
61	Amadjuak L.	65 0N	71 0W
36	Amagasaki	34 42N	135 20E
36	Amakusa-Shotō, Is.	32 15N	130 10E
21	Åmål	59 2N	12 40E
32	Amalner	21 5N	75 5E
24	Amangeldy	50 10N	65 10E
79	Amapá	2 5N	50 50W
79	Amapá □	1 40N	52 0W
79	Amarante	6 14S	42 50W
79	Amargosa	13 2S	39 36W
71	Amarillo	35 14N	101 46W
18	Amaro, Mt.	42 5N	14 6E
53	Amassama	5 1N	6 2E
30	Amasya	40 40N	35 50E
57	Amatikulu	29 3S	31 33E
74	Amatitlán	14 29N	90 38W
79	Amazon= Amazonas, R.	2 0S	53 30W
79	Amazonas, R.	2 0S	53 30W
78	Amazonas □	4 20S	64 0W
32	Ambala	30 23N	76 56E
57	Ambalavao	21 50S	46 56E
57	Ambanja	13 40S	48 27E
25	Ambarchik	69 40N	162 20E
57	Ambaro, B. d'	13 23S	48 38E
57	Ambata-Boéni	16 28S	46 43E
78	Ambato	1 5S	78 42W
57	Ambatofinandrahana	20 33S	46 48E
57	Ambatolampy	19 20S	47 35E
57	Ambatondrazaka	17 55S	48 28E
19	Ámbelos, Ákra	39 56N	23 55E
14	Amberg	49 25N	11 52E
74	Ambergris Cay	18 0N	88 0W
47	Amberley	43 9S	172 44E
33	Ambikapur	23 15N	83 15E
6	Ambleside	54 26N	2 58W
57	Ambohimanga du Sud	20 52S	47 36E
12	Amboise	47 25N	0 59E
35	Ambon	3 35S	128 20E
57	Ambositra	20 31S	47 25E
57	Ambovombé	25 11S	46 5E
73	Amboy	34 33N	115 51W
57	Ambre, C. d'	12 40S	49 10E
43	Amby	26 30S	148 11E
24	Amderma	69 45N	61 30E
74	Ameca	20 30N	104 0W
11	Ameland, I.	53 27N	5 45E
25	Amen	68 45N	180 0E
72	American Falls	42 46N	112 56E
47	American Samoa, I.	14 20S	170 0W
69	Americus	32 0N	84 10W
11	Amersfoort, Neth	52 9N	5 23E
57	Amersfoort, S. Afr.	26 59S	29 53E
45	Amery, Australia	31 9S	117 5E
65	Amery, Canada	56 45N	94 0W
70	Ames	42 0N	93 40W
25	Amga, R.	62 38N	134 32E
25	Amgu	45 45N	137 15E
33	Amherst, Burma	16 0N	97 40E
63	Amherst, Canada	45 48N	64 8W
62	Amherstburg	42 6N	83 6W
12	Amiens	49 54N	2 16E
27	Amirantes, Is.	6 0S	53 0E
6	Amlwch	53 24N	4 21W
28	'Ammān	32 0N	35 52E
28	Ammi'ad	32 55N	35 32E
19	Amorgós	36 50	25 57E
62	Amos	48 35N	78 5W
39	Amoy=Hsiamen	24 25N	118 4E
57	Ampanihy	24 40S	44 45E
53	Amper	9 25N	9 40E
63	Amqui	48 28N	67 27W
32	Amroati	20 55N	77 45E
32	Amreli	21 35N	71 17E
32	Amritsar	31 35N	74 57E
32	Amroha	28 53N	78 30E
11	Amsterdam, Neth.	52 23N	4 54E
57	Amsterdam, S. Afr.	26 35S	30 45E
68	Amsterdam, U.S.A.	42 58N	74 10W
3	Amsterdam, I.	37 30S	77 30E
24	Amu Darya, R.	43 40N	59 1E
60	Amukta Pass.	52 25N	172 0W
60	Amundsen G.	70 30N	123 0W
2	Amundsen Sea	72 0S	115 0W
25	Amur, R.	52 56N	141 10E
30	An Najaf	32 3N	44 15E
30	An Nasiriyah	31 0N	46 15E
34	An Nhon	13 53N	109 6E
30	An Nu'ayriyah	27 30N	48 30E
9	An Uaimh	53 39N	6 40W
28	Anabta	32 19N	35 7E
72	Anaconda	46 7N	113 0W
72	Anacortes	48 30N	122 40W
71	Anadarko	35 4N	98 15W
30	Anadolu, Reg.	38 0W	39 0E
25	Anadyr	64 35N	177 20E
25	Anadyr, R.	64 55N	176 5E
64	Anahim Lake	52 28N	125 18W
33	Anakapalle	17 42N	83 6E
42	Anakie	23 32S	147 45E
57	Analalava	14 35S	48 0E
34	Anambas, Kep.	3 20N	106 30E
53	Anambra □	6 30N	7 30E
36	Anan	33 54N	134 40E
32	Anantnag	33 45N	75 10E
79	Anápolis	16 15S	48 50W
31	Anar	30 55N	55 13E
30	Anatolia, Reg.= Anadolu, Reg.	38 0N	39 0E
80	Añatuya	28 20S	62 50W
60	Anchorage	61 10N	149 50W
78	Ancohuma, Mt.	16 0S	68 50W
18	Ancona	43 37N	13 30E
80	Ancud	42 0S	73 50W
80	Ancud, G. de	42 0S	73 0W
20	Andalsnes	62 35N	7 43E
13	Andalusia	31 51N	86 30W
27	Andaman Is.	12 30N	92 30E
11	Andenne	50 30N	5 5E
72	Anderson, Calif.	40 30N	122 19W
68	Anderson, Ind.	40 5N	85 40W
69	Anderson, S.C.	34 32N	82 40W
60	Anderson, R.	69 43N	128 58W
76	Andes, Mts.	20 0S	68 0W
57	Andevorante	18 57S	49 6E
32	Andhra Pradesh □	15 0N	80 0E
24	Andizhan	41 10N	72 0E
31	Andkhui	36 52N	65 8E
13	Andorra ■	42 30N	1 30E
13	Andorra	42 31N	1 32E
7	Andover	51 13N	1 29W
79	Andradina	20 54S	51 23W
60	Andreanof Is.	51 0N	178 0W
18	Ándria	41 13N	16 17E
57	Andriba	17 30S	46 58E
75	Andros, I.	24 30N	78 4W
19	Ándros I.	37 50N	24 50E
75	Andros Town	24 43N	77 47W
13	Andújar	38 3N	4 5W
53	Anécho	6 12N	1 34E
75	Anegada I.	18 45N	64 20W
75	Anegada Pass.	18 15N	63 45W
13	Aneto, Pico de	42 37N	0 40E
80	Angamos, Pta.	23 1S	70 32W
38	Anganki	47 9N	123 48E
25	Angara, R.	58 6N	93 0E
25	Angarsk	52 30N	104 0E
43	Angaston	34 30S	139 8E
20	Ånge	62 31N	15 35E
74	Angel de la Guarda, I.	29 30N	113 30W
35	Angeles	15 9N	120 35E
21	Ängelholm	56 15N	12 58E
73	Angels Camp	38 8N	120 30W
20	Ångermanälven, R.	62 48N	17 56E
12	Angers	47 30N	0 35E
6	Anglesey, I.	53 17N	4 20W
54	Ango	4 10N	26 5E
55	Angoche	16 8S	40 0E
80	Angol	37 48S	72 43W
55	Angola ■	12 0S	18 0E
12	Angoulême	45 39N	0 10E
12	Angoumois, Reg.	45 30N	0 25E
24	Angren	41 1N	69 45E
75	Anguilla, I.	8 14N	63 5W
42	Angurugu	14 0S	136 25E
8	Angus, Braes of	56 51N	3 0W
39	Anhsien	31 30N	104 35E
39	Anhwei □	33 15N	116 50E
53	Anie	7 42N	1 8E
57	Anivorzno	18 44S	48 58E
12	Anjou, Reg.	47 20N	0 15W
57	Anjozorobé	18 22S	47 52E
38	Anju	39 36N	125 40E
53	Anka	12 13N	5 58E
39	Ankang	32 38N	109 5E
30	Ankara	40 0N	32 54E
57	Ankaramina	21 57S	46 39E
57	Ankazoaba	22 18S	44 31E
57	Ankazobé	18 20S	47 10E
39	Anking	30 31N	117 2E
68	Ann Arbor	42 17N	83 45W
44	Anna Plains	19 17S	121 37E
50	Annaba	36 50N	7 46E
34	Annam, Reg.= Trung-Phan, Reg.	16 30N	107 30E
8	Annan	54 59N	3 16W
8	Annan, R.	54 59N	3 16W
68	Annapolis	38 59N	76 30W
63	Annapolis Royal	44 44N	65 32W
12	Annecy	45 55N	6 8E
37	Anning	24 58N	102 30E
69	Anniston	33 45N	85 50W
49	Annobón=Pagalu	1 35S	3 35E
70	Anoka	45 10N	93 26W
57	Anorotsangana	13 56S	47 55E
39	Anping	23 0N	120 6E
14	Ansbach	49 17N	10 34E
38	Anshan	41 3N	122 58E
39	Anshun	26 2N	105 57E
37	Ansi	40 21N	96 10E
44	Anson, B.	13 20S	130 6E
53	Ansongo	15 25N	0 35E
62	Ansonville	48 46N	80 43W
8	Anstruther	56 14N	2 40W
35	Ansuda	2 11S	139 22E
38	Anta	46 18N	125 34E
30	Antakya	36 14N	36 10E
57	Antalaha	14 57S	50 20E
30	Antalya	36 52N	30 45E
30	Antalya Körfezi	36 15N	31 30E
57	Antananarivo	18 55S	47 35E
1	Antarctica	90 0S	0 0
2	Antarctic Pen.	67 0S	60 0W
13	Antequera	37 5N	4 33W
73	Anthony	32 1N	106 37W
42	Anthony Lagoon	18 0S	135 30E
63	Anticosti I.	49 20N	62 40W
70	Antigo	45 8N	89 5W
63	Antigonish	45 38N	61 58W
74	Antigua	14 34N	90 41W
75	Antigua, I.	17 0N	61 50W
75	Antilla	20 40N	75 50W
73	Antimony	38 7N	112 0W
78	Antioquia	6 40N	75 55W
3	Antipodes Is.	49 45S	178 40E
80	Antofagasta	23 50S	70 30W
57	Antongil, B. d'	15 30S	49 50E
57	António Enes= Angoche	16 8S	40 0E
9	Antrim	54 43N	6 13W
9	Antrim □	54 55N	6 10W
9	Antrim, Mts. of	54 57N	6 10W
57	Antsalova	18 40S	44 37E
57	Antsirabe	19 55S	47 2E
57	Antsohihy	14 50S	47 50E
38	Antung	40 10N	124 18E
11	Antwerp= Antwerpen	51 13N	4 25E
11	Antwerpen	51 13N	4 25E
11	Antwerpen □	51 15N	4 40E
32	Anupgarh	29 10N	73 10E

Anuppur Australian Alps, Mts

33 Anuppur 22 58N 81 44E
32 Anuradhapura 8 22N 80 28E
11 Anvers= Antwerpen 51 13N 4 25E
60 Anvik 62 40N 160 12W
38 Anyang 36 7N 114 26E
35 Anyer-Lor 6 6S 105 56E
39 Anyi 28 50N 115 31E
24 Anzhero Sudzhensk 56 10N 83 40E
18 Ánzio 41 28N 12 37E
36 Aomori 40 45N 140 45E
36 Aomori □ 40 45N 140 40E
18 Aosta 45 43N 7 20E
51 Aozou 21 49N 17 25E
53 Apam 5 17N 0 44W
53 Apapa 6 25N 3 25E
35 Aparri 18 22N 121 38E
74 Apatzingán 19 0N 102 20W
11 Apeldoorn 52 13N 5 57E
34 Apenam 8 35S 116 13E
18 Apennines, Mts.= Appennini, Mts. 41 0N 15 0E
47 Apia 14 0S 171 55W
74 Apizaco 19 26N 98 9W
51 Apollonia= Marsa Susa 32 52N 21 59E
70 Apostle Is. 47 0N 90 30W
80 Apóstoles 27 55S 55 45W
78 Apoteri 4 2N 58 32W
58 Appalachian Mts. 38 0N 80 0W
6 Appleby 54 35N 2 29W
68 Appleton 44 17N 88 25W
79 Approuagne 4 20N 52 0W
80 Apucarana 23 55S 51 33W
31 Aq Chah 37 0N 66 5E
30 'Aqaba 29 31N 35 0E
30 'Aqaba, Khalîj al 28 15N 33 20E
51 Aqiq 18 14N 38 12E
28 Aqraba 32 9N 35 20E
79 Aquidauana 20 30S 55 50W
29 Ar Rab' al Khālī 21 0N 51 0E
28 Ar-Ramthā 32 34N 36 0E
30 Ar Raqqah 35 56N 39 1E
30 Ar Riyâd 24 41N 46 42E
31 Ar Ruska 23 35N 53 30E
30 Ar Ruṭbah 33 0N 40 15E
51 Arab, Bahr el, R. 9 2N 29 28E
26 Arabia, Reg. 25 0N 45 0E
48 Arabian Des. 28 0N 32 30E
26 Arabian Sea 16 0N 65 0E
79 Aracajú 10 55S 37 4W
78 Aracataca 10 38N 74 9W
79 Aracati 4 30S 37 44W
79 Araçatuba 21 10S 50 30W
13 Aracena 37 53N 6 58W
79 Araçuai 16 52S 42 4W
28 'Arad 31 17N 35 12E
15 Arad 46 10N 21 20E
26 Arafura Sea 10 0S 135 0E
13 Aragón, R. 42 13N 1 44W
13 Aragon, Reg. 41 0N 1 0W
79 Araguacema 8 50S 49 20W
79 Araguaia, R. 5 21S 48 41W
79 Araguari 18 38S 48 11W
30 Arak 34 0N 49 40E
33 Arakan Coast 19 0N 94 0E
33 Arakan Yoma, Mts. 20 0N 94 30E
23 Araks, R. 40 1N 48 28E
24 Aral Sea= Aralskoye More 44 30N 66 0E
24 Aralsk 46 50N 61 20E
24 Aralskoye More 44 30N 60 0E
9 Aran, I. 55 0N 8 30W
9 Aran Is. 53 5N 9 42W
13 Aranjuez 40 1N 3 40W
71 Aransas P. 28 0N 97 9W
34 Aranyaprathet 13 41N 102 30E
80 Arapongas 23 29S 51 28W
80 Araranguá 29 0S 49 30W
79 Araraquara 21 50S 48 0W
46 Ararat 37 16S 143 0E
30 Ararat, Mt.= Ağri Daği, Mt. 39 50N 44 15E
80 Arauca 7 0N 70 40W
79 Araxá 19 35S 46 55W
78 Araya, Pen. de 10 40N 64 0W
18 Arbatax 39 57N 9 42E
30 Arbıl 36 15N 44 5E
8 Arbroath 56 34N 2 35W
12 Arcachon 44 40N 1 10W
70 Arcadia 44 13N 91 29W
72 Arcata 40 55N 124 4W
22 Archangel= Arkhangelsk 64 40N 41 0E
52 Archers Post 0 35N 37 35E
65 Arcola 49 40N 102 30W
13 Arcos de los Frontera 36 45N 5 49W
32 Arcot 12 53N 79 20E
79 Arcoverde 8 25S 37 4W
61 Arctic Bay 73 2N 85 11W
3 Arctic Ocean 78 0N 160 0W
60 Arctic Red River 67 15N 134 0W
19 Arda, R. 41 39N 26 29E
30 Ardabīl 38 15N 48 18E
12 Ardèche □ 44 42N 4 16E
9 Ardee 53 51N 6 32W
11 Ardennes, Reg. 49 30N 5 10E
12 Ardennes □ 49 35N 4 40E
31 Ardestan 33 20N 52 25E
8 Ardgour, Reg. 56 45N 5 25W
46 Ardlethan 34 22S 146 53E
71 Ardmore, Australia 21 39S 139 11E
71 Ardmore, U.S.A. 34 10N 97 5W
9 Ardnacrusha 52 43N 8 38W
8 Ardnamurchan Pt. 56 44N 6 14W
8 Ardrossan 55 39N 4 50W
9 Ards □ 54 35N 5 30W
9 Ards Pen. 54 30N 5 25W
75 Arecibo 18 29N 66 42W
79 Areia Branca 5 0S 37 0W
13 Arenal 39 28N 2 47E
21 Arendal 58 28N 8 46E
78 Arequipa 16 20S 71 30W
54 Arero 4 41N 38 50E
13 Arévalo 41 3N 4 43W
18 Arezzo 43 28N 11 50E
63 Argentia 47 18N 53 58W
76 Argentine Basin, Reg. 44 0S 51 0E
80 Argentina ■ 35 0S 66 0W
80 Argentino, L. 50 10S 73 0W
15 Arges, R. 44 10N 26 45E
51 Argo 19 28N 30 30E
19 Argolikós Kól. 37 20N 22 52E
12 Argonne, Mts. 49 0N 5 20E
19 Árgos 37 40N 22 43E
19 Argostólion 38 12N 20 33E
73 Arguello, Pt. 34 34N 120 40W
25 Argun, R. 43 22N 45 55E
53 Argungu 12 40N 4 31E
44 Argyle, L. 16 20S 128 40E
21 Århus 56 8N 10 11E
78 Arica, Chile 18 32S 70 20W
78 Arica, Col. 1 30S 75 30W
45 Arid, C. 34 1S 123 10E
36 Arida 33 29N 135 44E
12 Ariège □ 42 56N 1 30E
75 Arima 10 38N 61 17W
8 Arisaig 56 50N 5 40W
80 Arizona 35 45S 65 25W
73 Arizona □ 34 20N 111 30W
78 Arjona 10 14N 75 22W
25 Arka 60 15N 142 0E
37 Arka Tagh, Mts. 36 30N 90 0E
71 Arkadelphia 34 5N 93 0W
8 Arkaig, L. 56 58N 5 10W
71 Arkansas, R. 33 48N 91 4W
71 Arkansas □ 35 0N 92 30W
71 Arkansas City 37 4N 97 3W
22 Arkhangelsk 64 40N 41 0E
9 Arklow 52 48N 6 10W
12 Arles 43 41N 4 40E
57 Arlington, S. Afr. 28 1S 27 53E
71 Arlington, U.S.A. 44 25N 97 4W
11 Arlon 49 42N 5 49E
45 Armadale 32 12S 116 0E
9 Armagh 54 22N 6 40W
9 Armagh □ 54 16N 6 35W
12 Armagnac, Reg. 43 44N 0 10E
23 Armavir 45 2N 41 7E
78 Armenia 4 35N 75 45W
23 Armenian S.S.R. □ 40 0N 41 10E
46 Armidale 30 30S 151 40E
64 Armstrong, B.C. 50 25N 119 10W
62 Armstrong, Ont. 50 20N 89 0W
11 Arnhem 51 58N 5 55E
42 Arnhem, B. 12 20S 136 10E
40 Arnhem Land 13 0S 135 0E
18 Arno, R. 43 31N 10 17E
62 Arnprior 45 23N 76 25W
43 Arrabury 26 45S 141 0E
33 Arrah 25 35N 84 32E
8 Arran, I. 55 34N 5 12W
12 Arras 50 17N 2 46E
50 Arrecife 28 59N 13 40W
12 Arrée, Mts. d' 48 26N 3 55W
45 Arrino 29 30S 115 40E
64 Arrowhead 50 40N 117 55W
47 Arrowtown 44 57S 168 50E
38 Arshan 46 59N 120 0E
19 Árta 39 8N 21 2E
61 Artemovsk 48 35N 37 55E
71 Artesia 32 55N 104 25W
42 Arthur, Pt. 22 7S 150 3E
80 Artigas 30 20S 56 30W
12 Artois, Reg. 50 20N 2 30E
30 Artvin 41 14N 41 44E
35 Aru, Kep. 6 0S 134 30E
52 Arua 3 1N 30 58E
79 Aruanã 15 0S 51 10W
75 Aruba, I. 12 30N 70 0W
33 Arunachal Pradesh □ 28 0N 95 0E
52 Arusha 3 20S 36 40E
72 Arvada 44 43N 106 6W
38 Arvayheer 46 15N 102 48E
63 Arvida 48 16N 71 14W
20 Arvidsjaur 65 35N 19 10E
21 Arvika 59 40N 12 36E
24 Arys 42 26N 68 48E
22 Arzamas 55 27N 43 55E
50 Arzew 35 50N 0 23W
28 As Salt 32 2N 35 43E
30 As Samawah 31 15N 45 15E
30 As Sulaimānīyah 24 8N 47 10E
30 As Sulamānīyah 35 35N 45 29E
31 As Suwaih 22 10N 59 33E
30 As Suwayda 32 40N 36 30E
30 As Suwayrah 32 55N 45 0E
53 Asaba 6 12N 6 38E
36 Asahikawa 43 45N 142 30E
53 Asamankese 5 50N 0 40W
33 Asansol 23 40N 87 1E
63 Asbestos 45 47N 71 58W
68 Asbury Park 40 15N 74 1W
74 Ascensión, B. de la 19 50N 87 20W
49 Ascension, I. 8 0S 14 15W
14 Aschaffenburg 49 58N 9 8E
18 Ascoli Piceno 42 51N 13 34E
29 Aseb 13 0N 42 40E
73 Ash Fork 35 14N 112 32W
30 Ash Shāmiyah 31 55N 44 35E
30 Ash Sharma 28 1N 35 18E
28 Ash Shuna 32 32N 35 34E
22 Asha 35 10N 33 38E
53 Ashanti □ 7 30N 2 0W
47 Ashburton 43 53S 171 48E
44 Ashburton, R. 37 52S 145 5E
44 Ashburton Downs 23 25S 117 4E
6 Ashby-de-la-Zouch 52 45N 1 29W
28 Ashdod 31 39N 34 35E
28 Ashdot Yaaqov 32 39N 35 35E
69 Asheboro 35 43N 79 46W
69 Asheville 35 39N 82 30W
7 Ashford 51 8N 0 53E
36 Ashikaga 36 28N 139 29E
6 Ashington 55 12N 1 35W
24 Ashkhabad 38 0N 57 50E
68 Ashland, Ky. 38 25N 82 40W
68 Ashland, Ohio 40 52N 82 20W
72 Ashland, Oreg. 42 10N 122 38W
70 Ashland, Wis. 46 40N 90 52W
28 Ashquelon 31 42N 34 55E
68 Ashtabula 41 52N 80 50W
72 Ashton 44 6N 111 30W
6 Ashton-under-Lyne 53 30N 2 8W
1 Asia 45 0N 75 0E
50 Asilah 35 29N 6 0W
18 Asinara, G. dell' 41 0N 8 30E
18 Asinara, I. 41 5N 8 15E
24 Asino 57 0N 86 0E
29 Asir, Ras 11 55N 51 0E
29 Asir, Reg. 18 40N 42 30E
28 Asira esh Shamaliya 32 16N 35 16E
21 Askersund 58 58N 14 8E
31 Asmar 35 10N 71 27E
51 Asmera 15 19N 38 55E
47 Aspiring, Mt. 44 23S 168 46W
33 Assam □ 25 45N 92 30E
11 Asse 50 54N 4 6E
11 Assen 53 0N 6 35E
65 Assiniboia 49 40N 106 0W
64 Assiniboine, Mt. 50 52N 115 39W
65 Assiniboine, R. 49 53N 97 8W
79 Assis 22 40S 50 20W
18 Assisi 43 4N 12 36E
8 Assynt, L. 58 25N 5 10W
23 Astara 38 30N 48 50E
18 Asti 44 54N 8 11E
19 Astipálaia, I. 36 32N 26 22E
13 Astorga 42 29N 6 8W
72 Astoria 46 16N 123 50W
23 Astrakhan 46 25N 48 5E
13 Asturias, Reg. 43 15N 6 0W
80 Asunción 25 21S 57 30W
51 Aswân 24 4N 32 57E
51 Aswân High Dam 24 5N 32 54E
51 Asyût 27 11N 31 4E
30 At Ta'if 21 5N 40 27E
80 Atacama Des. 24 0S 69 20W
80 Atacama, Pune de 25 0S 67 30W
80 Atacama, Salar de 24 0S 68 20W
53 Atakpamé 7 31N 1 13E
36 Atami 35 0N 139 55E
50 Atar 20 30N 13 5W
25 Atara 63 10N 129 10E
24 Atasu 48 30N 71 0E
51 Atbara 17 42N 33 59E
51 'Atbara, Nahr, R 17 40N 33 56E
24 Atbasar 51 48N 68 20E
70 Atchison 39 40N 95 0W
11 Ath 50 38N 3 47E
64 Athabasca 54 45N 113 20W
65 Athabasca, L. 59 10N 109 30W
65 Athabasca, R. 58 40N 110 50W
9 Athboy 53 37N 6 55W
9 Athenry 53 18N 8 45W
69 Athens, Ala. 34 49N 86 58W
69 Athens, Ga. 33 56N 83 24W
68 Athens, Ohio 39 52N 82 64W
71 Athens, Tex. 32 11N 95 48W
19 Athens=Athínai 37 58N 23 46E
42 Atherton 17 17S 145 30E
52 Athi River 1 29S 36 58E
53 Athiéme 6 37N 1 40E
19 Athínai 37 58N 23 46E
9 Athlone 53 26N 7 57W
68 Athol 42 36N 72 14W
8 Atholl, Forest of 56 51N 3 50W
63 Atholville 48 5N 67 5W
19 Athos, Mt. 40 9N 24 22E
9 Athy 53 0N 7 0W
25 Atka 60 50N 151 48E
60 Atka I. 52 15N 174 30W
69 Atlanta 33 50N 84 24W
70 Atlantic 41 25N 95 0W
68 Atlantic City 39 25N 74 25W
2 Atlantic Ocean 0 0 30 0W
50 Atlas, Anti, Mts. 30 0N 8 0½
50 Atlas, Moyen, Mts. 37 0N 5 0W
50 Atlas Saharien, Mts. 34 10N 3 30E
64 Atlin 59 31N 133 41W
28 Atlit 32 42N 34 56E
69 Atmore 31 2N 87 30W
78 Atocha 21 0S 66 10W
74 Atotonilco 20 20N 98 40W
62 Attawapiskat 53 0N 82 30W
62 Attawapiskat L. 52 20N 88 0W
62 Attawapiskat, R. 52 57N 82 18W
28 Attil 32 23N 35 4E
68 Attleboro 41 56N 71 18W
32 Attock 33 52N 72 20E
34 Attopeu 14 56N 106 50E
60 Attu I. 52 55N 173 0E
52 Atura 2 5N 32 17E
70 Atwood 39 52N 101 3W
56 Auasberg 22 45S 17 22E
12 Aube, R. 48 34N 3 43E
12 Aube □ 48 15N 4 0E
69 Auburn, Ala. 32 57N 85 30W
72 Auburn, Calif. 38 50N 121 10W
69 Auburn, Me. 44 6N 70 14W
12 Aubusson 45 57N 2 11E
12 Auch 43 39N 0 36E
53 Auchi 7 6N 6 13E
47 Auckland 36 52S 174 46E
3 Auckland Is. 51 0S 166 0E
12 Aude, R. 43 13N 3 14E
12 Aude □ 44 13N 3 15E
62 Auden 50 17N 87 54W
43 Augathella 25 48S 146 35E
14 Augsburg 48 22N 10 54E
45 Augusta, Australia 34 22S 115 10E
18 Augusta, Italy 37 14N 15 12E
69 Augusta, U.S.A. 33 29N 81 59W
69 Augusta 44 20N 69 46W
55 Augusto Cardoso 12 44S 34 50E
15 Augustów 53 51N 23 0E
45 Augustus, Mt. 24 20S 116 50E
42 Augustus Downs 18 35S 139 55E
53 Auna 10 9N 4 42E
12 Aunis, Reg. 46 0N 0 50W
32 Aurangabad, Maharashtra 19 50N 75 23E
12 Aurillac 44 55N 2 26E
70 Aurora, Colo. 39 44N 104 55W
68 Aurora, Ill. 41 42N 88 20W
21 Aust-Agde □ 58 55N 7 40E
70 Austin, Minn. 43 37N 92 59W
72 Austin, Nev. 39 30N 117 1W
71 Austin, Tex. 30 20N 97 45W
40 Australia ■ 23 0S 135 0E
46 Australian Alps, Mts. 36 30S 148 8E

Australian Capital Terr. □ Barat Daja, Kep.

46 Australian Capital Terr. □ 35 15s 149 8E
3 Australian Dependency □ 73 0s 90 0E
14 Austria ■ 47 0N 14 0E
74 Autlán 19 40N 104 30w
12 Autun 46 58N 4 17E
44 Auvergne 15 39s 130 1E
12 Auvergne, Mts. 45 20N 2 45E
12 Auvergne, Reg. 45 30N 3 20E
12 Auxerre 47 48N 3 32E
12 Avallon 47 30N 3 53E
63 Avalon Pen. 47 0N 53 20w
79 Aveiro, Brazil 3 10s 55 5w
13 Aveiro, Port. 40 37N 8 38w
80 Avellaneda 34 50s 58 10w
18 Avellino 40 54N 14 46E
18 Aversa 40 58N 14 11E
78 Aves, Is. de 12 0N 67 40w
21 Avesta 60 9N 16 10E
12 Aveyron □ 44 22N 2 45E
80 Aviá Terai 26 45s 60 50w
8 Aviemore 57 11N 3 50w
12 Avignon 43 57N 4 50E
13 Ávila 40 39N 4 43w
13 Avilés 43 35N 5 57w
46 Avoca 37 5s 143 28E
9 Avoca, R. 52 48N 6 10w
64 Avola, Canada 51 45N 119 30w
45 Avon, R, Australia 31 40s 116 7E
7 Avon, R., Avon 51 30N 2 43w
7 Avon, R., Dorset 50 43N 1 46w
7 Avon, R., Gloucester 51 59N 2 10w
7 Avon □ 51 30N 2 40w
7 Avonmouth 51 30N 2 42w
12 Avranches 48 40N 1 20w
36 Awaji-Shima, I. 34 30N 134 50E
31 Awali 26 0N 50 30E
54 Awash 9 1N 40 10E
47 Awatere, R. 41 37s 174 10E
8 Awe, L. 56 15N 5 15w
53 Awgu 6 4N 7 24E
51 Awjilah 29 8N 21 7E
53 Awka 6 12N 7 5E
58 Axel Heiberg Ld. 80 0N 90 0w
53 Axim 4 41N 2 15w
7 Axminster 50 47N 3 1w
36 Ayabe 35 20N 135 20E
80 Ayacucho, Arg. 37 5s 58 20w
78 Ayacucho, Peru 13 0s 74 0w
24 Ayaguz 48 10N 80 0E
13 Ayamonte 37 12N 7 24w
25 Ayan 56 30N 138 16E
22 Aykin 62 20N 49 56E
65 Aylesbury, Canada 50 55N 105 53w
7 Aylesbury, U.K. 51 48N 0 49w
60 Aylmer, L. 64 0N 109 0w
42 Ayr, Australia 19 35s 147 25E
8 Ayr, U.K. 55 28N 4 37w
8 Ayr, R. 55 29N 4 28w
6 Ayre, Pt. of 54 27N 4 21w
19 Aytos 42 47N 27 16E
30 Ayvalik 39 20N 26 46E
28 Az Zahiriya 31 25N 34 58E
30 Az Zahrān 26 10N 50 7E
28 Az-Zarqā' 32 5N 36 4E
30 Az Zilfi 26 12N 44 52E
30 Az Zubayr 30 20N 47 50E
33 Azamgarh 26 35N 83 13E
30 Āzārbāijān □ 37 0N 44 30E
53 Azare 11 55N 10 10E
50 Azbine=Aïr 18 0N 8 0E
23 Azerbaijan S.S.R. □ 40 20N 48 0E
28 Azor 32 2N 34 48E
2 Azores, Is. 38 44N 29 0w
23 Azov 47 3N 39 25E
23 Azov Sea= Azovskoye More 46 0N 36 30E
23 Azovskoye More 46 0N 36 30E
24 Azovy 64 55N 64 35E
73 Aztec 36 55N 108 0w
75 Azua 18 25N 70 44w
13 Azuaga 38 16N 5 39w
75 Azuero, Pen. de 7 40N 80 30w
80 Azul 36 42s 59 43w

B

34 Ba Don 17 45N 106 26E
31 Baba, Koh-i-, Mts. 34 40N 67 20E
78 Babahoyo 1 40s 79 30w
45 Babakin 32 11s 117 52E
53 Babana 10 31N 5 9E
52 Babati 4 13s 35 45E
35 Babelthuap, I. 7 30N 134 36E
42 Babinda 17 27s 146 0E
35 Babo 2 30s 133 30E
31 Bābol 36 40N 52 50E
31 Babol Sar 36 45N 52 45E
53 Babura 12 51N 8 59E
35 Babuyan Chan. 18 58N 122 0E
39 Babuyan Is. 19 0N 122 0E
30 Babylon 32 40N 44 30E
79 Bacabal 5 20s 56 45w
35 Bacan, I. 1 0s 127 30E
24 Bachelina 57 45N 67 20E
60 Back, R. 67 15N 95 15w
35 Bacolod 10 50N 123 0E
14 Bad Ischl 47 44 13 38E
32 Badagara 11 35N 75 40E
53 Badagri 6 25N 2 55E
13 Badajoz 38 50N 6 59w
31 Badakhshan □ 36 30N 71 0E
13 Badalona 41 26N 2 15E
31 Badalzal 29 50N 65 35E
30 Badanah 30 58N 41 30E
34 Badas 4 20N 114 37E
14 Baden 48 1N 16 13E
14 Baden-Baden 48 45N 8 14E
14 Baden Württemberg □ 48 40N 9 0E
8 Badenoch, Reg. 57 0N 4 0w
14 Badgastein 47 7N 13 9E
31 Badghis □ 35 0N 63 0E
32 Badin 24 38N 68 54E
13 Baeza 37 57N 3 25w
53 Bafang 5 9N 10 11E
61 Baffin B. 72 0N 65 0w
61 Baffin I. 68 0N 77 0w
53 Bafia 4 40N 11 10E
53 Bafilo 9 22N 1 22E
53 Bafoussam 5 2N 10 25E
30 Bafra 41 34N 35 54w
31 Bāft 29 15N 56 38w
52 Bagamoyo 6 28s 38 55E
25 Bagdarin 54 26N 113 36E
30 Baghdād 32 20N 44 30E
31 Baghīn 30 12N 56 45E
31 Baghlan 36 12N 69 0E
31 Baghlan □ 36 0N 68 30E
63 Bagotville 48 22N 70 54w
37 Bagrash Kol, L. 42 0N 87 0E
35 Baguio 16 26N 120 34E
75 Bahamas ■ 24 0N 74 0w
32 Bahawalpur 29 37N 71 40E
32 Bahawalpur □ 29 5N 71 3E
52 Bahi 5 58s 35 21E
79 Bahia= Salvador 13 0s 38 30w
75 Bahia, Is. de la 16 45N 86 15w
79 Bahia □ 12 0N 42 0E
80 Bahia Blanca 38 35s 62 13w
78 Bahia de Caráquez 0 40s 80 27w
80 Bahia Laura 48 10s 66 30w
78 Bahia Negra 20 5s 58 5w
51 Bahr el Ghazâl □ 7 0N 28 0E
33 Bahraich 27 38N 81 50E
31 Bahrain ■ 26 0N 50 35E
15 Baia Mare 47 40N 23 37E
79 Baião 2 50s 49 15w
63 Baie Comeau 49 12N 68 10w
63 Baie T. Paul 47 28N 70 32w
30 Ba 'iji 35 0N 43 30E
9 Baile Atha Cliath=Dublin 53 20N 6 18w
69 Bainbridge 30 53N 84 34w
60 Baird Mts. 67 10N 160 15w
46 Bairnsdale 37 48s 147 36E
13 Baixo-Alentejo, Reg. 38 0N 8 40w
15 Baja 46 12N 18 59E
74 Baja California Norte □ 30 0N 116 0w
74 Baja California Sur □ 26 0N 112 0w
43 Bajimba, Mt. 29 17s 152 6E
53 Bajoga 10 57N 11 20E
42 Bajool 24 30s 150 35E
24 Bakchar 57 0N 82 5E
72 Baker, Calif. 36 16N 116 2w
70 Baker, Mont. 46 22N 104 12w
2 Baker I. 0 10N 176 35E
60 Baker L. 64 0N 97 0w
72 Baker, Mt. 48 50N 121 49w
60 Baker Lake 64 20N 96 10w
62 Baker's Dozen Is. 57 30N 79 0w
73 Bakersfield 35 25N 119 0w
30 Bakhtiari □ 32 0N 49 0E
23 Bakinskikh Komissarov 39 20N 49 15E
15 Bakony Forest= Bakony Hegyseg, Reg. 47 10N 17 30E
53 Bakori 11 34N 7 27E
23 Baku 40 25N 49 45E
28 Bal'a 32 20N 35 6E
6 Bala, L. 52 53N 3 38w
34 Balabac I. 8 0N 117 0E
34 Balabac Str. 7 53N 117 5E
32 Balaghat 21 49N 80 12E
32 Balaghat Ra. 18 50N 76 30E
13 Balaguer 41 50N 0 50E
43 Balaklava, Australia 34 7s 138 22E
23 Balaklava, U.S.S.R. 44 30N 33 30E
22 Balakovo 52 4N 47 55E
22 Balashov 51 30N 43 10E
33 Balasore 21 35N 87 3E
15 Balaton, L. 46 50N 17 40E
74 Balboa 9 0N 79 30w
9 Balbriggan 53 35N 6 10w
80 Balcarce 38 0s 58 10w
47 Balclutha 46 15s 169 45E
45 Bald, Hd. 35 6s 118 1E
73 Baldy Pk. 33 55N 109 35w
13 Baleares, Is. 39 30N 3 0E
13 Balearic Is.= Baleares, Is. 39 30N 3 0E
42 Balfe's Creek 20 12s 145 55E
57 Balfour 26 38s 28 35E
53 Bali 5 54N 10 0E
34 Bali, I. 8 20s 115 0E
30 Balikesir 39 35s 27 58E
34 Balikpapan 1 10s 116 55E
39 Balintang Chan. 19 50N 122 0E
33 Balipara 26 50N 92 45E
79 Baliza 16 0s 52 20w
4 Balkan Pen. 42 0N 22 0E
4 Balkans, Mts. 42 45N 25 0E
31 Balkh □ 36 30N 67 0E
24 Balkhash 46 50N 74 50E
24 Balkhash, Oz. 46 0N 74 50E
8 Ballachulish 56 40N 5 10w
45 Balladonia 32 27s 123 51E
46 Ballarat 37 33s 143 50E
45 Ballard, L. 29 20s 120 10E
8 Ballater 57 2N 3 2w
45 Ballidu 30 35s 116 45E
43 Ballina, Australia 28 50s 153 31E
9 Ballina, Mayo 54 7N 9 10w
9 Ballina, Tipperary 52 49N 8 27w
9 Ballinasloe 53 20N 8 12w
71 Ballinger 31 45N 99 58w
9 Ballinrobe 53 36N 9 13w
9 Ballycastle 55 12N 6 15w
9 Ballymena 54 53N 6 18w
9 Ballymena □ 54 53N 6 18w
9 Ballymoney 55 5N 6 30w
9 Ballymoney □ 55 5N 6 30w
9 Ballyshannon 54 30N 8 10w
80 Balmaceda 46 0s 71 50w
8 Balmoral 57 3N 3 13w
55 Balovale 13 30s 23 15E
33 Balrampur 27 30N 82 20E
46 Balranald 34 38s 143 33E
74 Balsas, R. 17 55N 102 10w
23 Balta 48 2N 29 45E
4 Baltic Sea 56 0N 20 0E
9 Baltimore, Eire 51 29N 9 22w
68 Baltimore, U.S.A. 39 18N 76 37w
32 Baluchistan, Reg. 27 30N 65 0E
31 Bam 29 7N 58 14E
53 Bama 11 33N 13 33E
50 Bamako 12 34N 7 55w
54 Bambari 5 40N 20 35E
42 Bambaroo 18 50s 146 10E
14 Bamberg 49 54N 10 53E
53 Bamenda 5 57N 10 11E
31 Bāmian □ 35 0N 67 0E
31 Bampur 27 15N 60 21E
34 Ban Kantang 7 25N 99 35E
31 Banadar Daryay Oman □ 25 30N 56 0E
54 Banalia 1 32N 25 5E
50 Banamba 13 29N 7 22w
42 Banana 24 32s 150 12E
79 Bananal, I. de 11 30s 50 30w
33 Banaras=Varanasi 25 22N 83 8E
51 Bânâs, Ras 23 57N 35 50E
15 Banat, Reg. 45 30N 21 30E
9 Banbridge 54 26N 6 16w
9 Banbridge □ 54 21N 6 16w
7 Banbury 52 4N 1 21w
8 Banchory 57 3N 2 30w
62 Bancroft 45 3N 77 51w
31 Band-e Charak 26 45N 54 20E
31 Band-e Nakhīlu 26 58N 53 30E
32 Banda 25 30N 80 26E
34 Banda Aceh 5 35N 95 20E
43 Banda Banda, Mt. 31 10s 152 28E
35 Banda Sea 6 0s 130 0E
33 Bandar= Machilipatnam 16 12N 81 12E
31 Bandar Abbas 27 15N 56 15E
34 Bandar Maharani 2 3N 102 34E
34 Bandar Seri Begawan 4 52N 115 0E
31 Bandar-e Bushetir 28 55N 50 55E
31 Bandar-e Lengeh 26 35N 54 58E
30 Bandar-e Ma'shur 30 35N 49 10E
30 Bandar-e-Pahlavi 37 30N 49 30E
31 Bandar-e Rig 29 30N 50 45E
31 Bandar-e Shāh 37 0N 54 10E
30 Bandar-e Shahpur 30 30N 49 5E
52 Bandawe 11 58s 34 5E
79 Bandeira, Pico da 20 26s 41 47w
80 Bandera 28 55s 62 20w
53 Bandiagara 14 12N 3 29w
30 Bandirma 40 20N 28 0E
9 Bandon 51 44N 8 45w
9 Bandon, R. 51 40N 8 35w
54 Bandundu 3 15s 17 22¼
35 Bandung 6 36s 107 48E
75 Banes 20 58N 75 43w
64 Banff, Canada 51 20N 115 40w
8 Banff, U.K. 57 40N 2 32w
64 Banff Nat. Park 51 38N 116 22w
34 Bang Saphan 11 14N 99 28E
55 Bangala Dam 21 7s 31 25E
32 Bangalore 12 59N 77 40E
54 Bangassou 4 55N 23 55E
51 Banghazı 32 11N 20 3E
35 Bangil 7 36s 112 50E
34 Bangka, I., Selatan 3 30s 105 30E
35 Bangka, I., Utara 1 50N 125 5E
35 Bangkalan 7 2s 112 46E
34 Bangkok=Krung Thep 13 45N 100 31E
33 Bangladesh ■ 24 0N 90 0E
6 Bangor, Gwynedd 53 13N 4 9w
9 Bangor, N. Down 54 40N 5 40w
69 Bangor, Me. 44 48N 68 42w
35 Bangued 17 40N 120 37E
54 Bangui 4 23N 18 35E
54 Bangweulu, L. 11 0s 30 0E
75 Bani 18 16N 70 22w
28 Bani Na'im 31 31N 35 10E
51 Banınah 32 0N 20 12E
18 Banja Luka 44 49N 17 26E
35 Banjar 7 24s 108 30E
34 Banjarmasin 3 20s 114 35E
35 Banjarnegara 7 24s 109 42E
50 Banjul 13 28N 16 40w
42 Banka Banka 18 50s 134 0E
33 Bankipore 25 35N 85 10E
58 Banks I. 73 30N 120 0w
47 Banks, Pen. 43 45s 173 15E
33 Bankura 23 11N 87 18E
9 Bann, R. 55 2N 6 35w
73 Banning 48 44N 91 56w
32 Bannu 33 0N 70 18s
8 Bannockburn 56 5N 3 55w
15 Banská Bystrica 48 46N 19 14E
32 Banswara 23 32N 74 24E
35 Banten 6 5s 106 8E
9 Bantry 51 40N 9 28w
9 Bantry, B. 51 35N 9 50w
35 Bantul 7 55s 110 19E
33 Bapatla 15 55N 80 30E
28 Baqa el Gharbiya 32 25N 35 2E
19 Bar 42 8N 19 8E
34 Barabai 2 32s 115 34E
24 Barabinsk 55 20N 78 20E
70 Baraboo 43 28N 89 46w
75 Baracoa 20 20N 74 30w
75 Barahona 18 13N 71 7w
33 Barail Ra. 25 15N 93 20E
36 Barak □ 38 20N 140 0E
33 Barakhola 25 0N 92 45E
32 Baramula 34 15N 74 20E
32 Baran 25 9N 76 40E
64 Baranof 57 0N 135 10w
64 Baranof I. 57 0N 135 10w
22 Baranovichi 53 10N 26 0E
35 Barat □, Java 7 0s 107 0E
34 Barat □, Kalimantan 0 0s 111 0E
34 Barat □, Sumatera 1 0s 101 0E
35 Barat Daja, Kep. 7 30s 128 0E

Barbacena Bencubbin

79 Barbacena 21 15s 43 56w
78 Barbacoas 1 45N 78 0w
75 Barbados ■ 13 0N 59 30w
57 Barberton, S. Africa 25 42s 31 2E
68 Barberton, U.S.A. 41 0N 81 40w
75 Barbuda, I. 17 30N 61 40w
42 Barcaldine 22 33s 145 13E
51 Barce=Al Marj 32 25N 20 40E
13 Barcelona, Sp. 41 21N 2 10E
78 Barcelona, Ven. 10 10N 64 40w
78 Barcelos 1 0s 63 0w
51 Bardaî 21 25N 17 0E
29 Bardera 2 20N 42 0s
51 Bardiyah 31 45N 25 0E
6 Bardsey I. 52 46N 4 47w
32 Bareilly 28 22N 79 27E
4 Barents Sea 73 0N 39 0E
12 Barfleur, Pte. de 49 42N 1 17w
29 Bargal 11 25N 51 0E
42 Bargara 24 50s 152 25E
25 Barguzin 53 37N 109 37E
18 Bari 41 6N 16 52E
32 Bari Doab, Reg. 30 20N 73 0E
32 Bari Sadri 24 25N 74 29E
78 Barinas 8 36N 70 15w
60 Baring, C. 70 0N 116 30w
51 Bârîs 24 42N 30 31E
33 Barisal 22 30N 90 20E
34 Barisan, Bukit, Mts. 3 30s 102 15E
34 Barito, R. 4 0s 114 50E
31 Barkah 24 30N 58 0E
37 Barkha 31 0N 81 45E
56 Barkly East 30 58s 27 33E
42 Barkly Tableland 19 50s 138 40E
56 Barkly West 28 38s 24 11E
12 Bar-le-Duc 48 47N 5 10E
45 Barlee, L. 29 15s 119 30E
18 Barletta 41 20N 16 17E
46 Barmedman 34 9s 147 21E
32 Barmer 25 45N 71 20E
43 Barmera 34 15s 140 28E
6 Barmouth 52 44N 4 3w
6 Barnard Castle 54 33N 1 55w
24 Barnaul 53 20N 83 40E
70 Barnesville 33 6N 84 9w
7 Barnet 51 37N 0 15w
11 Barneveld 52 7N 5 36E
6 Barnsley 53 33N 1 29w
7 Barnstaple 51 5N 4 3w
32 Baroda= Vadodara 22 20N 73 10E
33 Barpeta 26 20N 91 10E
51 Barqa 27 0N 20 0E
78 Barquisimeto 9 58N 69 13w
79 Barra 11 5s 43 10w
8 Barra, I. 57 0N 7 30w
79 Barra de Corda 5 30s 45 10w
79 Barra do Piraí 22 30s 43 50w
43 Barraba 30 21s 150 35E
78 Barranca 10 45s 77 50w
78 Barrancabermeja 7 0N 73 50w
78 Barrancas 8 55N 62 5w
13 Barrancos 38 10N 6 58w
80 Barranqueras 27 30s 59 0w
78 Barranquilla 11 0N 74 50w
79 Barras 1 45s 73 13w
62 Barraute 47 30N 76 50w
68 Barre 44 15N 73 30w
79 Barreiras 12 8s 45 0w
79 Barreirinhas 2 30s 42 50w
13 Barreiro 38 40N 9 6w
79 Barreiros 8 49s 35 12w
79 Barretos 20 30s 48 35w
64 Barrhead 54 10N 114 30w
62 Barrie 44 25N 79 45w
6 Barrow, U.K. 54 8N 3 15w
60 Barrow, U.S.A. 71 16N 156 50w
44 Barrow, I. 20 45s 115 20E
9 Barrow, R. 52 46N 7 0w
42 Barrow Creek 21 30s 133 55E
7 Barry 51 23N 3 19w
62 Barry's Bay 45 30N 77 40w
52 Barsaloi 1 20N 36 52E
32 Barsi 18 10N 75 50E
73 Barstow 34 58N 117 2w
78 Bartica 6 25N 58 40w
71 Bartlesville 36 50N 95 58w
45 Barton Siding 30 31s 132 39E
6 Barton-upon-Humber 53 41N 0 27w
69 Bartow 27 53N 81 49w
38 Baruun Urt 46 46N 113 15E
12 Bas Rhin □ 48 40N 7 30E
14 Basel 47 35N 7 35E
22 Bashkir A.S.S.R. □ 54 0N 57 0E
35 Basilan, I. 6 35N 122 0E
35 Basilan City= Lamitan 6 37N 122 0E
35 Basilan Str. 13 10s 122 0E
7 Basildon 51 34N 0 29E
18 Basilicata □ 40 30N 16 0E
32 Basim 20 4N 77 4E
7 Basingstoke 51 15N 1 5w
62 Baskatong Res. 46 46N 75 50w
14 Basle=Basel 47 35N 7 35E
54 Basoka 1 16N 23 40E
13 Basque □ 42 50N 2 45w
30 Basra=Al Basrah 30 30N 47 55E
8 Bass Rock 56 5N 2 40w
42 Bass, Str. 39 15s 146 30E
18 Bassano del Grappa 45 45N 11 45E
53 Bassari 9 19N 0 57E
55 Bassas da India, I. 22 0s 39 0E
75 Basse Terre 16 0N 61 40w
33 Bassein, Burma 16 45N 94 30E
75 Basseterre 17 17N 62 43w
70 Bassett 42 37N 99 30w
12 Bassigny, Reg. 48 0N 5 10E
31 Bastak 27 15N 54 25E
33 Basti 26 52N 82 55E
12 Bastia 42 40N 9 30E
11 Bastogne 50 1N 5 43E
57 Basutoland■= Lesotho ■ 29 40s 28 0E
28 Bat Yam 32 2N 34 44E
54 Bata 1 57N 9 50E
35 Bataan, Pen. 14 38N 120 30E
75 Barabanó, G. de 22 30N 82 30w
25 Batagoy 67 38N 134 38E
13 Batalha 39 40N 8 50w
25 Batamay 63 30N 129 15E
39 Batan Is. 20 25N 121 59E
35 Batang 6 55s 109 40E
35 Batangas 13 35N 121 10E
15 Bataszék 46 12N 18 44E
68 Batavia 43 0N 78 10w
44 Batchelor 13 4s 131 1E
71 Batesville 35 48N 91 40w
7 Bath, U.K. 51 22N 2 22w
68 Bath, N.Y. 42 20N 77 17w
8 Bathgate 55 54N 3 38w
50 Bathurst=Banjul 13 28N 16 40w
46 Bathurst, Australia 33 25s 149 31E
63 Bathurst, Canada 47 37N 65 43w
60 Bathurst, C. 70 30N 128 30w
44 Bathurst, I., Australia 11 30s 130 10E
58 Bathurst I., Canada 76 30N 130 10w
60 Bathurst Inlet 67 15N 108 30w
63 Bathurst Mines 47 30N 65 47w
31 Batinah, Reg. 24 0N 57 0E
50 Batna 35 34N 6 15E
71 Baton Rouge 30 30N 91 5w
54 Batouri 4 30N 14 25E
34 Battambang 13 7N 103 12E
32 Batticaloa 7 43N 81 45E
28 Battir 31 44N 35 8E
7 Battle 50 55N 0 30E
65 Battle, R. 52 45N 108 15w
68 Battle Creek 42 20N 85 10w
63 Battle Harbour 52 13N 55 42w
72 Battle Mountain 40 45N 117 0w
65 Battleford 52 45N 108 15w
34 Batu, Kep. 0 30s 98 25E
34 Batu Pahat= Bandar Penggaram 1 50N 102 56E
23 Batumi 41 30N 41 30E
34 Baturadja 4 11s 104 15E
79 Baturité 4 28s 38 45w
35 Baubau 5 25s 123 50E
53 Bauchi 10 22N 9 48E
53 Bauchi □ 10 25N 10 0E
42 Bauhinia Downs 24 35s 149 18E
79 Bauru 22 10s 49 0w
79 Baus 18 22s 52 47½
14 Bautzen 51 11N 14 25w
14 Bavaria□= Bayern □ 49 7N 11 30E
33 Bawdwin 23 5N 97 50E
34 Bawean, I. 5 46s 112 35E
53 Bawku 11 3N 0 19w
33 Bawlake 19 11N 97 21E
68 Bay City, Mich. 43 35N 83 51w
71 Bay City, Tex. 28 59N 95 55w
68 Bay Shore 40 44N 73 15w
47 Bay View 39 25w 176 50E
75 Bayamón 18 24N 66 10w
38 Bayan 47 20N 107 55E
37 Bayan Kara Shan, Mts. 34 0N 98 0E
38 Bayan-Uul 49 6N 112 12E
24 Bayanaul 50 45N 75 45E
38 Bayantsogt 47 58N 105 1E
14 Bayern □ 49 7N 11 30E
12 Bayeux 49 17N 0 42w
25 Baykal, Oz. 53 0N 108 0E
25 Baykal, L.= Baykal, Oz. 53 0N 108 0s
25 Baykir 61 50N 95 50E
24 Baykonur 47 48N 65 50E
56 Baynes Mts. 22 40s 12 50E
12 Bayonne 43 30N 1 28E
14 Bayreuth 49 56N 11 35E
30 Bayrūt 33 53N 35 31E
28 Bayt Aula 31 37N 35 2E
28 Bayt Jālā 31 43N 35 11E
28 Bayt Lahm 31 43N 35 12E
28 Bayt Sāhūr 31 42N 35 13E
28 Baytin 31 56N 35 14E
71 Baytown 29 42N 94 57w
13 Baza 37 30N 2 47w
57 Bazaruto, I. do 21 40s 35 28E
65 Beach 46 57N 104 0w
7 Beachy Hd. 50 44N 0 16E
45 Beacon, Australia 30 20s 117 55E
68 Beacon, U.S.A. 41 32N 73 58w
80 Beagle 55 0s 68 30w
47 Bealey 43 2s 171 36E
62 Beardmore 49 36N 87 59w
70 Beardstown 40 0N 90 25w
12 Béarn, Reg 43 28N 0 36w
70 Beatrice 40 20N 96 40w
12 Beauce, Reg. 48 10N 2 0E
63 Beauceville 46 13N 70 46w
43 Beaudesert 27 59s 153 0E
34 Beaufort, Malaysia 5 30N 115 40E
46 Beaufort, Australia 37 25s 143 25E
69 Beaufort, U.S.A. 34 45N 76 40w
58 Beaufort Sea 70 30N 146 0w
56 Beaufort West 32 18s 22 36E
62 Beauharnois 45 20N 73 20w
12 Beaujolais, Reg. 46 0N 4 25E
8 Beauly 57 29N 4 27w
6 Beaumaris 53 16N 4 7w
71 Beaumont 30 5N 94 8w
12 Beaune 47 2N 4 50E
65 Beausejour 50 5N 96 35E
12 Beauvais 49 25N 2 8E
65 Beauval 55 9N 107 35w
60 Beaver, U.S.A. 66 40N 147 50w
70 Beaver Dam 43 28N 88 50w
68 Beaver Falls 40 44N 80 20w
32 Beawar 26 3N 74 18E
7 Beccles 52 27N 1 33E
50 Béchar 31 38N 2 18E
56 Bechuanaland■= Botswana ■ 23 0s 24 0E
56 Bechuanaland, Reg.= Betsjoeanaland, Reg. 26 30s 22 30E
68 Beckley 37 50N 81 8w
62 Bedford, Canada 45 10N 73 0w
56 Bedford, S. Africa 32 40s 26 10E
7 Bedford, U.K. 52 8N 0 29w
68 Bedford, Ohio 41 23N 81 32w
68 Bedford, Ind. 38 50N 86 30w
7 Bedford □ 52 4N 0 28w
64 Bednesti 53 50N 123 10w
42 Bedourie 24 30s 139 30E
43 Beenleigh 27 43s 153 10E
28 Be'er Sheva 31 15N 34 48E
28 Be'erotayim 32 19N 34 59E
6 Beeston 52 55N 1 11w
71 Beeville 28 27N 97 44w
46 Bega 36 41s 149 51E
53 Begoro 6 23N 0 23w
30 Behbehan 30 30N 50 15E
31 Behshahr 36 45N 53 35E
11 Beilen 52 52N 6 27E
57 Beira 19 50s 34 52E
13 Beira-Alta, Reg. 41 0N 7 20w
13 Beira-Baixa, Reg. 40 0N 7 30w
13 Beira Litoral, Reg. 40 0N 8 30w
30 Beirut=Bayrut 33 53N 35 31E
28 Beit Hanun 31 32N 34 32E
28 Beit'Ur et Tahta 31 54N 35 5E
57 Beitbridge 22 12s 30 0E
28 Beituniya 31 54N 35 10E
13 Beja, Port. 38 2N 7 53w
50 Béja, Tunisia 36 10N 9 0E
50 Béjaîa 36 42N 5 2E
15 Békéscsaba 46 40N 21 10E
57 Bekily 24 13s 45 19E
53 Bekwai 6 25N 1 37w
33 Bela, India 25 50N 82 0E
32 Bela, Pak. 26 12N 66 20E
79 Bela Vista 17 0s 49 0w
34 Belawan 3 33N 98 32E
23 Belaya Tserkov 49 45N 30 10E
62 Belcher Is. 56 20N 79 20w
22 Belebey 54 72N 54 7E
79 Belém 1 20s 48 30w
80 Belén 27 40s 67 5w
73 Belen 34 40N 106 50w
29 Belet Uen 4 30N 45 5E
57 Belfast, S. Afr. 25 42s 30 2E
9 Belfast, U.K. 54 35N 5 56w
69 Belfast, U.S.A. 44 30N 69 0w
9 Belfast, L. 54 40N 5 50w
9 Belfast □ 54 35N 5 56w
12 Belfort 47 38N 6 50E
12 Belfort, Terr. de □ 47 38N 6 52E
32 Belgaum 15 55N 74 35E
11 Belgium ■ 51 30N 5 0E
9 Belgooly 51 44N 8 30w
23 Belgorod 50 35N 36 35E
23 Belgorod-Dnestrovskiy 46 11N 30 23E
19 Belgrade= Beograd 44 50N 20 37E
34 Belitung, Pulau, I. 3 10s 107 50E
74 Belize ■ 17 0N 88 30w
74 Belize City 17 25N 88 0w
80 Bell Ville 32 40s 62 40w
64 Bella Coola 52 25N 126 40w
80 Bella Vista 28 33s 59 0w
68 Bellaire 40 1N 80 46w
32 Bellary 15 10N 76 56E
43 Bellata 29 53s 149 46E
12 Belle I. 47 20N 3 10w
63 Belle I, Str. of 51 30N 56 30w
70 Belle Fourche 44 43N 103 52w
69 Belle Glade 26 43N 80 38w
68 Bellefontaine 40 20N 83 45E
62 Belleville, Canada 44 15N 77 37w
70 Belleville, U.S.A. 38 30N 90 0w
64 Bellevue 46 35N 84 10w
61 Bellin 60 0N 70 0w
43 Bellingen 30 25s 152 50E
72 Bellingham 48 45N 122 27w
2 Bellingshausen Sea 66 0s 80 0w
14 Bellinzona 46 11N 9 1E
68 Bellows Falls 43 10N 72 30w
18 Belluno 46 8N 12 6E
13 Bélmez 38 17N 5 17w
46 Belmont 33 4s 151 42E
79 Belmonte, Brazil 16 0s 39 0w
74 Belmopan 17 18N 88 30w
9 Belmullet 54 13N 9 58w
79 Belo Horizonte 19 55s 43 56w
25 Belogorsk 51 0N 128 20E
70 Beloit 42 35N 89 0w
22 Belomorsk 64 35N 34 30E
22 Beloretsk 53 58N 58 24E
57 Belo-sur-Tsiribihina 19 40s 44 30E
24 Belovo 54 30N 86 0E
22 Beloye, Oz. 60 10N 37 35E
22 Beloye More 66 0N 38 0E
22 Belozersk 60 0N 37 30E
23 Belsty 47 48N 28 0E
43 Beltana 30 48s 138 25E
79 Belterra 2 45s 55 0w
71 Belton 31 4N 97 30w
9 Belturbet 54 6N 7 28w
70 Belvidere 42 15N 88 55w
24 Belyy Os. 73 30N 71 0E
24 Belyy Yar 58 26N 84 30E
70 Bemidji 47 30N 94 50w
8 Ben Cruachan, Mt. 56 26N 5 8w
51 Ben Gardane 33 11N 11 11E
8 Ben Hope, Mt. 58 24N 4 36w
8 Ben Lawers, Mt. 56 33N 4 13w
43 Ben Lomond, Mt., Australia 30 1s 151 43E
8 Ben Lomond, Mt., U.K. 56 12N 4 39w
8 Ben Macdhui, Mt. 57 4N 3 40w
8 Ben More, Mt. 56 26N 6 2w
8 Ben More Assynt, Mt. 58 7N 4 51w
8 Ben Nevis, Mt. 56 48N 5 0w
8 Ben Wyvis, Mt. 57 40N 4 35w
53 Bena 11 20N 5 50E
54 Bena Dibele 4 4s 22 50E
46 Benalla 36 30s 146 0E
33 Benares=Varanasi 25 22N 83 8E
8 Benbecula, I. 57 26N 7 20w
43 Benbonyathe Hill 30 25s 139 11E
45 Bencubbin 30 48s 117 52E

Bend Bodmin

72 Bend ... 44 2N 121 15W
53 Bendel □ ... 6 0N 5 40 E
29 Bender Beila ... 9 30N 50 48 E
45 Bendering ... 32 23 S 118 18 E
23 Bendery ... 46 50N 29 50 E
46 Bendigo ... 36 40 S 144 15 E
28 Bene Beraq ... 32 5N 34 50 E
57 Benenitra ... 23 27 S 45 5 E
18 Benevento ... 41 7N 14 45 E
26 Bengal, B. of ... 15 0N 90 0 E
51 Benghazi= Banghazı ... 32 11N 20 3 E
34 Bengkalis ... 1 30N 102 10 E
34 Bengkulu ... 3 50 S 102 12 E
34 Bengkulu □ ... 3 50 S 102 10 E
65 Bengough ... 49 25N 105 10W
55 Benguela ... 12 37 S 13 25 E
54 Beni ... 32 11 S 148 43 E
51 Beni Mazar ... 28 32N 30 44 E
50 Beni Mellal ... 32 21N 6 21W
51 Benî Suêf ... 29 5N 31 6 E
13 Benidorm ... 38 33N 0 9W
53 Benin ■ ... 8 0N 2 0 E
53 Benin, B. of ... 5 0N 3 0 E
53 Benin City ... 6 20N 5 31 E
78 Benjamin Constant 4 40 S 70 15W
42 Benlidi ... 24 35 S 144 50 E
69 Bennettsville ... 34 38N 79 39W
68 Bennington ... 42 52N 73 12W
57 Benoni ... 26 11 S 28 18 E
73 Benson ... 31 59N 110 19W
35 Benteng ... 6 10 S 120 30 E
71 Benton, Ark. ... 34 30N 92 35W
70 Benton, Ill. ... 38 0N 88 55W
68 Benton Harbor ... 42 10N 86 28W
53 Benue, R. ... 7 47N 6 45 E
53 Benue □ ... 7 20N 8 20 E
19 Beograd ... 44 50N 20 37 E
36 Beppu ... 33 15N 131 30 E
28 Ber Dagan ... 32 1N 34 49 E
19 Berati ... 40 43N 19 59 E
51 Berber ... 18 0N 34 0 E
29 Berbera ... 10 30N 45 2 E
54 Berbérati ... 4 15N 15 40 E
23 Berdicher ... 49 57N 28 30 E
24 Berdsk ... 54 47N 83 2 E
23 Berdyansk ... 46 45N 36 50 E
29 Bereda ... 11 45N 51 0 E
53 Berekum ... 7 29N 2 34W
65 Berens River ... 52 25N 97 0W
57 Berevo ... 19 44 S 44 58 E
22 Berezniki ... 59 24N 56 46 E
24 Berezovo ... 64 0N 65 0 E
18 Bérgamo ... 45 42N 9 40 E
11 Bergen, Neth. ... 52 40N 4 42 E
21 Bergen, Norway ... 60 23N 5 27 E
11 Bergen-op-Zoom ... 51 30N 4 18 E
12 Bergerac ... 44 51N 0 30 E
11 Bergum ... 53 13N 5 59 E
33 Berhampore ... 24 2N 88 27 E
33 Berhampur ... 19 15N 84 54 E
60 Bering Sea ... 59 0N 175 0W
60 Bering Str. ... 66 0N 170 0W
11 Beringen ... 51 3N 5 14 E
25 Beringovskiy ... 63 3N 179 19 E
13 Berja ... 36 50N 2 56W
72 Berkeley ... 38 0N 122 20W
2 Berkner I. ... 79 30 S 50 0W
7 Berkshire □ ... 51 30N 1 20W
14 Berlin, Germany ... 52 32N 13 24W
68 Berlin, U.S.A. ... 44 29N 71 10W
80 Bermejo, R. ... 26 51 S 58 23W
2 Bermuda, I. ... 32 45N 65 0W
14 Bern ... 46 57N 7 28 E
73 Bernalillo ... 35 17N 106 37W
80 Bernardo de Irigoyen ... 26 15 S 53 40W
14 Bernburg ... 51 48N 11 44 E
45 Bernier, I. ... 24 50 S 113 12 E
14 Bernina, Piz ... 46 20N 9 54 E
14 Beroun ... 49 57N 14 5 E
46 Berowra ... 33 35 S 151 12 E
50 Berrechid ... 33 18N 7 36W
43 Berri ... 34 14 S 140 35 E
46 Berrigan ... 35 38 S 145 49 E
12 Berry, Reg. ... 47 0N 2 0 E
54 Bertoua ... 4 30N 13 45 E
68 Berwick ... 41 4N 76 17W
6 Berwick-upon-Tweed ... 55 47N 2 0W
6 Berwyn Mts. ... 52 54N 3 26W
57 Besalampy ... 16 43 S 44 29 E
12 Besançon ... 47 9N 6 0 E
23 Beskids, Mts.= Vychodné Beskydy ... 49 30N 22 0 E
69 Bessemer ... 46 27N 90 0W
12 Bessin, Reg. ... 49 21N 1 0W
28 Bet Ha 'Emeq ... 32 58N 35 8 E
28 Bet Ha Shitta ... 32 31N 35 27 E
28 Bet Ha'tmeq ... 32 58N 35 8 E
28 Bet Oren ... 32 43N 34 59 E
28 Bet Qeshet ... 32 41N 35 21 E
28 Be't She'an ... 32 30N 35 30 E
28 Bet Shemesh ... 31 45N 35 0 E
28 Bet Yosef ... 32 34N 35 33 E
57 Betafo ... 19 50 S 46 51 E
54 Bétaré-Oya ... 5 40N 14 5 E
57 Bethal ... 26 27 S 29 28 E
55 Bethanien ... 26 31 S 17 8 E
28 Bethany= Eizariya ... 31 47N 35 15 E
28 Bethlehem, Jordan= Bayt Lahm ... 31 43N 35 12 E
57 Bethlehem, S. Africa ... 28 14 S 28 18 E
68 Bethlehem, U.S.A. 40 39N 75 24W
56 Bethulie ... 30 30 S 25 29 E
57 Betioky ... 23 48 S 44 20 E
42 Betoota ... 25 40 S 140 42 E
57 Betroka ... 23 16 S 46 6 E
56 Betsjoeanaland, Reg. ... 26 30 S 22 30 E
33 Bettiah ... 26 48N 84 33 E
32 Betul ... 21 48N 77 59 E
36 Betung ... 2 0 S 103 10 E
46 Beulah, Australia ... 35 58 S 142 29 E
65 Beulah, Canada ... 50 16N 101 2W
45 Beverley, Australia ... 32 9 S 116 56 E
6 Beverley, U.K. ... 53 52N 0 26W
64 Beverly ... 53 36N 113 21W
73 Beverly Hills ... 34 4N 118 29W
11 Beverwijk ... 52 28N 4 38 E
50 Beyla ... 8 30N 8 38W
7 Bexhill ... 50 51N 0 29 E
24 Beyneu ... 45 10N 55 3 E
30 Beypazari ... 40 10N 31 48 E
30 Beyşehir Gólú, L. ... 37 40N 31 45 E
28 Bezet ... 33 4N 35 8 E
22 Bezhitsa ... 53 19N 34 17 E
12 Béziers ... 43 20N 3 12 E
32 Bhachau ... 23 10N 70 15W
33 Bhadgaon ... 27 42N 85 27 E
33 Bhadrakh ... 21 10N 86 30 E
33 Bhagalpur ... 25 10N 87 0 E
33 Bhamo ... 24 15N 97 15 E
32 Bhandara ... 21 5N 79 42 E
32 Bhanrer Ra. ... 23 40N 79 45 E
32 Bharatpur ... 27 15N 77 30 E
32 Bharuch ... 21 47N 73 0 E
32 Bhatinda ... 30 15N 74 57 E
33 Bhatpara ... 22 50N 88 25 E
32 Bhavnagar ... 21 45N 72 10 E
32 Bhilwara ... 25 25N 74 38 E
32 Bhima, R. ... 17 20N 76 30 E
33 Bhimavaram ... 16 30N 81 30 E
32 Bhind ... 26 30N 78 46 E
32 Bhiwandi ... 19 15N 73 0 E
32 Bhiwani ... 28 50N 76 9 E
32 Bhopal ... 23 20N 77 53 E
32 Bhubaneswar ... 20 15N 85 50 E
32 Bhusaval ... 21 1N 75 56 E
33 Bhutan ■ ... 27 25N 89 50 E
48 Biafra, B. of= Bonny, B. of ... 4 0N 8 0 E
15 Biała Podlaska ... 52 4N 23 6 E
15 Białystok ... 53 10N 23 10 E
12 Biarritz ... 43 29N 1 33W
14 Biberach ... 48 5N 9 49 E
53 Bibiani ... 6 30N 2 8W
63 Bic ... 48 20N 68 41W
53 Bida ... 9 3N 5 58 E
7 Bicester ... 51 53N 1 9W
32 Bidar ... 17 55N 77 35 E
69 Biddeford ... 43 30N 70 28 E
7 Bideford ... 51 1N 4 13W
55 Bié ... 12 22 S 16 55 E
55 Bié Plat. ... 12 0 S 16 0 E
72 Bieber ... 41 4N 121 6W
14 Biel ... 47 8N 7 14 E
15 Bielé Karpaty, Mts. ... 49 5N 18 0 E
14 Bielefeld ... 52 2N 8 31 E
18 Biella ... 45 33N 8 3 E
15 Bielsko-Biała ... 49 50N 19 8 E
34 Biên Hoa ... 10 57N 106 49 E
62 Big Beaver House ... 52 59N 89 50W
71 Big Bend Nat. Park ... 29 15N 103 15W
60 Big Delta ... 64 15N 145 0W
68 Big Rapids ... 43 42N 85 27W
65 Big River ... 53 50N 107 0W
60 Big Salmon ... 61 50N 136 0W
71 Big Spring ... 32 10N 101 25W
69 Big Stone Gap ... 36 52N 82 45W
62 Big Trout L. ... 53 40N 90 0W
65 Biggar, Canada ... 52 10N 108 0W
8 Biggar, U.K. ... 55 38N 3 31W
44 Bigge, I. ... 14 35 S 125 10 E
43 Biggenden ... 25 31 S 152 4 E
72 Bighorn Mts. ... 44 30N 107 20W
12 Bigorre, Reg. ... 43 5N 0 2 E
72 Bigtimber ... 45 33N 110 0W
18 Bihác ... 44 49N 15 57 E
33 Bihar ... 25 5N 85 40 E
33 Bihar □ ... 25 0N 86 0 E
52 Biharamulo ... 2 25 S 31 25 E
50 Bijagos, Arquipélago dos 11 15N 16 10W
32 Bijapur ... 26 2N 77 36 E
32 Bijnor ... 29 27N 78 11 E
32 Bikaner ... 28 2N 73 18 E
25 Bikin ... 46 50N 134 20 E
32 Bilara ... 26 14N 73 53 E
33 Bilaspur ... 22 2N 82 15 E
13 Bilbao ... 43 16N 2 56W
30 Bilecik ... 40 5N 30 5 E
25 Bilibino ... 68 3N 166 20 E
25 Bilir ... 65 40N 131 20 E
45 Billabalong ... 27 25 S 115 49 E
44 Billiluna ... 19 37 S 127 41 E
6 Billingham ... 54 36N 1 18W
72 Billings ... 45 43N 108 29W
51 Bilma ... 18 50N 13 30 E
42 Biloela ... 24 34 S 150 31 E
71 Biloxi ... 30 30N 89 0W
51 Biltine ... 14 40N 20 50 E
42 Bilyana ... 18 5 S 145 50 E
35 Bima ... 8 22 S 118 49 E
32 Bina-Etawah ... 24 13N 78 14 E
35 Binalbagan ... 10 12N 122 50 E
34 Binatang ... 2 10N 111 40 E
42 Binbee ... 20 19 S 147 56 E
11 Binche ... 50 26N 4 10 E
45 Bindi Bindi ... 30 37 S 116 22 E
57 Bindura ... 17 18 S 31 18 E
43 Bingara, N.S.W. ... 29 40 S 150 40 E
43 Bingara, Queens. ... 28 10 S 144 37 E
72 Bingham Canyon ... 40 31N 112 10W
68 Binghamton ... 42 9N 75 54W
34 Binh Son ... 15 20N 104 40 E
34 Binjai ... 3 50N 98 30 E
28 Binyamina ... 32 32N 34 56 E
50 Binzerte ... 37 15N 9 50 E
51 Bir Atrun ... 18 15N 26 40 E
28 Bir Nabala ... 31 52N 35 12 E
51 Bîr Shalatein ... 23 5N 35 25 E
28 Bir Zeit ... 31 59N 35 11 E
65 Birch Hills ... 53 10N 105 10W
46 Birchip ... 35 52 S 143 0 E
41 Bird, I. ... 22 20 S 155 20 E
42 Birdsville ... 25 51 S 139 20 E
44 Birdum ... 15 50 S 133 0 E
34 Bireuen ... 5 14N 96 39 E
31 Birjand ... 32 57N 59 10 E
6 Birkenhead ... 53 24N 3 1W
15 Bîrlad ... 46 15N 27 38 E
7 Birmingham, U.K. ... 52 30N 1 55W
69 Birmingham, U.S.A. ... 33 31N 86 50W
53 Birni Ngaouré ... 13 5N 2 51 E
53 Birni Nkonni ... 13 55N 5 15 E
53 Birnin Gwari ... 11 0N 6 45 E
53 Birnin-Kebbi ... 12 32N 4 12 E
53 Birnin Kuku ... 11 30N 9 29 E
25 Birobidzhan ... 48 50N 132 50 E
9 Birr ... 53 7N 7 55W
65 Birtle ... 50 30N 101 5W
73 Bisbee ... 31 30N 110 0W
12 Biscay, B. of ... 45 0N 2 0W
73 Bishop ... 37 20N 118 26W
6 Bishop Auckland ... 54 40N 1 40W
63 Bishop's Falls ... 49 2N 55 24W
7 Bishop's Stortford ... 51 52 0 11 E
50 Biskra ... 34 50N 5 52 E
70 Bismarck ... 46 49N 100 49W
41 Bismark Arch. ... 3 30 S 148 30 E
20 Bispfors ... 63 2N 16 40 E
50 Bissau ... 11 45N 15 45W
65 Bissett ... 46 14N 78 4W
15 Bistrita ... 47 9N 24 35 E
15 Bistrita, R. ... 46 30N 26 57 E
19 Bitola ... 41 5N 21 21 E
55 Bitterfontein ... 31 0 S 18 32 E
72 Bitterroot Ra. ... 46 0N 114 20W
53 Bittou ... 11 17N 0 18W
53 Biu ... 10 40N 12 3 E
36 Biwa-Ko, L. ... 35 15N 135 45 E
24 Biysk ... 52 40N 85 0 E
36 Bizen ... 34 44N 134 9 E
50 Bizerte=Binzerte ... 37 15N 9 50 E
18 Bjelovar ... 45 56N 16 49 E
14 Black Forest= Schwarzwald ... 48 0N 8 0 E
70 Black Hills, Mts ... 44 0N 103 50W
7 Black Mts. ... 51 52N 3 50W
4 Black Sea ... 43 30N 35 0 E
53 Black Volta, R. ... 8 41N 1 33W
42 Blackall ... 24 26 S 145 27 E
42 Blackbull ... 18 0 S 141 7 E
6 Blackburn ... 53 44N 2 30W
72 Blackfoot ... 43 13N 112 12W
46 Blackheath ... 33 39 S 150 17 E
6 Blackpool ... 53 48N 3 3W
63 Blacks Harbour ... 45 3N 66 49W
63 Blackville ... 47 5N 65 58W
42 Blackwater ... 23 35 S 149 0 E
9 Blackwater, R., Cork ... 51 51N 7 50W
9 Blackwater, R., Dungannon ... 54 31N 6 34W
9 Blackwater, R., Meath ... 53 39N 6 43W
71 Blackwell ... 36 55N 97 20W
6 Blaenau Ffestiniog ... 53 0N 3 57W
23 Blagodarnoye ... 45 7N 43 37 E
25 Blagoveshchensk ... 50 20N 127 30 E
65 Blaine Lake ... 52 51N 106 52W
42 Blair Atholl, Australia ... 22 42 S 147 31 E
8 Blair Atholl, U.K. ... 56 46N 3 50W
8 Blairgowrie ... 56 36N 3 20W
64 Blairmore ... 49 40N 114 25W
50 Blanc, C.= Ras Nouadhibou 37 15N 9 56 E
12 Blanc, Mt. ... 45 50N 6 52 E
80 Blanca, B. ... 39 10 S 61 30W
73 Blanca Pk. ... 37 35N 105 29W
56 Blanco ... 33 57 S 22 24 E
7 Blandford ... 50 52N 2 10W
73 Blanding ... 37 35N 109 30W
55 Blantyre ... 15 45 S 35 0 E
9 Blarney ... 51 57N 8 35W
21 Blåvands Huk ... 55 33N 8 5 E
6 Blaydon ... 54 56N 1 47W
46 Blayney ... 33 32 S 149 14 E
14 Bleiburg ... 46 35N 14 49 E
21 Blekinge □ ... 56 15N 15 15 E
47 Blenheim ... 41 38 S 174 5 E
7 Bletchley ... 51 59N 0 54W
50 Blida ... 36 30N 2 49 E
62 Blind River ... 46 15N 83 0W
35 Blitar ... 8 5 S 112 11 E
53 Blitta ... 8 23N 1 6 E
68 Block I. ... 41 13N 71 35W
56 Bloemfontein ... 29 6 S 26 14 E
56 Bloemhof ... 27 38 S 25 32 E
12 Blois ... 47 35N 1 20 E
70 Bloomington, Ill. ... 40 25N 89 0W
68 Bloomington, Ind. ... 39 10N 86 30W
68 Bloomsburg ... 41 0N 76 30W
68 Blue Island ... 41 40N 87 41W
42 Blue Mud, B. ... 13 30 S 136 0 E
68 Blue Mts. ... 45 15N 119 0W
51 Blue Nile, R.= Nîl el Azraq, R. ... 10 30N 35 0 E
58 Blue Ridge, Mts ... 36 30N 80 15W
68 Bluefield ... 37 18N 81 14W
75 Bluefields ... 12 0N 83 50W
42 Bluff, Australia ... 23 40 S 149 0 E
47 Bluff, N.Z. ... 46 36 S 168 21 E
45 Bluff Knoll, Mt. ... 34 23 S 118 20 E
68 Bluffton ... 40 43N 85 9W
80 Blumenau ... 27 0 S 49 0W
6 Blyth ... 55 8N 1 32W
73 Blythe ... 33 40N 114 33W
71 Blytheville ... 35 56N 89 55W
50 Bo ... 7 55N 11 50W
78 Boa Vista ... 2 48N 60 30W
75 Boaco ... 12 29N 85 35W
54 Boali ... 4 48N 18 7 E
13 Bobadilla ... 36 58N 5 10W
33 Bobbili ... 18 35N 83 30 E
62 Bobcaygeon ... 44 33N 78 35W
50 Bobo-Dioulasso ... 11 8N 4 13W
22 Bobruysk ... 53 10N 29 15 E
79 Bocaiuva ... 17 7 S 43 49W
75 Bocas del Toro ... 9 15N 82 20W
14 Bocholt ... 51 50N 6 35 E
14 Bochum ... 51 28N 7 12 E
54 Boda ... 4 19N 17 26 E
25 Bodaybo ... 57 50N 114 0 E
45 Boddington ... 32 50 S 116 30 E
20 Boden ... 65 50N 21 42 E
14 Bodensee, L. ... 47 35N 9 25 E
32 Bodhan ... 18 40N 77 55 E
53 Bodinga ... 12 58N 5 10 E
7 Bodmin ... 50 28N 4 44W

Bodmin Moor, Reg. Brusque

7 Bodmin Moor, Reg. 50 33N 4 36W
20 Bodø 67 17N 14 27 E
15 Bodrog, R. 48 15N 21 35 E
71 Bogalusa 30 50N 89 55W
46 Bogan Gate 33 6s 147 44 E
42 Bogantungan 23 41s 147 17 E
55 Bogenfels 27 25s 15 25 E
43 Boggabri 30 45s 150 0 E
7 Bognor Regis 50 47N 0 40W
35 Bogor 6 36s 106 48 E
25 Bogorodskoye 52 22N 140 30 E
78 Bogota 4 34N 74 0W
24 Bogotal 56 15N 89 50 E
33 Bogra 24 26N 89 22 E
25 Boguchany 58 40N 97 30 E
14 Bohemia □ 49 50N 14 0 E
14 Bohemian Forest= Böhmerwald 14 30N 12 40 E
14 Böhmerwald, Mts. 49 30N 12 40 E
35 Bohol, I. 9 58N 124 20 E
29 Bohotleh 8 20N 46 25 E
53 Boi 9 34N 9 27 E
63 Boiestown 46 27N 66 26W
72 Boise 43 43N 116 9W
65 Boissevain 49 15N 100 0W
35 Bojonegoro 7 9s 111 52 E
53 Boju 7 22N 7 55 E
50 Boké 10 56N 14 17W
53 Bokkos 9 19N 9 1 E
21 Bokna, Fd. 59 12N 5 30 E
54 Bokote 0 12s 21 8 E
34 Bokpyin 11 18N 98 42 E
31 Bol, Kuh-e 30 40N 52 45 E
50 Bolama 11 30N 15 30W
32 Bolan Pass 29 50N 67 20 E
33 Bolangir 20 42N 83 20 E
12 Bolbec 49 30N 0 30 E
53 Bolgatanga 10 44N 0 53W
78 Bolívar, Arg. 36 2s 60 53W
72 Bolívar, Col. 2 0N 77 0W
78 Bolivia ■ 17 6s 64 0W
76 Bolivian Plat. 19 0s 69 0W
21 Bollnäs 61 22N 16 28 E
18 Bologna 44 30N 11 20 E
22 Bologoye 57 55N 34 0 E
18 Bolsena, L. di 42 35N 11 55 E
25 Bolshevik, Os. 78 30N 102 0 E
23 Bolshoi Kavkaz 42 50N 44 0 E
24 Bolshoy Atlym 62 25N 66 50 E
25 Bolshoy Shantar, Os. 55 0N 137 42 E
6 Bolton 53 35N 2 26W
18 Bolzano 46 30N 11 20 E
79 Bom Despacho 19 46s 45 15W
79 Bom Jesus da Lapa 13 10s 43 30W
54 Boma 5 50s 13 4 E
46 Bomaderry 34 52s 150 37 E
53 Bomadi 5 9N 6 0 E
46 Bombala 36 56s 149 15 E
32 Bombay 18 55N 72 50 E
54 Bomboma 2 25N 18 55 E
37 Bomda 29 59N 96 25 E
51 Bon, C. 37 1N 11 2 E
75 Bonaire, I. 12 10N 68 15W
44 Bonaparte Arch. 15 0s 124 30 E
63 Bonaventure 48 5N 63 32W
63 Bonavista 48 40N 53 5W
63 Bonavista B. 48 58N 53 25W
50 Bondoukoro 9 51N 4 25W
53 Bondoukou 8 2N 2 47W
35 Bondowoso 7 56s 113 49 E
35 Bone, Teluk, G. 4 10s 120 50 E
8 Bo'ness 56 0N 3 38W
51 Bongor 10 35N 15 20 E
71 Bonham 33 30N 96 10W
12 Bonifacio 41 24N 9 10 E
18 Bonifacio, Bouches de 41 23N 9 10 E
14 Bonn 50 43N 7 6 E
72 Bonners Ferry 48 38N 116 21W
45 Bonnie Rock 30 29s 118 22 E
53 Bonny, R. 4 20N 7 10 E
48 Bonny, B. of 4 0N 8 0 E
65 Bonnyville 54 20N 110 45W
34 Bontang 0 10N 117 30 E
35 Bonthain 5 34s 119 56 E
11 Boom 51 6N 4 20 E
43 Boonah 28 0s 152 35 E
70 Boone 42 5N 93 46W
68 Boonville, Ind 38 3N 87 13W
70 Boonville, Mo. 38 57N 92 45W
68 Boonville, N.Y. 43 31N 75 20W
61 Boothia, G. of 70 0N 90 0W
60 Boothia Pen. 70 30N 95 0W
6 Bootle 53 28N 3 1W
54 Booué 0 5s 11 55 E
43 Bopeechee 29 35s 137 30 E
21 Borås 57 42N 13 1 E
78 Borba 4 12s 59 34W
12 Bordeaux 44 50N 0 36W
45 Borden, Australia 34 3s 118 12 E
63 Borden, Canada 46 18N 63 47W
8 Borders □ 55 30N 3 0W
46 Bordertown 36 14s 140 58 E
11 Borger, Neth. 52 54N 7 33 E
71 Borger, U.S.A. 35 40N 101 20W
21 Borgholm 56 54N 16 48 E
23 Borisoglebsk 51 27N 42 5 E
22 Borisov 54 17N 28 28 E
78 Borja 4 20s 77 40W
51 Borkou 18 15N 18 50 E
21 Borlänge 60 28N 14 33 E
34 Borneo, I. 1 0N 115 0 E
21 Bornholm, I. 55 8N 14 55 E
53 Borno □ 12 0N 12 0 E
53 Bornu Yassu 12 14N 12 25 E
25 Borogontsy 62 42N 131 8 E
53 Boromo 11 45N 2 58W
22 Borovichi 58 25N 35 55 E
42 Borroloola 16 4s 136 17 E
22 Borsod-Abaüj-Zemplên □ 48 20N 21 0 E
30 Borujerd 33 55N 48 50 E
25 Borzya 50 24N 116 31 E
18 Bosa 40 17N 8 32 E
18 Bosanska Gradiška 45 9N 17 15 E
29 Bosaso 11 13N 49 8 E
7 Boscasble 50 42N 4 42W
56 Boshof 28 31s 25 13 E
19 Bosna, R. 45 4N 18 29 E
18 Bosna i Hercegovina □ 44 0N 18 0 E
30 Bosporus, Str.= Karadeniz Boğazi 41 10N 29 5 E
54 Bossangoa 6 35N 17 30 E
71 Bossier City 32 28N 93 38W
53 Bosso 13 30N 13 15 E
6 Boston, U.K. 52 59N 0 2W
68 Boston, U.S.A. 42 20N 71 0W
46 Botany B. 34 2s 151 6 E
56 Bothaville 27 23s 26 34 E
20 Bothnia, G. 63 0N 21 0 E
42 Bothwell 42 37N 81 54W
56 Botletle, R. 20 10s 24 10 E
15 Botoşani 47 42N 26 41 E
56 Botswana ■ 23 0s 24 0 E
79 Botucatu 22 55s 48 30W
63 Botwood 49 6N 55 23W
50 Bou Saâda 35 11N 4 9 E
50 Bouaké 7 40N 5 2W
54 Bouar 6 0N 15 40 E
50 Bouârfa 32 32N 1 58 E
12 Bouches-du-Rhône 43 37N 5 2 E
44 Bougainville, C. 13 57s 126 4 E
50 Bougouni 11 30N 7 20W
53 Boukombé 10 11N 1 6 E
70 Boulder 40 3N 105 10W
73 Boulder City 36 0N 114 58W
42 Boulia 22 52s 139 51 E
12 Boulogne-sur-Mer 50 42N 1 36 E
53 Boulsa 12 39N 0 34W
53 Bouna 9 10N 3 0N
72 Bountiful 40 57N 111 58W
12 Bourbonnais, Reg. 46 28N 3 0 E
53 Bourem 17 0N 0 24W
12 Bourg en Bresse 46 13N 5 12 E
12 Bourges 47 5N 2 22 E
12 Bourgogne, Reg. 47 0N 4 30 E
43 Bourke 30 8s 145 55 E
62 Bourlamaque 48 5N 77 56W
7 Bournemouth 50 43N 1 53W
3 Bouvet, I. 55 0s 3 30 E
64 Bow Island 49 50N 111 23W
45 Bowelling 33 25s 116 30 E
42 Bowen 20 0s 148 16 E
73 Bowie 32 15N 109 30W
6 Bowland Forest 54 0N 2 30W
68 Bowling Green, Ky. 37 0N 86 25W
68 Bowling Green, Ohio 41 22N 83 40W
42 Bowling Green, C. 19 19s 147 25 E
70 Bowman 46 12N 103 21W
62 Bowmanville 43 55N 78 40W
8 Bowmore 55 45N 6 18W
64 Bowness 50 55N 114 25W
46 Bowser 36 19s 146 23 E
65 Bowsman 52 15N 101 12W
11 Boxtel 51 36N 5 9 E
9 Boyle 53 58N 8 19W
9 Boyne, R. 53 40N 6 34W
48 Boyoma, Chutes 0 12N 25 25 E
45 Boyup Brook 33 47s 116 40 E
72 Bozeman 45 40N 111 0W
54 Bozoum 6 25N 16 35 E
11 Brabant □ 49 15N 5 20 E
18 Brac, I. 43 20N 16 40 E
62 Bracebridge 45 5N 79 20W
20 Bräcke 62 42N 15 32 E
15 Brad 46 10N 22 50 E
69 Bradenton 27 25N 82 35W
6 Bradford, U.K. 53 47N 1 45W
68 Bradford, U.S.A. 41 58N 78 41W
63 Bradore Bay 51 27N 57 18W
71 Brady 31 8N 99 25W
8 Braemar 57 2N 3 20W
13 Braga 41 35N 8 32W
79 Bragança, Brazil 1 0s 47 2W
13 Bragança, Port. 41 48N 6 50W
33 Brahmanbaria 23 50N 91 15 E
33 Brahmani, R. 21 0N 85 15 E
33 Brahmaputra, R. 26 30N 93 30 E
6 Braich-y-Pwll, Pt. 52 47N 4 46W
15 Brăila 45 19N 27 59 E
70 Brainerd 46 20N 94 10W
7 Braintree 51 53N 0 34 E
56 Brak, R. 29 35s 22 55 E
64 Bralorne 50 50N 123 15W
62 Brampton 43 42N 79 46W
78 Branco, R. 1 30N 61 15W
14 Brandenburg 52 24N 12 33 E
65 Brandon 49 50N 100 0W
56 Brandvlei 30 25s 20 30 E
15 Braniewo 54 25N 19 50 E
15 Brańsk 52 45N 22 51 E
62 Brantford 43 15N 80 15W
46 Branxholme 37 52s 141 49 E
79 Brasília 15 55s 47 40W
79 Brasilia Legal 3 45s 55 40W
15 Braşov 45 7N 25 39 E
11 Brasschaat 51 19N 4 27 E
14 Bratislava 48 10N 17 7 E
25 Bratsk 56 10N 101 3 E
68 Brattleboro 42 53N 72 37W
14 Braunschweig 52 17N 10 28 E
7 Braunton 51 6N 4 9W
29 Brava 1 20N 44 8 E
73 Brawley 32 58N 115 30W
9 Bray 53 12N 6 6W
12 Bray, Reg. 49 40N 1 40 E
77 Brazil ■ 10 0s 50 0W
68 Brazil 39 30N 87 8W
76 Brazilian Highlands, Mts. 18 0s 46 30W
71 Brazol, R. 30 30N 96 20W
54 Brazzaville 4 9s 15 12 E
42 Breadalbane 23 48s 139 33 E
8 Breadalbane, Reg. 56 30N 4 15W
47 Bream, B. 35 56s 174 35 E
47 Bream Head 35 51s 174 36 E
35 Brebes 6 52s 109 3 E
8 Brechin 56 44N 2 40W
71 Breckenridge 32 48N 98 55W
7 Breckland, Reg. 52 30N 0 40 E
7 Brecon 51 57N 3 23W
7 Brecon Beacons, Mts. 51 53N 3 27W
11 Breda 51 35N 4 45 E
56 Bredasdorp 34 33s 20 2 E
46 Bredbo 35 38s 149 10 E
14 Bregenz 47 30N 9 45 E
20 Breidafjördur 65 20N 23 0W
79 Brejo 3 41s 42 50W
14 Bremen 53 4N 8 47 E
14 Bremerhaven 53 34N 8 35 E
72 Bremerton 47 30N 122 48W
71 Brenham 30 5N 96 27W
14 Brenner P. 47 0N 11 30 E
62 Brent, Canada 46 0N 78 30W
7 Brent, U.K. 51 33N 0 18W
7 Brentwood 51 37N 0 19W
18 Bréscia 45 33N 10 13 E
14 Breslau=Wrocław 51 5N 17 5 E
18 Bressanone 46 43N 11 40 E
8 Bressay, I. 60 10N 1 5W
12 Bresse, Reg. 46 20N 5 10 E
12 Brest, Fr. 48 24N 4 31W
22 Brest, U.S.S.R. 52 10N 23 40 E
12 Bretagne, Reg. 48 0N 3 0W
15 Bretçu 46 7N 26 18 E
47 Brett, C. 35 10s 174 20 E
79 Breves 1 38s 50 25W
43 Brewarrina 30 0s 146 51 E
69 Brewer 44 43N 68 50W
69 Brewton 31 9N 87 2W
57 Breyten 26 16s 30 0 E
54 Bria 6 30N 21 58 E
12 Briançon 44 54N 6 39 E
57 Brickaville 18 49s 49 4 E
7 Bridgend 51 30N 3 35W
68 Bridgeport 41 12N 73 12W
68 Bridgeton 39 29N 75 10W
45 Bridgetown, Australia 33 58s 116 7 E
75 Bridgetown, Barbados 13 0N 59 30W
63 Bridgetown, Can. 44 55N 65 12W
46 Bridgewater, Australia 36 36s 143 59 E
63 Bridgewater, Can. 44 25N 64 31W
7 Bridgnorth 52 33N 2 25W
7 Bridgwater 51 7N 3 0W
6 Bridlington 54 4N 0 10W
7 Bridport 50 43N 2 45W
12 Brie, Reg. 48 35N 3 10 E
14 Brig 46 18N 7 59 E
6 Brigg 53 33N 0 30W
72 Brigham City 41 30N 112 1W
43 Brighton, Australia 35 1s 138 30 E
62 Brighton, Canada 44 3N 77 44W
7 Brighton, U.K. 50 50N 0 9W
19 Bríndisi 40 39N 17 55 E
43 Brisbane 27 25s 152 54 E
7 Bristol, U.K. 51 26N 2 35W
68 Bristol, Conn. 41 44N 72 37W
60 Bristol B. 58 0N 159 0W
7 Bristol Chan. 51 18N 3 30W
71 Bristow 35 5N 96 28W
2 British Antarctic Terr. 66 0s 45 0W
64 British Columbia □ 55 0N 125 15W
74 British Honduras■= Belize ■ 17 0N 88 30W
10 British Is. 55 0N 4 0W
57 Brits 25 37s 27 48 E
56 Britstown 30 37s 23 30 E
62 Britt 45 46N 80 35W
12 Brittany, Reg.= Bretagne, Reg. 48 0N 3 0W
70 Britton 45 50N 97 47W
42 Brixton 23 32s 144 52 E
14 Brno 49 10N 16 35 E
45 Broad Arrow 30 23s 121 15 E
8 Broad Law, Mt. 55 30N 3 22W
46 Broadford 37 14s 145 4 E
6 Broads, The 52 30N 1 15 E
65 Brock 51 27N 108 42W
14 Brocken, Mt. 51 48N 10 40 E
68 Brockton 42 8N 71 2W
62 Brockville 44 37N 75 38W
19 Brod 41 35N 21 17 E
61 Brodeur Pen. 72 0N 88 0W
8 Brodick 55 34N 5 9W
70 Broken Bow 41 25N 99 35W
46 Broken Hill 31 58s 141 29 E
7 Bromley 51 20N 0 5 E
21 Brönderslev 57 17N 9 55 E
53 Brong-Ahafo □ 7 50N 2 0W
57 Bronkhorstspruit 25 46s 28 45 E
42 Bronte Pk. 42 8s 146 30 E
70 Brookfield 39 50N 92 50W
71 Brookhaven 31 40N 90 25W
70 Brookings 44 19N 96 48W
60 Brooks Ra. 68 40N 147 0W
45 Brookton 32 22N 116 57 E
68 Brookville 41 10N 79 6W
8 Broom, L. 57 55N 5 15W
44 Broome 18 0s 122 15W
45 Broomehill 33 40s 117 36 E
8 Brora 58 0N 3 50W
9 Brosna, R. 53 8N 8 0W
61 Broughton I. 67 35N 63 50W
8 Broughty Ferry 56 29N 2 50W
7 Brown Willy, Mt. 50 35N 4 34W
71 Brownfield 33 10N 102 15W
72 Browning 48 35N 113 10W
65 Brownlee 50 43N 105 59N
71 Brownsville 25 54N 97 30W
71 Brownwood 31 45N 99 0W
44 Bruce, Mt. 22 31s 118 6 E
62 Bruce Mines 46 20N 83 45W
45 Bruce Rock 31 51s 118 2 E
14 Bruck 47 24N 15 16 E
7 Brue, R. 51 10N 2 50W
11 Brugge 51 13N 3 13 E
64 Brule 53 15N 117 38W
79 Brumado 14 13s 41 40W
34 Brunei ■ 4 52N 115 0 E
42 Brunette Downs 18 38s 135 57 E
14 Brünn=Brno 49 10N 16 35 E
47 Brunner 42 27s 171 20 E
65 Bruno 52 20N 105 30W
11 Brunssum 50 57N 5 59 E
69 Brunswick, Ga. 31 10N 81 30W
69 Brunswick, Me. 43 53N 69 50W
80 Brunswick, Pen. 53 30s 71 30W
45 Brunswick Junction 33 15s 115 50 E
80 Brusque 27 5s 49 0W

11 Brussel 50 51N 4 21E
46 Bruthen 37 43S 147 48E
11 Bruxelles= Brussel 50 51N 4 21E
68 Bryan, Ohio 41 30N 84 30W
71 Bryan, Tex. 30 40N 96 27W
22 Bryansk 53 13N 34 25E
21 Bryne 58 45N 5 36E
15 Brzeg 50 52N 17 30E
30 Bucak 37 28N 30 36E
78 Bucaramanga 7 0N 73 0W
8 Buchan, Reg. 57 32N 2 8W
8 Buchan Ness, Pt. 57 29N 1 48W
65 Buchanan, Canada 51 40N 102 45W
50 Buchanan, Liberia 5 57N 10 2W
63 Buchans 49 0N 57 2W
15 Bucharest = Bucureşti 44 27N 26 10E
73 Buckeye 33 28N 112 40W
68 Buckhannon 39 2N 80 10W
8 Buckie 57 40N 2 58W
7 Buckingham, U.K. 52 0N 0 59W
62 Buckingham, U.S.A. 45 37N 75 24W
7 Buckinghamshire □ 51 50N 0 55W
63 Buctouche 46 30N 64 45W
15 Bucureşti 44 27N 26 10E
68 Bucyrus 40 48N 83 0W
33 Budalin 22 20N 95 10E
15 Budapest 47 29N 19 5E
32 Budaun 28 5N 79 10E
7 Bude 50 49N 4 33W
53 Buea 4 10N 9 9E
78 Buenaventura 29 15S 69 40W
80 Buenos Aires 34 30S 58 20W
80 Buenos Aires, L. 46 35S 72 30W
65 Buffalo, Canada 50 49N 110 42W
68 Buffalo, U.S.A. 42 55N 78 50W
65 Buffalo Narrows 55 52N 108 28W
15 Bug, R. 51 20N 23 40E
78 Buga 4 0N 77 0W
52 Bugondo 1 33N 33 10E
22 Bugulma 54 38N 52 40E
53 Buguma 4 42N 6 55E
38 Bugun Shara, Mts. 48 30N 102 0E
22 Buturuslan 53 39N 52 26E
22 Bui 58 23N 41 27E
7 Builth Wells 52 10N 3 26W
52 Bujumbura 3 16S 29 18E
25 Bukachacha 52 55N 116 50E
52 Bukavu 2 20S 28 52E
52 Bukene 4 15S 32 48E
24 Bukhara 39 50N 64 10E
34 Bukit Mertajam 5 22N 100 28E
34 Bukittinggi 0 20S 100 20E
52 Bukoba 1 20S 31 49E
52 Bukombe 3 31S 32 3E
53 Bukuru 9 42N 8 48E
37 Bulak 45 2N 82 5E
57 Bulawayo 20 7S 28 32E
19 Bulgaria ■ 42 35N 25 30E
29 Bulhar 10 25N 44 30E
45 Bullabulling 31 0S 120 55E
44 Bullara 22 30S 114 2E
45 Bullaring 32 28S 117 40E
42 Bullock Creek 17 40S 144 30E
47 Bulls 40 10S 175 24E
29 Bulo Burti 3 50N 45 33E
32 Bulsar 20 40N 72 58E
56 Bultfontein 28 18S 26 10E
25 Bulun 70 37N 127 30E
32 Bulundshahr 28 30N 77 45E
54 Bumba 2 13N 22 30E
53 Bumbum 14 0N 8 10E
33 Bumhpa Bum, Mt. 26 40N 97 20E
45 Bunbury 33 20S 115 35E
9 Buncrana 55 8N 7 28W
43 Bundaberg 24 54S 152 22E
32 Bundi 25 30N 75 35E
43 Bundooma 24 54S 134 16E
52 Bunia 1 35N 30 20E
53 Bununu Dass 10 6N 9 25E
53 Bununu Kasa 9 51N 9 32E
53 Bunza 12 8N 4 0E
52 Bura 1 6S 39 57E
52 Bura Hills 3 20S 38 20E
33 Burdwan 23 16N 87 54E
6 Bure, R. 52 38N 1 38E
19 Burgas 42 33N 27 29E
14 Burgenland □ 47 20N 16 20E
63 Burgeo 47 36N 57 34W
56 Burgersdorp 31 0S 26 20E
13 Burgos 42 21N 3 41W
21 Burgsvik 57 3N 18 19E
35 Burias, I. 13 5N 122 55E
75 Burica, Pta 8 3N 82 51W
28 Burin 32 11N 35 15E
34 Buriram 15 0N 103 0E
42 Burketown 17 45S 139 33E
62 Burks Falls 45 37N 79 10W
72 Burley 42 37N 113 55W
62 Burlington, Canada 43 25N 79 45W
70 Burlington, Colo. 39 21N 102 18W
70 Burlington, Iowa 40 50N 91 5W
70 Burlington, Kans. 38 15N 95 47W
69 Burlington, N.C. 36 7N 79 27W
68 Burlington, N.J. 40 5N 74 50W
68 Burlington, Vt. 44 27N 73 14W
72 Burlington, Wash. 48 29N 122 19W
24 Burlyu-Tyube 46 30N 79 10E
33 Burma ■ 21 0N 96 30E
45 Burngup 33 0S 118 35E
42 Burnie 41 4S 145 56E
6 Burnley 53 47N 2 15W
72 Burns 43 40N 119 4W
64 Burns Lake 54 20N 125 45W
65 Burntwood, L. 55 35N 99 40W
28 Burqa 32 18N 35 11E
43 Burra 33 40S 138 55E
46 Burrendong Res. 32 45S 149 10E
80 Burruyacú 26 30S 64 45W
7 Burry Port 51 41N 4 17W
30 Bursa 40 15N 29 5E
6 Burton-on-Trent 52 48N 1 39W
35 Buru, I. 3 30S 126 3E
52 Burundi ■ 3 15S 30 0E
34 Burung 0 21N 108 25E
53 Burutu 5 20N 5 29E
6 Bury 53 36N 2 19W
7 Bury St. Edmunds 52 15N 0 42E
25 Buryat A.S.S.R. □ 53 0N 110 0E
52 Busembatia 0 45N 33 32E
52 Bushenyi 0 32S 30 11E
52 Busia 0 25N 34 6E
21 Buskerud □ 60 20N 9 0E
45 Busselton 33 42S 115 15E
11 Bussum 52 16N 5 10E
18 Busto Arsizio 45 38N 8 50E
54 Busu-Djanoa 1 50N 21 5E
35 Busuanga, I. 12 10N 120 0E
54 Buta 2 50N 24 53E
52 Butare 2 31S 29 52E
8 Bute, I. 55 48N 5 2W
54 Butembo 0 9N 29 18E
52 Butere 0 14N 34 51E
52 Butiaba 1 50N 31 20E
68 Butler 40 52N 79 52W
8 Butt of Lewis, Pt. 58 30N 6 20W
72 Butte, Mont. 46 0N 112 31W
70 Butte, Neb. 42 56N 98 54W
34 Butterworth 5 24N 100 23E
35 Butuan 8 52N 125 36E
35 Butung, I. 5 0S 122 45E
23 Buturlinovka 50 50N 40 35E
56 Buxton, S. Afr. 27 38S 24 42E
6 Buxton, U.K. 53 16N 1 54W
25 Buyaga 59 50N 127 0E
38 Buyr Nuur, L. 47 50N 117 35E
15 Buzău 45 10N 26 50E
15 Buzău, R. 45 10N 27 20E
36 Buzen 33 35N 131 5E
22 Buzuluk 52 48N 52 12E
68 Buzzards Bay 41 45N 70 38W
15 Bydgoszcz 53 10N 18 0E
22 Byelorussian S.S.R. □ 53 30N 27 0E
73 Bylas 33 11N 110 9W
61 Bylot I. 73 0N 78 0W
2 Byrd Ld. 79 30S 125 0W
43 Byrock 30 40S 146 27E
43 Byron Bay 28 30S 153 30E
20 Byske 64 59N 21 17E
25 Byrranga, Gory 75 0N 100 0E
15 Bytom 50 25N 19 0E
52 Byumba 1 35S 30 4E

C

63 Cabana 8 25S 78 5W
35 Cabanatuan 15 30N 121 5E
79 Cabedelo 7 0S 34 50W
78 Cabimas 10 30N 71 25W
54 Cabinda 5 40S 12 11E
72 Cabinet Mts. 48 8N 115 46W
80 Cabo Blanco 47 56S 65 47W
79 Cabo Frio 22 51S 42 3W
62 Cabonga Res. 47 35N 76 40W
43 Caboolture 27 5S 152 47E
55 Cabora Bassa Dam 15 30S 32 40E
74 Caborca 30 40N 112 10W
63 Cabot Str. 47 15N 59 40W
13 Cabrera, I. 39 6N 2 59E
65 Cabri 50 35N 108 25W
13 Cabriel, R. 39 14N 1 3W
78 Cabruta 7 50N 66 10W
19 Čačak 43 54N 20 20E
13 Cáceres 39 26N 6 23W
62 Cache Bay 46 26N 80 0W
62 Cache Lake 49 55N 74 35W
80 Cachinal 24 59S 69 35W
79 Cachoeira 12 30S 39 0W
79 Cachoeiro de Itapemirim 20 51S 41 7W
80 Cachoeira do Sul 30 3S 52 53W
55 Caconda 13 48S 15 8E
62 Cadillac, Canada 49 45N 108 0W
68 Cadillac, U.S.A. 44 16N 85 25W
35 Cadiz, Philippines 11 30N 123 15E
13 Cádiz, Sp. 36 30N 6 20W
13 Cádiz, G. de 36 35N 6 20W
64 Cadomin 52 59N 117 28½
45 Cadoux 30 47S 117 8E
12 Caen 49 10N 0 22W
6 Caernarfon 53 8N 4 17W
6 Caernarfon B. 53 4N 4 40W
7 Caerphilly 51 34N 3 13W
28 Caesarea=Qesari 32 30N 34 53E
79 Caetité 13 50S 42 50W
35 Cagayan de Oro 8 30N 124 40E
18 Cágliari 39 15N 9 6E
18 Cágliari, G. di 39 8N 9 10E
75 Caguas 18 14N 66 4W
9 Caher 52 23N 7 56W
9 Cahirciveen 51 57N 10 13W
9 Cahore Pt. 52 34N 6 11W
12 Cahors 44 27N 1 27E
75 Caibarién 22 30N 79 30W
78 Caicara 7 50N 66 10W
79 Caicó 6 20S 37 0W
75 Caicos Is. 21 40N 71 40W
8 Cairn Gorm, Mt. 57 7N 3 40W
8 Cairngorm Mts. 57 6N 3 42W
42 Cairns 16 55S 145 51E
51 Cairo, Egypt= El Qâhira 30 1N 31 14E
69 Cairo, Ga. 30 52N 84 12W
71 Cairo, Mo. 37 0N 89 10W
78 Cajamarca 7 5S 78 28W
79 Cajazeiras 7 0S 38 30W
13 Cala Millor 39 34N 3 18E
53 Calabar 4 57N 8 20E
78 Calaboza 9 0N 67 20W
18 Calabria □ 39 4N 16 30E
80 Calafate 50 25S 72 25W
13 Calahorra 42 18N 1 59W
12 Calais 50 57N 1 56E
78 Calama 22 30S 68 55W
78 Calamar 10 15N 74 55W
35 Calamian Group, Is. 11 50N 119 55E
13 Calamocha 40 50N 1 17W
15 Călăraşi 44 14N 27 23E
13 Calatayud 41 20N 1 40W
35 Calauag 13 55N 122 15E
33 Calcutta 22 36N 88 24E
6 Calder R. 53 44N 1 21W
80 Caldera 27 5S 70 55W
72 Caldwell 43 45N 116 42W
56 Caledon 34 14S 19 26E
56 Caledon, R. 30 31S 26 5E
13 Calella 41 37N 2 40E
6 Calf of Man, I. 54 4N 4 48W
64 Calgary 51 0N 114 10W
78 Cali 3 25N 76 35W
32 Calicut 11 15N 75 43E
73 Caliente 37 43N 114 34W
73 California □ 37 25N 120 0W
74 California, G. de 27 0N 111 0W
74 California, Baja, Reg. 30 0N 115 0W
80 Calingasta 31 15S 69 30W
73 Calipatria 33 8N 115 30W
56 Calitzdorp 33 30S 21 41E
9 Callan 52 33N 7 25W
78 Callao 12 0S 77 0W
42 Callide 24 23S 150 33E
42 Calliope 24 0S 151 16E
57 Calo 31 37S 27 33E
43 Caloundra 26 45S 153 10E
18 Calatagirone 37 13N 14 30E
18 Caltanissetta 37 30N 14 3E
12 Calvados □ 49 5N 0 15W
12 Calvi 42 34N 8 45E
56 Calvinia 31 28S 19 45E
7 Cam, R. 52 21N 0 15E
75 Camagüey 21 20N 78 0W
80 Camarones 44 50S 66 0W
32 Cambay 22 23N 72 33E
32 Cambay, G. of 20 45N 72 30E
34 Cambodia ■ 12 15N 105 0E
7 Camborne 50 13N 5 18W
12 Cambrai 50 11N 3 14E
7 Cambrian Mts. 52 10N 3 52W
62 Cambridge, Canada 43 23N 80 19W
47 Cambridge, N.Z. 37 54S 175 29E
7 Cambridge, U.K. 52 13N 0 8E
68 Cambridge, Mass. 42 20N 71 8W
68 Cambridge, Ohio 40 1N 81 22W
7 Cambridge □ 52 21N 0 5E
60 Cambridge B. 69 10N 105 0W
44 Cambridge, G. 14 45S 128 0E
46 Camden, Australia 34 5S 150 38E
69 Camden, Ala. 31 59N 87 15W
71 Camden, Ark. 33 30N 92 50W
69 Camden, S.C. 34 17N 80 34W
71 Cameron 30 53N 97 0W
51 Cameroon ■ 3 30N 12 30E
53 Cameroun, Mt. 4 45N 8 55E
79 Cametá 2 0S 49 30W
13 Caminha 41 50N 8 50W
43 Camira Creek 29 15S 153 10E
79 Camocim 2 55S 40 50W
42 Camooweal 19 56S 138 7E
79 Camopi 3 45N 52 50W
18 Campania □ 40 50N 14 45E
80 Campana, I. 48 20S 75 10W
3 Campbell I. 52 30S 169 0E
64 Campbell River 50 1N 125 15W
42 Campbell Town 41 52S 147 30E
46 Campbelltown, Australia 34 5S 150 48E
63 Campbellton, N.B. 47 57N 66 43W
64 Campbellton, Alta. 53 32N 113 15W
8 Campbeltown 55 25N 5 36W
74 Campeche 19 50N 90 32W
74 Campeche □ 19 50N 90 32W
74 Campeche, B. de 19 30N 93 0W
46 Camperdown 38 4S 143 12E
79 Campino Grande 7 20S 35 47W
79 Campinas 22 50S 47 0W
79 Campo Formoso 10 30S 40 20W
80 Campo Gallo 26 35S 62 50W
79 Campo Grande 20 25S 54 40W
79 Campo Maior, Brazil 4 50S 42 12W
78 Campalegre 2 48N 75 20W
18 Campobasso 41 34N 14 40E
79 Campos 21 50S 41 20W
79 Campos Belos 13 10S 46 45W
64 Camrose 53 0N 112 50W
34 Can Tho 10 2N 105 46E
60 Canada ■ 60 0N 100 0W
80 Cañada de Gómez 32 55S 61 30W
71 Canadian, R. 35 27N 95 3W
74 Canal Zone 9 10N 79 48W
74 Cananea 31 0N 110 20W
50 Canarias, Is. 29 30N 17 0W
75 Canarreos, Arch. de los 21 35N 81 40W
50 Canary Is.= Canarias, Is. 29 30N 17 0W
69 Canaveral, C. 28 28N 80 31W
79 Canavieiras 15 45S 39 0W
46 Canberra 35 15S 149 8E
19 Candia=Iráklion 35 20N 25 12E
60 Candle 65 55N 161 56W
80 Canelones 34 32S 56 10W
80 Cañete 37 50S 73 10W
55 Cangamba 13 40S 19 54W
13 Cangas de Narcea 43 10N 6 32W
79 Canguaretama 6 20S 35 5W
80 Canguçu 31 22S 52 43W
34 Canipaan 8 33N 117 15E
64 Canmore 51 7N 115 18W
46 Cann River 37 35S 149 6E
8 Canna, I. 57 3N 6 33W
30 Cannakale 40 5N 27 20E
30 Cannakale Boğazi= Dardenelles, Str. 40 10N 27 20E
32 Cannanore 11 53N 75 27E
12 Cannes 43 32N 7 0E
6 Cannock 52 42N 2 2W
70 Canon City 39 30N 105 20W
65 Canora 51 40N 102 30W
63 Canso 45 20N 61 0W
13 Cantabrian Mts.= Cantábrica, Cord. 43 0N 5 10W
13 Cantábrica, Cord. 43 0N 5 10W
12 Cantal □ 45 4N 2 45E
47 Canterbury □ 43 45S 117 19E
42 Canterbury, Australia 33 55S 151 7E
7 Canterbury, U.K. 51 17N 1 5E
47 Canterbury Bight 44 16S 171 55E

Charente □ Clarkston

12 Charente □ 45 50N 0 36W
12 Charente-Maritime □ 45 50N 0 35W
51 Chari, R. 12 58N 14 31E
31 Charikar 35 0N 69 10E
37 Charkhlikh 39 16N 88 17E
11 Charleroi 50 24N 4 27E
68 Charles, C. 37 10N 75 52W
70 Charles City 43 2N 92 41W
71 Charleston, Mass. 34 2N 90 3W
69 Charleston, S.C. 32 47N 79 56W
68 Charleston, W.Va. 38 24N 81 36W
75 Charlestown, Nevis 17 8N 62 37W
57 Charlestown, S. Afr. 27 30S 29 55E
43 Charleville, Australia 26 24S 146 15E
9 Charleville, Eire= Rath Luire 52 21N 8 40W
43 Charleville 26 24S 146 15E
12 Charleville-Mézières 49 44N 4 40E
69 Charlotte 35 16N 80 46W
75 Charlotte Amalie 18 22N 64 56W
14 Charlottenburg 52 31N 13 16E
68 Charlottesville 38 1N 78 30W
63 Charlottetown 46 19N 63 3W
46 Charlton 36 16S 143 24E
70 Charlton 40 59N 93 20W
62 Charlton I. 52 0N 79 20W
63 Charny 46 43N 71 15W
12 Charolles 46 27N 4 16E
42 Charters Towers 20 5S 146 13E
12 Chartres 48 29N 1 30E
80 Chascomús 35 30S 58 0W
60 Chatanika 65 7N 147 31W
12 Château Salins 48 49N 6 30E
12 Châteaubriant 47 43N 1 23W
12 Châteauroux 46 50N 1 40E
12 Châtellerault 46 50N 0 30E
7 Chatham, U.K. 51 22N 0 32E
63 Chatham, N.B. 47 2N 65 28W
62 Chatham, Ont. 42 23N 82 15W
68 Chatham, Alas. 57 30N 135 0W
2 Chatham Is. 44 0S 176 40W
64 Chatham Str. 57 0N 134 40W
33 Chatrapur 19 21N 85 0E
69 Chattahoochee 30 43N 84 51W
69 Chattanooga 35 2N 85 17W
12 Chaumont 48 7N 5 8E
79 Chaves, Brazil 0 15S 49 55W
13 Chaves, Port. 41 45N 7 32W
14 Cheb 50 9N 12 20E
22 Cheboksary 56 8N 47 30E
68 Cheboygan 45 38N 84 29W
38 Chefoo=Yentai 37 30N 121 21E
25 Chegdomyn 51 7N 132 52E
72 Chehallis 46 44N 122 59W
39 Cheju 33 28N 126 30E
39 Cheju Do, I. 33 29N 126 34E
39 Chekiang □ 29 30N 120 0E
80 Chelforó 39 0S 66 40W
24 Chelkar 47 40N 59 32E
24 Chelkar Tengiz Solonchak 48 0N 62 30E
15 Chełm 51 8N 23 30E
15 Chełmno 53 20N 18 30E
7 Chelmsford 51 44N 0 29E
15 Chełmza 53 10N 18 39E
46 Chelsea 38 5S 145 8E
7 Cheltenham 51 55N 2 5W
24 Chelyabinsk 55 10N 61 35E
64 Chemainus 48 54N 123 41W
57 Chemba 17 11S 34 53E
22 Chemikovsk 54 58N 56 0W
14 Chemnitz= Karl Marx Stadt 50 50N 12 55E
72 Chemult 43 14N 121 54W
32 Chenab, R. 29 23N 71 2E
39 Chengchou= Chengchow 34 47N 113 46E
39 Chengchow 34 47N 113 46E
37 Chengkiang 24 58N 102 59E
38 Chengteh 41 0N 117 55E
38 Chengting 38 8N 114 37E
37 Chengtu 30 45N 104 0E
38 Chengyang 36 20N 120 16E
39 Chenhsien 25 45N 112 37E
39 Chenning 25 57N 105 51E
38 Chentung 46 2N 123 1E
39 Chenyuan 27 0N 108 20E
75 Chepo 9 10N 79 6W
7 Chepstow 51 39N 2 41W
70 Chequamegon B. 46 40N 90 30W
12 Cher, R. 47 21N 0 29E
12 Cher □ 47 10N 2 30E
12 Cherbourg 49 39N 1 40W
50 Cherchell 36 35N 21 63E
22 Cherdyn 60 20N 56 20E
25 Cheremkhovo 53 32N 102 40E
24 Cherepanovo 54 15N 83 30E
22 Cherepovets 59 5N 37 55E
23 Cherkassy 49 30N 32 0E
22 Chernigov 51 28N 31 20E
23 Chernovtsy 48 0N 26 0E
25 Chernoye 70 30N 89 10E
70 Cherokee 42 40N 95 30W
22 Cheropovets 59 5N 37 55E
80 Cherquenco 38 35S 72 0W
33 Cherrapunji 25 17N 91 47E
25 Cherskogo Khrebet 65 0N 143 0E
7 Cherwell, R. 51 44N 1 15W
68 Chesapeake B. 38 0N 76 12W
6 Cheshire □ 53 14N 2 30W
6 Chester, U.K. 53 12N 2 53W
68 Chester, Pa. 39 54N 75 20W
69 Chester, S.C. 34 44N 81 13W
6 Chesterfield 53 14N 1 26W
60 Chesterfield Inlet 63 30N 91 0W
41 Chesterfield Is. 19 52S 158 15E
74 Chetumal 18 30N 88 20W
74 Chetumal, B. de 18 40N 88 10W
6 Cheviot, The, Mt. 55 28N 2 8W
6 Cheviot Hills 55 20N 2 30W
54 Chew Bahir, L. 4 40N 30 50E
72 Chewelah 48 25N 117 56W
70 Cheyenne 41 9N 104 49W
70 Cheyenne, R. 44 40N 101 15W
32 Chhindwara 22 2N 78 59E
34 Chi, R. 15 13N 104 45E
39 Chiai 23 29N 120 25E
55 Chianje 15 35S 13 40E
74 Chiapas □ 17 0N 92 45W
18 Chiávari 44 20N 9 20E
18 Chiavenna 46 18N 9 23E
36 Chiba 35 30N 140 7E
36 Chiba □ 35 30N 140 20E
55 Chibemba 15 48S 14 8E
62 Chibougamau 49 56N 74 24W
53 Chibuk 10 52N 12 50E
68 Chicago 41 45N 87 40W
68 Chicago Heights 41 29N 87 37W
64 Chichagof I. 58 0N 136 0W
7 Chichester 50 50N 0 47W
74 Chichén Itzá 20 40N 88 34W
36 Chichibu 36 5N 139 10E
38 Chichirin 50 35N 123 45E
71 Chickasha 35 0N 98 0W
13 Chiclana de la Frontera 36 26N 6 9W
78 Chiclayo 6 42S 79 50W
72 Chico 39 45N 121 54W
80 Chico, R. 43 50S 66 25W
68 Chicopee 42 6N 72 37W
63 Chicoutimi 48 28N 71 5W
61 Chidley, C. 60 30N 64 15W
54 Chiengi 8 38S 29 10E
37 Chiengmai 18 55N 98 55E
18 Chieti 42 22N 14 10E
78 Chiguana 21 0S 67 50W
38 Chihfeng 42 10N 118 56E
39 Chihing 25 2N 113 45E
39 Chihkiang 27 21N 109 45E
38 Chihli, G. of= Po Hai, G. 38 30N 119 0E
39 Chihsien 35 29N 114 1E
74 Chihuahua 28 40N 106 3W
74 Chihuahua □ 28 40N 106 3W
24 Chiilí 44 10N 66 55E
32 Chilas 35 25N 74 5E
43 Childers 25 15S 152 17E
71 Childress 34 30N 100 50W
77 Chile ■ 35 0S 71 15W
80 Chilecito 29 0S 67 40W
78 Chilete 7 10S 78 50W
55 Chililabombwe 12 18S 27 43E
38 Chilin=Kirin 43 58N 126 31E
33 Chilka L. 19 40N 85 25E
80 Chillán 36 40S 72 10W
70 Chillicothe, Mo. 39 45N 93 30W
68 Chillicothe, Ohio. 39 53N 82 58W
64 Chilliwack 49 10N 122 0W
80 Chiloé, I. de 42 50S 73 45W
74 Chilpancingo 17 30N 99 40W
46 Chiltern 36 10S 146 36E
7 Chiltern Hills 51 44N 0 42W
52 Chilumba 10 28N 34 12E
39 Chilung 25 3N 121 45E
55 Chilwa, L. 15 15S 35 40E
37 Chimai 34 0N 101 39E
52 Chimala 8 55S 34 4E
78 Chimborazo, Mt. 1 20S 78 55W
78 Chimbote 9 0S 78 35W
24 Chimkent 42 40N 69 25E
33 Chin □ 22 0N 93 0E
37 China ■ 35 0N 100 0E
38 Chinan=Tsinan 34 50N 105 40E
75 Chinandega 12 30N 87 0W
78 Chincha Alta 13 20S 76 0W
43 Chinchilla 26 45S 150 38E
38 Chinchow 41 10N 121 2E
57 Chinde 18 45S 36 30E
33 Chindwin, R. 21 26N 95 15E
39 Ching Ho, R. 34 20N 109 0E
55 Chingola 12 31S 27 53E
55 Chingole 13 4S 34 17E
38 Ch'ingtao= Tsingtao 36 0N 120 25E
38 Chinhae 35 9N 128 58E
32 Chiniot 31 45N 73 0E
38 Chinju 35 12N 128 2E
39 Chinkiang 32 2N 119 29E
73 Chino Valley 34 54N 112 28W
12 Chinon 47 10N 0 15E
65 Chinook, Canada 51 28N 110 59W
72 Chinook, U.S.A. 48 35N 109 19W
52 Chintheche 11 50S 34 5E
38 Chinwangtao 40 0N 119 31E
18 Chióggia 45 13N 12 15E
19 Chios, I.= Khíos, I. 38 20N 26 0E
64 Chip Lake 53 35N 115 35W
55 Chipata 13 38S 32 28E
57 Chipinga 20 13S 32 36E
7 Chippenham 51 27N 2 7W
70 Chippewa, R. 44 25N 92 10W
70 Chippewa Falls 44 56N 91 24W
74 Chiquimula 14 51N 89 37W
78 Chiquinquira 5 37N 73 50W
32 Chirala 15 50N 80 20E
24 Chirchik 81 58N 69 15E
60 Chirikof I. 55 50N 155 35W
75 Chiriquí, G. de 8 0N 82 10W
75 Chiriquí, L. de 9 10N 82 0W
75 Chiriqui, Mt. 8 55N 82 35W
57 Chiromo 16 30S 35 7E
55 Chisamba 14 55S 28 20E
25 Chita 52 0N 113 25E
55 Chitembo 13 30S 16 50E
32 Chitorgarh 24 52N 74 43E
75 Chitré 7 59N 80 27W
33 Chittagong 22 19N 91 55E
33 Chittagong □ 24 5N 91 25E
32 Chittoor 13 15N 79 5E
18 Chiusi 43 1N 11 58E
18 Chivasso 45 10N 7 52E
80 Chivilcoy 35 0S 60 0W
52 Chiwanda 11 22S 34 54E
56 Chobe Nat. Park 18 25S 24 15E
80 Choele Choel 39 11S 65 40W
15 Choinice 53 42N 17 40E
12 Cholet 47 4N 0 52W
75 Choluteca 13 20N 87 14W
56 Choma 16 48S 26 59E
14 Chomutov 50 28N 13 23E
34 Chon Buri 13 21N 101 1E
38 Chonan 36 56N 127 3E
78 Chone 0 40S 80 0W
38 Chongjin 41 51N 129 58E
38 Chŏngju, N. Korea 39 41N 125 13E
38 Chŏngju, S. Korea 36 39N 127 27E
38 Chŏnju 35 50N 127 4E
80 Chonos, Arch. de los 45 0S 75 0W
6 Chorley 53 39N 2 39W
15 Chorzow 50 18N 19 0E
80 Chos-Malal 37 20S 70 15W
36 Chóshi 35 45N 140 45E
14 Choszczno 53 7N 15 25E
72 Choteau 47 50N 112 10W
32 Chotila 22 25N 71 11E
38 Choybalsan 48 3N 114 28E
47 Christchurch, N.Z. 43 33S 172 47W
7 Christchurch, U.K. 50 44N 1 47W
56 Christiana 27 52S 25 8E
44 Christmas Creek 18 29S 125 23E
3 Christmas I. Indian Oc. 10 0S 105 40E
2 Christmas I. Pacific Oc. 1 58N 157 27W
24 Chu 43 36N 73 42E
39 Chu Kiang, R. 24 50N 113 37E
39 Chuanchow 24 57N 118 31E
39 Chuanhsien 25 50N 111 12E
36 Chûbu □ 36 45N 137 0E
80 Chubut, R. 43 20S 65 5W
38 Chucheng 36 0N 119 16E
39 Chuchow 27 56N 113 3E
22 Chudskoye, Oz. 58 13N 27 30E
60 Chugiak 61 25N 149 30W
36 Chûgoku □ 35 0N 133 0E
36 Chûgoku-Sanchi, Mts. 35 0N 133 0E
39 Chuhsien 30 51N 107 1E
52 Chuka 0 23S 37 38E
34 Chukai 4 13N 103 25E
25 Chukotskiy Khrebet 68 0N 175 0E
25 Chukotskoye More 68 0N 175 0W
73 Chula Vista 33 44N 117 8W
39 Chumatien 33 0N 114 4E
80 Chumbicha 29 0S 66 10W
25 Chumikan 54 40N 135 10E
34 Chumphon 10 35N 99 14E
38 Chunchŏn 37 58N 127 44E
39 Ch'ungch'ing= Chungking 29 30N 106 30E
39 Chunghsien 30 17N 108 4E
39 Chungking 29 30N 106 30E
37 Chungtien 28 0N 99 30E
38 Chungwei 37 35N 105 10E
52 Chunya 8 30S 33 27E
14 Chur 46 52N 9 32E
65 Churchill 58 45N 94 5W
65 Churchill, R., Man. 58 47N 94 12W
63 Churchill, R., Newf. 53 30N 60 10W
64 Churchill Pk. 58 10N 125 10W
32 Churu 28 20N 75 0E
39 Chusan, I. 30 0N 122 20E
22 Chuvash A.S.S.R. □ 53 30N 48 0E
22 Chuvovoy 58 15N 57 40E
35 Cianjur 6 81S 107 7E
35 Cibatu 7 8S 107 59E
68 Cicero 41 48N 87 48W
15 Ciechańow □ 53 0N 20 0E
75 Ciego de Avila 21 50N 78 50W
78 Ciénaga 11 0N 74 10W
75 Cienfuegos 22 10N 80 30W
15 Cieszyn 49 45N 18 35E
13 Cieza 38 17N 1 23W
35 Cilacap 7 43S 109 0E
71 Cimarron, R. 36 10N 96 17W
35 Cimahi 6 53S 107 33E
15 Cîmpina 45 10N 25 45E
15 Cîmpulung 45 17N 25 3E
13 Cinca, R. 41 26N 0 21E
68 Cincinnati 39 10N 84 26W
12 Cinto, Mt. 42 24N 8 54E
60 Circle 47 26N 105 35W
68 Circleville, Ohio 39 35N 82 57W
73 Circleville, Utah 38 12N 112 24W
35 Cirebon 6 45S 108 32E
7 Cirencester 51 43N 1 59W
71 Cisco 32 25N 99 0W
74 Citlaltepetl, Mt. 19 0N 97 20W
56 Citrusdal 32 35S 19 0E
74 Ciudad Acuña 29 20N 101 10W
75 Ciudad Bolívar 8 5N 63 30W
74 Ciudad Camargo 27 41N 105 10W
74 Ciudad de Valles 22 0N 98 30W
74 Ciudad del Carmen 18 20N 97 50W
78 Ciudad Guayana 8 20N 62 35W
74 Ciudad Guzmán 19 40N 103 30W
74 Ciudad, Juárez 31 40N 106 28W
74 Ciudad Madero 22 19N 97 50W
74 Ciudad Mante 22 50N 99 0W
74 Ciudad Obregón 27 28N 109 59W
78 Ciudad Piar 7 27N 63 19W
13 Ciudad Real 38 59N 3 55W
13 Ciudad Rodrigo 40 35N 6 32W
74 Ciudad Victoria 23 41N 99 9W
18 Civitanova Marche 43 18N 13 41E
18 Civitavécchia 42 6N 11 46E
30 Çivril 38 20N 29 55E
45 Clackline 31 40S 116 32E
7 Clacton 51 47N 1 10E
56 Clanwilliam 32 11S 18 52E
9 Clara 53 20N 7 38W
43 Clare 33 20S 143 50E
9 Clare □ 52 52N 8 55W
9 Clare, R. 53 20N 9 3W
68 Claremont 43 23N 72 20W
71 Claremore 36 20N 95 20W
9 Claremorris 53 45N 9 0W
80 Clarence, I. 54 0S 72 0W
44 Clarence, Str. 12 0S 131 0E
47 Clarence, R. 42 10S 173 56E
71 Clarendon 34 41N 91 20W
63 Clarenville 48 10N 54 1W
64 Claresholm 50 0N 113 45W
70 Clarinda 40 45N 95 0W
72 Clark Fork, R. 48 9N 116 15W
73 Clarkdale 34 53N 112 3W
63 Clarke City 50 12N 66 38W
63 Clarkes Harbour 43 25N 65 38W
68 Clarksburg 39 18N 80 21W
71 Clarksdale 34 12N 90 33W
72 Clarkston 46 28N 117 2W

Cotopaxi, Mt. Dee,, R., Wales

78 Cotopaxi, Mt. 0 30S 78 30W
7 Cotswold Hills 51 42N 2 10W
72 Cottage Grove 43 48N 123 2W
14 Cottbus 51 44N 14 20E
73 Cottonwood 34 48N 112 1W
72 Coulee City 47 44N 119 12W
60 Council, Alas. 64 55N 163 45W
72 Council, Id. 44 45N 116 30W
70 Council Bluffs 41 20N 95 50W
64 Courtenay 49 45N 125 0W
7 Coventry 52 25N 1 32W
13 Covilhã 40 17N 7 31W
69 Covington, Ga. 33 36N 83 50W
68 Covington, Ky. 39 5N 84 30W
65 Cowan 52 5N 100 45W
45 Cowan, L. 31 45S 121 45E
46 Cowangie 35 12S 141 26E
62 Cowansville 45 14N 72 46W
8 Cowdenbeath 56 7N 3 20W
43 Cowell 33 38S 136 40E
7 Cowes 50 45N 1 18W
46 Cowra 33 49S 148 42E
79 Coxim 18 30S 54 55W
33 Cox's Bazar 21 25N 92 3E
74 Cozumel, I. de 20 30N 86 40W
15 Cracow= Kraków 50 4N 19 57E
56 Cradock 32 8S 25 36E
72 Craig 40 32N 107 44W
9 Craigavon □ 54 27N 6 26W
15 Craiova 44 21N 23 48E
54 Crampel 7 8N 19 8E
65 Cranberry Portage 54 36N 101 22W
42 Cranbrook, Tas. 42 0S 148 5E
45 Cranbrook, W. Australia 34 20S 117 35E
64 Cranbrook Canada 49 30N 115 55W
79 Crateús 5 10S 40 50W
79 Crato, Brazil 7 10S 39 25W
68 Crawfordsville 40 2N 86 51W
7 Crawley 51 7N 0 10W
12 Crécy 48 50N 2 53E
65 Cree L. 57 30N 107 0W
18 Cremona 45 8N 10 2E
18 Cres, I. 44 58N 14 25E
72 Crescent City 41 45N 124 12W
62 Cressman 47 40N 72 55W
64 Creston, Canada 49 10N 116 40W
70 Creston, U.S.A. 41 0N 94 20W
69 Crestview 30 45N 86 35W
4 Crete, I. 35 10N 25 0E
13 Creus, C. 42 20N 3 19E
12 Creuse □ 46 0N 2 0E
12 Creuse, R. 47 0N 0 34E
6 Crewe 53 6N 2 28W
80 Criciúma 28 40S 49 23W
8 Crieff 56 22N 3 50W
23 Crimea= Krymskaya, Reg. 45 0N 34 0E
8 Crinan 56 4N 5 30W
74 Cristóbal 9 10N 80 0W
15 Crişul Alb, R. 46 42N 21 17E
15 Crişul Negru, R. 46 42N 21 16E
19 Crna, R. 41 35N 21 59E
19 Crna Gora □ 42 40N 19 20E
19 Crna Gora, Mts. 42 20N 21 30E
71 Crockett 31 20N 95 30W
44 Croker, I. 11 12S 132 32E
8 Cromarty 57 40N 4 2W
6 Cromer 52 56N 1 18E
47 Cromwell 45 3S 169 14E
46 Cronulla 34 3S 151 8E
75 Crooked I. 22 50N 74 10W
70 Crookston 47 50N 96 40W
6 Cross Fell, Mt. 54 44N 2 29W
53 Cross River □ 6 20N 8 20E
9 Crosshaven 51 48N 8 19W
18 Crotone 39 5N 17 6E
72 Crow Agency 45 40N 107 30W
9 Crow Hd. 51 34N 10 9W
71 Crowley 30 15N 92 20W
64 Crowsnest P. 49 40N 114 40W
42 Croydon, Australia 18 15S 142 14E
7 Croydon, U.K. 51 18N 0 5W
3 Crozet Is. 46 27S 52 0E
80 Cruz Alta 28 40S 53 32W
80 Cruz del Eje 30 45S 64 50W
79 Cruzeiro 22 50S 45 0W
78 Cruzeiro do Sul 7 35S 72 35W
43 Crystal Brook 33 21S 138 13E
71 Crystal City 38 15N 90 23W
15 Csongrád 46 43N 20 12E
55 Cuamba 14 45S 36 22E
55 Cuando, R. 14 0S 19 30E
75 Cuba ■ 22 0N 79 0W
45 Cuballing 32 50S 117 15E
56 Cubango, R. 18 50S 22 25E
78 Cucui 1 10N 66 50W
78 Cúcuta 7 54N 72 31W
32 Cuddalore 11 46N 79 45E
32 Cuddapah 14 30N 78 47E
45 Cue 27 20S 117 55E
78 Cuenca, Ecuador 2 50S 79 9W
13 Cuenca, Sa. de 39 55N 1 50W
74 Cuernavaca 18 50N 99 20W
71 Cuero 29 5N 97 17W
13 Cuevas de Almanzora 37 18N 1 58W
79 Cuiabá 15 30S 56 0W
8 Cuillin Hills 57 14N 6 15W
56 Cuito, R. 18 1S 20 48E
74 Cuitzeo, L. 19 55N 101 5W
46 Culcairn 35 41S 147 3E
13 Culebra, Sa. de la 41 55N 6 20W
74 Culiacán 24 50N 107 40W
8 Cullen 57 45N 2 50W
44 Cullen, Pt. 11 50S 141 47E
13 Cullera 39 9N 0 17W
8 Culloden Moor 57 29N 4 7W
47 Culverden 42 47S 172 49E
78 Cumaná 10 30N 64 5W
64 Cumberland, Canada 49 40N 125 0W
68 Cumberland, U.S.A. 39 40N 78 43W
61 Cumberland Pen. 67 0N 65 0W
58 Cumberland Plat. 36 0N 84 30W
61 Cumberland Sd. 65 30N 66 0W
6 Cumbria □ 54 44N 2 55W
6 Cumbrian, Mts. 54 30N 3 0W
32 Cumbum 15 40N 79 10E
45 Cunderdin 31 39S 117 15E
56 Cunene, R. 17 20S 11 50E
18 Cúneo 44 23N 7 32E
43 Cunnamulla 28 4S 145 41E
65 Cupar, Canada 51 0N 104 10W
8 Cupar, U.K. 56 20N 3 0W
78 Cupica, G. de 6 25N 77 30W
75 Curaçao 12 10N 69 0W
78 Curiapo 8 33N 61 5W
80 Curicó 34 55S 71 20W
80 Curitiba 25 20S 49 10W
79 Currais Novos 6 13S 36 30W
79 Curralinho 1 35S 49 30W
42 Currawilla 25 10S 141 20E
72 Currie 40 16N 114 45W
42 Curtis, I. 23 40S 151 15E
79 Curuçá 0 35S 47 50W
79 Cururupu 1 50S 44 50W
80 Curuzú Cuatiá 29 50S 58 5W
79 Curvelo 18 45S 44 27W
46 Curya 35 53S 142 54E
71 Cushing 31 43N 94 50W
70 Custer 43 45N 103 38W
72 Cut Bank 48 40N 112 15W
33 Cuttack 20 25N 85 57E
45 Cuvier, C. 23 14S 113 22E
14 Cuxhaven 53 52N 8 42E
68 Cuyahoga Falls 41 8N 81 30W
78 Cuzco, Mt. 20 0S 66 50W
78 Cuzco 13 32S 72 0W
19 Cyclades, Is.= Kikládhes, Is. 37 20N 24 30E
42 Cygnet 43 8S 147 1E
30 Cyprus ■ 35 0N 33 0E
51 Cyrenaica=Barqa Reg. 27 0N 20 0E
51 Cyrene=Shahhat 32 39N 21 18E
14 Czechoslovakia ■ 49 0N 17 0E
15 Częstochowa 50 49N 19 7E

D

37 Da, R. 16 0N 107 0E
34 Da Lat 12 3N 108 32E
34 Da Nang 16 10N 108 7E
53 Dabai 11 25N 5 15E
50 Dabakala 8 15N 4 20W
14 Dąbie 53 27N 14 45E
50 Dabola 10 50N 11 5W
33 Dacca 23 43N 90 26E
33 Dacca □ 24 0N 90 0E
78 Dadanawa 3 0N 59 30W
53 Dadiya 9 35N 11 24E
32 Dadu 26 45N 67 45E
23 Dagesta A.S.S.R. □ 42 30N 47 0E
35 Dagupan 16 3N 120 33E
50 Dahomey ■= Benin ■ 8 0N 2 0E
9 Daingean 53 18N 7 15W
38 Dairen=Talien 39 0N 121 31E
51 Dairût 27 34N 30 43E
45 Dairy Creek 25 12S 115 48E
36 Daisetsu-Zan, Mt. 43 30N 142 57E
42 Dajarra 21 42S 139 30E
50 Dakar 14 34N 17 29W
50 Dakhla 23 50N 15 53W
23 Dakhovskaya 44 13N 40 13E
53 Dakingari 11 37N 4 1E
38 Dalai Nor, L. 49 0N 117 50E
21 Dalälven, R. 60 38N 17 27E
38 Dalandzadgad 43 35N 104 30E
21 Dalarö 59 8N 18 24E
32 Dalbandin 28 53N 64 25E
8 Dalbeattie 54 56N 3 49W
43 Dalby 27 11S 151 16E
71 Dalhart 36 4N 102 31W
63 Dalhousie 48 0N 66 26W
28 Daliyat el Karmel 32 41N 35 3E
8 Dalkeith 55 54N 3 4W
71 Dallas 32 47N 96 48W
31 Dalma, I. 24 30N 52 20E
18 Dalmacija, Reg. 43 0N 17 0E
18 Dalmatia, Reg.= Dalmacija, Reg. 43 0N 17 0E
8 Dalmellington 55 20N 4 25W
25 Dalnerechensk 45 50N 133 40E
50 Daloa 6 53N 6 27W
62 Dalton, Canada 60 10N 137 0N
69 Dalton, Neb. 41 27N 103 0W
44 Daly, R. 13 20S 130 19E
42 Daly Waters 16 15S 133 22E
32 Daman 20 25N 72 57E
32 Daman, Dadra & Nagar Haveli □ 20 25N 72 58E
51 Damanhûr 31 2N 30 28E
56 Damaraland, Reg. 22 33S 17 6E
30 Damascus= Dimashq 33 30N 36 18E
53 Damataru 11 45N 11 55E
31 Damāvand 35 45N 52 10E
31 Damāvand, Qolleh-ye, Mt. 35 56N 52 8E
15 Dâmboviţa, R. 44 40N 26 0E
31 Dāmāghan 36 10N 54 17E
51 Damietta= Dumyât 31 24N 31 48E
28 Damiya 32 6N 35 34E
32 Damoh 23 50N 79 28E
44 Dampier 20 39S 116 45E
35 Dampier, Selat 0 40S 130 40E
28 Dan 33 13N 35 39E
53 Dan Dume 11 28N 7 8E
53 Dan Gulbi 11 40N 6 15E
53 Dan Yashi 12 0N 8 5E
50 Danané 7 16N 8 9W
68 Danbury 41 23N 73 29W
46 Dandenong 37 52S 145 12E
53 Dangora 11 25N 8 7E
63 Daniel's Harbour 50 13N 57 35W
22 Danilov 58 16N 40 13E
53 Danja 11 29N 7 30E
53 Dankama 13 20N 7 44E
32 Dankhar Gompa 32 9N 78 10E
21 Dannemora 60 11N 16 49E
47 Dannevirke 40 12S 176 8E
57 Dannhauser 28 0S 30 3E
68 Dansville 42 32N 77 41W
15 Danube, R. (Donau) =Dunárea, R. 45 20N 29 40E
68 Danville, Ill. 40 10N 87 45W
68 Danville, Ky. 37 40N 84 45W
69 Danville, Va. 36 40N 79 20W
15 Danzig= Gdánsk 54 22N 18 40E
53 Dapango 10 52N 0 12E
46 Dapto 34 30S 150 47E
28 Dar'a 32 37N 36 6E
52 Dar-es-Salaam 6 50S 39 12E
31 Dārāb 28 50N 54 30E
53 Darazo 11 1N 10 24E
32 Darband 34 30N 72 50E
33 Darbhanga 26 15N 86 3E
64 D'Arcy 50 35N 122 30W
30 Dardanelles= Cannakale Boğazi, Str. 40 0N 26 20E
51 Dârfûr □ 15 35N 25 0E
51 Dârfûr, Reg. 12 35N 25 0E
32 Dargai 34 25N 71 45E
24 Dargan Ata 40 40N 62 20E
47 Dargaville 35 57S 173 52E
38 Darhan 49 27N 105 57E
78 Darién, G. del 9 0N 77 0W
14 Darmstadt 49 51N 8 40E
57 Darnall 29 23S 31 18E
60 Darnley, B. 69 30N 124 30W
42 Darr 24 34S 144 52E
7 Dart, R. 50 34N 3 56W
46 Dartmoor 37 56S 141 19E
7 Dartmoor, Reg. 50 36N 4 0W
42 Dartmouth, Australia 23 30S 144 40E
63 Dartmouth Canada 44 40N 63 30W
7 Dartmouth, U.K. 50 21N 3 35W
33 Darjeeling 27 3N 88 18E
63 Dark Cove 49 54N 54 5W
45 Darkan 33 19S 116 37E
46 Darling, R. 34 4S 141 54E
43 Darling Downs 27 30S 150 30E
45 Darling Ra. 32 0S 116 30E
6 Darlington 54 33N 1 33W
14 Darłowo 54 26N 16 23E
24 Darvaza 40 12N 58 24E
44 Darwin 12 20S 130 50E
44 Darwin River 12 49S 130 58E
30 Daryācheh-ye Reza'iyeh, L. 37 30N 45 30E
31 Das 35 5N 75 4E
51 Dashen, Ras, Mt. 13 10N 38 26E
38 Dashinchilen 47 50N 103 60E
32 Dasht, R. 25 10N 61 40E
31 Dasht-e Kavir, Des. 34 30N 55 0E
31 Dasht-e Lút, Des. 31 30N 58 0E
32 Datia 25 39N 78 27E
22 Daugavpils 55 53N 26 32E
31 Daulat Yar 34 33N 65 46E
65 Dauphin 51 15N 100 5W
12 Dauphiné, Reg. 45 15N 5 25E
53 Daura 13 2N 8 21E
32 Davangere 14 25N 75 50E
35 Davao 7 0N 125 40E
35 Davao G. 6 30N 125 48E
70 Davenport, Iowa 41 30N 90 40W
72 Davenport, Wash. 47 40N 118 5W
7 Daventry 52 16N 1 10W
75 David 8 30N 82 30W
60 Davis, Alas. 51 52N 176 39W
72 Davis, Calif. 38 39N 121 45W
63 Davis Inlet 55 50N 60 45W
2 Davis Str. 68 0N 58 0W
14 Davos 46 48N 9 50E
60 Dawson 64 4N 139 25W
64 Dawson Creek 55 46N 120 14W
80 Dawson, I. 53 50S 70 50W
28 Dayr al-Ghusūn 32 21N 35 5E
30 Dayr az Zawr 35 20N 40 9E
28 Dayral Balah 31 25N 34 21E
68 Dayton, Ohio 39 45N 84 10W
72 Dayton, Wash. 46 20N 118 0W
69 Daytona Beach 29 14N 81 0W
45 D'Entrecasteaux, Pt. 34 50S 116 0E
56 De Aar 30 39S 24 0E
44 De Grey 20 30S 120 0E
44 De Grey, R. 20 12S 119 11E
70 De Kalb 41 55N 88 45W
69 De Land 29 1N 81 19W
71 De Ridder 30 48N 93 15W
70 De Soto 38 8N 90 34W
28 Dead Sea= Miyet, Bahr el 31 30N 35 30E
70 Deadwood 44 25N 103 43W
45 Deakin 30 46S 129 0E
7 Deal 51 13N 1 25E
7 Dean, Forest of 51 50N 2 35W
80 Deán Funes 30 20S 64 20W
60 Dease Arm, B. 66 45N 120 6W
64 Dease Lake 58 40N 130 5W
73 Death Valley 36 0N 116 40W
73 Death Valley Nat. Mon. 36 30N 117 0W
73 Death Valley Junction 36 15N 116 30W
53 Deba Habe 10 14N 11 20E
51 Debre Markos 10 20N 37 40E
51 Debre Tabor 11 50N 38 5E
15 Debrecen 47 33N 21 42E
69 Decatur, Ala. 34 35N 87 0W
69 Decatur, Ga. 33 47N 84 17W
70 Decatur, Ill. 39 50N 89 0W
68 Decatur, Ind. 40 52N 85 28W
26 Deccan, Reg. 18 0N 77 0E
70 Decorah 43 20N 91 50W
53 Dédougou 12 30N 3 35W
8 Dee, R., Scot. 57 4N 3 7W
6 Dee, R., Wales 53 15N 3 7W

E

Ellen Mt. Felipe Carillo Puerto

73 Ellen Mt. 38 4N 110 56W
44 Ellendale, Australia 17 56S 124 48E
70 Ellendale, U.S.A. 46 3N 98 30W
72 Ellensburg 47 0N 120 30W
58 Ellesmere I. 79 30N 80 0W
6 Ellesmere Port 53 17N 2 55W
3 Ellice Is= Tuvalu ■ 8 0S 176 0E
57 Elliot 31 22S 27 48E
62 Elliot Lake 46 35N 82 35W
42 Elliott 41 5S 145 38E
43 Elliston 33 39S 134 55E
8 Ellon 57 21N 2 5W
33 Ellore=Eluru 16 48N 81 8E
70 Ellsworth 38 47N 98 15W
2 Ellsworth Ld. 75 30S 80 0W
68 Ellwood City 40 52N 80 19W
72 Elma 47 0N 123 30E
30 Elmali 36 44N 29 56E
52 Elmenteita 0 32S 36 14E
68 Elmhurst 41 52N 87 58W
53 Elmina 5 5N 1 21W
68 Elmira 42 8N 76 49W
46 Elmore 36 30S 144 37E
65 Elrose 51 20N 108 0W
73 Elsinore 33 40N 117 15W
47 Eltham 39 26S 174 19E
33 Eluru 16 48N 81 8E
13 Elvas 38 50N 7 17W
21 Elverum 60 55N 11 34E
68 Elwood 40 20N 85 50W
7 Ely, U.K. 52 24N 0 16E
70 Ely, U.S.A. 47 54N 91 52W
28 Elyashiv 32 23N 34 55E
68 Elyria 41 22N 82 8W
24 Emba 48 50N 58 8E
80 Embarcación 23 10S 64 0W
52 Embu 0 32S 37 38E
14 Emden 53 22N 7 12E
42 Emerald 23 30S 148 11E
65 Emerson 49 0N 97 10W
18 Emilia Romagna □ 44 33N 10 40E
11 Emmen 52 48N 6 57E
72 Emmett 24 45S 144 30W
74 Empalme 28 1N 110 49W
57 Empangeni 28 50S 31 52E
80 Empédrado 28 0S 58 46W
70 Emporia, Kans. 38 25N 96 16W
69 Emporia, Va. 36 41N 77 32W
68 Emporium 41 30N 78 17W
14 Ems, R. 51 9N 9 26E
28 'En Kerem 31 47N 35 6E
51 En Nahud 12 45N 28 25E
28 'En Yahav 30 37N 35 11E
36 Ena 35 25N 137 25E
80 Encarnación 27 15S 56 0W
74 Encarnación de Diaz 21 30N 102 20W
53 Enchi 5 53N 2 48W
78 Encontrados 9 3N 72 14W
35 Ende 8 45S 121 30E
42 Endeavour, Str. 10 45S 142 0E
64 Enderby 50 35N 119 10W
44 Enderby, I. 20 35S 116 30E
3 Enderby Ld. 66 0S 53 0E
68 Endicott 42 6N 76 2W
7 Enfield 51 38N 0 4W
75 Engaño, C., Dom. Rep. 18 30N 68 20W
35 Engaño, C., Philippines 18 35N 122 23E
57 Engcobo 31 39S 28 1E
22 Engels 51 28N 46 6E
34 Enggano 5 20S 102 40E
10 England ■ 53 0N 2 0W
63 Englee 50 45N 56 5W
62 Englehart 47 49N 79 52W
70 Englewood, Colo. 39 39N 104 59W
65 English, R. 50 12N 95 0W
33 English Bazar 24 58N 88 21E
4 English Chan. 50 0N 2 30W
71 Enid 36 26N 97 52W
57 Enkeldoorn 19 2S 30 52E
11 Enkhuizen 52 42N 5 17E
18 Enna 37 34N 14 15E
51 Ennedi 17 15N 22 0E
9 Ennis, Eire 52 51N 8 59W
71 Ennis, U.S.A. 32 15N 96 40W
9 Enniscorthy 52 30N 6 35W
9 Enniskillen 54 20N 7 40W
9 Ennistymon 52 56N 9 18W
20 Enontekio 68 23N 23 38E
11 Enschede 52 13N 6 53E
52 Entebbe 0 4N 32 28E
72 Enterprise 45 25N 117 17W
55 Entre Rios 14 57S 37 20E
80 Entre Rios, Reg. 30 0S 58 30W
53 Enugu 6 30N 7 30E
53 Enugu Ezike 7 0N 7 29E
18 Eólie o Lípari, I. 38 30N 14 50E
11 Epe, Neth. 52 21N 5 59E
53 Epe, Nigeria 6 36N 3 59E
12 Épernay 49 3N 3 56E
72 Ephraim 39 30N 111 37W
12 Épinal 48 19N 6 27E
7 Epping 51 42N 0 8E
54 Equatorial Guinea ■ 2 0N 8 0E
51 Er Rahad 12 45N 30 32E
50 Er Rif 35 1N 4 1W
51 Er Roseires 11 55N 34 30E
45 Eradu 28 40S 115 2E
25 Ercha 69 45N 147 20E
38 Erdene 44 30N 111 10E
38 Erdenedalay 46 3N 105 1E
80 Erechim 27 35S 52 15W
30 Ereğli 41 15N 31 30E
14 Erfurt 50 58N 11 2E
30 Ergani 38 26N 39 49E
23 Ergeni Vozvyshennost 47 0N 44 0E
38 Erhlien 43 42N 112 2E
8 Eriboll, I. 58 28N 4 41W
68 Erie 42 10N 80 7W
68 Erie, L. 42 30N 82 0W
29 Erigavo 10 35N 47 35E
65 Eriksdale 50 52N 98 5W
19 Erímanthos, Mt. 37 57N 21 50E
64 Erith 53 25N 116 46W
51 Eritrea □ 14 0N 41 0E
14 Erlangen 49 35N 11 0E
42 Erldunda 25 14S 133 12E
11 Ermelo, Neth. 52 35N 5 35E
57 Ermelo, S. Afr. 26 31S 29 59E
32 Ernakulam 9 59N 76 19E
9 Erne, L. 54 14N 7 30W
9 Erne, R. 54 30N 8 16W
32 Erode 11 24N 77 45E
32 Erramala Hills 15 30N 78 15E
53 Eruwa 7 33N 3 26E
14 Erzgebirge Mts. 50 25N 13 0E
30 Erzurum 39 57N 41 15E
51 Es Sider 30 50N 18 21E
21 Esbjerg 55 29N 8 29E
68 Escanaba 45 44N 87 5W
11 Esch 49 32N 6 0E
73 Escondido 33 9N 117 4W
74 Escuintla 14 20N 90 48W
31 Esfahan 32 40N 51 38E
31 Esfahan □ 33 0N 53 0E
51 Esh Shimâliya □ 20 0N 31 0E
57 Eshowe 28 50S 31 30E
28 Eshta'ol 31 47N 35 0E
6 Esk, R., Eng. 54 29N 0 37W
8 Esk, R., Scot. 54 58N 3 2W
21 Eskilstuna 59 22N 16 32E
65 Eskimo Point 61 10N 94 15W
30 Eskisehir 39 50N 30 35E
13 Esla, R. 41 29N 6 3W
78 Esmeraldas 1 0N 79 40W
62 Espanola 46 15N 81 46W
24 Espe 44 0N 74 5E
45 Esperance 33 51S 121 53E
45 Esperance, B. 33 48S 121 55E
83 Esperanza 31 29S 61 3W
13 Espichel, C. 38 22N 9 16W
78 Espinal 4 9N 74 53W
79 Espinhaço, Sa. do 17 30S 43 30W
74 Espíritu Santo, B. del 19 15N 79 40W
79 Espíritu Santo □ 19 30S 40 30W
80 Esquel 42 40S 71 20W
50 Essaouira 31 32N 9 42W
11 Essen, Belgium 51 28N 4 28E
14 Essen, W. Germany 51 28N 6 59E
7 Essex □ 51 48N 0 30E
14 Esslingen 48 43N 9 19E
12 Essonne □ 48 30N 2 20E
80 Estados, I. de los 54 40S 64 30W
79 Estância, Brazil 11 15S 37 30W
73 Estancia, U.S.A. 34 50N 106 1W
57 Estcourt 28 58S 29 53E
75 Estelí 13 9N 86 22W
65 Esterhazy 50 37N 102 5W
65 Estevan 49 10N 103 0W
70 Estheville 43 25N 94 50W
22 Estonian S.S.R. □ 48 30N 25 30E
13 Estoril 38 42N 9 23W
13 Estrêla, Sa. da 40 10N 7 45W
13 Estremadura, Reg. 39 0N 9 0W
79 Estrondo, Sa. de 7 20S 48 0W
15 Esztergom 47 47N 18 44E
32 Etawah 26 48N 79 6E
44 Ethel Creek 22 55S 120 11E
65 Ethelbert 51 32N 100 25W
29 Ethiopia ■ 8 0N 40 0E
48 Ethiopian Highlands, Mts. 10 0N 37 0E
8 Etive, L. 56 30N 5 12W
18 Etna, Mt. 37 45N 15 0E
56 Etoshapan 18 40S 16 30E
8 Ettrick, R. 55 31N 2 55W
74 Etzatlán 20 48N 104 5W
68 Euclid 41 32N 81 31W
46 Eucumbene, L. 36 2S 148 40E
69 Eufaula 31 55N 85 11W
72 Eugene 44 0N 123 8W
71 Eunice 30 35N 92 28W
11 Eupen 50 37N 6 3E
30 Euphrates, R.= Furat, Nahr al 33 30N 43 0E
12 Eure □ 49 6N 1 0E
72 Eureka, Calif. 40 50N 124 0W
72 Eureka, Nev. 39 32N 116 2W
72 Eureka, Utah 40 0N 112 0W
12 Eure-et-Loir □ 48 22N 1 30E
46 Euroa 36 44S 145 35E
55 Europa, Île 22 20S 40 22E
13 Europa, Picos de 43 10N 5 0W
13 Europa, Pta. de 36 3N 5 21W
5 Europe 50 0N 20 0E
11 Europoort 51 57N 4 10E
43 Evans Head 29 7S 153 27E
68 Evanston, Ill. 42 0N 87 40W
72 Evanston, Wyo. 41 10N 111 0W
68 Evansville 38 0N 87 35W
70 Eveleth 47 35N 92 40W
28 Even Yehuda 32 16N 34 53E
33 Everest, Mt. 28 5N 86 58E
72 Everett 48 0N 122 10W
69 Everglades Nat. Park 25 50N 80 40W
7 Evesham 52 6N 1 57W
13 Evora 38 33N 7 57W
12 Évreux 49 0N 1 8E
28 Evron 32 59N 35 6E
19 Evvoia □ 38 40N 23 40E
8 Ewe, L. 57 49N 5 38W
70 Excellsior Springs 39 20N 94 10W
7 Exe, R. 50 37N 3 25W
7 Exeter 50 43N 3 31W
7 Exmoor, Reg. 51 10N 3 55W
44 Exmouth, Australia 22 6S 114 0E
7 Exmouth, U.K. 50 37N 3 24W
44 Exmouth, G. 22 15S 114 15E
13 Extremadura, Reg. 39 30N 6 5W
75 Exuma Sd. 24 30N 76 20W
52 Eyasi, L. 3 30S 35 0E
8 Eye Pen. 58 20N 0 51E
8 Eyemouth 55 53N 2 5W
43 Eyre, L. 28 30S 136 45E
43 Eyre, Pen. 33 30S 137 17E

F

73 Fabens 31 30N 106 8W
18 Fabriano 43 20N 12 52E
78 Facatativa 4 49N 74 22W
53 Fada N'Gourma 12 10N 0 30E
18 Faenza 44 17N 11 53E
53 Fafa 15 22N 0 48E
53 Fagam 11 1N 10 1E
15 Făgăraş 45 48N 24 58E
21 Fagernes 61 0N 9 16E
21 Fagersta 61 1N 15 46E
80 Fagnano, L. 54 30S 68 0W
31 Fahraj 29 0N 59 0E
39 Fahsien 21 19N 110 33E
31 Fahud 22 18N 56 28E
68 Fair Haven 43 36N 76 16W
73 Fairbank 31 44N 110 12W
60 Fairbanks 64 59N 147 40W
70 Fairbury 40 5N 97 5W
46 Fairfield, Australia 37 45S 175 17E
69 Fairfield, Ala. 33 30N 87 0W
72 Fairfield, Calif. 38 14N 122 1W
70 Fairfield, Ill. 38 20N 88 20W
70 Fairfield, Iowa 41 0N 91 58W
71 Fairfield, Tex. 31 40N 96 0W
47 Fairlie 44 5S 170 49E
70 Fairmont, Minn. 43 37N 94 30W
68 Fairmont, W. Va. 39 29N 80 10W
68 Fairport 43 8N 77 29W
42 Fairview, Australia 15 31S 144 17E
64 Fairview, Canada 56 5N 118 25W
60 Fairweather, Mt. 58 55N 137 45W
31 Faizabad, Afghanistan 37 7N 70 33E
33 Faizabad, India 26 45N 82 10E
75 Fajardo 18 20N 65 39W
6 Fakenham 52 50N 0 51E
35 Fakfak 3 0S 132 15E
38 Faku 42 31N 123 26E
12 Falaise 48 54N 0 12W
33 Falam 23 0N 93 45E
18 Falcone, C. 41 0N 8 10E
71 Falfurrias 27 8N 98 8E
21 Falkenberg 56 54N 12 30E
8 Falkirk 56 0N 3 47W
80 Falkland, Sd. 52 0S 60 0W
80 Falkland Is. □ 51 30S 59 0W
2 Falkland Is. Dependencies □ 57 0S 40 0N
21 Falköping 58 12N 13 33E
68 Fall River 41 45N 71 5W
72 Fallon 39 31N 118 51W
70 Falls City 40 0N 95 40W
75 Falmouth, Jamaica 18 30N 77 40W
7 Falmouth, U.K. 50 9N 5 5W
75 Falso, C. 17 45N 71 40W
21 Falster, I. 54 48N 11 58E
21 Falsterbo 55 23N 12 50E
21 Falun 60 37N 15 37E
30 Famagusta 35 8N 33 55E
57 Fandriana 20 14S 47 21E
39 Fangcheng 31 2N 118 13E
2 Fanning I. 3 51N 159 22W
18 Fano 43 50N 13 0E
64 Fanshaw 57 11N 133 30W
52 Faradje 3 50N 29 45E
57 Farafangana 22 49S 47 50E
50 Faranah 10 2N 10 45W
31 Farar 32 30N 62 17E
31 Farar □ 32 25N 62 10E
29 Farasān, Jazā'ir, I. 16 45N 41 55E
57 Faratsiho 19 24S 46 57E
7 Fareham 50 52N 1 11W
61 Farewell, C., Greenland= Farvel, K. 66 0N 44 0W
47 Farewell, C., N.Z. 40 29S 172 43E
70 Fargo 47 0N 97 0W
70 Faribault 44 15N 93 19W
33 Faridpur 23 36N 89 53E
43 Farina 30 3S 138 15E
73 Farmington, N. Mex. 36 45N 108 28W
72 Farmington, Utah 41 0N 111 58W
7 Farnborough 51 17N 0 46W
6 Farne Is. 55 38N 1 37W
79 Faro, Brazil 2 0S 56 45W
13 Faro, Port. 37 2N 7 55W
4 Faroe Is. 62 0N 7 0W
45 Farquhar, C. 23 38S 113 36E
31 Farrāshband 28 57N 52 5E
68 Farrell 41 13N 80 29W
43 Farrell Flat 33 48S 138 48E
31 Fars □ 29 30N 55 0E
21 Farsund 58 5N 6 55E
53 Faru 12 48N 6 12E
61 Farvel, K. 60 0N 44 0W
31 Faryab □ 36 0N 65 0E
9 Fastnet Rock 51 22N 9 27W
32 Fatehgarh 27 25N 79 35E
32 Fatehpur, Rajasthan 28 0N 75 4E
33 Fatehpur, Ut.P. 27 8N 81 7E
39 Fatshan 23 0N 113 4E
70 Faulkton 45 4N 99 8W
45 Faure, I. 25 52S 113 50E
55 Fauresmith 29 44S 25 17E
20 Fauske 67 17N 15 25E
18 Favara 37 19N 13 39E
18 Favignana, I. 37 56N 12 18E
20 Faxaflói, B. 64 29N 23 0W
71 Fayetteville, Ark. 36 0N 94 5W
69 Fayetteville, N.C. 35 0N 78 58W
32 Fazilka 30 27N 74 2E
50 F'Dérik 22 40N 12 45E
9 Feale, R. 52 26N 9 28W
69 Fear, C. 33 45N 78 0W
47 Featherston 41 6S 175 20E
12 Fécamp 49 45N 0 22E
14 Fehmarn, I. 54 26N 11 10E
14 Fehmarn Bælt 54 35N 11 20E
47 Feilding 40 13S 175 35E
79 Feira de Santana 12 15S 38 57W
14 Feldkirch 47 15N 9 37E
74 Felipe Carillo Puerto 19 38N 88 3W

Felixstowe Fulton, N.Y.

7 Felixstowe 51 58N 1 22W
20 Femund, L. 62 5N 11 55E
38 Fen Ho, R. 35 36N 110 42E
57 Fénérive 17 22S 49 25E
39 Fencheng 28 2N 115 46E
38 Fengcheng, Heilungkiang 45 41N 128 54E
38 Fengcheng, Liaoning 40 28N 124 4E
39 Fenghsien 33 56N 106 41E
39 Fengkieh 31 0N 109 33E
38 Fengtai 39 57N 116 21E
39 Fengyuan 24 10N 120 45E
57 Fenoarivo 18 26S 46 34E
6 Fens, Reg. 52 45N 0 2E
38 Fenyang 37 19N 111 46E
23 Feodosiya 45 2N 35 28E
24 Fergana 40 23N 71 46E
62 Fergus 43 43N 80 24W
70 Fergus Falls 46 25N 96 0W
62 Ferland 50 19N 88 27W
9 Fermanagh □ 54 21N 7 40W
9 Fermoy 52 4N 8 18W
2 Fernando de Noronha, Is. 4 0S 33 10W
53 Fernando Póo, I.= Macias Nguema Biyoga 3 30N 8 4E
64 Fernie 49 30N 115 5W
42 Fernlees 23 51S 148 7E
32 Ferozepore 30 55N 74 40E
18 Ferrara 44 50N 11 36E
50 Fès 34 0N 5 0½W
8 Fetlar, I. 60 36N 0 52W
51 Fezzan 27 0N 15 0E
57 Fianarantsoa 21 26S 47 5E
57 Fianarantsoa □ 21 30S 47 0E
14 Fichtelgebirge, Mts. 50 10N 12 0E
57 Ficksburg 28 51S 27 53E
53 Fiditi 7 45N 3 53E
15 Fier, Portile de 44 42N 22 30E
8 Fife □ 56 13N 3 2W
12 Figeac 44 37N 2 2E
57 Figtree 20 22S 28 20E
13 Figueira da Foz 40 7N 8 54W
13 Figueras 42 18N 2 58E
50 Figuig 32 5N 1 11W
57 Fihaonana 18 36S 47 12E
47 Fiji ■ 17 20S 179 0E
6 Filey 54 13N 0 10W
19 Filiatrá 37 9N 21 35E
53 Filingué 14 21N 3 19E
21 Filipstad 59 43N 14 9E
73 Fillmore 34 23N 118 58W
8 Findhorn 57 30N 3 45W
68 Findlay 41 0N 83 41W
12 Finistère □ 48 20N 4 20W
13 Finisterre, C. 42 50N 9 19W
42 Finke 25 34S 134 35E
20 Finland ■ 70 0N 27 0E
22 Finland, G. of 60 0N 26 0¼E
46 Finley 35 38S 145 35E
64 Finnegan 51 7N 112 5W
42 Finnigan, Mt. 15 49S 145 17E
43 Finniss, C. 33 38S 134 51E
20 Finnmark □ 69 30N 25 0E
18 Firenze 43 47N 11 15E
32 Firozabad 27 10N 78 25E
31 Firūzābād 28 52N 52 35E
31 Firūzkūh 35 50N 52 40E
45 Fisher 30 30S 131 0E
7 Fishguard 51 59N 4 59W
68 Fitchburg 42 35N 71 47W
80 Fitz Roy 47 10S 67 0W
69 Fitzgerald 31 45N 83 10W
42 Fitzroy, R., Queens. 23 32S 150 52E
44 Fitzroy, R., W. Australia 17 31S 138 35E
44 Fitzroy Crossing 18 9S 125 38E
54 Fizi 4 17S 28 55E
73 Flagstaff 35 10N 111 40W
21 Flåm 60 52N 7 14E
6 Flamborough Hd. 54 8N 0 4W
72 Flaming Gorge L. 41 15N 109 30W
11 Flanders= Flandres, Plaines des 51 10N 3 15E
11 Flandre Occidentale □ 51 0N 3 0E
11 Flandre Orientale □ 51 0N 4 0E
11 Flandres, Plaines des 51 10N 3 15E
8 Flannan Is. 58 9N 7 52W
72 Flathead L. 47 50N 114 0W
42 Flattery, C., Australia 14 58S 145 21E
72 Flattery, C., U.S.A. 48 21N 124 31W
6 Fleetwood 53 55N 3 .1W
21 Flekkefjord 58 18N 6 39E
14 Flensburg 54 46N 9 28E
7 Fletton 52 34N 0 13W
65 Flin Flon 54 46N 101 53W
45 Flinders, B. 34 19S 114 9E
42 Flinders, I. 40 0S 148 0E
43 Flinders, Ras. 31 30S 138 30E
6 Flint, U.K. 53 15N 3 7W
68 Flint, U.S.A. 43 0N 83 40W
1 Flint I. 11 26S 151 48W
6 Flodden 55 37N 2 8W
70 Flora 38 40N 88 30W
18 Florence, Italy= Firenze 43 47N 11 15E
69 Florence, Ala. 34 50N 87 50W
73 Florence, Ariz. 33 0N 111 25W
72 Florence, Oreg. 44 0N 124 3W
69 Florence, S.C. 34 5N 79 50W
78 Florencia 1 36N 75 36W
74 Flores 16 50N 89 40W
35 Flores, I. 8 35S 121 0¼E
35 Flores Sea 6 30S 124 0E
79 Floriano 6 50S 43 0W
80 Florianópolis 27 30S 48 30W
80 Florida 34 7S 56 10W
69 Florida □ 28 30N 82 0W
59 Florida Str. 25 0N 80 0W
19 Flórina 40 48N 21 26E
21 Florø 61 35N 5 1E
11 Flushing= Vlissingen 51 26N 3 34E
41 Fly, R. 7 50S 141 20E
65 Foam Lake 51 40N 103 15W
15 Focşani 45 41N 27 15E
18 Fóggia 41 28N 15 31E
53 Foggo 11 21N 9 57E
63 Fogo 49 43N 54 17W
12 Foix, Reg. 43 0N 1 30E
62 Foleyet 48 15N 82 25W
18 Foligno 42 58N 12 40E
7 Folkestone 51 5N 1 11E
65 Fond du Lac, Canada 59 20N 107 10W
70 Fond-du-Lac, U.S.A. 43 46N 88 26W
18 Fondi 41 21N 13 25E
13 Fonsagrada 43 8N 7 4W
74 Fonseca, G. de 13 10N 87 40W
12 Fontainebleau 48 24N 2 40E
78 Fonte Boa 2 25S 66 0W
53 Fontem 5 32N 9 52E
12 Fontenay-le-Comte 46 28N 0 48W
39 Foochow 26 5N 119 18E
46 Forbes 33 22S 148 0E
64 Forest Lawn 51 4N 114 0W
64 Forestburg 52 35N 112 1W
63 Forestville 48 48N 69 20W
12 Forez, Mts. du 45 40N 3 50E
8 Forfar 56 40N 2 53W
18 Forlì 44 14N 12 2E
6 Formby Pt. 53 33N 3 7W
13 Formentera, I. 38 40N 1 30E
79 Formiga 20 27S 45 25W
80 Formosa, Arg. 26 15S 58 10W
79 Formosa, Brazil 15 32S 47 20W
39 Formosa= Taiwan ■ 24 0N 121 0E
79 Formosa, Sa. 12 0S 55 0W
39 Formosa Str. 24 40N 124 0E
8 Forres 57 37N 3 38W
45 Forrest 38 22S 143 40E
71 Forrest City 35 1N 90 47W
42 Forsayth 18 33S 143 34E
14 Forst 51 43N 15 37E
72 Forsyth 46 14N 106 37W
62 Fort Albany 52 15N 81 35W
51 Fort-Archambault =Sarh 9 5N 18 23E
64 Fort Assinboine 54 20N 114 45W
8 Fort Augustus 57 9N 4 40W
56 Fort Beaufort 32 46S 26 40E
72 Fort Benton 47 50N 110 40W
72 Fort Bragg 39 28N 123 50W
72 Fort Bridger 41 22N 110 20W
61 Fort Chimo 58 9N 68 12W
65 Fort Chipewyan 58 46N 111 9W
70 Fort Collins 40 30N 105 4W
62 Fort Coulonge 45 50N 76 45W
57 Fort-Dauphin 25 2S 47 0E
70 Fort Dodge 42 29N 94 10W
65 Fort Frances 48 35N 93 25W
60 Fort Franklin 65 30N 123 45W
62 Fort George 53 40N 79 0W
62 Fort George, R. 53 50N 77 0W
60 Fort Good Hope 66 14N 128 40W
64 Fort Graham 56 38N 124 35W
73 Fort Hancock 31 19N 105 56W
62 Fort Hope 51 30N 88 10W
63 Fort Kent 47 12N 68 30W
51 Fort-Lamy= Ndjamena 12 4N 15 8E
70 Fort Laramie 42 15W 104 30W
69 Fort Lauderdale 26 10N 80 5W
64 Fort Liard 60 20N 123 30W
64 Fort Mackay 57 12N 111 41W
63 Fort McKenzie 56 50N 69 0W
64 Fort Macleod 49 45N 113 30W
50 Fort MacMahon 29 51N 1 45E
60 Fort McPherson 67 30N 134 55W
70 Fort Madison 40 39N 91 20W
50 Fort Mirabel 29 31N 2 55E
70 Fort Morgan 40 10N 103 50W
32 Fort Munro 30 0N 69 55E
69 Fort Myers 26 30N 82 0W
64 Fort Nelson 58 50N 122 30W
60 Fort Norman 64 57N 125 30W
69 Fort Payne 34 25N 85 44W
72 Fort Peck 47 1N 105 30W
72 Fort Peck Res. 47 40N 107 0W
69 Fort Pierce 27 29N 80 19W
52 Fort Portal 0 40N 30 20E
64 Fort Providence 61 20N 117 30W
65 Fort Qu'Appelle 50 45N 103 50W
64 Fort Resolution 61 10N 114 40W
54 Fort-Rousset 0 29S 15 55E
62 Fort Rupert 51 30N 78 40W
64 Fort St. James 54 30N 124 10W
64 Fort St. John 56 15N 120 50W
32 Fort Sandeman 31 20N 69 25E
64 Fort Saskatchewan 53 40N 113 15W
71 Fort Scott 38 0N 94 40W
60 Fort Selkirk 62 43N 137 22W
62 Fort Severn 56 0N 87 40W
64 Fort Simpson 61 45N 121 30W
24 Fort Shevchenko 44 30N 50 10E
71 Fort Smith 35 25N 94 25W
71 Fort Stockton 30 48N 103 2W
71 Fort Sumner 34 24N 104 8W
69 Fort Valley 32 33N 83 52W
64 Fort Vermilion 58 30N 115 57W
57 Fort Victoria 20 8S 30 55E
68 Fort Wayne 41 5N 85 10W
62 Fort William, Canada= Thunder Bay 48 20N 89 10W
8 Fort William, U.K. 56 48N 5 8W
71 Fort Worth 32 45N 97 25W
60 Fort Yukon 66 35N 145 12W
79 Fortaleza 3 35S 38 35W
75 Fort-de-France 14 36N 61 5W
44 Fortescue, R. 21 20S 116 5E
8 Forth, Firth of 56 5N 2 55W
8 Fortrose 57 35N 4 10W
72 Fortuna 48 38N 124 8W
60 Forty Mile 64 20N 140 30W
68 Fostoria 41 8N 83 25W
12 Fougères 48 21N 1 14W
8 Foula, I. 60 10N 2 5W
7 Foulness, I. 51 26N 0 55E
53 Foumban 5 45N 10 50E
44 Fourcroy, C. 11 45S 130 2E
57 Fouriesburg 28 38S 28 14E
50 Fouta Djalon, Mts. 11 20N 12 10W
47 Foveaux, Str. 46 42S 168 10E
7 Fowey 50 20N 4 39W
45 Fowlers, B. 31 59S 132 34E
39 Fowning 33 30N 119 40E
65 Fox Valley 50 30N 109 25W
61 Foxe Basin 68 30N 77 0W
61 Foxe Chan. 66 0N 80 0W
61 Foxe Pen. 65 0N 76 0W
47 Foxton 40 29S 175 18E
9 Foyle, L. 55 6N 7 18W
9 Foynes 52 37N 9 6W
80 Foz do Iguaçu 25 30S 54 30W
79 Franca 20 25S 47 30W
19 Francavilla Fontana 40 32N 17 35E
12 France ■ 47 0N 3 0E
54 Franceville 1 38S 13 35E
12 Franche Comté, Reg. 46 30N 5 50E
63 Francis Harbour 52 34N 55 44W
57 Francistown 21 11S 27 32E
63 François 47 34N 56 44W
14 Franconia 50 0N 9 0E
57 Frankfort, S. Afr. 27 16S 28 30E
68 Frankfort, Ind. 40 20N 86 33W
68 Frankfort, Ky. 38 12N 85 44W
14 Frankfurt am Main 50 7N 8 40E
14 Frankfurt an der Oder 52 50N 14 31E
14 Fränkishe Alb. 49 20N 11 30E
70 Franklin, Nebr. 40 9N 98 55W
68 Franklin, N.H. 43 28N 71 39W
68 Franklin, Pa. 41 22N 79 45W
69 Franklin, Tenn. 35 54N 86 53W
68 Franklin, W. Va. 38 38N 79 21W
60 Franklin, Reg. 71 0N 99 0W
72 Franklin D. Roosevelt L. 48 30N 118 16W
60 Franklin Mts. 66 0N 125 0W
60 Franklin Str. 72 0N 96 0W
46 Frankston 38 8S 145 8E
24 Frantsa Iosifa, Zemlya, Is. 76 0N 62 0E
62 Franz 48 25N 85 30W
43 Fraser, I. 25 15S 153 10E
64 Fraser, R. 49 9N 123 12W
64 Fraser Lake 54 0N 124 50W
56 Fraserburg 31 55S 21 30E
8 Fraserburgh 47 41N 2 0½W
80 Fray Bentos 33 10S 58 15W
44 Frazier Downs 18 48S 121 42E
21 Fredericia 55 34N 9 45E
68 Frederick, Md. 39 25N 77 23W
71 Frederick, Okla. 34 22N 99 0W
68 Fredericksburg 38 16N 77 29W
63 Fredericton 45 57N 66 40W
21 Frederikshavn 57 28N 10 31E
68 Fredonia 42 26N 79 20W
21 Fredrikstad 59 13N 10 57E
75 Freeport, Bahamas 26 30N 78 35W
70 Freeport, Ill. 42 18N 89 40W
68 Freeport, N.Y. 40 39N 73 35W
71 Freeport, Tex. 28 55N 95 22W
50 Freetown 8 30N 13 10W
14 Freiburg 48 0N 7 50E
80 Freire 39 0S 72 50W
14 Freising 48 24N 11 27E
14 Freistadt 48 30N 14 30E
12 Fréjus 43 25N 6 44E
45 Fremantle 32 1S 115 47E
70 Fremont, Nebr. 41 30N 96 30W
68 Fremont, Ohio 41 20N 83 5W
46 French, I. 38 20S 145 22E
79 French Guiana ■ 4 0N 53 0W
29 French Terr. of the Afars & Issas■= Djibouti ■ 11 30N 42 15E
79 Fresco, R. 6 39S 51 59W
74 Fresnillo 23 10N 103 0W
73 Fresno 36 47N 119 50W
42 Frewena 19 50S 135 50E
80 Frías 28 40S 65 5W
14 Fribourg 46 49N 7 9E
14 Friedrichshafen 47 39N 9 29E
47 Friendly Is.= Tonga Is. 20 0S 173 0W
11 Friesian Is.= Waddeniladen 53 30N 5 30E
11 Friesland □ 53 5N 5 50E
55 Frio, C. 18 0S 12 0E
18 Friuli Venezia Giulia □ 46 0N 13 0E
61 Frobisher B. 63 0N 67 0W
7 Frome 51 16N 2 17W
68 Front Royal 38 55N 78 10W
74 Frontera 18 30N 92 40W
18 Frosinone 41 38N 13 20E
68 Frostburg 39 43N 78 57W
24 Frunze 42 54N 74 36E
79 Frutal 20 0S 49 0W
15 Frýdek Místek 49 40N 18 20E
38 Fuchin 47 10N 132 0E
39 Fuchou=Foochow 26 5N 119 18E
39 Fuchow 27 50N 116 14E
36 Fuchu 34 34N 133 14E
39 Fuchun Kiang, R. 30 10N 120 9E
13 Fuente Ovejuna 38 15N 5 25W
13 Fuentes de Oñoro 40 33N 6 52W
50 Fuerteventura, I. 28 30N 14 0W
31 Fujaira 25 7N 56 18E
36 Fuji 35 9N 138 39E
36 Fuji-san, Mt. 35 22N 138 44E
36 Fuji-no-miya 35 20N 138 40E
36 Fujisawa 35 22N 139 29E
39 Fukien □ 26 0N 117 30E
36 Fukuchiyama 35 25N 135 9E
36 Fukui 36 0N 136 10E
36 Fukui □ 36 0N 136 12E
36 Fukuoka 33 30N 130 30E
36 Fukuoka □ 33 30N 131 0E
36 Fukushima 37 30N 140 15E
36 Fukushima □ 37 30N 140 15E
36 Fukuyama 34 35N 133 20E
14 Fulda 50 32N 9 41E
73 Fullerton 33 52N 117 58W
70 Fulton, Mo. 38 50N 91 55W
68 Fulton, N.Y. 43 20N 76 22W

Funabashi Glendale, Oreg.

36 Funabashi 35 45N 140 0E
3 Funafuti, I. 8 30S 179 0E
50 Funchal 32 45N 16 55W
78 Fundación 10 31N 74 11W
13 Fundão 40 8N 7 30W
63 Fundy, B. of 45 0N 66 0W
53 Funtua 11 31N 7 17E
30 Furat, Nahr al, R. 33 30N 43 0E
6 Furness 54 14N 3 8W
14 Fürth 49 29N 11 0E
61 Fury & Hecla Str. 69 40N 81 0W
78 Fusagasugá 4 21N 74 22W
38 Fushan 37 30N 121 5E
38 Fushun 42 0N 123 59E
38 Fusin 42 12N 121 33E
39 Futing 27 15N 120 10E
39 Futsing 25 46N 119 29E
39 Fuyang 30 5N 119 56E
38 Fuyu 45 10N 124 50E
21 Fyen, I.=Fyn, I. 55 20N 10 30E
6 Fylde, R. 53 47N 2 56W
21 Fyn, I. 55 20N 10 30E
8 Fyne, L. 56 0N 5 20W

G

53 Gaanda 10 10N 12 27E
50 Gabès 33 53N 10 2E
51 Gabès, G. de 34 0N 10 30E
54 Gabon ■ 0 10S 10 0E
56 Gaborone 24 37S 25 57E
19 Gabrovo 42 52N 25 27E
31 Gach-Sarán 30 15N 50 45E
53 Gada 13 38N 5 36E
32 Gadag 15 30N 75 45E
32 Gadarwara 22 50N 78 50E
32 Gadhada 22 0N 71 35E
69 Gadsden, Ala. 34 1N 86 0W
73 Gadsden, Ariz. 32 35N 114 47W
32 Gadwal 16 10N 77 50E
18 Gaeta 41 12N 13 35E
69 Gaffney 35 10N 81 31W
50 Gafsa 34 24N 8 51E
63 Gagetown 45 46N 66 29W
50 Gagnoa 6 4N 5 55W
63 Gagnon 51 50N 68 5W
69 Gainesville, Fla. 29 38N 82 20W
69 Gainesville, Ga. 34 17N 83 47W
71 Gainesville, Tex. 33 40N 97 10W
6 Gainsborough 53 23N 0 46W
43 Gairdner, L. 32 0S 136 0E
8 Gairloch, L. 57 43N 5 45W
53 Gajiram 12 29N 13 9E
55 Galangue 13 48S 16 3E
2 Galápagos, Is. 0 0N 89 0W
8 Galashiels 55 37N 2 50W
15 Galaţi 45 27N 28 2E
19 Galatina 40 10N 18 10E
69 Galax 36 42N 80 57W
21 Galdhøpiggen, Mt. 61 45N 8 40E
45 Galena 27 50S 114 41E
70 Galesburg 40 57N 90 23W
22 Galich 58 23N 42 18E
13 Galicia, Reg. 42 43N 8 0W
28 Galilee= Hagalil, Reg. 32 53N 35 18E
28 Galilee, Sea of= Kinneret, Yam 32 49N 35 36E
69 Gallatin 36 24N 86 27W
32 Galle 6 5N 80 10E
13 Gállego, R. 41 39N 0 51W
80 Gallegos, R. 51 35S 69 0W
78 Gallinas, Pta. 12 28N 71 40W
19 Gallipoli 40 8N 18 0E
68 Gallipolis 38 50N 82 10W
20 Gällivare 67 7N 20 32E
8 Galloway, Reg. 55 0N 4 25W
8 Galloway, Mull of 54 38N 4 50W
73 Gallup 35 30N 108 54W
62 Galt= Cambridge 43 23N 80 19W
9 Galty Mts. 52 20N 8 10W
71 Galveston 29 15N 94 48W
71 Galveston B. 29 30N 94 50W
80 Gálvez 32 0S 61 20W
9 Galway 53 16N 9 4W
9 Galway, B. 53 10N 9 20W
9 Galway □ 53 16N 9 3W
36 Gamagori 34 50N 137 14E
53 Gamawa 12 10N 10 31E
53 Gambaga 10 30N 0 28W
50 Gambia ■ 13 20N 15 45W
50 Gambia, R. 13 28N 16 34W
44 Gambier, C. 11 56S 130 57E
74 Gamboa 9 8N 79 42W
73 Gamerco 35 33N 108 56W
56 Gamtoos, R. 33 58S 25 1E
28 Gan Shamu'el 32 28N 34 56E
28 Gan Yavne 31 48N 34 42E
62 Gananoque 44 20N 76 10W
11 Gand=Gent 51 2N 3 37E
33 Gandak, R. 25 32N 85 5E
63 Gander 49 1N 54 33W
53 Gandi 12 55N 5 49E
33 Ganga, R. 23 22N 90 32E
32 Ganganagar 29 56N 73 56E
33 Gangaw 22 5N 94 15E
33 Ganges, R.= Ganga, R. 23 22N 90 32E
33 Gangtok 27 20N 88 40E
53 Gao 18 0N 1 0E
53 Gaoua 10 20N 3 8W
50 Gaoual 11 45N 13 25W
12 Gap 44 33N 6 5E
79 Garanhuns 8 50S 36 30W
72 Garberville 40 11N 123 50W
57 Garcia 25 32S 32 13E
12 Gard □ 44 2N 4 10E
18 Garda, L. di 45 40N 10 40E
71 Garden City 38 0N 100 45W
31 Gardez 33 31N 68 59E
72 Gardiner 45 3N 110 53W
68 Gardner 42 35N 72 0W
29 Gardo 9 18N 49 20E
72 Garfield 47 3N 117 8W
18 Gargano, Mte. 41 43N 15 40E
52 Garissa 0 25S 39 40E
53 Garkida 10 27N 12 36E
53 Garko 11 45N 8 53E
72 Garland 41 47N 112 10W
24 Garm 39 0N 70 20E
31 Garmsar 35 20N 52 25E
29 Garoe 8 35N 48 40E
12 Garonne, R. 45 2N 0 36W
53 Garoua 9 19N 13 21E
72 Garrison 46 37N 112 56W
70 Garrison Res. 47 30N 102 0W
60 Garry, L. 65 40N 100 0W
62 Garson 50 5N 96 50W
37 Gartok 31 59N 80 30E
35 Garut 7 14S 107 53E
47 Garvie, Mts. 45 27S 169 59E
68 Gary 41 35N 87 20W
78 Garzón 2 10N 75 40W
17 Gascogne, Reg. 43 45N 0 20E
12 Gascogne, G. de 44 0N 2 0W
12 Gascony, Reg.= Gascogne, Reg. 43 45N 0 20E
45 Gascoyne, R. 24 52S 113 37E
45 Gascoyne Junction 25 3S 115 12E
50 Gashaka 7 20N 11 29E
53 Gashua 12 54N 11 0E
63 Gaspé 48 52N 64 30W
63 Gaspé, C. 48 48N 64 7W
63 Gaspé Pass. 49 10N 64 0W
63 Gaspé Pen. 48 45N 65 40W
63 Gaspesian Prov. Park 49 0N 66 45W
69 Gastonia 35 17N 81 10W
80 Gastre 42 10S 69 15W
13 Gata, C. de 36 41N 2 13W
13 Gata, Sa. de 40 20N 6 20W
8 Gatehouse of Fleet 54 53N 4 10W
6 Gateshead 54 57N 1 37W
57 Gaths 26 2S 30 32E
62 Gatineau Nat. Park 45 30N 75 52W
57 Gatooma 18 21S 29 55E
74 Gatun 9 16N 79 55W
74 Gatun L. 9 7N 79 56W
33 Gauhati 26 5N 91 55E
20 Gaula, R. 63 21N 10 14E
31 Gavater 25 10N 61 23E
21 Gavle 60 41N 17 13E
21 Gävleborgs □ 61 20N 16 15E
32 Gawilgarh Hills 21 15N 76 45E
43 Gawler 34 30S 138 42E
33 Gaya, India 24 47N 85 4E
53 Gaya, Nigeria 11 57N 9 0E
43 Gayndah 25 35S 151 39E
28 Gaza 31 30N 34 28E
57 Gaza □ 23 0S 33 0E
28 Gaza Strip 31 29N 34 25E
53 Gazaoua 13 32N 7 55E
30 Gaziantep 37 6N 37 23E
53 Gboko 7 17N 9 4E
53 Gbongan 7 28N 4 20E
57 Gcuwa 32 20S 28 11E
15 Gdańsk 54 22N 18 40E
15 Gdańska, Zatoka 54 30N 19 15E
15 Gdynia 54 35N 18 33E
51 Gebeit Mine 21 3N 36 29E
51 Gedaref 14 2N 35 28E
28 Gedera 31 49N 34 46E
21 Gedser 54 35N 11 55E
46 Geelong 38 2S 144 20E
45 Geelvink, Chan. 28 30S 114 10E
11 Geeraadsbergen 50 45N 3 53E
53 Geidam 12 57N 11 57E
51 Geili 16 1N 32 37E
52 Geita 2 48S 32 12E
18 Gela 37 3N 14 15E
11 Gelderland □ 52 5N 6 10E
11 Geldrop 51 25N 5 32E
11 Geleen 50 57N 5 49E
30 Gelibolu 40 28N 26 43E
14 Gelsenkirchen 51 30N 7 5E
34 Gemas 2 37N 102 36E
11 Gembloux 50 34N 4 43E
54 Gemena 3 20N 19 40E
80 General Acha 37 20S 64 38W
80 General Alvear 36 0S 60 0W
80 General Belgrano 36 0S 58 30W
80 General Guido 36 40S 57 40W
80 General Juan Madariaga 37 0S 57 0W
80 General Paz 27 45S 57 36W
80 General Pico 35 45S 63 50W
80 General Pinedo 27 15S 61 30W
80 General Roca 30 0S 67 40W
80 General Villegas 35 0S 63 0W
14 Geneva, Switz.= Genève 46 12N 6 9E
68 Geneva, U.S.A. 42 53N 77 0W
14 Geneva, L.= Léman, L. 46 26N 6 30E
14 Genève 46 12N 6 9E
13 Genil, R. 37 42N 5 19W
12 Genissiat 46 1N 5 48E
11 Genk 50 58N 5 32E
18 Genoa=Genova 44 24N 8 56E
18 Genova 44 24N 8 56E
18 Génova, G. di 44 0N 9 0E
11 Gent 51 2N 3 37E
45 Geographe, B. 33 30S 115 15E
45 Geographe, Chan. 24 30S 113 0E
56 George 33 58S 22 29E
68 George, L. 43 30N 73 30W
61 George R.=Port Nouveau-Quebec 58 30N 65 50W
42 George Town Australia 41 5S 148 55E
34 George Town, W. Malaysia 5 25N 100 19E
42 Georgetown, Australia 18 17S 143 33E
62 Georgetown, Ont. 43 40N 80 0W
63 Georgetown, P.E.I. 46 13N 62 24W
50 Georgetown, Gambia 13 30N 14 47W
78 Georgetown, Guyana 6 50N 58 12W
69 Georgetown, U.S.A. 33 22N 79 15W
69 Georgia □ 32 0N 82 0W
64 Georgia Str. 49 20N 124 0W
62 Georgian B. 45 15N 81 0W
23 Georgian S.S.R. □ 41 0N 45 0E
23 Georgiu-Dezh 51 3N 39 20E
23 Georgiyevsk 44 12N 43 28E
14 Gera 50 53N 12 5E
45 Geraldton, Australia 28 48S 114 32E
62 Geraldton, Canada 49 44N 86 59W
60 Gerdine, Mt. 61 32N 152 50W
30 Gerede 40 45N 32 10E
29 Gerlogubi 6 53N 45 3E
64 Germansen Landing 55 43N 124 40W
57 Germiston 26 15S 28 5E
36 Gero 35 48N 137 14E
13 Gerona 41 58N 2 46E
12 Gers □ 43 35N 0 38E
12 Gevaudan, Reg. 44 40N 3 40E
72 Geyser 47 17N 110 30W
20 Geysir 64 19N 20 18W
28 Gezer 31 52N 34 55E
33 Ghaghara, R. 25 45N 84 40E
53 Ghana ■ 6 0N 1 0W
50 Ghardaïa 32 31N 3 37E
30 Ghat 24 59N 10 19E
51 Ghazal, Bahr el, R. 9 31N 30 25E
50 Ghazaouet 35 8N 1 50W
32 Ghaziabad 28 42N 77 35E
33 Ghazipur 25 38N 83 35E
31 Ghazni 33 30N 68 17E
31 Ghazni □ 33 0N 68 0E
11 Ghent=Gent 51 2N 3 37E
31 Ghor □ 34 0N 64 20E
62 Ghost River 51 25N 83 20W
50 Ghudames 30 11N 9 29E
32 Ghugus 19 55N 79 15E
32 Ghulam Mohammed Barr. 25 30N 67 0E
31 Ghurian 34 17N 61 25E
14 Giant Mts.= Krkonose 50 50N 16 10E
9 Giant's Causeway 55 15N 6 30W
18 Giarre 37 44N 15 10E
75 Gibara 21 0N 76 20W
55 Gibeon 25 7S 17 45E
13 Gibraltar ■ 36 7N 5 22W
13 Gibraltar, Str. of 35 55N 5 40W
45 Gibson, Des. 24 0S 126 0E
14 Giessen 50 34N 8 40E
36 Gifu 35 30N 136 45E
36 Gifu □ 36 0N 137 0E
74 Giganta, Sa. de la 25 30N 111 30W
8 Gigha, I. 55 42N 5 45W
13 Gijón 43 32N 5 42W
73 Gila, R. 32 43N 114 33W
73 Gila Bend 32 57N 112 43W
30 Gilan □ 37 0N 49 0E
53 Gilbedi 13 40N 5 45E
3 Gilbert Is. 1 0N 176 0E
65 Gilbert Plains 51 9N 100 28W
42 Gilbert River 18 9S 142 50E
45 Gilgai 31 15S 119 56E
46 Gilgandra 31 42S 148 39E
52 Gilgil 0 30S 36 20E
32 Gilgit 35 50N 74 15E
65 Gillam 56 20N 94 40W
42 Gilliat 20 40S 141 28E
7 Gillingham 51 23N 0 34E
62 Gilmour 44 48N 77 37W
73 Gilroy 37 10N 121 37W
42 Gindie 23 45S 148 10E
45 Gingin 31 22S 115 37E
28 Ginnosar 32 51N 35 32E
35 Giong, Teluk, B. 4 50N 118 20E
78 Girardot 4 18N 74 48W
8 Girdle Ness 57 9N 2 2W
30 Giresun 40 45N 38 30E
51 Girga 26 17N 31 55E
33 Giridih 24 10N 86 21E
31 Girishk 31 47N 64 24E
12 Gironde, R. 45 30N 1 0W
12 Gironde □ 44 45N 0 30W
8 Girvan 55 15N 4 50W
47 Gisborne 38 39S 178 5E
52 Gisenyi 1 41S 29 30E
52 Gitega 3 26S 29 56E
15 Giurgiu 43 52N 25 57E
28 Giv'at Olga 32 28N 34 53E
28 Giv'atayim 32 4N 34 49E
51 Giza=El Gîza 30 0N 31 10E
31 Gizhiga 62 0N 150 27E
25 Gizhiginskaya Guba 61 0N 158 0E
15 Gîzycko 54 2N 21 48E
60 Gjoa Haven 68 20N 96 0W
21 Gjøvik 60 47N 10 43E
63 Glace Bay 46 11N 59 58W
64 Glacier B. Nat. Monument 58 45N 136 30W
72 Glacier Nat. Park 48 40N 114 0W
71 Gladewater 32 30N 94 58W
42 Gladstone, Queens. 23 52S 151 16E
43 Gladstone, S. Australia 33 17S 138 22E
65 Gladstone, Canada 50 20N 99 0W
21 Glåma, R. 59 12N 10 57E
8 Glasgow, U.K. 55 52N 4 14W
68 Glasgow, U.S.A. 37 2N 85 55W
7 Glastonbury 51 9N 2 42W
14 Glauchau 50 50N 12 33E
22 Glazov 58 0N 52 30E
64 Gleichen 50 50N 113 0W
8 Glen Affric 57 15N 5 0W
73 Glen Canyon Dam 37 0N 111 25W
73 Glen Canyon Nat. Recreation Area 37 30N 111 0W
8 Glen Coe 56 40N 5 0W
8 Glen Garry 57 3N 5 7W
8 Glen More 57 12N 4 30E
46 Glen Thompson 37 38S 142 35E
46 Glenalbyn 36 30S 143 48E
47 Glenbrook 33 46S 150 37E
57 Glencoe 28 11S 30 11E
57 Glendale 17 22S 31 5E
73 Glendale, Ariz. 33 40N 112 8W
73 Glendale, Calif. 34 7N 118 18W
72 Glendale, Oreg. 42 44N 123 29W

Glendive Guadalajara, Mexico

70 Glendive 47 7N 104 40W
43 Glenelg 34 58S 138 30E
46 Glenelg, R. 38 3S 141 9E
9 Glengariff 51 45N 9 33W
42 Glengyle 24 48S 139 37E
43 Glenn Innes 29 44S 151 44E
46 Glennies Creek 32 30S 151 8E
42 Glenorchy 36 55S 142 41E
42 Glenore 17 50S 141 12E
42 Glenormiston 22 55S 138 50E
72 Glenrock 42 53N 105 55W
8 Glenrothes 56 12N 3 11W
68 Glens Falls 43 20N 73 40W
9 Glenties 54 48N 8 18W
64 Glenwood, Canada 49 21N 113 24W
70 Glenwood, U.S.A. 45 38N 95 21W
72 Glenwood Springs 39 39N 107 15W
15 Gliwice 50 22N 18 41E
73 Globe 33 25N 110 53W
14 Głogów 51 37N 16 5E
57 Glorieuses, Is. 11 30S 47 20E
6 Glossop 53 27N 1 56W
46 Gloucester, Australia 32 0S 151 59E
7 Gloucester, U.K. 51 52N 2 15W
7 Gloucestershire □ 51 44N 2 10W
68 Gloversville 43 5N 74 18W
14 Glückstadt 53 46N 9 28E
14 Gmünd 48 45N 15 0E
14 Gmunden 47 55N 13 48E
15 Gniezno 52 30N 17 35E
45 Gnowangerup 33 58S 117 59E
34 Gô Công 10 12N 107 0E
32 Goa 15 33N 73 59E
32 Goa □ 15 33N 73 59E
53 Goaso 6 48N 2 30W
8 Goat Fell, Mt. 55 37N 5 11W
54 Goba 7 1N 39 59E
56 Gobabis 22 16S 19 0E
38 Gobi, Des. 44 0N 111 0E
33 Godavari, R. 16 37N 82 18E
33 Godavari Pt. 17 0N 82 20E
63 Godbout 49 20N 67 38W
62 Goderich 43 45N 81 41W
75 Golfito 8 41N 83 5W
32 Godhra 22 49N 73 40E
65 Gods L. 54 40N 94 10W
2 Godthåb 64 10N 51 46W
56 Goei Hoop, K.die =Good Hope, C. of 34 24S 18 30E
11 Goeree 51 50N 4 0E
11 Goes 51 30N 3 55E
62 Gogama 47 35N 81 35W
42 Gogango 23 40S 150 2E
51 Gogriâl 8 30N 28 0E
79 Goiânia 16 35S 49 20W
79 Goias □ 12 10S 48 0W
36 Gojo 34 21N 135 42E
32 Gojra 31 10N 72 40E
33 Gokteik 22 26N 97 0E
53 Gold Coast 4 0N 1 40W
64 Golden, Canada 51 20N 117 0W
70 Golden, U.S.A. 39 42N 105 30W
47 Golden B. 40 40S 172 50E
65 Goldfields 37 45N 117 13W
69 Goldsboro 35 24N 77 59W
44 Goldsworthy 20 21S 119 30E
14 Goleniów 53 35N 14 50E
75 Golfito 8 41N 83 5W
18 Golfo Aranci 41 0N 9 38E
8 Golspie 57 58N 3 58W
54 Goma 1 37S 29 10E
53 Gombe 10 19N 11 2E
22 Gomel 52 28N 31 0E
50 Gomera, I. 28 10N 17 5W
74 Gómez Palacio 25 40N 104 40W
31 Gonābād 34 15N 58 45E
75 Gonaïves 19 20N 72 50W
33 Gonda 27 9N 81 58E
51 Gonder 12 23N 37 30E
32 Gondia 21 30N 80 10E
28 Gonen 33 7N 35 39E
56 Gongola, R. 9 30N 12 10E
53 Goniri 11 30N 12 15E
52 Gonja 4 15S 38 0E
71 Gonzales 29 30N 97 30W
56 Good Hope, C. of 34 24S 18 30E
6 Goole 53 42N 0 52W
46 Goolgowi 33 58S 154 39E
45 Goomalling 31 19S 116 49E
43 Goondiwindi 28 30S 150 21E
11 Goor 52 13N 6 33E
63 Goose Bay 53 15N 60 20W
32 Gop 22 5N 69 50E
33 Gorakhpur 26 47N 83 32E
75 Gorda, Pta. 14 10N 83 10W
70 Gordon 42 49N 102 6W
45 Gordon River 34 10S 117 15E
56 Gordonia, Reg. 28 13S 21 10E
42 Gordonvale 17 5S 145 50E
43 Gore, Australia 28 17S 151 29E
54 Gore, Ethiopia 8 12N 35 32E
47 Gore, N.Z. 46 5S 168 58E
9 Gorey 52 41N 6 18W
78 Gorgona, I. 3 0N 78 10W
23 Goris 39 31N 46 23E
18 Gorízia 45 56N 13 37E
22 Gorki=Gorkiy 56 20N 44 0E
22 Gorkiy 56 20N 44 0E
22 Gorkovskoye Vdkhr 57 2N 43 4E
14 Görlitz 51 10N 14 59E
23 Gorlovka 48 25N 37 58E
19 Gorna Oryakhovitsa 43 7N 25 40E
24 Gorno Filinskoye 60 5N 70 0E
22 Gornyatski 67 49N 64 20E
35 Gorontalo 0 35N 123 13E
53 Goronyo 13 29N 5 39E
9 Gort 53 4N 8 50W
22 Goryn, R. 52 8N 27 17E
14 Gorzów Wielkopolski 52 43N 15 15E
46 Gosford 33 23S 151 18E
68 Goshen 41 36N 85 46W
14 Goslar 51 55N 10 23E
18 Gospič 44 35N 15 23E
7 Gosport 50 48N 1 8W
21 Göta kanal 58 45N 14 15E
21 Göteborg 57 43N 11 59E
21 Göteborgs och Bohus □ 58 30N 11 30E
14 Gotha 50 56N 10 42E
21 Gothenburg= Göteborg 57 43N 11 59E
21 Gotland, I. 57 30N 18 30E
21 Götland, Reg. 58 0N 14 0E
36 Gōtsu 35 0N 132 14E
14 Göttingen 51 31N 9 55E
15 Gottwaldov 49 14N 17 40E
11 Gouda 52 1N 4 42E
2 Gough, I. 40 10S 9 45W
62 Govin Res. 48 35N 74 40W
46 Goulburn 32 22S 149 31E
53 Goundam 16 25N 3 45W
51 Gounou-Gaya 9 38N 15 31E
75 Governor's Harbour 25 10N 76 14W
7 Gower, Pen. 51 35N 5 10W
80 Goya 29 10S 59 10W
18 Gozo, I. 36 0N 14 13E
56 Graaff-Reinet 32 13S 24 32E
18 Gračac 44 18N 15 57E
75 Gracias a Dios, C. 15 0N 83 20W
13 Grado 45 40N 13 20E
43 Grafton, Australia 29 35S 152 0E
70 Grafton, U.S.A. 48 30N 97 25W
62 Graham, Canada 49 20N 90 30W
69 Graham, N.C. 36 5N 79 22W
71 Graham, Tex. 33 7N 98 38W
64 Graham I. 53 40N 132 30W
2 Graham Ld. 65 0S 64 0W
65 Grahamdale 51 30N 98 34W
56 Grahamstown 33 19S 26 31E
48 Grain Coast, Reg. 4 20N 10 0W
79 Grajaú 5 50S 46 30W
8 Grampian □ 57 20N 2 45W
8 Grampian Highlands, Mts. 56 50N 4 0W
50 Gran Canaria, I. 27 55N 15 35W
80 Gran Chaco, Reg. 25 0S 61 0W
18 Gran Paradiso, Mt. 49 33N 7 17E
18 Gran Sasso d'Italia, Mts. 42 25N 13 30E
75 Granada, Nic. 11 58N 86 0W
13 Granada, Sp. 37 10N 3 35W
9 Granard 53 47N 7 30W
62 Granby 45 25N 72 45W
75 Grand Bahama I. 26 40N 78 30W
63 Grand Bank 47 6N 55 48W
50 Grand Bassam 5 10N 3 49W
75 Grand Bourg 15 53N 61 19W
73 Grand Canyon 36 10N 112 45W
73 Grand Canyon Nat. Park 36 15N 112 20W
75 Grand Cayman, I. 19 20N 81 20W
72 Grand Coulee Dam 48 0N 118 50W
63 Grand Falls 47 2N 67 46W
64 Grand Forks, Canada 49 0N 118 30W
70 Grand Forks, U.S.A. 48 0N 97 3W
68 Grand Haven 43 3N 86 13W
70 Grand Island 40 59N 98 25W
73 Grand Junction 39 0N 108 30W
50 Grand Lahou 5 10N 5 0W
70 Grand Marais 47 45N 90 25W
62 Grand' Mère 46 36N 72 40W
65 Grand Rapids, Canada 53 12N 99 19W
68 Grand Rapids, Mich. 42 57N 85 40W
70 Grand Rapids, Minn. 47 19N 93 29W
14 Grand St-Bernard, Col. du 45 53N 7 11E
72 Grand Teton, Mt. 43 45N 110 57W
80 Grande, B. 50 30S 68 20W
66 Grande, R. 25 57N 97 9W
63 Grand Baie 48 19N 70 52W
63 Grande-Entrée 47 30N 61 40W
64 Grande Prairie 55 15N 118 50W
63 Grande Rivière 48 26N 64 30W
8 Grangemouth 56 1N 3 43W
72 Grangeville 45 57N 116 4W
70 Granite City 38 45N 90 3W
47 Granity 41 39S 171 51E
79 Granja 3 17S 40 50W
13 Granollers 41 39N 2 18E
6 Grantham 52 55N 0 39W
8 Grantown-on-Spey 57 19N 3 36W
73 Grants 35 14N 107 57W
72 Grants Pass 42 30N 123 22W
72 Grantsville 40 35N 112 32W
12 Granville, France 48 50N 1 35W
68 Granville, U.S.A. 43 24N 73 16W
57 Graskop 24 56S 30 49W
72 Grass Valley 39 18N 121 0W
12 Grasse 43 38N 6 56E
65 Gravelbourg 49 50N 105 35W
62 Gravenhurst 44 52N 79 20W
43 Gravesend, Australia 29 35S 150 20E
7 Gravesend, U.K. 51 25N 0 22E
7 Grays 51 28N 0 23E
65 Grayson 50 45N 102 40W
14 Graz 47 4N 15 27E
75 Great Abaco I. 26 15N 77 10W
42 Great Australian Basin 24 30S 143 0E
45 Great Australian Bight 33 30S 130 0E
75 Great Bahama Bank 23 15N 78 0W
47 Great Barrier I. 37 12S 175 25E
42 Great Barrier Reef 19 0S 149 0E
72 Great Basin 40 0N 116 30W
60 Great Bear L. 65 0N 120 0W
70 Great Bend 38 25N 98 55W
51 Great Bitter Lake 30 15N 32 40E
9 Great Blasket, I. 52 5N 10 30W
56 Great Bushman Land 29 20S 19 0E
46 Great Divide, Mts. 23 0S 146 0E
42 Great Dividing Range 25 0S 147 0E
75 Great Exuma I. 23 30N 75 50W
72 Great Falls 47 27N 111 12W
57 Great Fish, R. 33 30S 27 8E
75 Great Inagua I. 21 0N 73 20W
32 Great Indian Des. 28 0N 72 0E
34 Great L.= Tonlé Sap 13 0N 104 0E
56 Great Namaqualand= Groot Namaqualand 26 0S 18 0E
6 Great Orme's Hd. 53 20N 3 52W
6 Great Ouse, R. 52 47N 0 22E
58 Great Plains 42 0N 100 0W
52 Great Ruaha, R. 7 56S 37 52E
72 Great Salt L. 41 0N 112 30W
72 Great Salt Lake Des. 40 20N 113 50W
44 Great Sandy Des. 21 0S 124 0E
64 Great Slave L. 61 30N 114 20W
69 Great Smoky Mt. Nat. Park 35 39N 83 30W
45 Great Victoria Des. 29 30S 126 30E
62 Great Whale, R. 55 20N 77 45E
62 Great Whale River=Poste de la Baleine 55 20N 77 40E
6 Great Whernside, Mt. 54 9N 1 59W
6 Great Yarmouth 52 40N 1 45E
75 Greater Antilles 20 0N 74 0W
6 Greater Manchester □ 53 35N 2 15W
34 Greater Sunda Is. 4 30S 113 0E
13 Gredos, Sa. de 40 20N 5 0W
19 Greece ■ 40 0N 23 0E
70 Greeley 40 30N 104 40W
68 Green Bay 44 30N 88 0W
68 Green B. 45 0N 87 30W
47 Green Island 45 54S 170 27E
73 Green River, Utah 39 0N 110 10W
72 Green River, Wyo. 41 32N 109 28W
68 Greencastle 39 40N 86 48W
69 Greeneville 31 50N 86 38W
68 Greenfield, Ind. 39 47N 85 51W
68 Greenfield, Mass. 42 38N 72 38W
2 Greenland ■ 66 0N 45 0W
8 Greenock 55 57N 4 45W
9 Greenore 54 2N 6 8W
45 Greenough, R. 28 51S 114 38E
69 Greensboro 36 7N 79 46W
68 Greensburg, Ind. 39 20N 85 30W
68 Greensburg, Pa. 40 18N 79 31W
50 Greenville, Liberia 5 7N 9 6W
68 Greenville, Mich. 43 12N 85 14W
71 Greenville, Miss. 33 25N 91 0W
69 Greenville, N.C. 35 37N 77 26W
68 Greenville, Pa. 41 23N 80 22W
69 Greenville, S.C. 34 54N 82 24W
71 Greenville, Tex. 33 5N 96 5W
7 Greenwich, U.K. 51 28N 0 0
71 Greenwood, Miss. 33 30N 90 4W
69 Greenwood, S.C. 34 13N 82 13W
42 Gregory Downs 18 35S 138 45E
44 Gregory L. 20 10S 127 30E
14 Greifswalder Bodden 54 12N 13 35E
22 Gremikha 67 50N 39 40E
71 Grenada 33 45N 89 50W
75 Grenada, I. 12 10N 61 40W
46 Grenfell 33 52S 148 8E
21 Grenen, C. 57 46N 10 34E
12 Grenoble 45 12N 5 42E
35 Gresik 9 13S 112 38E
71 Gretna 30 0N 90 2W
8 Gretna Green 55 0N 3 3W
11 Grevenmacher 49 41N 6 26E
47 Grey, R. 42 27S 171 12E
63 Grey Res. 48 20N 56 30W
72 Greybull 44 30N 108 3W
47 Greymouth 42 29S 171 13E
47 Greytown, N.Z. 41 5S 175 29E
57 Greytown, S. Africa 29 1S 30 36E
72 Gridley 39 27N 121 47W
56 Griekwastad 28 49S 23 15E
69 Griffin 33 15N 84 16W
46 Griffith 34 14S 145 46E
65 Griffith Mine 50 47N 93 25W
6 Grimsby 53 35N 0 5W
20 Grimsey, I. 66 33N 18 0W
64 Grimshaw 56 10N 117 40W
21 Grimstad 58 22N 8 35E
70 Grinnell 41 45N 92 50W
57 Griqualand East, Reg. 30 30S 29 0E
56 Griqualand West, Reg. 28 40S 23 30E
12 Gris Nez, C. 50 50N 1 35E
57 Groblersdal 25 15S 29 25E
22 Grodno 53 42N 23 52E
14 Grodzisk Mãzowiecki 52 7N 20 37E
20 Grong 64 25N 12 8E
11 Groningen 53 15N 6 35E
11 Groningen □ 53 16N 6 40E
56 Groot-Brakrivier 34 2S 22 18E
56 Groot Karasberge, Mts. 27 10S 18 45E
56 Groot Karoo, Reg. 32 35S 23 0E
57 Groot Kei, R. 32 41S 28 22E
55 Groot Namakwaland= Namaland, Reg. 26 0S 18 0E
56 Groot Winterberg, Mt. 32 45S 26 50E
42 Groote Eylandt, I. 14 0S 136 50E
56 Grootfontein 19 31S 18 6E
14 Gross Glockner, Mt. 47 5N 12 40E
18 Grosseto 42 45N 11 7E
68 Groveton 44 34N 71 30W
23 Groznyy 43 20N 45 45E
15 Grudziądz 53 30N 18 47E
22 Gryazi 52 30N 39 58E
33 Gua 22 13N 85 20E
80 Guachípas 25 40S 65 30W
75 Guacanayabo, G. de 20 40N 77 20W
74 Guadalajara, Mexico 20 40N 103 20W

Hauts-de-Seine □ Hualien

12 Hauts-de-Seine □ . 48 52N 2 15 E
75 Havana=
La Habana 23 0N 82 41W
7 Havant 50 51N 0 59W
14 Havel, R. .... 52 53N 11 58 E
62 Havelock 44 26N 77 53W
47 Havelock North ... 39 42S 176 53 E
7 Haverfordwest 51 48N 4 59W
68 Haverhill 42 50N 71 2W
7 Havering .... 51 33N 0 20 E
14 Havlíckuv Brod ... 49 36N 15 33 E
72 Havre 48 40N 109 34W
63 Havre St. Pierre ... 50 18N 63 33W
30 Havza .... 41 0N 35 35 E
66 Hawaii □ 20 0N 155 0W
66 Hawaii, I. 20 0N 155 0W
47 Hawea, L. .... 44 28S 169 19 E
47 Hawera .... 39 35S 174 19 E
8 Hawick 55 25N 2 48W
62 Hawk Junction 48 5N 84 35W
47 Hawke, B. .... 39 25S 177 20 E
43 Hawker .... 31 59S 138 22 E
47 Hawke's Bay □ ... 39 45S 176 35 E
63 Hawke's Harbour . 53 2N 55 50W
63 Hawkesbury,
Nova Scotia 45 40N 61 10W
62 Hawkesbury, Ont. . 45 35N 74 40W
72 Hawthorne 38 37N 118 47W
46 Hay, Australia .... 34 30S 144 51 E
7 Hay, U.K. 52 4N 3 9W
64 Hay River 60 50N 115 50W
73 Hayden 40 30N 107 22W
42 Haydon .... 18 0S 141 30 E
60 Hayes, Mt. 63 37N 146 43W
65 Hayes, R. 57 3N 92 9W
7 Hayling I. 50 40N 1 0W
70 Hays 38 55N 99 25W
7 Haywards Heath .. 51 0N 0 5W
31 Hazārān,
Kūh-e, Mt. ..... 29 35N 57 20 E
68 Hazard 37 18N 83 10W
33 Hazaribagh .... 23 58N 85 26 E
64 Hazelton 55 20N 127 42W
68 Hazleton 40 58N 76 0W
28 Hazor .... 33 2N 35 2 E
31 Hazrat Imam ..... 37 15N 68 50 E
57 Headlands .... 18 15S 32 2 E
72 Healdsburg 38 33N 122 51W
6 Heanor 53 1N 1 20W
3 Heard I. .... 53 0S 74 0 E
62 Hearst 49 40N 83 41W
63 Heart's Content ... 47 54N 53 27W
63 Heath Steele 46 48N 66 20W
43 Hebel .... 28 59S 147 48 E
63 Hebertville 47 0N 71 30W
8 Hebrides, Inner, Is. 57 20N 6 40W
8 Hebrides, Outer, Is. 57 50N 7 25W
61 Hebron, Canada .. 58 10N 62 50W
28 Hebron, Jordan ... 31 32N 35 6 E
64 Hecate Str. 53 10N 130 30W
52 Hedaru .... 4 30S 37 54 E
20 Hede .... 62 22N 13 43 E
21 Hedemora .... 60 18N 15 48 E
21 Hedmark □ .... 61 45N 11 0 E
11 Heemstede .... 52 19N 4 37 E
11 Heerde .... 52 24N 6 2 E
11 Heerenveen ...... 52 57N 5 55 E
11 Heerlen .... 50 55N 6 0 E
56 Heidelberg,
C. Prov. .... 34 6S 20 59 E
57 Heidelberg, Trans. . 26 30S 28 23 E
14 Heidelberg,
W. Germ. ...... 49 23N 8 41 E
57 Heilbron .... 27 16S 27 59 E
14 Heilbronn .... 49 8N 9 13 E
38 Heilungkiang □ ... 47 30N 129 0 E
21 Heinola .... 61 13N 26 10 E
65 Heinsburg 53 50N 110 30W
33 Heinze Is. .... 14 25N 97 45 E
20 Hekla, Mt. 63 56N 19 35W
71 Helena, Ark. 34 30N 90 35W
72 Helena, Mont. 46 40N 112 0W
8 Helensburgh 56 0N 4 44W
47 Helensville .... 36 41S 174 29 E
28 Helez .... 31 36N 34 39 E
14 Heligoland, I. ..... 54 10N 7 51 E
55 Hell-Ville .... 13 25S 48 16 E
11 Hellendoorn ...... 52 24N 6 27 E
13 Hellín 38 31N 1 40W
31 Helmand, Hamun . 31 0N 61 0 E
31 Helmand □ .... 31 0N 64 0 E
31 Helmand, R. ...... 31 12N 61 34 E
11 Helmond .... 51 29N 5 41 E
8 Helmsdale 58 7N 3 40W
21 Helsingborg ...... 56 3N 12 42 E
21 Helsingfors=
Helsinki .... 60 15N 25 3 E
21 Helsingør .... 56 2N 12 35 E
21 Helsinki .... 60 15N 25 3 E
7 Helston 50 7N 5 17W
6 Helvellyn, Mt. 54 31N 3 1W
51 Helwân .... 29 50N 31 20 E
7 Hemel
Hempstead 51 45N 0 28W
68 Hempstead 40 42N 73 37W
21 Hemse .... 57 15N 18 20 E
13 Henares, R. 40 24N 3 30W
13 Hendaye 43 23N 1 47W
68 Henderson, Ky. 37 50N 87 38W
69 Henderson, N.C. ... 36 18N 78 23W
71 Henderson, Tex. .. 32 5N 94 49W
69 Hendersonville 35 21N 82 28W
43 Hendon .... 28 5S 151 50 E
56 Hendrik Verwoerd
Dam .... 30 38S 25 30 E
11 Hengelo .... 52 15N 6 48 E
39 Hengyang .... 26 57N 112 28 E
62 Henrietta Maria, C. 55 10N 82 30W
54 Henrique de
Carvalho .... 9 39S 20 24 E
71 Henryetta 35 2N 96 0W
46 Henty .... 35 30N 147 0 E
33 Henzada .... 17 38N 95 35 E
72 Heppner 45 27N 119 34W
31 Herat .... 34 20N 62 7 E
31 Herat □ .... 34 20N 62 7 E
12 Hérault □ .... 43 34N 3 15 E
65 Herbert 50 30N 107 10W
42 Herbert Downs ... 23 0S 139 11 E
19 Hercegnovi .... 42 30N 18 33 E
19 Hercegovina □ .... 43 20N 18 0 E
7 Hereford, U.K. 52 4N 2 42W
71 Hereford, U.S.A. .. 34 50N 102 28W
7 Hereford and
Worcester □ 52 14N 1 42W
11 Herentals .... 51 12N 4 51 E
14 Herford .... 52 7N 8 40 E
56 Hermanus .... 34 27S 19 12 E
46 Hermidale .... 31 30S 146 42 E
72 Hermiston 45 50N 119 16W
47 Hermitage .... 43 44S 170 5 E
80 Hermite, I. 55 50S 68 0W
30 Hermon, Mt.=
Sheikh, Jabal ash 33 20N 26 0 E
74 Hermosillo 29 10N 111 0W
15 Hernad R. .... 47 56N 21 8 E
7 Herne Bay .... 51 22N 1 8 E
21 Herning .... 56 8N 9 0 E
62 Heron Bay 48 40N 85 25W
30 Herowabad .... 37 37N 48 32 E
13 Herrera del
Duque 39 10N 5 3W
71 Herrin 37 50N 89 0W
11 Herstal .... 50 40N 5 38 E
7 Hertford 51 47N 0 4W
7 Hertford □ 51 51N 0 5W
28 Herzliyya .... 32 10N 34 50 E
14 Hessen □ .... 50 57N 9 20 E
61 Hewett, C. 70 30N 68 0W
6 Hexham 54 58N 2 7W
6 Heysham 54 5N 2 53W
46 Heywood .... 38 8S 141 37 E
70 Hibbing 47 30N 93 0W
69 Hickory 35 46N 81 17W
36 Hida Sammyaku,
Mts. .... 36 0N 137 10 E
74 Hidalgo □ 20 30N 99 10W
74 Hidalgo del Parral . 26 10N 104 50W
50 Hierro, I. 27 57N 17 56W
39 Hifung .... 22 59N 115 17 E
36 Higashiōsaka ..... 34 39N 135 35 E
45 Higginsville ...... 31 42S 121 38 E
52 High Lava Plat. ... 3 40N 36 45 E
69 High Point 35 57N 79 58W
64 High Prairie 55 30N 116 30W
64 High River 50 30N 113 50W
7 High Wycombe ... 51 37N 0 45W
48 High Veld .... 26 30S 30 0 E
8 Highland □ 57 30N 4 50W
68 Highland Park, Ill. . 42 10N 87 50W
68 Highland Park,
Mich. 42 25N 83 6W
30 Hijāz, Reg. .... 26 0N 37 30 E
36 Hikari .... 33 58N 131 56 E
36 Hikone .... 35 15N 136 10 E
47 Hikurangi .... 37 54S 178 5 E
14 Hildersheim ...... 52 9N 9 55 E
11 Hillegom .... 52 18N 4 35 E
7 Hillingdon 51 33N 0 29W
70 Hillsboro, Kan. ... 38 28N 97 10W
72 Hillsboro, Oreg. ... 45 31N 123 0W
71 Hillsboro, Tex. 32 0N 97 10W
62 Hillsport 49 27N 85 34W
46 Hillston .... 33 30S 145 31 E
66 Hilo 19 44N 155 5W
11 Hilversum .... 52 14N 5 10 E
32 Himachal
Pradesh □ ...... 31 30N 77 0 E
26 Himalaya, Mts. .... 29 0N 84 0 E
32 Himatnagar .... 23 36N 72 58 E
36 Himeji .... 34 50N 134 40 E
36 Himi .... 36 50N 137 0 E
30 Hims=Homs ...... 34 40N 36 45 E
42 Hinchinbrook, I. .. 18 20S 146 15 E
7 Hinckley 52 33N 1 21W
46 Hindmarsh, L. .... 35 50S 141 55 E
32 Hindubagh .... 30 56N 67 57 E
31 Hindukush, Mts. .. 36 0N 71 0 E
32 Hindupur .... 13 49N 77 32 E
64 Hines Creek 56 20N 118 40W
39 Hingan .... 25 39N 110 43 E
38 Hingcheng .... 40 21N 120 10 E
72 Hingham 48 40N 110 29W
37 Hingi .... 25 4N 105 2 E
39 Hingning .... 24 2N 115 55 E
32 Hingoli .... 19 41N 77 15 E
39 Hingwa Wan, G. .. 25 0N 120 0 E
20 Hinnoy, I. .... 68 40N 16 28 E
64 Hinton, Canada ... 53 26N 117 28W
68 Hinton, U.S.A. 37 40N 80 51W
33 Hirakud Dam ..... 21 32N 83 45 E
36 Hiratsuka .... 35 40N 139 36 E
36 Hirosaki .... 40 35N 140 25 E
36 Hiroshima .... 34 30N 132 30 E
36 Hiroshima □ ...... 34 30N 133 0 E
75 Hispaniola, I. 19 0N 71 0W
32 Hissar .... 29 12N 75 45 E
36 Hita .... 33 42N 130 52 E
36 Hitachi .... 36 40N 140 35 E
7 Hitchin 51 57N 0 16W
36 Hitoyoshi .... 32 13N 130 45 E
20 Hitra, I. .... 63 30N 8 45 E
21 Hjälmaren, L. ..... 59 18N 15 40 E
21 Hjørring .... 57 29N 9 59 E
53 Ho .... 6 37N 0 27 E
64 Hoadley 52 45N 114 30W
34 Hoai Nhon .... 14 28N 103 37 E
42 Hobart, Australia . 42 50S 147 21 E
71 Hobart, U.S.A. ... 35 0N 99 5W
71 Hobbs 32 40N 103 3W
11 Hoboken .... 51 11N 4 21 E
21 Hobro .... 56 39N 9 46 E
39 Hichih .... 24 43N 107 43 E
39 Hochwan .... 30 0N 106 15 E
36 Hodaka-Dake, Mt. 36 20N 137 30 E
29 Hodeida .... 14 50N 43 0 E
65 Hodgson 51 20N 97 40W
15 Hódmezővásárhely 46 28N 20 22 E
50 Hodna, Chott el ... 35 30N 5 0 E
14 Hodonin .... 48 50N 17 0 E
11 Hoek van Holland . 52 0N 4 7 E
57 Hoëveld .... 26 30S 30 0 E
39 Hofei .... 31 45N 116 36 E
36 Hōfu .... 34 0N 130 30 E
50 Hoggar=
Ahaggar, Mts. .. 23 0N 6 30 E
38 Hohpi .... 35 59N 114 13 E
52 Hoima .... 1 26N 31 21 E
38 Hokang .... 47 36N 130 28 E
38 Hokien .... 38 30N 116 2 E
47 Hokitika .... 42 42S 171 0 E
36 Hokkaidō □ ...... 43 30N 143 0 E
36 Hokkaidō, I. ...... 43 30N 143 0 E
37 Hokow .... 22 39N 103 57 E
38 Holan Shan .... 38 40N 105 50 E
46 Holbrook,
Australia .... 35 42S 147 18 E
73 Holbrook, U.S.A. .. 35 0N 110 0W
71 Holdenville 35 5N 96 25W
6 Holderness, Pen. .. 53 45N 0 5W
75 Holguín 20 50N 76 20W
55 Hollams Bird I. ... 24 40S 14 30 E
11 Holland ■=
Netherlands ■ .. 52 0N 5 30 E
68 Holland 42 47N 86 0W
35 Hollandia=
Jayapura .... 2 28N 140 38 E
73 Hollywood, Calif. . 34 0N 118 10W
68 Hollywood, Fla. ... 26 0N 80 9W
60 Holman Island 70 43N 117 43W
20 Holmsund .... 63 41N 20 20 E
28 Holon .... 32 2N 34 47 E
21 Holstebro .... 56 22N 8 33 E
60 Holy Cross 62 12N 159 47W
6 Holy, I., Eng. 55 42N 1 48W
6 Holy, I., Wales 53 17N 4 37W
6 Holyhead 53 18N 4 38W
68 Holyoke 42 14N 72 37W
33 Homalin .... 24 55N 95 0 E
53 Hombori .... 15 20N 1 38 E
42 Home Hill .... 19 43S 147 25 E
72 Homedale 43 42N 116 59W
60 Homer 59 40N 151 35W
42 Homestead .... 20 20S 145 40 E
30 Homs .... 34 40N 36 45 E
39 Honan □ .... 33 50N 113 15 E
78 Honda 5 12N 74 45W
53 Hohoe .... 7 8N 0 32 E
55 Hondeklipbaai .... 30 19S 17 17 E
74 Hondo, R. 19 26N 99 13W
75 Honduras ■ 14 40N 86 30W
74 Honduras, G. de .. 16 50N 87 0W
21 Hønefoss .... 60 10N 10 12 E
12 Honfleur .... 49 25N 0 10 E
37 Hongha, R. .... 22 0N 104 0 E
39 Hong Kong ■ ..... 22 11N 114 14 E
7 Honiton 50 48N 3 11W
66 Honolulu 21 19N 157 52W
36 Honshū, I. .... 36 0N 138 0 E
45 Hood, Pt. .... 34 23S 119 34 E
11 Hoogeveen .... 52 44N 6 30 E
11 Hoogezand .... 53 11N 6 45 E
33 Hooghly, R. ...... 21 56N 88 4 E
9 Hook Hd. 52 8N 6 57W
64 Hoonah 58 15N 135 30W
68 Hoopeston 40 30N 87 40W
11 Hoorn .... 52 38N 5 4 E
73 Hoover Dam 36 0N 114 45W
64 Hope, Canada .... 49 25N 121 25 E
71 Hope, U.S.A. 33 40N 93 30W
60 Hope, Pt. 68 20N 166 40W
75 Hope Town 26 30N 76 30W
56 Hopefield .... 33 3S 18 22 E
38 Hopei □ .... 39 25N 116 45 E
56 Hopetown .... 29 34S 24 3 E
46 Hopetoun, Vic. ... 35 48S 142 25 E
45 Hopetoun,
W. Australia .... 33 54S 120 6 E
68 Hopkinsville 36 52N 87 26W
39 Hoppo .... 21 32N 109 6 E
72 Hoquiam 47 0N 123 55W
21 Hordaland □ ..... 60 25N 6 45 E
31 Hormoz .... 27 35N 55 0 E
31 Hormoz, Jazireh-ye 27 4N 56 28 E
31 Hormoz, Kūh-e ... 27 40N 55 30 E
31 Hormuz, Str. of ... 26 30N 56 30 E
14 Horn .... 48 39N 15 40 E
80 Horn, C.=
Hornos, C. de ... 55 50S 67 30W
6 Horncastle 53 13N 0 8W
68 Hornell 42 23N 77 41W
62 Hornepayne 49 14N 84 48W
80 Hornos, C. de 55 50S 67 30W
46 Hornsby .... 33 42S 151 2 E
6 Hornsea 53 55N 0 10W
80 Horqueta 23 15S 56 55W
21 Horsens .... 55 52N 9 51 E
46 Horsham,
Australia .... 36 44S 142 13 E
7 Horsham, U.K. ... 51 4N 0 20W
21 Horten .... 59 25N 10 32 E
32 Hoshangabad ..... 22 45N 77 44 E
32 Hoshiarpur .... 31 30N 75 58 E
32 Hospet .... 15 15N 76 20 E
13 Hospitalet de
Llobregat .... 41 21N 2 6 E
80 Hoste, I. 55 0S 69 0W
60 Hot Springs, Alas. . 64 55N 150 10W
71 Hot Springs, Ark. . 34 30N 93 0W
70 Hot Springs, S.D. . 43 25N 103 30W
37 Hotien .... 37 6N 79 59 E
20 Hoting .... 64 8N 16 15 E
6 Houghton-le-
Spring 54 51N 1 28W
47 Houhora .... 34 49S 173 9 E
69 Houlton 46 5N 68 0W
71 Houma 29 35N 90 50W
8 Hourne, L. 57 7N 5 35W
71 Houston 29 50N 5 20W
7 Hove 50 50N 0 10W
38 Hövsgöl Nuur, L. .. 51 0N 100 30 E
43 Howard .... 25 16S 152 32 E
45 Howatharra .... 28 29S 114 33 E
46 Howe, C. .... 37 30S 150 0 E
57 Howick .... 29 28S 30 14 E
33 Howrah .... 22 37N 88 27 E
9 Howth Hd. 53 21N 6 0W
8 Hoy, I. 58 50N 3 15W
21 Høyanger .... 61 25N 6 50 E
14 Hradec Králové ... 50 15N 15 50 E
15 Hron, R. .... 47 49N 18 45 E
18 Hrvatska □ .... 45 20N 16 0 E
33 Hsenwi .... 23 22N 97 55 E
39 Hsiamen .... 24 28N 118 7 E
39 Hsian=Sian .... 34 2N 109 0 E
39 Hsiao Shan .... 34 0N 111 30 E
39 Hsinchow .... 19 37N 109 17 E
39 Hsinchu .... 24 55N 121 0 E
39 Hsuchang .... 34 2N 114 0 E
39 Hsüchou=Suchow . 34 10N 117 20 E
78 Huacho 11 10S 77 35W
39 Hualien .... 24 0N 121 30 E

Huancane Irshih

78 Huancane 15 10s 69 50w
78 Huancavelica 12 50s 75 5w
78 Huancayo 12 5s 75 0w
39 Huangliu 18 30N 108 46E
78 Huánuco 9 55s 76 15w
78 Huaraz 9 30s 77 32w
78 Huascarán, Mt. 9 0s 77 30w
80 Huasco 28 24s 71 15w
74 Huatabampo 26 50N 109 50w
32 Hubli 15 22N 75 15E
39 Huchow 30 57N 120 1E
74 Huchuetenango 15 25N 91 30w
6 Huddersfield 53 38N 1 49w
21 Hudiksvall 61 43N 17 10E
68 Hudson 42 15N 73 46w
68 Hudson, R. 40 42N 74 2w
61 Hudson B. 60 0N 86 0w
68 Hudson Falls 43 18N 73 34w
64 Hudson Hope 56 0N 121 54w
61 Hudson Str. 62 0N 70 0w
34 Hué 16 30N 107 35E
13 Huelva 37 18N 6 57w
13 Huesca 42 8N 0 25w
42 Hughenden 20 52s 144 10E
45 Hughes, Australia 30 40s 129 30E
60 Hughes, U.S.A. 66 3N 154 16w
38 Huhehot 40 52N 111 36E
78 Huila, Mt. 3 0N 76 0w
39 Huiling Shan, I. 21 35N 111 57E
80 Huinca Renancó 34 51s 64 22w
74 Huixtla 15 9N 92 28w
33 Hukawng Valley 26 30N 96 30E
39 Hukow 29 38N 116 25E
38 Hulan 46 0N 126 44E
28 Hūlda 31 50N 34 51E
38 Hulin 45 45N 133 0E
62 Hull, Canada 45 20N 75 40w
6 Hull, U.K. 53 45N 0 20w
6 Hull, R. 53 44N 0 19w
38 Huma 51 44N 126 42E
38 Huma, R. 51 40N 126 44E
80 Humahuaca 23 10s 65 25w
78 Humaitá 7 35s 62 40w
56 Humansdorp 34 2s 24 46E
6 Humber, R. 53 32N 0 8E
6 Humberside □ 53 45N 0 20w
65 Humboldt, Canada 52 15N 105 9w
71 Humboldt, U.S.A. 35 50N 88 55w
72 Humboldt, R. 40 2N 118 31w
51 Hūn 29 2N 16 0E
20 Hunaflói, B. 65 50N 21 0w
39 Hunan □ 27 30N 111 30E
38 Hunchun 42 49N 130 31E
15 Hunedoara 45 40N 22 50E
39 Hung Ho, R. 33 0N 117 0E
15 Hungary ■ 47 20N 19 20E
39 Hunghai Wan, G. 20 30N 115 0E
39 Hungshui Ho, R. 23 70N 110 30E
39 Hunghu 29 49N 113 30E
39 Hungkiang 27 0N 109 49E
38 Hungnam 39 59N 127 40E
39 Hungtze Hu, L. 33 20N 118 35E
56 Hunsberge 27 45s 17 12E
14 Hunsruck, Mts. 50 0N 7 30E
6 Hunstanton 52 57N 0 30E
45 Hunter, R. 32 50s 151 40E
47 Hunterville 39 56s 175 35E
62 Huntingdon, Canada 45 10N 74 10w
7 Huntingdon, U.K. 52 20N 0 11w
68 Huntingdon, U.S.A. 40 28N 78 1w
68 Huntington, Ind. 40 52N 85 30w
68 Huntington, W. Va. 38 20N 82 30w
73 Huntington Beach 34 40N 118 0w
73 Huntington Park 33 58N 118 15w
47 Huntly, N.Z. 37 34s 175 11E
8 Huntly, U.K. 57 27N 2 48w
62 Huntsville, Canada 45 20N 79 14w
69 Huntsville, Ala. 34 45N 86 35w
71 Huntsville, Tex. 30 50N 95 35w
42 Huonville 43 0s 147 5E
39 Hupei □ 31 5N 113 5E
70 Huron 44 30N 98 20w
68 Huron, L. 45 0N 83 0w
73 Hurricane 37 10N 113 12w
47 Hurunui, R. 42 54s 173 18E
20 Húsavik 66 3N 17 13w
21 Huskvarna 57 47N 14 15E
28 Hussein Bridge 31 53N 35 33E
38 Hutag 49 25N 102 34E
71 Hutchinson 38 3N 97 59w
28 Huwarā 32 9N 35 15E
11 Huy 50 31N 5 15E
18 Hvar, I. 43 11N 16 28E
20 Hvítá, R., Iceland 63 50N 21 0w
20 Hvítá, R., Iceland 64 40N 22 0w
39 Hwainan 32 44N 117 1E
38 Hwang Ho, R. 37 32N 118 19E
39 Hwangshih 30 27N 115 0E
39 Hweian 25 2N 118 56E
37 Hweitseh 26 32N 103 6E
38 Hwo Shan, Mts. 37 0N 112 30E
38 Hwohsien 36 30N 111 42E
68 Hyannis 42 3N 101 45w
37 Hyargas Nuur, L. 49 0N 92 30E
64 Hydaburg 55 15N 132 45w
45 Hyden 32 24s 118 46E
32 Hyderabad, India 17 10N 78 29E
32 Hyderabad, Pak. 25 23N 68 36E
32 Hyderabad □ 25 3N 68 24E
12 Hyères 43 8N 6 9E
12 Hyères, Îs. d' 43 0N 6 28E
72 Hyndman Pk. 44 4N 114 0w
36 Hyōgo □ 35 15N 135 0E
72 Hyrum 41 35N 111 56w
7 Hythe 51 4N 1 5E
21 Hyvinkää 60 38N 25 0E

I

57 Iakora 23 6s 46 40E
15 Ialomiţa, R. 44 42N 27 51E
15 Iaşi 47 10N 27 40E
78 Iaurête 0 30N 69 5w
53 Ibadan 7 22N 3 58E
78 Ibagué 4 27N 73 14w
19 Ibar, R. 43 43N 20 45E
78 Ibarra 0 21N 78 7w
29 Ibb 14 1N 44 10E
4 Iberian Pen. 40 0N 5 0w
62 Iberville 5 19N 73 17w
80 Ibicuy 33 55s 59 10w
13 Ibiza 38 54N 1 26E
13 Ibiza, I. 39 0N 1 30E
35 Ibonma 3 22s 133 31E
36 Ibusuki 31 16N 130 39E
78 Icá 14 0s 75 30w
78 Içana 0 21N 67 19w
35 Iceland ■ 65 0N 19 0w
25 Icha 55 30N 156 0E
39 Ichang 30 48N 111 29E
33 Ichchapuram 19 10N 84 40E
36 Ichihara 35 35N 140 6E
36 Ichinomiya 35 20N 136 50E
38 Ichun 47 42N 129 8E
53 Idah 6 10N 6 40E
72 Idaho □ 44 10N 114 0w
72 Idaho Falls 43 30N 112 10w
72 Idaho Springs 39 49N 105 30w
51 Idd el Ghanam 11 30N 24 25E
51 Idehan Marzúq 24 50N 13 51E
51 Idfû 25 0N 32 49E
34 Idi 4 55N 97 45E
52 Idi Amin Dada, L. 0 25s 29 40E
30 Idlip 35 55N 36 38E
28 Idna 31 34N 34 58E
57 Idutywa 32 8s 28 18E
11 Ieper 50 51N 2 53E
52 Ifakara 8 10s 36 35E
57 Ifanadiana 21 29s 47 39E
53 Ife 7 30N 4 31E
53 Ifon 6 58N 5 40E
79 Igarapava 20 3s 47 47w
79 Igarapé Açu 1 4s 47 33w
25 Igarka 67 30N 87 20E
32 Igawa 8 45s 34 23E
53 Igbetti 8 44N 4 8E
53 Igbo-Ora 7 10N 3 15E
53 Igboho 8 40N 3 50E
53 Igbor 7 30N 8 32E
21 Iggesund 61 39N 17 10E
18 Iglésias 39 19N 8 27E
61 Igloolik Island 69 20N 81 30w
65 Ignace 49 30N 91 40w
80 Iguaçu, R. 25 30s 53 10w
80 Iguaçu Falls 25 40s 54 33w
74 Iguala 18 20N 99 40w
13 Igualada 41 37N 1 37E
80 Iguape 24 43s 47 33w
79 Iguatu 6 20s 39 18w
53 Ihiala 5 40N 6 55E
57 Ihosy 22 24s 46 8E
38 Ihsien 41 45N 121 3E
36 Iida 35 35N 138 0E
20 Iisalmi 63 32N 27 10E
36 Iizuka 33 38N 130 42E
53 Ijebu-Igbo 6 56N 4 1E
53 Ijebu-Ode 6 47N 3 52E
11 Ijmuiden 52 28N 4 35E
11 Ijsel, R. 52 30N 6 0E
11 Ijsselmeer, L. 52 45N 5 20E
19 Ikaría, I. 37 35N 26 10E
36 Ikeda 34 1N 133 48E
27 Ikeja 6 28N 3 45E
53 Ikerre-Ekiti 7 25N 5 19E
36 Iki, I. 33 45N 129 42E
53 Ikire 7 10N 4 15E
53 Ikom 6 0N 8 42E
53 Ikot Ekpene 5 12N 7 40E
53 Ikurun 7 55N 4 41E
53 Ila 8 0N 4 51E
35 Ilagan 17 9N 121 53E
38 Ilan 46 14N 129 33E
25 Ilanskiy 56 14N 96 3E
53 Ilaro 6 53N 3 3E
42 Ilbilbie 21 45s 149 20E
12 Île de France, Reg. 49 0N 2 20E
54 Ilebo 4 17s 20 47E
53 Ilero 8 0N 3 20E
53 Ilesha 8 57N 3 28E
42 Ilfracombe, Australia 23 30s 144 30E
7 Ilfracombe, U.K. 51 13N 4 8w
80 Ilha Grande, B. da. 23 10s 44 30w
79 Ilhéus 15 0s 39 10w
60 Iliamna L. 59 30N 155 0w
60 Iliamna, Mt. 60 5N 153 9w
24 Ilich 41 0N 68 10E
68 Ilion 43 0N 75 3w
24 Iliysk=Kapchagai 44 10N 77 20E
6 Ilkeston 52 59N 1 19w
38 Ilkhuri Shan, Mts. 51 30N 124 0E
80 Illapel 32 0s 71 10w
12 Ille-et-Vilaine □ 48 10 1 30w
78 Illimani, Mt. 16 30s 67 50w
70 Illinois, R. 38 58N 90 27w
70 Illinois □ 40 15N 89 30w
50 Illizi 26 31N 8 32E
22 Ilmen, Oz. 58 15N 31 10E
78 Ilo 17 40s 71 20w
53 Ilobu 7 45N 4 25E
35 Iloilo 10 45N 122 33E
52 Ilongero 4 45s 34 55E
53 Ilora 7 45N 3 50E
53 Ilorin 8 30N 4 35E
35 Ilwaki 7 55s 126 30E
36 Imabari 34 4N 133 0E
25 Iman 45 50N 133 40E
22 Imandra, Oz. 67 45N 33 0E
36 Imari 33 15N 129 52E
6 Immingham 53 37N 0 12w
53 Imo □ 4 15N 7 30E
18 Imola 44 20N 11 42E
79 Imperatriz 5 30s 47 29w
18 Impéria 43 52N 8 0E
65 Imperial, Canada 51 21N 105 28w
73 Imperial, U.S.A. 32 52N 115 34w
73 Imperial Dam 32 50N 114 30w
54 Impfondo 1 40N 18 0E
33 Imphal 24 15N 94 0E
28 Imwas 31 51N 34 59E
50 In Salah 27 10N 2 32E
47 Inangahua Junction 41 52s 171 59E
20 Inari 68 54N 27 5E
20 Inari, L. 69 0N 28 0E
13 Inca 39 43N 2 54E
38 Inchŏn 37 32N 126 45E
33 Indaw 24 15N 96 5E
71 Independence, Kans. 37 10N 95 50w
70 Independence, Mo. 39 3N 94 25w
72 Independence, Oreg. 44 53N 123 6w
32 India ■ 23 0N 77 30E
64 Indian Cabin 59 50N 117 12w
65 Indian Head 50 30N 103 35w
1 Indian Ocean 5 0s 75 0E
68 Indiana 40 38N 79 9w
68 Indiana □ 40 0N 86 0w
68 Indianapolis 39 42N 86 10w
70 Indianola 41 20N 93 38w
22 Indiga 67 50N 48 50E
34 Indonesia ■ 5 0s 115 0E
32 Indore 22 42N 75 53E
35 Indramaju 6 21s 108 20E
32 Indravati, R. 18 43N 80 17E
12 Indre □ 46 45N 1 30E
12 Indre-et-Loire □ 47 12N 0 40E
32 Indus, R. 24 20N 67 47E
30 Inebolu 41 55N 33 40E
30 Inegöl 40 5N 29 31E
62 Ingersoll 43 4N 80 55w
42 Ingham 18 43s 146 10E
6 Ingleborough, Mt. 54 11N 2 23w
43 Inglewood, N.S.W. 28 25s 151 8E
46 Inglewood, Vic. 36 29s 143 53E
47 Inglewood, N.Z. 39 9s 174 14E
73 Inglewood 33 58N 118 27w
14 Ingolstadt 48 45N 11 26w
23 Ingulec 47 42N 33 4E
57 Inhambane 23 54s 35 30E
57 Inhambane □ 22 30s 34 20E
55 Inharrime 24 30s 35 0E
39 Ining, Kwangsi-Chuang 25 8N 109 57E
37 Ining Sinkiang-Uigur 43 57N 81 20E
9 Inishmore, I. 53 8N 9 45w
9 Inishowen, Pen. 55 14N 7 15w
36 Inland Sea= Setonaikai 34 10N 133 10E
14 Inn, R. 48 35N 13 28E
38 Inner Mongolian Autonomous Rep. □ 44 50N 117 40E
42 Innisfail, Australia 17 33s 146 5E
64 Innisfail, Canada 52 0N 114 0w
14 Innsbruck 47 16N 11 23E
15 Inowrocław 52 50N 18 20E
45 Inscription, C. 25 29s 112 59E
33 Insein 16 46N 96 18E
22 Inta 66 2N 60 8E
14 Interlaken 46 41N 7 50E
70 International Falls 48 30N 93 25w
80 Intiyaco 28 50s 60 0w
80 Inútil, B. 53 30s 70 15w
60 Inuvik 68 25N 133 30w
8 Inveraray 56 13N 5 5w
8 Inverbervie 56 50N 2 17w
47 Invercargill 46 24s 168 24E
43 Inverell 29 48s 151 36E
8 Invergordon 57 41N 4 10w
64 Invermere 50 51N 116 9w
63 Inverness, Canada 46 15N 61 19w
8 Inverness, U.K. 57 29N 4 12w
8 Inverurie 57 15N 2 21w
44 Inverway 17 50s 129 38E
43 Investigator, Str. 35 30s 137 0E
57 Inyangani, Mt. 18 20s 32 20E
73 Inyokern 35 37N 117 54w
22 Inza 53 55N 46 25E
19 Ioánnina 39 42N 20 55E
71 Iola 38 0N 95 20w
8 Iona, I. 56 20N 6 25w
68 Ionia 42 59N 85 7w
19 Ionian Is.= Iónioi Nísoi 38 40N 20 8E
19 Ionian Sea 37 30N 17 30E
19 Iónioi Nísoi, Is. 38 40N 20 8E
19 Íos, I. 36 41N 25 20E
70 Iowa □ 42 18N 93 30w
70 Iowa City 41 40N 91 35w
70 Iowa Falls 42 30N 93 15w
79 Ipameri 17 44s 48 9w
78 Ipiales 1 0N 77 45w
37 Ipin 28 58N 104 45E
19 Ipiros □ 39 30N 20 30E
34 Ipoh 4 36N 101 4E
43 Ipswich, Australia 27 38s 152 37E
7 Ipswich, U.K. 52 4N 1 9E
79 Ipu 4 23s 40 44w
78 Iquique 20 19s 70 5w
78 Iquitos 3 45s 73 10w
79 Iracoubo 53 .N 53 10w
19 Iráklion 35 20N 25 12E
31 Iran ■ 33 0N 53 0E
26 Iran, Plat. of 32 0N 57 0E
31 Iranshahr 27 75N 60 40E
74 Irapuato 20 40N 101 40w
30 Iraq ■ 33 0N 44 0E
28 Irbid 32 35N 35 48E
75 Ireland, I., Bermuda 32 19N 64 50w
9 Ireland, I., Europe 53 0N 8 0w
53 Irele 7 40N 5 40E
25 Iret 60 10N 154 5E
38 Iri 35 59N 127 0E
35 Irian Jaya □ 5 0s 140 0E
51 Iriba 15 7N 22 15E
52 Iringa 7 48s 33 43E
79 Iriri, R. 3 52s 52 37w
9 Irish Republic ■ 53 0N 8 0E
10 Irish Sea 54 0N 145 12E
25 Irkineyeva 58 30N 96 49E
25 Irkutsk 52 10N 104 20E
70 Iron Mountain 45 49N 88 4w
7 Ironbridge 52 38N 2 29w
68 Ironton 38 35N 82 40w
70 Ironwood 46 30N 90 10w
62 Iroquois Falls 48 40N 80 40w
33 Irrawaddy, R. 15 50N 95 6E
38 Irshih 47 8N 119 57E

Jyekundo Keeling Is. = Cocos Is.

37 Jyekundo 33 0N 96 50 E
21 Jylland, Reg. 56 25N 9 30 E
20 Jyväskylä 62 12N 25 47 E

K

32 K2, Mt. 36 0N 77 0 E
55 Kaap Plato 28 30s 24 0 E
56 Kaapstad= Cape Town 33 55s 18 22 E
35 Kabaena, I. 5 15s 122 0 E
52 Kabale 9 38N 11 37w
54 Kabalo 6 0s 27 0 E
54 Kabambare 4 41s 27 39 E
54 Kabarega Falls 2 15s 31 38 E
52 Kabarnet 0 35N 35 50 E
53 Kabba 7 57N 6 3 E
54 Kabinda 6 23s 24 38 E
54 Kabongo 7 22s 25 33 E
42 Kabra 23 25s 150 25 E
31 Kabul 34 28N 69 18 E
31 Kabul □ 34 0N 68 30 E
55 Kabwe 14 30s 28 29 E
33 Kachin □ 26 0N 97 0 E
24 Kachiry 53 10N 75 50 E
52 Kachung 1 48N 32 50 E
34 Kadan Kyun 12 30N 98 20 E
53 Kade 6 7N 0 56w
43 Kadina 34 0s 137 43 E
23 Kadiyerka 48 35N 38 30 E
53 Kaduna 10 30N 7 21 E
53 Kaduna □ 11 0N 7 30 E
53 Kaelé 10 15N 14 15 E
32 Kaerh 31 45N 80 22 E
50 Kaesŏng 37 58N 126 35 E
53 Kafanchan 9 40N 8 20 E
52 Kafulwe 9 0s 29 1 E
51 Kafia Kingi 9 20N 24 25 E
19 Kafirévs, Akra 38 9N 24 8 E
28 Kafr Kanna 32 45N 35 20 E
28 Kafr Ra'i 32 23N 35 9 E
55 Kafue, R. 15 56s 28 55 E
52 Kafulwe 9 0s 29 1 E
24 Kagan 39 43N 64 33 E
36 Kagawa □ 34 15N 134 0 E
36 Kagoshima 31 36N 130 40 E
36 Kagoshima □ 30 0N 130 0 E
52 Kahama 4 8s 32 30 E
52 Kahe 3 30s 37 25 E
35 Kai, Kep 5 55s 132 45 E
47 Kaiapoi 42 24s 172 40 E
39 Kaifeng 34 50N 114 27 E
47 Kaikohe 35 25s 173 49 E
47 Kaikoura 42 25s 173 43 E
66 Kailua 21 24N 157 44w
53 Kainji Res. 10 1N 4 40 E
47 Kaipara, Harbour 36 25s 174 14 E
38 Kaiping 40 28N 122 10 E
50 Kairouan 35 45N 10 5 E
14 Kaiserslautern 49 30N 7 43 E
47 Kaitaia 35 8s 173 17 E
47 Kaitangata 46 17s 169 51 E
38 Kaiyuan 42 33N 124 4 E
20 Kajaani 64 17N 27 46 E
52 Kajiado 1 53s 36 48 E
52 Kakamega 0 20N 34 46 E
36 Kake 34 6N 132 19 E
36 Kakegawa 34 45N 138 1 E
23 Kakhovka 46 46N 34 28 E
33 Kakinada= Cocanada 16 50N 82 11 E
36 Kakogawa 34 46N 134 51 E
53 Kala 12 2N 14 40 E
32 Kalabagh 33 0N 71 28 E
35 Kalabahi 8 13s 124 31 E
19 Kalabáka 39 42N 21 39 E
23 Kalach 50 22N 41 0 E
33 Kaladan, R. 20 9N 92 57 E
56 Kalahari, Des. 24 0s 22 0 E
25 Kalakan 55 15N 116 45 E
19 Kalamata 37 3N 22 10 E
68 Kalamazoo 42 20N 85 35w
45 Kalamunda 32 0s 116 0 E
30 Kalan 39 7N 39 32 E
45 Kalannie 30 22s 117 5 E
32 Kalat 29 8N 66 31 E
31 Kalat-i-Ghilzai 32 15N 66 58 E
52 Kalemie 5 55s 29 9 E
33 Kalewa 22 41N 95 32 E
45 Kalgoorlie 30 40s 121 22 E
19 Kaliakra, Nos. 43 21N 28 30 E
35 Kalibo 11 43N 122 22 E
34 Kalimantan □ 0 0 115 0 E
19 Kálimnos, I. 37 0N 27 0 E
22 Kalinin 56 55N 35 55 E
22 Kaliningrad 54 44N 20 32 E
72 Kalispell 48 10N 114 22 E
15 Kalisz 53 17N 15 55 E
52 Kaliua 5 5s 31 48 E
28 Kallia 31 46N 35 30 E
53 Kalmalo 13 40N 5 20 E
21 Kalmar 56 40N 16 20 E
21 Kalmar □ 57 25N 16 15 E
23 Kalmyk A.S.S.R. □ 46 5N 46 1 E
24 Kalmykovo 49 0N 51 35 E
15 Kalocsa 46 32N 19 0 E
56 Kalomo 17 0s 26 30 E
60 Kaltag 64 20N 158 44w
56 Kaltungo 9 48N 11 19 E
22 Kaluga 54 35N 36 10 E
21 Kalundborg 55 41N 11 5 E
22 Kama, R. 55 45N 52 0 E
52 Kamachumu 1 37s 31 37 E
36 Kamaishi 39 20N 142 0 E
29 Kamaran, I. 15 28N 42 35 E
52 Kamba 11 50N 3 45 E
45 Kambalda 31 10s 121 37 E
22 Kambarka 56 17N 54 12 E
25 Kamchatka Pol. 57 0N 160 0 E
52 Kamembe 2 29s 28 54 E
24 Kamen 53 50N 81 30 E
23 Kamenets Podolskiy 48 40N 26 30 E
22 Kamenka 65 58N 44 0 E
23 Kamensk Shakhtinskiy 48 23N 40 20 E
24 Kamensk Uralskiy 56 28N 61 54 E
25 Kamenskoye 62 45N 165 30 E
36 Kameoka 35 0N 135 35 E
54 Kamina 8 45s 25 0 E
64 Kamloops 50 40N 120 20w
52 Kampala 0 20N 32 30 E
11 Kampen 52 33N 5 53 E
34 Kampot 10 36N 104 10 E
34 Kampuchea ■ = Cambodia ■ 12 15N 105 0 E
65 Kamsack 51 35N 101 50w
22 Kamskoye Vdkhr. 58 0N 56 0 E
23 Kamyshin 50 10N 45 30 E
39 Kan Kiang, R. 29 45N 116 10 E
73 Kanab 27 3N 112 29w
54 Kananga 5 55s 22 18 E
22 Kanash 55 48N 47 32 E
36 Kanazawa 36 30N 136 38 E
34 Kanchanaburi 14 8N 99 31 E
33 Kanchenjunga, Mt. 27 50N 88 10 E
32 Kanchipuram 12 52N 79 45 E
39 Kanchow 25 51N 114 59 E
38 Kanchwan 36 29N 109 24 E
24 Kandagach 49 20N 57 15 E
31 Kandahar 31 32N 65 30 E
31 Kandahar □ 31 0N 65 0 E
22 Kandalaksha 67 9N 32 30 E
22 Kandalakshskiy Zaliv 66 0N 35 0 E
34 Kandangan 2 50s 115 20 E
47 Kandavu, I. 19 0s 178 15 E
53 Kandi, Benin 11 7N 2 55 E
32 Kandi, India 23 58N 88 5 E
32 Kandy 7 42N 80 37 E
68 Kane 41 39N 78 53w
58 Kane Basin 79 0N 70 0w
34 Kangar 6 27N 100 12 E
43 Kangaroo, I. 35 45s 137 0 E
30 Kangāvar 34 40N 48 0 E
38 Kangnŭng 37 45N 128 54 E
39 Kangshan 22 43N 120 14 E
37 Kangsu □ 38 0N 101 40 E
33 Kangto, Mt. 27 50N 92 35 E
22 Kanin, Pol. 68 0N 45 0 E
46 Kaniva 36 22s 141 18 E
68 Kankakee 41 6N 87 50w
68 Kankakee, R. 41 23N 88 16w
50 Kankan 10 30N 9 15w
69 Kannapolis 35 32N 80 37w
53 Kano 12 2N 8 30 E
53 Kano □ 12 0N 8 30 E
36 Kanoya 31 23N 130 51 E
33 Kanpetlet 21 10N 93 59 E
32 Kanpur 26 35N 80 20 E
32 Kanrach 25 35N 65 20 E
70 Kansas, R. 39 7N 94 36w
70 Kansas □ 38 40N 98 0w
70 Kansas City, Kans. 39 0N 94 40w
70 Kansas City, Mo. 39 3N 94 30w
25 Kansk 56 20N 96 37 E
53 Kantché 13 31N 8 30 E
36 Kantō □ 36 0N 120 0 E
37 Kantse 31 30N 100 29 E
9 Kanturk 52 10N 8 55w
36 Kanuma 36 44N 139 42 E
56 Kanye 25 0s 25 28 E
39 Kanyu 34 53N 119 9 E
39 Kaohsiung 22 35N 120 16 E
56 Kaokoveld 19 0s 13 0 E
50 Kaolack 14 5N 16 8w
38 Kaomi 36 25N 119 45 E
38 Kaoping 35 48N 112 55 E
39 Kaoyu Hu, L. 32 50N 119 25 E
18 Kapela, Ra. 45 0N 15 15 E
14 Kapfenberg 47 26N 15 18 E
55 Kapiri Mposha 13 59s 28 43 E
31 Kapisa □ 34 45N 69 30 E
56 Kapps 22 32s 17 18 E
52 Kapsabet 0 14N 35 5 E
34 Kapuas, R. 0 25s 109 24 E
43 Kapunda 34 20s 138 56 E
62 Kapuskasing 49 25N 82 30w
43 Kaputar, Mt. 30 15s 130 10 E
52 Kaputir 2 5N 35 28 E
24 Kara 69 10N 65 25 E
24 Kara Bogaz Gol, Zaliv 41 0N 53 30 E
24 Kara Kalpak A.S.S.R. □ 43 0N 59 0 E
24 Kara Sea 75 0N 70 0 E
30 Karabük 41 12N 32 37 E
24 Karabutak 49 59N 60 14 E
32 Karachi □ 25 30N 67 0 E
32 Karad 17 54N 74 10 E
30 Karadeniz Bogaži 41 10N 29 5 E
30 Karadeniz Dağlari, Mts. 41 30N 35 0 E
24 Karaganda 49 50N 73 0 E
24 Karagayly 49 26N 76 0 E
32 Karaikkudi 10 0N 78 45 E
31 Karaj 35 4N 51 0 E
24 Karakas 48 20N 83 30 E
38 Karakorum, Mts. 35 20N 76 0 E
32 Karakoram P. 35 33N 77 46 E
30 Karaköse 39 44N 43 3 E
25 Karalon 57 5N 115 50 E
34 Karambu 3 53s 116 6 E
56 Karasburg 28 0s 18 44 E
24 Karasino 66 50N 86 50 E
20 Karasjok 69 27N 25 30 E
24 Karasuk 53 44N 78 2 E
24 Karatau 43 10N 70 28 E
24 Karatau Ra. 44 0N 69 0 E
36 Karatsu 33 30N 130 0 E
18 Karawanken, Mts. 46 30N 14 40 E
24 Karazhal 48 2N 70 49 E
30 Karbalā 32 47N 44 3 E
15 Karcag 47 19N 21 1 E
56 Kareeberge 30 50s 22 0 E
22 Karelian A.S.S.R. □ 65 30N 32 30 E
24 Kargasok 59 3N 80 53 E
24 Kargat 55 10N 80 15 E
32 Kargil 34 32N 76 12 E
22 Kargopol 61 30N 38 58 E
57 Kariba L. 16 40s 28 25 E
32 Karikal 10 59N 79 50 E
53 Karima 18 30N 21 40 E
34 Karimata, Selat, Str. 2 0s 108 20 E
32 Karimnagar 18 26N 79 10 E
36 Kariya 34 58N 137 1 E
24 Karkaralinsk 49 30N 75 10 E
23 Karkinitskiy Zaliv 45 36N 32 35 E
28 Karkur 32 29N 34 57 E
14 Karl-Marx-Stadt 50 50N 12 55 E
18 Karlovac 45 31N 15 36 E
14 Karlovy Vary 50 13N 12 51 E
21 Karlsborg 58 33N 14 33 E
21 Karlshamn 56 10N 14 51 E
21 Karlskoga 59 22N 14 33 E
21 Karlskrona 56 10N 15 35 E
14 Karlsruhe 49 3N 8 23 E
21 Karlstad 59 23N 13 30 E
60 Karluk 57 30N 155 0w
32 Karnal 29 42N 77 2 E
33 Karnaphuli Res. 22 40N 92 20 E
32 Karnataka □ 13 15N 77 0 E
14 Karnische Alpen, Mts. 46 36N 13 0 E
14 Kärnten □ 46 52N 13 30 E
54 Karonga 9 57s 33 55 E
43 Karoonda 35 1s 139 59 E
19 Kárpathos, I. 35 37N 27 10 E
22 Karpogory 63 59N 44 27 E
30 Kars 40 40N 43 5 E
24 Karsakpay 47 55N 66 40 E
24 Karshi 38 53N 65 48 E
24 Kartaly 53 3N 60 40 E
52 Karumo 2 25s 32 50 E
52 Karungu 0 50s 34 10 E
32 Karur 10 59N 78 2 E
32 Karwar 14 44N 74 5 E
54 Kasai, R. 3 2s 16 57 E
52 Kasama 10 16s 31 9 E
54 Kasangulu 4 15s 15 15 E
32 Kasaragod 12 30N 74 58 E
52 Kasenyi 1 24N 30 26 E
52 Kasese 0 13N 30 3 E
31 Kāshān 34 5N 5130¼
37 Kashgar 39 46N 75 52 E
39 Kashing 30 45N 120 41 E
27 Kashmir □ 34 0N 78 0 E
22 Kasimov 54 55N 41 20 E
64 Kaslo 49 55N 117 0w
54 Kasongo 4 30s 26 33 E
19 Kásos, I. 35 20N 26 55 E
51 Kassala 15 23N 36 26 E
51 Kassalâ □ 15 20N 36 26 E
14 Kassel 51 19N 9 32 E
35 Kassue 6 58s 139 21 E
30 Kastamonu 41 25N 33 43 E
52 Kasulu 4 37s 30 5 E
32 Kasur 31 5N 74 25 E
25 Kata 58 46N 102 40 E
54 Katako Kombe 3 25s 24 20 E
49 Katanga, Reg.= Shaba, Reg. 8 30s 25 0 E
45 Katanning 33 40s 117 33 E
33 Katha 24 10N 96 30 E
44 Katherine 14 27s 132 20 E
32 Kathiawar, Reg. 22 0N 71 0 E
34 Katiet 2 21s 99 14 E
33 Katihar 25 34N 87 36 E
56 Katima Mulilo 17 28s 24 13 E
60 Katmai Mt. 58 20N 154 59w
33 Katmandu 27 45N 85 12 E
55 Katombora 18 0s 25 30 E
54 Katompi 6 2s 26 23 E
46 Katoomba 33 41s 150 19 E
15 Katowice 50 17N 19 5 E
8 Katrine, L. 56 15N 4 30 E
21 Katrineholm 59 9N 16 12 E
53 Katsina 7 10N 9 20 E
31 Kattawaz Urgan □ 32 10N 62 20 E
21 Kattegat, Str. 57 0N 11 20 E
11 Katwijk-aan-Zee 52 12N 4 22 E
66 Kauai, I. 19 30N 155 30w
56 Kaukauveld 20 0s 20 15 E
20 Kaukonen 67 42N 24 58 E
22 Kaunas 54 54N 23 54 E
53 Kaura Namoda 12 37N 6 33 E
20 Kautokeino 69 0N 23 4 E
25 Kavacha 60 16N 169 51 E
19 Kavála 40 57N 24 28 E
79 Kaw 4 30N 52 15w
36 Kawagoe 35 55N 139 29 E
36 Kawaguchi 35 52N 138 45 E
66 Kawaihae 20 5N 155 50w
52 Kawambwa 9 48s 29 3 E
36 Kawanoe 34 1N 133 34 E
36 Kawasaki 35 35N 138 42 E
62 Kawene 48 45N 91 15w
47 Kawerau 38 7s 176 42 E
47 Kawhia Harbour 38 4s 174 49 E
33 Kawnro 22 48N 99 8 E
34 Kawthaung 10 5N 98 36 E
33 Kawthoolei □ 18 0N 97 30 E
53 Kaya 13 25N 1 10w
33 Kayah □ 19 15N 97 15 E
52 Kayambi 9 28s 31 59 E
73 Kayenta 36 46N 110 15 E
50 Kayes 14 25N 11 30w
43 Kayrunnera 30 40s 142 30 E
30 Kayseri 38 45N 35 30 E
34 Kayuagung 3 28s 104 46 E
25 Kazachye 70 52N 135 58 E
24 Kazakh S.S.R. □ 50 0N 58 0 E
22 Kazan 55 48N 49 3 E
19 Kazanlŭk 42 38N 25 35 E
23 Kazbek, Mt. 42 30N 44 30 E
31 Kāzerūn 29 38N 51 40 E
24 Kazym, R. 63 54N 65 50 E
19 Kéa, I. 37 30N 24 22 E
70 Kearney 40 45N 99 3w
20 Kebnekaise, Mt. 67 48N 18 30 E
29 Kebri Dehar 6 45N 44 17w
35 Kebumen 7 42s 109 40 E
15 Kecskemet 46 57N 19 35 E
63 Kedgwick 47 40N 67 20w
35 Kediri 7 51s 112 -1 E
3 Keeling Is.= Cocos Is. 12 12s 96 54 E

Keelung = Chilung Kishangarh

39 Keelung=Chilung 25 3N 121 45E
68 Keene 42 57N 72 17W
56 Keetmanshoop 26 35S 18 8E
65 Keewatin 47 23N 93 0W
60 Keewatin, Reg. 63 20N 94 40W
19 Kefallinía, I. 38 28N 20 30E
35 Kefamenanu 9 28S 124 38E
28 Kefar Gil'adi 33 14N 35 35E
28 Kefar Sava 32 11N 34 54E
28 Kefar Szold 33 11N 35 34E
28 Kefar Tavor 32 42N 35 24E
28 Kefar Vitkin 32 22N 34 53E
28 Kefar Yona 32 20N 34 54E
28 Kefar Zetim 32 49N 35 27E
53 Keffi 8 55N 7 43E
20 Keflavík 64 2N 22 35W
6 Keighley 53 52N 1 54W
56 Keimoes 28 41S 21 0E
53 Keita 14 46N 5 46E
43 Keith, Australia 36 0S 140 20E
8 Keith, U.K. 57 33N 2 58W
60 Keith Arm, B. 65 30N 122 0W
25 Kël 69 30N 124 10E
34 Kelang 3 2N 101 26E
51 Kelibia 36 50N 11 3E
45 Kellerberrin 31 36S 117 38E
72 Kellogg 47 30N 116 5W
9 Kells=Ceanannas Mor 53 42N 6 53W
64 Kelowna 49 50N 119 25W
64 Kelsey Bay 50 25N 126 0W
47 Kelso, N.Z. 45 54S 169 15E
8 Kelso, U.K. 55 36N 2 27W
72 Kelso, U.S.A. 46 10N 122 57W
34 Keluang 2 3N 103 18E
65 Kelvington 52 20N 103 30W
22 Kem 65 0N 34 38E
22 Kem, R. 64 57N 34 41E
24 Kemerovo 55 20N 85 50E
20 Kemi 65 47N 24 32E
20 Kemijärvi 66 43N 27 22E
20 Kemijoki, R. 65 47N 24 30E
72 Kemmerer 41 52N 110 30W
43 Kempsey 31 1S 152 50E
14 Kempten 47 42N 10 18E
62 Kemptville 45 0N 75 38W
8 Ken, R. 54 50N 4 4W
35 Kendal, Indonesia 6 56S 110 14E
6 Kendal, U.K. 54 19N 2 44W
35 Kendari 3 50S 122 30E
53 Kende 11 30N 4 12E
45 Kendenup 34 30S 117 38E
60 Kendi 60 30N 151 0W
33 Kendrapara 20 35N 86 30E
50 Kenema 7 50N 11 14W
33 Keng Tawng 20 45N 98 18E
33 Keng Tung 21 0N 99 30E
38 Kenho 50 43N 121 30E
50 Kenitra 34 15N 6 40W
9 Kenmare 51 52N 9 35W
69 Kennedy, C.= Canaveral, C. 28 28N 80 31W
7 Kennet, R. 51 28N 0 57W
71 Kennett 36 7N 90 0W
72 Kennewick 46 11N 119 2W
60 Keno Hill 63 57N 135 25W
65 Kenora 49 50N 94 35W
68 Kenosha 42 33N 87 48W
63 Kensington 46 25N 63 34W
68 Kent 41 8N 81 20W
7 Kent □ 51 12N 0 40E
60 Kent Pen. 68 30N 107 0W
24 Kentau 43 32N 68 36E
68 Kenton 40 40N 83 35W
68 Kentucky, R. 38 41N 85 11W
68 Kentucky □ 37 20N 85 0W
63 Kentville 45 6N 64 29W
52 Kenya ■ 2 20N 38 0E
54 Kenya, Mt. 0 10S 37 18E
70 Keokuk 40 25N 91 30W
19 Kephallinia, I.= Kefallinía, I. 38 28N 20 30E
32 Kerala □ 11 0N 76 15E
46 Kerang 35 40S 143 55E
31 Keray 26 15N 57 30E
23 Kerch 45 20N 36 20E
28 Kerem Maharal 32 39N 34 59E
3 Kerguelan, I. 48 15S 69 10E
52 Kericho 0 22S 35 15E
34 Kerinci, Mt. 2 5S 101 0E
51 Kerkenna, Is. 34 48N 11 1E
24 Kerki 37 10N 65 0E
19 Kérkira 39 38N 19 50E
19 Kérkira, I. 39 35N 19 45E
11 Kerkrade 50 53N 6 4E
2 Kermadec Is. 31 8S 175 16W
31 Kermān 30 15N 57 1E
31 Kermān □ 30 0N 57 0E
30 Kermānshāh 34 23N 47 0E
30 Kermānshāh □ 34 0N 46 30E
71 Kermit 31 56N 103 3W
52 Kerripi 3 55N 31 52E
65 Kerrobert 52 0N 109 11W
71 Kerrville 30 1N 99 8W
9 Kerry □ 52 7N 9 35W
9 Kerry Hd. 52 26N 9 56W
38 Kerulen, R. 48 48N 117 0E
50 Kerzaz 29 29N 1 25W
20 Keski-Suomen □ 63 0N 25 0E
57 Kestell 28 17S 28 42E
6 Keswick 54 35N 3 9W
53 Keta 5 49N 1 0E
53 Keta Lagoon 5 50N 1 0E
34 Ketapang 1 55S 110 0E
64 Ketchikan 55 25N 131 40W
53 Kete Krachi 7 55N 0 1W
15 Kętrzyn 54 7N 21 22E
7 Kettering 52 24N 0 44W
72 Kettle Falls 48 41N 118 2W
70 Kewanee 41 18N 90 0W
70 Keweenaw B. 47 0N 88 0W
70 Keweenaw Pt. 47 26N 87 40W
67 Key West 24 40N 82 15W
68 Keyser 39 26N 79 0W
25 Kezhma 59 15N 100 57E
24 Khabarovo 69 30N 60 30E
25 Khaborovsk 48 20N 135 0E
33 Khairagarh 21 27N 81 2E
32 Khairpur 27 32N 68 49E
31 Khalij-e Fars 28 20N 51 45E
19 Khalkís 38 27N 23 42E
22 Khalmer Yu 67 58N 65 1E
22 Khalturin 58 40N 48 50E
56 Khamas Country 21 45S 26 30E
29 Khamir 16 10N 43 45E
37 Khan Tengri, Mt. 42 25N 80 10E
28 Khān Yūnis 31 21N 34 18E
31 Khanabad 36 45N 69 5E
30 Khānaqin 34 23N 45 25E
33 Khandwa 21 49N 76 22E
25 Khandyga 62 30N 134 50E
32 Khanewal 30 20N 71 55E
19 Khaniá 35 30N 24 4E
19 Khaníon, Kól. 35 33N 23 55E
25 Khanka, Oz. 45 0N 132 30E
24 Khanty-Mansiysk 61 0N 69 0E
25 Khapcheranga 49 40N 112 0E
33 Kharagpur 22 20N 87 25E
30 Kharfa 22 0N 46 35E
23 Kharkov 49 58N 36 20E
22 Kharovsk 59 56N 40 13E
32 Kharsaniya 27 10N 49 10E
51 Khartoum=El Khartûm 15 31N 32 35E
31 Khasab 26 14N 56 15E
31 Khāsh 28 15N 61 5E
51 Khashm el Girba 14 59N 35 58E
32 Khashmor 28 30N 69 31E
19 Khaskovo 41 56N 25 30E
25 Khatanga 72 0N 102 20E
25 Khatanga, R. 73 30N 109 0E
30 Khavari □ 37 20N 46 0E
32 Khed Brahma 24 2N 73 3E
50 Khemis Miliana 36 11N 2 14E
50 Khenchela 35 28N 7 11E
50 Khenifra 32 58N 5 46W
23 Kherson 46 35N 32 35E
37 Khetinsiring 32 54N 92 50E
25 Khilok 51 30N 110 45E
19 Khíos 38 27N 26 9E
19 Khíos, I. 38 20N 26 0E
24 Khiva 41 30N 60 18E
23 Khmelnitisky 49 23N 27 0E
32 Khojak P. 30 55N 66 30E
22 Kholm 57 10N 31 15E
25 Kholmsk 35 5N 139 48E
34 Khong, R. 14 7N 105 51E
34 Khonh Hung 9 37N 105 50E
25 Khonu 66 30N 143 25E
22 Khoper, R. 52 0N 43 20E
31 Khorasan □ 34 0N 58 0E
34 Khorat=Nakhon Ratchasima 14 59N 102 12E
24 Khorog 37 30N 71 36E
30 Khorramābād 33 30N 48 25E
30 Khorromshahr 30 29N 48 15E
50 Khouribga 32 58N 6 50W
31 Khugiani 31 28N 66 14E
33 Khulna 22 45N 89 34E
33 Khulna □ 22 45N 89 35E
32 Khushab 32 20N 72 20E
30 Khuzestan □ 31 0N 50 0E
31 Khvor 33 45N 55 0E
31 Khvormūj 28 40N 51 30E
30 Khvoy 38 35N 45 0E
31 Khyber P. 34 10N 71 8E
39 Kialing Kiang, R. 30 2N 106 18E
46 Kiama 34 40S 150 50E
46 Kiamal 34 58S 142 18E
52 Kiambu 1 8S 36 50E
38 Kiamusze 46 45N 130 30E
39 Kian 27 1N 114 58E
39 Kiangling 30 28N 113 16E
39 Kiangsi □ 27 45N 115 0E
39 Kiangsu □ 33 0N 119 50E
39 Kiangyin 31 51N 120 0E
38 Kiaohsien 36 20N 120 0E
52 Kibau 8 35S 35 18E
52 Kiberege 7 55S 36 53E
52 Kibiti 7 40S 38 54E
52 Kibombo 3 57S 25 53E
52 Kibwezi 2 27S 37 57E
25 Kichiga 59 50N 163 5E
64 Kicking Horse P. 51 27N 116 25W
7 Kidderminster 52 24N 2 13W
52 Kidete 6 25S 37 17E
52 Kidugallo 6 49S 38 15E
14 Kiel 54 16N 10 8E
14 Kieler B. 54 30N 10 30E
39 Kienko 31 50N 105 30E
39 Kienow 27 0N 118 16E
37 Kienshui 23 57N 102 45E
39 Kiensi 26 58N 106 0E
39 Kienteh 29 30N 119 28E
39 Kienyang 27 30N 118 0E
23 Kiev=Kiyev 50 30N 30 28E
50 Kiffa 16 50N 11 15W
52 Kigali 1 5S 30 4E
52 Kigoma-Ujiji 5 30S 30 0E
52 Kihurio 4 32S 38 5E
36 Kii-Suido, Chan. 33 0N 134 50E
52 Kijabe 0 56S 36 33E
39 Kikiang 28 58N 106 44E
19 Kikinda 45 50N 20 30E
19 Kikládhes, Is. 37 20N 24 30E
19 Kikládhes □ 37 20N 24 30E
43 Kilcoy 26 59S 152 30E
9 Kildare 53 10N 6 50W
9 Kildare □ 53 10N 6 50W
52 Kilembe 0 15N 30 3E
71 Kilgore 32 22N 94 40W
52 Kilifi 3 40S 39 48E
52 Kilimanjaro, Mt. 3 7S 37 20E
52 Kilimatinde 5 55S 34 58E
52 Kilindini 4 4S 39 40E
30 Kilis 36 50N 37 10E
9 Kilkee 52 41N 9 40W
9 Kilkenny 52 40N 7 17W
9 Kilkenny □ 52 35N 7 15W
9 Killala 54 13N 9 12W
9 Killaloe 52 48N 8 28W
65 Killarney, Canada 49 10N 99 40W
9 Killarney, Eire 52 2N 9 30W
9 Killary Harbour 53 38N 9 52W
8 Killiecrankie, P. of 56 44N 3 46W
8 Killin 56 27N 4 20W
9 Killybegs 54 38N 8 26W
46 Kilmany 38 8S 146 55E
8 Kilmarnock 55 36N 4 30W
46 Kilmore 37 25S 144 53E
52 Kilosa 6 48S 37 0E
9 Kilrush 52 39N 9 30W
52 Kilwa Kisiwani 8 58S 39 32E
52 Kilwa Kivinje 8 45S 39 25E
43 Kimba 33 8S 136 23E
70 Kimball 41 17N 103 20W
65 Kimberley, Canada 49 40N 116 10W
56 Kimberley, S. Africa 28 43S 24 46E
44 Kimberley Downs 17 24S 124 22E
72 Kimberly 42 33N 114 25W
38 Kimchaek 40 41N 129 12E
38 Kimchon 36 11N 128 4E
22 Kimry 56 55N 37 15E
34 Kinabalu, Mt. 6 0N 116 0E
65 Kincaid 49 40N 107 0W
62 Kincardine 44 10N 81 40W
65 Kindersley 51 30N 109 10W
50 Kindia 10 0N 12 52W
54 Kindu 2 55S 25 50E
22 Kineshma 57 30N 42 5E
42 King, I. 39 50S 144 0E
42 King, Mt. 25 10S 147 31E
44 King Edward, R. 14 14S 126 35E
80 King George B. 51 30S 60 30W
61 King George Is. 53 40N 80 30W
44 King Leopold, Ras. 17 20S 124 20E
44 King Sd. 16 50S 123 20E
60 King William I. 69 0N 98 0W
56 King William's Town 32 51S 27 22E
43 Kingaroy 26 32S 151 51E
37 Kingku 23 49N 100 30E
73 Kingman 35 12N 114 2W
43 Kingoonya 30 54N 135 18E
38 Kingpeng 43 30N 117 25E
73 Kings Canyon Nat. Park 37 0N 118 45W
6 Kings Lynn 52 45N 0 25E
7 Kingsbridge 50 14N 3 46W
9 Kingscourt 53 55N 6 48W
62 Kingston, Canada 44 20N 76 30W
75 Kingston, Jamaica 18 0N 76 50W
47 Kingston, N.Z. 45 20S 168 43E
68 Kingston, N.Y. 41 55N 74 0W
68 Kingston, Pa. 41 19N 75 58W
43 Kingston South East 36 52S 139 51E
75 Kingstown 13 10N 61 10W
62 Kingsville, Canada 42 3N 82 45W
71 Kingsville, U.S.A. 27 30N 97 53W
38 Kingtai 37 4N 103 59E
39 Kingtehchen 29 8N 117 21E
39 Kingtzekwan 33 25N 111 10E
8 Kingussie 47 5N 4 2W
38 Kinhsien 36 6N 107 49E
39 Kinhwa 29 5N 119 32E
65 Kinistino 52 59N 105 0W
54 Kinkala 4 18S 14 49E
36 Kinki □ 33 30N 136 0E
47 Kinleith 38 20S 175 56E
47 Kinloch 44 51S 168 20E
39 Kinmen, I. 24 25N 118 24E
28 Kinneret 32 44N 35 34E
28 Kinneret, Yam, L. 32 49N 35 36E
8 Kinross 56 13N 3 25W
9 Kinsale 51 42N 8 31W
9 Kinsale, Old Hd. 51 37N 8 32W
37 Kinsha, R. 32 30N 98 0E
54 Kinshasa 4 20S 15 15E
39 Kinsiang 35 4N 116 25E
69 Kinston 35 18N 77 35W
52 Kintiku 6 0S 35 20E
8 Kintyre, Pen. 55 30N 5 35W
52 Kinyangiri 4 35S 24 37E
52 Kioga, L. 1 35N 33 0E
39 Kioshan 32 50N 114 0E
19 Kiparissía 37 15N 21 40E
19 Kiparissiakós Kól. 37 25N 21 25E
62 Kipawa Reserve Prov. Park 47 0N 78 30W
52 Kipembawe 7 38S 33 23E
52 Kipengere Ra. 9 12S 34 15E
52 Kipili 7 28S 30 32E
52 Kipini 2 30S 40 32E
25 Kirensk 57 50N 107 55E
24 Kirgiz S.S.R. □ 42 0N 75 0E
30 Kirikkale 39 51N 33 32E
22 Kirillov 59 51N 38 14E
38 Kirin 43 58N 126 31E
38 Kirin □ 43 45N 125 20E
8 Kirkcaldy 56 7N 3 10W
8 Kirkcudbright 54 50N 4 3W
32 Kirkee 18 34N 73 56E
20 Kirkenes 69 40N 30 5E
8 Kirkintilloch 55 57N 4 10W
62 Kirkland Lake 48 15N 80 0W
70 Kirksville 40 8N 92 35W
30 Kirkūk 35 30N 44 21E
8 Kirkwall 58 59N 2 59W
56 Kirkwood 33 22S 25 15E
22 Kirov 58 35N 49 40E
23 Kirovabad 40 45N 46 10E
23 Kirovakan 41 0N 44 0E
23 Kirovograd 48 35N 32 20E
22 Kirovsk 67 48N 33 50E
25 Kirovskiy 45 51N 48 11E
8 Kirriemuir 56 41N 3 0W
22 Kirsanov 52 35N 42 40E
32 Kirthar Ra. 27 0N 67 0E
20 Kiruna 67 50N 20 20E
45 Kirup 33 40S 115 50E
36 Kiryū 36 25N 139 20E
52 Kisaki 7 27S 37 40E
54 Kisangani 0 35N 25 15E
34 Kisaran 2 47N 99 29E
36 Kisaratzu 35 25N 139 59E
24 Kiselevsk 54 5N 86 6E
54 Kisengwa 6 0S 25 50E
52 Kiserawe 6 53S 39 0E
52 Kishanda 1 42S 31 34E
33 Kishanganj 26 3N 88 14E
32 Kishangarh 27 50N 70 30E

Kishi Kuningan

53 Kishi 9 1N 3 45 E
23 Kishinev 47 0N 28 50 E
36 Kishiwada 34 28N 135 22 E
28 Kishon 32 33N 35 12 E
32 Kishtwar 33 20N 75 48 E
38 Kisi 45 21N 131 0 E
52 Kisii 0 40S 34 45 E
52 Kisiju 7 23S 39 19 E
60 Kiska I. 52 0N 177 30 E
15 Kiskörös 46 37N 19 20 E
15 Kiskunfélegyháza 46 42N 19 53 E
15 Kiskunhalas 46 28N 19 37 E
23 Kislovodsk 43 50N 42 45 E
36 Kiso-Gawa, R. 35 2N 136 45 E
52 Kisoro 1 17S 29 48 E
50 Kissidougou 9 5N 10 0W
33 Kistna, R.= Krishna, R. 15 43N 80 55 E
52 Kisumu 0 3S 34 45 E
37 Kitai 44 0N 89 27 E
36 Kitaibaraki 36 50N 140 45 E
36 Kitakyūshū 33 50N 130 50 E
52 Kitale 1 0N 35 12 E
52 Kitangari 10 40S 39 20 E
45 Kitchener, Australia 30 55S 124 8 E
62 Kitchener, Canada 43 30N 80 30W
54 Kitega 3 30S 29 58 E
52 Kitgum 3 17N 32 52 E
19 Kíthira 36 9N 23 0 E
19 Kíthira, I. 36 10N 23 0 E
19 Kíthnos, I. 37 26N 24 27 E
64 Kitimat 53 55N 129 0W
52 Kitoma 1 5N 30 55 E
36 Kitsuki 33 35N 131 37 E
68 Kittanning 40 49N 79 30W
52 Kitui 1 17S 38 0 E
55 Kitwe 12 54S 28 7 E
39 Kityang 23 30N 116 29 E
39 Kiukiang 29 37N 116 2 E
39 Kiuling Shan, Mts. 28 40N 115 0 E
39 Kiungchow 19 57N 110 17 E
39 Kiungchow-Haihsia, Str. 20 40N 110 0 E
52 Kivu, L. 1 48S 29 0 E
39 Kiyang 26 36N 111 42 E
23 Kiyev 50 30N 30 28 E
23 Kiyevskoye, Vdkhr. 51 0N 30 0 E
22 Kizel 59 3N 57 40 E
23 Kizlyar 43 51N 46 40 E
23 Kizyl-Arvat 38 58N 56 15 E
24 Kizyl Kiva 40 20N 72 35 E
14 Kladno 50 10N 14 7 E
14 Klagenfurt 46 38N 14 20 E
22 Klaipeda 55 43N 21 10 E
72 Klamath Falls 42 20N 121 50W
21 Klarälven, R. 59 23N 13 32 E
35 Klaten 7 43S 110 36 E
14 Klatovy 49 23N 13 18 E
64 Klawak 55 35N 133 0W
56 Klawer 31 44S 18 36 E
64 Kleena Kleene 52 0N 124 50W
56 Klein Karoo 33 45S 21 30 E
56 Klerksdorp 26 51S 26 38 E
56 Klipplaat 33 0S 24 22 E
14 Kłodzko 50 28N 16 38 E
64 Klondike 64 0N 139 40W
53 Klouto 6 57N 0 44 E
60 Kluane, L. 61 25N 138 50W
6 Knaresborough 54 1N 1 29W
7 Knighton 52 21N 3 2W
11 Knokke 51 20N 3 17 E
70 Knoxville, Iowa 41 20N 93 5W
69 Knoxville, Tenn. 35 58N 83 57W
56 Knysna 34 2S 23 2 E
61 Koartac 61 5N 69 36W
35 Koba 6 37S 134 37 E
18 Kobarid 46 15N 13 30 E
36 Kobe 34 45N 135 10 E
21 København 55 41N 12 34 E
14 Koblenz 50 21N 7 36 E
19 Kočani 41 55N 22 25 E
18 Kočevje 45 39N 14 50 E
36 Kōchi 33 30N 133 35 E
36 Kōchi □ 33 40N 133 30 E
60 Kodiak 57 48N 152 23W
60 Kodiak I. 57 30N 152 45 E
51 Kodok 9 53N 32 7 E
56 Koffiefontein 29 22S 24 58 E
53 Koforidua 6 3N 0 17W
36 Kōfu 35 40N 138 30 E
53 Kogin Baba 7 55N 11 35 E
32 Kohat 33 40N 71 29 E
33 Kohima 25 35N 94 10 E
45 Kojonup 33 48S 117 10W
24 Kokand 40 30N 70 57 E
64 Kokanee Glacier Prov. Park 49 47N 117 10W
24 Kokchetav 53 20N 69 10 E
28 Kokhav Mikha'el 31 37N 34 40 E
37 Kokiu 23 22N 103 6 E
20 Kokkola 63 50N 23 8 E
53 Koko 11 28N 4 29 E
37 Koko Nor, L. 37 0N 100 0 E
68 Kokomo 40 30N 86 6W
61 Koksoak, R. 58 30N 68 10W
57 Kokstad 30 32S 29 29 E
25 Kokuora 61 30N 145 0 E
22 Kola 68 45N 33 8 E
38 Kolan 38 43N 111 32 E
32 Kolar 13 12N 78 15 E
32 Kolar Gold Fields 12 58N 78 16 E
19 Kolarovgrad 43 27N 26 42 E
32 Kolayat 27 51N 72 59 E
21 Kolding 55 30N 9 29 E
35 Kolepom, I. 8 0S 138 30 E
22 Kolguyev 69 20N 48 30 E
32 Kolhapur 16 43N 74 15 E
14 Kolín 50 2N 15 9 E
14 Köln 50 56N 9 58 E
15 Koło 52 14N 18 40 E
14 Kołobrzeg 54 10N 15 35 E
22 Kołomna 55 8N 38 45 E
23 Kolomyya 48 31N 25 2 E
33 Kolosib 24 15N 92 45 E
24 Kolpashevo 58 20N 83 5 E
22 Kolskiy Pol. 67 30N 38 0 E
22 Kolskiy Zaliv 69 23N 34 0 E
54 Kolwezi 10 40S 25 25 E
25 Kolyma, R. 64 40N 153 0 E
3 Komandorskiye Is. 55 0N 167 0 E
15 Komárno 47 49N 18 5 E
57 Komatipoort 25 25S 31 57 E
36 Komatsu 36 25N 136 30 E
53 Komenda 5 4N 1 28W
57 Komga 32 37S 27 56 E
22 Komi A.S.S.R. 64 0N 55 0 E
36 Komoro 36 19N 138 26 E
19 Komotiri 41 9N 25 26 E
34 Kompong Bang 12 24N 104 40 E
34 Kompong Cham 11 54N 105 30 E
34 Kompong Som 10 38N 103 30 E
56 Komsberge 32 40S 20 45 E
25 Komsomolets, Os. 80 30N 95 0 E
25 Komsomolsk 50 30N 137 0 E
25 Kondakovo 69 20N 151 30 E
45 Kondinin 32 34S 118 8 E
52 Kondoa 4 0S 36 0 E
53 Konduga 11 35N 13 26 E
50 Koudougou 12 10N 2 20W
25 Kondratyevo 57 30N 98 30 E
34 Kong, Koh 11 20N 103 0 E
38 Kongju 36 30N 127 0 E
33 Konglu 27 13N 97 57 E
39 Kongmoon 22 35N 113 1 E
54 Kongolo 5 22S 27 0 E
21 Kongsberg 59 39N 9 39 E
22 Königsberg= Kaliningrad 54 42N 20 32 E
21 Kongsvinger 60 12N 12 2 E
52 Kongwa 6 11S 36 26 E
3 Kønig Haakon VII Sea 66 0S 35 0 E
15 Konin 52 12N 18 15 E
19 Konjic 43 42N 17 58 E
53 Konongo 6 40N 1 15W
22 Konosha 61 0N 40 5 E
23 Konotop 51 12N 33 7 E
15 Końskie 51 15N 20 23 E
14 Konstanz 47 39N 9 10 E
53 Kontagora 10 23N 5 27 E
30 Konya 37 52N 32 35 E
52 Konza 1 45S 37 0 E
45 Kookynie 29 17S 121 22 E
44 Kooline 22 57S 116 20 E
45 Koolyanobbing 30 48S 119 46 E
45 Koonibba 31 58S 133 27 E
45 Koorda 30 48S 117 35 E
64 Kootenay Nat. Park 51 0N 116 0W
46 Koo-wee-rup 38 13S 145 28 E
19 Kopaonik Planina, Mts. 43 10N 21 0 E
21 Kopervik 59 17N 5 17 E
24 Kopeysk 55 7N 61 37 E
21 Köping 59 31N 16 3 E
21 Kopparberg 59 53N 14 59 E
21 Kopparbergs □ 61 20N 14 15 E
19 Korça 40 37N 20 50 E
18 Korčula, I. 42 57N 17 0 E
30 Kordestān □ 36 0N 47 0 E
51 Kordofân □ 13 0N 29 0 E
38 Korea B. 39 0N 124 0 E
50 Korhogo 9 29N 5 28 E
19 Korinthiakós Kól. 38 16N 22 30 E
19 Kórinthos 37 26N 22 55 E
36 Kōriyama 37 24N 140 23 E
37 Korla 41 45N 86 4 E
53 Koro 14 1N 2 58W
47 Koro Sea 17 30S 179 45W
52 Korogwe 5 5S 38 25 E
46 Koroit 38 18S 142 24 E
15 Körös, R. 46 30N 142 42 E
25 Korsakov 46 30N 142 42 E
21 Korsør 55 20N 11 9 E
11 Kortrijk 50 50N 3 17 E
46 Korumburra 38 26S 145 50 E
25 Koryakskiy Khrebet, Mts. 61 0N 171 0 E
19 Kos, I. 36 50N 27 15 E
14 Kościan 52 5N 16 40 E
71 Kosciusko 33 3N 89 34W
64 Kosciusko I. 56 0N 133 40W
46 Kosciusko, Mt. 36 27S 148 16 E
15 Košice 48 42N 21 15 E
22 Koslan 63 28N 48 52 E
19 Kosovska-Mitrovica 42 54N 20 52 E
56 Koster 25 52S 26 54 E
51 Kôstî 13 8N 32 43 E
22 Kostroma 57 50N 41 58 E
14 Kostrzyn 52 24N 17 14 E
14 Koszalin 54 12N 16 8 E
32 Kota 25 14N 75 49 E
34 Kota Baharu 6 7N 102 14 E
34 Kota Kinabalu 6 0N 116 12 E
34 Kota Tinggi 1 44N 103 53 E
34 Kotabaru 3 20S 116 20 E
34 Kotabumi 4 49S 104 46 E
34 Kotawaringin 2 28S 111 27 E
22 Kotelnich 58 20N 48 10 E
21 Kotka 60 28N 26 55 E
22 Kotlas 61 15N 47 0 E
60 Kotlik 63 2N 163 33W
19 Kotor 42 25N 18 47 E
33 Kottagudem 17 30N 80 40 E
32 Kottayam 9 35N 76 33 E
32 Kotturu 14 45N 76 13 E
60 Kotzebue 66 53N 162 39W
53 Koudougou 12 10N 2 20W
56 Kougaberge 33 40S 23 55 E
54 Koula-Moutou 1 15S 12 25 E
42 Koumala 21 38S 149 15 E
24 Kounradskiy 47 20N 75 0 E
79 Kourou 5 9N 52 39W
50 Kouroussa 10 45N 9 45W
53 Kouvé 6 30N 1 30 E
22 Kovdor 67 34N 30 22 E
22 Kovel 51 10N 25 0 E
22 Kovrov 56 25N 41 25 E
39 Kowloon 22 20N 114 15 E
39 Koyiu 23 2N 112 28 E
60 Koyukuk, R. 64 56N 157 30W
19 Kozáni □ 40 20N 21 45 E
32 Kozhikode= Calicut 11 15N 75 43 E
22 Kozhva 65 10N 57 0 E
50 Kpandu 7 2N 0 18 E
53 Kpessi 7 50N 1 25 E
34 Kra, Isthmus of= Kra, Kho Khot 10 15N 99 30 E
34 Kra, Kho Khot 10 15N 99 30 E
15 Kracków 50 4N 19 57 E
21 Kragerø 58 56N 9 30 E
19 Kragujevac 44 2N 20 56 E
35 Krakatau, I.= Rakatau, P. 6 10S 105 20 E
35 Kraksaan 7 43S 113 23 E
19 Kraljevo 43 44N 20 41 E
23 Kramatorsk 48 50N 37 30 E
20 Kramfors 62 55N 17 48 E
18 Kras, Reg 45 30N 14 0 E
22 Krasavino 60 58N 46 26 E
25 Kraskino 42 45N 130 58 E
15 Krasnik 50 55N 22 5 E
23 Krasnodar 45 5N 38 50 E
22 Krasnokamsk 58 0N 56 0 E
24 Krasnoselkupsk 65 20N 82 10 E
24 Krasnoturinsk 59 39N 60 1 E
22 Krasnoufimsk 56 30N 57 37 E
22 Krasnouralsk 58 0N 60 0 E
24 Krasnovodsk 40 0N 52 52 E
22 Krasnovishersk 60 23N 56 59 E
25 Krasnoyarsk 56 8N 93 0 E
23 Krasnyy Yar 46 43N 48 23 E
34 Kratie 12 32N 106 10 E
14 Krefeld 51 20N 6 22 E
23 Kremenchug 49 5N 33 25 E
23 Kremenchugskoye, Vdkhr. 49 20N 32 30 E
15 Kremnica 48 45N 18 50 E
33 Krishna, R. 15 43N 80 55 E
33 Krishnanagar 23 24N 88 33 E
21 Kristiansand 58 5N 7 50 E
21 Kristianstad 56 5N 14 7 E
21 Kristianstads □ 56 0N 14 0 E
20 Kristiansund 63 10N 7 45 E
21 Kristinehamn 59 18N 14 13 E
20 Kristinestad 62 18N 21 25 E
19 Kriti, I. 35 15N 25 0 E
19 Kriti □ 35 15N 25 0 E
23 Krivoy Rog 47 51N 33 20 E
18 Krk, I. 45 5N 14 56 E
14 Krkonose, Mts. 50 50N 16 10 E
57 Krokodil, R. 25 26S 32 0 E
21 Kronobergs □ 56 45N 14 30 E
22 Kronshtadt 60 5N 29 35 E
56 Kroonstad 27 43S 27 19 E
25 Kropotkin 58 50N 115 10 E
15 Krosno 49 35N 21 56 E
15 Krotoszyn 51 42N 17 23 E
57 Krugersdorp 26 5S 27 46 E
56 Kruisfontein 34 0S 24 43 E
34 Krung Thep 13 45N 100 35 E
9 Kruševac 43 35N 21 28 E
23 Krymskaya 44 57N 37 50 E
50 Ksar El Boukhari 35 5N 2 52 E
50 Ksar-el-Kebir 35 0N 6 0W
34 Kuala 2 46N 105 47 E
34 Kuala Dungun 4 46N 103 25 E
34 Kuala Kerai 5 32N 102 12 E
34 Kuala Kubu Baharu 3 35N 101 38 E
34 Kuala Lipis 4 22N 102 5 E
34 Kuala Lumpur 3 9N 101 41 E
34 Kuala Selangor 3 20N 101 15 E
34 Kuala Terengganu 5 20N 103 8 E
34 Kualakapuas 2 55S 114 20 E
34 Kualakurun 1 10S 113 50 E
34 Kualapembuang 3 14S 112 38 E
34 Kualasimpang 4 16N 98 4 E
34 Kuantan 3 49N 103 20 E
23 Kuba 41 21N 48 22 E
32 Kubak 27 10N 63 10 E
23 Kuban, R. 45 20N 37 30 E
36 Kubokawa 33 12N 133 8 E
37 Kucha 41 50N 82 30 E
34 Kuching 1 33N 110 25 E
36 Kuchinotsu 32 36N 130 11 E
32 Kuda 23 10N 71 18 E
34 Kudat 7 0N 116 42 E
35 Kudus 6 48N 110 51 E
39 Kueiyang= Kweiyang 25 30N 106 35 E
51 Kufra, El Wâhât et 24 17N 23 15 E
14 Kufstein 47 35N 12 11 E
31 Kūhpāyeh 32 44N 52 20 E
53 Kukawa 12 58N 13 27 E
45 Kukerin 33 13S 118 0 E
42 Kulgera 25 50S 133 18 E
45 Kulin 32 40S 118 2 E
45 Kulja 30 35S 117 31 E
24 Kulsary 46 59N 54 1 E
52 Kululu 9 28N 33 1 E
24 Kulunda 52 45N 79 15 E
24 Kulyab 37 55N 69 50 E
37 Kum Darya, R. 41 0N 89 0 E
24 Kum Tekei 43 10N 79 30 E
53 Kumaganum 13 8N 10 38 E
34 Kumai 2 52S 111 45 E
36 Kumamoto 32 45N 130 45 E
36 Kumamoto □ 32 30N 130 40 E
47 Kumara 42 37S 171 12 E
45 Kumari 32 45S 121 30 E
53 Kumasi 6 41N 1 38 E
53 Kumba 4 36N 9 24 E
43 Kumbarilla 27 15S 150 55 E
53 Kumbo 6 15N 10 36 E
36 Kumagaya 36 9N 139 22 E
22 Kumertau 52 46N 55 47 E
52 Kumi 1 30N 33 58 E
21 Kumla 59 8N 15 10 E
53 Kumo 10 1N 11 12 E
33 Kumon Bum, Mts. 26 0N 97 15 E
31 Kunar □ 35 15N 71 0 E
45 Kundip 33 42S 120 10 E
31 Kunduz 36 50N 68 50 E
31 Kunduz □ 36 50N 68 50 E
56 Kunene, R. 17 20S 11 50 E
38 Kungchuling 43 31N 124 58 E
37 Kungho 36 28N 100 45 E
24 Kungrad 43 6N 58 54 E
33 Kungram 25 45N 89 35 E
21 Kungsbacka 57 30N 12 7 E
39 Kunhsien 32 30N 111 17 E
35 Kuningan 6 59S 108 29 E

Kunlong Las Flores

33 Kunlong 23 20N 98 50E
26 Kunlun Shan, Mts. 36 0N 82 0E
37 Kunming 25 11N 102 37E
38 Kunsan 35 59N 126 35E
44 Kununurra 15 40s 128 39E
42 Kunwarara 22 25s 150 7E
20 Kuopio 62 53N 27 35E
20 Kuopio □ 63 25N 27 10E
18 Kupa, R. 45 28N 16 24E
35 Kupang 10 19s 123 39E
64 Kupreanof I. 56 50N 133 30W
23 Kura, R. 39 24N 49 24E
36 Kurashiki 34 40N 133 50E
36 Kurayoshi 35 26N 133 50E
36 Kure 34 14N 132 32E
24 Kurgaldzhino 50 35N 70 20E
24 Kurgan 55 30N 65 0E
25 Kurilskiye Os. 45 0N 150 0E
36 Kurino 31 57N 130 43E
32 Kurnool 15 45N 78 0E
47 Kurow 44 4s 170 29E
46 Kurri Kurri 32 50s 151 28E
22 Kursk 51 42N 36 11E
36 Kurume 33 15N 130 30E
32 Kurunegala 7 30N 80 18E
25 Kurya 61 15N 108 10E
38 Kushan 39 58N 123 30E
36 Kushikino 31 44N 130 16E
36 Kushima 31 29N 131 14E
36 Kushimoto 33 28N 135 47E
36 Kushiro 43 0N 144 30E
31 Kushk 34 55N 62 30E
24 Kushka 35 20N 62 18E
33 Kushtia 23 55N 89 5E
60 Kuskokwim, R. 60 17N 162 27W
60 Kuskokwim B. 59 45N 162 25W
24 Kustanai 53 20N 63 45E
34 Kut, Ko 11 40N 102 35E
30 Kutahya 39 25N 29 59E
23 Kutaisi 42 19N 42 40E
34 Kutaraja=Banda Aceh 5 35N 95 20E
32 Kutch, G. of. 22 50N 69 15E
32 Kutch, Rann of, Reg. 24 0N 70 0N
15 Kutno 52 15N 19 23E
42 Kuttabul 21 5s 148 48E
51 Kutum 14 20N 24 10E
30 Kuwait ■ 29 30N 47 30E
36 Kuwana 35 0N 136 43E
38 Kuyang 41 8N 110 1E
22 Kuybyshev, Kuyb. Obl. 53 12N 50 9E
22 Kuybyshev, Tatar A.S.S.R. 54 57N 49 5E
24 Kuybyshev, Novosibirsk Obl. 55 27N 78 19E
22 Kuybyshevskoye Vdkhr. 55 2N 49 30E
25 Kuyumba 61 10N 97 10E
22 Kuyto, Oz. 64 40N 31 0E
22 Kuznetsk 53 12N 46 40E
22 Kuzomen 66 22N 36 50E
18 Kvarner, G. 44 50N 14 10E
18 Kvarneric 44 43N 14 37E
57 Kwabhaca 30 51s 29 0E
79 Kwakoegron 5 25N 55 25W
52 Kwale 4 15s 39 31E
56 Kwando, R. 16 48s 22 45E
39 Kwangan 30 35N 106 40E
39 Kwangchou= Kwangchow 23 10N 113 10E
39 Kwangchow 23 10N 113 10E
39 Kwangchow Wan, G. 21 0N 111 0E
38 Kwangju 35 10N 126 45E
37 Kwangnan 24 10N 105 0E
39 Kwangsi-Chuang Aut.Dist. □ 23 30N 108 55E
39 Kwangtseh 27 30N 117 25E
39 Kwangtung □ 23 35N 114 0E
39 Kwangyuan 32 30N 105 49E
37 Kwanhsien 30 59N 103 40E
37 Kwantung 25 12N 101 37E
53 Kwara □ 8 30N 5 0E
35 Kwatisore 3 7s 139 59E
39 Kwei Kiang, R. 23 30N 110 30E
39 Kweichih 30 40N 117 30E
39 Kweichow= Fengkieh 31 0N 109 33E
39 Kweichow □ 26 40N 107 0E
39 Kweihsien 22 59N 109 44E
39 Kweiki 28 10N 117 8E
39 Kweilin 25 16N 110 15E
39 Kweiping 23 12N 110 0E
39 Kweiting 26 0N 113 35E
39 Kweiyang 25 30N 106 35E
15 Kwidzyń 54 5N 18 58E
60 Kwiguk Island 62 45N 164 28W
45 Kwinana 32 15s 115 47E
39 Kwo Ho, R. 33 20N 116 50E
35 Kwoka, Mt. 0 31s 132 27E
53 Kwolla 8 55N 9 18E
25 Kyakhta 50 30N 106 25E
43 Kyancutta 33 8s 135 34E
33 Kyaukpadaung 20 52N 95 8E
33 Kyaukpyu 19 28N 93 30E
33 Kyaukse 21 36N 96 10E
52 Kyenjojo 0 40N 30 37E
55 Kyle Dam 20 14s 31 0E
42 Kynuna 21 35s 141 55E
54 Kyoga, L. 1 35N 33 0E
43 Kyogle 28 40s 153 0E
38 Kyongju 35 59N 129 26E
33 Kyonpyaw 17 12N 95 10E
36 Kyōto 35 0N 135 45E
36 Kyōto □ 35 15N 135 30E
30 Kyrínia 35 20N 33 19E
25 Kystatyam 67 15N 123 0E
25 Kytal Ktakh 65 30N 123 40E
33 Kyunhla 23 25N 95 15E
36 Kyūshū, I. 32 30N 131 0E
36 Kyūshū □ 32 30N 131 0E
19 Kyustendil 42 25N 22 41E
25 Kyusyur 70 30N 127 0E
25 Kyzyl 51 50N 94 30E
24 Kzyl Orda 44 50N 65 10E

L

13 La Alcarria, Reg. 40 31N 2 45W
78 La Asunción 11 2N 63 53W
80 La Banda 27 45s 64 10W
74 La Barca 20 20N 102 40W
78 La Blanquilla, I. 11 51N 64 37W
74 La Boca 9 0N 79 30E
80 La Calera 32 50s 71 10W
80 La Carlota 33 30s 63 20W
13 La Carolina 38 17N 3 38W
75 La Ceiba, Honduras 15 40N 86 50W
78 La Ceiba, Ven. 9 30N 71 0W
14 La Chaux-de-Fonds 47 7N 6 50E
80 La Cocha 27 50s 65 40W
13 La Coruña 43 20N 8 25W
70 La Crosse 43 48N 91 13W
78 La Dorada 5 30N 74 40W
13 La Estrada 42 43N 8 27W
68 La Fayette 40 22N 86 52W
69 La Folette 36 23N 84 9W
72 La Grande 45 15N 118 0W
69 La Grange 33 4N 85 0W
78 La Guaira 10 36N 66 56W
75 La Habana 23 0N 82 41W
75 La Mabana 23 8N 82 22W
71 La Junta 38 0N 103 30W
13 La Linea de la Concepción 36 15N 5 23W
65 La Loche 56 29N 109 27W
11 La Louvière 50 27N 4 10E
63 La Malbaie 47 40N 70 10W
13 La Mancha, Reg. 39 10N 2 54W
60 La Martre, L. 63 0N 118 0W
73 La Mesa 32 48N 117 5W
78 La Orchila, I. 12 30N 67 0W
78 La Oroya 11 32s 75 54W
13 La Palma 37 21N 6 38W
75 La Palma 8 15N 78 0W
50 La Palma, I. 28 40N 17 52W
78 La Paragua 6 50N 63 20W
80 La Paz, Arg. 30 50s 59 45W
78 La Paz, Bolivia 16 20s 68 10W
74 La Paz, Mexico 24 10N 110 20W
78 La Pedrera 1 18s 69 43W
36 La Perouse, Str. 45 40N 142 0E
74 La Piedad 20 20N 102 1W
72 La Pine 40 53N 80 45W
80 La Plata 35 0s 57 55W
68 La Porte 41 40N 86 40W
62 La Reine 48 50N 79 30W
80 La Rioja 29 20s 67 0W
13 La Rioja, Reg. 42 20N 2 20W
13 La Robla 42 50N 5 41W
12 La Roche-sur-Yon 46 40N 1 25W
12 La Rochelle 46 10N 1 9W
13 La Roda 39 13N 2 15W
75 La Romana 18 27N 68 57W
70 La Salle 41 20N 89 5W
62 La Sarre 48 45N 79 15W
80 La Serena 29 55s 71 10W
18 La Spézia 44 8N 9 50E
78 La Tagua 0 3N 74 40W
78 La Tortuga, I. 10 56N 65 20W
62 La Tuque 47 30N 72 50W
80 La Unión, Chile 40 10s 73 0W
74 La Union, Salvador 13 20N 87 50W
78 La Urbana 7 8N 66 56W
75 La Vega 19 20N 70 30W
78 La Vela 11 30N 69 30W
62 La Verendrye Prov. Park 47 15N 77 10W
78 La Victoria 10 14N 67 20W
21 Laaland= Lolland, I. 54 45N 11 30E
53 Labbézenga 14 57N 0 42E
50 Labé 11 24N 12 16W
34 Labis 2 22N 103 2E
80 Laboulaye 34 10s 63 30W
58 Labrador, Reg. 53 20N 61 0W
63 Labrador City 52 42N 67 0W
35 Labuha 0 30s 127 30E
35 Labuhan 6 26s 105 50E
64 Lac la Biche 54 45N 111 50W
65 Lac Seul 50 28N 92 0W
27 Laccadive Is. 10 0N 72 30E
62 Lachine 45 30N 73 40W
46 Lachlan, R. 34 21s 143 57E
62 Lachute 45 39N 74 21W
68 Lackawanna 42 49N 78 50W
64 Lacombe 52 30N 113 50W
68 Laconia 43 32N 71 30W
32 Ladakh Ra. 34 0N 78 0E
56 Ladismith 33 28s 21 15E
31 Lādiz 28 55N 61 15E
22 Ladozhskoye, Oz. 61 15N 30 30E
3 Ladrone Is. 17 0N 145 0E
56 Lady Grey 30 43s 27 13E
56 Ladybrand 29 9s 27 29E
64 Ladysmith, Canada 49 0N 124 0W
57 Ladysmith, S. Africa 28 32s 29 46E
21 Laesø, I. 57 15N 10 53E
71 Lafayette 30 18N 92 0W
53 Lafia 8 30N 8 34E
53 Lafiagi 8 52N 5 20E
62 Laforest 47 4N 81 12W
21 Lågen, R. 61 8N 10 25E
31 Laghman □ 34 20N 70 0E
50 Laghouat 33 50N 2 59E
35 Lagonoy G. 13 50N 123 50E
53 Lagos, Nigeria 6 25N 3 27E
13 Lagos, Port. 37 5N 8 41W
53 Lagos □ 6 25N 3 35E
74 Lagos de Moreno 21 21N 101 55W
44 Lagrange 14 13s 125 46E
80 Laguna 28 30s 48 50E
73 Laguna Beach 33 31N 117 52W
78 Lagunas 21 0s 69 45W
38 Laha 48 9N 124 30E
35 Lahad Datu 5 0N 118 30E
66 Lahaina 20 52N 156 41W
34 Lahat 3 45s 103 30E
30 Lahijan 37 12N 50 1E
14 Lahn, R. 50 18N 7 37E
21 Laholm 56 30N 13 2E
32 Lahore 31 32N 74 22E
32 Lahore □ 31 55N 74 5E
37 Lai Chau 22 5N 103 3E
38 Laichow Wan, G. 37 30N 119 30E
43 Laidley 27 39s 152 20E
30 Laila 22 10N 46 40E
56 Laingsburg 33 9s 20 52E
39 Laipin 23 42N 109 16E
8 Lairg 58 1N 4 24W
34 Lais 3 35s 102 0E
56 Laisamis 1 38N 37 50E
38 Laiyang 36 58N 120 41E
80 Lajes 27 48s 50 20W
71 Lake Charles 31 10N 93 10W
69 Lake City, Fla. 30 10N 82 40W
69 Lake City, S.C. 33 51N 79 44W
45 Lake Grace 33 7s 118 28E
61 Lake Harbour 62 30N 69 50W
73 Lake Havasu City 34 25N 114 20W
45 Lake King 33 5s 119 45E
73 Lake Mead Nat. Rec. Area 36 20N 114 30W
42 Lake Nash 20 57s 138 0E
62 Lake Superior Prov. Park 47 45N 85 0W
62 Lake Traverse 45 56N 78 4W
69 Lake Worth 26 36N 80 3W
62 Lakefield 44 25N 78 16W
69 Lakeland 28 0N 82 0W
72 Lakeport 39 1N 122 56W
46 Lakes Entrance 37 50s 148 0E
72 Lakeview 34 12N 109 59W
68 Lakewood 41 28N 81 50W
33 Lakhimpur 27 14N 94 7E
19 Lakonikós Kól. 36 40N 22 40E
20 Lakselv 70 2N 24 56E
33 Lala Ghat 24 30N 92 40E
13 Lalín 42 40N 8 5W
38 Lalin 45 14N 126 52E
32 Lalitpur 24 42N 78 28E
53 Lama-Kara 9 30N 1 15E
33 Lamaing 15 25N 97 53E
54 Lambaréné 0 20s 10 12E
50 Lame 10 27N 9 12E
13 Lamego 41 5N 7 52W
43 Lameroo 35 19s 140 33E
71 Lamesa 32 45N 101 57W
19 Lamía 38 55N 22 41E
35 Lamitan 6 40N 122 10E
8 Lammermuir Hills 55 50N 24 0W
35 Lamon B. 14 30N 122 20E
18 Lampedusa, I. 35 36N 12 40E
7 Lampeter 52 6N 4 6W
65 Lampman 49 25N 102 50W
34 Lampung □ 5 30s 105 0E
52 Lamu 2 10s 40 55E
8 Lanark 55 40N 3 48W
6 Lancashire □ 53 40N 2 30W
63 Lancaster, Canada 45 17N 66 10W
6 Lancaster, U.K. 54 3N 2 48W
73 Lancaster, Calif. 34 47N 118 8W
68 Lancaster, Ky. 37 40N 84 40W
68 Lancaster, N.H. 44 29N 71 34W
69 Lancaster, S.C. 34 45N 80 47W
61 Lancaster Sd. 74 0N 84 0W
39 Lanchi 29 11N 119 30E
38 Lanchou= Lanchow 36 4N 103 44E
38 Lanchow 36 4N 103 44E
38 Lanciano 42 15N 14 22E
14 Landeck 47 9N 10 34E
72 Lander 42 50N 108 49W
12 Landes □ 43 57N 0 48W
12 Landes, Reg. 44 0N 1 5W
32 Landi Kotal 34 7N 71 6E
10 Land's End 50 4N 5 42W
14 Landshut 48 31N 12 10E
21 Landskrona 56 53N 12 50E
69 Lanett 33 0N 85 15W
39 Langchung 31 31N 105 58E
56 Langeberg 33 55s 21 20E
38 Langfeng 48 4N 121 10E
8 Langholm 55 9N 2 59W
34 Langkawi, Pulau 6 25N 99 45E
63 Langlade, I. 46 50N 56 20W
13 Langreo 43 13N 5 42W
12 Langres 47 52N 5 20E
12 Langres, Plat. de 47 45N 5 20E
34 Langsa 4 30N 97 57E
37 Langson 21 52N 106 42E
12 Languedoc, Reg. 43 58N 3 22E
62 Lansdowne House 52 5N 88 0W
63 L'Anse au Loup 51 32N 56 50W
68 Lansing 42 47N 84 32W
50 Lanzarote, I. 29 0N 13 40W
37 Lao Cai 22 30N 103 57E
35 Laoag 18 7N 120 34E
35 Laoang 12 32N 125 8E
9 Laois □ 53 0N 7 20W
12 Laon 49 33N 3 35E
34 Laos ■ 17 45N 105 0E
68 Lapeer 43 3N 83 20W
20 Lappi □ 64 33N 25 10E
20 Lappland, Reg. 68 7N 24 0E
25 Laptev Sea 76 0N 125 0E
18 L'Aquila 42 21N 13 24E
31 Lār 27 40N 54 14E
50 Larache 35 10N 6 5W
70 Laramie 41 15N 105 29W
62 Larder Lake 48 5N 79 40W
71 Laredo 27 34N 99 29W
51 Largeau 17 58N 19 6E
8 Largs 55 48N 4 51W
19 Lárisa 39 38N 22 28E
32 Larkana 27 32N 68 2E
30 Lárnax 35 0N 33 35E
9 Larne 54 52N 5 50W
9 Larne □ 54 55N 5 55W
44 Larrimah 15 35s 133 12E
21 Larvik 59 4N 10 0E
24 Laryak 61 15N 80 0E
29 Las Anod 8 26N 47 19E
73 Las Cruces 32 25N 106 50W
80 Las Flores 36 0s 59 0W

Liverpool, Canada — Mackenzie, R.

63 Liverpool, Canada 44 5N 64 41W
6 Liverpool, U.K. 53 25N 3 0W
74 Livingston, Guatemala 15 50N 88 50W
72 Livingston, U.S.A. 45 40N 110 40W
56 Livingstone 17 46S 25 52E
52 Livingstone Mts. 9 40S 34 20E
52 Livingstonia 10 38S 34 5E
22 Livny 52 30N 37 30E
18 Livorno 43 32N 10 18E
52 Liwale 9 48S 37 58E
7 Lizard Pt. 49 57N 5 11W
18 Ljubljana 46 4N 14 33E
20 Ljungan, R. 62 19N 17 23E
21 Ljungby 56 49N 13 55E
21 Ljusdal 61 46N 16 3E
21 Ljusnan, R. 61 12N 17 8E
7 Llandeilo 50 54N 4 0W
7 Llandovery 51 59N 3 49W
7 Llandrindod Wells 52 15N 3 23W
6 Llandudno 53 19N 3 51W
7 Llanelli 51 41N 4 11W
13 Llanes 43 25N 4 50W
6 Llangollen 52 58N 3 10W
7 Llanidloes 52 28N 3 31W
58 Llano Estacado, Reg. 34 0N 103 0W
76 Llanos, Reg. 3 25N 71 35W
80 Llanquihue, L. 41 10S 72 50W
13 Lloret de Mar 41 41N 2 53E
65 Lloydminster 53 20N 110 0W
80 Llullaillaco, Mt. 24 30S 68 30W
55 Lobatse 25 12S 25 40E
80 Lobería 38 10S 58 40W
55 Lobito 12 18S 13 35E
14 Locarno 46 10N 8 47E
8 Lochaber, Reg. 56 55N 5 0W
8 Lochalsh, Kyle of 57 17N 5 43W
8 Lochboisdale 57 10N 7 20W
8 Lochgilphead 56 2N 5 37W
8 Lochmaddy 57 36N 7 10W
8 Lochnagar, Mt. 56 57N 3 14W
8 Lochy, L. 56 58N 4 55W
43 Lock 33 34S 135 46E
63 Lockeport 43 47N 65 4W
8 Lockerbie 55 7N 3 21W
71 Lockhart 29 55N 97 40W
28 Lod 31 57N 34 54E
72 Lodi 38 12N 121 16W
54 Lodja 3 30S 23 23E
52 Lodwar 3 10N 35 40E
15 Łódź 51 45N 19 27E
20 Lofoten, Is. 68 10N 13 0E
68 Logan, Ohio 39 35N 82 22W
72 Logan, Utah 41 45N 111 50W
68 Logan, W. Va. 37 51N 81 59W
60 Logan, Mt. 60 40N 140 0W
68 Logansport 31 58N 93 58W
31 Logar □ 33 50N 69 0E
13 Logrono 42 28N 2 32W
29 Loheia 15 45N 42 40E
39 Loho 33 33N 114 5E
21 Loimaa 60 50N 23 5E
12 Loir, R. 47 33N 0 32W
12 Loir-et-Cher □ 47 40N 1 20E
12 Loire □ 45 40N 4 5E
12 Loire, R. 47 16N 2 11W
12 Loire-Atlantique □ 47 25N 1 40W
12 Loiret □ 47 58N 2 10E
78 Loja, Ecuador 3 59S 79 16W
13 Loja, Sp. 37 10N 4 10W
11 Lokeren 51 6N 3 59E
52 Lokitaung 4 12N 35 48E
20 Lokka, L. 68 0N 27 50E
20 Løkken 57 22N 9 41E
53 Lokoja 7 47N 6 45E
54 Lokolama 2 35S 19 50E
39 Lokwei 19 12N 110 30E
21 Lolland, L. 54 45N 11 30E
19 Lom 43 48N 23 20E
54 Lomami, R. 0 46N 24 16E
18 Lombardia □ 45 35N 9 45E
35 Lomblen, I. 8 30S 116 20E
34 Lombok, I. 8 35S 116 20E
53 Lomé 6 9N 1 20E
54 Lomela 2 5S 23 52E
54 Lomela, R. 0 14S 20 42E
64 Lomond 50 24N 112 36W
8 Lomond, L. 56 8N 4 38W
73 Lompoc 34 41N 120 32W
15 Łomza 53 10N 22 2E
80 Loncoche 39 20S 72 50W
52 Londiani 0 10S 35 33E
62 London, Canada 43 0N 81 15W
7 London, U.K. 51 30N 0 5W
7 London □ 51 30N 0 5W
9 Londonderry 55 0N 7 20W
9 Londonderry □ 55 0N 7 20W
44 Londonderry, C. 13 45S 126 55E
80 Londonderry, I. 55 0S 71 0W
80 Londrina 23 0S 51 10W
73 Lone Pine 36 35N 118 2W
73 Long Beach 33 46N 118 12W
6 Long Eaton 52 54N 1 16W
75 Long I., Bahamas 23 20N 75 10W
62 Long I., Canada 44 23N 66 19W
68 Long I., U.S.A. 40 50N 73 20W
63 Long Range Mts. 48 0N 58 30W
34 Long Xuyen 10 19N 105 28E
9 Longford 53 43N 7 50W
9 Longford □ 53 42N 7 45W
34 Longiram 0 5S 115 45E
70 Longmont 40 10N 105 4W
42 Longreach 23 28S 144 14E
71 Longview, Tex. 32 30N 94 45W
72 Longview, Wash. 46 9N 122 58W
12 Lons-le-Saunier 46 40N 5 31E
20 Lønsdal 66 46N 15 26E
7 Looe 50 21N 4 26W
65 Loomis 49 15N 108 45W
65 Loon Lake 44 50N 77 15W
45 Loongana 30 52S 127 5E
9 Loop Hd. 52 34N 9 55W
37 Lop Nor, L. 40 30N 90 30E
54 Lopez, C. 0 47S 8 40E
68 Lorain 41 20N 82 5W
32 Loralaï 30 29N 68 30E
13 Lorca 37 41N 1 42W
3 Lord Howe I. 31 33S 159 6E
73 Lordsburg 32 15N 108 45W
30 Lorestan □ 33 0N 48 30E
79 Loreto, Brazil 7 5S 45 30W
18 Loreto, Italy 43 26N 13 36E
12 Lorient 47 45N 3 23N
8 Lorn, Firth of 56 20N 5 40W
8 Lorne, Reg. 56 26N 5 10W
12 Lorraine, Reg. 49 0N 6 0E
62 Lorrainville 47 21N 79 23W
52 Lorugumu 2 50N 35 15E
73 Los Alamos 35 57N 106 17W
80 Los Andes 32 50S 70 40W
80 Los Angeles, Chile 37 28S 72 23W
73 Los Angeles, U.S.A. 34 0N 118 10W
73 Los Angeles Aqueduct 35 0N 118 20W
73 Los Banos 37 8N 120 56W
80 Los Blancos 23 45S 62 30W
78 Los Hermanos, Is. 11 45N 64 25W
80 Los Lagos 39 51S 72 50W
74 Los Mochis 25 45N 109 5W
78 Los Roques, Is. 11 50N 66 45W
78 Los Testigos, Is. 11 23N 63 6W
80 Los Vilos 32 0S 71 30W
25 Loshkalakh 62 45N 147 20E
18 Losinj 44 35N 14 28E
8 Lossiemouth 57 43N 3 17W
12 Lot □ 44 39N 1 40E
12 Lot, R. 44 18N 0 20E
12 Lot-et-Garonne □ 44 22N 0 30E
80 Lota 37 5S 73 10W
52 Lotagipi Swamp 4 55N 35 0E
8 Lothian □ 55 55N 3 35W
54 Loto 28 50S 22 28E
6 Loughborough 52 46N 1 11W
9 Loughrea 53 11N 8 33W
57 Louis Trichardt 23 0S 25 55E
63 Louisbourg 45 55N 60 0W
62 Louiseville 46 20N 73 0W
3 Louisiade Arch. 11 10S 153 0E
71 Louisiana □ 30 50N 92 0W
68 Louisville, Ky. 38 15N 85 45W
71 Louisville, Miss. 33 7N 89 3W
13 Loulé 37 9N 8 0W
70 Loup City 41 19N 98 57E
12 Lourdes 43 6N 0 3W
57 Lourenço Marques= Maputo 25 58S 32 32E
43 Louth, Australia 30 30S 145 8E
9 Louth, Eire 53 47N 6 33W
6 Louth, U.K. 53 23N 0 0
9 Louth □ 53 55N 6 30W
65 Love 53 29N 104 9W
70 Loveland 40 27N 105 4W
72 Lovelock 40 17N 118 25W
21 Lovisa 60 28N 26 12E
68 Lowell 42 38N 71 19W
47 Lower Hutt 41 10S 174 55E
7 Lowestoft 52 29N 1 44E
15 Łowicz 52 6N 19 55E
68 Lowville 43 48N 75 30W
43 Loxton 34 28S 140 31E
39 Loyang 34 41N 112 28E
39 Loyung 24 25N 109 25E
12 Lozère □ 44 35N 3 30E
38 Lu-ta 39 0N 121 31E
54 Lualaba, R. 0 26N 25 20E
54 Luanda 8 58S 13 9E
37 Luang Prabang 19 45N 102 10E
55 Luangwa, R. 15 40N 30 25E
55 Luanshya 13 3S 28 28E
13 Luarca 43 32N 6 32W
35 Lubang Is. 13 50N 120 12E
28 Lubban 32 9N 35 14E
71 Lubbock 33 40N 102 0W
14 Lübeck 53 52N 10 41E
54 Lubefu 4 47S 24 27E
15 Lublin 51 12N 22 38E
30 Lubnân, Mts. 34 0N 36 0E
34 Lubuklinggau 3 15S 102 55E
34 Lubuksikaping 0 10N 100 15E
55 Lubumbashi 11 32S 27 28E
52 Lubushi 10 32S 30 30E
54 Lubutu 0 45S 26 30E
60 Lucania, Mt. 60 48N 141 25W
18 Lucca 43 50N 10 30E
8 Luce B. 54 45N 4 48W
35 Lucena, Philippines 13 56N 121 37E
13 Lucena, Sp. 37 27N 4 31W
15 Lučenec 48 18N 19 42E
14 Lucerne=Luzern 43 3N 8 13E
39 Luchow 29 2N 105 10E
14 Luckenwalde 52 5N 13 11E
33 Lucknow 26 50N 81 0E
56 Lüderitz 26 41S 15 8E
32 Ludhiana 30 57N 75 56E
68 Ludington 43 58N 86 27W
7 Ludlow 52 23N 2 42W
21 Ludvika 60 8N 15 14E
14 Ludwigsburg 48 53N 9 11E
14 Ludwigshafen 49 27N 8 27E
71 Lufkin 31 25N 94 40W
22 Luga 58 40N 29 55E
14 Lugano 46 0N 8 57E
23 Lugansk= Voroshilovgrad 48 35N 39 29E
52 Lugazi 0 32N 30 42E
29 Lugh Ganana 3 48N 42 40E
13 Lugo 43 2N 7 35W
15 Lugoj 45 42N 21 57E
24 Lugovoy 43 0N 72 20E
79 Luis Correia 3 0S 41 35W
80 Luján 34 45S 59 5W
39 Lukang 24 0N 120 19E
15 Łuków 51 56N 22 23E
55 Lukulu 14 35S 23 25E
20 Luleå 65 35N 22 10E
54 Lulonga, R. 0 43N 18 23E
54 Lulua, R. 5 2S 21 7E
54 Luluabourg= Kananga 5 55S 22 18E
69 Lumberton 34 37N 78 59W
52 Lumbwa 0 12S 35 28E
47 Lumsden 45 44S 168 27E
38 Lun 47 55N 105 1E
21 Lund 55 41N 13 12E
55 Lundazi 12 20S 33 7E
7 Lundy, I. 51 10N 4 41W
6 Lune, R. 54 2N 2 50W
14 Lüneburg 53 15N 10 23E
14 Lüneburger Heide, Reg. 53 0N 10 0E
63 Lunenburg 44 22N 64 18W
12 Lunéville 48 36N 6 30E
38 Lunghwa 41 15N 117 51E
38 Lungkiang 47 22N 123 4E
38 Lungkow 37 40N 120 25E
33 Lungleh 22 55N 92 45E
38 Lungsi 35 0N 104 35E
32 Luni 26 0N 73 6E
32 Luni, R. 24 40N 71 15E
54 Luofu 0 1S 29 15E
18 Luqa 35 35N 14 28E
9 Lurgan 54 28N 6 20W
55 Lusaka 15 28S 28 16E
52 Lushoto 4 47S 38 20E
38 Lushun 38 48N 121 16E
55 Luso 11 47S 19 52E
38 Lü-ta 39 0N 122 0E
7 Luton 51 53N 0 24W
34 Lutong 4 30N 114 0E
22 Lutsk 50 50N 25 15E
52 Luwingu 10 15S 30 4E
11 Luxembourg 49 37N 6 9E
11 Luxembourg ■ 50 0N 6 0E
11 Luxembourg □ 49 58N 5 30E
51 Luxor=El Uqsur 25 41N 32 38E
22 Luza 60 39N 47 10E
14 Luzern 47 3N 8 18E
79 Luziania 16 20S 48 0W
35 Luzon, I. 16 0N 121 0E
23 Lvov 49 40N 24 0E
38 Lwanhsien 39 45N 118 45E
52 Lwasamaire 0 53S 30 7E
25 Lyakhovskiye Os. 73 40N 141 0E
32 Lyallpur 31 30N 73 5E
8 Lybster 58 18N 3 16W
20 Lycksele 64 38N 18 40E
28 Lydda=Lod 31 57N 34 54E
57 Lydenburg 25 10S 30 29E
47 Lyell 41 48S 172 4E
47 Lyell, Ra. 41 38S 172 20E
7 Lyme Regis 50 44N 2 57W
7 Lymington 50 46N 1 32W
68 Lynchburg 37 23N 79 10W
46 Lyndhurst, N.S.W. 33 41N 149 2E
42 Lyndhurst, Queens. 18 56S 144 30E
68 Lyndonville 44 32N 72 1W
68 Lynn 42 28N 70 57W
65 Lynn Lake 56 51N 101 3W
7 Lynton 51 14N 3 50W
12 Lyon 45 46N 4 50E
12 Lyonnais, Reg. 45 45N 4 15E
12 Lyons=Lyon 45 46N 4 50E
12 Lyons, G. of= Lion, G. du 43 0N 4 0E
45 Lyons, R. 25 2N 115 9W
22 Lysra 57 7N 57 47E
6 Lytham St. Annes 53 45N 2 58W
47 Lyttelton 43 35S 172 44E

M

28 Ma'ad 32 37N 35 36E
39 Maanshan 31 40N 118 30E
11 Maas, R. 51 49N 5 1E
11 Maastricht 50 50N 5 40E
6 Mablethorpe 53 21N 0 14E
52 Mabuki 2 57S 33 12E
79 Macaé 20 20S 41 55W
71 McAllen 26 12N 98 15W
71 McAlester 34 57N 95 40W
79 Macapá 0 5N 51 10W
42 McArthur, R. 15 54S 136 40E
79 Macau 5 0S 36 40W
39 Macau ■ 22 16N 113 35E
64 McBride 53 20N 120 10W
72 McCammon 42 41N 112 11W
6 Macclesfield 53 16N 2 9W
65 McClintock 57 45N 94 15W
60 M'Clintock Chan. 71 0N 103 0W
71 McComb 31 20N 90 30W
70 McCook 40 15N 100 35W
3 McDonald I. 54 0S 73 0E
44 Macdonnell, Ras. 23 40S 133 0E
60 Macdougall, L. 66 20N 98 30W
8 Macduff 57 40N 2 30W
62 Mace 48 55N 80 0W
19 Macedonia □, Greece= Makedhonia □ 40 39N 22 0E
19 Macedonia □, Y.-slav.= Makedonija □ 41 53N 21 40E
79 Maceió 9 40S 35 41W
50 Macenta 8 35N 9 20W
18 Macerata 43 19N 13 28E
72 McGill 35 27N 114 50W
9 Macgillycuddy's Reeks, Mts. 52 2N 9 45W
32 Mach 29 50N 67 20E
52 Machakos 1 30S 37 15E
78 Machala 3 10S 79 50W
25 Macheřna 61 20N 172 20E
33 Machilipatnam 16 11N 81 8E
78 Machiques 10 4N 72 34W
7 Machynlleth 52 36N 3 51W
53 Macias Nguema Biyoga, I. 3 30N 8 40E
43 Macintyre, R. 28 38S 150 47E
42 Mackay, Australia 21 36S 148 39E
72 Mackay, U.S.A. 43 58N 113 37W
44 Mackay, L. 22 40S 128 35E
68 McKeesport 40 29N 79 50W
60 Mackenzie, Reg. 61 30N 144 30W
64 Mackenzie 55 20N 123 5W
42 Mackenzie, R. 23 30S 150 0E
60 Mackenzie, R. 69 15N 134 8W

Mackenzie City Maputo, B. de

78 Mackenzie City 6 0N 58 10W
60 Mackenzie Mts. 64 0N 130 0W
42 McKinlay 21 16S 141 17E
60 McKinley, Mt. 63 10N 151 0W
71 McKinney 33 10N 96 40W
52 Mackinnon Road 3 40S 39 0E
65 Macklin 52 20N 109 56W
43 Macksville 30 40S 152 56E
43 Maclean 29 26S 153 16E
57 Maclear 31 2S 28 23E
43 Macleay, R. 30 52S 153 1E
64 McLennan 55 42N 116 50W
45 McLeod, L. 24 9S 113 47E
64 McLure 50 55N 120 20W
58 M'Clure Str. 74 40N 117 30W
72 McMinnville, Oreg. 45 16N 123 11W
69 McMinnville, Tenn. 35 43N 85 45W
65 McMurray 56 45N 111 27W
73 McNary 34 4N 109 53W
70 Macomb 40 25N 90 40W
12 Mâcon 46 19N 4 50E
69 Macon 32 50N 83 37W
70 McPherson 38 25N 97 40W
3 Macquarie Is. 54 36S 158 55E
46 Macquarie, R. 30 7S 147 24E
9 Macroom 51 54N 8 57W
30 Madā'in Sālih 26 51N 37 58E
53 Madagali 10 56N 13 33E
53 Madagascar ■ 20 0S 47 0E
51 Madama 22 0N 14 0E
3 Madang 5 0S 145 46E
53 Madaoua 14 5N 6 27E
53 Madara 11 45N 10 35E
33 Madaripur 23 2N 90 15E
33 Madauk 17 56N 96 52E
33 Madaya 22 20N 96 10E
74 Madden L. 9 20N 79 37W
50 Madeira, I. 32 50N 17 0W
78 Madeira, R. 3 22S 58 45W
73 Madera 37 0N 120 1W
32 Madhya Pradesh □ 21 50N 81 0E
29 Madinat al Shaab 12 50N 45 0E
54 Madingou 4 10S 13 33E
68 Madison, Ind. 38 42N 85 20W
70 Madison, S.D. 44 0N 97 8W
70 Madison, Wis. 43 5N 89 25W
68 Madisonville 37 42N 86 30W
35 Madiun 7 38S 111 32E
52 Mado Gashi 0 47N 39 12E
32 Madras, India 13 8N 80 19E
72 Madras, U.S.A. 44 40N 121 10W
74 Madre, Laguna 25 0N 97 30W
78 Madre de Dios, R. 10 59S 66 8W
80 Madre de Dios, I. 50 20S 75 10W
74 Madre del Sur, Sa. 17 30N 100 0W
74 Madre Occidental, Sa. 27 0N 107 0W
74 Madre Oriental, Sa. 25 0N 100 0W
13 Madrid 40 25N 3 45W
35 Madura, I. 7 0N 113 20E
35 Madura, Selat 7 30S 113 20E
45 Madura Motel 31 55S 127 0E
32 Madurai 9 55N 78 10E
32 Madurantakam 12 30N 79 50E
34 Mae Sot 16 43N 98 34E
36 Maebashi 36 23N 139 4E
7 Maesteg 51 36N 3 40W
75 Maestra, Sa. 20 15N 77 0W
13 Maestrazgo, Mts. de 40 30N 0 25W
57 Maevatanana 16 56S 46 49E
65 Mafeking, Canada 52 40N 101 10W
56 Mafeking, S.Africa 25 50S 25 38E
52 Mafia I. 7 45S 39 50E
80 Mafra, Brazil 26 7S 49 49W
13 Mafra, Port. 38 56N 9 20W
52 Mafupa 10 30S 29 7E
25 Magadan 59 30N 151 0E
52 Magadi 1 54S 36 19E
80 Magallanes, Estrecho de, Str. 52 30S 75 0W
78 Magangue 9 14N 74 45W
63 Magdalen Is. 47 30N 61 40W
80 Magdalena, Arg. 35 4S 57 32W
74 Magdalena, Mexico 30 50N 112 0W
73 Magdalena, U.S.A. 34 10N 107 20W
80 Magdalena, I., Chile 44 42S 73 10W
74 Magdalena, I., Mexico 24 40N 112 15W
14 Magdeburg 52 8N 11 36E
28 Magdi'el 32 10N 34 54E
9 Magee, I. 54 48N 5 44W
35 Magelang 7 29S 110 13E
80 Magellan's Str.= Magallanes, Estrecho de 52 30S 75 0W
18 Maggiore, L. 46 0N 8 35E
28 Maghar 32 54N 35 24E
9 Magherafelt 54 45N 6 36W
9 Magherafelt □ 54 45N 6 36W
24 Magnitogorsk 53 20N 59 0E
71 Magnolia 33 18N 93 12W
63 Magog 45 18N 72 9W
64 Magrath 49 25N 112 50W
79 Maguarinho, C. 0 15S 48 30W
33 Magwe 20 10N 95 0E
30 Mahābād 36 50N 45 45E
57 Mahabo 20 23S 44 40E
29 Mahaddei Uen 3 0N 45 32E
52 Mahagi 2 20N 31 0E
52 Mahagi Port 2 3N 31 17E
56 Mahalapye 23 1S 26 51E
31 Mahallāt 33 55N 50 30E
33 Mahanadi, R. 20 0N 86 25E
57 Mahanoro 19 59S 48 48E
32 Maharashtra □ 19 30N 75 30E
32 Mahbubnagar 16 45N 77 59E
51 Mahdia 35 28N 11 0E
52 Mahenge 8 45S 36 35E
47 Maheno 45 10S 170 50E
47 Mahia Pen. 39 9S 177 55E
13 Mahón 39 50N 4 18E
63 Mahone Bay 44 27N 64 23W
52 Mahuta 11 32N 4 58E
54 Mai-Ndombe, L. 2 0S 18 0E
7 Maidenhead 51 31N 0 42W
65 Maidstone, Canada 53 5N 109 20W
7 Maidstone, U.K. 51 16N 0 31E
53 Maiduguri 12 0N 13 20E
33 Maijdi 22 48N 91 10E
33 Maikala Ra. 22 0N 81 0E
9 Main, R. 54 43N 6 18W
14 Main, R. 50 0N 8 18E
69 Maine □ 45 20N 69 0W
12 Maine, Reg. 48 0N 0 0E
12 Maine-et-Loire □ 47 31N 0 30W
33 Maingkwan 26 15N 96 45E
8 Mainland, I., Orkney 59 0N 3 10W
8 Mainland, I., Shetland 60 15N 1 22W
32 Mainpuri 27 18N 79 4E
57 Maintirano 18 3S 44 5E
14 Mainz 50 0N 8 17E
80 Maipú 37 0S 58 0W
78 Maiquetía 10 36N 66 57W
33 Mairabari 26 30N 92 30E
75 Maisí, C. 20 10N 74 10W
46 Maitland 32 44S 151 36E
57 Maiyema 12 5N 4 25E
36 Maizuru 35 25N 135 22E
35 Majalengka 6 55S 108 14E
28 Majd el Kurum 32 56N 35 15E
35 Majene 3 27S 118 57E
13 Majorca, I.= Mallorca, I. 39 30N 3 0E
57 Majunga 17 0S 47 0E
57 Majunga □ 16 30S 46 30E
52 Makania 4 21S 37 49E
25 Makarovo 57 40N 107 45E
35 Makasar, Selat, Str. 1 0S 118 20E
24 Makat 47 39N 53 19E
19 Makedhona □ 40 39N 22 0E
19 Makedonija □ 41 53N 21 40E
50 Makeni 8 55N 12 5W
23 Makeyevka 48 0N 38 0E
56 Makgadikgadi Salt Pans 20 40S 25 45E
23 Makhachkala 43 0N 47 15E
52 Makindu 2 17S 37 49E
24 Makinsk 52 37N 70 26E
30 Makkah 21 30N 39 54E
63 Makkovik 55 0N 59 10W
25 Maklakovo 58 16N 92 29E
15 Makó 46 14N 20 33E
54 Makokou 0 40N 12 50E
52 Makongolosi 8 23S 33 10E
32 Makran Coast Ra. 25 40N 4 0E
52 Maktau 3 25S 38 2E
30 Māku 39 15N 44 31E
36 Makurazaki 31 15N 130 20E
53 Makurdi 7 45N 8 32E
23 Mal Usen, R. 48 50N 49 39E
32 Malabar Coast, Reg. 11 0N 75 0E
34 Malacca=Melaka 2 15N 102 15E
34 Malacca, Str. of 3 0N 101 0E
72 Malad City 41 10N 112 20W
13 Maladetta, Mt. 42 40N 0 30E
13 Málaga 36 43N 4 23W
52 Malagarasi 5 5S 30 50E
55 Malagasy Rep.= Madagascar ■ 19 0S 46 0E
57 Malaimbandy 20 20S 45 36E
51 Malakâl 9 33N 31 50E
32 Malakand 34 40N 71 55E
25 Malamyzh 50 0N 136 50E
35 Malang 7 59S 112 35E
52 Malangali 8 33S 34 57E
54 Malanje 9 30S 16 17E
21 Mälaren, L. 59 30N 17 10E
80 Malargüe 35 40S 69 30W
62 Malartic 48 9N 78 9W
30 Malatya 38 25N 38 20E
55 Malawi ■ 13 0S 34 0E
55 Malawi, L. 12 30S 34 30E
34 Malaya □ 4 0N 102 0E
30 Malayer 28 22N 56 38E
34 Malaysia ■ 5 0N 110 0E
42 Malbon 21 5S 140 17E
15 Malbork 54 3N 19 10E
45 Malcolm 28 51S 121 25E
2 Malden I. 4 3S 154 59W
27 Maldive Is. 2 0N 73 0W
80 Maldonado 35 0S 55 0W
19 Malea, Ákra 36 58N 23 7E
32 Malegaon 20 30N 74 30E
51 Malha 15 8N 26 12E
13 Malhão, Sa. do 37 20N 8 0W
50 Mali ■ 15 0N 10 0W
52 Malimba Mts. 7 30S 29 30E
9 Malin Hd. 55 18N 7 16W
52 Malindi 3 12S 40 5E
35 Malingping 6 45S 106 2E
34 Maliwun 10 14N 98 37E
46 Mallacoota, Inlet 34 40S 149 40E
8 Mallaig 57 0N 5 50W
51 Mallawi 27 44N 30 44E
13 Mallorca, I. 39 30N 3 0E
9 Mallow 52 8N 8 39W
20 Malmberget 67 11N 20 40E
11 Malmédy 50 26N 6 2E
56 Malmesbury 33 28S 18 41E
21 Malmö 55 36N 12 59E
21 Malmöhus □ 55 45N 13 30E
35 Malolos 14 50N 21 2E
68 Malone 44 50N 74 19W
72 Malta 48 20N 107 55W
18 Malta ■ 35 50N 14 30E
6 Malton 54 9N 0 48W
35 Maluku, Js. 3 0S 128 0E
53 Malumfashi 11 48N 7 39E
32 Malvan 16 2N 73 30E
7 Malvern, U.K. 52 7N 2 19W
71 Malvern, U.S.A. 34 22N 92 50W
7 Malvern Hills 52 0N 2 19W
80 Malvinas, Is.= Falkland Is. □ 51 30S 59 0W
79 Mamanguape 6 50S 35 4W
35 Mamasa 2 55S 119 20E
52 Mambrui 3 5S 40 5E
53 Mamfe 5 50N 9 15E
73 Mammoth 32 46N 110 43W
39 Mamoi 26 0N 119 25E
78 Mamoré, R. 10 23S 65 53W
50 Mamou 10 15N 12 0W
34 Mampawah 0 30N 109 5E
50 Man 7 30N 7 40W
6 Man, I. of 54 15N 4 30W
33 Man Na 23 27N 97 19E
79 Mana 5 45N 53 55W
78 Manacapuru 3 10S 60 50W
13 Manacor 39 32N 3 12E
35 Manado 1 40N 124 45E
75 Managua 12 0N 86 20W
75 Managua, L. de 12 20N 86 30W
57 Manakara 22 8S 48 1E
57 Mananjary 21 13S 48 20E
57 Manantenina 24 17S 47 19E
78 Manaos=Manaus 3 0S 60 0W
47 Manapouri, L. 45 32S 167 32E
37 Manass 44 20N 86 21E
33 Manaung Kyun, I. 18 45N 93 40E
78 Manaus 3 0S 60 0W
12 Manche □ 49 10N 1 20W
6 Manchester, U.K. 53 30N 2 15W
68 Manchester, U.S.A. 42 58N 71 29W
38 Manchouli 49 46N 117 24E
27 Manchuria, Reg. 44 0N 126 0E
52 Manda 10 30S 34 40E
21 Mandal 58 2N 7 25E
35 Mandala, Puncak, Mt. 4 30S 141 0E
33 Mandalay 22 0N 96 10E
38 Mandalgovi 45 40N 106 22E
30 Mandali 33 52N 45 28E
70 Mandan 46 50N 101 0W
35 Mandar, Teluk, G. 3 35S 119 4E
32 Mandasaur 24 4N 75 4E
55 Mandimba 14 22S 35 33E
57 Mandoto 19 34S 46 17E
57 Mandritsara 15 50S 48 49E
45 Mandurah 32 32S 115 43E
32 Mandya 12 30N 77 0E
53 Manengouba, Mts. 5 15N 9 15E
51 Manfalût 27 20N 30 52E
18 Manfredónia, G. di 41 30N 16 10E
32 Mangalore 12 55N 74 47E
47 Mangaweka 39 48S 175 47E
34 Manggar 2 50S 108 10E
32 Mangla Dam 33 32N 73 50E
35 Mangole, I. 1 50S 125 55E
47 Mangonui 35 1S 173 32E
80 Mangueira, L. 33 0S 52 50W
37 Mangyai 38 6N 91 37E
24 Mangyshlak Pol. 43 40N 52 30E
70 Manhattan 39 10N 96 40W
79 Manhuaçu 20 15S 42 2W
57 Manica et Sofala □ 19 10S 33 45E
57 Manicaland □ 19 0S 32 30E
78 Manicoré 6 0S 61 10W
63 Manicouagan, L. 51 25N 68 15W
2 Manihiki, I. 11 0S 161 0W
33 Manikpur 25 5N 81 5E
35 Manila 14 40N 121 3E
35 Manila B. 14 0N 120 0E
46 Manildra 33 11S 148 41E
43 Manilla 30 45S 150 43E
33 Manipur □ 24 30N 94 0E
30 Manisa 38 38N 27 30E
68 Manistee 44 15N 86 20W
68 Manistique 45 59N 86 18W
65 Manitoba □ 55 30N 97 0W
65 Manitoba, L. 50 40N 98 30W
70 Manitou Springs 38 52N 104 55W
62 Manitoulin I. 45 40N 82 30W
68 Manitowoc 44 8N 87 40W
78 Manizales 5 5N 75 32W
57 Manja 21 26S 44 20E
57 Manjakandriana 18 55S 47 47E
32 Manjhand 25 50N 68 10E
30 Manjil 36 46N 49 30E
45 Manjimup 34 15S 116 6E
32 Manjra, R. 18 49N 77 52E
70 Mankato, Kans. 39 49N 98 11W
70 Mankato, Minn. 44 8N 93 59W
50 Mankono 8 10N 6 10W
32 Mankulam 9 7N 80 26E
46 Manly 33 48S 151 14E
32 Manmad 20 18N 74 28E
43 Mannahill 32 26S 139 59E
32 Mannar, G. of 8 30N 79 0E
32 Mannar, I. 9 4N 79 45E
14 Mannheim 49 28N 8 29E
64 Manning 56 53N 117 39W
43 Mannum 34 57S 139 12E
35 Manokwari 0 54N 134 0E
57 Manombo 22 57S 43 28E
54 Manono 7 18S 27 25E
54 Mansa, Zambia 11 13S 28 55E
61 Mansel I. 62 0N 80 0W
46 Mansfield, Australia 37 0S 146 0E
6 Mansfield, U.K. 53 8N 1 12W
68 Mansfield, U.S.A. 40 45N 82 30W
51 Mansura= El Mansura 31 0N 31 19E
78 Manta 1 0S 80 40W
73 Manteca 37 50N 121 12W
12 Mantes-la-Jolie 49 0N 1 41E
72 Manti 39 23N 111 32W
79 Mantiqueira, Sa. da 22 0S 44 0W
18 Mántova 45 10N 10 47E
18 Mantua =Mantova 45 9N 10 48E
35 Manukan 8 14N 123 3E
47 Manukau 37 2S 174 54E
23 Manych-Gudilo, Oz. 46 24N 42 38E
52 Manyoni 5 45S 34 55E
32 Manzai 32 20N 70 15E
13 Manzanares 39 0N 3 22W
75 Manzanillo, Cuba 20 20N 77 10W
74 Manzanillo, Mexico 19 0N 104 20W
75 Manzanillo, Pta. 9 30N 79 40W
57 Manzini 26 30S 31 25E
51 Mao 14 4N 15 19E
65 Maple Creek 49 55N 109 27W
70 Maplewood 38 33N 90 18W
57 Maputo 25 58S 32 32E
57 Maputo, B. de 26 0S 32 50E

Maputo □ Mende

57 Maputo □ 26 30s 32 40 E
30 Maqnā 28 25N 34 50 E
80 Maquinchao 41 15s 68 50w
80 Mar Sa. do 25 30s 49 0w
80 Mar Chiquita, L. 30 40s 62 50w
80 Mar del Plata 38 0s 57 30w
52 Mara 1 30s 34 32 E
79 Marabá 5 20s 49 5w
78 Maracaibo 10 40N 71 37w
78 Maracaibo, L. de 9 40N 71 30w
78 Maracay 10 15N 67 36w
51 Maradah 29 4N 19 4 E
53 Maradi 13 35N 8 10 E
30 Maragheh 37 30N 46 12 E
79 Marajó, I. de 1 0s 49 30w
52 Maralal 1 0N 36 58 E
56 Maramba = Livingstone 17 50N 25 50 E
30 Marand 38 30N 45 45 E
57 Marandellas 18 5s 31 42 E
79 Maranguape 3 55s 38 50w
79 Maranhão=São Luís 2 39s 44 15w
79 Maranhão □ 5 0s 46 0w
78 Marañón, R. 4 50s 75 35w
30 Maraş 37 37N 36 53 E
19 Marathón 38 11N 23 58 E
42 Marathon 20 51s 143 32 E
29 Marbat 17 0N 54 45 E
44 Marble Bar 21 9s 119 44 E
7 March 57 33N 0 5 E
18 Marche □ 43 22N 13 10 E
12 Marche, Reg. 46 5N 2 10 E
11 Marche-en-Famenne 50 14N 5 19 E
13 Marchena 37 18N 5 23w
32 Mardan 34 12N 72 2 E
30 Mardin 37 20N 40 36 E
8 Maree, L. 57 40N 5 30w
42 Mareeba 16 59s 145 28 E
64 Margaret Bay 51 20N 127 20w
44 Margaret River 18 0s 126 30 E
78 Margarita, Is. de 11 0N 64 0w
57 Margate, S. Afr. 30 50s 30 20 E
7 Margate, U.K. 51 23N 1 24 E
52 Margherita, Mt. 0 22N 29 51 E
22 Mari A.S.S.R. □ 56 30N 48 0 E
47 Maria van Diemen, C. 34 29s 172 40 E
52 Mariakani 3 50s 39 27 E
3 Mariana Is. 17 0N 145 0 E
75 Marianao 23 8N 82 24w
69 Marianna 30 45N 85 15w
55 Mariano Machado 13 2s 14 40 E
29 Marib 15 25N 45 20 E
18 Maribor 46 36N 15 40 E
61 Maricourt 61 36N 71 57w
75 Marie-Galante, I. 15 56N 61 16w
21 Mariehamn 60 5N 19 57 E
56 Mariental 24 36s 18 0 E
21 Mariestad 58 43N 13 50 E
69 Marietta, Ga. 34 0N 84 30w
68 Marietta, Ohio 39 27N 81 27w
75 Marigot 15 32N 61 18w
24 Marniisk 56 10N 87 20 E
79 Marília 22 0s 50 0w
13 Marin 42 23N 8 42w
35 Marinduque, I. 13 25N 122 0 E
68 Marinette 45 4N 87 40w
80 Maringá 23 35s 51 50w
71 Marion, Ill. 37 45N 88 55w
68 Marion, Ind. 40 35N 85 40w
70 Marion, Iowa 42 2N 91 36w
68 Marion, Ohio 40 38N 83 8w
69 Marion, S.C. 34 11N 79 22w
69 Marion, Va. 36 51N 81 29w
19 Maritsa 42 1N 25 50 E
31 Marjan 32 5N 68 20 E
6 Market Drayton 52 55N 2 30w
7 Market Harborough 52 29N 0 55w
6 Market Rasen 53 24N 0 20w
22 Marks 51 45N 46 50 E
42 Marlborough 22 46s 149 52 E
47 Marlborough □ 41 45s 173 33 E
7 Marlborough Downs 51 25N 1 55w
71 Marlin 31 25N 96 50w
32 Marmagao 15 25N 73 56 E
30 Marmara Denizi, Sea 40 45N 28 15 E
62 Marmora 44 28N 77 41w
12 Marne □ 49 0N 4 10 E
12 Marne, R. 48 49N 2 24 E
57 Maroantsetra 15 26s 49 44 E
43 Maroochydore 26 35s 153 10w
53 Maroua 10 40N 14 20 E
57 Marovoay 16 6s 46 39 E
57 Marquard 28 40s 27 28 E
2 Marquesas Is. 9 0s 139 30w
68 Marquette 46 30N 87 21w
51 Marra, J. 7 20N 27 35 E
50 Marrakech 31 40N 8 0w
50 Marrakesh= Marrakech 31 40N 8 0w
42 Marrawah 40 56s 144 41 E
43 Marree 29 39s 138 1 E
51 Marsa Brega 30 30N 19 20 E
51 Marsa Susa 32 52N 21 59 E
52 Marsabit 2 18N 38 0 E
18 Marsala 37 48N 12 25 E
46 Marsden 33 47N 147 32 E
12 Marseille 43 18N 5 23 E
12 Marseilles= Marseille 43 18N 5 23 E
70 Marshall, Minn. 44 25N 95 45w
70 Marshall, Mo. 39 8N 93 15w
71 Marshall, Tex. 32 29N 94 20w
3 Marshall Is. 9 0N 171 0 E
70 Marshalltown 42 0N 93 0w
70 Marshfield 44 42N 90 10w
33 Martaban 16 30N 97 35 E
33 Martaban, G. of 15 40N 96 30 E
34 Martapura, Kalimantan 3 22s 114 56 E
34 Martapura, Sumatera 4 19s 104 22 E
53 Marte 12 23N 13 46 E
43 Marthaguy Creek 30 16s 147 35 E
68 Martha's Vineyard 41 25N 70 35w
14 Martigny 46 6N 7 3 E
75 Martinique, I. 14 40N 61 0w
75 Martinique Pass. 15 15N 61 0w
68 Martins Ferry 40 5N 80 46w
68 Martinsburg 39 30N 77 57w
68 Martinsville, Ind. 39 29N 86 23w
69 Martinsville, Va. 36 41N 79 52w
47 Marton 40 4s 175 23 E
13 Martos 37 44N 3 58w
53 Maru 12 22N 6 22 E
36 Marugame 34 15N 133 55 E
46 Marulan 34 43s 150 3 E
52 Marungu Mts. 7 30s 30 0 E
32 Marwar 25 43N 73 45 E
24 Mary 37 40N 61 50 E
42 Mary Kathleen 20 35s 139 48 E
61 Mary River 70 30N 78 0w
43 Maryborough, Queens. 25 31s 152 37 E
46 Maryborough, Vic. 37 0s 143 44 E
68 Maryland □ 39 10N 76 40w
6 Maryport 54 43N 3 30w
63 Marystown 47 10N 55 10w
73 Marysvale 38 25N 112 17w
72 Marysville 39 14N 121 40w
69 Maryville 35 50N 84 0w
51 Marzūq 25 53N 14 10 E
52 Masai Steppe 4 30s 36 30 E
52 Masaka 0 21s 31 45 E
53 Masakali 13 2N 12 32 E
35 Masamba 2 30s 120 15 E
38 Masan 35 11N 128 32 E
31 Masandam, Ras. 26 30N 56 30 E
52 Masasi 10 45s 38 52 E
75 Masaya 12 0N 86 7w
53 Masba 10 35N 13 1 E
35 Masbate 12 20N 123 30 E
35 Masbate, I. 12 20N 123 30 E
50 Mascara 35 26N 0 6 E
56 Maseru 29 18s 27 30 E
31 Mashhad 36 20N 59 35 E
53 Mashi 13 0N 7 54 E
62 Mashkode 47 2N 84 7w
57 Mashonaland North □ 16 30s 30 0 E
57 Mashonaland South □ 18 0s 31 30 E
52 Masindi 1 40N 41 43 E
52 Masindi Port 1 43N 32 2 E
52 Masisi 1 23s 28 49 E
30 Masjed Soleyman 31 55N 49 25 E
9 Mask, L. 53 36N 9 24w
57 Masoala, C. 15 59s 50 13 E
70 Mason City 48 0N 119 0w
31 Masqat 23 37N 58 36 E
18 Massa 44 2N 10 7 E
68 Massachusetts □ 42 25N 72 0w
51 Massawa=Mitsiwa 15 35N 39 25 E
68 Massena 44 52N 74 55w
64 Masset 54 0N 132 0w
12 Massif Central Reg. 45 30N 2 21 E
68 Massillon 40 47N 81 30w
47 Masterton 40 56s 175 39 E
32 Mastung 29 50N 66 42 E
30 Mastura 23 7N 38 52 E
36 Masuda 34 40N 131 51 E
15 Masurian Lakes= Mazurski, Pojezierze 53 50N 21 0 E
57 Matabeleland □ 20 0s 27 30 E
35 Mataboor 1 41s 138 3 E
62 Matachewan 47 50N 80 55w
38 Matad 47 12N 115 29 E
54 Matadi 5 52s 13 31 E
75 Matagalpa 13 10N 85 40w
62 Matagami 49 45N 77 34w
32 Matale 7 30N 80 44 E
74 Matamoros 18 2N 98 17w
63 Matane 48 50N 67 33w
60 Matanuska 61 38N 149 0w
75 Matanzas 23 0N 81 40w
34 Mataram 8 41s 116 10 E
44 Mataranka 14 55s 133 4 E
13 Mataró 41 32N 2 29 E
57 Matatiele 30 20s 28 49 E
47 Mataura 46 11s 168 51 E
74 Matehuala 23 40N 100 50w
57 Mateke Hills 21 48s 31 0 E
18 Matera 40 40N 16 37 E
32 Mathura 27 30N 77 48 E
6 Matlock 53 8N 1 32w
50 Matmata 33 30N 9 59 E
79 Mato Grosso □ 14 0s 54 0w
52 Matombo 7 3s 37 46 E
48 Matopo 20 36s 28 20 E
57 Matopo Hills 20 36s 28 20 E
13 Matozinhos 41 11N 8 42w
31 Matrah 23 37N 58 30 E
51 Matrûh 31 19N 27 9 E
53 Matsena 13 5N 10 5 E
39 Matsu, I. 26 9N 119 56 E
36 Matsue 35 25N 133 10 E
36 Matsumoto 36 15N 138 0 E
36 Matsusaka 34 34N 136 32 E
36 Matsuyama 33 45N 132 45 E
32 Mattancheri 9 50N 76 15 E
62 Mattawa 46 20N 78 45w
14 Matterhorn, Mt. 45 58N 7 39 E
75 Matthew Town 20 57N 73 40w
70 Mattoon 39 30N 88 20w
34 Matua 2 58s 110 52 E
78 Maturín 9 45N 63 11w
32 Mau Ranipur 25 16N 79 8 E
78 Maués 3 20s 57 45w
66 Maui, I. 20 45N 156 20 E
33 Maulamyaing 16 30N 97 40 E
35 Maumere 8 38s 122 13 E
56 Maun 20 0s 23 26 E
66 Mauna Loa, Mt. 19 50N 155 28 E
63 Maungmagan Is. 41 0s 97 48 E
52 Maungu 3 32s 38 42 E
50 Mauritania ■ 20 50N 10 0w
49 Mauritius 20 0s 57 0 E
12 Maurienne, Reg. 45 15N 6 20 E
28 Mavqi'im 31 38N 34 32 E
33 Mawkmai 20 14N 97 50 E
33 Mawlaik 23 40N 94 26 E
42 Maxwelton 39 51s 174 49 E
75 May Pen 17 58N 77 15w
74 Maya Mts. 16 30N 89 0w
75 Mayaguana I. 21 30N 72 44w
75 Mayagüez 18 12N 67 9w
45 Mayanup 33 58s 116 25 E
42 Maydena 42 45s 146 39 E
12 Mayenne 48 20N 0 38w
12 Mayenne □ 48 10N 0 40w
64 Mayerthorpe 53 57N 115 15w
69 Mayfield 36 45N 88 40w
23 Maykop 44 35N 40 25 E
62 Maynooth, Canada 45 14N 77 56w
9 Maynooth, Eire 53 22N 6 38w
60 Mayo 63 38N 135 57w
9 Mayo □ 53 47N 9 7w
68 Maysville 38 43N 84 16w
54 Mayumba 3 25s 10 39 E
25 Mayya 61 44N 130 18 E
55 Mazabuka 15 52s 27 44 E
79 Mazagão 0 20s 51 50w
64 Mazama 49 43N 120 8w
31 Mazan Deran □ 36 30N 53 30 E
31 Mazar-i-Sharif 36 41N 67 0 E
80 Mazarredo 47 10s 66 50w
13 Mazarrón 37 38N 1 19w
74 Mazatenango 14 35N 91 30w
74 Mazatlán 23 10N 106 30w
15 Mazurski, Pojezierze 53 50N 21 0 E
57 Mbabane 26 18s 31 6 E
54 M'Baiki 3 53N 18 1 E
52 Mbala 8 46s 31 17 E
52 Mbale 1 8N 34 12 E
53 Mbalmayo 3 33N 11 33 E
52 Mbamba Bay 11 13s 34 49 E
54 Mbandaka 0 1s 18 18 E
53 Mbanga 4 30N 9 33 E
52 Mbarara 0 35s 30 25 E
52 Mbeya 8 54s 33 29 E
54 Mbuji-Mayi 6 9s 23 40 E
52 Mbulamuti 0 57N 33 0 E
52 Mbulu 3 45s 35 30 E
52 Mchinja 9 46s 39 45 E
55 Mchinji 13 47s 32 58 E
18 Mdina 35 51N 14 25 E
73 Mead, L. 36 10N 114 10w
45 Meadow 26 35s 114 30 E
65 Meadow Lake 54 10N 108 10w
65 Meadow Lake Prov. Park 52 25N 109 0w
68 Meadville 41 39N 80 9w
62 Meaford 44 40N 80 36w
9 Meath □ 53 32N 6 40w
12 Meaux 48 58N 2 50 E
30 Mecca=Makkah 21 30N 39 54 E
11 Mechelen 51 2N 4 29 E
14 Mecklenburger, B. 54 20N 11 40 E
44 Meda P.O. 17 20s 123 59 E
34 Medan 3 40N 98 38 E
80 Medanosa, Pta. 48 0s 66 0w
50 Médéa 36 12N 2 50 E
78 Medellín 6 15N 75 35w
50 Médenine 33 21N 10 30 E
50 Mederdra 17 0N 15 38w
72 Medford 42 20N 122 52w
15 Mediaş 46 9N 24 22 E
72 Medicine Bow 41 56N 106 11w
72 Medinine Bow Ra. 41 10N 106 25w
65 Medicine Hat 50 0N 110 45w
68 Medina 43 15N 78 27w
13 Medina del Campo 41 18N 4 55w
13 Medina-Sidonia 36 28N 5 57w
16 Mediterranean Sea 35 0N 15 0 E
12 Médoc, Reg. 45 10N 0 56w
23 Medveditsa, R. 49 0N 43 58 E
25 Medvezhi Oshova 71 0N 161 0 E
22 Medvezhyegorsk 63 0N 34 25 E
7 Medway, R. 51 27N 0 44 E
45 Meeberrie 26 57s 116 0 E
45 Meekatharra 26 32s 118 29 E
32 Meerut 29 1N 77 50 E
54 Mega 3 57N 38 30 E
63 Mégantic 45 36N 70 56w
19 Mégara 37 58N 23 22 E
33 Meghalaya □ 25 50N 91 0 E
28 Megiddo 32 36N 15 11 E
15 Mehadia 44 56N 22 23 E
32 Mehsana 23 39N 72 26 E
38 Meihokow 42 37N 125 46 E
39 Meihsien 24 20N 116 0 E
33 Meiktila 21 0N 96 0 E
14 Meissen 51 10N 13 29 E
80 Mejillones 23 10s 70 30w
51 Mekele 13 33N 39 30 E
32 Mekhtar 30 33N 69 20 E
50 Meknès 33 57N 5 33w
53 Meko 7 30N 3 0 E
34 Mekong, R. 10 33N 105 24 E
34 Melaka 2 15N 102 15 E
34 Melalap 5 10N 116 5 E
46 Melbourne 37 40s 145 0 E
74 Melchor Múzquiz 27 50N 101 40w
22 Melekess= Dimitrovgrad 54 25N 49 33 E
65 Melfort, Canada 52 50N 105 40w
57 Melfort, Rhod. 18 0s 31 25 E
50 Melilla 35 21N 2 57w
28 Melilot 31 22N 34 37 E
65 Melita 49 15N 101 5w
23 Melitopol 46 50N 35 22 E
14 Melk 48 13N 15 20 E
21 Mellerud 58 41N 12 28 E
80 Melo 32 20s 54 10w
8 Melrose 55 35N 2 44w
6 Melton Mowbray 52 46N 0 52w
12 Melun 48 32N 2 39 E
65 Melville 32 2s 115 48 E
44 Melville, I., Australia 11 30s 131 0 E
58 Melville, I., Canada 75 30N 111 0w
63 Melville, L. 53 45N 59 40w
61 Melville Pen. 68 0N 84 0w
57 Memel 27 38s 29 36 E
22 Memel=Klaipeda 55 43N 21 10 E
14 Memmingen 47 59N 10 12 E
71 Memphis 35 7N 90 0w
6 Menai Str. 53 7N 4 20w
53 Ménaka 15 59N 2 18 E
70 Menasha 44 13N 88 27w
34 Menate 0 12s 112 47 E
39 Mencheng 33 27N 116 45 E
12 Mende 44 31N 3 30 E

Mendip Hills — Molucca Sea

7 Mendip Hills 51 17N 2 40W
72 Mendocino 39 26N 123 50W
73 Mendota 36 46N 120 24W
80 Mendoza 32 50S 68 52W
78 Mene de Mauroa 10 45N 70 50W
78 Mene Grande 9 49N 70 56W
30 Menemen 38 36N 27 4E
11 Menen 50 47N 3 7E
18 Menfi 37 36N 12 57E
34 Menggala 4 20S 105 15E
37 Mengtz 23 20N 103 20E
46 Menindee 32 20N 142 25E
70 Menominee 45 9N 87 39W
70 Menomonie 44 50N 91 54W
13 Menor, Mar 37 40N 0 45W
13 Menorca, I. 40 0N 4 0E
34 Mentawai, Kep. 2 0S 99 0E
12 Menton 43 50N 7 29E
51 Menzel Temime 36 46N 11 0E
22 Menzelinsk 55 43N 53 8E
45 Menzies 29 40S 120 58E
28 Me'ona 33 1N 35 15E
11 Meppel 52 42N 6 12E
35 Merak 5 55S 106 1E
18 Merano 46 40N 11 10E
35 Merauke 8 29S 120 24E
29 Merca 1 48N 44 50E
32 Mercara 12 30N 75 45E
73 Merced 37 25N 120 30W
80 Mercedes, Buenos Aires 34 40S 59 30W
80 Mercedes, Corrientes 29 10S 58 5W
80 Mercedes, San Luis 33 40S 65 30W
80 Mercedes, Uruguay 33 12S 58 0W
80 Merceditas 28 20S 70 35W
47 Mercer 37 16S 175 5E
61 Mercy, C. 65 0N 62 30W
7 Mere 51 5N 2 16W
80 Meredith, C. 52 15S 60 40W
34 Mergui 12 30N 98 35E
34 Mergui Arch.= Myeik Kyunzu 11 0N 98 0E
74 Mérida, Mexico 20 50N 89 40W
13 Mérida, Sp. 38 55N 6 25W
78 Mérida, Ven. 8 36N 71 8W
68 Meriden 41 33N 72 47W
72 Meridian, Id. 43 41N 116 20W
71 Meridian, Miss. 32 20N 88 42W
79 Meriruma 1 15N 54 50W
11 Merksem 51 16N 4 25E
51 Merowe 18 29N 31 46E
45 Merredin 31 28S 118 18E
70 Merrill 45 11N 89 41W
64 Merritt 50 10N 120 45W
45 Merroe 27 53S 117 50E
54 Mersa Fatma 14 57N 40 17E
7 Mersea I. 51 48N 0 55E
14 Merseburg 51 20N 12 0E
6 Mersey, R. 53 25N 3 0W
6 Merseyside □ 53 25N 2 55W
30 Mersin 36 51N 34 36E
34 Mersing 2 25N 103 50E
7 Merthyr Tydfil 51 45N 3 23W
13 Mértola 37 40N 7 40E
71 Mertzon 31 17N 100 48W
52 Meru 0 3N 37 40E
52 Meru, Mt. 3 15S 36 46E
73 Mesa 33 20N 111 56W
31 Meshed=Mashhad 36 20N 59 35E
73 Mesilla 32 20N 107 0W
19 Mesolóngion 38 27N 21 28E
30 Mesopotamia, Reg.=Al Jazirah, Reg. 33 30N 44 0E
57 Messina, S.Africa 22 20S 30 12E
18 Messina, Str. di 38 5N 15 35E
19 Messíni 37 4N 22 1E
19 Messiniakós Kól. 36 45N 22 5E
19 Mesta, R. 40 41N 24 44E
78 Meta, R. 6 12N 67 28W
62 Metagama 47 0N 81 55W
80 Metán 25 30S 65 0W
47 Methven 43 38S 171 40E
64 Metlakatla 55 8N 131 35W
71 Metropolis 37 10N 88 47W
28 Metulla 33 17N 35 34E
12 Metz 49 8N 6 10E
34 Meulaboh 4 11N 96 3E
34 Meureudu 5 19N 96 10E
12 Meurthe-et-Moselle □ 48 52N 6 0E
12 Meuse □ 49 8N 5 25E
11 Meuse, R. 51 49N 5 1E
71 Mexia 31 38N 96 32W
79 Mexiana, I. 0 0 49 30W
74 Mexicali 32 40N 115 30W
74 Mexico, Mexico 19 20N 99 10W
70 Mexico, U.S.A. 39 10N 91 55W
74 Mexico ■ 20 0N 100 0W
74 México □ 19 20N 99 10W
22 Mezen, R. 66 11N 43 59E
22 Mezen 65 50N 44 20E
15 Mezökövesd 47 49N 20 35E
15 Mezötur 47 0N 20 41E
57 Mhlaba Hills 18 30S 30 30E
32 Mhow 22 33N 75 50E
74 Miahuatlán 16 21N 96 36W
69 Miami 25 52N 80 15W
69 Miami Beach 25 49N 80 6W
30 Miandowāb 37 0N 46 5E
57 Miandrivaso 19 31S 45 28E
30 Mīāneh 37 30N 47 40E
32 Mianwali 32 38N 71 28E
39 Miaoli 24 34N 120 48E
24 Miass 54 59N 60 6E
60 Michelson, Mt. 69 19N 144 17W
68 Michigan □ 44 40N 85 40W
68 Michigan, L. 44 0N 87 0W
68 Michigan City 41 42N 86 56W
63 Michikamau L. 54 0N 6 0W
62 Michipicoten I. 47 55N 85 45W
62 Michipicoten River 47 50N 84 58W
74 Michoacán □ 19 0N 102 0W
22 Michurinsk 52 58N 40 27E
7 Mid Glamorgan □ 51 40N 3 25W
11 Middelburg, Neth. 51 30N 3 36E
57 Middelburg, C. Prov. 31 30S 25 0E
56 Middelburg, Trans. 25 49S 29 28E
56 Middelveld, Reg. 26 30S 26 0E
63 Middle Brook 48 40N 54 20W
68 Middlebury 44 0N 73 9W
69 Middlesboro 36 40N 83 40W
6 Middlesbrough 54 35N 1 14W
68 Middletown, Conn. 41 37N 72 40W
68 Middletown, N.Y. 41 28N 74 28W
68 Middletown, Ohio 39 29N 84 25W
63 Middleton 44 50N 65 5W
42 Middleton P.O. 22 22S 141 32E
12 Midi, Canal du 43 45N 1 21E
45 Midland, Australia 31 54S 115 59E
62 Midland, Canada 44 45N 79 50W
68 Midland, Mich. 43 37N 84 17W
71 Midland, Tex. 32 0N 102 3W
57 Midlands □ 19 0S 29 30E
33 Midnapore 22 25N 87 21E
57 Midongy du Sud 23 35S 47 1E
2 Midway Is. 28 13N 177 22W
72 Midwest 43 27N 106 11W
36 Mie □ 34 20N 136 20E
14 Międzychod 52 35N 15 53E
15 Międzyrzec Podlaski 51 58N 22 45E
39 Mienyang 31 18N 104 26E
15 Miercurea Ciuc 46 21N 25 48E
13 Mieres 43 18N 5 48W
28 Migdal 32 51N 35 30E
28 Migdal Ha'Emeq 32 41N 35 14E
36 Mihara 34 25N 133 5E
52 Mikese 6 48S 37 55E
52 Mikindani 10 15S 40 2E
20 Mikkeli □ 61 56N 28 0E
22 Mikun 62 20N 50 0E
78 Milagro 2 0S 79 30W
18 Milan=Milano 45 28N 9 10E
43 Milang 35 20S 138 55E
18 Milano 45 28N 9 10E
18 Milazzo 38 13N 15 13E
7 Mildenhall 52 20N 0 30E
46 Mildura 34 13S 142 9E
43 Miles 26 37S 150 10E
70 Miles City 46 30N 105 50W
65 Milestone 50 0N 104 30W
59 Milford, Conn. 41 13N 73 4W
68 Milford, Del. 38 52N 75 26W
73 Milford, Utah 38 20N 113 0W
7 Milford Haven 51 43N 5 2W
45 Miling 30 30S 116 17E
12 Millau 44 8N 3 4E
63 Millertown Junction 48 49N 56 28W
43 Millicent 37 34S 140 21E
69 Millinocket 45 45N 68 45W
6 Millom 54 13N 3 16W
68 Millville 39 22N 74 0W
61 Milne Inlet 72 30N 80 0W
64 Milo 24 28N 103 23E
19 Mílos, I. 36 44N 24 25E
47 Milton, N.Z. 46 7S 169 59E
68 Milton, U.S.A. 41 0N 76 53W
7 Milton Keynes 52 3N 0 42W
9 Miltown Malbay 52 51N 9 25W
68 Milwaukee 43 9N 87 58W
72 Milwaukie 45 33N 122 39W
30 Minā al Ahmadī 29 5N 48 10E
30 Mina Saud 28 45N 48 20E
31 Mīnāb 27 10N 57 1E
36 Minamata 32 10N 130 30E
80 Minas 34 20S 55 15W
13 Minas de Rio Tinto 37 42N 6 22W
79 Minas Gerais □ 18 50S 46 0W
74 Minatitlán 17 58N 94 35W
33 Minbu 20 10N 95 0E
8 Minch, Little, Chan. 57 40N 6 50W
8 Minch, North, Chan. 58 0N 6 0W
35 Mindanao, I. 8 0N 125 0E
35 Mindanao Sea 9 0 124 0E
35 Mindanao Trench 8 0N 128 0E
14 Minden 52 18N 8 54E
71 Minden 32 40N 93 20W
35 Mindoro, I. 13 0N 121 0E
35 Mindoro Str. 12 30N 120 30E
7 Minehead 51 12N 3 29W
71 Mineral Wells 32 50N 98 5W
63 Mingan 50 20N 64 0W
23 Mingechaurskoye, Vdkhr. 40 56N 47 20E
42 Mingela 19 52S 146 38E
45 Mingenew 29 12S 115 21E
13 Minho, R. 41 52N 8 51W
13 Minho Reg. 41 40N 8 30W
39 Minhow=Foochow 26 5N 119 18E
45 Minilya 23 55S 114 0E
39 Min Kiang, R. 26 0N 119 30E
39 Minkiang 32 30N 114 10E
53 Minna 9 37N 6 30E
70 Minneapolis 44 58N 93 20W
65 Minnedosa 50 20N 99 50W
70 Minnesota □ 46 40N 94 0W
43 Minnipa 32 51S 135 9E
36 Mino 35 32N 136 55E
13 Minorca, I.= Menorca, I. 40 0N 4 0E
70 Minot 48 10N 101 15W
22 Minsk 53 52N 27 30E
15 Mińsk Mazowiecki 52 10N 21 33E
63 Minto 34 1S 150 51E
61 Minto, L. 48 0N 84 45W
72 Minturn 39 45N 106 25W
25 Minusinsk 53 50N 91 20E
33 Minutang 28 15N 96 30E
37 Minya Konka, Mt. 29 34N 101 53E
63 Miquelon, I. 47 8N 56 24W
32 Miraj 16 50N 74 45E
79 Miranda 20 10S 50 15W
13 Miranda de Ebro 42 41N 2 57W
13 Miranda do Douro 41 30N 6 16W
34 Miri 4 18N 114 0E
42 Miriam Vale 24 20S 151 39E
80 Mirim, L. 32 45S 52 50W
32 Mirpur Khas 25 30N 69 0E
33 Mirzapur 25 10N 82 45E
38 Mishan 45 31N 132 2E
68 Mishawaka 41 40N 86 8W
36 Mishima 35 10N 138 52E
28 Mishmar Alyalon 31 52N 34 57E
28 Mishmar Ha 'Emeq 32 37N 35 7E
28 Mishmar Ha Negev 31 22N 34 48E
28 Mishmar Ha Yarden 33 0N 35 56E
31 Miskīn 2344⅛ 56 52E
75 Miskitos, Cayos 14 26N 82 50W
15 Miskolc 48 7N 20 50E
35 Misool, I. 2 0S 130 0E
51 Misrātah 32 18N 15 3E
71 Mission 26 15N 98 30W
64 Mission City 49 10N 122 15W
71 Mississippi □ 33 0N 90 0W
71 Mississippi, R. 29 0N 89 15W
71 Mississippi, Delta of the 29 10N 89 15W
72 Missoula 47 0N 114 0W
70 Missouri □ 38 25N 92 30W
70 Missouri, Plat. du Coteau du 46 0N 99 30W
70 Missouri, R. 38 50N 90 8W
62 Mistassini, L. 51 0N 73 40W
43 Mitchell, Australia 26 29S 147 58E
70 Mitchell, U.S.A. 43 40N 98 0W
69 Mitchell, Mt. 35 40N 82 20W
9 Mitchelstown 52 16N 8 18W
19 Mitylene, I.= Lésvos, I. 39 0N 26 20E
19 Mitilíni 39 6N 26 35E
74 Mitla 16 55N 96 17W
36 Mito 36 20N 140 30E
57 Mitsinjo 16 1S 45 52E
51 Mitsiwa 15 35N 39 25E
43 Mittagong 34 28S 150 29E
46 Mittyack 35 8S 142 36E
54 Mitumba, Chaîne des 10 0S 26 20E
52 Mityana 0 24N 32 3E
36 Miyagi □ 38 15N 140 45E
36 Miyako 39 40N 141 75E
36 Miyakonojo 31 32N 131 5E
36 Miyazaki 31 56N 131 30E
36 Miyazaki 32 0N 131 30E
28 Miyet, Bahr el 31 30N 35 30E
36 Miyoshi 34 48N 132 32E
38 Miyun 40 22N 116 49E
9 Mizen Hd., Cork 51 27N 9 50W
9 Mizen Hd., Wicklow 52 52N 6 4W
33 Mizoram □ 23 0N 92 40E
28 Mizpe Ramon 20 36N 34 48E
52 Mjanji 0 17N 33 59E
21 Mjölby 58 20N 15 10E
21 Mjøsa, L. 60 45N 11 0E
52 Mkobela 10 57S 38 5E
55 Mkushi 14 20S 29 20E
52 Mkwaya 6 17S 35 40E
14 Mladá Boleslav 50 27N 14 53E
15 Mława 53 9N 20 25E
48 Mlanje, Mt. 16 2S 35 33E
53 Mme 6 18N 10 14E
20 Mo 66 15N 14 8E
35 Moa, I. 8 0S 128 0E
73 Moab 38 40N 109 35W
46 Moama 36 3S 144 45E
52 Moba 7 3S 29 47E
54 Mobaye 4 25N 21 5E
70 Moberly 39 25N 92 25W
62 Mobert 48 41N 85 40W
69 Mobile 30 41N 88 3W
52 Mobutu Sese Seko, L. 1 30N 31 0E
55 Moçambique 15 3S 40 42E
55 Moçâmedes 16 35S 12 30E
56 Mochudi 24 27S 26 7E
52 Moçimboa da Praia 11 25S 40 20E
78 Mocoa 1 15N 76 45W
74 Moctezuma, R. 21 59N 98 34W
55 Mocuba 16 54S 37 25E
12 Modane 45 12N 6 40E
56 Modderrivier 29 2S 24 38E
18 Módena 44 39N 10 55E
73 Modesto 37 43N 121 0W
18 Módica 36 52N 14 45E
46 Moe 38 12S 146 19E
79 Moengo 5 45N 54 20W
54 Moero, L. 9 0S 28 45E
8 Moffat 55 20N 3 27W
29 Mogadiscio 2 2N 45 25E
29 Mogadishu= Mogadiscio 2 2N 45 25E
50 Mogador= Essaouira 31 32N 9 42W
33 Mogaung 25 20N 97 0E
80 Mogi das Cruzes 23 45S 46 20W
79 Mogi Mirim 22 20S 47 0W
22 Mogilev 53 55N 30 18E
23 Mogilev Podolskiy 48 20N 27 40E
25 Mogocha 53 40N 119 50E
73 Mogollon Mesa 43 40N 110 0W
45 Mogumber 31 2S 116 3E
15 Mohács 45 58N 18 41E
38 Moho 53 15N 122 27E
52 Mohoro 8 6S 39 8E
24 Mointy 47 40N 73 45E
73 Mojave 35 8N 118 8W
73 Mojave Des. 35 0N 117 30W
35 Mojokerto 7 29S 112 25E
47 Mokau, R. 38 42S 174 37E
39 Mokpo 34 50N 126 30E
53 Mokwa 9 18N 5 2E
11 Mol 51 11N 5 5E
6 Mold 53 10N 3 10W
23 Moldanan S.S.R. □ 47 0N 28 0E
20 Molde 62 46N 7 12E
56 Molepolole 24 28S 25 28E
18 Molfetta 41 12N 16 35E
70 Moline 41 30N 90 30W
18 Molise □ 41 45N 14 30E
78 Mollendo 17 0S 72 0W
21 Mölndal 57 40N 12 3E
66 Molokai, I. 21 8N 156 0W
46 Molong 33 5S 148 54E
56 Molopo, R. 28 30S 20 13E
56 Molteno 31 22S 26 22E
35 Molucca Sea 4 0S 124 0E

Moluccas, Is. = Maluku, Is. Mundo Novo

35 Moluccas, Is.= Maluku, Is. 1 0s 127 0e
57 Moma 16 47s 39 4e
52 Mombasa 4 2s 39 43e
52 Mombo 4 57s 38 20e
78 Mompos 9 14n 74 26w
21 Møn, I. 54 57n 12 15e
75 Mona, Pta. 9 37n 82 36w
75 Mona, I. 18 5n 67 54w
8 Monach Is. 57 32n 7 40w
12 Monaco ■ 43 46n 7 23e
8 Monadhliath Mts. 57 10n 4 4w
9 Monaghan 54 15n 6 58w
9 Monaghan □ 54 10n 7 0w
71 Monahans 31 35n 102 50w
51 Monastir 35 50n 10 49e
22 Monchegorsk 67 54n 32 58e
14 Mönchengladbach 51 12n 6 23e
13 Monchique 37 19n 8 38w
74 Monclava 26 50n 101 30w
63 Moncton 46 7n 64 51w
13 Mondego, R. 40 9n 8 52w
18 Mondovì 44 23n 7 56e
68 Monessen 40 9n 79 50w
62 Monet 48 10n 75 40w
13 Monforte de Lemos 42 31n 7 33w
33 Mong Kung 21 35n 97 35e
33 Mong Pan 20 19n 98 22e
33 Mong Pawk 22 4n 99 16e
33 Mong Ton 20 25n 98 45e
33 Mong Wa 21 26n 100 27e
33 Mong Yai 22 28n 98 3e
45 Monger, L. 29 25s 117 5e
33 Monghyr 25 23n 86 30e
51 Mongo 12 14n 18 43e
37 Mongolia ■ 47 0n 103 0e
53 Mongonu 12 40n 13 32e
55 Mongu 15 16s 23 12e
65 Monk 47 7n 69 59w
42 Monkira 24 46s 140 30e
7 Monmouth, U.K. 51 48n 2 43w
70 Monmouth, U.S.A. 40 50n 90 40w
75 Mono, Pta. del 12 0n 83 30w
18 Monópoli 40 57n 17 18e
71 Monroe, La. 32 32n 92 4w
68 Monroe, Mich. 41 55n 83 26w
69 Monroe, N.C. 35 2n 80 37w
70 Monroe, Wis. 42 38n 89 40w
50 Monrovia, Liberia 6 18n 10 47w
73 Monrovia, U.S.A. 34 7n 118 1w
11 Mons 50 27n 3 58e
64 Mont Joli 48 37n 68 10w
62 Mont Laurier 46 35n 75 30w
12 Mont St. Michel 48 40n 1 30w
62 Mont Tremblant Prov. Park 46 30n 74 30w
56 Montagu 33 45s 20 8e
63 Montague 46 10n 62 39w
74 Montague, I. 31 40n 144 46w
13 Montalbán 40 50n 0 45w
72 Montana □ 6 0s 73 0w
12 Montargis 48 0n 2 43e
12 Montauban 44 0n 1 21e
68 Montauk Pt. 41 4n 71 52w
12 Montbéliard 47 31n 6 48e
12 Mont-de-Marsan 43 54n 0 31w
79 Monte Alegre 2 0s 54 0w
79 Monte Azul 15 9s 42 53w
12 Monte Carlo 43 46n 7 23e
80 Monte Caseros 30 10s 57 50w
80 Monte Comán 34 40s 68 0w
18 Monte Sant 'Angelo 41 42n 15 59e
62 Montebello 45 40n 74 55w
78 Montecristi 1 0s 80 40w
75 Montego Bay 18 30n 78 0w
44 Montejinnie 16 40s 131 45e
12 Montélimar 44 33n 4 45e
74 Montemorelos 25 11n 99 42w
19 Montenegro□= Crna Gora 42 40n 19 20e
73 Monterey 36 35n 121 57w
78 Montería 8 46n 75 53w
74 Monterrey 25 40n 100 30w
79 Montes Claros 16 30s 43 50w
72 Montesano 47 0n 123 39w
80 Montevideo 34 50s 56 11w
7 Montgomery, U.K. 52 34n 3 9w
69 Montgomery, U.S.A. 32 20n 86 20w
32 Montgomery= Sahiwal 30 45n 73 8e
73 Monticello, Utah 37 55n 109 27w
13 Montijo 38 52n 6 39w
13 Montilla 37 36n 4 40w
70 Montivideo 44 55n 95 40w
12 Montluçon 46 22n 2 36e
63 Montmagny 46 58n 70 43e
63 Montmorency 46 53n 71 11w
42 Monto 24 52s 151 12e
13 Montoro 38 1n 4 27w
72 Montpelier, Id. 42 15n 11 29w
68 Montpelier, Vt. 44 15n 72 38w
12 Montpellier 43 37n 3 52e
62 Montreal 45 31n 73 34w
12 Montreuil 50 27n 1 45e
14 Montreux 46 26n 6 55e
8 Montrose, U.K. 56 43n 2 28w
73 Montrose, U.S.A. 38 30n 107 52w
75 Montserrat, I. 16 40n 62 10w
33 Monywa 22 7n 95 11e
57 Monze 16 17s 27 29e
32 Monze, C. 24 47n 66 37e
13 Monzón 41 52n 0 10e
45 Mooliabeenee 31 20s 116 2e
62 Moonbeam 49 20n 82 10w
43 Moonie 27 46s 150 20e
43 Moonta 34 6s 137 32e
45 Moora 30 37s 115 58e
42 Mooraberree 25 13s 140 54e
45 Moorarie 25 56s 117 35e
45 Moore, L. 29 50s 117 35e
45 Moore River 31 6s 115 32e
56 Moorreesburg 33 6s 18 38e
8 Moorfoot Hills 55 44n 3 8w
70 Moorhead 47 0n 97 0w
62 Moose, R. 43 37n 75 22w
62 Moose Factory 52 20n 80 40w
65 Moose Jaw 50 30n 105 30w
70 Moose Lake 46 27n 92 48w
65 Moosomin 50 9n 101 40w
62 Moosonee 51 25n 80 51w
55 Mopeia Velha 17 30s 35 40e
50 Mopti 14 30n 4 0w
78 Moquegua 17 15s 70 46w
21 Mora, Sweden 61 2n 14 38e
32 Moradabad 28 50n 78 50e
57 Moramanga 18 56s 48 12e
75 Morant Pt. 17 55n 76 12w
8 Morar, L. 56 57n 5 40w
32 Moratuwa 6 45n 79 55e
19 Morava, R. 48 10n 16 59e
45 Morawa 29 13s 116 0e
78 Morawhanna 8 30n 59 40w
8 Moray Firth 57 50n 3 30w
12 Morbihan □ 47 55n 2 50w
65 Morden 49 15n 98 10w
46 Mordialloc 38 1s 145 6e
22 Mordovian A.S.S.R. □ 54 20n 44 30e
20 Møre og Romsdal □ 63 0n 9 0e
6 Morecambe 54 5n 2 52w
6 Morecambe B. 54 7n 3 0w
43 Moree 29 28s 149 54e
69 Moorhead City 34 46n 76 44w
14 Moravian Hts.= Ceskomoravská V. 49 20n 15 30e
19 Morea□= Pelopónnisos 37 40n 22 15e
74 Morelia 19 40n 101 11w
42 Morella 23 0s 143 47e
74 Morelos □ 18 40n 99 10w
13 Morena, Sa. 38 20n 4 0w
73 Morenci 33 7n 109 20w
43 Moreton, I. 27 10s 153 25e
71 Morgan City 29 40n 91 15w
69 Morganton 35 46n 81 48w
68 Morgantown 39 39n 75 58w
57 Morgenzon 26 45s 29 36e
53 Moriki 12 52n 6 30e
64 Morinville 53 49n 113 41w
36 Morioka 39 45n 141 8e
12 Morlaix 48 36n 3 52w
42 Mornington, I., Australia 16 30s 139 30e
80 Mornington, I., Chile 49 50s 75 30w
35 Moro G. 6 30n 123 0e
50 Morocco ■ 32 0n 5 50w
52 Morogoro 6 50s 37 40e
74 Moroleón 20 8n 101 32w
57 Morombé 21 45s 43 22e
75 Morón 22 0n 78 30w
38 Mörön, R. 47 14n 110 37e
13 Morón de la Frontera 37 6n 5 28w
57 Morondavo 20 17s 44 27e
35 Morotai, I. 2 10n 128 30e
52 Moroto 2 28n 34 42e
52 Moroto, Mt. 2 30n 34 43e
6 Morpeth 55 11n 1 41w
71 Morrilton 35 10n 92 45w
79 Morrinhos 17 45s 49 10w
47 Morrinsville 37 40s 175 32e
65 Morris 49 25n 97 30w
45 Morris, Mt. 26 9s 131 4e
62 Morrisburg 44 55n 75 7w
69 Morristown, Tenn. 36 18n 83 20w
73 Morro Bay 35 27n 120 54w
78 Morrosquillo, G. de 9 35n 75 40w
22 Morshansk 53 28n 41 50e
80 Morteros 30 50s 62 0w
79 Mortes, R. 11 45s 50 44w
46 Mortlake 38 5s 142 50e
46 Morundah 34 57s 146 19e
43 Morven 26 22s 147 5e
8 Morvern, Reg. 56 38n 5 44w
46 Morwell 38 10s 146 22e
33 Moscos Is. 14 0n 97 45e
72 Moscow 46 45n 116 59w
22 Moscow=Moskva 55 45n 37 35e
14 Mosel, R. 50 22n 7 36e
12 Moselle, R. 50 22n 7 36e
12 Moselle □ 48 59n 6 33e
47 Mosgiel 45 53s 170 21e
52 Moshi 3 22s 37 18e
20 Mosjøen 65 51n 13 12e
22 Moskva 55 45n 27 35e
22 Moskva, R. 55 5n 38 50e
78 Mosquera 2 35n 78 30w
75 Mosquitos, G. de los 9 15n 81 0w
21 Moss 59 27n 10 40e
46 Moss Vale 34 32s 150 25e
65 Mossbank 50 0n 106 0w
47 Mossburn 45 41s 168 15e
56 Mosselbaai 34 11s 22 8e
54 Mossendjo 2 55s 12 42e
46 Mossgiel 33 15s 144 30e
42 Mossman 16 28s 145 23e
79 Mossoró 5 10s 37 15w
55 Mossuril 14 58s 40 42e
14 Most 50 31n 13 38e
18 Mosta 35 53n 14 26e
50 Mostaganem 35 54n 0 5e
19 Mostar 43 22n 17 50e
80 Mostardas 31 2s 50 51w
30 Mosul=Al Mawsil 36 20n 43 5e
21 Motala 58 32n 15 1e
8 Motherwell 55 48n 4 0w
33 Motihari 26 37n 85 1e
13 Motril 36 44n 3 37w
47 Motueka 41 7s 173 1e
54 Mouila 1 50s 11 0e
12 Moulins 46 35n 3 19¼
33 Moulmein= Maulamyaing 16 30n 97 40e
69 Moultrie 31 11n 83 47w
51 Moundou 8 40n 16 10e
68 Moundsville 39 53n 80 43w
69 Mount Airy 36 31n 80 37w
43 Mount Barker 34 38s 117 40e
68 Mount Carmel, Ill. 38 20n 87 48w
68 Mount Carmel, Pa. 40 46n 76 25w
42 Mount Coolon 21 25s 147 25e
55 Mount Darwin 16 47s 31 38e
42 Mount Douglas 21 35s 146 50e
47 Mount Eden 36 53s 174 46e
64 Mount Edgecumbe 57 3n 135 21w
44 Mount Elizabeth 16 0s 125 50e
62 Mount Forest 43 59n 80 43w
46 Mount Gambier 37 50s 140 46e
42 Mount Garnet 17 41s 145 7e
43 Mount Hope 34 7s 135 23e
42 Mount Isa 20 42s 139 26e
45 Mount Keith 27 15s 120 30e
42 Mount Larcom 23 48s 150 59e
32 Mount Lavinia 6 50n 79 50e
45 Mount Magnet 28 2s 117 47e
47 Mount Maunganui 37 40s 176 14e
42 Mount Molloy 16 42s 145 20e
42 Mount Morgan 23 40s 150 25e
45 Mount Narryer 26 30s 115 55e
44 Mount Newman 23 18s 119 45e
70 Mount Pleasant, Iowa 41 0n 91 35w
68 Mount Pleasant, Mich. 43 38n 84 46w
71 Mount Pleasant, Texas 33 5n 95 0w
72 Mount Pleasant, Utah 39 40n 111 29w
72 Mount Rainier Nat. Park 46 50n 121 20w
64 Mt. Revelstoke Nat. Park 51 6n 118 0w
64 Mount Robson 52 56n 119 15w
68 Mount Sterling 38 0n 84 0w
42 Mount Surprise 18 10s 144 17e
70 Mount Vernon, Ill. 38 19n 88 55w
68 Mount Vernon, N.Y. 40 57n 73 49w
68 Mount Vernon, Ohio 40 20n 82 30w
72 Mount Vernon, Wash. 48 27n 122 18w
43 Mount Willoughby 27 58s 134 8e
72 Mountain Home 43 3n 115 52w
64 Mountain Park 52 50n 117 15w
73 Mountain View 37 26n 122 5w
73 Mountainair 34 35n 106 15w
9 Mountmellick 53 7n 7 20w
42 Moura, Australia 24 35s 149 58e
78 Moura, Brazil 1 25s 61 45w
51 Mourdi, Depression du 18 10n 23 0e
53 Mouri 5 6n 1 14w
9 Mourne, Mts. 54 10n 6 0w
9 Mourne, R. 54 45n 7 25w
11 Mouscron 50 45n 3 12e
47 Moutohora 38 27s 177 32e
39 Mowming 21 50n 110 32e
38 Mowping 37 25n 121 34e
52 Moyale 3 30n 39 0e
9 Moyle □ 55 10n 6 15w
28 Moza 31 48n 35 8e
55 Mozambique ■ 19 0s 35 0e
48 Mozambique Chan. 20 0s 39 0e
22 Mozyr 52 0n 29 15e
52 Mpanda 6 23s 31 40e
55 Mpika 11 51s 31 25e
52 Mporokoso 9 25s 30 5e
52 Mpulungu 8 51s 31 5e
52 Mpwapwa 6 30s 36 30e
51 Msaken 35 49n 10 33e
55 Msoro 13 35s 31 50e
52 Mtito Andei 2 41s 38 12e
52 Mtwara 10 20s 40 20e
79 Muaná 1 25s 49 15w
37 Muang Chiang Rai 19 52n 99 50e
34 Muar=Bandar Maharani 2 3n 102 34e
34 Muarabungo 1 40s 101 10e
34 Muarakaman 0 2s 116 45e
34 Muaratembesi 1 42s 103 2e
34 Muaratewe 0 50s 115 0e
30 Mubairik 23 22n 39 8e
52 Mubende 0 33n 31 22e
53 Mubi 10 18n 13 16e
8 Muck, I. 56 50n 6 15w
79 Mucuri 18 0s 40 0w
52 Mueda 11 36s 39 28e
55 Mufulira 12 32s 28 15w
51 Muhammad Qol 20 53n 37 9e
52 Muheza 5 9s 38 48e
14 Mühlhausen 51 12n 10 29e
9 Muine Bheag 52 42n 6 59w
29 Mukalla 14 33n 49 2e
38 Mukden=Shenyang 41 48n 123 27e
29 Mukeiras 13 59n 45 52e
45 Mukinbudin 30 55s 118 5e
34 Mukomuko 2 20s 101 10e
52 Mukono 0 28n 32 37e
32 Muktsar 30 30n 74 30e
75 Mulatas, Arch. de las 6 51n 78 31w
80 Mulchén 37 45s 72 20w
14 Mulde, R., 51 10n 12 48e
52 Muleba 1 50s 31 37e
63 Mulgrave 45 38n 61 31w
13 Mulhacén, Mt. 37 4n 3 20w
14 Mülheim 51 26n 6 53w
12 Mulhouse 47 40n 7 20e
8 Mull of Galloway, Pt. 54 40n 4 55w
8 Mull of Kintyre, Pt. 55 20n 5 45w
8 Mull, I. 56 27n 6 0w
46 Mullengudgery 31 43s 147 29e
9 Mullet, Pen. 54 10n 10 2w
45 Mullewa 28 29s 115 30e
9 Mullingar 53 31n 7 20w
43 Mullumbimby 28 30s 153 30e
32 Multan 30 15n 71 30e
46 Mulwala 35 59s 146 0e
52 Mumias 0 20n 34 29e
34 Mun, R. 15 19n 105 31e
35 Muna, I. 5 0s 122 30e
32 Munabao 25 45n 70 17e
14 München 48 8n 11 33e
68 Muncie 40 10n 85 20w
14 Münden 51 25n 9 42e
44 Mundiwindi 23 47s 120 9e
79 Mundo Novo 11 50s 40 29w

Mundrabilla Neosho

45 Mundrabilla 31 52S 127 51E
43 Mungallala 26 25S 147 34E
42 Mungana 17 8S 144 27E
43 Mungindi 28 58S 149 1E
55 Munhango 12 9S 18 36E
14 Munich=München 48 8N 11 33E
80 Muñoz Gamero, Pen. 52 30S 73 5E
9 Munster □ 52 20N 8 40W
14 Münster 51 58N 7 37E
45 Muntadgin 31 48S 118 30E
34 Muntok 2 5S 105 10E
20 Muonio, R. 67 48N 23 25E
14 Mur, R. 46 18N 16 53E
80 Murallón, Mt. 49 55S 73 30W
52 Murangá 0 45S 37 9E
52 Muranisgar Mts. 3 0N 35 0E
22 Murashi 59 30N 49 0E
46 Murchison, Australia 36 39S 145 14E
47 Murchison, N.Z. 41 49S 172 21E
45 Murchison, R. 26 1S 117 6E
13 Murcia 38 2N 1 10W
13 Murcia, Reg. 38 35N 1 50W
15 Mureş, R. 46 15N 20 13E
69 Murfreesboro 35 50N 86 21W
24 Murgab 38 10N 73 59E
43 Murgon 26 15S 151 54E
14 Muritz See 53 25N 12 40E
22 Murmansk 68 57N 33 10E
22 Murom 55 35N 42 3E
36 Muroran 42 25N 141 0E
71 Murphysboro 37 50N 89 20W
69 Murray, Ky. 36 40N 88 20W
72 Murray, Utah 40 41N 111 58W
43 Murray, R. 35 22S 139 22E
43 Murray Bridge 35 6S 139 14E
56 Murraysburg 31 58S 23 47E
46 Murrayville 35 16S 141 11E
32 Murree 33 56N 73 28E
45 Murrin Murrin 28 50S 121 45E
46 Murrumbidgee, R. 34 43S 143 12E
46 Murrurundi 31 42S 150 51E
46 Murtoa 36 35S 142 28E
47 Murupara 38 30S 178 40E
33 Murwara 23 46N 80 28E
43 Murwillumbah 28 18S 153 27E
14 Mürzzuschlag 47 36N 15 41E
19 Musala, Mt. 41 13N 23 27E
31 Muscat=Masqat 23 37N 58 36E
70 Muscatine 41 25N 91 5W
52 Mushao 2 2S 29 20E
54 Mushie 2 56S 17 4E
53 Mushin 6 32N 3 21E
68 Muskegon 43 15N 86 17W
68 Muskegon Heights 43 12N 86 17W
71 Muskogee 35 50N 95 25W
51 Musmar 18 6N 35 40E
52 Musoma 1 30S 33 48E
8 Musselburgh 55 57N 3 3W
80 Musters, L. 45 20S 69 25W
46 Muswellbrook 32 16S 150 56E
51 Mût 25 28N 28 58E
38 Mutankiang 44 35N 129 30E
42 Muttaburra 22 38S 144 29E
63 Mutton Bay 50 50N 59 2W
25 Muya 56 27N 115 39E
32 Muzaffarabad 34 25N 73 30E
32 Muzaffarnagar 29 26N 77 40E
32 Muzaffarpur 26 7N 85 32E
24 Muzhi 65 25N 64 40E
37 Muztagh, Mt. 36 30N 87 22E
54 Mvadhi Ousye 1 13N 13 12E
52 Mvomero 6 18S 37 28E
52 Mwanza, Tanzania 2 30S 32 58E
54 Mwanza, Zaire 7 55S 26 43E
52 Mwaya 9 32S 33 55E
54 Mweka 4 50S 21 40E
54 Mweru, L. 9 0S 28 45E
52 Mwirasandu 0 56S 30 22E
34 My Tho 10 29N 106 23E
33 Myanaung 18 25N 95 10E
33 Myaungmya 16 30N 95 0E
34 Myeik Kyunzu 11 0N 98 0E
33 Myingyan 21 30N 95 30E
33 Myitkyina 25 30N 97 26E
33 Mymensingh=Nasirabad 24 42N 90 30E
72 Myrtle Creek 43 0N 123 19W
72 Myrtle Point 43 0N 124 4W
32 Mysore 12 17N 76 41E
20 Mývatn, L. 65 36N 17 0W
57 Mzimvubu, R. 31 30S 29 30E

N

28 Na'an 31 53N 34 52E
21 Naantali 60 27N 21 57E
9 Naas 53 12N 6 40W
56 Nababeep 29 36S 17 46E
33 Nabadwip 23 34N 88 20E
51 Nabenl 36 30N 10 51E
28 Nabi Rubin 31 56N 34 44E
57 Naboomspruit 24 32S 28 40E
28 Nābulus 32 14N 35 15E
52 Nachingwea 10 49S 38 49E
43 Nackara 32 48S 139 12E
71 Nacogdoches 31 33N 95 30W
74 Nacozari 30 30N 109 50W
32 Nadiad 22 41N 72 56E
31 Nadūshan 32 2N 53 35E
22 Nadvoitsy 63 52N 34 15E
24 Nadym 63 35N 72 42E
53 Nafada 11 8N 11 20E
35 Naga 13 38N 123 15E
33 Nagaland □ 26 0N 95 0E
36 Nagano 36 40N 138 10E
36 Nagano □ 36 15N 138 0E
36 Nagaoka 32 27N 138 51E
32 Nagappattinam 10 46N 79 51E
36 Nagasaki 32 47N 129 50E
36 Nagasaki □ 3250⅛ 129 40E
36 Nagato 36 15N 138 16E
32 Nagaur 27 15N 73 45E
32 Nagercoil 8 12N 77 33E
25 Nagornyy 55 58N 124 57E
36 Nagoya 35 10N 136 50E
32 Nagpur 21 8N 79 10E
14 Nagykanizsa 46 28N 17 0E
15 Nagykörös 47 2N 19 48E
39 Naha 26 12N 127 40E
60 Nahannai Butte 61 5N 123 30W
28 Nahariyya 33 1N 35 5E
30 Nahavand 34 10N 48 30E
28 Nahf 32 56N 35 18E
80 Nahuel Huapi, L. 41 0S 71 32W
65 Naicam 52 30N 104 30W
63 Nain 56 34N 61 40W
32 Nainpur 22 26N 80 6E
8 Nairn 57 35N 3 54W
52 Nairobi 1 17S 36 48E
52 Naivasha 0 40S 36 30E
31 Najafabād 32 40N 51 15E
30 Najd, Reg. 26 30N 42 0E
32 Najibabad 29 40N 78 20E
36 Nakamura 33 0N 133 0E
52 Nakasongola 1 19N 32 28E
30 Nakhi Mubarak 24 10N 38 10E
23 Nakhichevan 39 14N 45 30E
25 Nakhodka 43 10N 132 45E
34 Nakhon Phanom 17 23N 104 43E
34 Nakhon Ratchasima 14 59N 102 12E
34 Nakhon Sawan 15 35N 100 12E
34 Nakhon Si Thammarat 8 29N 100 0E
62 Nakina 50 10N 86 40W
21 Nakskov 54 50N 11 8E
52 Nakuru 0 15S 35 5E
64 Nakusp 50 20N 117 45W
32 Nal, R. 26 2N 65 19E
38 Nalayh 47 43N 107 22E
23 Nalchik 43 30N 43 33E
32 Nalgonda 17 6N 79 15E
32 Nallamalai Hills 15 30N 78 50E
51 Nalūt 31 54N 11 0E
37 Nam Dinh 20 25N 106 5E
34 Nam-Phan, Reg. 10 30N 106 0E
34 Nam Tok 14 21N 99 0E
37 Nam Tso, L. 30 40N 90 30E
56 Namaland, Reg. 29 43S 19 5E
24 Namangan 41 30N 71 30E
55 Namapa 13 43S 39 50E
52 Namasagali 1 2N 33 0E
55 Namber 1 2S 134 57E
43 Nambour 26 38S 152 49E
43 Nambucca Heads 30 40S 152 48E
37 Namcha Barwa, Mt. 29 30N 95 10E
56 Namib Des.=Namibwoestyn 22 30S 15 0W
55 Namibia ■=S.W. Africa ■ 22 0S 18 0E
56 Namibwoestyn 22 30S 15 0W
35 Namlea 3 10S 127 5E
72 Nampa 43 40N 116 40W
55 Nampula 15 6S 39 7E
35 Namrole 3 46S 126 46E
20 Namsen, R. 64 27N 11 28E
20 Namsos 64 29N 11 30E
33 Namtu 23 5N 97 28E
11 Namur 50 27N 4 52E
11 Namur □ 50 17N 5 0E
55 Namutoni 18 49S 16 55E
55 Namwala 15 44S 26 30E
39 Namyung 25 15N 114 5E
37 Nan 18 48N 100 46E
37 Nan Shan, Mts. 38 0N 98 0E
64 Nanaimo 49 10N 124 0W
43 Nanango 26 40S 152 0E
36 Nanao 37 0N 137 0E
39 Nanchang 28 34N 115 48E
39 Nancheng 27 30N 116 28E
39 Nancheng=Hanchung 33 10N 107 2E
39 Nanching=Nanking 32 10N 118 50E
39 Nanchung 30 47N 105 59E
12 Nancy 48 42N 6 12E
32 Nanda Devi, Mt. 30 30N 80 30E
32 Nander 19 10N 77 20E
47 Nandi 17 25S 176 50E
32 Nandurbar 21 20N 74 15E
32 Nandyal 15 30N 78 30E
53 Nanga-Eboko 4 40N 12 26E
32 Nanga Parbat, Mt. 35 10N 74 35E
32 Nangal Dam 31 25N 76 38E
31 Nangarhar □ 34 15N 70 30E
39 Nankang 25 42N 114 35E
39 Nanking 32 10N 118 50E
36 Nankoku 33 39N 133 44E
45 Nannine 26 51S 118 18E
39 Nanning 22 51N 108 18E
45 Nannup 33 59S 115 45E
39 Nanping 26 45N 118 5E
36 Nansei-Shotō, Is. 29 0N 129 0E
45 Nanson 28 34S 114 46E
39 Nantan 25 0N 107 35E
12 Nantes 47 12N 1 33W
68 Nanticoke 41 12N 76 1W
64 Nanton 50 20N 113 50W
39 Nantou 23 57N 120 35E
58 Nantucket I. 41 16N 70 3W
39 Nantung 32 0N 120 50E
79 Nanuque 17 50S 40 21W
39 Nanyang 33 2N 112 35E
38 Nanyuan 39 48N 116 23E
52 Nanyuki 0 2N 37 4E
13 Nao, C. de la 38 44N 0 14E
36 Naoetsu 37 12N 138 10E
72 Napa 38 18N 122 17W
62 Napanee 44 15N 77 0W
47 Napier 39 30S 176 56E
44 Napier Broome, B. 14 0S 127 0E
44 Napier Downs 16 20S 124 30E
18 Naples=Nápoli 40 50N 14 5E
78 Napo, R. 3 20S 72 40W
70 Napoleon 46 32N 99 49W
18 Nápoli 40 50N 14 5E
36 Nara 34 40N 135 49E
36 Nara □ 34 30N 136 0E
46 Naracoorte 36 50S 140 44E
33 Narasapur 16 26N 81 50E
33 Narayanganj 23 31N 90 33E
32 Narayanpet 16 45N 77 30E
12 Narbonne 43 11N 3 0E
45 Narembeen 32 4S 118 24E
45 Naretha 31 0S 124 50E
32 Narmada, R. 21 35N 72 35E
52 Narok 1 20S 33 30E
46 Narrabri 30 19S 149 46E
43 Narran, R. 29 45S 147 20E
46 Narrandera 34 42S 146 31E
45 Narrogin 32 58S 117 14E
46 Narromine 32 12S 148 12E
32 Narsinghpur 22 54N 79 14E
36 Naruto 35 36N 140 25E
20 Narvik 68 28N 17 26E
24 Narym 59 0N 81 58E
24 Narymskoye 49 10N 84 15E
24 Naryn 41 30N 76 10E
50 Nasarawa 8 32N 7 41E
51 Naser, Buheiret en 23 0N 32 30E
72 Nashua, Mont. 48 10N 106 25W
68 Nashua, N.H. 42 50N 71 25W
69 Nashville 36 12N 86 46W
32 Nasik 20 2N 73 50E
33 Nasirabad, Bangladesh 26 15N 74 45E
32 Nasirabad, Pak. 28 25N 68 25E
75 Nassau 25 0N 77 30W
80 Nassau, B. 55 20S 68 0W
51 Nasser, L.=Naser, Buheiret en 23 0N 32 30E
21 Nässjö 57 38N 14 45E
62 Nastapoka Is. 57 0N 77 0W
33 Nat Kyizio 14 55N 98 0E
78 Natagaima 3 37N 75 6W
79 Natal, Brazil 5 47S 35 13W
34 Natal, Indonesia 0 35N 99 0E
57 Natal □ 28 30S 30 30E
63 Natashquan 50 14N 61 46W
63 Natashquan, R. 50 6N 61 49W
71 Natchez 31 35N 91 25W
71 Natchitoches 31 47N 93 4W
46 Natimuk 36 35S 141 59E
53 Natitingou 10 20N 1 26E
73 National City 32 45N 117 7W
79 Natividade 11 43S 47 47W
52 Natron, L. 2 20S 36 0E
34 Natuna Besar, Kep. 4 0N 108 0E
34 Natuna Selatan, Kep. 3 0N 109 55E
14 Naumburg 51 10N 11 48E
32 Naushahra 33 9N 74 15E
33 Nautanwa 27 26N 83 25E
73 Navajo Res. 36 55N 107 30W
13 Navalcarnero 40 17N 4 5W
9 Navan=An Uaimh 53 39N 6 40W
80 Navarino, I. 55 0S 67 30W
13 Navarra, Reg. 42 40N 1 40W
75 Navassa, I. 18 30N 75 0W
24 Navoi 40 9N 65 22E
74 Navojoa 27 0N 109 30W
22 Navolok 62 33N 39 57E
19 Návpaktos 38 23N 21 42E
19 Navplion 37 33N 22 50E
32 Navsari 20 57N 72 59E
32 Nawabshah 26 15N 68 25E
32 Nawalgarh 27 50N 75 15E
19 Náxos, I. 37 5N 25ʻ30E
31 Nāy Band 27 20N 52 40E
25 Nayakhan 62 10N 159 0E
74 Nayarit □ 22 0N 105 0W
79 Nazaré, Brazil 13 0S 39 0W
28 Nazareth, Israel 32 42N 35 17E
33 Nazir Hat 22 35N 91 55E
52 Ndala 4 46S 33 16E
54 N'Délé 8 25N 20 36E
54 Ndendé 2 29S 10 46E
51 Ndjamena 12 4N 15 8E
55 Ndola 13 0S 28 34E
52 Ndumbwe 10 14S 39 58E
52 Ndungu 4 28S 38 4E
9 Neagh, L. 54 35N 6 25W
60 Near Is. 53 0N 172 0W
7 Neath 51 39N 3 49W
42 Nebo 39 27N 90 47W
70 Nebraska □ 41 30N 100 0W
70 Nebraska City 40 40N 95 52W
18 Nebrodi, Monti 37 55N 14 35E
14 Neckar, R. 49 31N 8 26E
80 Necochea 38 30S 58 50W
73 Needles 34 50N 114 35W
32 Neemuch 24 30N 74 50E
70 Neenah 44 10N 88 30W
65 Neepawa 50 20N 99 30W
50 Nefta 33 53N 7 58E
23 Neftyannyye Kamni 40 20N 50 55E
6 Nefyn 52 57N 4 31W
68 Negaunee 46 30N 87 36W
15 Negoiu, Mt. 45 48N 24 32E
32 Negombo 7 12N 79 50E
19 Negotin 44 16N 22 37E
35 Negra Pt. 18 40N 120 50E
78 Negra, Pta. 6 6S 81 10W
80 Negro, R., Arg. 41 2S 62 47W
78 Negro, R., Brazil 3 10S 59 58W
35 Negros, I. 10 0N 123 0E
31 Nehbandān 31 35N 60 5E
39 Neikiang 29 35N 105 10E
14 Neisse, R. 52 4N 14 47E
78 Neiva 2 56N 75 18W
51 Nekemte 9 4N 36 30E
21 Neksø 55 4N 15 8E
25 Nelkan 57 50N 136 15E
32 Nellore 14 27N 79 59E
25 Nelma 47 30N 139 0E
64 Nelson, Canada 49 30N 117 20W
47 Nelson, N.Z. 41 18S 173 16E
6 Nelson, U.K. 53 50N 2 14W
47 Nelson □ 42 11S 172 15E
80 Nelson, Estrecho 51 30S 75 0W
65 Nelson, R. 55 30N 96 50W
64 Nelson Forks 59 30N 124 0W
57 Nelspruit 25 29S 30 59E
50 Néma 16 40N 7 15W
36 Nemuro 43 20N 145 35E
36 Nemuro-Kaikyō, Str. 43 30N 145 30E
25 Nemuy 55 40N 135 55E
9 Nenagh 52 52N 8 11W
60 Nenana 63 34N 149 7W
6 Nene, R. 52 48N 0 13E
71 Neosho 35 59N 95 10W

Nepal ■ Northern Mid-Atlantic Ridge

33 Nepal ■ 28 0N 84 30 E
33 Nepalganj 28 0N 81 40 E
72 Nephi 39 43N 111 52W
25 Nerchinsk 52 0N 116 39 E
25 Nerchinskiyzavod 51 10N 119 30 E
13 Nerva 37 42N 6 30W
28 Nes Ziyyona 31 56N 34 48W
28 Nesher 32 45N 35 3 E
8 Ness, L. 57 15N 4 30W
21 Nesttun 60 19N 5 21 E
28 Netanya 32 20N 34 51 E
11 Netherlands ■ 52 0N 5 30 E
61 Nettilling L. 66 30N 71 0W
14 Neu Brandenburg 53 33N 13 17 E
14 Neuchâtel 47 0N 6 55 E
14 Neuchâtel, L. de 46 53N 6 50 E
14 Neumünster 54 4N 9 58 E
14 Neunkirchen 49 23N 7 6 E
80 Neuquén 38 0S 68 0 E
14 Neustrelitz 53 22N 13 4 E
71 Nevada 37 20N 94 40W
72 Nevada □ 39 20N 117 0W
13 Nevada, Sa. 37 3N 3 15W
78 Nevada de Sta. Marta, Sa. 10 55N 73 50W
25 Nevanka 56 45N 98 55 E
12 Nevers 47 0N 3 9 E
46 Nevertire 31 50S 147 44 E
75 Nevis, I. 17 0N 62 30W
68 New Albany 38 20N 85 50W
78 New Amsterdam 6 15N 57 30W
68 New Bedford 41 40N 70 52W
69 New Bern 35 8N 77 3W
71 New Braunfels 29 43N 98 9W
47 New Brighton 43 29S 172 43 E
68 New Britain 41 41N 72 47W
3 New Britain, I. 6 0S 151 0 E
68 New Brunswick 40 30N 74 28W
63 New Brunswick □ 46 50N 66 30W
53 New Bussa 9 55N 4 33 E
3 New Caledonia, I. 21 0S 165 0 E
13 New Castille= Castilla la Nueva 39 45N 3 20W
68 New Castle, Ind. 39 55N 85 23W
68 New Castle, Pa. 41 0N 80 20W
32 New Delhi 28 37N 77 13 E
64 New Denver 50 0N 117 25W
7 New Forest, Reg. 50 53N 1 40W
63 New Glasgow 45 35N 62 36W
41 New Guinea, I. 5 0S 141 0 E
68 New Hampshire □ 43 40N 71 40W
57 New Hanover 29 22S 30 31 E
68 New Haven 41 20N 72 54W
3 New Hebrides, I. 15 0S 168 0 E
71 New Iberia 30 2N 91 54W
3 New Ireland, I. 3 0S 151 30 E
68 New Jersey □ 39 50N 74 10W
68 New Kensington 40 36N 79 43W
62 New Liskeard 47 31N 79 41W
68 New London 41 23N 72 8W
73 New Mexico □ 34 30N 106 0W
45 New Norcia 30 58S 116 13 E
47 New Norfolk 42 46S 147 2 E
71 New Orleans 30 0N 90 5W
68 New Philadelphia 40 29N 81 25W
47 New Plymouth 39 4S 174 5 E
75 New Providence I. 25 0N 77 30W
7 New Radnor 52 15N 3 10W
7 New Romney 50 59N 0 57 E
41 New South Wales □ 33 0S 146 0 E
70 New Ulm 44 15W 94 30W
63 New Waterford 46 13N 60 4W
64 New Westminster 49 10N 122 52W
68 New York 40 45N 74 0W
68 New York □ 42 40N 76 0W
47 New Zealand ■ 40 0S 173 0 E
52 Newala 10 58S 39 10 E
6 Newark, U.K. 53 6N 0 48W
68 Newark, N.J. 40 41N 74 12W
68 Newark, N.Y. 43 2N 77 10W
69 Newberry 46 20N 85 32W
68 Newburgh 41 30N 74 1W
7 Newbury 51 24N 1 19W
68 Newburyport 42 48N 70 50W
46 Newcastle, Australia 32 52S 151 49 E
63 Newcastle, Canada 47 1N 65 38W
9 Newcastle, Eire 52 27N 9 3W
57 Newcastle, S.Africa 27 45S 29 58 E
9 Newcastle, N. Ireland 54 13N 5 54W
6 Newcastle, Tyne and Tees 54 59N 1 37W
7 Newcastle Emlyn 52 2N 4 29W
42 Newcastle Waters 17 30S 133 28 E
6 Newcastle-under-Lyme 53 2N 2 15W
45 Newdegate 33 17N 118 58 E
28 Newe Etan 32 30N 35 32 E
28 Newe Sha'anan 32 47N 34 59 E
28 Newe Zohar 31 9N 35 21 E
60 Newenham, C. 58 37N 162 12W
63 Newfoundland □ 48 28N 56 0W
63 Newfoundland, I. 48 30N 56 0W
7 Newhaven 50 47N 0 4 E
44 Newman, Mt. 23 20S 119 34 E
9 Newmarket, Eire 52 13N 9 0W
7 Newmarket, U.K. 52 15N 0 23 E
69 Newnan 33 22N 84 48W
7 Newport, Gwent 51 35N 3 0W
7 Newport, I. of Wight 50 42N 1 18W
71 Newport, Ark. 35 38N 91 15W
68 Newport, Ky. 39 5N 84 23W
72 Newport, Oreg. 44 41N 124 2W
68 Newport, Rhode I. 41 30N 71 19W
68 Newport, Vt. 44 57N 72 17W
73 Newport Beach 33 40N 117 58W
68 Newport News 37 2N 76 54W
7 Newquay 50 24N 5 6W
9 Newry 54 10N 6 20W
9 Newry & Mourne □ 54 10W 6 20W
70 Newton, Iowa 41 40N 93 3W
71 Newton, Kans. 38 2N 97 30W
68 Newton, Mass. 42 21N 71 10W
68 Newton, N.J. 41 3N 74 46W
7 Newton Abbot 50 32N 3 37W
8 Newton Stewart 54 57N 4 30W
8 Newtonmore 57 4N 4 7W
46 Newtown, Australia 54 37N 5 40W
7 Newtown, U.K. 52 31N 3 19W
9 Newtownabbey □ 54 40N 5 55W
9 Newtownards 54 37N 5 40W
22 Neya 58 21N 43 49 E
31 Neyshābūr 36 10N 58 20 E
23 Nezhin 51 5N 31 55 E
53 Ngala 12 15N 14 15 E
55 Ngami Depression 20 30S 22 46 E
57 Ngamo 19 3S 27 25 E
35 Nganjuk 7 32S 111 55 E
53 Ngaoundéré 7 15N 13 35 E
47 Ngapara 44 57S 170 46 E
35 Ngawi 7 24S 111 26 E
52 Ngerengere 6 47S 38 10 E
52 Ngomba 8 20S 32 53 E
52 Ngong 1 25S 36 39 E
37 Ngoring Nor, L. 34 50N 98 0 E
52 Ngorongoro Crater 3 11S 35 32 E
52 Ngudu 2 58S 33 25 E
53 Nguru 12 56N 10 29 E
52 Nguru Mts. 6 0S 37 30 E
34 Nha Trang 12 16N 109 10 E
46 Nhill 36 18S 141 40 E
62 Niagara Falls, Canada 43 7N 79 5W
68 Niagara Falls, U.S.A. 43 5N 79 0W
34 Niah 3 58S 113 46 E
53 Niamey 13 27N 2 6 E
54 Niangara 3 50N 27 50 E
34 Nias, I. 1 0N 97 40 E
75 Nicaragua ■ 11 40N 85 30W
18 Nicastro 39 0N 16 18 E
12 Nice 43 42N 7 14 E
36 Nichinan 31 28N 131 26 E
44 Nicholson Ra. 27 12S 116 40 E
27 Nicobar Is. 9 0N 93 0 E
64 Nicola 50 8N 120 40W
62 Nicolet 46 17N 72 35W
30 Nicosia=Levkosia, Cyprus 35 10N 33 25 E
75 Nicoya, G. de 10 0N 85 0W
75 Nicoya, Pen. de 9 45N 85 40W
6 Nidd, R. 54 1N 1 12W
14 Nieder-Osterreich □ 48 25N 15 40 E
14 Niedersachsen □ 52 45N 9 0 E
14 Nienburg 52 38N 9 15 E
79 Nieuw Amsterdam 5 53N 55 5W
79 Nieuw Nickerie 6 0N 57 10W
12 Nièvre □ 47 10N 5 40 E
30 Niğde 37 59N 34 42 E
57 Nigel 26 27S 28 25 E
50 Niger ■ 13 30N 10 0 E
53 Niger, R. 5 33N 6 33 E
53 Niger Delta 4 0N 5 30 E
53 Niger □ 10 0N 5 30 E
53 Nigeria ■ 8 30N 8 0 E
47 Nightcaps 45 57S 168 14 E
36 Niigata 37 58N 139 0 E
36 Niigata □ 37 15N 138 45 E
36 Niihama 33 55N 133 10 E
66 Niihau, I. 21 55N 160 10W
36 Niimi 34 59N 133 28 E
11 Nijkerk 52 13N 5 30 E
11 Nijmegen 51 50N 5 52 E
53 Nike 6 26N 7 29 E
35 Nikiniki 9 40S 124 30 E
53 Nikki 9 58N 3 21 E
23 Nikolayev 46 58N 32 7 E
23 Nikolayevsk 50 10N 45 35 E
25 Nikolayevskna-Am 53 40N 140 50 E
23 Nikopol 47 35N 34 25 E
51 Nîl, Nahr en, R. 30 10N 31 6 E
51 Nîl el Abyad, R. 15 40N 32 30 E
51 Nîl el Azraq, R. 11 40N 32 30 E
51 Nîl el Azraq □ 12 30N 34 30 E
73 Niland 33 16N 115 30W
51 Nile, R.= Nîl, Nahren, R. 30 10N 31 6 E
68 Niles 41 8N 80 40W
12 Nîmes 43 50N 4 23 E
46 Nimmitabel 36 29S 149 15 E
25 Nimneryskiy 58 0N 125 10 E
52 Nimule 3 32N 32 3 E
46 Ninety Mile Beach, The 38 30S 147 10 E
30 Nineveh 36 25N 43 10 E
39 Ningming 22 10N 107 59 E
39 Ningpo 29 50N 121 30 E
38 Ningsia Hui □ 37 45N 106 0 E
39 Ningteh 26 45N 120 0 E
38 Ningwu 39 2N 112 15 E
37 Ninh Binh 20 15N 105 55 E
11 Ninove 50 51N 4 2 E
70 Niobrara, R. 42 45N 98 0W
50 Nioro 13 40N 15 50W
12 Niort 46 19N 0 29W
65 Nipawin 53 20N 104 0W
65 Nipawin Prov. Park 54 0N 104 40W
62 Nipigon 49 0N 88 17W
62 Nipigon, L. 49 40N 88 30W
79 Niquelandia 14 27S 48 27W
36 Nirasaki 35 42N 138 27 E
19 Niš 43 19N 21 58 E
29 Nisab 14 25N 46 29 E
36 Nishinomiya 34 45N 135 20 E
79 Niterói 22 52S 43 0W
8 Nith, R. 55 0N 3 35W
15 Nitra 48 19N 18 4 E
15 Nitra, R. 47 46N 18 10 E
11 Nivelles 50 35N 4 20 E
12 Nivernais, Reg. 47 0N 3 40 E
32 Nizamabad 18 45N 78 7 E
33 Nizamghat 28 20N 95 45 E
25 Nizhne Kolymsk 68 40N 160 55 E
24 Nizhne-Vartovskoye 60 56N 76 38 E
25 Nizhneangarsk 56 0N 109 30 E
25 Nizhneudinsk 55 0N 99 20 E
24 Nizhniy Tagil 57 45N 60 0 E
30 Nizip 37 1N 37 46 E
15 Nizké Tatry, Mts. 48 55N 20 0 E
28 Nizzanim 31 42N 34 37 E
52 Njombe 9 0S 34 35 E
53 Nkambe 6 35N 10 40 E
53 Nkawkaw 6 36N 0 49W
52 Nkhata Bay 11 33S 34 16 E
55 Nkhota Kota 12 55S 34 15 E
52 Nkonge 0 15N 31 10 E
53 Nkongsamba 4 55N 9 55 E
33 Noakhali=Maijdi 22 48N 91 10 E
60 Noatak 67 34N 162 59W
36 Nobeoka 32 36N 131 41 E
18 Nocera Inferiore 40 45N 14 37 E
36 Noda 47 30N 142 5 E
74 Nogales, Mexico 31 36N 94 29W
73 Nogales, U.S.A. 31 33N 110 59W
36 Nōgata 33 48N 130 54 E
45 Noggerup 33 32S 116 5 E
25 Noginsk 55 50N 38 25 E
12 Noire, Mts. 48 11N 3 40W
12 Noirmoutier, Î. de 46 58N 2 10W
32 Nok Kundi 28 50N 62 45 E
25 Nokhhuysk 60 0N 117 45 E
60 Nome 64 30N 165 30W
42 Nonda 20 40S 142 28 E
34 Nong Khai 17 50N 102 46 E
44 Noonamah 12 38S 131 4 E
43 Noondoo 28 35S 148 30 E
11 Noord Beveland, I. 51 45N 3 50 E
11 Noord Brabant □ 51 40N 5 0 E
11 Noord Holland □ 52 30N 4 45 E
11 Noordoost-Polder 52 45N 5 45 E
11 Noordwijk 52 14N 4 26 E
64 Nootka I. 49 40N 126 50W
62 Noranda 48 20N 79 0 E
12 Nord □ 50 15N 3 30 E
14 Nord-Ostsee Kanal 54 5N 9 15 E
64 Nordegg 52 29N 116 5W
20 Nordkapp 71 11N 25 48 E
20 Nordland □ 65 40N 13 0 E
14 Nordrhein Westfalen □ 51 45N 7 30 E
25 Nordvik 73 40N 110 57 E
9 Nore, R. 52 25N 6 58W
70 Norfolk, Nebr. 42 3N 97 25W
68 Norfolk, Va. 36 52N 76 15W
6 Norfolk □ 52 39N 1 0 E
3 Norfolk I. 28 58S 168 3 E
25 Norilsk 69 20N 88 0 E
70 Normal 40 30N 89 0W
71 Norman 35 12N 97 30W
60 Norman Wells 65 40N 126 45W
12 Normandie, Reg. 48 45N 0 10 E
62 Normandin 48 49N 72 31W
12 Normandy, Reg.= Normandie, Reg. 48 45N 0 10 E
42 Normanton 17 40S 141 10 E
45 Nornalup 35 0S 116 49 E
80 Norquinco 41 51S 70 55W
20 Norrbotten □ 66 45N 23 0 E
21 Nørresundby 57 5N 9 52 E
68 Norristown 40 9N 75 15W
21 Norrköping 58 37N 16 11 E
20 Norrland, Reg. 64 25N 18 0 E
21 Norrtälje 59 46N 18 42 E
45 Norseman 32 8S 121 43 E
25 Norsk 52 30N 130 0 E
79 Norte, C. do 1 40N 49 55W
47 North, C. 34 23S 173 4 E
47 North I. 38 0S 176 0 E
68 North Adams 42 42N 73 6W
1 North America 45 0N 100 0W
65 North Battleford 52 50N 108 10W
62 North Bay 46 20N 79 30W
62 North Belcher Is. 56 30N 79 0W
64 North Bend, Canada 49 50N 121 35W
72 North Bend, Oreg 43 28N 124 7W
8 North Berwick 56 4N 2 44W
34 North Borneo □= Sabah □ 6 0N 117 0 E
69 North Carolina □ 35 30N 80 0W
8 North Channel 55 0N 5 30W
68 North Chicago 42 19N 87 50W
70 North Dakota □ 47 30N 100 0W
45 North Dandalup 32 31S 115 58 E
9 North Down □ 54 40N 5 45W
7 North Downs 51 17N 0 30W
33 North East Frontier Agency= Arunachal Pradesh 28 0N 95 0 E
8 North Esk, R. 56 54N 2 38W
4 North European Plain 55 0N 25 0 E
7 North Foreland, Pt. 51 22N 1 28 E
52 North Horr 3 20N 37 8 E
64 North Kamloops 50 40N 120 25W
38 North Korea ■ 40 0N 127 0 E
33 North Lakhimpur 27 15N 94 10 E
2 North Magnetic Pole 76 5N 101 3W
8 North Minch 58 5N 5 55W
70 North Platte 41 10N 100 50W
8 North Ronaldsay, I. 59 20N 2 30W
65 North Saskatchewan, R. 53 15N 105 6W
4 North Sea 55 0N 5 0 E
63 North Sydney 46 12N 60 21W
68 North Tonawanda 43 5N 78 50W
20 N.-Trøndelag □ 64 30N 12 30 E
71 North Truchas Pk. 36 0N 105 30W
6 North Tyne, R. 54 59N 2 8W
8 North Uist, I. 57 40N 7 15W
64 North Vancouver 49 25N 123 20W
75 North Village 32 15N 64 45W
6 North Walsham 52 49N 1 22 E
44 North West, C. 21 45S 114 9 E
8 North West Highlands, Mts. 57 35N 5 2W
60 North West Territories □ 65 0N 100 0W
6 North York Moors 54 25N 0 50W
6 North Yorkshire □ 54 10N 1 25W
6 Northallerton 54 20N 1 26W
45 Northam 31 35S 116 42 E
45 Northampton, Australia 28 21S 114 33 E
7 Northampton, U.K. 52 14N 0 54W
68 Northampton, Mass. 42 22N 72 39W
7 Northampton □ 52 16N 0 55W
42 Northampton Downs 24 35S 145 48 E
45 Northcliffe 34 36S 116 7 E
53 Northern □ 9 0N 1 30W
33 Northern Circars, Reg. 17 30N 82 30 E
9 Northern Ireland ■ 54 45N 7 0W
1 Northern Mid-Atlantic Ridge 30 0N 40 0W

Northern Rhodesia ■ = Zambia Opp

55 Northern Rhodesia■= Zambia ■ 15 0s 28 0e
40 Northern Territory □ 16 0s 133 0e
70 Northfield 44 37n 93 10w
6 Northumberland □ 55 12n 2 0w
42 Northumberland, Is. 21 45s 150 20e
63 Northumberland Str. 46 20n 64 0w
6 Northwich 53 16n 2 30w
57 Norton 17 52s 30 40e
60 Norton Sd. 64 0n 165 0w
68 Norwalk, Conn. 41 7n 73 27w
68 Norwalk, Ohio 41 15n 82 37w
20 Norway ■ 67 0n 11 0e
65 Norway House 53 55n 98 50w
3 Norwegian Dependency 75 0s 15 0e
4 Norwegian Sea 66 0n 1 0e
6 Norwich, U.K. 52 38n 1 17e
68 Norwich, N.Y. 42 32n 75 30w
24 Nosok 70 10n 82 20e
31 Nosratabad 29 55n 60 0e
8 Noss Hd. 58 29n 3 4w
56 Nossob, R. 26 55s 20 37e
57 Nosy Bé, I. 13 20s 48 15e
57 Nosy-Varika 20 35s 48 32e
14 Noteć R. 52 44n 15 26e
64 Notikewin 57 15n 117 5w
18 Noto 36 52n 15 4e
63 Notre Dame B. 49 45n 55 30w
61 Notre Dame de Koartac=Koartac 60 55n 69 40w
61 Notre Dame d'Ivugivik= Ivugivik 62 20n 78 0w
62 Nottawasaga B. 44 40n 80 30w
6 Nottingham 52 57n 1 10w
6 Nottinghamshire □ 53 10n 1 0w
50 Nouadhibou 21 0n 17 0w
50 Nouakchott 18 20n 15 50w
3 Nouméa 22 17s 166 30e
56 Noupoort 31 10s 24 57e
62 Nouveau Comptoir 53 2n 78 55w
79 Nova Cruz 6 28s 35 25w
79 Nova Friburgo 22 10s 42 30w
79 Nova Granada 20 29s 49 19w
79 Nova Lima 20 5s 44 0w
55 Nova Lisboa= Huambo 12 42s 15 54e
63 Nova Scotia □ 45 10n 63 0w
55 Nova Sofola 20 7s 34 48e
79 Nova Venecia 18 45s 40 24e
18 Novara 45 27n 8 36e
22 Novaya Ladoga 60 7n 32 16e
24 Novaya Lyalya 58 50n 60 35e
25 Novaya Sibir, Os. 75 10n 150 0e
24 Novaya Zemlya, I. 75 0n 56 0e
15 Nové Zámky 47 59n 18 11e
22 Novgorod 58 30n 31 25e
19 Novi-Sad 45 18n 19 52e
54 Novo Redondo 11 10s 13 48e
23 Novocherkassk 47 27n 40 5e
24 Novokazalinsk 45 40n 61 40e
22 Novokiybyshevsk 53 7n 49 58e
24 Novo-kuznetsk 54 0n 87 10e
22 Novomoskovsk 54 5n 38 15e
23 Novorossiyk 44 43n 37 52e
23 Novoshakhtinsk 47 39n 39 58e
24 Novosibirsk 55 0n 83 5e
25 Novosibirskiye Os. 75 0n 140 0e
22 Novotroitsk 51 10n 58 15e
23 Novouzensk 50 32n 48 17e
18 Novska 45 19n 17 0e
31 Now Shahr 36 40n 51 40e
46 Nowa Nowa 37 44s 148 3e
33 Nowgong 26 20n 92 50e
46 Nowra 34 53s 150 35e
15 Nowy Sącz 49 40n 20 41e
14 Nowy Tomyśl 52 19n 16 10e
12 Noyon 49 34n 3 0e
57 Nsanje 16 55s 35 12e
53 Nsawam 5 50n 0 24w
53 Nsukka 7 0n 7 50e
57 Nuanetsi 21 22s 30 45e
57 Nuanetsi, R. 22 40s 31 50e
53 Nuatja 7 0n 1 10e
48 Nubian Des. 21 30n 33 30e
51 Nûbîya, Es Sahrâ en 21 30n 33 30e
74 Nueva Rosita 28 0n 101 20w
80 Nueve de Julio 35 30s 60 50w
75 Nuevitas 21 30n 77 20w
80 Nuevo, G. 43 0s 64 30w
74 Nuevo Laredo 27 30n 99 40w
74 Nuevo León □ 25 0n 100 0w
47 Nuhaka 39 3s 177 45e
51 Nukheila 19 1n 26 21e
24 Nukus 42 20n 59 40e
60 Nulato 64 43n 158 6w
44 Nullagine 21 53s 120 6e
45 Nullarbor 31 26s 130 55e
45 Nullarbor Plain 31 20s 128 0e
53 Numan 9 29n 12 3e
36 Numata 36 38n 139 3e
36 Numazu 35 7n 138 51e
46 Numurkah 36 0s 145 26e
7 Nuneaton 52 32n 1 29w
60 Nunivak I. 60 0n 166 0w
38 Nunkiang 49 11n 125 12e
11 Nunspeet 52 21n 5 45e
18 Núoro 40 20n 9 20e
14 Nuremburg= Nürnberg 49 26n 11 5e
14 Nürnberg 49 26n 11 5e
34 Nusa Tenggara Barat 8 50s 117 30e
35 Nusa Tenggara Timur □ 9 30s 122 0e
32 Nushki 29 35n 65 59e
61 Nutak 57 30n 61 59w
56 Nuweveldberge 32 10s 21 45e
45 Nyabing 33 30s 118 7e
52 Nyahanga 2 20s 33 37e
52 Nyahua 5 25s 33 23e
52 Nyahururu 0 2n 36 27e
52 Nyakanazi 3 2s 31 10e
52 Nyakanyazi 1 10s 31 13e
53 Nyakrom 5 40n 0 50w
51 Nyâlâ 12 2n 24 58e
52 Nyalikungu 2 35s 33 27e
52 Nyanguge 2 30s 33 12e
52 Nyanza 2 20s 29 42e
55 Nyasa, L. 12 0s 34 30e
21 Nybro 56 44n 15 55e
24 Nyda 66 40n 73 10e
37 Nyenchen, Ra. 30 30n 95 0e
52 Nyeri 0 23s 36 56e
52 Nyika Plat. 10 30s 36 0e
15 Nyíregyháza 48 0n 21 47e
20 Nykarleby 63 32n 22 31e
21 Nykøbing 54 56n 11 52e
21 Nyköping 58 45n 17 0e
57 Nylstroom 24 42s 28 22e
21 Nynäshamn 58 54n 17 57e
46 Nyngan 31 30s 147 8e
53 Nyong, R. 3 17n 9 54e
46 Nyora 38 20s 145 41e
15 Nysa 50 40n 17 22e
14 Nysa, R. 52 4n 14 46e
25 Nyurba 63 17n 118 20e
52 Nzega 4 10s 33 12e
50 Nzérékoré 7 49n 8 48w

O

70 Oahe Dam 44 28n 100 25w
70 Oahe Res. 45 30n 100 15w
66 Oahu, I. 21 30n 158 0w
72 Oak Creek 40 15n 106 59w
68 Oak Park 41 55n 87 45w
69 Oak Ridge 36 1n 84 5w
71 Oakdale 30 50n 92 28w
6 Oakengates 52 42n 2 29w
72 Oakesdale 47 11n 117 9w
43 Oakey 27 25s 151 43e
6 Oakham 52 40n 0 43w
73 Oakland 37 50n 122 18w
46 Oakleigh 37 54s 145 6e
44 Oakover, R. 20 43s 120 33e
72 Oakridge 43 47n 122 31w
65 Oakville, Man. 49 56n 97 58w
47 Oamaru 45 6s 170 58e
74 Oaxaca □ 17 0n 97 0w
24 Ob, R. 62 40n 66 0e
62 Oba 49 4n 84 7w
8 Oban 56 25n 5 30w
64 Obed 53 30n 117 10w
14 Ober-Österreich □ 48 10n 14 0e
14 Oberhausen 51 28n 6 50e
53 Obiaruku 5 51n 6 9e
36 Obihiro 42 55n 143 10e
25 Obluchye 49 10n 130 50e
24 Obskaya Guba 70 0n 73 0e
53 Obuasi 6 17n 1 40w
53 Obudu 6 40n 9 10e
69 Ocala 29 11n 82 5w
78 Ocaña, Col. 8 15n 73 20w
13 Ocaña, Sp. 39 55n 3 30w
78 Occidental, Cord. 5 0n 76 0w
68 Ocean City 39 18n 74 34w
64 Ocean Falls 52 25n 127 40w
72 Oceanlake 45 0n 124 0w
73 Oceanside 33 13n 117 26w
8 Ochil Hills 56 14n 3 40w
70 Oconto 44 52n 87 53w
74 Ocatlán 20 21n 102 42w
78 Ocumare del Tuy 10 7n 66 46w
35 Ocussi 9 20s 124 30e
53 Ōda 5 50n 1 5w
20 Odáďahraun 65 5n 17 0w
36 Odawara 35 20n 139 6e
21 Odda 60 3n 6 35e
29 Oddur 4 0n 43 35e
30 Ödemiş 38 15n 28 0e
56 Odendaalsrus 27 48s 26 43e
21 Odense 55 22n 10 23e
14 Oder=Odra R. 53 33n 14 38e
14 Oder Haff 53 46n 14 14e
23 Odessa 46 30n 30 45e
71 Odessa 31 51n 102 23w
50 Odienné 9 30n 7 34w
14 Odra, R. 53 33n 14 38e
55 Odzi 18 58s 32 23e
79 Oeiras 7 0s 42 8w
70 Oelwein 42 39n 91 55w
44 Oenpelli 12 20s 133 4e
53 Offa 8 13n 4 42e
9 Offaly □ 53 20n 7 30w
14 Offenbach 50 6n 8 46e
13 Ofir 41 30n 8 52w
62 Ogahalla 50 6n 85 51w
36 Ōgaki 35 25n 136 35e
70 Ogallala 50 6n 85 51w
53 Ogbomosho 8 1n 3 29e
72 Ogden 41 13n 112 1w
68 Ogdensburg 44 40n 75 27w
18 Oglio, R. 45 15n 10 15e
42 Ogmore 22 37s 149 35e
53 Ogoja 6 38n 8 39e
62 Ogoki 51 35n 86 0w
54 Ogooué, R. 1 0s 10 0e
53 Ogun □ 6 55n 3 38e
53 Oguta 5 44n 6 44e
53 Ogwashi-Uku 6 15n 6 30e
80 O'Higgins, L. 49 0s 72 40w
47 Ohakune 39 24s 175 24e
71 Ohio, R. 38 0n 86 0w
68 Ohio □ 40 20n 83 0w
14 Ohre, R. 50 10n 12 30e
19 Ohrid 41 8n 20 52e
19 Ohrid, L.= Ohridsko, J. 41 8n 20 52e
19 Ohridsko, J. 41 8n 20 52e
57 Ohrigstad 24 41s 30 36e
79 Oiapoque 3 50n 51 50w
68 Oil City 41 26n 79 40w
12 Oise □ 49 28n 2 30e
36 Ōita 33 15n 131 36e
80 Ojos del Salado, Cerro, Mt. 27 0s 68 40w
56 Okahandja 22 0s 16 59e
72 Okanagan 48 24n 119 24w
47 Okarito 43 15s 170 9e
55 Okavango, R. 17 40s 19 30e
56 Okavango Swamps 19 30s 23 0e
36 Okaya 36 0n 138 10e
36 Okayama 34 40n 133 54e
36 Okayama □ 35 0n 133 50e
36 Okazaki 34 36n 137 0e
53 Oke-Iho 8 1n 3 18e
69 Okeechobee, L. 21 0n 80 50w
69 Okefenokee Swamp. 30 50n 82 15w
7 Okehampton 50 44n 4 1w
53 Okene 7 32n 6 11e
25 Okha 53 40n 143 0e
25 Okhotsk 59 20n 143 10e
25 Okhotsk, Sea of 55 0n 145 0e
25 Okhotskiy Perevoz 61 52n 135 35e
25 Oknotsko kolymskoy 63 0n 157 0e
36 Oki-Shotō 36 15n 133 15e
56 Okiep 29 39s 17 53e
53 Okigwi 5 52n 7 20e
53 Okija 5 54n 6 55e
39 Okinawa, I. 26 40n 128 0e
39 Okinawa-guntō, Is. 26 0n 127 30e
53 Okitipupa 6 31n 4 50e
71 Oklahoma □ 35 20n 97 30w
71 Oklahoma City 35 25n 97 30w
71 Okmulgee 35 38n 96 0w
53 Okrika 4 47n 7 4e
25 Oktyabriskoy Revolyutsii Os. 79 30n 97 0e
22 Oktyabrski 53 11n 48 40e
47 Okura 43 55s 168 55e
36 Okushiri-To, I. 42 15n 139 30e
53 Okuta 9 14n 3 12e
21 Öland, I. 56 45n 16 50e
43 Olary 32 17s 140 19e
70 Olathe 38 50n 94 50w
80 Olavarría 36 55s 60 20w
18 Ólbia 40 55n 9 30e
13 Old Castille= Castilla la Vieja 39 45n 3 20w
60 Old Crow 67 35n 139 50w
62 Old Factory 52 36n 78 43w
69 Old Town 45 0n 68 50w
9 Oldcastle 53 46n 7 10w
52 Oldeani 3 25s 35 35e
14 Oldenburg 53 10n 8 10e
11 Oldenzaal 52 19n 6 53e
64 Olds 51 50n 114 10w
68 Olean 42 8n 78 25w
25 Olekminsk 60 40n 120 30e
22 Olenegorsk 68 9n 33 15e
25 Olenek 68 20n 112 30e
12 Oléron, Î. d' 45 55n 1 15w
15 Oleśnica 51 13n 17 22e
25 Olga 43 50n 135 0e
45 Olga, Mt. 25 20s 130 40e
57 Olifants, R. 24 10s 32 40s
19 Olimbos, Oros 40 6n 22 23e
64 Oliver 49 20n 119 30w
78 Ollague 21 15s 68 10w
68 Olney 38 40n 88 0w
14 Olomouc 49 38n 17 12e
25 Olovyannaya 50 50n 115 10e
15 Olsztyn 53 48n 20 29e
15 Olt, R. 43 50n 24 40e
15 Oltenita 44 7n 26 42e
72 Olympia 47 0n 122 58w
72 Olympic Mts. 48 0n 124 0w
72 Olympic Nat. Park 47 35n 123 30w
72 Olympus Mt. 47 52n 123 40w
9 Omagh 54 36n 7 20w
9 Omagh □ 54 35n 7 20w
70 Omaha 41 15n 96 0w
72 Omak 48 25n 119 24w
29 Oman ■ 23 0n 58 0e
31 Oman, G. of 24 30n 58 30e
56 Omaruru 21 26s 16 0e
78 Omate 16 45s 71 0w
35 Ombai, Selat, Str 8 30s 124 50e
51 Omdurmân 15 40n 32 28e
28 Omez 32 22n 35 0e
36 Ōmiya 35 54n 139 38e
54 Omo, R. 8 48n 37 14e
24 Omsk 55 0n 73 38e
36 Ōmura 33 8n 130 0e
36 Ōmuta 33 0n 130 26e
13 Onda 39 55n 0 17w
55 Ondangua 17 57s 16 4e
53 Ondo 7 4n 4 47e
53 Ondo □ 7 0n 5 5e
38 Ondörhaan 47 22n 110 31e
22 Onega 64 0n 38 10e
22 Onega, R. 63 0n 39 0e
47 Onehunga 36 55n 174 30e
68 Oneida 43 5n 75 40w
70 O'Neill 42 30n 98 38w
68 Oneonta 42 26n 75 5w
22 Onezhskaya Guba 64 30n 37 0e
22 Onezhskoye, Oz 62 0n 35 30e
47 Ongarue 38 42s 175 19e
45 Ongerup 33 58s 118 29e
32 Ongole 15 33n 80 2e
57 Onilahy, R. 23 34s 43 45e
53 Onitsha 6 6n 6 42e
36 Onoda 34 2n 131 10e
44 Onslow 21 40s 115 0e
11 Onstwedde 52 2n 7 4e
36 Ontake-San, Mt. 35 50n 137 15e
73 Ontario 34 2n 117 40w
68 Ontario, L. 43 40n 78 0w
62 Ontario □ 52 0n 88 10w
43 Oodnadatta 27 33s 135 30e
45 Ooldea 30 27s 131 50e
42 Oorindi 20 40s 141 1e
11 Oostende 51 15n 2 50e
11 Oosterhout 51 38n 4 51e
11 Oosterschelde, R. 51 30n 4 0e
32 Ootacamund 11 30n 76 44e
25 Opala, U.S.S.R. 52 15n 156 15e
54 Opala, Zaïre 0 37s 24 21e
52 Opari 2 56n 32 0e
15 Opava 49 57n 17 58e
71 Opelousas 30 35n 92 0w
60 Ophir 63 10n 156 31w
53 Opi 6 36n 7 28e
53 Opobo 4 35n 7 34e
15 Opole 50 42n 17 58e
13 Oporto=Pôrto 41 8n 8 40w
47 Opotiki 38 1s 177 19e
69 Opp 31 19e 86 13w

Parachilna Piedras Blancas Pt.

43 Parachilna 31 10s 138 21 E
72 Paradise 47 27N 114 54w
71 Paragould 36 5N 90 30w
78 Paraguaipoa 11 21N 71 57w
78 Paraguaná, Penide 12 0N 70 0w
80 Paraguari 25 36s 57 0w
80 Paraguay ■ 23 0s 57 0w
80 Paraguay, R. 27 18s 58 38w
79 Paraiba=
João Pessoa 7 10s 34 52w
79 Paraiba □ 7 0s 36 0w
21 Parainen 60 18N 22 18 E
53 Parakou 9 25N 2 40 E
79 Paramaribo 5 50N 55 10w
80 Paraná, Arg. 32 0s 60 30w
79 Paraná, Brazil 12 30s 47 40w
80 Paraná, R. 33 43s 59 15w
80 Paraná □ 24 30s 51 0w
80 Paranaguá 25 30s 48 30w
79 Paranapanema, R. 22 40s 53 9w
80 Paranapiacaba,
Sa. do 24 31s 48 35w
79 Paratinga 12 40s 43 10w
43 Paratoo 32 42s 139 22 E
32 Parbhani 19 8N 76 52 E
28 Pardes Hanna 32 28N 34 57 E
14 Pardubice 50 3N 15 45 E
35 Pare 7 43s 112 12 E
52 Pare Mts. 4 0s 37 45 E
25 Paren 62 45N 163 0 E
62 Parent 47 55N 74 35w
35 Parepare 4 0s 119 40 E
55 Parfuri 22 28s 31 17 E
22 Parguba 62 58N 34 25 E
75 Paria, G. de 10 20N 62 0w
78 Pariaguan 8 51N 64 43w
34 Pariaman 0 47s 100 11 E
35 Parigi 0 50s 120 5 E
78 Parika 6 50N 58 20w
15 Paringul-Mare, Mt. 45 20N 23 37 E
79 Parintins 2 40s 56 50w
62 Paris, Canada 43 20N 80 25w
12 Paris, Fr. 48 50N 2 20 E
69 Paris, Tenn. 36 20N 88 20w
71 Paris, Tex. 33 40N 95 30w
12 Paris □ 48 0N 2 20 E
72 Park City 40 42N 111 35w
72 Park Ra. 40 0N 106 30w
57 Park Rynie 30 25s 30 35 E
20 Parkano 62 5N 23 0 E
73 Parker, Ariz 34 8N 114 16w
70 Parker, S.D. 43 25N 97 7w
68 Parkersburg 39 18N 81 31w
65 Parkerview 51 28N 103 18w
46 Parkes 33 9s 148 11 E
64 Parksville 49 20N 124 21w
18 Parma, Italy 44 50N 10 20 E
72 Parma, U.S.A. 43 49N 116 59w
79 Parnaguá 10 10s 44 10w
79 Parnaíba, Piauí 3 0s 41 40w
79 Parnaiba, São
Paulo 19 34s 51 14w
79 Parnaiba, R. 3 0s 41 50w
19 Parnassós, Mt. 38 17N 21 30 E
22 Pärnu 58 12N 24 33 E
19 Páros, I. 37 5N 25 12 E
73 Parowan 37 54N 112 56w
80 Parral 36 10s 72 0w
46 Parramatta 33 48s 151 1 E
74 Parras 25 30N 102 20w
7 Parrett, R. 51 13N 3 1w
63 Parrsboro 45 30N 64 10w
58 Parry Is. 77 0N 110 0w
62 Parry Sd. 42 20N 80 0w
71 Parsons 37 20N 95 10w
33 Parvatipuram 18 50N 83 25 E
31 Parwan □ 35 0N 69 0 E
57 Parys 26 52s 27 29 E
71 Pasadena, Calif. 34 5N 118 0w
73 Pasadena, Tex. 29 45N 95 14w
78 Pasaje 3 10s 79 40w
71 Pascagoula 30 30N 88 30w
72 Pasco 46 10N 119 0w
12 Pas-de-Calais □ 50 30N 2 30 E
34 Pasir Mas 6 2N 102 8 E
35 Pasirian 8 13s 113 8 E
45 Pasley, C. 33 52s 123 35 E
80 Paso de Indios 43 55s 69 0w
73 Paso Robles 35 40N 120 45w
63 Paspébiac 48 3N 65 17w
9 Passage West 51 52N 8 20w
14 Passau 48 34N 13 27 E
18 Passero, C. 36 42N 15 8 E
80 Passo Fundo 28 10s 52 30w
79 Passos 20 45s 46 29w
78 Pasto 1 13N 77 17w
35 Pasuruan 7 40s 112 53 E
76 Patagonia, Reg. 45 0s 69 0w
68 Patchogue 40 46N 73 1w
47 Patea 39 45s 174 30 E
53 Pategi 8 50N 5 45 E
56 Patensie 33 46s 24 49 E
18 Paterno 37 34N 14 53 E
68 Paterson 40 55N 74 10w
32 Pathankot 32 18N 75 45 E
72 Pathfinder Res. 42 0N 107 0w
32 Patan 23 52N 72 4 E
35 Patani 0 20N 128 50 E
38 Pataokiang 41 58N 126 30 E
32 Patiala 30 23N 76 26 E
33 Patkai Bum, Mts. 27 0N 95 30 E
19 Patmos, I. 37 21N 26 36 E
33 Patna 25 35N 85 18 E
80 Patos, L. dos 31 20s 51 0w
79 Patos de Minas 18 35s 46 32w
19 Pátrai 38 14N 21 47 E
19 Pátraikos Kól. 38 17N 21 30 E
79 Patrocínio 18 57s 47 0w
34 Pattani 6 48N 101 15 E
18 Patti 31 17N 74 54 E
75 Patuca, R. 15 50N 84 18w
74 Pátzcuaro 19 30N 101 40w
12 Pau 43 19N 0 25w
12 Pauillac 45 11N 0 46w
33 Pauk 21 55N 94 30 E
79 Paulistana 8 9s 41 9w
79 Paulo Afonso 9 21s 38 15w
57 Paulpietersburg 27 23s 30 50 E
71 Paul's Valley 34 40N 97 17w
18 Pavia 45 10N 9 10 E
24 Pavlodar 52 33N 77 0 E
23 Pavlograd 48 30N 35 52 E
22 Pavlovo, Gorkiy 55 58N 43 5 E
25 Pavlovo, Yakut
A.S.S.R. 63 5N 115 25 E
23 Pavlovsk 50 26N 40 5 E
68 Pawtucket 41 51N 71 22w
34 Payakumbah 0 20s 100 35 E
72 Payette 44 0N 117 0w
61 Payne Bay=Bellin 60 0N 70 0w
61 Payne L. 59 30N 74 30w
45 Paynes Find 29 15s 117 42 E
80 Paysandú 32 19s 58 8w
72 Payson 40 8N 111 41w
19 Pazardzhik 42 12N 24 20 E
72 Pe Ell 46 30N 122 59w
65 Peace, R. 59 30N 111 30w
64 Peace River 56 15N 117 18w
64 Peace River, Res. 55 40N 123 40w
6 Peak, The., Mt. 53 24N 1 53w
42 Peak Downs Mine 22 17s 148 11 E
46 Peak Hill 32 39s 148 11 E
43 Peake 35 25s 140 0 E
66 Pearl City 21 21N 158 0w
66 Pearl Harbor 21 20N 158 0w
56 Pearston 32 33s 25 7 E
57 Pebane 17 10s 38 8 E
78 Pebas 3 10s 71 55w
19 Peć 42 40N 20 17 E
22 Pechenga 69 30N 31 25 E
22 Pechora 65 15N 57 0 E
22 Pechora, R. 68 13N 54 10 E
22 Pechorskaya Guba 68 40N 54 0 E
71 Pecos 31 25N 103 35w
71 Pecos, R. 29 42N 101 22w
15 Pécs 46 5N 18 15 E
79 Pedra Asul 16 1s 41 16w
75 Pedregal 8 22N 82 27w
79 Pedro Afonso 9 0s 48 10w
79 Pedro Juan
Caballero 22 30s 55 40w
8 Peebles 55 40N 3 12w
68 Peekskill 41 18N 73 57w
6 Peel 54 14N 4 40w
60 Peel, R. 67 0N 135 0w
47 Pegasus, B. 43 20s 173 10 E
33 Pegu 17 20N 96 29 E
33 Pegu Yoma, Mts. 19 0N 96 0 E
39 Peh Kiang, R. 23 10N 113 10 E
38 Pehan 48 17N 120 31 E
39 Pehpei 29 44N 106 29 E
80 Pehuajó 36 0s 62 0w
38 Peiping 39 45N 116 25 E
79 Peixe 12 0s 48 40w
35 Pekalongan 6 53s 109 40 E
70 Pekin 40 35N 89 40w
38 Peking=Peiping 39 45N 116 25 E
35 Pelabuhan Ratu,
Teluk, G. 7 0s 106 32 E
35 Pelabuhanratu 7 5s 106 30 E
15 Peleaga, Mt. 45 22N 22 55 E
35 Peleng, I. 1 20s 123 30 E
65 Pelican Narrows 55 12N 102 55 E
64 Pelican Portage 55 51N 113 0w
65 Pelican Rapids 52 38N 100 42 E
60 Pelly, R. 62 47N 137 19w
61 Pelly Bay 68 53N 89 51w
19 Peloponnese□=
Pelopónnisos □ 37 40N 22 15 E
19 Pelopónnisos □ 37 40N 22 15 E
18 Peloro, C. 38 15N 15 40 E
47 Pelorus, Sd. 40 59s 173 59 E
80 Pelotas 31 42s 52 23w
12 Pelvoux, Massif du 44 52N 6 20 E
35 Pemalang 6 53s 109 23 E
34 Pematang 0 12s 102 4 E
34 Pematangsiantar 2 57N 99 5 E
55 Pemba 16 31s 27 22 E
52 Pemba I. 5 0s 39 45 E
45 Pemberton,
Australia 34 30s 116 0 E
64 Pemberton, Canada 50 25N 122 50w
62 Pembroke, Canada 45 50N 77 15w
47 Pembroke, N.Z.=
Wanaka 44 33s 169 9 E
7 Pembroke, U.K. 51 41N 4 57w
34 Penang□=
Pinang □ 5 25N 100 15 E
79 Penápolis 21 24s 50 4w
13 Peñas, C. de 43 42N 5 52w
80 Penas, G. de 47 0s 75 0w
50 Pendembu 8 6N 10 45w
72 Pendleton 45 35N 118 50w
79 Penedo 10 15s 36 36w
62 Penetanguishene 44 50N 79 55w
32 Penganga, R. 19 53N 79 9 E
39 Penghu, I. 23 30N 119 30 E
38 Penglai 37 49N 120 47 E
39 Pengpu 33 0N 117 25 E
42 Penguin 41 8s 146 6 E
57 Penhalonga 18 54s 32 40 E
13 Peniche 39 19N 9 22w
8 Peniciuk 55 50N 3 14w
38 Penki 41 20N 132 50 E
68 Penn Yan 42 40N 77 3w
6 Pennine Ra. 54 50N 2 20w
68 Pennsylvania □ 40 50N 78 0w
64 Penny 53 58N 121 1w
69 Penobscot, R. 44 30N 68 50w
46 Penola 37 25s 140 47 E
75 Penonomé 8 37N 80 25w
2 Penrhyn Is. 9 0s 150 30w
46 Penrith, Australia 33 43s 150 38 E
6 Penrith, U.K. 54 40N 2 45w
69 Pensacola 30 30N 87 10w
64 Penticton 49 30N 119 30w
42 Pentland 20 32s 145 25 E
8 Pentland Firth 58 43N 3 10w
8 Pentland Hills 55 48N 3 25w
6 Pen-y-Ghent, Mt. 54 10N 2 15w
22 Penza 53 15N 45 5 E
7 Penzance 50 7N 5 32w
70 Peoria 40 40N 89 40w
34 Perabumilih 3 27s 104 15 E
12 Perche, Reg. 48 30N 1 0 E
44 Percival Lakes 21 25s 125 0 E
42 Percy, Is. 21 39s 150 16 E
12 Perdu, Mt. 42 40N 0 1 E
78 Pereira 4 49N 75 43w
23 Perekop 46 0N 33 0 E
45 Perenjori 29 26s 116 16 E
23 Pereyaslav
khmelnitskiy 50 3N 31 28 E
74 Pérez, I. 22 40N 89 30w
80 Pergamino 33 52s 60 30w
63 Peribonca, R. 48 45N 72 5w
80 Perico 24 25s 65 10w
12 Perigord, Reg. 45 0N 0 40 E
12 Périgueux 45 10N 0 42 E
29 Perim, I. 12 39N 43 25 E
22 Perm 58 0N 57 10 E
79 Pernambuco=
Recife 8 0s 35 0w
79 Pernambuco □ 8 0s 37 0w
19 Pernik 42 36N 23 2 E
45 Peron, C. 25 30s 113 30 E
12 Perpignan 42 42N 2 53 E
70 Perry, Iowa 41 48N 94 5w
71 Perry, Okla. 36 20N 97 20w
31 Persia=Iran ■ 35 0N 50 0 E
31 Persian G. 27 0N 50 0 E
45 Perth, Australia 31 57s 115 52 E
62 Perth, Canada 44 55N 76 20w
8 Perth, U.K. 56 24N 3 27w
68 Perth Amboy 40 31N 74 16w
78 Peru ■ 8 0s 75 0w
70 Peru, Ill. 41 18N 89 12w
68 Peru, Ind. 40 42N 86 0w
18 Perúgia 43 6N 12 24 E
23 Pervomaysk 48 5N 30 55 E
24 Pervouralsk 56 55N 60 0 E
18 Pésaro 43 55N 12 53 E
18 Pescara 42 28N 14 13 E
32 Peshawar 34 2N 71 37 E
32 Peshawar □ 35 0N 72 50 E
79 Pesqueira 8 20s 36 42w
28 Petah Tiqwa 32 6N 34 53 E
72 Petaluma 38 13N 122 45w
11 Petange 49 33N 5 55 E
55 Petauke 14 14s 31 12 E
62 Petawawa 45 54N 77 17w
74 Petén Itzá, L. 16 58N 89 50w
62 Peterbell 48 36N 83 21w
43 Peterborough,
Australia 32 58s 138 51 E
62 Peterborough, Can. 44 20N 78 20w
7 Peterborough, U.K. 52 35N 1 14w
8 Peterhead 57 30N 1 49w
6 Peterlee 54 45N 1 18w
64 Petersburg, Alas. 56 50N 133 0w
68 Petersburg, Va. 37 17N 77 26w
63 Petit Cap 48 58N 63 58w
75 Petit Goâve 18 27N 72 51w
12 Petit St. Bernard,
Col du 45 41N 6 53 E
63 Petitcodiac 45 57N 65 11w
63 Petite Saguenay 47 59N 70 1w
32 Petlad 22 30N 72 45 E
47 Petone 41 13s 174 53 E
68 Petoskey 45 21N 84 55w
19 Petrich 41 24N 23 13 E
79 Petrolandia 9 5s 38 20w
62 Petrolia 52 54N 82 9w
79 Petrolina 9 24s 40 30w
24 Petropavlovsk 55 0N 69 0 E
25 Petropavlovsk-
kamchatskiy 53 16N 159 0 E
79 Petrópolis 22 33s 43 9w
19 Petrovaradin 45 16N 19 55 E
22 Petrovsk 52 22N 45 19 E
25 Petrovsk-
Zdbaykalskiy 51 17N 108 50 E
22 Petrozavodsk 61 41N 34 20 E
56 Petrusburg 29 8s 25 27 E
34 Peureulak 4 48N 97 45 E
25 Pevek 69 15N 171 0 E
14 Pforzheim 48 53N 8 43 E
32 Phagwara 31 13N 75 47 E
55 Phala 23 45s 26 50 E
32 Phalodi 27 12N 72 24 E
34 Phan Rang 11 34N 108 59 E
34 Phan Thiet 11 1N 108 9 E
34 Phangan, Ko 9 45N 100 4 E
34 Phangna 8 28N 98 30 E
34 Phanh Bho
Ho Chi Minh 10 58N 106 40 E
37 Pharo Dzong 27 45N 89 14 E
34 Phatthalung 7 39N 100 6 E
69 Phenix City 32 30N 85 0w
34 Phetchabun 16 24N 101 11 E
34 Phetchaburi 16 25N 101 8 E
68 Philadelphia 40 0N 75 10w
19 Philippi 41 0N 24 19 E
35 Philippines ■ 12 0N 123 0 E
56 Philippolis 30 19s 25 13 E
56 Philipstown 30 26s 24 29 E
46 Phillip, I. 38 30s 145 12 E
43 Phillott 27 53s 145 50 E
72 Philomath 44 28N 123 21w
34 Phitsanulok 16 50N 100 12 E
34 Phnom Dangrek
Ra. 14 15N 105 0 E
34 Phnom Penh 11 33N 104 55 E
73 Phoenix 33 30N 112 10w
2 Phoenix Is. 3 30s 172 0w
37 Phong Saly 21 41N 102 6 E
34 Phra Nakhon Si
Ayutthaya 14 25N 100 30 E
34 Phu Quoc, I. 10 15N 104 0 E
34 Phuket 8 0N 98 28 E
34 Phuoc Le 10 30N 107 10 E
18 Piacenza 45 2N 9 42 E
43 Pialba 25 20s 152 45 E
43 Pian Creek 30 2s 148 12 E
15 Piatra Neamț 46 56N 26 22 E
79 Piani □ 7 0s 43 0w
12 Picardie, Reg. 50 0N 2 15 E
12 Picardy, Reg.=
Picardie, Reg. 50 0N 2 15 E
71 Picayune 30 40N 89 40w
80 Pichilemú 34 23s 72 2 E
6 Pickering 54 15N 0 46w
62 Pickle Crow 51 30N 90 0w
80 Pico Truncado 46 40s 68 10w
46 Picton, Australia 34 12s 150 34 E
62 Picton, Canada 44 1N 77 9w
47 Picton, N.Z. 41 18s 174 3 E
63 Pictou 45 41N 62 42w
64 Picture Butte 49 55N 112 45w
80 Picún Leufú 39 30s 69 5w
32 Pidurutalagala, Mt. 7 10N 80 50 E
73 Piedras Blancas Pt. 35 45N 121 18w

Piedras Negras Potrerillos

74 Piedras Negras 28 35N 100 35W
18 Piermonte □ ...... 45 0N 7 30 E
70 Pierre 44 23N 100 20W
57 Piet Retief .... 27 1 S 30 50 E
57 Pietermaritzburg .. 29 35 S 30 25 E
57 Pietersburg .... 23 54 S 29 25 E
15 Pietrosu, Mt. ...... 47 8N 25 11 E
15 Pietrosul, Mt. ..... 47 36N 24 38 E
62 Pigeon River 48 1N 89 42W
80 Pigüé .... 37 36 S 62 25W
56 Piketberg .... 32 55 S 18 40 E
68 Pikeville 37 30N 82 30W
14 Piła .... 53 10N 16 48 E
80 Pilar .... 26 50 S 58 10W
79 Pilar .... 14 30 S 49 45W
80 Pilcomayo, R. ...... 25 21 S 57 42W
32 Pilibhit .... 28 40N 78 50 E
15 Pilica, R. .... 51 52N 21 17 E
19 Pilos .... 36 55N 21 42 E
14 Pilsen=Plzeń ..... 49 45N 13 22 E
14 Pilzen=Plzeń ..... 49 45N 13 22 E
73 Pima 32 54N 109 50W
43 Pimba .... 31 18 S 136 46 E
34 Pinang, I. .... 5 25N 100 15 E
75 Pinar del Rio 22 26N 83 40W
65 Pinawa 50 15N 95 50W
64 Pincher Creek 49 30N 113 35W
15 Pinczów .... 50 32N 20 35 E
45 Pindar .... 28 30 S 115 47 E
53 Pindiga .... 9 58N 10 53 E
19 Pindos Óros ...... 40 0N 21 0 E
19 Pindus Mts.=
Pindos Óros .... 40 0N 21 0 E
63 Pine, C. 46 37N 53 30W
71 Pine Bluff 34 10N 92 0W
44 Pine Creek .... 13 49 S 131 49 E
65 Pine Falls 50 51N 96 11W
64 Pine Point 60 50N 114 40W
22 Pinega, R. .... 64 8N 41 54 E
42 Pinehill .... 23 38 S 146 57 E
18 Pinerolo .... 44 47N 7 21 E
18 Pinetown .... 29 48 S 30 54 E
71 Pineville 31 22N 92 30W
34 Ping, R. .... 15 42N 100 9 E
45 Pingaring .... 32 40 S 118 32 E
45 Pingelly .... 32 29 S 116 59 E
39 Pingkiang .... 28 45N 113 30 E
38 Pingliang .... 35 32N 106 50 E
39 Pingsiang .... 22 2N 106 55 E
39 Pingtingshan ...... 33 43N 113 28 E
39 Pingtung .... 22 38N 120 30 E
38 Pingyao .... 37 12N 112 10 E
13 Pinhel 40 18N 7 0W
38 Pinhsien .... 35 10N 108 10 E
19 Pinios, R. .... 39 54N 22 45 E
45 Pinjarra .... 32 37 S 115 52 E
38 Pinkiang=
Harbin .... 45 46N 126 51 E
46 Pinnaroo .... 35 13 S 140 56 E
75 Pinos, I. de 21 40N 82 40W
73 Pinos, Pt. 36 50N 121 57W
35 Pinrang .... 3 46 S 119 34 E
22 Pinsk .... 52 10N 26 8 E
65 Pinto Butte, Mt. ... 49 22N 107 25W
45 Pintumba .... 31 50 S 132 18 E
39 Pinyang .... 23 12N 108 35 E
22 Pinyug .... 60 5N 48 0 E
73 Pioche 38 0N 114 35N
18 Piombino .... 42 54N 10 30 E
15 Piotrków
Trybunalski ..... 51 23N 19 43 E
70 Pipestone 44 0N 96 20W
80 Pipinas .... 35 30N 57 19 E
63 Pipmuacan Res. ... 49 40N 70 25W
44 Pippingarra .... 20 27 S 118 42 E
68 Piqua 40 10N 84 10W
79 Piracicaba .... 22 45 S 47 30W
79 Piracuruca .... 3 50 S 41 50W
19 Piraeus=
Piraiévs .... 37 57N 23 42 E
19 Piraiévs .... 37 57N 23 42 E
80 Pirané .... 25 44 S 59 7W
19 Pirgos .... 37 40N 21 25 E
79 Piripiri .... 4 15 S 41 46W
35 Piru .... 3 3 S 128 12 E
18 Pisa .... 43 43N 10 23 E
78 Pisagua .... 19 40 S 70 15W
18 Pisciotta .... 40 7N 15 12 E
78 Pisco .... 13 50 S 76 5W
14 Pisek .... 49 19N 14 10 E
18 Pistóia .... 43 57N 10 53 E
2 Pitcairn I. .... 25 5 S 130 5W
20 Pitea .... 65 20N 21 25 E
15 Piteşti .... 44 52N 24 54 E
33 Pithapuram .... 17 10N 82 15 E
45 Pithara .... 30 20 E 116 35 E
8 Pitlochry 56 43N 3 43W
72 Pittsburg, Calif. ... 38 1N 121 50W
71 Pittsburg, Kans. ... 37 21N 94 43W
68 Pittsburgh, Pa. 40 25N 79 55W
71 Pittsburgh, Tex. ... 32 59N 94 58W
68 Pittsfield 42 28N 73 17W
68 Pittston 41 19N 75 50W
43 Pittsworth .... 27 41 S 151 37 E
78 Piura .... 5 5 S 80 45W
18 Pizzo .... 38 44N 16 10 E
63 Placentia 47 20N 54 0W
72 Placerville 38 47N 120 51W
75 Placetas 22 15N 79 44W
68 Plainfield 40 37N 74 28W
71 Plainview 34 10N 101 40W
71 Plaquemine 30 20N 91 15W
13 Plasencia 40 3N 6 8W
63 Plaster Rock 46 53N 67 22W
80 Plata, R. de la .... 34 45 S 57 30W
80 Plate, R.=
Plata, R. de la .. 34 35 S 57 30W
53 Plateau □ .... 8 30N 8 45 E
78 Plato 9 47N 74 47W
70 Platte, R. 41 4N 95 53W
70 Platteville 40 18N 104 47W
68 Plattsburgh 44 41N 73 30W
70 Plattsmouth 41 0N 96 0W
14 Plauen .... 50 29N 12 9 E
68 Pleasantville 39 25N 74 30W
47 Plenty, B. of ...... 37 45 S 177 0 E
22 Plesetsk .... 62 40N 40 10 E
63 Plessisville 46 14N 71 46W
19 Pleven .... 43 26N 24 37 E
15 Płock .... 52 32N 19 40 E
15 Ploieşti .... 44 57N 26 5 E
19 Plovdiv .... 42 8N 24 44 E
57 Plumtree .... 20 27 S 27 55 E
75 Plymouth,
Montserrat 16 42N 62 13W
7 Plymouth, U.K. ... 50 23N 4 9W
68 Plymouth, Ind. 41 20N 86 19W
14 Plzeň .... 49 45N 13 22 E
53 Pô 11 10N 1 9W
18 Po, R. .... 44 57N 12 4 E
38 Po Hai, G. .... 38 40N 119 0 E
53 Pobé .... 6 58N 2 41 E
25 Pobedino .... 49 51N 142 49 E
72 Pocatello 42 50N 112 25W
79 Poços de
Caldas .... 21 50 S 46 45W
25 Podkamenndya
Tunguska .... 61 50N 90 26 E
22 Podolsk .... 55 30N 37 30 E
22 Podporozny .... 60 55N 34 2 E
56 Pofadder .... 29 10 S 19 22 E
38 Pohang .... 36 8N 129 23 E
62 Point Edward 43 10N 82 30W
54 Pointe-Noire ...... 4 48 S 12 0 E
75 Pointe-à-Pitre 16 10N 61 30W
12 Poitiers .... 46 35N 0 20 E
12 Poitou, Reg. 46 25N 0 15W
32 Pokaran .... 26 55N 71 55 E
43 Pokataroo .... 29 30 S 148 34 E
54 Poko .... 3 7N 26 52 E
38 Pokotu .... 48 46N 121 54 E
25 Pokrovsk .... 61 29N 129 6 E
73 Polacca 35 52N 110 25W
15 Poland ■ .... 52 0N 20 0 E
80 Polcura .... 37 17 S 71 43W
7 Polden Hills 51 7N 2 50W
38 Poli .... 8 34N 12 54 E
35 Polillo Is. .... 14 56N 122 0 E
19 Poljanovgrad ..... 42 35N 26 58 E
32 Pollachi .... 10 35N 77 0 E
24 Polnovat .... 63 50N 66 5 E
22 Polotsk .... 55 30N 28 50 E
72 Polson 47 45N 114 12W
23 Poltava .... 49 35N 34 35 E
22 Polyarny .... 69 8N 33 20 E
79 Pombal, Brazil .... 6 55 S 37 50W
13 Pombal, Port. 39 55N 8 40W
73 Pomona 34 2N 117 49W
69 Pompano 26 12N 80 6W
71 Ponca City 36 40N 97 5W
75 Ponce 18 1N 66 37W
61 Pond Inlet 72 30N 75 0W
32 Pondicherry ...... 11 59N 79 50 E
57 Pondoland .... 31 10 S 29 30 E
13 Ponferrada 42 32N 6 35W
33 Ponnyadaung, Mts. 22 0N 94 10 E
22 Ponoi .... 67 0N 41 0 E
64 Ponoka 52 35N 113 40W
35 Ponorogo .... 7 52 S 111 29 E
63 Pont Lafrance 47 40N 64 58W
80 Ponta Grossa ..... 25 0 S 50 10W
12 Pontarlier .... 46 54N 6 20 E
71 Pontchartrain, L. .. 30 12N 90 0W
79 Ponte Nova .... 20 25 S 42 54W
18 Pontedera .... 43 40N 10 37 E
6 Pontefract 53 42N 1 19W
65 Ponteix 49 46N 107 29W
13 Pontevedra 42 26N 8 40W
70 Pontiac, Ill. 40 50N 88 40W
68 Pontiac, Mich. 42 40N 83 20W
34 Pontianak .... 0 3 S 109 15 E
30 Pontine Mts.=
Karadeniz
Dağlari, Mts. ... 41 30N 35 0 E
7 Pontypool 51 42N 3 1W
7 Ponytpridd .... 51 36N 3 21 S
18 Ponziane, Ís. ...... 40 55N 13 0 E
43 Poochera .... 32 43 S 134 51 E
7 Poole 50 42N 2 2W
32 Poona=Pune ..... 18 29N 73 57 E
78 Poopó, L. .... 18 30 S 67 35W
45 Popanyinning ..... 32 40 S 117 2 E
78 Popayán 2 27N 76 36W
11 Poperinge .... 50 51N 2 42 E
25 Popigay .... 71 55N 110 47 E
71 Poplar Bluff 36 45N 90 22W
74 Popocatepetl, Mt. . 19 10N 98 40W
32 Porbandar .... 21 44N 69 43 E
60 Porcupine, R. 66 35N 145 15W
21 Pori .... 61 29N 21 48 E
20 Porjus .... 66 57N 19 50 E
21 Porkkala .... 59 59N 24 26 E
78 Porlamar 10 57N 63 51W
25 Poronaysk .... 49 20N 143 0 E
43 Port Adelaide ..... 34 46 S 138 30 E
64 Port Alberni 49 15N 124 50W
32 Port Albert
Victor .... 21 0N 71 30 E
63 Port Alfred, Canada 48 18N 70 53W
56 Port Alfred, S. Afr. 33 6 S 26 55 E
64 Port Alice 50 25N 127 25W
68 Port Allegany 41 49N 78 17W
72 Port Angeles 48 0N 123 30W
62 Port Arthur,
Canada=
Thunder Bay ... 48 25N 89 10W
38 Port Arthur, China=
Lushun .... 38 48N 121 16 E
71 Port Arthur,
U.S.A. 30 0N 94 0W
62 Port Arthur=
Thunder Bay ... 48 25N 89 10W
43 Port Augusta ..... 32 30 S 137 50 E
63 Port aux Basques .. 47 32N 59 8W
57 Port-Bergé Vaovao 15 33 S 47 40 E
13 Port Bou .... 42 25N 3 9 E
43 Port Broughton ... 33 37 S 137 56 E
33 Port Canning ..... 22 18N 88 40 E
63 Port Cartier 50 10N 66 50W
47 Port Chalmers .... 45 49 S 170 30 E
68 Port Chester 41 0N 73 41W
62 Port Colborne 42 50N 79 10W
64 Port Coquitlam ... 49 20N 122 45W
43 Port Darwin ...... 12 18 S 130 55 E
75 Port de Paix 19 50N 72 50W
34 Port Dickson ..... 2 30N 101 49 E
42 Port Douglas ..... 16 30 S 145 30 E
64 Port Edward 54 14N 130 18W
62 Port Elgin 44 25N 81 25W
56 Port Elizabeth .... 33 58 S 25 40 E
8 Port Ellen 55 39N 6 12W
6 Port Erin 54 5N 4 45W
50 Port Étienne=
Nouadhibou 21 0N 17 0W
46 Port Fairy .... 38 22 S 142 12 E
54 Port-Gentil .... 0 47 S 8 40 E
8 Port Glasgow 55 57N 4 40W
53 Port Harcourt ..... 4 43N 7 5 E
64 Port Hardy 50 41N 127 30W
61 Port Harrison=
Inoucdouac 58 25N 78 15W
44 Port Hedland ..... 20 25 S 118 35 E
68 Port Henry 44 0N 73 30W
63 Port Hood 46 0N 61 32W
62 Port Hope 44 0N 78 20W
68 Port Jefferson 40 57N 73 4W
34 Port Kelang ...... 3 0N 101 24 E
46 Port Kembla ...... 34 29 S 150 56 E
9 Port Laoise 53 2N 7 20W
71 Port Lavaca 28 38N 96 38W
43 Port Lincoln ...... 34 42 S 135 52 E
50 Port-Lyautey=
Kenitra 34 15N 6 40W
43 Port Macquarie ... 31 25 S 152 54 E
63 Port Maitland 44 0N 66 2W
64 Port Mellon 49 32N 123 31W
63 Port Menier 49 51N 64 15W
60 Port Moller 00 00N 00 00W
3 Port Moresby ..... 9 24 S 147 8 E
65 Port Nelson 57 5N 92 56W
56 Port Nolloth ...... 29 17 S 16 52 E
61 Port Nouveau-
Quebec 58 30N 65 50W
75 Port of Spain 10 40N 61 20W
72 Port Orchard 47 31N 122 47W
62 Port Perry 44 6N 78 56W
43 Port Pirie .... 33 10 S 137 58 E
60 Port Radium 66 10N 117 40W
51 Port Said=
Bûr Sa'îd .... 31 16N 32 18 E
57 Port St. Johns=
Umzimvubu .... 31 38 S 29 33 E
63 Port St. Servain ... 51 21N 58 0W
57 Port Shepstone .... 30 44 S 30 28 E
64 Port Simpson 54 30N 130 20W
62 Port Stanley 42 40N 81 10W
51 Port Sudan=
Bûr Sûdân ...... 19 32N 37 9 E
7 Port Talbot 51 35N 3 48W
72 Port Townsend 48 0N 122 50W
12 Port-Vendres ..... 42 32N 3 8 E
22 Port Vladimir ..... 69 25N 33 6 E
43 Port Wakefield .... 34 12 S 138 10 E
34 Port Weld .... 4 50N 100 38 E
9 Portadown 54 27N 6 26W
70 Portage 43 31N 89 25W
65 Portage la Prairie .. 49 58N 98 18W
13 Portalegre 39 19N 7 25W
71 Portales 34 12N 103 25W
9 Portarlington 53 10N 7 10W
75 Port-au-Prince 18 40N 72 20W
56 Porterville, S. Afr. . 33 0 S 19 0 E
73 Porterville, U.S.A. . 36 5N 119 0W
7 Porthcawl 51 28N 3 42W
13 Portimão 37 8N 8 32W
46 Portland,
Australia .... 33 13 S 149 59 E
69 Portland, Me. 43 40N 70 15W
72 Portland, Oreg. ... 45 35N 122 30W
7 Portland Bill 50 31N 2 27W
7 Portland I. 50 32N 2 25W
61 Portland
Promontory 59 0N 78 0W
8 Portmadoc 52 51N 4 8W
63 Portneuf 46 43N 71 55W
13 Porto, Port. 41 8N 8 40W
80 Pôrto Alegre ...... 30 5 S 51 3W
55 Porto Amélia=
Pemba .... 12 58 S 40 30 E
79 Pôrto de Móz ..... 1 41 S 52 22W
18 Porto Empédocle .. 37 18N 13 30 E
79 Porto Franco ..... 9 45 S 47 0W
79 Porto Grande 0 42N 51 24W
80 Pôrto Mendes ..... 24 30 S 54 15W
78 Pôrto Murtinho ... 21 45 S 57 55W
79 Porto Nacional .... 10 40 S 48 30W
53 Porto-Novo .... 6 23N 2 42 E
79 Porto Seguro ..... 16 20 S 39 0W
18 Porto Torres ...... 40 50N 8 23 E
80 Pôrto União ...... 26 10 S 51 0W
12 Porto-Vecchio .... 41 35N 9 16 E
78 Porto Velho ...... 8 46 S 63 54W
18 Portoferráio ...... 42 50N 10 20 E
72 Portola 39 49N 120 28W
18 Portoscuso .... 39 12N 8 22 E
78 Portoviejo .... 1 0 S 80 20W
8 Portpatrick 54 50N 5 7W
8 Portree 57 25N 6 11W
9 Portrush 55 13N 6 40W
7 Portsmouth, U.K. . 50 48N 1 6W
68 Portsmouth, N.H. . 43 5N 70 45W
68 Portsmouth, Ohio . 38 45N 83 0W
68 Portsmouth, Va. ... 36 50N 76 50W
8 Portsoy 57 41N 2 41W
20 Porttipahta, I. ..... 68 5N 26 40 E
13 Portugal ■ 40 0N 7 0W
50 Portuguese
Guinea■=
Guinea Bissau ■ 12 0N 15 0W
9 Portumna 53 5N 8 12W
80 Porvenir .... 53 10 S 70 30W
21 Provoo .... 60 27N 25 50 E
80 Posadas .... 27 30 S 56 0W
39 Poseh .... 23 50N 106 0 E
38 Poshan=Tzepo .... 36 28N 117 58 E
35 Poso .... 1 20 S 120 55 E
79 Posse .... 14 4 S 46 18W
62 Poste de la Baleine 55 20N 77 40W
50 Poste Maurice
Cortier .... 22 14N 1 2 E
56 Postmasburg ...... 28 18 S 23 5 E
18 Postojna .... 45 46N 14 12 E
56 Potchefstroom .... 26 41 S 27 7 E
18 Potenza .... 40 40N 15 50 E
57 Potgietersrus ..... 24 10 S 29 3 E
23 Poti .... 42 10N 41 38 E
53 Potiskum .... 11 39N 11 2 E
68 Potomac, R. 38 0N 76 20W
78 Potosí .... 19 38 S 65 50W
35 Potatan .... 10 56N 122 38 E
38 Potow .... 38 8N 116 31 E
80 Potrerillos .... 26 26 S 69 29W

Potsdam, E. Germany Raglan, Australia

14 Potsdam, E. Germany 52 23N 13 4E
68 Potsdam, U.S.A. 44 40N 74 59W
68 Pottstown 40 15N 75 38W
68 Pottsville 40 39N 76 12W
64 Pouce Coupe 55 40N 120 10W
68 Poughkeepsie 41 40N 73 57W
47 Poverty B. 38 43S 178 0E
13 Póvoa de Varzim 41 25N 8 46W
22 Povenets 62 48N 35 0E
62 Powassan 46 5N 79 25W
70 Powder, R. 46 44N 105 26W
72 Powder River 43 5N 107 0W
72 Powell 44 45N 108 45W
73 Powell, L. 37 25N 110 45W
64 Powell River 49 48N 125 20W
7 Powys □ 52 20N 3 30W
39 Poyang 28 59N 116 40E
39 Poyang Hu, L. 29 10N 116 10E
25 Poyarkovo 49 38N 128 45E
19 Požarevac 44 35N 21 18E
14 Poznań 52 25N 17 0E
78 Pozo Almonte 20 10S 69 50W
53 Pra, R. 5 1N 1 37W
34 Prachuap Khiri Khan 11 48N 99 47E
79 Prado 17 20S 39 20W
14 Prague=Praha 50 5N 14 22E
14 Praha 50 5N 14 22E
79 Prainha 1 45S 53 30W
42 Prairie 20 50S 144 35E
72 Prairie City 45 27N 118 44W
70 Prairie du Chien 43 1N 91 9W
70 Prairies,Coteau des. 44 0N 97 0W
34 Praja 8 39S 116 37E
79 Prata 19 25S 49 0W
18 Prato 43 5 11 5E
71 Pratt 37 40N 98 45W
13 Pravia 43 30N 6 12W
65 Preeceville 52 0N 102 50W
64 Premier 56 4N 130 1W
14 Prenzlau 53 19N 13 51E
19 Prepansko, J. 40 45N 21 0E
15 Prerov 49 28N 17 27E
62 Prescott, Canada 44 45N 75 30W
73 Prescott, U.S.A. 34 35N 112 30W
80 Presidencia Roque Saenz Peña 26 50S 60 30W
79 Presidente Epitácio 21 46S 52 6W
79 Presidente Prudente 15 45S 54 0W
15 Prešov 49 0N 21 15E
69 Presque Isle 46 40N 68 0W
14 Pressburg= Bratislava 48 10N 17 7E
53 Prestea 5 22N 2 7W
7 Presteign 52 17N 3 0W
6 Preston 53 46N 2 42W
8 Prestonpans 55 58N 3 0W
8 Prestwick 55 30N 4 38W
57 Pretoria 25 44S 28 12E
19 Préveza 38 57N 20 47E
60 Pribilov Is. 56 0N 170 0W
14 Příbram 49 41N 14 2E
72 Price 39 40N 110 48W
56 Prieska 29 40S 22 42E
23 Prikaspiyskaya Nizmennost 47 30N 50 0E
23 Prikumsk 44 30N 44 10E
19 Prilep 41 21N 21 37E
23 Priluki 50 30N 32 15E
65 Prince Albert 53 15N 105 50W
65 Prince Albert Nat. Park 54 0N 106 25W
60 Prince Albert Pen. 72 0N 116 0W
60 Prince Albert Sd. 70 25N 115 0W
60 Prince Charles I. 68 0N 76 0W
3 Prince Edward Is. 45 15S 39 0E
63 Prince Edward I. □ 44 2N 77 20W
64 Prince George 53 50N 122 50W
58 Prince of Wales, C. 53 50N 131 30W
42 Prince of Wales, I., Australia 10 35S 142 0E
60 Prince of Wales I., Canada 73 0N 99 0W
64 Prince of Wales I., U.S.A. 53 30N 131 30W
64 Prince Rupert 54 20N 130 20W
42 Princess Charlotte, B. 14 15S 144 0E
64 Princeton, Canada 49 27N 120 30W
68 Princeton, Ind. 38 20N 87 35W
68 Princeton, Ky. 37 6N 87 55W
68 Princeton, W.Va. 37 21N 81 8W
49 Principé, I. 1 37N 7 25E
56 Prins Albert 33 12S 22 2E
22 Priozersk 61 2N 30 4E
22 Pripet, R.= Pripyat, R. 51 20N 30 20E
22 Pripyat, R. 51 20N 30 20E
19 Priština 42 40N 21 13E
69 Pritchard 30 47N 88 5W
35 Probolinggo 7 46S 113 13E
32 Proddatur 14 45N 78 30E
74 Progreso 21 20N 89 40W
24 Prokopyevsk 54 0N 87 3E
33 Prome 18 45N 95 30E
79 Propriá 10 13S 36 51W
42 Proserpine 20 21S 148 36E
72 Prosser 46 11N 119 52W
14 Prostějov 49 30N 17 9E
12 Provence, Reg. 43 40N 5 45E
68 Providence 41 41N 71 15W
62 Providence Bay 45 41N 82 15W
75 Providencia, I. de 13 25N 81 26W
25 Provideniya 64 23N 173 18W
64 Provincial Cannery 51 33N 127 36W
12 Provins 48 33N 3 15E
72 Provo 40 16N 111 37W
65 Provost 52 25N 110 20W
42 Prudhoe, I. 21 23S 149 45E
60 Prudhoe Bay 70 10N 148 0W
65 Prudhomme 52 22N 105 47W
15 Pruszków 52 9N 20 49E
23 Prut, R. 45 28N 28 12E
15 Przemysl 49 50N 22 45E
15 Przeworsk 50 6N 22 32E
24 Przhevalsk 42 30N 78 20E
22 Pskov 57 50N 28 25E
80 Puán 37 30S 63 0W
78 Pucallpa 8 25S 74 30W
39 Puchi 29 42N 113 54E
32 Pudukkottai 10 28N 78 47E
74 Puebla 19 0N 98 10W
74 Puebla □ 18 30N 98 0W
70 Pueblo 38 20N 104 40W
80 Pueblo Hundido 26 20S 69 30W
13 Pueblonuevo 38 20N 5 15W
80 Puelches 38 5S 66 0W
80 Puente Alto 33 32S 70 35W
13 Puente Genil 37 22N 4 47W
37 Puerh 23 11N 100 56E
75 Puerto Armuelles 8 20N 83 10W
78 Puerto Asís 0 30N 76 30W
78 Puerto Ayacucho 5 40N 67 35W
74 Puerto Barrios 15 40N 88 40W
78 Puerto Berrío 6 30N 74 30W
78 Puerto Bolívar 3 10S 79 55W
78 Puerto Cabello 10 28N 68 1W
75 Puerto Cabezas 14 0N 83 30W
78 Puerto Carreño 6 12N 67 22W
78 Puerto Casado 22 19S 57 56W
75 Puerto Cortes 15 51N 88 0W
74 Puerto Cortés 8 20N 82 20W
80 Puerto Coyle 50 54S 69 15W
78 Puerto Cumarebo 11 29N 69 21W
13 Puerto de Santa María 36 35N 6 15W
50 Puerto del Rosario 28 30N 13 52W
80 Puerto Deseado 47 45S 66 0W
78 Puerto Páez 6 13N 67 28W
78 Puerto Leguizamo 0 12S 74 46W
80 Puerto Lobos 42 0S 65 3W
80 Puerto Madryn 42 48S 65 4W
80 Puerto Montt 41 28S 72 57W
80 Puerto Natales 51 45S 72 25W
75 Puerto Padre 21 13N 76 35W
80 Puerto Pirámides 42 35S 64 20W
78 Puerto Piritu 10 5N 65 0W
75 Puerto Plata 19 40N 70 45W
35 Puerto Princesa 9 55N 118 50E
80 Puerto Quellón 43 7S 73 37W
75 Puerto Rico, I. 18 15N 66 45W
80 Puerto Saavedra 38 47S 73 24W
78 Puerto Suárez 18 58S 57 52W
80 Puerto Varas 41 19S 72 59W
13 Puertollano 38 43N 4 7W
80 Pueyrredón, L. 47 20S 72 0W
22 Pugachev 52 0N 48 55E
72 Puget Sd. 47 15N 123 30W
18 Puglia □ 41 0N 16 30E
47 Pukaki, L. 44 5S 170 1E
65 Pukatawagan 55 45N 101 20W
47 Pukekohe 37 12S 174 55E
18 Pula 39 0N 9 0E
78 Pulacayo 20 25S 66 41W
38 Pulantien 39 25N 122 0E
68 Pulaski, N.Y. 43 32N 76 9W
69 Pulaski, Tenn. 35 10N 87 0W
68 Pulaski, Va. 37 4N 80 49W
15 Puławy 51 23N 21 59E
32 Pulicat L. 13 40N 80 15E
72 Pullman 46 49N 117 10W
34 Puloraja 4 55N 95 24E
15 Pułtusk 52 43N 21 6E
37 Puluntohai 47 2N 87 29E
32 Punch 33 48N 74 4E
32 Pune 18 29N 73 57E
32 Punjab □ 31 0N 76 0E
78 Puno 15 55S 70 3W
80 Punta Alta 38 53S 62 4W
80 Punta Arenas 53 0S 71 0W
80 Punta de Díaz 28 0S 70 45W
80 Punta Delgada 42 43S 63 38W
74 Punta Gorda 16 10N 88 45W
78 Punta Rieles 22 20S 59 40W
43 Puntabie 32 12S 134 5E
75 Puntarenas 10 0N 84 50W
78 Punto Fijo 11 42N 70 13W
78 Purace, Mt. 2 21N 76 23W
7 Purbeck, I. of 50 40N 2 5W
33 Puri 19 50N 85 58E
33 Purnea 25 45N 87 31E
34 Pursat 12 34N 103 50E
33 Purulia 23 17N 86 33E
78 Purus, R. 3 42S 61 28W
35 Purwakarta 6 35S 107 29E
35 Purwodadi, Jawa 7 7S 110 55E
35 Purwodadi, Jawa 7 51S 110 0E
35 Purwokerto 7 25S 109 14E
35 Purworedjo 7 43S 110 2E
38 Pusan 35 5N 129 0E
25 Pushchino 54 20N 158 10E
23 Pushkino 51 16N 47 9E
33 Putao 27 28N 97 30E
47 Putaruru 38 3S 175 47E
38 Putehachi 48 4N 122 45E
39 Putien 22 28N 119 0E
32 Puttalam 8 4N 79 50E
14 Puttgarden 54 28N 11 15E
78 Putumayo, R. 3 7S 67 58E
12 Puy de Dôme, Mt. 45 46N 2 57E
72 Puyallup 47 10N 122 22W
12 Puy-de-Dôme □ 45 47N 3 0E
52 Pweto 8 25S 28 51E
23 Pyatigorsk 44 2N 43 0E
33 Pyinmana 19 45N 96 20E
38 Pyŏngyang 39 0N 125 30E
4 Pyrenees, Mts. 42 45N 0 20E
12 Pyrénées-Atlantiques □ 43 15N 0 45W
12 Pyrénées-Orientales □ 42 35N 2 25E
33 Pyu 18 30N 96 35E

Q

28 Qabatiya 32 25N 35 16E
31 Qadam 32 55N 66 45E
30 Qadhima 22 20N 39 13E
30 Qal'at al Mu'azzam 27 43N 37 27E
30 Qal'at Sālih 31 31N 47 16E
30 Qal'at Sura 26 10N 38 40E
31 Qala-i-Kirta 32 15N 63 0E
31 Qala Nau 35 0N 63 5E
28 Qalqīlya 32 12N 34 58E
51 Qâra 29 38N 26 30E
31 Qasr-e Qand 26 15N 60 45E
51 Qasr Farâfra 27 0N 28 1E
29 Qasr Hamam 21 5N 46 5E
31 Qatar ■ 25 30N 51 15E
51 Qattara Depression= Qattara, Munkhafed el 29 30N 27 30E
51 Qattara, Munkhafed el 29 30N 27 30E
30 Qazvin 36 15N 50 0E
51 Qena 26 10N 32 43E
28 Qesari 32 30N 34 53E
31 Qeshm 26 55N 56 10E
31 Qeshm, I. 26 50N 56 0E
31 Qeys, Jazireh-ye 26 32N 53 56E
28 Qezi'ot 30 52N 34 28E
32 Qila Safed 29 0N 61 30E
32 Qila Saifullah 30 45N 68 17E
28 Qiryat Bialik 32 50N 35 5E
28 Qiryat 'Eqron 31 52N 34 49E
28 Qiryat Gat 31 36N 35 47E
28 Qiryat Hayyim 32 49N 35 4E
28 Qiryat Mal'akhi 31 44N 34 45E
28 Qiryat Shemona 33 13N 35 35E
28 Qiryat Tiv'om 32 43N 35 8E
28 Qiryat Yam 32 51N 35 4E
29 Qīzān 16 57N 42 3E
31 Qom 34 40N 51 4E
45 Quairading 32 0S 117 21E
45 Qualeup 33 48S 116 48E
34 Quan Long 9 7N 105 8E
34 Quang Ngai 15 13N 108 58E
34 Quang Tri 16 45N 107 13E
7 Quantock Hills 51 8N 3 10W
80 Quaraí 30 15S 56 20W
31 Qūchān 37 10N 58 27E
57 Que Que 18 58S 29 48E
46 Queanbeyan 35 17S 149 14E
63 Québec 46 52N 71 13W
63 Québec □ 50 0N 70 0W
64 Queen Charlotte 53 28N 132 2W
64 Queen Charlotte Is. 53 10N 132 0W
64 Queen Charlotte Str. 51 0N 128 0W
58 Queen Elizabeth Is. 75 0N 95 0W
60 Queen Maud G. 68 15N 102 0W
41 Queensland □ 15 0S 142 0E
42 Queenstown, Australia 42 4S 145 35E
47 Queenstown, N.Z. 45 1S 168 40E
56 Queenstown, S.Africa 31 52S 26 52E
79 Queimadas 11 0S 39 38W
54 Quela 9 10S 16 56E
57 Quelimane 17 53S 36 58E
39 Quemoy, I. = Kinmen, I. 24 25N 118 25E
80 Quequén 38 30S 58 30W
74 Querêtaro 20 40N 100 23W
74 Querêtaro □ 20 30N 100 30W
64 Quesnel 53 5N 122 30W
62 Quetico 48 45N 90 55W
62 Quetico Prov. Park 48 15N 91 45W
32 Quetta 30 15N 66 55E
32 Quetta □ 30 15N 68 30E
74 Quezaltenango 14 40N 91 30W
35 Quezon City 14 38N 121 0E
34 Qui Nhon 13 40N 109 13E
78 Quibdo 5 42N 76 40W
12 Quiberon 47 29N 3 9W
80 Quilân, C. 43 15S 74 30W
55 Quilengues 14 12S 15 12E
80 Quillota 32 54S 71 16W
32 Quilon 8 50N 76 38E
43 Quilpie 26 35S 144 11E
80 Quimilí 27 40S 62 30W
12 Quimper 48 0N 4 9W
12 Quimperlé 47 53N 3 33W
68 Quincy, Mass. 42 14N 71 0W
69 Quincy.Fla. 30 34N 84 34W
70 Quincy, Ill. 39 55N 91 20W
80 Quines 32 14S 65 48W
74 Quintana Roo □ 19 0E 88 0W
13 Quintanar de la Orden 39 36N 3 5W
80 Quintero 32 45S 71 30W
78 Quito 0 15S 78 35W
79 Quixadá 4 55S 39 0W
28 Qumran 31 43N 35 27N
44 Quoin, I. 14 54S 129 32E
43 Quorn 32 25S 138 0E
37 Qurug-Tagh, Mts. 41 30N 90 0E
51 Qûs 25 55N 32 50E
51 Quseir 26 7N 34 16E

R

28 Ra'anana 32 12N 34 52E
20 Raane 64 40N 24 28E
8 Raasay, I. 57 25N 6 4W
35 Raba 8 36S 118 55E
52 Rabai 3 50S 39 31E
50 Rabat 34 2N 6 48W
3 Rabaul 4 24S 152 18E
30 Rabigh 22 50N 39 5E
63 Race, C. 46 40N 53 18W
15 Racibórz 50 7N 18 18E
68 Racine 42 41N 87 51W
68 Radford 37 8N 80 32W
15 Radom 51 23N 21 12E
19 Radomir 42 37N 23 4E
15 Radomsko 51 5N 19 28E
7 Radstock 51 17N 2 25W
65 Radville 49 30N 104 15W
64 Rae 62 45N 115 50W
33 Rae Bareli 26 18N 81 20E
61 Rae Isthmus 66 40N 87 30W
47 Raetihi 39 25S 175 17E
80 Rafaela 31 10S 61 30W
30 Rafhā 29 35N 43 35E
31 Rafsanjān 30 30N 56 5E
51 Râgâ 8 28N 25 41E
32 Ragama 7 0N 79 54E
42 Raglan, Australia 23 42S 150 49E

Raglan, N.Z. Rockford, Ill.

47 Raglan, N.Z. 37 55s 174 55 E
18 Ragusa 36 56N 14 42 E
51 Rahad el Bardi 11 20N 23 40 E
32 Raichur 16 10N 77 20 E
33 Raigarh 21 56N 83 25 E
42 Railton 41 25s 146 28 E
72 Rainier, Mt. 46 50N 121 50W
65 Rainy River 48 50N 94 30W
33 Raipur 21 17N 81 45 E
62 Raith 48 50N 90 0W
33 Raj Nandgaon 21 5N 81 5 E
33 Rajahmundry 17 1N 81 48 E
32 Rajapalaiyam 9 25N 77 35 E
32 Rajasthan □ 26 45N 73 30 E
32 Rajgarh 24 2N 76 45 E
32 Rajkot 22 15N 70 56 E
33 Rajshahi 24 22N 88 39 E
33 Rajshahi □ 25 0N 89 0 E
47 Rakaia 43 45s 172 1 E
47 Rakaia, R. 43 54s 172 12 E
35 Rakatau, P. 6 10s 105 20 E
65 Raleigh, Australia 30 27s 153 2 E
69 Raleigh, Canada 49 30N 92 5W
28 Rám Alláh 31 55N 35 10 E
46 Ram Head 37 47s 149 30 E
28 Rama 32 56N 35 21 E
32 Ramanathapuram 9 25N 78 55 E
28 Ramat Gan 32 4N 34 48 E
28 Ramat Ha Sharon 32 7N 34 50 E
28 Ramat Ha Shofet 32 36N 35 5 E
33 Rambre Kyun, I. 19 0N 94 0 E
35 Ramelau, Mt. 8 55s 126 22 E
33 Ramgarh 23 39N 85 31 E
30 Rāmhormoz 31 15N 49 35 E
52 Ramisi 4 35s 39 15 E
28 Ramla 31 55N 34 52 E
32 Ramnad 9 25N 78 55 E
73 Ramona 33 1N 116 56W
56 Ramoutsa 24 50s 25 52 E
60 Rampart 65 30N 150 10W
32 Rampur 23 25N 73 53 E
33 Rampur Hat 24 10N 87 50 E
62 Ramsey, Canada 47 25N 82 20W
6 Ramsey, U.K. 54 20N 4 21W
7 Ramsgate 51 20N 1 25 E
33 Ranaghat 23 15N 88 35 E
80 Rancagua 34 10s 70 50W
72 Ranchester 44 57N 107 12W
33 Ranchi 23 19N 85 27 E
80 Ranco, L. 40 15s 72 25W
21 Randers 56 29N 10 1 E
57 Randfontein 26 8s 27 45 E
68 Randolph 43 55N 72 39W
20 Råneå 65 53N 22 18 E
47 Rangaunu, B. 34 51s 173 15 E
33 Rangia 26 15N 91 20 E
47 Rangitaiki, R. 37 54s 176 53 E
47 Rangitata, R. 44 11s 171 30 E
35 Rangkasbitung 6 22s 106 16 E
33 Rangon=
Rangoon 16 45N 96 20 E
33 Rangoon 16 45N 96 20 E
33 Rangpur 25 42N 89 22 E
33 Raniganj 23 40N 87 15 E
32 Raniwara 24 47N 72 10 E
60 Rankin Inlet 62 30N 93 0W
46 Rankins Springs 33 49s 146 14 E
8 Rannoch 56 41N 4 20W
8 Rannoch, L. 56 41N 4 20W
57 Ranohira 22 29s 45 24 E
34 Ranong 9 56N 98 40 E
34 Rantauprapat 2 15N 99 50 E
35 Rantemario, Mt. 3 15s 119 57 E
28 Rantis 32 4N 35 3 E
68 Rantoul 40 18N 88 10W
2 Rapa Iti, Is. 27 35s 144 20W
35 Rapang 3 45s 119 55 E
70 Rapid City 44 0N 103 0W
2 Rarotonga, I. 21 30s 160 0W
80 Rasa, Pte. 40 55s 63 20N
31 Ras al Khaima 25 50N 56 5 E
51 Ra's Al-Unuf 30 25N 18 15 E
30 Ra's al Tannurah 26 40N 50 10 E
51 Rashad 11 55N 31 0 E
51 Rashîd 31 21N 30 22 E
30 Rasht 37 20N 49 40 E
60 Rat Is. 51 50N 178 15 E
32 Ratangarh 28 5N 74 35 E
9 Rath Luirc 52 21N 8 40W
9 Rathdrum, Eire 52 57N 6 13W
72 Rathdrum, U.S.A 47 50N 116 58W
14 Rathenow 52 38N 12 23 E
9 Rathkeale 52 32N 8 57W
9 Rathlin, I. 55 18N 6 14W
14 Ratisbon=
Regensburg 49 1N 12 7 E
32 Ratlam 23 20N 75 0 E
32 Ratnagiri 16 57N 73 18 E
71 Raton 37 0N 104 30W
8 Rattray Hd. 57 38N 1 50W
47 Raukumara, Ra. 38 5s 177 55 E
21 Rauma 61 10N 21 30 E
31 Ravar 31 20N 56 51 E
18 Ravenna 44 28N 12 15 E
14 Ravensburg 47 48N 9 38 E
42 Ravenshoe 17 37s 145 29 E
45 Ravensthorpe 33 35s 120 2 E
32 Ravi, R. 30 35N 71 38 E
52 Ravine 0 15N 36 15 E
32 Rawalpindi 33 38N 73 8 E
32 Rawalpindi □ 33 38N 73 8 E
62 Rawdon 46 3N 73 40W
47 Rawene 35 25s 173 32 E
45 Rawlinna 30 58s 125 28 E
72 Rawlins 41 50N 107 20W
80 Rawson 43 15s 65 0W
63 Ray, C. 47 33N 59 15W
33 Rayagada 19 15N 83 20 E
25 Raychikhinsk 49 46N 129 25 E
64 Raymond, Canada 49 30N 112 35W
72 Raymond, U.S.A. 46 45N 123 48W
71 Raymondville 26 30N 97 50W
65 Raymore 51 25N 104 31W
71 Rayne 30 16N 92 16W
12 Raz, Pte. du 48 2N 4 47W
12 Ré, I. de 46 12N 1 30W
7 Reading, U.K. 51 27N 0 57W
68 Reading, U.S.A. 40 20N 75 53W
80 Realicó 35 0s 64 15W
35 Rebi 5 30s 134 7 E
79 Recife 8 0s 35 0W
80 Reconquista 29 10s 59 45W
80 Recreo 29 25s 65 10W
71 Red, R. 48 10N 97 0W
72 Red Bluff 40 11N 122 11W
64 Red Deer 52 20N 113 50W
65 Red Lake 51 1N 94 1W
70 Red Oak 41 0N 95 10W
48 Red Sea 20 0N 39 0 E
70 Red Wing 44 32N 92 35W
7 Redbridge 51 35N 0 7 E
6 Redcar 54 37N 1 4W
65 Redcliff 50 10N 110 50W
43 Redcliffe 27 12s 153 0 E
46 Redcliffs 34 16s 142 10 E
72 Redding 40 30N 122 25W
7 Redditch 52 18N 1 57W
73 Redlands 34 0N 117 0W
45 Redmond,
Australia 34 55s 117 40 E
72 Redmond, U.S.A. 44 19N 121 11W
75 Redonda, I. 16 58N 62 19W
13 Redondela 42 15N 8 38W
13 Redondo 38 39N 7 37W
73 Redondo Beach 33 52N 118 26W
7 Redruth 50 14N 5 14W
64 Redstone 52 8N 123 42W
65 Redvers 49 35N 101 40W
64 Redwater 53 55N 113 0W
73 Redwood City 37 30N 122 15W
9 Ree, L. 53 35N 8 0W
73 Reedley 34 40N 119 27W
72 Reedsport 43 45N 124 4W
47 Reefton 42 6s 171 51 E
28 Regavim 32 32N 35 2 E
14 Regensburg 49 1N 12 7 E
18 Reggio nell'Emilia 44 42N 10 38 E
18 Réggio di Calábria 38 7N 15 38 E
65 Regina 50 30N 104 35W
31 Registan, Reg. 30 15N 65 0 E
56 Rehoboth 17 55s 15 5 E
28 Rehovot 31 54N 34 48 E
14 Reichenbach 50 36N 12 19 E
45 Reid 35 17s 149 8 E
42 Reid River 19 40s 146 48 E
69 Reidsville 36 21N 79 40W
7 Reigate 51 14N 0 11W
12 Reims 49 15N 4 0 E
28 Reina 32 43N 35 18 E
80 Reina
Adelaida, Arch. 52 20s 74 0W
65 Reindeer L. 57 20N 102 20W
47 Reinga, C. 34 25s 172 43 E
13 Reinosa 43 2N 4 15W
14 Reisengebirge 50 40N 15 45 E
57 Reitz 27 48s 28 29 E
25 Rekinniki 60 38N 163 50 E
79 Remanso 9 41s 42 4W
35 Rembang 6 42s 111 21 E
31 Remeshk 26 55N 58 50 E
14 Remscheid 51 11N 7 12 E
14 Rendsburg 54 18N 9 41 E
25 Rene 66 2N 179 25W
62 Renfrew, Canada 45 30N 76 40W
8 Renfrew, U.K. 55 52N 4 24W
34 Rengat 0 30s 102 45 E
51 Renk 11 47N 32 49 E
11 Renkum 51 58N 5 43 E
43 Renmark 34 11s 140 43 E
12 Rennes 48 7N 1 41W
72 Reno 39 30N 119 0W
72 Renton 47 30N 122 9W
70 Republican, R. 39 3N 96 48W
61 Repulse Bay 66 30N 86 30W
65 Reserve 33 50N 108 54W
80 Resistencia 27 30s 59 0W
15 Reşiţa 45 18N 21 53 E
61 Resolution I.,
Canada 61 30N 65 0W
47 Resolution, I., N.Z. 45 40s 166 40 E
57 Ressano Garcia 25 25s 32 0 E
74 Retalhulen 14 33N 91 46W
19 Réthímnon 35 15N 24 40 E
49 Réunion, Í. 22 0s 56 0 E
13 Reus 41 10N 1 5 E
14 Reutlingen 48 28N 9 13 E
64 Revelstoke 51 0N 118 0W
2 Revilla Gigedo Is. 18 40N 112 0W
33 Rewa 24 33N 81 25 E
32 Rewari 28 15N 76 40 E
72 Rexburg 43 45N 111 50W
53 Rey Malabo 3 45N 8 50 E
20 Reykanes, Pen. 63 48N 22 40W
20 Reykjavik 64 10N 21 57 E
74 Reynosa 26 5N 98 18W
30 Reza'iyeh 37 40N 45 0 E
7 Rhayader 52 19N 3 30W
11 Rheden 52 0N 6 3 E
14 Rhein, R. 51 42N 6 20 E
14 Rhein-Donau-Kanal 49 45N 11 0 E
14 Rheine 52 17N 7 25 E
14 Rheinland-Pfalz □ 50 50N 7 0 E
14 Rhine, R. =
Rhein, R. 51 42N 6 20 E
70 Rhinelander 45 38N 89 29W
50 Rhir, C. 30 38N 9 54W
68 Rhode Island □ 41 38N 71 37W
19 Rhodes, I.=
Ródhos, I. 36 15N 28 10 E
57 Rhodesia ■ 20 0s 28 30 E
19 Rhodope, Mts. =
Rhodopi Planina 41 40N 24 20 E
19 Rhodopi Planina 41 40N 24 20 E
14 Rhön, Mts. 50 25N 10 0 E
7 Rhondda 51 39N 3 30W
12 Rhône □ 45 54N 4 35 E
12 Rhône, R. 43 28N 4 42 E
8 Rhum, I. 57 0N 6 20W
6 Rhyl 53 19N 3 29W
79 Riachão 7 20s 46 37W
34 Riau □ 1 0N 102 35 E
34 Riau, Kep. 0 30N 104 20 E
13 Ribadeo 43 35N 7 5W
79 Ribas do Rio Pardo 20 27s 53 46W
13 Ribatejo, Reg. 39 15N 8 30W
6 Ribble, R. 54 13N 2 20W
21 Ribe 55 19N 8 44 E
79 Ribeirão Prêto 21 10s 47 50W
47 Riccarton 43 32s 172 37 E
70 Rice Lake 44 10N 78 10W
55 Richards B. 28 48s 32 6 E
63 Richibucto 46 42N 64 54W
72 Richland 44 49N 117 9W
42 Richmond,
Australia 20 43s 143 8 E
47 Richmond, N.Z. 41 4s 173 12 E
56 Richmond, C. Prov 31 23s 23 56 E
57 Richmond, Natal
S. Africa 29 54s 30 8 E
7 Richmond, Surrey 51 28N 0 18W
6 Richmond, Yorks. 54 24N 1 43W
72 Richmond, Calif. 38 0N 122 30W
68 Richmond, Ind. 39 50N 84 50W
68 Richmond, Ky. 37 40N 84 20W
72 Richmond, Utah 41 55N 111 48W
68 Richmond, Va. 37 33N 77 27W
62 Richmond Gulf, L. 56 20N 75 50W
68 Richwood 38 17N 80 32W
65 Ridgedale 53 0N 104 10W
62 Ridgetown 42 26N 81 52W
68 Ridgway 41 25N 78 43W
65 Riding Mountain
Nat. Park 50 55N 100 25W
14 Ried 48 14N 13 30 E
56 Riet, R. 29 0s 23 54 E
18 Rieti 42 23N 12 50 E
72 Rifle 39 40N 107 50W
22 Riga 56 53N 24 8 E
63 Rigolet 54 10N 58 23W
53 Rijau 11 7N 5 14 E
18 Rijeka 45 20N 14 21 E
11 Rijssen 52 19N 6 30 E
11 Rijswijk 52 4N 4 22 E
72 Riley 39 18N 96 50W
53 Rima, R. 13 10N 5 15 E
53 Rimi 12 58N 7 43 E
18 Rímini 44 3N 12 33 E
15 Rîmnicu Sărat 45 26N 27 3 E
15 Rîmnicu Vîlcea 45 9N 24 21 E
63 Rimouski 48 27N 68 30W
9 Rineanna 52 42N 85 7W
53 Ringim 12 8N 9 10 E
21 Ringkøbing 56 5N 8 15 E
79 Rio Amazonas,
Estuario do 1 0N 49 0W
78 Rio Branco, Brazil 9 58s 67 49W
80 Rio Branco,
Uruguay 32 34s 53 25W
75 Rio Claro 10 20N 61 25W
80 Rio Cuarto 33 10s 64 25W
79 Rio de Janeiro 23 0s 43 12W
79 Rio de Janeiro □ 22 50s 43 0W
80 Rio do Sul 27 95s 49 37W
80 Rio Gallegos 51 35s 69 15W
80 Rio Grande, Brazil 32 0s 52 20W
66 Rio Grande, R. 37 47N 106 15W
79 Rio Grande do
Norte □ 5 45s 36 0W
80 Rio Grande do
Sul □ 30 0s 54 0W
79 Rio Largo 9 28s 35 50W
78 Rio Mulatos 19 40s 66 50W
54 Rio Muni □ 1 30N 10 0 E
80 Rio Negro 26 0s 50 0W
79 Rio Verde, Brazil 17 43s 50 56W
74 Río Verde,
Mexico 21 56N 99 59W
72 Rio Vista 38 11N 121 44W
78 Riobamba 1 50s 78 45W
78 Ríohacha 11 33N 72 55W
78 Ríosucio 5 30N 75 40W
78 Rioscio 7 27N 77 7W
6 Ripon, U.K. 54 8N 1 31W
70 Ripon, U.S.A. 43 51N 88 50W
28 Rishon Le Zion 31 58N 34 48 E
28 Rishpon 32 12N 34 49 E
21 Risør 58 43N 9 13 E
53 Riti 7 57N 9 41 E
72 Ritzville 47 10N 118 21W
18 Riva 45 53N 10 50 E
80 Rivadavia, Arg. 24 5s 63 0W
80 Rivadavia, Chile 29 50s 70 35W
75 Rivas 11 30N 85 50W
80 Rivera 31 0s 55 50W
68 Riverhead 40 53N 72 40W
65 Riverhurst 50 55N 106 50W
53 Rivers □ 5 0N 6 30 E
56 Riversdale 34 7s 21 15 E
73 Riverside, Calif. 34 0N 117 15W
72 Riverside, Wyo. 41 12N 106 57W
43 Riverton, Australia 34 10s 138 46 E
65 Riverton, Canada 51 5N 97 0W
47 Riverton, N.Z. 46 21s 168 0 E
72 Riverton, U.S.A. 43 1N 108 27W
18 Riviera di Levante 44 23N 9 15 E
18 Riviera di Ponente 43 50N 7 58 E
63 Rivière Bleue 47 26N 69 2W
63 Rivière du Loup 47 50N 69 30W
63 Rivière Pentecôte 49 57N 67 1W
30 Riyadh = Ar Riyád 24 41N 46 42 E
30 Rize 41 0N 40 30 E
21 Rjukan 59 54N 8 33 E
12 Roanne 46 3N 4 4 E
69 Roanoke, Ala. 33 9N 85 23W
68 Roanoke, Va 37 19N 79 55W
68 Roanoke Rapids 36 36N 77 42W
75 Roatán, I. de 16 23N 86 26W
56 Robertson 33 46s 19 50 E
62 Roberval 48 32N 72 15W
65 Roblin 51 21N 101 25W
64 Robson, Mt. 53 10N 119 10W
71 Robstown 27 47N 97 40W
13 Roca, C. da 38 40N 9 31W
56 Rocadas 16 45s 15 0 E
79 Rocas, Is. 4 0s 34 1W
80 Rocha 34 30s 54 25W
6 Rochdale 53 36N 2 10W
12 Rochefort 45 56N 0 57W
70 Rochelle 41 55N 89 5W
64 Rocher River 61 12N 114 0W
46 Rochester,
Australia 36 22s 144 41 E
7 Rochester, U.K. 51 22N 0 30 E
70 Rochester, Minn. 44 1N 92 28W
68 Rochester, N.H. 43 19N 70 57W
68 Rochester, N.Y. 43 10N 77 40W
69 Rock Hill 34 55N 81 2W
70 Rock Island 41 30N 90 35W
75 Rock Sound 24 54N 76 12W
72 Rock Springs 46 55N 106 11W
4 Rockall, I. 57 37N 13 42W
70 Rockford, Ill. 42 20N 89 0W

Rockford, Mich. St. Lawrence, I.

70 Rockford, Mich. 43 7N 85 33W
42 Rockhampton 23 22S 150 32E
45 Rockingham 32 15S 115 38E
69 Rockland, Mass. 44 6N 69 8W
68 Rockville, Md. 39 7N 77 10W
45 Rocky Gully 34 30S 117 0E
69 Rocky Mount 35 55N 77 48W
64 Rocky Mountain House 52 22N 114 55W
58 Rocky Mts. 48 0N 113 0W
64 Rockyford 51 13N 113 8W
21 Rødbyhavn 54 39N 11 22E
63 Roddickton 50 51N 56 8W
12 Rodez 44 21N 2 33E
19 Ródhos 36 15N 28 10E
19 Ródhos, I. 36 15N 28 10E
47 Rodney, C. 36 17S 174 50E
3 Rodriguez, I. 20 0S 65 0E
44 Roebourne 20 44S 117 9E
44 Roebuck, B. 18 5S 122 20E
44 Roebuck Plains P.O. 17 56S 122 28E
11 Roermond 51 12N 6 0E
61 Roes Welcome Sd. 65 0N 87 0W
11 Roeselare 50 57N 3 7E
21 Rogaland □ 59 12N 6 20E
71 Rogers 36 20N 94 0W
62 Roggan River 54 24N 78 5W
56 Roggeveldberge 32 10S 20 10E
32 Rohri 27 45N 68 51E
32 Rohtak 28 55N 76 43E
80 Rolândia 23 5S 52 0W
71 Rolla 38 0N 91 42W
42 Rollingstone 19 2S 146 24E
42 Rolleston 43 35S 172 24E
75 Rolleville 23 41N 76 0W
43 Roma, Australia 26 32S 148 49E
18 Roma, Italy 41 54N 12 30E
21 Roma, Sweden 57 32N 18 28E
15 Roman 43 8N 23 54E
15 Romania■= Rumania ■ 46 0N 25 0E
60 Romanzof, C. 61 49N 165 56W
18 Rome, Italy = Roma 41 54N 12 30E
69 Rome, Ga. 34 20N 85 0W
68 Rome, N.Y. 43 14N 75 29W
7 Romney Marsh 51 0N 1 0E
12 Romorantin-Lanthenay 47 21N 1 45E
20 Romsdalen, R. 62 25N 7 50E
8 Ronaldsay, North I. 59 23N 2 26W
8 Ronaldsay, South I. 58 47N 2 56W
79 Roncador, S. do 12 30S 52 30W
13 Roncevoux 43 0N 1 23W
13 Ronda 36 46N 5 12W
78 Rondônia □ 11 0S 63 0W
79 Rondonópolis 16 28S 54 38W
52 Rongai 0 10S 35 51E
21 Rønne 55 6N 14 44E
45 Ronsard, C. 24 46S 113 10E
11 Ronse 50 45N 3 35E
55 Roodepoort-Maraisburg 26 11S 27 54E
32 Roorkee 29 52N 77 59E
11 Roosendaal 51 32N 4 29E
73 Roosevelt Res. 33 46N 111 0W
42 Roper, R. 14 43S 135 27E
78 Roraima □ 2 0N 61 30W
78 Roraima, Mt. 5 10N 60 40W
14 Rosa, Mte. 45 57N 7 53E
80 Rosario, Arg. 33 0S 60 50W
79 Rosário, Brazil 3 0S 44 15W
74 Rosario, Mexico 23 0S 105 52W
80 Rosario de la Frontera 25 50S 65 0W
80 Rosário do Sul 30 15S 54 55W
13 Rosas 42 19N 3 10E
13 Rosas, G. de 42 10N 3 15E
9 Roscommon 53 38N 8 11W
9 Roscommon □ 53 40N 8 15W
9 Roscrea 52 57N 7 47W
63 Rose Blanche 47 38N 58 45W
64 Rose Harbour 52 15N 131 10W
65 Rose Valley 52 19N 103 49W
75 Roseau 48 56N 96 0W
71 Rosenberg 29 30N 95 48W
72 Rosebud 31 5N 97 0W
72 Roseburg 43 10N 123 10W
46 Rosedale 38 11S 146 48E
65 Rosetown 57 33N 108 0E
51 Rosetta = Rashîd 31 21N 30 22E
72 Roseville 38 46N 121 41W
43 Rosewood 35 38S 147 52E
28 Rosh Ha'Ayin 32 5N 34 47E
28 Rosh Pinna 32 58N 35 32E
78 Rosignol 6 15N 57 30W
21 Roskilde 55 38N 12 3E
22 Roslavl 53 57N 32 55E
47 Ross, N.Z. 42 53S 170 49E
7 Ross, U.K. 51 55N 2 34W
9 Ross □ 70 0S 170 5W
2 Ross Dependency □ 70 0S 170 0W
3 Ross Sea 74 0S 178 0E
64 Rossland 49 6N 117 50W
9 Rosslare 52 17N 6 23W
50 Rosso 16 30N 15 49W
23 Rossosh 50 15N 39 20E
65 Rosthern 52 40N 106 20W
14 Rostock 54 4N 12 9E
23 Rostov 47 15N 39 45E
71 Roswell 33 26N 104 32W
8 Rosyth 56 2N 3 26W
7 Rother, R. 50 59N 0 40W
6 Rotherham 53 26N 1 21W
8 Rothes 57 31N 3 12W
8 Rothesay 55 50N 5 3W
35 Roti, I. 10 50S 123 0E
46 Roto 33 0S 145 30E
47 Rotorua 38 9S 176 16E
47 Rotorua, L. 38 5S 176 18E
11 Rotterdam 51 55N 4 30E
45 Rottnest, I. 32 0S 115 27E
14 Rottweil 48 9N 8 38E
3 Rotuma, I. 12 25S 177 5E
12 Roubaix 50 40N 3 10E
12 Rouen 49 27N 1 4E
12 Rouergue, Reg. 44 20N 2 20E
15 Roumania■= Rumania ■ 46 0N 25 0E
43 Round, Mt. 30 26S 152 16E
72 Roundup 46 25N 108 35W
8 Rousay, I. 59 10N 3 2W
12 Roussillon, Reg. 45 24N 4 49E
56 Rouxville 30 11S 26 50E
62 Rouyn 48 20N 79 0W
20 Rovaniemi 66 29N 25 41E
18 Rovereto 45 53N 11 3E
18 Rovigo 45 4N 11 48E
18 Rovinj 45 18N 13 40E
23 Rovno 50 40N 26 10E
35 Roxas 11 36N 122 49E
47 Roxburgh 45 33S 169 19E
44 Roy Hill 22 37S 119 58E
68 Royal Oak 42 30N 83 5W
70 Royale, I. 48 0N 89 0W
12 Royan 45 37N 1 2W
22 Rtishchevo 52 35N 43 50E
47 Ruapehu, Mt. 39 18S 175 35E
52 Rubeho Mts. 6 50S 36 25E
78 Rubio 7 43N 72 22W
24 Rubtsovsk 51 30N 80 50E
60 Ruby 38 27S 145 55E
43 Rudall 33 43S 136 17E
22 Rudnichny 59 38N 52 26E
25 Rudnogorsk 57 15N 103 42E
24 Rudnyy 52 57N 63 7E
52 Rudolf, L. = Turkana, L. 4 10N 36 10E
51 Rufa'a 14 44N 33 32E
52 Rufiji, R. 8 0S 39 20E
80 Rufino 34 20S 62 50W
50 Rufisque 14 43N 17 17W
7 Rugby, U.K. 52 23N 1 16W
70 Rugby, U.S.A. 48 21N 100 0W
14 Rügen, I. 54 22N 13 25E
28 Ruhâma 31 31N 34 43E
52 Ruhengeri 1 30S 29 36E
14 Ruhr, R. 51 27N 6 44E
54 Ruki, R. 0 5N 18 17E
52 Rukungiri 0 53S 29 58E
52 Rukwa, L. 7 50S 32 10E
44 Rum Jungle 13 0S 130 59E
15 Rumania ■ 46 0N 25 0E
42 Rumbalara 25 20S 134 29E
68 Rumford 44 30N 70 30W
36 Rumoi 43 56N 141 39W
52 Rumuruti 0 17N 36 32E
47 Runanga 42 25S 171 15E
6 Runcorn 53 20N 2 44W
52 Rungwa 6 55S 33 32E
52 Rungwe, Mt. 9 11S 33 32E
53 Runka 12 28N 7 20E
34 Rupat, I. 1 45N 101 40E
62 Rupert House = Fort Rupert 51 30N 78 40W
57 Rusape 18 35S 32 8E
19 Ruse 43 48N 25 59E
7 Rushden 52 17N 0 37W
68 Rushville 39 38N 85 22W
46 Rushworth 36 32S 145 1E
79 Russas 4 56S 37 58W
65 Russell, Canada 50 50N 101 20W
70 Russell, U.S.A. 38 56N 98 55W
69 Russellville, Ala. 34 30N 87 44W
71 Russellville, Ark. 35 15N 93 0W
24 Russian Soviet Federal Socialist Rep. 60 0N 80 0E
24 Russkaya Polyana 53 47N 73 53E
56 Rustenburg 25 41S 27 14E
71 Ruston 32 30N 92 40W
35 Ruteng 8 26S 120 30E
72 Ruth 39 15N 115 1W
46 Rutherglen, Australia 36 5S 146 29E
8 Rutherglen, U.K. 55 50N 4 11W
68 Rutland 43 38N 73 0W
52 Rutshuru 1 13S 29 25E
52 Ruvu 6 49S 38 43E
52 Ruvuma, R. 10 29S 40 28E
52 Ruwenzori, Mts. 0 30N 29 55E
15 Ruzomberok 49 3N 19 17E
52 Rwanda ■ 2 0S 30 0E
8 Ryan, L. 55 0N 5 2W
22 Ryazan 54 38N 39 44E
22 Ryazhsk 53 40N 40 7E
24 Rybache 46 40N 81 20E
22 Rybachiy Pol. 69 43N 32 0E
22 Rybinsk 58 3N 38 52E
22 Rybinskoye, Vdkhr. 58 30N 38 25E
7 Ryde 50 44N 1 9W
7 Rye 50 57N 0 46E
6 Rye, R. 54 12N 0 53W
15 Rypin 53 3N 19 32E
39 Ryūkyū, Is. 26 0N 128 0E
15 Rzeszów 50 5N 21 58E
22 Rzhev 56 15N 34 18E

S

28 Sa'ad 31 28N 34 33E
31 Sa'ādatābād 30 10N 53 5E
14 Saale, R. 51 57N 11 55E
14 Saar, R. 49 20N 6 45E
14 Saarbrücken 49 15N 6 58E
22 Saaremaa, I. 58 30N 22 30E
14 Saarland □ 49 20N 0 75E
75 Saba, I. 17 30N 63 10W
13 Sabadell 41 28N 2 7E
34 Sabah □ 6 0N 117 0E
30 Sabalan, Kuhha-ye 38 15N 47 49E
78 Sabanalargo 10 38N 74 55W
34 Sabang 5 50N 95 15E
79 Sabará 19 55S 43 55W
28 Sabastiya 32 17N 35 12E
18 Sabáudia 41 17N 13 2E
51 Sabhah 27 9N 14 29E
57 Sabie 25 4S 30 48E
74 Sabinas 27 50N 101 10W
74 Sabinas Hidalgo 26 40N 100 10W
71 Sabine, R. 30 0N 93 45W
59 Sable, C., Canada 43 29N 65 38W
63 Sable, C., U.S.A. 25 5N 81 0W
63 Sable I. 44 0N 60 0W
53 Sabou 12 1N 2 28W
31 Sabzevār 36 15N 57 40E
31 Sabzvāran 28 45N 57 50E
69 Saco 43 29N 70 28W
72 Sacramento 38 39N 121 30E
72 Sacramento, R. 38 3N 121 56W
73 Sacramento Mts. 32 30N 105 30W
13 Sádaba 2 19N 1 12W
51 Sadd el Aali 24 5N 32 54E
53 Sade 11 22N 10 45E
36 Sado, I. 38 15N 138 30E
30 Safaniya 28 5N 48 42E
31 Safed Koh 34 15N 64 0E
73 Safford 32 54N 109 52W
7 Saffron Walden 52 5N 0 15E
50 Safi 32 20N 9 17W
35 Saga, Indonesia 2 40S 132 55E
36 Saga, Japan 33 15N 130 18E
36 Saga □ 33 15N 130 20E
33 Sagaing 22 0N 96 0E
32 Sagar 23 50N 78 50E
37 Sagil 50 15N 91 15E
68 Saginaw 43 26N 83 55W
68 Saginaw B. 43 50N 83 40W
61 Saglouc 62 30N 74 15W
13 Sagres 37 0N 8 58W
75 Sagua la Grande 22 50N 80 10W
73 Saguache 38 10N 106 4W
63 Saguenay, R. 48 10N 69 45W
13 Sagunto 39 42N 0 18W
13 Sahagun 42 18N 5 2W
50 Sahara 23 0N 5 0W
32 Saharanpur 29 58N 77 33E
32 Sahiwal 30 45N 73 8E
31 Sa'idābād 29 30N 55 45E
32 Saidapet 13 0N 80 15E
32 Saidu 34 50N 72 15E
31 Saighan 35 10N 67 55E
34 Saigon=Phan Bho Ho Chi Minh 10 58N 106 40E
29 Saihut 15 12N 51 10E
36 Saijo 34 0N 133 5E
36 Saiki 32 35N 131 50E
8 St. Abbs Hd. 55 55N 2 10W
7 St. Albans, U.K. 51 46N 0 21W
68 St. Albans, U.S.A. 44 49N 73 5W
7 St. Albans Hd. 50 34N 2 3W
57 St. André, C. 16 10S 44 27E
8 St. Andrews 56 20N 2 48W
46 St. Arnaud 36 32S 143 16E
6 St. Asaph 53 15N 3 27W
63 St. Augustin 51 19N 58 48W
69 St. Augustine 29 52N 81 20W
7 St. Austell 50 20N 4 48W
75 St. Barthelémy, I. 17 50N 62 50W
6 St. Bees Hd. 54 30N 3 38E
65 St. Boniface 49 50N 97 10W
7 St. Bride's B. 51 48N 5 15W
12 St. Brieuc 48 30N 2 46W
7 St. Catherine's Pt. 50 34N 1 18W
70 St. Charles 38 46N 90 30W
75 St. Christopher, I. 17 20N 62 40W
62 St. Clair, L. 42 30N 82 45W
65 St. Claude 49 40N 98 22W
70 St. Cloud 45 30N 94 11W
63 St. Cœur de Marie 48 39N 71 43W
45 St. Cricq, C. 25 17S 113 6E
75 St. Croix, I. 17 30N 64 40W
7 St. Davids 51 54N 5 16W
7 St. David's Hd. 51 54N 5 16W
75 St. David's I. 32 22N 64 39W
12 St. Denis 48 56N 2 22E
60 St. Elias, Mt. 60 20N 141 59W
12 St. Étienne 45 27N 4 22E
62 St. Félicien 48 40N 72 25W
63 St. Fintan's 48 10N 58 50W
12 St. Flour 45 2N 3 6E
56 St. Francis, C. 34 14S 24 49E
62 St. Gabriel de Brandon 46 17N 73 24W
14 St. Gallen 47 25N 9 23E
43 St. George, Australia 28 1S 148 41E
75 St. George, Bermuda 32 24N 64 42W
63 St. George, Canada 45 11N 66 57W
73 St. George, U.S.A. 37 10N 113 35W
69 St. George, C. 29 36N 85 2W
46 St. George Hd. 35 11S 150 45E
65 St. George West 50 33N 96 7W
11 St. Georges, Belgium 50 37N 4 20E
62 St. Georges, Canada 46 42N 72 35W
79 St. George's, Fr. Guiana 4 0N 52 0W
75 St. Georges, Grenada 12 5N 61 43W
63 St. George's B. 48 20N 59 0W
10 St. George's Chan. 52 0N 6 0W
75 St. George's I. 32 22N 64 40W
49 St. Helena, I. 15 55S 5 44W
56 St. Helenabaai 32 40S 18 10E
42 St. Helens, Australia 41 20S 148 15E
6 St. Helens, U.K. 53 28N 2 44W
72 St. Helens, U.S.A. 45 55N 122 50W
62 St. Hyacinthe 45 40N 72 58W
7 St. Ives, Cambridge 52 20N 0 5W
7 St. Ives, Cornwall 50 13N 5 29W
62 St. Jean 45 20N 73 50W
65 St. Jean Baptiste 49 15N 97 20W
62 St. Jérôme 45 55N 74 0W
63 St. John 45 20N 66 8W
63 St. John, L. 48 40N 72 0W
75 St. John's, Antigua 17 6N 61 51W
63 St. John's, Canada 47 45N 52 40W
68 St. Johnsbury 44 25N 72 1W
68 St. Joseph, Mich. 42 6N 86 29W
70 St. Joseph, Mo. 39 46N 94 51W
62 St. Jovite 46 8N 74 38W
47 St. Kilda 45 53S 170 31E
10 St. Kilda, I. 57 50N 8 40W
75 St. Kitts, I.= St. Christopher, I. 17 20N 62 40W
65 St. Laurent 50 25N 97 58W
63 St. Lawrence 46 54N 55 23W
63 St. Lawrence, G. of 48 25N 62 0W
60 St. Lawrence, I. 63 0N 170 0W

St. Lawrence, R. Sanlúcar-la-Mayor

63 St. Lawrence, R. . . 49 15N 67 0W
63 St. Leonard 47 12N 67 58W
62 St. Lin 45 44N 73 46W
12 St. Lô 49 7N 1 5W
12 St. Louis, France . . 47 35N 7 34E
50 St. Louis, Senegal . 16 8N 16 27W
70 St. Louis, U.S.A. . . 38 40N 90 20W
57 St. Lucia, C. 28 32S 32 29E
75 St. Lucia, I. 14 0N 60 50W
57 St. Lucia, L. 28 5S 32 30E
75 St. Lucia Chan. . . . 14 15N 61 0W
75 St. Maarten, I. . . . 18 0N 63 5W
12 St. Malo 48 39N 2 1W
75 St. Marc 19 10N 72 5W
72 St. Maries 47 17N 116 34W
75 St. Martin, I. 18 0N 63 0W
63 St. Martins 45 22N 65 38W
42 St. Marys, Australia 41 32S 148 11E
68 St. Marys, U.S.A. . 41 30N 78 33W
7 St. Marys, I. 49 55N 6 17W
60 St. Matthew I. . . . 60 30N 172 45W
7 St. Michael's Mt. . . 50 7N 5 30W
14 St. Moritz 46 30N 9 50E
12 St. Nazaire 47 17N 2 12W
7 St. Neots 52 14N 0 16W
11 St. Niklaas 51 10N 4 8E
12 St. Omer 50 45N 2 15E
63 St. Pacôme 47 24N 69 58W
63 St. Pamphile 46 58N 69 48W
63 St. Pascal 47 32N 69 48W
64 St. Paul, Canada . . 51 34N 57 47W
70 St. Paul, U.S.A. . . . 44 54N 93 5W
2 St. Paul, I., Atlantic Oc. 0 50N 31 40W
3 St. Paul, I., Indian Oc. 30 40S 77 34E
70 St. Peter 44 15N 93 57W
7 St. Peter Port 49 27N 2 31W
69 St. Petersburg 27 45N 82 40W
63 St. Pierre 46 40N 56 0W
62 St. Pierre, L. 46 10N 72 50W
63 St. Pierre et Miquelon □ 46 49N 56 15W
12 St. Quentin 49 50N 3 16E
63 St. Siméon 47 51N 69 54W
63 St. Stephen 45 16N 67 17W
62 St. Thomas, Canada 42 47N 81 12W
75 St. Thomas, Virgin Is. 18 21N 64 56W
62 St. Tite 46 45N 72 40W
12 St. Tropez 43 17N 6 38E
11 St. Troud 50 48N 5 10E
12 St. Valéry 50 10N 1 38E
75 St. Vincent, I. 13 10N 61 10W
75 St. Vincent Pass. . . 13 30N 61 0W
65 St. Walburg 53 39N 109 12W
63 Ste. Anne de Beaupré 47 2N 70 58W
63 Ste. Cecile 47 56N 64 34W
75 Ste. Marie 14 48N 61 1W
57 Ste. Marie, C. 25 36S 45 8E
63 Ste. Marie de la Madeleine 46 26N 71 0W
75 Ste. Rose 16 20N 61 45W
65 Ste. Rose du lac . . . 51 10N 99 30W
12 Saintes 45 45N 0 37W
12 Saintonge, Reg. . . . 45 40N 0 50W
34 Sairang 23 50N 92 45E
36 Saitama □ 36 25N 137 0E
78 Sajama, Mt. 18 6S 68 54W
52 Saka 0 11S 39 30E
36 Sakai 34 30N 135 30E
36 Sakaide 34 32N 133 50E
36 Sakaiminato 35 33N 133 15E
36 Sakata 38 55N 139 56E
53 Sakété 6 40N 2 32E
25 Sakhalin 51 0N 143 0E
28 Sakhnin 32 52N 35 12E
39 Sakishima-gunto, Is. 24 30N 124 0E
55 Sakrivier 30 54S 20 28E
21 Sala 59 58N 16 35E
2 Sala-y-Gomez, I. . . 26 28S 105 28W
80 Saladillo 35 40S 59 55W
80 Salado, R., Buenos Aires . . . 36 0S 57 30W
80 Salado, R., Sta. Fe. 31 40S 60 41W
50 Salaga 8 31N 0 31W
80 Salamanca, Chile . . 32 0S 71 25W
13 Salamanca, Sp. 40 58N 5 39W
68 Salamanca, U.S.A. . 42 10N 78 42W
19 Salamis 37 56N 23 30E
35 Salatiga 7 19S 110 30E
22 Salavat 53 21N 55 55E
78 Salaverry 8 15S 79 0W
35 Salawati, I. 1 7S 130 54E
54 Salazar 9 18S 14 54E
56 Saldanha 33 0S 17 58E
46 Sale, Australia 38 7S 147 0E
6 Sale, U.K. 53 26N 2 19W
50 Salé 34 3N 6 48W
24 Salekhard 66 30N 66 25E
32 Salem, India 11 40N 78 11E
68 Salem, Mass. 42 29N 70 53W
68 Salem, Ohio 40 52N 80 50W
72 Salem, Oreg. 45 0N 123 0W
68 Salem, Va. 37 19N 80 8W
21 Sälen 64 41N 11 27E
18 Salerno 40 40N 14 44E
6 Salford 53 30N 2 17W
30 Salihli 38 29N 28 9E
55 Salima 13 47S 34 26E
70 Salina 38 50N 97 40W
18 Salina I. 38 35N 14 50E
74 Salina Cruz 16 10N 95 10W
79 Salinas, Brazil 16 20S 42 10W
73 Salinas, U.S.A. . . . 36 40N 121 38W
75 Salinas, B. de 11 4N 85 45W
80 Salinas Grandes . . . 29 30S 65 0W
79 Salinópolis 0 40S 47 20W
43 Salisbury, Australia 34 46S 138 38E
57 Salisbury, Rhodesia 17 50S 31 2E
7 Salisbury, U.K. 51 4N 1 48W
68 Salisbury, Md. 38 20N 75 38W
69 Salisbury, N.C. 35 42N 80 29W
7 Salisbury Plain 51 13N 2 0W
72 Salmon 45 12N 113 56W
72 Salmon, R. 45 51N 116 46W
64 Salmon Arm 50 40N 119 15W
45 Salmon Gums 32 59S 121 38E
72 Salmon River Mts. 45 0N 114 30W
21 Salo 60 22N 23 3E
19 Salonica= Thessaloniki 40 38N 23 0E
15 Salonta 46 49N 21 42E
7 Salop □ 52 36N 2 45W
23 Salsk 46 28N 41 30E
72 Salt Lake City 40 45N 111 58W
80 Salta 24 47S 65 25W
8 Saltcoats 55 38N 4 47W
74 Saltillo 25 30N 100 57W
80 Salto 31 20S 58 10W
73 Salton Sea 33 20N 116 0W
53 Saltpond 5 15N 1 3W
64 Saltspring 48 54N 123 37W
51 Salûm 31 31N 25 7E
33 Salur 18 27N 83 18E
18 Saluzzo 44 39N 7 29E
79 Salvador, Brazil . . . 13 0S 38 30W
65 Salvador, Canada . . 52 20N 109 25W
74 Salvador ■ 13 50N 89 0W
33 Salween, R. 16 31N 97 37E
14 Salzburg 47 48N 13 2E
14 Salzburg □ 47 25N 13 15E
14 Salzgitter 52 2N 10 22E
71 Sam Rayburn Res. 31 15N 94 20W
24 Sama 60 10N 60 15E
25 Samagaltai 50 36N 95 3E
31 Samangan □ 36 15N 67 40E
35 Samar, I. 12 0N 125 0E
28 Samaria, Reg.= Shomron, Reg. . . 32 15N 35 13E
34 Samarinda 0 30S 117 9E
24 Samarkand 39 40N 67 0E
33 Sambalpur 21 28N 83 58E
32 Sambhal 28 35N 78 37E
32 Sambhar 26 52N 75 5E
18 Sambiase 38 57N 16 17E
11 Sambre, R. 50 28N 4 52E
38 Samchŏk 37 27N 129 10E
52 Same 4 2S 37 38E
47 Samoa Is. 14 0S 171 0W
19 Sámos, I. 37 45N 26 50E
19 Samothráki, I. . . . 40 28N 25 38E
80 Sampacho 33 20S 64 50W
35 Sampang 7 11S 113 13E
34 Sampit 2 20S 113 0E
39 Samshui 23 7N 112 58E
30 Samsun 41 15N 36 15E
34 Samui, Ko 9 30N 100 0E
34 Samut Prakan 13 32N 100 40E
34 Samut Songkhram . 13 24N 100 1E
50 San 13 15N 4 45W
34 San, R., Cambodia 13 32N 105 57E
15 San, R., Poland . . . 50 45N 21 51E
2 San Ambrosio, I. . . 26 21S 79 52W
75 San Andrés, I. de . 12 42N 81 46W
74 San Andrés Tuxtla 18 30N 95 20W
71 San Angelo 31 30N 100 30W
80 San Antonio, Chile 33 40S 71 40W
13 San Antonio, Sp. . . 38 58N 1 27E
71 San Antonio, U.S.A. 29 30N 98 30W
80 San Antonio, C., Arg. 36 15S 56 40W
75 San Antonio, C., Cuba 21 50N 84 57W
75 San Antonio de los Banos 22 54N 82 31W
80 San Antonio Oeste 40 40S 65 0W
18 San Benedetto 45 2N 10 57E
71 San Benito 26 5N 97 32W
73 San Bernardino . . . 34 7N 117 18W
35 San Bernardino Str. 12 37N 124 12E
80 San Bernardo 33 40S 70 50W
78 San Bernardo, I. de 9 45N 75 50W
75 San Blas, Cord. de 9 15N 78 30W
80 San Carlos, Arg. . . 33 50S 69 0W
35 San Carlos, Philippines 10 29N 123 25E
80 San Carlos, Uruguay 34 46S 54 58W
78 San Carlos, Ven. . . 1 55N 67 4W
78 San Carlos, Ven. . . 9 40N 68 36W
80 San Carlos de Bariloche 41 10S 71 25W
78 San Carlos del Zulía 9 1N 71 55W
73 San Carlos L. 33 13N 110 24W
73 San Clemente, U.S.A. 33 29N 117 45W
73 San Clemente I. . . . 33 0N 118 30W
75 San Cristóbal, Dom. Rep. 18 25N 70 6W
80 San Cristóbal, Arg. 30 20S 61 10W
78 San Cristóbal, Ven. 7 46N 72 14W
74 San Cristóbal de las Casas 16 50N 92 33W
73 San Diego 32 50N 117 10W
80 San Diego, C. 54 40S 65 10W
80 San Felipe, Chile . . 32 43S 70 50W
78 San Felipe, Ven. . . 10 20N 68 44W
13 San Felíu de Guíxals 41 45N 3 1E
77 San Felix, I. 26 30S 80 0W
35 San Fernando, Philippines 15 5N 120 37E
35 San Fernando, Philippines 16 40N 120 23E
13 San Fernando, Sp. . 36 22N 6 17W
75 San Fernando, Trinidad 10 20N 61 30W
73 San Fernando, U.S.A. 34 15N 118 29W
78 San Fernando de Apure 7 54N 67 28W
78 San Fernando de Atabapo 4 3N 67 42W
80 San Francisco, Arg. 31 30S 62 5W
73 San Francisco, U.S.A. 37 35N 122 30W
73 San Francisco, R. . . 32 59N 109 22W
75 San Francisco de Macoris 19 19N 70 15W
80 San Francisco de Monte del Oro . . 32 36S 66 8W
74 San Francisco del Oro 26 52N 105 50W
78 San Gil 6 33N 73 8W
14 San Gottardo, P. del 46 33N 8 33E
80 San Ignacio 26 52S 57 3W
72 San Joaquin, R. . . . 36 43N 121 50W
80 San Jorge, G. de, Arg. 46 0S 66 0W
75 San José, Costa Rica 10 0N 83 57W
74 San José, Guatemala 14 0N 90 50W
35 San Jose, Philippines 15 45N 120 55E
35 San Jose, Philippines 10 50N 122 5E
73 San Jose, U.S.A. . . 37 20N 122 0W
80 San José, G. 42 20S 64 20W
80 San José de Jáchal . 30 5S 69 0W
80 San José de Mayo . 34 27S 56 27W
78 San José de Ocune 4 15N 70 20W
80 San José del Boquerón 26 5S 63 38W
74 San José del Cabo . 23 0N 109 50W
78 San José del Guaviare 2 35N 72 38W
79 San José do Rio Prêto 21 0S 49 30W
80 San Juan, Arg. 31 30S 68 30W
75 San Juan, Dom. Rep. 18 49N 71 12W
74 San Juan, Mexico . 21 20N 102 50W
75 San Juan, Puerto Rico 18 40N 66 11W
73 San Juan, R. 37 18N 110 28W
73 San Juan Capistrano 33 29N 117 46W
78 San Juan de los Morros 9 55N 67 21W
75 San Juan del Norte, B. de 11 30N 83 40W
73 San Juan Mts. 38 30N 108 30W
80 San Julián 49 15S 68 0W
80 San Justo 30 55S 60 30W
73 San Leandro 37 40N 122 6W
78 San Lorenzo, Ecuador 1 15N 78 50W
80 San Lorenzo, Mt. . . 47 40S 72 20W
74 San Lucas, C. de . . 22 50N 110 0W
80 San Luis 33 20S 66 20W
74 San Luis de la Paz . 21 18N 100 31W
73 San Luis Obispo . . 35 17N 120 40W
74 San Luis Potosí . . . 22 9N 100 59W
74 San Luis Potosí □ . 22 30N 100 30W
74 San Marcos, Guatemala 14 59N 91 52W
71 San Marcos, U.S.A. 29 53N 98 0W
18 San Marino 43 56N 12 25E
18 San Marino ■ 43 56N 12 25E
73 San Mateo 37 32N 122 25W
80 San Matías, G. 41 30S 64 0W
74 San Miguel, Salvador 13 30N 88 12W
80 San Miguel de Tucumán 26 50S 65 20W
80 San Nicolás de los Arroyas 33 17S 60 10W
80 San Pedro, Arg. . . . 24 10S 57 15W
75 San Pedro, Dom. Rep. 18 30N 69 18W
74 San Pedro de las Colonias 25 50N 102 59W
80 San Pedro del Paraná 26 43S 56 13W
74 San Pedro Sula 15 30N 88 0W
35 San Quintin 16 1N 120 56E
80 San Rafael 34 40S 68 30W
18 San Remo 43 48N 7 47E
80 San Roque 28 15S 58 45W
80 San Rosendo 37 10S 72 50W
74 San Salvador 13 40N 89 20W
75 San Salvador, I. . . . 24 0N 74 40W
80 San Salvador de Jujuy 23 30S 65 40W
80 San Sebastián, Arg. 53 10S 68 30W
13 San Sabastián, Spain 43 17N 1 58W
18 San Severo 41 41N 15 23E
73 San Simon 32 14N 109 16W
80 San Valentín, Mt. . 46 30S 73 30W
13 San Vicente de la Barquera 43 30N 4 29W
29 Sana 15 27N 44 12E
18 Sana, R. 45 3N 16 23E
53 Sanaga, R. 3 35N 9 38E
35 Sanana 2 5S 125 50E
30 Sanandaj 35 25N 47 7E
75 Sancti Spíritus 21 52N 79 33W
62 Sand Lake 47 46N 84 31W
71 Sand Springs 36 12N 96 5W
34 Sandakan 5 53N 118 10E
8 Sanday, I. 59 14N 2 30W
73 Sanders 35 12N 109 25W
43 Sandgate 27 20S 153 5E
30 Sandikli 38 30N 30 20E
21 Sandnes 58 50N 5 45E
15 Sandomierz 50 40N 21 43E
33 Sandoway 18 20N 94 30E
72 Sandpoint 48 20N 116 40W
6 Sandringham 52 50N 0 30E
45 Sandstone 28 0S 119 15E
68 Sandusky 41 25N 82 40W
56 Sandveld 32 0S 18 15E
21 Sandviken 60 38N 16 46E
33 Sandwip Chan. 22 35N 91 35E
42 Sandy, C. 24 41S 153 8E
69 Sanford, Fla. 28 45N 81 20W
69 Sanford, N.C. 35 30N 79 10W
60 Sanford, Mt. 62 30N 143 0W
73 Sanger 36 47N 119 35W
34 Sanggau 0 5N 110 30E
35 Sangihe, Pulau 3 45N 125 30E
32 Sangli 16 55N 74 33E
54 Sangmelina 2 57N 12 1E
13 Sangonera, R. 37 59N 1 4W
71 Sangre de Cristo Mts. 37 0N 105 0W
37 Sangsang 29 30N 86 0E
54 Sangwa 5 30S 26 0E
13 Sanlucar de Barrameda 36 47N 6 21W
13 Sanlúcar-la-Mayor 37 26N 6 18W

Sivas Stellaland

30 Sivas 39 43N 36 58E
30 Siverek 37 50N 39 25E
51 Siwa 29 11N 25 31E
33 Siwalik Ra. 28 0N 83 0E
7 Sizewell 52 13N 1 38E
21 Sjaelland, I. 55 30N 11 30E
19 Skadarsko, Jezero, L. 42 10N 19 15E
21 Skagen 57 43N 10 35E
21 Skagerrak, Str. 57 30N 9 0E
64 Skagway 59 30N 135 20W
21 Skara 58 25N 13 30E
21 Skaraborg □ 58 20N 13 30E
32 Skardu 35 20N 73 35E
64 Skeena, R. 54 15N 130 5W
64 Skenna Mts. 56 40N 128 0W
6 Skegnwss 53 9N 0 20E
78 Skeldon 6 0N 57 20W
20 Skellefteå 64 45N 20 59E
20 Skelleftehamn 64 41N 21 14E
9 Skibbereen 51 33N 9 16W
6 Skiddaw, Mt. 54 39N 3 9W
21 Skien 59 12N 9 35E
15 Skierniewice 51 58N 20 19E
50 Skikda 36 50N 6 58E
6 Skipton 53 57N 2 1W
19 Skíros, I. 38 55N 24 34E
21 Skive 56 33N 9 2E
21 Skoghall 59 20N 13 30E
19 Skopje 42 1N 21 32E
19 Skoplje=Skopje 42 1N 21 32E
21 Skövde 58 24N 13 50E
25 Skovorodino 53 59N 123 55E
69 Skowhegan 44 49N 69 40W
21 Skudeneshavn 59 10N 5 10E
9 Skull 51 32N 9 40W
14 Skwierzyna 52 46N 15 30E
8 Skye, I. 57 15N 6 10W
9 Slaney, R. 52 52N 6 45W
14 Slask, Reg. 51 0N 16 45E
15 Slatina 44 28N 24 22E
71 Slaton 33 27N 101 38W
53 Slave Coast 6 0N 2 30E
64 Slave Lake 55 25N 114 50W
24 Slavgorod 53 10N 78 50E
23 Slavyansk 45 15N 38 11E
6 Sleaford 53 0N 0 22W
8 Sleat, Sd. of 57 5N 5 47W
11 Sliedrecht 51 50N 4 45E
18 Sliema 35 55N 14 29E
9 Sligo 54 17N 8 28W
9 Sligo □ 54 10N 8 40W
21 Slite 57 42N 18 45E
22 Slobodskoy 58 40N 50 6E
7 Slough 51 30N 0 35W
18 Slovenia □ = Slovenija 45 58N 14 30E
18 Slovenija □ 45 58N 14 30E
15 Slovenské Rudohorie, Mts. 50 25N 13 0E
14 Słupsk 54 28N 17 1E
25 Slyudyanka 51 40N 103 30E
65 Smeaton 53 30N 105 49W
19 Smederevo 44 40N 20 57E
64 Smith 55 10N 114 0W
60 Smith Arm, B. 66 30N 123 0W
64 Smithers 54 45N 127 10W
56 Smithfield, S. Afr 30 13S 26 32E
69 Smithfield, U.S.A. 35 31N 78 16W
62 Smiths Falls 44 55N 76 0W
42 Smithton 40 53S 145 6E
62 Smoky Falls 50 10N 82 10W
70 Smoky Hill, R. 39 3N 96 48W
22 Smolensk 54 45N 32 0E
19 Smolikas, Mt. 40 9N 20 58E
62 Smooth Rock Falls 49 17N 81 37W
6 Snaefell, Mt. 54 18N 4 26W
20 Snaefellsjökull.Mt. 64 50N 23 49W
72 Snake, R. 46 12N 119 2W
72 Snake River Plain 43 13N 113 0W
11 Sneek 53 2N 5 40E
56 Sneeuberg 31 46S 24 20E
14 Sněžka, Mt. 50 41N 14 55E
20 Snøhetta, Mt. 62 19N 9 16E
65 Snow Lake 54 53N 101 2W
6 Snowdon, Mt. 53 4N 4 8W
73 Snowflake 34 30N 110 4W
72 Snowshoe Pk. 48 13N 115 41W
46 Snowy, Mts. 36 15S 148 20E
71 Snyder 32 45N 100 57W
57 Soalala 16 6S 45 20E
72 Soap Lake 47 29N 119 31W
79 Sobral 3 50S 40 30W
37 Soche 38 24N 77 20E
23 Sochi 43 35N 39 40E
2 Society Is. 17 0S 151 0W
78 Socorro, Col. 6 29N 73 16W
73 Socorro, U.S.A. 34 3N 106 58W
29 Socotra, I. 12 30N 54 0E
64 Soda Creek 52 25N 122 10W
72 Soda Springs 42 4N 111 40W
21 Söderhamn 61 18N 17 10E
21 Söderköping 58 31N 16 35E
21 Södermanlands □ 59 10N 16 30E
21 Södertälje 59 12N 17 50E
54 Sodo 7 0N 37 57E
57 Soekmekaar 23 30S 29 55E
11 Soest, Neth. 52 9N 5 19E
55 Sofala = Beira 19 50S 34 52E
19 Sofia=Sofiya 42 45N 23 20E
19 Sofiya 42 45N 23 20E
78 Sogamoso 5 43N 72 56W
21 Sogn og Fjordane □ 61 40N 6 0E
51 Sohâg 26 27N 31 43E
11 Soignes 50 35N 4 5E
12 Soissons 49 25N 3 19E
30 Soke 37 48N 27 28E
53 Sokodé 9 0N 1 11E
22 Sokol 59 30N 40 5E
15 Sokólka 53 25N 23 30E
53 Sokoto 13 2N 5 16E
53 Sokoto, R. 11 20N 4 10E
53 Sokoto □ 11 40N 5 15E
52 Solai 0 2N 36 12E
35 Solano 16 25N 121 15E
78 Soledad, Col. 10 55N 74 46W
73 Soledad, U.S.A. 36 27N 121 16W
78 Soledad, Ven. 8 10N 63 34W
7 Solent 50 45N 1 25W
22 Soligalich 59 5N 42 10E
22 Solikamsk 59 38N 56 50E
20 Sollefteå 63 10N 17 20E
13 Sóller 39 43N 2 45E
12 Sologne, Reg. 47 40N 2 0E
34 Solok 0 55S 100 40E
74 Sololá 14 49N 91 10E
3 Solomon Is. 8 0S 159 0E
14 Solothurn 47 13N 7 32E
31 Soltānābād 36 29N 58 5E
30 Soltāniyeh 36 20N 48 55E
21 Sölvesborg 56 5N 14 35E
22 Solvychegodsk 61 21N 46 52E
55 Solwezi 12 20S 26 26E
8 Solway Firth 54 45N 3 38W
57 Somabula 19 40S 29 38E
29 Somali Rep. ■ 7 0N 47 0E
75 Somerset, Bermuda 32 20N 64 55W
68 Somerset, Ky. 37 5N 84 40W
7 Somerset □ 51 9N 3 0W
56 Somerset East 32 42S 25 35E
56 Somerset West 34 8S 18 50E
75 Somerset I., Bermuda 32 20N 64 55W
60 Somerset I., Canada 73 30N 93 0W
15 Someş, R. 47 9N 23 55E
12 Somme □ 40 0N 2 15E
12 Somme, R. 50 11N 1 39E
19 Somovit 43 45N 24 48E
13 Somport, Pto. de 42 48N 0 31W
56 Sondags, R. 33 44S 25 51E
21 Sønderborg 54 55N 9 49E
2 Søndre Strømfjord 66 30N 50 52W
32 Sonepat 29 0N 77 5E
33 Sonepur 20 55N 83 50E
52 Songea 10 40S 35 40E
21 Songefjorden 61 10N 5 30E
34 Songkhla 7 13N 100 37E
32 Sonmiani 25 25N 66 40E
71 Sonora 30 33N 100 37W
74 Sonora □ 37 59N 120 27W
74 Sonsonate 13 45N 89 45W
39 Soochow 31 18N 120 41E
15 Sopot 54 27N 18 31E
14 Sopron 47 41N 16 37E
63 Sop's Arm 49 46N 56 56W
20 Sør Trøndelag □ 63 0N 11 0E
78 Sorata 15 50S 68 50W
62 Sorel 46 0N 73 10W
18 Sorgono 40 1N 9 7E
13 Soria 41 43N 2 32W
31 Sorkh, Kuh-e 35 40N 58 30E
80 Sorocaba 23 31S 47 35W
35 Sorong 0 55S 131 15E
52 Soroti 1 43N 33 35E
20 Sørøya, I. 70 35N 22 45E
18 Sorrento 40 38N 14 23E
20 Sorsele 65 31N 17 30E
22 Sortavala 61 42N 30 41E
22 Sosnogorsk 63 37N 53 51E
25 Sosnovka 54 9N 109 35E
15 Sosnowiec 50 20N 19 10E
54 Souanke 2 10N 14 10E
19 Soúdas, Kol. 35 28N 24 10E
38 Soul 37 33N 126 58E
57 Sources, Mt. aux 28 45S 28 50E
79 Soure 0 35S 48 30W
65 Souris 49 40N 100 20W
65 Souris, R. 49 39N 99 34W
79 Sousa 7 0S 38 10W
79 Sousel 2 38S 52 29W
51 Sousse 35 50N 10 33E
56 South Africa ■ 30 0S 25 0E
1 South America 10 0S 60 0W
40 South Australia □ 32 0S 139 0E
68 South Bend, Ind. U.S.A. 41 38N 86 20W
72 South Bend, Wash. 46 44N 123 52W
69 South Boston 36 42N 78 58W
69 South Carolina □ 33 45N 81 0W
68 South Charleston 38 20N 81 40W
26 South China Sea 10 0N 111 0E
70 South Dakota □ 45 0N 100 0W
9 South Esk, R. 56 40N 2 40W
2 South Georgia, I. 54 30S 37 0W
7 South Glamorgan □ 51 28N 3 26W
43 South Grafton 42 11S 71 42W
68 South Haven 42 22N 86 20W
52 South Horr 2 12N 36 56E
47 South Invercargill 46 26S 168 23E
47 South Island 43 50S 171 0E
38 South Korea ■ 36 0N 128 0E
3 South Magnetic Pole 66 30S 139 30E
68 South Milwaukee 42 50N 87 52W
2 South Orkney Is. 63 0S 45 0W
70 South Platte, R. 41 7N 100 42W
62 South Porcupine 48 30N 81 12W
62 South River 45 52N 79 21W
2 South Sandwich Is. 57 0S 27 0W
65 South Saskatchewan, R. 53 15N 105 5W
2 South Shetland Is. 62 0S 59 0W
6 South Shields 54 59N 1 26W
70 South Sioux City 42 30N 96 30W
6 South Tyne, R. 54 59N 2 8W
9 South Uist, I. 57 10N 7 10W
56 South West Africa 22 0S 18 0E
29 South Yemen ■ 15 0N 48 0E
6 South Yorkshire □ 52 45N 1 25W
62 Southampton, Canada 44 30N 81 25W
7 Southampton, U.K. 50 54N 1 23W
68 Southampton, U.S.A. 40 54N 72 22W
61 Southampton I. 64 30N 84 0W
7 Southend 51 32N 0 43E
47 Southern Alps, Mts. 43 41S 170 11E
45 Southern Cross 31 12S 119 15E
1 Southern Mid-Atlantic Ridge 30 0S 15 0W
3 Southern Ocean 62 0S 160 0W
8 Southern Uplands, Mts. 55 30N 4 0W
43 Southport, Australia 28 0S 153 25E
6 Southport, U.K. 53 38N 3 1W
7 Southwold 52 19N 1 41E
57 Soutpansberge 22 55S 29 30E
22 Sovetsk 57 38N 48 53E
25 Sovetskaya Gavan 48 50N 140 0E
13 Spain ■ 40 0N 5 0W
6 Spalding 52 47N 0 9W
14 Spandau 52 32N 13 13E
63 Spaniard's Bay 47 38N 53 20W
72 Spanish Fork 40 10N 111 37W
75 Spanish Pt. 32 12N 64 45W
75 Spanish Town 18 0N 77 20W
72 Sparks 39 30N 119 45W
70 Sparta 43 55N 91 10W
69 Spartanburg 35 0N 82 0W
19 Spárti 37 5N 22 25E
18 Spartivento, C., Italy 37 56N 16 4E
18 Spartivento, C., Sardinia 38 52N 8 50E
25 Spassk-Dal'niy 44 40N 132 40E
19 Spátha, Ákra 35 42N 23 43E
70 Spearfish 44 32N 103 52W
46 Speed 35 21S 142 27E
75 Speightstown 13 18N 59 30W
52 Speke G. 2 20S 32 50E
60 Spenard 61 0N 149 50W
60 Spence Bay 69 32N 93 31W
70 Spencer 43 5N 95 3W
43 Spencer, G. 34 30S 137 0E
47 Spenser, Mts. 42 15S 172 45E
9 Sperrin Mts. 54 50N 7 0W
8 Spey, R. 57 40N 3 6W
14 Speyer 49 19N 8 26E
18 Spezia=La Spezia 44 8N 9 50E
18 Spinazzola 40 58N 16 5E
64 Spirit River 55 45N 119 0W
7 Spithead 50 46N 1 12W
18 Split 43 31N 16 26E
72 Spokane 47 45N 117 25W
18 Spoleto 42 44N 12 44E
19 Sporades, Is.= Sporádhes, Voríai 39 15N 23 30E
19 Sporádhes, Voríai 39 15N 23 30E
14 Spree, R. 52 32N 13 13E
56 Springbok 29 42S 17 54E
47 Springburn 43 40S 171 32E
63 Springdale, Canada 49 30N 56 6W
71 Springdale, U.S.A. 36 10N 94 5W
73 Springerville 34 10N 109 16W
47 Springfield, N.Z. 43 19S 171 56E
70 Springfield, Ill. 39 58N 89 40W
68 Springfield, Mass. 42 8N 72 37W
71 Springfield, Mo. 37 15N 93 20W
68 Springfield, Ohio 39 50N 83 48W
72 Springfield, Ore. 44 2N 123 0W
69 Springfield, Tenn. 36 35N 86 55W
56 Springfontein 30 15S 25 40E
63 Springhill 45 40N 64 4W
57 Springs 26 13S 28 25E
42 Springsure 24 8S 148 6E
42 Springvale, Queens. 23 33S 140 42E
44 Springvale, W.Australia 17 48S 127 41E
68 Springville, N.Y. 42 31N 78 41W
72 Springville, Utah 40 14N 111 35W
6 Spurn Hd. 53 34N 0 8W
64 Squamish 49 45N 123 10W
18 Squillace 38 45N 16 28E
35 Sragen 7 28S 110 59E
25 Sredinnyy Khrebet 57 0N 160 0E
25 Sredne Tamborskoye 50 55N 137 45E
25 Srednekolymsk 67 20N 154 40E
25 Srednevilyuysk 63 50N 123 5E
19 Sremska Mitrovica 44 58N 19 37E
34 Srépok, R. 13 33N 106 16E
25 Sretensk 52 10N 117 40E
32 Sri Lanka ■ 7 30N 80 50E
33 Srikakulam 18 14N 84 4E
32 Srinagar 34 12N 74 50E
18 Srnetica 44 25N 16 33E
8 Staffa, I. 56 26N 6 21W
6 Stafford 52 49N 2 9W
6 Stafford □ 52 53N 2 10W
7 Staines 51 26N 0 30W
23 Stalingrad = Volgograd 48 40N 44 25E
6 Stalybridge 53 29N 2 2W
42 Stamford, Australia 21 15S 143 46E
7 Stamford, U.K. 52 39N 0 29W
68 Stamford, Conn. 41 5N 73 30W
71 Stamford, Tex. 32 58N 99 50W
57 Standerton 26 55S 29 13E
57 Stanger 29 18S 31 21E
19 Stanke Dimitrov 42 27N 23 9E
42 Stanley, Australia 40 46S 145 19E
80 Stanley, Falkland Is. 51 40S 58 0W
72 Stanley, U.S.A. 44 10N 114 59W
48 Stanley Falls = Chutes Boyoma 0 12N 25 25E
54 Stanleyville = Kisangani 0 41N 52 11E
74 Stann Creek 17 0N 88 20W
25 Stanovoy Khrebet 55 0N 130 0E
43 Stanthorpe 28 36S 151 59E
60 Stanton 69 45N 128 52W
19 Stara Planina 43 15N 23 0E
19 Stara Zagora 42 26N 25 39E
22 Staraya Russa 57 58N 31 10E
2 Starbuck I. 5 37S 155 55W
14 Stargard Szczecinski 53 20N 15 0E
71 Starkville 37 10N 104 31W
7 Start Pt. 50 13N 3 38W
25 Staryy Keydzhan 60 0N 144 50E
68 State College 40 47N 77 49W
69 Statesboro 32 26N 81 46W
69 Statesville 35 48N 80 51W
68 Staunton 38 7N 79 4W
21 Stavanger 58 57N 5 40E
23 Stavrapol 45 2N 41 59E
46 Stawell 36 58S 142 47E
72 Steamboat Springs 40 30N 106 58W
68 Steelton 40 17N 76 50W
64 Steen River 59 40N 117 12W
45 Steep, Pt. 26 8S 113 8E
54 Stefanie, L. = Chew Bahir 4 40N 30 50E
14 Steiermark □ 47 26N 15 0E
56 Steilrandberg 17 30S 13 0E
65 Steinbach 49 32N 96 40W
20 Steinkjer 63 59N 11 31E
56 Stellaland 26 45S 24 50E

Stellarton Tak

63 Stellarton 45 34N 62 40W
56 Stellenbosch 33 58S 18 50E
18 Stelvio, P. de 46 32N 10 27E
14 Stendal 52 36N 11 50E
23 Stepanakert 40 0N 46 25E
70 Stephen 48 30N 96 53W
46 Stephens Creek 31 50S 141 30E
63 Stephenville, Canada 48 31N 58 30W
71 Stephenville, U.S.A. 32 12N 98 12W
23 Stepnoi = Elista 46 25N 44 17E
19 Stereá Ellas □ 38 55N 22 0E
56 Sterkstroom 31 32S 26 32E
70 Sterling, Colo. 40 40N 103 15W
70 Sterling, Ill. 41 45N 89 45W
22 Sterlitamak 53 40N 56 0E
15 Stettin=Szczecin 53 27N 14 27E
64 Stettler 52 25N 112 40W
68 Steubenville 40 21N 80 39W
70 Stevens Point 44 32N 89 34W
80 Stewart, I., Chile 54 50S 71 30W
47 Stewart, I., N.Z. 46 58S 167 54E
60 Stewart River 63 25N 139 30W
56 Steynsburg 31 15S 25 49E
14 Steyr 48 3N 14 25E
56 Steytlerville 33 17S 24 19E
64 Stikine, R. 56 40N 132 30W
56 Stilfontein 26 50S 26 50E
70 Stillwater, Minn. 45 3N 92 47W
71 Stillwater, Okla. 36 5N 97 3W
72 Stillwater Mts. 39 45N 118 6W
19 Štip 41 42N 22 10E
8 Stirling 56 17N 3 57W
14 Stockerau 48 24N 16 12E
21 Stockholm 59 17N 18 3E
21 Stockholms □ 59 40N 18 45E
6 Stockport 53 25N 2 11W
46 Stockton, Australia 32 56S 151 47E
6 Stockton, U.K. 54 34N 1 20W
73 Stockton, U.S.A. 38 0N 121 20W
6 Stoke-on-Trent 53 1N 2 11W
62 Stokes Bay 45 0N 81 22W
25 Stolbovaya 64 50N 153 50E
42 Stonehenge, Australia 24 22S 143 17E
7 Stonehenge, U.K. 51 9N 1 45W
8 Stonehaven 56 58N 2 11W
65 Stonewall 50 10N 96 50W
20 Storavan, L. 65 45N 18 10E
21 Store Baelt 55 28N 11 0E
20 Støren 63 3N 10 18E
70 Storm Lake 42 35N 95 5W
56 Stormberg 31 16S 26 17E
8 Stornoway 58 12N 6 23W
20 Storsjön, L. 60 35N 16 45E
65 Stoughton 49 40N 103 0W
7 Stour, R., Dorset 50 43N 1 46W
7 Stour, R., Hereford and Worcester 52 20N 2 15W
7 Stour, R., Kent 51 18N 1 22E
7 Stour, R., Suffolk 51 52N 1 16E
7 Stourbridge 52 28N 2 8W
7 Stowmarket 52 11N 1 0E
9 Strabane 54 50N 7 28W
9 Strabane □ 54 50N 7 28W
42 Strahan 42 8S 145 24E
14 Stralsund 54 17N 13 5E
56 Strand 34 9S 18 48E
9 Strangford, L. 54 30N 5 37W
8 Stranraer 54 54N 5 0W
65 Strasbourg, Canada 51 10N 104 55W
12 Strasbourg, Fr. 48 35N 7 42E
46 Stratford, Australia 37 59S 147 5E
62 Stratford, Canada 43 23N 81 0W
47 Stratford, N.Z. 39 20S 174 19E
7 Stratford-on-Avon 52 12N 1 42W
8 Strath Spey 57 15N 3 40W
43 Strathalbyn 35 13S 138 53E
8 Strathclyde □ 55 30N 5 0W
64 Strathmore 51 5N 113 25W
8 Strathmore, Reg. 58 23N 4 40W
62 Strathroy 42 58N 81 38W
8 Strathy, Pt. 58 35N 4 0W
43 Streaky Bay 32 51S 134 18E
70 Streator 41 9N 88 52W
25 Strelka 58 5N 93 10E
24 Strezhevoy 60 42N 77 34E
18 Strómboli, I. 38 48N 15 12E
8 Stromeferry 57 20N 5 33W
21 Strömstad 58 55N 11 15E
8 Stronsay, I. 59 8N 2 38W
7 Stroud 51 44N 2 12W
21 Struer 56 30N 8 35E
19 Struma, R. 40 47N 23 51E
68 Struthers 41 6N 80 38W
34 Stung Treng 13 26N 106 0E
68 Sturgeon Bay 44 52N 87 20W
62 Sturgeon Falls 46 25N 79 57W
44 Sturt Cr. 20 8S 127 24E
56 Stutterheim 32 33S 27 28E
71 Stuttgart, U.S.A. 34 30N 91 33W
14 Stuttgart, W.Germany 48 46N 9 10E
22 Styr, R. 52 7N 26 35E
51 Suakin 19 0N 37 20E
39 Suancheng 30 58N 118 57E
38 Suanhwa 40 35N 115 0E
39 Suao 24 32N 121 42E
35 Subang 7 30S 107 45E
19 Subotica 46 6N 19 29E
74 Suchitato 13 56N 89 0W
39 Suchou=Soochow 31 18N 120 41E
39 Suchow 34 10N 117 20E
9 Suck, R. 53 16N 8 3W
78 Sucre 19 0S 65 15W
51 Sudan ■ 15 0N 30 0E
62 Sudbury 46 30N 81 0W
51 Sûdd 8 20N 29 30E
14 Sudetes, Mts.= Sudety, Mts. 50 20N 16 45E
14 Sudety, Mts. 50 20N 16 45E
35 Sudirman, Pengunungan, Ra. 4 30S 137 0E
13 Sueca 39 12N 0 21W
51 Suez = El Suweis 28 40N 33 0E
68 Suffolk 36 47N 76 33W
68 Suffolk □ 52 16N 1 0E
37 Sufu 39 44N 75 53E
61 Sugluk = Saglouc 62 10N 75 40W
31 Suhar 24 20N 56 40E
38 Suhbaatar 50 17N 106 10E
39 Suhsien 33 28N 117 54E
38 Suichung 40 45N 120 46E
39 Suichwan 26 26N 114 32E
38 Suihwa 46 40N 126 57E
39 Suikhai 21 17N 110 19E
39 Suiping 33 15N 114 6E
9 Suir, R. 52 15N 7 0W
35 Sukabumi 6 56S 106 57E
34 Sukadana 1 10S 110 0E
23 Sukhumi 43 0N 41 0E
32 Sukkur 27 50N 68 46E
32 Sulaiman Ra. 30 30N 69 50E
28 Sulam Tsor 33 4N 35 6E
35 Sulawesi, I. 2 0S 120 0E
15 Sulina 45 10N 29 40E
20 Sulitälma 67 17N 17 28E
20 Sulitjelma 61 7N 16 8E
78 Sullana 5 0S 80 45W
68 Sullivan 39 5N 87 26W
73 Sulphur 30 20N 93 22W
71 Sulphur Springs 33 5N 95 30W
33 Sultanpur 26 18N 82 10E
35 Sulu Arch. 6 0N 121 0E
35 Sulu Sea 8 0N 120 0E
51 Suluq 31 44N 20 14E
35 Sumalata 1 0N 122 37E
34 Sumatera □ 0 40N 100 20E
34 Sumatera, I. 0 40N 100 20E
72 Sumatra 46 45N 107 37W
34 Sumatra, I. = Sumatera, I. 0 40N 100 20E
35 Sumba, Selat, Str. 9 0S 118 40E
35 Sumba, I. 9 45S 119 35E
35 Sumbawa, I. 8 34S 117 17E
34 Sumbawa Besar 8 30S 117 26E
52 Sumbawanga 7 57S 31 35E
38 Sümber 46 40N 108 50E
35 Sumbing, Mt. 7 19S 110 3E
35 Sumedang 6 49S 107 56E
35 Sumenep 7 3S 113 51E
63 Summerside 46 29N 63 41W
62 Summit 47 50N 72 20W
64 Summit Lake 54 20N 122 40W
73 Summit Pk. 37 20N 106 48W
36 Sumoto 34 21N 134 54E
14 Sumperk 49 59N 17 0E
69 Sumter 33 55N 80 10W
23 Sumy 50 57N 34 50E
8 Sunart, L. 56 42N 5 35W
68 Sunbury 40 50N 76 46W
39 Sunchon 34 52N 127 31E
34 Sunda, Selat 6 0S 105 45E
33 Sundarbans, Reg. 22 0N 89 0E
6 Sunderland 54 54N 1 22W
62 Sundridge 45 45N 79 25W
20 Sundsvall 62 23N 17 17E
34 Sungaigerung 4 58S 105 7E
34 Sungaipakning 1 19N 102 0E
34 Sungaipenuh 2 1S 101 20E
34 Sungaitiram 0 45S 117 8E
38 Sungari, R. 47 30N 132 30E
35 Sungguminasa 5 17S 119 30E
39 Sungkiang 31 0N 121 20E
37 Sungpan 32 50N 103 20E
39 Sungtzu Hu, L. 30 10N 111 45E
72 Sunnyside 46 24N 120 2W
46 Sunshine 37 48S 144 52E
53 Sunyani 7 21N 2 22W
33 Supaul 26 10N 86 40E
73 Superior, Ariz. 33 19N 111 9W
70 Superior, Wis. 46 45N 92 0W
62 Superior, L. 47 40N 87 0W
39 Supu 27 57N 110 15E
30 Sûr, Lebanon 33 19N 35 16E
31 Sûr, Oman 22 34N 59 32E
22 Sura, R. 56 6N 46 0E
35 Surabay 7 17S 112 45E
35 Surakarta 7 35S 110 48E
32 Surat 21 12N 72 55E
34 Surat Thani 9 3N 99 28E
32 Suratgarh 29 18N 73 55E
24 Surgut 61 20N 73 28E
33 Suri 23 50N 87 34E
28 Surif 31 40N 35 4E
77 Surinam ■ 4 0N 56 15W
7 Surrey □ 51 16N 0 30W
51 Surt 31 11N 16 46E
51 Surt, Khalij
20 Surtsey, I. 63 27N 20 15W
36 Suruga-Wan, G. 34 45N 138 30E
18 Susa 45 8N 7 3E
36 Susaki 33 22N 133 17E
25 Susanino 52 50N 140 14E
72 Susanville 40 28N 120 40W
68 Susquehanna, R. 39 33N 76 5W
80 Susques 23 35S 66 25W
63 Sussex 45 45N 65 37W
25 Susuman 62 47N 148 10E
65 Sutherland, Canada 52 15N 106 40W
56 Sutherland, S. Africa 32 33S 20 40E
32 Sutlej, R. 29 23N 71 2E
6 Sutton-in-Ashfield 52 8N 1 16W
47 Suva 17 40S 178 8E
15 Suwałki 54 8N 22 59E
69 Suwannee, R. 29 18N 83 9W
36 Suwanose-Jima, I. 29 26N 129 30E
2 Suwarrow Is. 13 15S 163 5W
28 Suweilih 32 2N 35 50E
51 Suweis, Kaĥg es 28 40N 33 0E
39 Suwen 20 27N 110 2E
38 Suwôn 37 17N 127 1E
22 Suzdal 56 29N 40 26E
36 Suzu 37 25N 137 17E
36 Suzuka 34 55N 136 36E
3 Svalbard, Is. 78 0N 17 0E
20 Svappavaara 67 40N 21 3E
20 Svartisen, Mt. 66 40N 14 16E
21 Svealand, Reg. 60 0N 15 0E
21 Sveg 62 2N 14 21E
21 Svendborg 55 4N 10 35E
24 Sverdlovks 56 50N 60 30E
58 Sverdrup Is. 79 0N 97 0W
19 Svishtov 43 36N 25 23E
25 Svobodnyy 51 20N 128 0E
20 Svolvaer 68 15N 14 34E
14 Swabian Mts.= Scwäbische Alb., Mts. 48 30N 9 30E
56 Swakop, R. 22 38S 14 36E
56 Swakopmund 22 37S 14 30E
6 Swale, R. 54 6N 1 20W
46 Swan Hill 35 15S 143 31E
64 Swan Hills 54 42N 115 49W
75 Swan Is. 17 22N 83 57W
65 Swan River 52 10N 101 25W
7 Swanage 50 36N 1 59W
46 Swansea, Australia 33 3S 151 35E
7 Swansea, U.K. 51 37N 3 57W
56 Swartberge 30 15S 29 23E
56 Swartruggens 25 39S 26 42E
39 Swatow = Shantow 23 25N 116 40E
57 Swaziland ■ 26 30S 31 30E
20 Sweden ■ 67 0N 15 0E
53 Swedru 5 32N 0 41W
71 Sweetwater 32 30N 100 28W
56 Swellendam 34 1S 20 26E
14 Swidnica 50 50N 16 30E
14 Swiebodzin 52 15N 15 37E
65 Swift Current 50 20N 107 45W
7 Swindon 51 33N 1 47W
14 Swinoujście 53 54N 14 16E
14 Switzerland ■ 46 30N 8 0E
9 Swords 53 27N 6 15W
46 Sydney, Australia 33 53S 151 10E
63 Sydney, Canada 46 7N 60 7W
63 Sydney Mines 46 18N 60 15W
22 Syktyvkar 61 45N 50 40E
69 Sylacauga 33 10N 86 15W
33 Sylhet 24 43N 91 55E
64 Sylvan Lake 52 20N 114 10W
24 Sym 60 20N 87 50E
24 Syr Darya, R. 46 3N 61 0E
68 Syracuse 38 0N 101 40W
30 Syria ■ 35 0N 38 0E
25 Syul'dzhyukyor 63 25N 113 40E
22 Syzran 53 12N 48 30E
14 Szczecin 53 27N 14 27E
39 Szechwan □ 30 15N 103 15E
15 Szeged 46 16N 20 10E
15 Székesfehérvár 47 15N 18 25E
15 Szekszárd 46 22N 18 42E
37 Szemao 22 50N 101 0E
39 Szengen 24 50N 108 0E
15 Szentes 46 39N 20 21E
38 Szeping 43 10N 124 18E
15 Szolnok 47 10N 20 15E
14 Szombathely 47 14N 16 38E

T

38 Ta Hingan Ling, Mts. 48 0N 120 0E
37 Ta Liang Shan, Mts. 28 0N 103 0E
80 Tabacal 23 15S 64 15W
53 Tabagné 7 53N 3 7W
8 Tabasco □ 17 45N 93 30W
64 Taber 49 48N 111 5W
35 Tablas, I. 12 20N 122 10E
56 Table Mt. 34 0S 18 22E
44 Tableland 17 16S 126 51E
42 Tabletop, Mt. 23 30S 147 0E
14 Tábor 49 25N 14 39E
52 Tabora 5 2S 32 57E
50 Tabou 4 30N 7 20W
30 Tabriz 38 7N 56 20E
30 Tabuk 28 30N 36 25E
78 Tachira 8 7N 72 21W
35 Tacloban 11 1N 125 0E
78 Tacna 18 0S 70 20W
72 Tacoma 47 15N 122 30W
80 Tacuarembó 31 45S 56 0W
50 Tademait, Plateau du 28 30N 2 30E
29 Tadjoura 11 50N 44 55E
47 Tadmor, N.Z. 41 27S 172 45E
30 Tadmor, Syria 34 30N 37 55E
63 Tadoussac 48 11N 69 42W
24 Tadzhik S.S.R. □ 35 30N 70 0E
38 Taegu 35 50N 128 25E
38 Taejon 35 30N 127 22E
13 Tafalla 42 30N 1 41W
56 Tafelbaai 33 35S 18 25E
7 Taff, R. 51 27N 3 9W
31 Taftan, Kūh-e, Mt. 28 36N 61 6E
23 Taganrog 47 12N 38 50E
35 Tagbilaran 9 42N 124 3E
18 Tagliamento, R. 45 38N 13 6E
79 Taguatinga 12 26S 45 40W
47 Tahakopa 46 30S 169 23E
34 Tahan, Gunong 4 38N 102 14E
37 Tahcheng 46 50N 83 1E
2 Tahiti, I. 17 45S 149 30W
72 Tahoe, L. 39 6N 120 0W
53 Tahoua 14 57N 5 16E
39 Tahsien 31 12N 108 13E
51 Tahta 26 44N 31 32E
39 Tai Hu 31 10N 120 0E
39 Taichow 32 30N 119 50E
39 Taichung 24 10N 120 35E
38 Taihan Shan, Mts. 36 0N 114 0E
47 Taihape 39 41S 175 48E
39 Taiho 26 50N 114 54E
38 Taiku 37 46N 112 28E
38 Tailai 46 28N 123 18E
43 Tailem Bend 35 12S 139 29E
30 Taima 27 35N 38 45E
8 Tain 57 49N 4 4W
39 Tainan 23 0N 120 15E
19 Taínaron, Ákra 36 22N 22 27E
39 Taipei 25 2N 121 30E
34 Taiping 4 50N 100 43E
80 Taitao, Pen. de 46 30S 75 0W
39 Taitung 22 43N 121 4E
39 Taiwan ■ 23 30N 121 0E
28 Taiyiba, Israel 32 36N 35 27E
28 Taiyiba, Jordan 31 55N 35 17E
38 Taiyuan 38 0N 112 30E
29 Ta'izz 13 38N 44 4E
13 Tajo, R. 38 40N 9 24W
51 Tājūra 32 51N 13 27E
34 Tak 17 0N 99 10E

Takachiho Thames, R., U.K.

36 Takachiho .... 32 42N 131 18 E
36 Takada .... 37 7N 138 15 E
47 Takaka .... 40 51 S 172 50 E
36 Takamatsu .... 34 20N 134 5 E
36 Takaoka .... 36 40N 137 0 E
47 Takapuna .... 36 47 S 174 47 E
36 Takasaki .... 36 20N 139 0 E
36 Takatsuki .... 34 40N 135 37 E
52 Takaungu .... 3 38 S 39 52 E
36 Takayama .... 36 10N 137 5 E
36 Takefu .... 35 50N 136 10 E
31 Takhar □ .... 36 30N 69 30 E
37 Takla Makan, Reg. 39 40N 85 0 E
53 Takoradi 4 58N 1 55W
53 Takum .... 7 18N 10 0 E
78 Talara .... 4 30 S 81 10W
53 Talata Mafara ..... 12 35N 6 2 E
35 Talaud, Kep. ...... 4 30N 127 10 E
13 Talavera de la Reina 39 55N 4 46W
80 Talca .... 35 20 S 71 46W
80 Talcahuano .... 36 40 S 73 10W
24 Taldy Kurgan ..... 45 10N 78 45 E
28 Talfit .... 32 5N 35 17 E
32 Talguppa .... 14 11N 74 51 E
39 Tali, Shensi .... 34 48N 109 48 E
37 Tali, Yunnan ..... 25 50N 100 0 E
35 Taliabu, I. .... 1 45 S 125 0 E
38 Talien .... 38 53N 121 35 E
34 Taliwang .... 8 50 S 116 55 E
60 Talkeetna 62 20N 149 50W
69 Talladega 33 28N 86 2W
69 Tallahassee 30 25N 84 15W
46 Tallangatta .... 36 10 S 147 14 E
22 Tallinn .... 59 29N 24 58 E
71 Tallulah 32 25N 91 12W
28 Talluza .... 32 17N 35 18 E
80 Taltal .... 25 23 S 70 40W
43 Talwood .... 28 27 S 149 20 E
53 Tamale 9 22N 0 50W
36 Tamano .... 34 35N 133 59 E
50 Tamanrasset ...... 22 56N 5 30 E
7 Tamar, R. 50 22N 4 10W
36 Tamashima .... 34 27N 133 18 E
53 Tamaské .... 14 55N 5 40 E
57 Tamatave .... 18 10 S 49 25 E
57 Tamatave □ ...... 18 0 S 49 0 E
74 Tamaulipas □ 24 0N 99 0W
50 Tambacounda 13 55N 13 45W
45 Tambellup .... 34 4 S 117 37 E
42 Tambo .... 24 54 S 146 14 E
34 Tambora, I. .... 8 14 S 117 55 E
22 Tambov .... 52 45N 41 20 E
50 Tamchaket 17 25N 10 40W
74 Tamiahua, Laguna de 21 30N 97 30W
32 Tamil Nadu □ .... 11 0N 77 0 E
38 Taming .... 36 20N 115 10 E
28 Tammun .... 32 18N 35 23 E
69 Tampa 27 57N 82 30W
21 Tampere .... 61 30N 23 50 E
74 Tampico 22 20N 97 50W
29 Tamra .... 32 51N 35 12 E
38 Tamsagbulag ...... 47 15N 117 5 E
43 Tamworth, Australia ...... 31 0 S 150 58 E
7 Tamworth, U.K. ... 52 38N 1 2W
20 Tana .... 70 23N 28 13 E
51 Tana, L. .... 12 0N 37 20 E
52 Tana, R. .... 2 32 S 40 31 E
36 Tanabe .... 33 44N 135 22 E
60 Tanacross 63 40N 143 30W
34 Tanahgrogot ...... 1 55 S 116 15 E
35 Tanahmeroh ...... 6 0 S 140 7 E
44 Tanami, Des. ..... 23 15 S 132 20 E
60 Tanana 65 10N 152 15W
60 Tanana, R. 64 25N 145 30W
57 Tananarive = Antananarivo ... 18 55 S 47 31 E
57 Tananarive □ ..... 19 0 S 47 0 E
18 Tánaro, R. ...... 44 9N 7 50 E
53 Tanda 7 48N 3 10W
80 Tandil .... 37 15 S 59 6W
32 Tando Adam ..... 25 45N 48 40 E
47 Taneatua .... 38 4 S 177 1 E
36 Tane-ga-Shima, I. . 30 30N 131 0 E
33 Tanen Tong Dan, Mts. ...... 19 40N 99 0 E
50 Tanezrouft .... 23 9N 0 11 E
52 Tanga .... 5 5 S 39 2 E
52 Tanganyika ■ = Tanzania ■ ..... 6 40 S 34 0 E
52 Tanganyika, L. .... 6 40 S 30 0 E
50 Tanger 35 50N 5 49W
35 Tangerang .... 6 12 S 106 39 E
37 Tanghla Shan, Mts. 33 10N 90 0 E
50 Tangiers = Tanger .. 35 50N 5 49W
39 Tangshan, Anhwei . 34 23N 116 34 E
38 Tangshan, Hopei .. 39 40N 118 10 E
39 Tangtu .... 31 37N 118 39 E
53 Tanguiéta .... 10 37N 1 16 E
39 Tangyang .... 30 50N 111 45 E
35 Tanimbar, Kep. .... 7 30 S 131 30 E
34 Tanjung .... 2 10 S 115 25 E
34 Tanjungbalai ...... 2 55N 99 44 E
34 Tanjungkarang .... 5 25 S 105 16 E
34 Tanjungpandan ... 2 45 S 107 39 E
34 Tanjungredeb ..... 2 12N 117 35 E
34 Tanjungselor ...... 2 55N 117 25 E
62 Tannin .... 49 40N 91 0 E
53 Tanout .... 14 58N 8 53 E
51 Tanta .... 30 45N 30 57 E
43 Tanunda .... 34 30 S 139 0 E
52 Tanzania ■ .... 6 40 S 34 0 E
38 Taonan .... 45 30N 122 20 E
39 Taoyuan .... 25 0N 121 4 E
39 Tapa Shan, Mts. ... 31 45N 109 30 E
74 Tapachula 14 54N 92 17W
34 Tapah .... 4 10N 101 17 E
34 Tapaktuan .... 3 30N 97 10 E
47 Tapanui .... 45 56N 169 18 E
32 Tapti, R. .... 21 5N 72 40 E
47 Tapuaenuka, Mt. .. 41 55 S 173 50 E
24 Tara .... 56 55N 74 30 E
24 Tara, R. .... 56 42N 74 36 E
25 Tarabagatay, Khrebet, Mts. ... 47 30N 84 0 E
30 Tarābulus, Lebanon 34 31N 35 52 E
51 Tarābulus, Libya .. 32 49N 13 7 E
46 Tarago .... 35 6 S 149 39 E
34 Tarakan .... 3 20N 117 35 E
47 Taranaki □ .... 39 5 S 174 51 E
32 Taranga Hill ...... 24 0N 72 40 E
18 Táranto .... 40 30N 17 11 E
18 Táranto, G. di .... 40 0N 17 15 E
78 Tarapaca .... 2 56 S 69 46W
78 Tarapoto .... 6 30 S 76 20W
47 Tarawera .... 39 2 S 176 36 E
47 Tarawera, L. ...... 38 13 S 176 27 E
8 Tarbat Ness 57 52N 3 48W
32 Tarbela Dam ..... 34 0N 72 52 E
8 Tarbert 57 54N 6 49W
12 Tarbes .... 43 15N 0 3 E
46 Taree .... 31 50 S 152 30 E
13 Tarifa 36 1N 5 36W
78 Tarija .... 21 30 S 64 40W
37 Tarim, R. .... 41 5N 86 40 E
56 Tarkastad .... 32 0 S 26 16 E
23 Tarkhankut, Mys. . 45 25N 32 30 E
24 Tarko Sale .... 64 55N 77 50 E
53 Tarkwa 5 20N 2 0W
35 Tarlac .... 15 30N 120 25 E
42 Tarlton Downs .... 22 40 S 136 45 E
12 Tarn, R. .... 44 5N 1 6 E
12 Tarn □ .... 43 50N 2 8 E
12 Tarn-et-Garonne □ 44 8N 1 20 E
15 Tarnobrzeg .... 50 35N 21 41 E
15 Tarnów .... 50 3N 21 0 E
15 Tarnowskie Góry .. 50 27N 18 54 E
31 Tarom .... 28 11N 55 42 E
13 Tarragona .... 41 5N 1 17 E
13 Tarrasa .... 41 26N 2 1 E
51 Tarso Emissi ...... 21 27N 18 36 E
30 Tarsus .... 36 58N 34 55 E
78 Tartagal .... 22 30 S 63 50W
22 Tartu .... 58 25N 26 58 E
30 Tartūs .... 34 55N 35 55 E
34 Tarutung .... 2 0N 99 0 E
51 Tasâwah .... 26 0N 13 37 E
62 Taschereau 48 40N 78 40W
24 Tashauz .... 42 0N 59 20 E
37 Tashigong .... 33 0N 79 30 E
24 Tashkent .... 41 20N 69 10 E
37 Tashkurgan .... 37 51N 74 57 E
31 Tashkurghan ...... 36 45N 67 40 E
24 Tashtagol .... 52 47N 87 53 E
35 Tasikmalaya ...... 7 18 S 108 12 E
25 Taskan .... 63 5N 150 5 E
47 Tasman, B. .... 40 59 S 173 25 E
47 Tasman Glacier ... 43 45 S 170 20 E
3 Tasman Sea ...... 42 30 S 168 0 E
42 Tasmania, I. □ .... 49 0 S 146 30 E
15 Tatabánya .... 47 32N 18 25 E
22 Tatar A.S.S.R. □ .. 55 30N 51 30 E
24 Tatarsk .... 55 50N 75 20 E
36 Tateyama .... 35 0N 139 50 E
39 Tatien .... 25 45N 118 0 E
15 Tatra Mts. = Tatry, Mts. ..... 49 20N 20 0 E
15 Tatry, Mts. .... 49 20N 20 0 E
37 Tatsaitan .... 37 55N 95 0 E
80 Tatui .... 23 25 S 48 0W
38 Tatung .... 40 10N 113 10 E
38 Tatungkow .... 39 55N 124 10 E
80 Taubaté .... 23 5 S 45 30W
47 Taumarunui ...... 38 53 S 175 15 E
78 Taumaturgo ...... 9 0 S 73 50W
56 Taung .... 27 33 S 24 47 E
33 Taungdwingyi ..... 20 1N 95 40 E
33 Taunggyi .... 20 50N 97 0 E
33 Taungup Taunggya 18 20N 93 40 E
7 Taunton, U.K. 51 1N 3 7W
68 Taunton, U.S.A. .. 41 54N 71 6W
14 Taunus, Mts. ...... 50 15N 8 20 E
47 Taupo .... 38 41 S 176 7 E
47 Taupo, L. .... 38 46 S 175 55 E
47 Tauranga .... 37 35 S 176 11 E
30 Taurus Mts. = Toros Daglari ... 37 0N 35 0 E
39 Tava Wan, G. ..... 22 40N 114 40 E
60 Tavani 62 10N 93 30W
24 Tavda 58 7N 65 8W
24 Tavda, R. .... 57 47N 67 16 E
52 Taveta .... 3 31N 37 37 E
47 Taveuni, I. .... 16 51 S 179 58W
13 Tavira 37 8N 7 40W
7 Tavistock 50 33N 4 9W
33 Tavoy .... 14 7N 98 18 E
7 Taw, R. 51 4N 4 11W
35 Tawitawi, I. .... 5 2N 120 0 E
8 Tay, Firth of 56 25N 3 8W
8 Tay, L. 56 30N 4 10W
8 Tay, R. 56 37N 3 58W
78 Tayabamba .... 8 15 S 77 10 E
71 Taylor 30 30N 97 30W
73 Taylor, Mt. 35 16N 107 50W
70 Taylorville 39 32N 29 20W
25 Taymyr Pol. ...... 75 0N 100 0 E
8 Tayport 56 27N 2 52W
25 Tayshet .... 55 58N 97 25 E
8 Tayside □ 56 30N 3 35W
35 Taytay .... 10 45N 119 30 E
39 Tayu .... 25 38N 114 9 E
37 Tayulehsze .... 29 15N 98 1 E
50 Taza 34 10N 4 0W
24 Tazovskiy .... 67 28N 78 42 E
23 Tbilisi .... 41 50N 44 50 E
51 Tchad ■ .... 12 30N 17 15 E
53 Tchad, L. .... 13 30N 14 30 E
54 Tchibanga .... 2 45 S 11 12 E
47 Te Anau, L. ...... 45 15 S 167 45 E
47 Te Aroha .... 37 32 S 175 44 E
47 Te Awamutu ..... 38 1 S 175 20 E
47 Te Horo .... 40 48 S 175 6 E
47 Te Kuiti .... 38 20 S 175 11 E
47 Te Puke .... 37 46 S 176 22 E
50 Tébessa .... 35 28N 8 9 E
34 Tebingtinggi ...... 3 38 S 102 1 E
74 Tecuala 22 24N 105 30W
15 Tecuci .... 45 51N 27 27 E
24 Tedzhen .... 37 23N 60 31 E
6 Tees, R. 54 34N 1 16W
6 Teesside 54 37N 1 13W
78 Tefé .... 3 25 S 64 50W
35 Tegal .... 6 52 S 109 8 E
11 Tegelen .... 51 20N 6 9 E
53 Tegina .... 10 5N 6 14 E
75 Tegucigalpa 14 10N 87 0W
38 Tehchow .... 37 28N 116 18 E
31 Tehrān .... 35 44N 51 30 E
31 Tehrān □ .... 35 30N 51 0 E
37 Tehtsin .... 28 45N 98 58 E
74 Tehuacán 18 20N 97 30W
74 Tehuantepec 16 10N 95 19W
74 Tehuntepec, Istmo de 17 0N 94 30W
7 Teifi, R. 52 7N 4 42W
7 Teign, R. 50 33N 3 29W
7 Teignmouth 50 33N 3 30W
55 Teixeira da Silva .. 12 12 S 15 52 E
54 Teixeira de Sousa . 10 42 S 22 12 E
13 Tejo, R. 38 40N 9 24W
47 Tekapo, L. .... 43 48 S 170 32 E
74 Tekax 20 20N 89 30W
24 Tekeli .... 44 50N 79 0 E
30 Tekirdag .... 40 58N 27 30 E
33 Tekkali .... 18 43N 84 24 E
28 Tel Aviv-Yafo .... 32 4N 34 48 E
28 Tel Mond .... 32 15N 34 56 E
74 Tela 15 40N 87 28W
34 Telanaipura = Jambi .... 1 38 S 103 30 E
23 Telavi .... 42 0N 45 30 E
64 Telegraph Creek .. 58 0N 131 10W
21 Telemark □ ...... 59 30N 8 30 E
6 Telford 52 42N 2 29W
38 Telisze .... 39 50N 112 0 E
64 Telkwa 54 41N 126 56W
68 Tell City 38 0N 86 44W
32 Tellicherry .... 11 45N 75 30 E
34 Telok Anson ...... 4 0N 101 10 E
80 Telsen .... 42 30 S 66 50W
34 Telukbetung ...... 5 29 S 105 17 E
34 Telukbutun .... 4 5N 108 7 E
34 Telukdalem .... 0 45N 97 50 E
53 Tema .... 5 41N 0 0 E
35 Temanggung ...... 7 18 S 110 10 E
57 Tembuland .... 31 30 S 28 20 E
7 Teme, R. 52 9N 2 18W
34 Temerloh .... 3 27N 102 25 E
24 Temir .... 49 8N 57 6 E
24 Temirtou .... 53 10N 87 20 E
62 Temiskaming 46 44N 79 5W
46 Temora .... 34 30 S 147 30 E
73 Tempe 33 26N 111 59W
34 Tempino .... 1 55 S 103 23 E
71 Temple 31 5N 97 28W
9 Templemore 52 48N 7 50W
80 Temuco .... 38 50 S 72 50W
47 Temuka .... 44 14 S 171 17 E
53 Tenado .... 12 6N 2 38 E
32 Tenali .... 16 15N 80 35 E
74 Tenancingo 18 98N 99 33W
74 Tenango 19 0N 99 40W
34 Tenasserim .... 12 6N 99 3 E
7 Tenby 51 40N 4 42W
12 Tenda, Col di ..... 44 9N 7 34 E
12 Tende .... 44 5N 7 34 E
50 Tenerife, I. 28 20N 16 40W
35 Tengah□, Java .... 7 0 S 110 0 E
34 Tengah□, Kalimantan ..... 2 20 S 113 0 E
37 Tengchung .... 24 58N 98 30 E
39 Tenghsien .... 35 10N 117 10 E
24 Tengiz, Oz. .... 50 30N 69 0 E
32 Tenkasi .... 8 55N 77 20 E
53 Tenkodogo 11 55N 0 20W
42 Tennant Creek .... 19 30 S 134 0 E
69 Tennessee, R. 37 0N 88 20W
69 Tennessee □ 36 0N 86 30W
36 Tenryū-Gawa, R. .. 34 39N 137 47 E
43 Tenterfield .... 29 0 S 152 0 E
79 Teófilo Otoni ..... 17 15 S 41 30W
74 Teotihuacan 19 44N 98 50W
74 Tepic 21 30N 104 54W
14 Teplice .... 50 39N 13 48 E
13 Ter, R. .... 42 1N 3 12 E
53 Téra .... 14 1N 0 50 E
46 Terang .... 38 3 S 142 59 E
23 Terek, R. .... 43 44N 46 33 E
79 Teresina .... 5 2 S 42 45W
24 Termez .... 37 0N 67 15 E
18 Términi Imerese .. 37 59N 13 51 E
74 Términos, L. de ... 18 35N 91 30W
18 Térmoli .... 42 0N 15 0 E
35 Ternate .... 0 45N 127 25 E
11 Terneuzen .... 51 20N 3 50 E
18 Terni .... 42 34N 12 38 E
43 Terowie .... 38 10 S 138 50 E
64 Terrace 54 30N 128 35W
18 Terracina .... 41 17N 13 12 E
18 Terralba .... 39 43N 8 37 E
3 Terre Adélie ...... 67 0 S 140 0 E
68 Terre Haute 46 30N 75 13W
71 Terrell 32 44N 96 19W
11 Terschelling, I. .... 53 25N 5 20 E
13 Teruel 40 22N 1 8W
20 Tervola .... 66 6N 24 59 E
50 Tessalit .... 20 12N 1 0 E
53 Tessaoua .... 13 45N 8 0 E
7 Test, R. 51 7N 1 30W
80 Tetas, Pta. .... 22 28 S 70 38W
57 Tete .... 16 13 S 33 33 E
57 Tete □ .... 16 20 S 32 30 E
50 Tetouan 35 30N 5 25W
25 Tetyukhe = Dalnergorsk .... 44 40N 135 50 E
80 Teuco, R. .... 25 35 S 60 11W
65 Teulon 50 30N 97 20W
14 Teutoburger Wald . 52 5N 8 15 E
18 Tevere, R. .... 41 44N 12 14 E
8 Teviot, R. 55 36N 2 26W
43 Tewantin .... 26 27 S 153 3 E
7 Tewkesbury 51 59N 2 8W
71 Texarkana, Ark. ... 33 25N 94 0W
71 Texarkana, Tex. ... 33 25N 94 0W
43 Texas .... 28 49 S 151 15 E
71 Texas □ 31 30N 98 30W
71 Texas City 27 20N 95 20W
11 Texel, I. .... 53 5N 4 50 E
74 Teziutlán 19 50N 97 30W
33 Tezpur .... 26 40N 92 45 E
57 Thabana Ntlenyana 29 30 S 29 9 E
56 Thabazimbi .... 24 40 S 26 4 E
34 Thailand ■ .... 16 0N 101 0 E
34 Thakhek .... 17 25 104 45 E
32 Thal .... 33 28N 70 33 E
32 Thal Desert .... 31 0N 71 30 E
43 Thallon .... 28 30 S 148 57 E
7 Thame, R. 51 52N 0 47W
47 Thames .... 37 7 S 175 34 E
62 Thames, R., Canada 42 19N 82 28W
7 Thames, R., U.K. . 51 28N 0 43 E

Trenque Lauquen — Umtali

80 Trenque Lauquen 36 0S 62 45W
6 Trent, R. 53 40N 0 40W
18 Trentino-Alto Adige □ 46 5N 11 0E
18 Trento 46 5N 11 8E
62 Trenton, Canada 44 10N 77 40W
68 Trenton, U.S.A. 40 15N 74 41W
63 Trepassey 46 43N 53 25W
80 Tres Arroyos 38 20S 60 20W
79 Três Corações 21 30S 45 30S
79 Três Lagoas 20 50S 51 50W
80 Tres Montes, C. 47 0S 75 35W
80 Tres Puentes 27 50S 70 15W
80 Tres Puntas, C. 47 0S 66 0W
79 Três Rios 22 20S 43 30W
21 Treungen 58 55N 8 27E
18 Treviso 45 40N 12 15E
42 Triabunna 42 28S 148 0E
32 Trichinopoly= Tiruchchirappalli 10 45N 78 45E
32 Trichur 10 20N 76 18E
14 Trier 49 45N 6 37E
18 Trieste 45 39N 13 45E
18 Triglav, Mt. 46 30N 13 45E
19 Tríkkala 39 34N 21 47E
35 Trikora, Puncak, Mt. 4 11S 138 0E
9 Trim 53 34N 6 48W
32 Trincomalee 8 38N 81 15E
2 Trindade, I. 20 20S 29 50W
78 Trinidad, Bolivia 14 54S 64 50W
75 Trinidad, Cuba 21 40N 80 0W
71 Trinidad, U.S.A. 37 15N 104 30W
80 Trinidad, Uruguay 33 30S 56 50W
80 Trinidad I., Arg. 39 10S 62 0W
75 Trinidad I., Trinidad & Tobago 10 30N 61 20W
75 Trinidad & Tobago ■ 10 30N 61 20W
71 Trinity, R. 29 47N 94 42W
60 Trinity Is. 56 33N 154 25W
30 Tripoli, Lebanon= Tarābulus 34 34N 35 52E
51 Tripoli, Libya= Tarābulus 32 49N 13 7E
19 Trípolis 37 31N 22 25E
33 Tripura □ 24 0N 92 0E
2 Tristan de Cunha, I. 37 6S 12 20W
32 Trivandrum 8 31N 77 0E
15 Trnava 48 23N 17 35E
63 Trois Pistoles 48 5N 69 10W
62 Trois Rivières 46 25N 72 40W
24 Troitsk 54 10N 61 35E
22 Troitsko Pechorsk 62 40N 56 10E
21 Trollhättan 58 17N 12 20E
56 Trompsburg 30 2S 25 5E
20 Troms □ 69 19N 19 0E
20 Tromsø 69 40N 19 0E
80 Tronador, Mt. 41 53S 71 0W
20 Trondheim 63 25N 10 25E
20 Trondheims, Fd. 63 40N 10 45E
30 Tróodos, Mt. 34 58N 32 55E
8 Troon 55 33N 4 40W
8 Trossachs, Reg. 56 14N 4 24W
8 Trotternish, Reg. 57 32N 6 15W
12 Trouville 49 21N 0 54E
7 Trowbridge 51 18N 2 12W
69 Troy, Ala. 31 50N 85 58W
68 Troy, N.Y. 42 45N 73 39W
68 Troy, Ohio 40 0N 84 10W
12 Troyes 48 19N 4 3E
72 Truckee 39 29N 120 12W
75 Trujillo, Honduras 16 0N 86 0W
78 Trujillo, Peru 8 0S 79 0W
13 Trujillo, Sp. 39 28N 5 55W
78 Trujillo, Ven. 9 22N 70 26W
3 Truk, I. 7 25N 151 46E
34 Trung-Phan, Reg. 16 0N 108 0E
63 Truro, Canada 45 21N 63 14W
7 Truro, U.K. 50 17N 5 2W
45 Truslove 33 20S 121 45E
73 Truth or Consequences 33 9N 107 16W
37 Tsaidam, Reg. 37 0N 95 0E
38 Tsanghsien 38 24N 116 57E
37 Tsangpo, R. 29 40N 89 0E
39 Tsaochwang 35 11N 115 28E
57 Tsaratanana 16 47S 47 39E
57 Tsaratanana, Mt. de 14 0S 49 0E
37 Tsaring Nor, L. 35 0N 97 0E
55 Tsau 20 12S 22 22E
52 Tsavo 3 0S 38 27E
24 Tselinograd 51 10N 71 30E
38 Tsetserleg 47 46N 101 32E
53 Tsévié 6 25N 1 13E
55 Tshabong 26 2S 22 29E
55 Tshane 24 5S 21 54E
55 Tshwane 22 24S 22 1N
39 Tsiaotso 35 11N 113 37E
57 Tsihombé 25 18S 45 29E
23 Tsimlyanskoye, Vdkhr. 47 45N 42 0E
39 Tsin Ling Shan, Mts. 34 0N 107 30E
38 Tsinan 34 50N 105 40E
38 Tsincheng 35 30N 113 0E
38 Tsinghai 38 56N 116 52E
37 Tsinghai □ 35 10N 96 0E
39 Tsingkiang, Kiangsi 27 50N 114 38E
39 Tsingkiang, Kiangsu 33 30N 119 2E
38 Tsingning 35 25N 105 50E
39 Tsingshih 29 43N 112 13E
38 Tsingtao 36 0N 120 25E
39 Tsining, Inner Mongolia 40 59N 112 59E
38 Tsining, Shantung 35 30N 116 35E
39 Tsinyang 35 2N 112 59E
57 Tsiroanomandidy 18 46S 46 2E
38 Tsitsihar 47 20N 124 0E
57 Tsivory 24 4S 46 5E
23 Tskhinvali 42 14N 44 1E
22 Tsna, R. 54 32N 42 5E
36 Tsu 34 45N 136 25E
36 Tsuchiura 36 12N 140 15E
36 Tsugaru-Kaikyo, Str. 41 30N 140 30E
38 Tsuiluan 47 58N 28 27E
56 Tsumeb 19 9S 17 44E
39 Tsungfa 23 35N 113 35E
39 Tsungtso 22 20N 107 25E
39 Tsunyi 27 40N 107 0E
36 Tsuruga 35 35N 136 0E
39 Tsushima-Kaikyō, Str. 34 20N 130 0E
36 Tsuyama 35 0N 134 0E
57 Tswana □ 24 0S 27 50E
35 Tual 5 30S 132 50E
9 Tuam 53 30N 8 50W
2 Tuamotu Arch. 17 0S 144 0W
23 Tuapse 44 5N 39 10E
47 Tuatapere 48 7S 167 43E
73 Tubac 31 45N 111 2W
35 Tuban 6 57S 112 4E
80 Tubarão 28 30S 49 0W
28 Tubas 32 20N 35 22E
30 Tubayq, Jabal at 29 40N 37 30E
14 Tübingen 48 31N 9 4E
53 Tubo, R. 10 25N 7 10E
51 Tubruq 32 7N 23 55E
2 Tubuai Is. 23 20S 151 0W
78 Tucacas 10 48N 68 19W
45 Tuckanarra 27 8S 118 1E
75 Tucker's Town 32 19N 64 43W
73 Tucson 32 14N 110 59W
71 Tucumcari 35 12N 103 45W
78 Tucupita 9 4N 62 0W
79 Tucurui 3 45S 49 48W
13 Tudela 42 4N 1 39W
57 Tugela, R. 29 14S 31 30E
35 Tuguegarao 17 35N 121 42E
25 Tugur 53 50N 136 45E
39 Tuhshan 25 40N 107 30E
60 Tuktoyaktuk 69 15N 133 0W
52 Tukuyu 9 17S 33 35E
53 Tula, Nigeria 9 51N 11 27E
22 Tula, U.S.S.R. 54 13N 37 32E
37 Tulan 37 24N 98 1E
73 Tulare 36 15N 119 26W
73 Tularosa 33 4N 106 1W
55 Tulbagh 33 16S 19 6E
78 Tulcán 0 48N 77 43W
15 Tulcea 45 13N 28 46E
57 Tuléar 23 21S 43 40E
57 Tuléar □ 21 0S 45 0E
55 Tuli 1 24S 122 26E
28 Tülkarm 32 19N 35 10E
69 Tullahoma 35 23N 86 12W
9 Tullamore 53 17N 7 30W
12 Tulle 45 16N 1 47E
9 Tullow 52 48N 6 45W
42 Tully 17 30S 141 0E
51 Tulymaythah 32 40N 20 55E
71 Tulsa 36 10N 96 0W
78 Tulua 4 6N 76 11W
25 Tulun 54 40N 100 10E
35 Tulungagung 8 5S 111 54E
75 Tuma, R. 13 6N 84 35W
78 Tumaco 1 50N 78 45W
78 Tumatumari 5 20N 58 55W
54 Tumba, L. 0 50S 18 0E
78 Tumbes 3 30S 80 20W
43 Tumby Bay 34 21S 136 8E
38 Tumen 42 46N 129 59E
78 Tumeremo 7 18N 61 30W
32 Tumkur 13 18N 77 12W
8 Tummel, L. 56 43N 3 55W
32 Tump 26 7N 62 16E
34 Tumpat 6 11N 102 10E
79 Tumucumaque South 2 0N 55 0W
46 Tumut 35 16S 148 13E
7 Tunbridge Wells 51 7N 0 16E
52 Tunduma 9 20S 32 48E
52 Tunduru 11 0S 37 25E
19 Tundzha, R. 41 40N 26 34E
32 Tungabhadra, R. 15 57N 78 15E
39 Tungcheng 31 0N 117 3E
38 Tungchow 39 58N 116 50E
39 Tungchuan 35 4N 109 2E
39 Tungfanghsien 18 50N 108 33E
38 Tunghwa 41 46N 126 0E
38 Tungkiang 47 40N 132 30E
39 Tungkwanshan 31 0N 117 45E
38 Tungliao 43 42N 122 11E
39 Tunglu 29 50N 119 35E
38 Tungping 35 50N 116 20E
39 Tungshan 29 36N 144 28E
39 Tungshan, I. 23 40N 117 31E
64 Tungsten 61 52N 128 1W
39 Tungtai 32 55N 120 15E
39 Tungting Hu, L. 28 30N 112 30E
39 Tungtze 27 59N 106 56E
38 Tunhwa 43 27N 128 16E
37 Tunhwang 40 5N 94 46E
50 Tunis 36 50N 10 11E
50 Tunisia ■ 33 30N 9 0E
78 Tunja 5 40N 73 25E
25 Tuoy-khaya 62 30N 111 0W
69 Tupelo 34 15N 88 42W
25 Tupik 54 26N 119 57E
78 Tupiza 21 30S 65 40W
68 Tupper Lake 44 18N 74 30W
80 Tupungato, Mt. 33 15S 69 50W
78 Túquerres 1 5N 77 37W
28 Tur 31 47N 35 14E
33 Tura, India 25 30N 90 16E
52 Tura, Tanz. 5 15S 33 48E
30 Turayf 31 45N 38 30E
78 Turbaco 10 20N 75 25W
78 Turbo 8 6N 76 43E
15 Turda 46 35N 23 48E
15 Turek 52 3N 18 30E
37 Turfan 43 6N 89 24E
37 Turfan Depression 43 0N 88 0E
19 Turgovishte 43 17N 26 38E
30 Turgutlu 38 30N 27 48E
30 Turhal 40 24N 36 19E
13 Turia, R. 39 27N 0 19W
79 Turiaçu 1 40S 45 28W
18 Turin=Torino 45 3N 7 40E
52 Turkana, L. 4 10N 36 10E
24 Turkestan 43 10N 68 10E
30 Turkey ■ 39 0N 36 0E
44 Turkey Creek P.O. 17 2S 128 12E
24 Turkmen S.S.R. 39 0N 59 0E
75 Turks Is. 21 20N 71 20W
21 Turku 60 27N 22 14E
73 Turlock 37 30N 122 55W
74 Turneffe Is. 17 20N 87 50W
11 Turnhout 51 19N 4 57W
19 Tûrnovo 43 5N 25 41E
15 Turnu Măgurele 43 46N 24 56E
15 Turnu-Severin 44 39N 22 41E
8 Turriff 57 32N 2 58W
65 Turtle 48 52N 92 40W
65 Turtleford 53 30N 108 50W
30 Turūbah 28 20N 43 15E
21 Turun ja Pori □ 61 0N 22 30E
69 Tuscaloosa 33 13N 87 31W
69 Tuskegee 32 26N 85 42W
79 Tutoja 2 45S 42 20W
14 Tuttlingen 47 59N 8 50E
35 Tutuala 8 25S 127 15E
2 Tutuila, I. 14 19S 170 50W
25 Turukhansk 65 55N 88 5E
25 Tava, A.S.S.R. 52 0N 95 0E
3 Tuvalu ■ 8 0S 176 0E
30 Tuwaiq, Jabal 23 0N 46 0E
74 Tuxpan 20 50N 97 30W
74 Tuxtla Gutiérrez 16 50N 93 10W
13 Tuy 42 3N 8 39W
39 Tuyun 26 5N 107 20E
30 Tuz Gölü 38 45N 33 30E
30 Tuz Khurmātu 34 50N 44 45E
6 Tweed, R. 55 46N 2 0W
64 Tweedsmuir Prov. Park 52 55N 126 5W
57 Tweeling 27 38S 28 30E
72 Twin Falls 42 30N 114 30W
68 Two Rivers 44 10N 87 31W
71 Tyler 32 20N 95 15W
25 Tyndinskiy 55 10N 124 43E
6 Tyne, R. 55 1N 1 26W
6 Tyne & Wear □ 54 55N 1 35W
6 Tynemouth 55 1N 1 27W
30 Tyre =Sur 33 19N 35 16E
46 Tyrendarra 38 12S 141 50E
21 Tyrifjorden 60 2N 10 3E
14 Tyrol, Reg.= Tirol, Reg. 46 50N 11 40E
18 Tyrrhenian Sea 40 0N 12 30E
24 Tyumen 57 0N 65 18E
7 Tywi, R. 51 46N 4 22W
57 Tzaneen 23 47S 30 9E
39 Tzeki 27 40N 117 5E
39 Tzekung 29 25N 104 30E
39 Tzekwei 31 0N 110 46E
38 Tzepo 36 28N 117 58E
38 Tzeyang 32 47N 108 58E

U

29 Uarsciek 2 28N 45 55E
78 Uaupés 0 8S 67 5W
79 Ubá 21 0S 43 0W
79 Ubaitaba 14 18S 39 20W
36 Ube 34 6N 131 20E
13 Ubeda 38 3N 3 23W
79 Uberaba 19 50S 48 0W
79 Uberlândia 19 0S 48 20W
53 Ubiaja 6 40N 6 20E
34 Ubon Ratchathani 15 15N 104 50E
54 Ubundu 0 22S 25 30E
78 Ucayali, R. 4 30S 73 30W
65 Uchi Lake 51 10N 92 40W
36 Uchiura-Wan, G. 42 25N 140 40E
64 Ucluelet 48 57N 125 32W
32 Udaipur 24 36N 73 44E
21 Uddevalla 58 21N 11 55E
20 Uddjaur, L. 65 55N 17 50E
53 Udi 6 23N 7 21E
18 Údine 46 5N 13 10E
32 Udipi 13 25N 74 42E
22 Udmurt A.S.S.R. □ 57 30N 52 30E
34 Udon Thani 17 29N 102 46E
52 Udzungwa Ra. 8 30S 35 30E
36 Ueda 36 30N 138 10E
25 Uelen 66 10N 170 0W
14 Uelzen 53 0N 10 33E
54 Uere, R. 3 42N 25 24E
22 Ufa 54 45N 55 55E
52 Uganda ■ 2 0N 32 0E
60 Ugashik Lakes 57 0N 157 0W
53 Ugep 5 50N 8 1E
25 Uglegorsk 49 10N 142 5E
56 Uitenhage 33 40S 25 28E
52 Ujiji=Kigoma-Ujiji 4 57S 29 40E
32 Ujjain 23 9N 75 43E
15 Ujpest 47 33N 19 6E
35 Ujung Pandang 5 10S 119 0E
25 Uka 57 50N 162 0E
52 Ukerewe I. 2 0S 33 0E
33 Ukhrul 25 10N 94 25E
22 Ukhta 63 55N 54 0E
72 Ukiah 39 10N 123 9W
23 Ukrainian S.S.R. □ 48 0N 35 0E
38 Ulaanbaatar 48 0N 107 0E
38 Ulan Bator = Ulaanbaatar 48 0N 107 0E
25 Ulan Ude 52 0N 107 30E
38 Ulanhot 46 5N 122 1E
32 Ulhasnagar 19 15N 73 10E
46 Ulladulla 35 21S 150 29E
8 Ullapool 57 54N 5 10W
6 Ullswater, L. 54 35N 2 52W
14 Ulm 48 23N 10 0E
21 Ulricehamn 57 46N 13 26E
68 Ulrichsville 40 27N 81 30W
9 Ulster □ 54 45N 6 30W
52 Uluguru Mts. 7 15S 37 30E
6 Ulverston 54 13N 3 7W
42 Ulverstone 41 11S 146 11E
22 Ulyanovsk 54 25N 48 25E
23 Uman 48 40N 30 12E
33 Umaria 23 31N 80 40E
18 Umbria □ 42 53N 12 30E
20 Umeå 63 45N 20 20E
57 Umfuli, R. 17 50S 29 40E
57 Umkomaas 30 13S 30 48E
31 Umm al Qaiwain 25 30N 55 35E
28 Umm el Fahm 32 31N 35 9E
51 Umm Keddada 13 36N 26 42E
30 Umm Lajj 25 0N 37 23E
60 Umnak I. 53 0N 168 0W
57 Umniati, R. 17 30S 29 23E
57 Umtali 18 58S 32 38E

Umtata | Vila Cabral = Lichinga

57 Umtata 31 36S 28 49E
53 Umuahia 5 33N 7 29E
57 Umvuma 19 16S 30 30E
57 Umzimvubu 31 38S 29 33E
57 Umzinto 30 15S 30 45E
18 Unac, R. 44 30N 16 9E
60 Unalakleet 63 53N 160 50W
60 Unalaska I. 54 0N 164 30W
73 Uncompahgre Pk. 38 5N 107 32W
46 Underbool 35 10S 141 51E
46 Ungarie 33 38S 146 56E
61 Ungava B. 59 30N 67 0W
61 Ungava Pen. 60 0N 75 0W
79 União 4 50S 37 50W
80 União da Vitoría 26 5S 51 0W
60 Unimak I. 54 30N 164 30W
69 Union 34 49N 81 39W
68 Union City, Pa. 41 53N 79 50W
71 Union City, Tenn. 36 35N 89 0W
72 Union Gap 46 38N 120 29W
27 Union of Soviet Socialist Republics ■ 60 0N 60 0E
56 Uniondale 33 39S 23 7E
68 Uniontown 39 54N 79 45W
31 United Arab Emirates ■ 24 0N 54 30E
10 United Kingdom ■ 55 0N 3 0W
66 United States of America ■ 37 0N 96 0W
65 Unity 52 30N 109 5W
8 Unst, I. 60 50N 0 55W
30 Ünye 41 5N 37 15E
36 Uozu 36 48N 137 24E
78 Upata 8 1N 62 24W
56 Upington 28 25S 21 15E
47 Upolu, I. 13 58S 172 0W
53 Upper □ 10 40N 2 0W
47 Upper Hutt 41 8S 175 5E
63 Upper Musquodoboit 45 10N 62 58W
53 Upper Volta ■ 12 0N 0 30W
21 Uppsala 59 53N 17 42E
21 Uppsala □ 60 0N 17 30E
30 Ur 30 55N 46 25E
78 Uracará 2 20S 57 50W
46 Ural, Mt. 33 21S 146 12E
22 Ural Mts. = Uralskie Gory 60 0N 59 0E
24 Ural, R. 47 0N 51 48E
43 Uralla 30 37S 151 29E
24 Uralsk 51 20N 51 20E
22 Uralskie Gory 60 0N 59 0E
42 Urandangi 21 32S 138 14E
65 Uranium City 59 28N 108 40W
36 Urawa 35 50N 139 40E
24 Uray 60 5N 65 15E
70 Urbana, Ill. 40 7N 88 12W
68 Urbana, Ohio 40 9N 83 44W
18 Urbino 43 43N 12 38E
6 Ure, R. 54 1N 1 12W
24 Urengoy 66 0N 78 0E
30 Urfa 37 12N 38 50E
14 Urfahr 48 19N 14 17E
24 Urgench 41 40N 60 30E
78 Uribia 11 43N 72 16W
28 Urim 31 18N 34 32E
30 Urmia, L. = Daryâcheh-ye Reza'iyeh 37 30N 45 30E
79 Uruaca 14 35S 49 16W
74 Uruapán 19 30N 102 0W
79 Uruçui 7 20S 44 28W
80 Uruguay ■ 32 30S 55 30W
80 Uruguay, R. 34 0S 58 30W
80 Uruguaiana 29 50S 57 0W
37 Urumchi= Wulumuchi 43 40N 87 50E
37 Urungu, R. 46 30N 88 50E
31 Uruzgan □ 33 30N 66 0E
22 Usa, R. 65 57N 56 55E
30 Uşak 38 43N 29 28E
56 Usakos 22 0S 15 31E
52 Usambara Mts. 4 50S 38 20E
14 Usedom, I. 53 50N 13 55E
30 Usfan 21 58N 39 27E
24 Ush-Tobe 45 16N 78 0E
12 Ushant, I.= Ouessant, I. d' 48 28N 5 6W
80 Ushuaia 54 50S 68 23W
25 Ushuman 52 47N 126 32E
7 Usk, R. 51 36N 2 58W
30 Üsküdar 41 0N 29 5E
22 Usman 52 5N 39 48E
52 Usoke 5 8S 32 24E
25 Usolye Sibirskoye 52 40N 103 40E
53 Usoro 5 34N 6 13E
80 Uspallata, P. 32 30S 69 28W
24 Uspenskiy 48 50N 72 55E
25 Ussuriysk 43 40N 131 50E
25 Ust-Ilga 55 5N 104 55E
25 Ust-Ilimsk 58 3N 102 39E
24 Ust Ishim 57 45N 71 10E
25 Ust-Kamchatsk 56 10N 162 0E
24 Ust Kamenogorsk 50 0N 82 20E
25 Ust-Kut 56 50N 105 10E
25 Ust Kuyga 70 1N 135 36E
25 Ust Maya 60 30N 134 20E
25 Ust Olenck 73 0N 120 10E
24 Ust Post 70 0N 84 10E
22 Ust Tsilma 65 25N 52 0E
25 Ust-Tungir 55 25N 120 15E
22 Ust Usa 66 0N 56 30E
25 Ustchaun 68 47N 170 30E
14 Ustí nad Labem 50 41N 14 3E
18 Ustica, I. 38 42N 13 10E
25 Ustye 55 30N 97 30E
74 Usulután 13 25N 88 28W
72 Utah □ 39 30N 111 30W
35 Utara □, Sulawesi 1 0N 120 3E
34 Utara □, Sumatera 2 0N 99 0E
52 Utete 7 59S 38 47E
30 Uthmaniya 25 5N 49 6E
68 Utica 43 5N 75 18W
11 Utrecht, Neth. 52 3N 5 8E
11 Utrecht, Neth. □ 52 6N 5 7E
57 Utrecht, S. Africa 27 38S 30 20E
13 Utrera 37 12N 5 48W
36 Utsunomiya 36 30N 139 50E
33 Uttar Pradesh □ 27 0N 80 0E
34 Uttaradit 17 36N 100 5E
6 Uttoxeter 52 53N 1 50W
21 Uudenmaa □ 60 25N 23 0E
38 Uuldza 49 8N 112 10E
21 Uusikaupunki 60 47N 21 28E
71 Uvalde 29 15N 99 48W
24 Uvat 59 5N 68 50E
52 Uvinza 5 5S 30 24E
54 Uvira 3 22S 29 3E
37 Uvs Nuur, L. 50 20N 92 30E
36 Uwajima 33 10N 132 35E
74 Uxmal 20 22N 89 46W
53 Uyo 5 1N 7 53E
78 Uyuni 20 35S 66 55W
24 Uzbek S.S.R. 40 5N 65 0E

V

56 Vaal, R. 29 4S 23 38E
20 Vaasa 63 10N 21 35E
20 Vaasa □ 63 6N 23 0E
15 Vác 47 49N 19 10E
32 Vadodara 22 20N 73 10E
20 Vadsø 70 3N 29 50E
15 Váh, R. 47 55N 18 0E
24 Vaigach 70 10N 59 0E
62 Val d'Or 48 7N 77 47W
65 Val Marie 49 15N 107 45W
15 Valahia, Reg. 44 35N 25 0E
80 Valchete 40 40S 66 20W
12 Val-d'Oise □ 49 5N 2 0E
12 Val-de-Marne □ 48 45N 2 28E
22 Valdayskaya Vozvyshennost 57 0N 33 40E
13 Valdepeņas, Ciudad Real 38 43N 3 25W
80 Valdés, Pen. 42 30S 63 45W
60 Valdez 61 14N 146 10W
80 Valdivia 39 50S 73 14W
69 Valdosta 30 50N 83 48W
79 Valença, Brazil 13 20S 39 5W
79 Valença da Piaui 6 20S 41 45W
12 Valence 44 57N 4 54E
13 Valencia, Sp. 39 27N 0 23W
78 Valencia, Ven. 10 11N 68 0W
13 Valencia, G. de 39 30N 0 20E
13 Valencia, Reg. 39 25N 0 45W
13 Valencia de Alcantara 39 25N 7 14W
12 Valenciennes 50 20N 3 34E
9 Valentia, I. 51 54N 10 22W
70 Valentine 42 50N 100 35W
78 Valera 9 19N 70 37W
11 Valkenswaard 51 21N 5 29E
74 Valladolid, Mexico 20 30N 88 20W
13 Valladolid, Sp. 41 38N 4 43W
18 Valle d'Aosta □ 45 45N 7 22E
78 Valle de la Pascua 9 13N 66 0W
74 Valle de Santiago 20 25N 101 15W
13 Vallecas 40 23N 3 41W
72 Vallejo 38 12N 122 15W
80 Vallenar 28 30S 70 50W
18 Valletta 35 54N 14 30E
70 Valley City 46 57N 98 0W
62 Valleyfield 45 15N 74 8W
64 Valleyview 55 5N 117 25W
13 Valls 41 18N 1 15E
12 Valognes 49 30N 1 28W
80 Valparaíso 33 2S 71 40W
56 Valsbaai 34 15S 18 40E
13 Valverde del Camino 37 35N 6 47W
71 Van Buren, Ark. 35 28N 94 18W
63 Van Buren, Me. 47 10N 68 1W
44 Van Diemen, C. 16 30S 139 46E
44 Van Diemen, G. 12 0S 132 0E
30 Van Gölü 38 30N 43 0E
68 Van Wert 40 52N 84 31W
64 Vancouver, Canada 49 20N 123 10W
72 Vancouver, U.S.A. 45 44N 122 41W
64 Vancouver I. 49 50N 126 30W
70 Vandalia 38 57N 89 4W
57 Vanderbijlpark 26 42S 27 54E
64 Vanderhoof 54 0N 124 0W
42 Vandyke 24 8S 142 45E
21 Vänern, L. 58 47N 13 50E
21 Vänersborg 58 26N 12 27E
54 Vanga 4 35S 39 12E
57 Vangaindrano 23 21S 47 36E
25 Vankarem 67 51N 175 50W
62 Vankleek Hill 45 32N 74 40W
20 Vännäs 63 58N 19 48E
12 Vannes 47 40N 2 47W
56 Vanrhynsdorp 31 36S 18 44E
21 Vansbro 60 32N 14 15E
47 Vanua Levu, I. 15 45S 179 10E
12 Var □ 43 27N 6 18E
33 Varanasi 25 22N 83 8E
18 Varaždin 46 20N 16 20E
21 Varberg 57 17N 12 20E
19 Vardar, R. 40 35N 22 50E
18 Varese 45 49N 8 50E
21 Värmlands □ 59 45N 13 0E
19 Varna 43 13N 27 56E
21 Värnamo 57 10N 14 3E
13 Vascongadas, Reg. 42 50N 2 45W
15 Vaslui 46 38N 27 42E
21 Västerås 59 37N 16 38E
20 Västerbotten □ 64 58N 18 0E
21 Västerdalälven, R. 60 33N 15 8E
20 Västernorrlands □ 63 30N 17 40E
21 Västervik 57 43N 16 43E
21 Västmanlands □ 89 5N 16 20E
18 Vasto 42 8N 14 40E
20 Vatnajökull 64 30N 16 30W
57 Vatomandry 19 20S 48 59E
15 Vatra-Dornei 47 22N 25 22E
21 Vättern, L. 58 25N 14 30E
12 Vaucluse □ 44 3N 5 10E
73 Vaughan 34 37N 105 12W
64 Vauxhall 50 5N 112 9W
21 Växjö 56 52N 14 50E
24 Vaygach, Os. 70 0N 60 0E
11 Vechte, R. 52 35N 6 5E
15 Vedea, R. 43 53N 25 59E
11 Veendam 53 5N 6 25E
11 Veenendaal 52 2N 5 34E
20 Vefsna, R. 65 50N 13 12E
20 Vegafjord 65 37N 12 0E
64 Vegreville 53 30N 112 5W
13 Vejer de la Frontera 36 15N 5 59W
21 Vejle 55 47N 9 30E
12 Velay, Mts. du 45 0N 3 40E
56 Velddrif 32 42S 18 11E
18 Velebit Planina, Mts. 44 50N 15 20E
78 Vélez 6 2N 73 43W
13 Vélez Málaga 36 48N 4 5W
13 Vélez Rubio 37 41N 2 5W
22 Velikiy Ustyug 60 47N 46 20E
22 Velikiye Luki 56 25N 30 32E
32 Velikonda Ra. 14 45N 79 10E
18 Velletri 41 43N 12 43E
32 Vellore 12 57N 79 10E
11 Velsen 52 27N 4 40E
22 Velsk 61 10N 42 5E
80 Venado Tuerto 33 50S 62 0W
12 Vendée □ 46 40N 1 20W
18 Veneto □ 45 30N 12 0E
18 Venézia 45 27N 12 20E
18 Venézia, G. di 45 20N 13 0E
78 Venezuela ■ 8 0N 65 0W
78 Venezuela, G. de 11 30N 71 0W
32 Vengurla 15 53N 73 45E
18 Venice=Venézia 45 27N 12 20E
11 Venlo 51 22N 6 11E
11 Venraij 51 31N 6 0E
7 Ventnor 50 35N 1 12W
22 Ventspils 57 25N 21 32E
73 Ventura 34 16N 119 25W
80 Vera, Arg. 29 30S 60 20W
13 Vera, Sp. 37 15N 1 15W
74 Veracruz 19 10N 96 10W
74 Veracruz □ 19 0N 96 15W
32 Veraval 20 53N 70 27E
18 Vercelli 45 19N 8 25E
80 Verde, R. 41 56S 65 5W
14 Verden 52 56N 9 15E
12 Verdun 49 12N 5 24E
57 Vereeniging 26 38S 27 57E
23 Verkhniy Baskunchak 48 5N 46 50E
25 Verkhoyansk 67 50N 133 50E
25 Verkhoyanskiy Khrebet 66 0N 129 0E
65 Vermilion 53 20N 110 50W
65 Vermilion, R. 53 44N 110 18W
65 Vermilion Bay 49 50N 93 20W
70 Vermillion 42 50N 96 56W
68 Vermont □ 43 40N 72 50W
72 Vernal 40 28N 109 35W
62 Verner 46 25N 80 8W
64 Vernon, Canada 50 20N 119 15W
71 Vernon, U.S.A. 34 0N 99 15W
18 Verona 45 27N 11 0E
12 Versailles 48 48N 2 8E
50 Verte, C. 14 45N 17 30W
57 Verulam 29 38S 31 2E
11 Verviers 50 37N 5 52E
23 Veselovskoye, Vdkhr. 47 0N 41 0E
12 Vesoul 60 40N 6 11E
21 Vest-Agde □ 58 30N 7 0E
21 Vestfold □ 59 15N 10 0E
20 Vestmannaejar, Is. 63 27N 20 15W
18 Vesuvio, Mt. 40 50N 14 22E
18 Vesuvius, Mt.= Vesuvio, Mt. 40 50N 14 22E
15 Veszprém 47 8N 17 57E
21 Vetlanda 57 24N 15 3E
12 Vexin, Reg. 49 20N 1 30E
78 Viacha 16 30S 68 5W
79 Viana 3 0S 44 40W
13 Viana do Castelo 41 42N 8 50W
79 Vianopolis 16 40S 48 35W
21 Viborg 56 27N 9 23E
18 Vicenza 45 32N 11 31E
13 Vich 41 58N 2 19E
12 Vichy 46 9N 3 26E
71 Vicksburg 32 22N 90 56W
79 Vicosa 9 28S 36 25W
43 Victor Harbour 35 30S 138 37E
41 Victoria, Australia 21 16S 149 3E
53 Victoria, Cameroon 4 1N 9 10E
64 Victoria, Canada 48 30N 123 25W
80 Victoria, Chile 38 22S 72 29W
39 Victoria, Hong Kong 22 25N 114 15E
34 Victoria, Malaysia 5 20N 115 20E
18 Victoria, Malta 36 2N 14 14E
71 Victoria, U.S.A. 28 50N 97 0W
52 Victoria, L. 1 0S 33 0E
44 Victoria, R. 15 12S 129 43E
57 Victoria □ 20 55S 31 50E
65 Victoria Beach 50 45N 96 32W
75 Victoria de las Tunas 20 58N 76 59W
56 Victoria Falls 17 58S 25 45E
60 Victoria I. 71 0N 11 0W
9 Victoria Ld. 75 0S 160 0E
52 Victoria Nile, R. 2 14N 31 26E
33 Victoria Taungdeik, Mt. 21 15N 93 55E
56 Victoria West 31 25S 23 4E
63 Victoriaville 46 4N 71 56W
80 Victorica 36 15S 65 30W
73 Victorville 34 32N 117 18W
80 Vicuña 30 2S 70 44W
69 Vidalia 32 13N 82 25W
19 Vidin 43 59N 22 52E
80 Viedma 40 50S 63 0W
80 Viedma, L. 49 30S 72 30W
14 Vienna = Wien 48 12N 16 22E
12 Vienne 45 31N 4 53E
12 Vienne, R. 47 13N 0 5E
12 Vienne □ 45 53N 0 42E
27 Vientiane 18 7N 102 35E
12 Vierzon 47 13N 2 5E
34 Vietnam ■ 16 0N 108 0E
35 Vigan 17 35N 120 28E
79 Vigia 0 50S 48 5W
13 Vigo 42 12N 8 41W
33 Vijayawada 16 31N 80 39E
24 Vikulovo 56 50N 70 40E
55 Vila Cabral = Lichinga 13 13S 35 11E

Vila da Maganja Wauwatosa

57 Vila da Maganja .. 17 18s 37 30E
57 Vila de Manica 18 58s 32 58E
13 Vila Franca de Xira 38 57N 8 59W
55 Vila Machado 19 15s 34 14E
13 Vila Real 41 17N 7 48W
13 Vila Real de Sto. António . 37 10N 7 28W
12 Vilaine, R. 47 30N 2 27W
25 Viliga 60 2N 156 56E
80 Villa Ángela 27 34s 60 45W
50 Villa Cisneros = Dakhla 23 50N 15 53W
80 Villa Colón 31 38s 68 20W
80 Villa Hayes 25 0s 57 20W
75 Villa Julia Molina . 19 5N 69 45W
80 Villa María 32 20s 63 10W
80 Villa Mazán 28 40s 66 10W
80 Villa Ocampo 28 30s 59 20W
14 Villach 46 37N 13 51E
80 Villa de Maria 29 55s 63 45W
13 Villagarcia de Arosa 42 34N 8 46W
80 Villaguay 32 0s 58 45W
74 Villahermosa, Mexico 17 45N 92 50W
13 Villalba 40 36N 3 59W
73 Villanueva 35 16N 105 31W
13 Villanueva de la Serena 38 59N 5 50W
13 Villarreal 39 55N 0 3W
80 Villarrica 39 15s 72 30W
78 Villavicencio 4 9N 73 37W
13 Villaviciosa 43 32N 5 27W
78 Villazón 22 0s 65 35W
62 Ville Marie 47 20N 79 30W
71 Ville Platte 30 45N 92 17W
13 Villena 38 39N 0 52W
57 Villiers 27 2s 28 36E
64 Vilna 54 7N 111 55W
22 Vilnius 54 38N 25 25E
11 Vilvoorde 50 56N 4 26E
25 Vilyuysk 63 40N 121 20E
80 Viña del Mar 33 0s 71 30W
13 Vinaroz 40 30N 0 27E
68 Vincennes 38 42N 87 29W
32 Vindhya Ra. 22 50N 77 0E
37 Vinh 18 45N 105 38E
34 Vinh Loi 17 4N 107 2E
71 Vinita 36 40N 95 12W
19 Vinkovci 45 19N 18 48E
23 Vinnitsa 49 15N 28 30E
46 Violet Town 36 19s 145 37E
35 Viqueque 8 42s 126 30E
32 Viramgam 23 5N 72 0E
65 Virden 49 50N 101 0W
80 Vírgenes, C. 52 19s 68 21W
75 Virgin Gorda, I. ... 18 45N 64 26W
75 Virgin Is., Br. 18 40N 64 30W
75 Virgin Is., U.S. ... 18 20N 64 50W
56 Virginia, S. Afr. ... 28 8s 26 55E
70 Virginia, U.S.A. ... 47 30N 92 32W
68 Virginia □ 37 45N 78 0W
68 Virginia Beach 36 54N 75 58W
72 Virginia City 45 25N 111 58W
11 Virton 49 35N 5 32E
32 Virudunagar 9 30N 78 0E
18 Vis, I. 43 0N 16 10E
73 Visalia 36 25N 119 18W
35 Visayan Sea 11 30N 123 30E
21 Visby 57 37N 18 18E
58 Viscount Melville Sd. 78 0N 108 0W
11 Visé 50 44N 5 41E
79 Viseu, Brazil 1 10s 46 20W
13 Viseu, Port. 40 40N 7 55W
33 Vishakhapatnam .. 17 45N 83 20E
56 Visrivier 31 45s 25 20E
15 Vistula, R.= Wisła, R. 54 22N 18 55E
18 Viso, Mte. 44 40N 7 7E
22 Vitebsk 55 10N 30 15E
18 Viterbo 42 25N 12 8E
47 Viti Levu, I. 17 30s 177 30E
25 Vitim 59 45N 112 25E
25 Vitim, R. 59 26N 112 34E
79 Vitoria, Brazil 20 20s 40 22W
13 Vitória, Sp. 42 50N 2 41W
79 Vitória da Conquista 14 51s 40 51W
79 Vitoria de Santo Antão 8 10s 37 20W
18 Vittória 36 58N 14 30E
18 Vittório Véneto ... 45 59N 12 18E
13 Vivero 43 39N 7 38W
33 Vizianagaram 18 6N 83 10E
11 Vlaardingen 51 55N 4 21E
22 Vladimir 56 0N 40 30E
25 Vladivostok 43 10N 131 53E
11 Vlissingen 51 26N 3 34E
19 Vlóra 40 32N 19 28E
35 Vogelkop, Mt.= Doberai, Djazirah 1 25s 133 0E
57 Vohémar 13 25s 50 0E
57 Vohipeno 22 22s 47 51E
52 Voi 3 25s 38 32E
23 Volga, R. 45 55N 47 52E
23 Volga Heights, Mts. 51 0N 46 0E
23 Volgograd 48 40N 44 25E
23 Volgogradskoye, Vdkhr. 50 0N 45 20E
57 Volksrust 27 24s 29 53E
11 Vollenhove 52 40N 5 58E
25 Volochanka 71 0N 94 28E
22 Vologda 59 25N 40 0E
19 Vólos 39 24N 22 59E
22 Volsk 52 5N 47 28E
53 Volta, L. 7 30N 0 15E
53 Volta, R. 5 46N 0 41E
50 Volta Noire, R. ... 8 41N 1 33W
79 Volta Redonda 22 31s 44 5W
18 Volterra 43 24N 10 50E
23 Volzhskiy 48 56N 44 46E
57 Vondrozo 22 49s 47 20E
11 Voorburg 52 5N 4 24E
14 Vor-Arlberg □ 47 15N 9 55E
22 Vorkuta 67 48N 64 20E
22 Voronezh 51 40N 39 10E
23 Voroshilovgrad 48 38N 39 15E
12 Vosges, Mts. 48 20N 7 10E
12 Vosges □ 48 12N 6 20E
21 Voss 60 38N 6 26E
25 Vostochnyy Sayan . 54 0N 96 0E
2 Vostok, I. 10 5s 152 23W
22 Votkinsk 57 0N 53 55E
22 Votkinskoye, Vdkhr. 57 30N 55 0E
22 Vozhe, Oz. 60 45N 39 0E
25 Voznesenka 46 51N 35 26E
23 Voznesensk 47 35N 31 15E
22 Voznesenye 61 0N 35 45E
25 Vrangelya, Os. 71 0N 180 0E
19 Vranje 42 34N 21 54E
19 Vratsa 43 13N 23 30E
57 Vrede 27 30s 29 6E
56 Vredefort 27 5s 27 16E
55 Vredenburg 32 51s 18 0E
56 Vredendal 31 41s 18 35E
19 Vršac 45 8N 21 18E
56 Vryburg 26 55s 24 45E
57 Vryheid 27 54s 30 47E
11 Vught 51 38N 5 20E
64 Vulcan 50 25N 113 15W
18 Vulcano, I. 38 27N 14 58E
22 Vyatskiye 56 5N 51 0E
22 Vyazma 55 10N 34 15E
22 Vyborg 60 42N 28 45E
15 Vychodné Beskydy 49 30N 22 0E
22 Vyg, Oz. 63 30N 34 0E
6 Vyrnwy, L. 52 48N 3 30W
22 Vyshniy Volochek . 57 30N 34 30E
22 Vytegra 61 15N 36 40E

W

53 Wa 10 7N 2 25W
11 Waal, R. 51 55N 4 30E
63 Wabana 47 40N 53 0W
68 Wabash 40 48N 85 46W
68 Wabash, R. 37 46N 88 2W
65 Wabowden 54 55N 98 35W
15 Wabrzeźno 53 16N 18 57E
63 Wabush City 52 40N 67 0W
71 Waco 31 33N 97 5W
51 Wad Banda 13 10N 27 50E
51 Wad Hamid 16 20N 32 45E
51 Wâd Medanî 14 28N 33 30E
36 Wadayama 35 19N 134 52E
11 Waddeniladen, Is. . 53 30N 5 30E
11 Waddenzee 53 15N 5 15E
45 Wadderin Hill 32 0s 118 25E
64 Waddington, Mt. .. 51 10N 125 20W
65 Wadena, Canada .. 52 0N 103 50W
70 Wadena, U.S.A. .. 46 25N 95 2W
51 Wadi Halfa 21 53N 31 19E
11 Wageningen 51 58N 5 40E
61 Wager Bay 66 0N 91 0W
46 Wagga Wagga 35 7s 147 24E
45 Wagin, Austral 33 17s 117 25E
53 Wagin, Nigeria 12 45N 7 8E
35 Wahai 2 48s 129 35E
70 Wahpeton 46 20N 96 35W
47 Waiau 42 39s 173 5E
47 Waiau, R. 42 46s 173 23E
35 Waigeo, I. 0 20s 130 40E
47 Waihi 37 23s 175 52E
47 Waihou, R. 37 10s 175 32E
47 Waikaremoana, L. . 38 49s 177 9E
47 Waikari 42 58s 72 41E
47 Waikato, R. 37 23s 174 43E
47 Waikerie 34 9s 140 0E
47 Waikokopu 39 3s 177 52E
47 Waikouaiti 45 36s 170 41E
47 Waimakariri, R. ... 43 24s 172 42E
47 Waimarino 40 40s 175 20E
47 Waimate 44 53s 171 3E
32 Wainganga, R. 18 50N 79 55E
35 Waingapu 9 35s 120 11E
65 Wainwright 52 50N 110 50W
47 Waiouru 39 29s 175 40E
47 Waipara 43 3N 172 46E
47 Waipawa 39 56s 176 38E
47 Waipiro 38 2s 176 22E
47 Waipu 35 59s 174 29E
47 Waipukurau 40 1s 176 33E
47 Wairakei 38 37s 176 6E
47 Wairau, .R. 41 32s 174 7E
47 Wairoa 39 3s 177 25E
47 Waitaki, R. 44 56s 171 7E
47 Waitara 38 59s 174 15E
47 Waiuku 37 15s 174 45E
39 Waiyeung 23 12N 11432E
36 Wajima 37 30N 137 0E
52 Wajir 1 42N 40 20E
36 Wakasa 35 20N 134 24E
36 Wakasa-Wan 34 45N 135 30E
47 Wakatipu, L. 45 6s 168 30E
65 Wakaw 52 39N 105 44W
36 Wakayama 34 15N 135 15E
36 Wakayama □ 34 50N 135 30E
3 Wake, I. 19 18N 166 36E
6 Wakefield, U.K. ... 53 41N 1 31W
47 Wakefield, N.Z. ... 41 24s 173 5E
61 Wakeham Bay = Maricourt 61 36N 71 57W
36 Wakkanai 45 28N 141 35E
57 Wakkerstroom 27 24s 30 10E
35 Wakre 0 30s 131 5E
15 Walachia, Reg.= Valahia, Reg. ... 44 35N 25 0E
14 Walbrzych 50 45N 16 18E
7 Walbury Hill 51 22N 1 28W
43 Walcha 30 55s 151 31E
11 Walcheren, I. 51 30N 3 35E
72 Walden 40 47N 106 20W
65 Waldron 50 53N 102 35W
45 Walebing 30 40s 116 15E
10 Wales ■ 52 30N 3 30W
43 Walgett 30 0s 148 5E
45 Walkaway 28 59s 114 48W
62 Walkerton 44 10N 81 10W
72 Walla Walla 46 3N 118 25W
72 Wallace 47 30N 116 0W
62 Wallaceburg 42 40N 82 30W
43 Wallal 26 32s 146 7E
44 Wallal Downs 19 47s 120 40E
45 Wallaroo 33 56s 137 39E
6 Wallasey 3 26s 3 2W
46 Wallerawang 33 25s 150 4E
42 Wallahallow 17 50s 135 50E
72 Wallowa 45 40N 117 35W
6 Wallsend 54 59N 1 30W
43 Wallumbilla 26 33s 149 9E
56 Walmer 33 57s 25 35E
6 Walney, I 54 5N 3 15W
46 Walpeup 35 10s 142 2E
7 Walsall 52 36N 1 59W
71 Walsenburg 37 42N 104 45W
62 Waltham 45 57N 76 57W
56 Walvisbaai 23 0s 14 28E
56 Walvis Bay = Walvisbaai 23 0s 14 28E
53 Wamba 2 10N 27 57E
47 Wanaka, L. 44 33s 169 7E
35 Wanapiri 4 30s 135 50E
43 Wanbi 34 46s 140 17E
57 Wanderer 19 37s 29 59E
43 Wandoan 26 5s 149 55E
47 Wanganui 39 35s 175 3E
46 Wangaratta 36 21s 146 19E
43 Wangary 34 33s 135 29E
38 Wangtu 38 42N 115 4E
39 Wanhsien 30 45N 108 20E
56 Wankie 18 18s 26 30E
65 Wanless 54 11N 101 21W
39 Wanning 18 45N 110 28E
39 Wantsai 28 1N 114 5E
39 Wanyang Shan, Mts. 26 30N 113 30E
39 Wanyuan 32 3N 108 16E
72 Wapato 46 30N 120 25W
29 Warandab 7 20N 44 2E
32 Warangal 17 58N 79 45E
47 Ward 41 49s 174 11E
31 Wardak □ 34 15N 68 0E
57 Warden 27 56s 29 0E
32 Wardha 20 45N 78 39E
43 Warialda 29 29s 150 33E
35 Warkopi 1 12s 134 9E
47 Warkworth 36 24s 174 41E
7 Warley 52 30N 2 0W
65 Warman 52 25N 106 30W
57 Warmbad 24 51s 28 19E
55 Warmbad, S.W. Africa 28 25s 18 42E
55 Warmbad, S.W. Africa 19 14s 13 51E
46 Warncoort 38 30s 143 45E
14 Warnemünde 54 9N 12 5E
72 Warner Ra. 41 30s 120 20W
69 Warner Robins 32 41N 83 36W
45 Waroona 32 50s 115 55E
46 Warracknabeal 36 9s 142 26E
46 Warragul 38 10s 145 58E
43 Warrego, R. 30 24s 145 21E
46 Warren, Australia . 31 42s 147 51E
68 Warren, Ohio 41 18N 80 52W
68 Warren, Pa. 41 52N 79 10W
71 Warren 33 35N 92 3W
9 Warrenpoint 54 7N 6 15W
70 Warrensburg 38 45N 93 45W
56 Warrenton, S. Africa 28 9s 24 47E
72 Warrenton, U.S.A. 46 11N 123 59W
53 Warri 5 30N 5 41E
6 Warrington, U.K. . 53 25N 2 38W
69 Warrington, U.S.A. 30 22N 87 16W
46 Warrnambool 38 25s 142 30E
32 Warsak Dam 34 10N 71 25E
68 Warsaw 41 14N 85 50W
15 Warsaw=Warszawa 52 13N 21 0E
15 Warszawa 52 13N 21 0E
15 Warta, R. 52 35N 14 39E
7 Warwick □ 52 20N 1 30W
43 Warwick, Australia 28 10s 152 1E
7 Warwick, U.K. 52 17N 1 36W
68 Warwick, U.S.A. .. 41 43N 71 25W
64 Wasa 49 45N 115 50W
58 Wasatch Mts. 40 30N 111 15W
57 Wasbank 28 15s 30 9E
73 Wasco, Calif. 35 37N 119 16W
72 Wasco, Oreg. 45 45N 120 46W
70 Waseca 44 3N 93 31W
6 Wash, The 52 58N 0 20W
72 Washington □ 47 45N 120 30W
68 Washington, D.C. . 38 52N 77 0W
68 Washington, Ind. .. 38 40N 87 8W
70 Washington, Iowa . 41 20N 91 45W
70 Washington, Mo. .. 38 33N 91 1W
69 Washington, N.C. .. 35 35N 77 1W
68 Washington, Ohio . 39 34N 83 26W
68 Washington, Pa. ... 40 10N 80 20W
68 Washington, Mt. .. 44 15N 71 18W
11 Wassenaar 52 8N 4 24E
62 Waswanipi 49 30N 77 0W
35 Watangpone 4 29s 120 25E
57 Waterberg 24 14s 28 0E
68 Waterbury 41 32N 73 0W
9 Waterford 52 16N 7 8W
9 Waterford □ 51 10N 7 40W
11 Waterloo, Belgium 50 43N 4 25E
62 Waterloo, Canada . 43 30N 80 32W
70 Waterloo, Iowa ... 42 27N 92 20W
68 Watertown, N.Y. .. 43 58N 75 57W
70 Watertown, S.D. .. 44 57N 97 5W
70 Watertown, Wis. .. 43 15N 88 45W
57 Waterval-Boven ... 25 40s 30 18E
68 Waterville 44 35N 69 40W
68 Watervliet 42 46N 73 43W
35 Wates 7 53s 110 6E
7 Watford 51 38N 0 23W
45 Watheroo 30 15s 116 0W
68 Watkins Glen 42 25N 76 55E
75 Watling, I. 24 0N 74 30W
65 Watrous 51 40N 105 25W
52 Watsa 3 4N 29 30E
45 Watson 30 19s 131 41E
64 Watson Lake 60 12N 129 0W
73 Watsonville 37 58N 121 49W
46 Waubra 37 21s 143 39E
46 Wauchope 31 28s 152 45E
65 Waugh 49 40N 95 20W
68 Waukegan 42 22N 87 54W
70 Waukesha 43 0N 88 15W
70 Waupun 43 38N 88 44W
70 Wausau 44 57N 89 40W
68 Wauwatosa 43 6N 87 59W

Wave Hill Wuntho

44 Wave Hill 17 32N 131 0E
7 Waveney, R. 52 28N 1 45E
47 Waverley 39 46S 174 37E
70 Waverly 42 40N 92 30W
11 Wavre 50 43N 4 38E
51 Wâw 7 45N 28 1E
71 Waxahachie 32 22N 96 53W
42 Wayatinah 42 19S 146 27E
69 Waycross 31 12N 82 25W
68 Waynesboro, Pa. 39 46N 77 32W
68 Waynesboro, Va. 38 4N 78 57W
69 Waynesville 35 31N 83 0W
31 Wazirabad, Afghanistan 36 44N 66 47E
32 Wazirabad, Pak. 32 30N 74 8E
7 Weald, The 51 7N 0 9E
6 Wear, R. 54 55N 1 22W
71 Weatherford 32 45N 97 48W
70 Webster City 42 30N 93 50W
70 Webster Green 38 38N 90 20W
35 Weda 0 30N 127 50E
80 Weddell I. 51 50S 61 0W
2 Weddell Sea 72 30S 40 0W
46 Wedderburn 36 20S 143 33E
63 Wedgeport 43 44N 65 59W
43 Wee Waa 30 11S 149 26E
72 Weed 41 29N 122 22W
57 Weenen 28 57S 30 3E
11 Weert 51 15N 5 43E
39 Wei Ho, R. 35 45N 114 30E
38 Weifang 36 47N 119 10E
38 Weihai 37 30N 122 10E
14 Weimar 51 0N 11 20E
39 Weinan 34 30N 109 35E
42 Weipa 12 24S 141 50E
65 Weir River 57 0N 94 10W
72 Weiser 44 10N 117 0W
15 Wejherow 54 35N 18 12E
65 Wekusko 54 45N 99 45W
68 Welch 37 29N 81 36W
56 Welkom 28 0S 26 50E
62 Welland 43 0N 79 10W
6 Welland, R. 52 53N 0 2E
42 Wellesley, Is. 17 20S 139 30E
7 Wellingborough 52 18N 0 41W
46 Wellington, Australia 32 30S 149 0E
62 Wellington, Canada 43 57N 77 20W
47 Wellington, N.Z. 41 19S 174 46E
6 Wellington, U.K. 52 42N 2 31W
71 Wellington, U.S.A. 37 15N 97 25W
47 Wellington □ 40 8S 175 36E
80 Wellington, I. 49 30S 75 0W
6 Wells, Norfolk 52 57N 0 51E
7 Wells, Somerset 51 12N 2 39W
72 Wells, U.S.A. 41 8N 115 0W
45 Wells, L. 26 44S 123 15W
68 Wellsboro 41 45N 77 16W
68 Wellsville, N.Y. 42 9N 77 57W
68 Wellsville, Ohio 40 36N 80 40W
14 Wels 48 9N 14 1E
46 Welshpool, Australia 38 42S 146 26E
7 Welshpool, U.K. 52 40N 3 9W
6 Wem 52 52N 2 45W
72 Wenatchee 47 30N 120 17W
39 Wenchang 19 38N 110 42E
53 Wenchi 7 46N 2 8W
39 Wenchou= Wenchow 28 0N 120 35E
39 Wenchow 28 0N 120 35E
72 Wendell 42 50N 114 51W
39 Wensiang 34 35N 110 40E
6 Wensleydale 54 20N 2 0W
37 Wensu 41 15N 80 14E
38 Wenteng 25 15S 23 16E
46 Wentworth 34 2S 141 54E
56 Wepener 29 42S 27 3E
55 Werda 25 15S 23 16E
14 Werra, R. 51 26N 9 39E
46 Werribee 37 54S 144 40E
46 Werris Creek 31 8S 150 38E
14 Weser, R. 53 32N 8 34E
63 Wesleyville 49 8N 53 36W
42 Wessel, Is. 11 10S 136 45E
68 West Bend 43 25N 88 10W
33 West Bengal □ 25 0N 90 0E
7 West Bromwich 52 32N 2 1W
70 West Des Moines 41 30N 93 45W
80 West Falkland, I. 51 30S 60 0W
70 West Frankfort 37 56N 89 0W
14 West Germany ■ 51 0N 9 0E
7 West Glamorgan □ 51 40N 3 55W
71 West Helena 34 30N 90 40W
2 West Indies 20 0N 65 0W
71 West Memphis 35 5N 90 3W
7 West Midlands □ 52 30N 2 0W
71 West Monroe 32 32N 92 7W
69 West Palm Beach 26 44N 80 3W
75 West Pt. 18 14N 78 30W
71 West Point, Miss. 33 36N 88 38W
68 West Point, Va. 37 35N 76 47W
7 West Sussex □ 50 55N 0 30W
68 West Virginia □ 39 0N 18 0W
46 West Wyalong 33 56S 147 10E
6 West Yorkshire □ 53 45N 1 40W
69 Westbrook 43 41N 70 21W
42 Westbury 41 30S 146 51E
53 Western □ 6 0N 2 20W
40 Western Australia □ 25 0S 118 0E
32 Western Ghats, Mts. 15 30N 74 30E
8 Western Isles □ 57 30N 7 10W
47 Western Samoa ■ 14 0S 172 0W
11 Westerschelde, R. 51 25N 4 0E
14 Westerwald, Mts. 50 39N 8 0E
47 Westland □ 43 33S 169 59E
64 Westlock 54 20N 113 55W
9 Westmeath □ 53 30N 7 30W
68 Westminster 39 34S 77 1W
73 Westmorland 33 2N 115 42W
34 Weston, Malaysia 5 10N 115 35E
68 Weston, U.S.A. 39 3N 80 29W
7 Weston-super-Mare 51 20N 2 59W
15 Westphalia□= Nordrhein-Westfalen □ 51 45N 7 30E
9 Westport, Eire 53 44N 9 31W
47 Westport, N.Z. 41 46S 171 37E
8 Westray, I. 59 18N 3 0W
64 Westview 49 50N 124 31W
72 Westwood 40 26N 121 0W
35 Wetar, I. 7 30S 126 30E
64 Wetaskiwin 52 55N 113 24W
11 Wetteren 51 0N 3 53E
14 Wetzlar 50 33N 8 30E
71 Wewaka 35 10N 96 35W
9 Wexford 52 20N 6 28W
9 Wexford □ 52 20N 6 40W
65 Weyburn 49 40N 103 50W
7 Weymouth, U.K. 50 36N 2 28W
47 Whakatane 37 57S 177 1E
61 Whale, R. 57 40N 67 0W
65 Whale Cove 62 10N 93 0W
8 Whalsay, I. 60 22N 1 0W
47 Whangamomona 39 8S 174 44E
47 Whangarei 35 43S 174 21E
47 Whangaroa, Harbour 35 4S 173 46E
6 Wharfe, R. 53 51N 1 7W
70 Wheatland 42 4N 105 58W
73 Wheeler Pk. 38 57N 114 15W
68 Wheeling 40 2N 80 41W
6 Whernside, Mt. 54 14N 2 24W
6 Whitby 54 29N 0 37W
68 White, R., Ind. 38 25N 87 44W
71 White, R., Ark. 33 53N 91 3W
43 White Cliffs 30 50S 143 10E
7 White Horse, Vale of 51 37N 1 30W
51 White Nile, R. = Nîl el Abyad 9 30N 31 40E
62 White River, Canada 48 35N 85 20W
57 White River, S. Afr. 25 20S 31 0E
22 White Sea= Beloye More 66 30N 38 0E
72 White Sulphur Springs 46 35N 111 0W
57 White Volta, R. 9 10N 1 15W
47 Whitecliffs 43 26S 171 55E
72 Whitefish 48 25N 114 22W
72 Whitehall, Wis. 44 20N 91 19W
6 Whitehaven 54 33N 3 35W
64 Whitehorse 60 45N 135 10W
65 Whiteshell Prov. Park 50 0N 95 25W
42 Whitewood 21 28S 143 30E
65 Whitewood 50 20N 102 20W
8 Whithorn 54 55N 4 25W
47 Whitianga 36 47S 175 41E
73 Whitney, Mt. 36 35N 118 14W
7 Whitstable 51 21N 1 2E
42 Whitsunday, I. 20 15S 149 4E
60 Whittier 60 46N 148 48W
63 Whittle, C. 50 11N 60 8W
43 Whyalla 33 2S 137 30E
62 Wiarton 44 50N 81 10W
53 Wiawso 6 12N 2 29W
71 Wichita 37 40N 97·29W
71 Wichita Falls 33 57N 98 30W
8 Wick 58 26N 3 5W
73 Wickenburg 33 58N 112 45W
45 Wickepin 32 50S 117 30E
9 Wicklow 53 0N 6 2W
9 Wicklow □ 52 59N 6 25W
9 Wicklow Mts. 53 0N 6 30W
45 Widgiemooltha 31 30S 121 34E
6 Widnes 53 22N 2 44W
15 Wieliczka 50 0N 20 5E
15 Wieluń 51 15N 18 40E
14 Wien 48 12N 16 22E
14 Wiener Neustadt 47 49N 16 16E
11 Wierden 52 22N 6 35E
14 Wiesbaden 50 7N 8 17E
6 Wigan 53 33N 2 38W
8 Wigtown 54 52N 4 27W
8 Wigtown B. 54 46N 4 15W
46 Wilcannia 31 30S 143 26E
68 Wildwood 39 5N 74 46W
14 Wilhelmshaven 53 30N 8 9E
68 Wilkes-Barre 41 15N 75 52W
3 Wilkes Ld. 69 0S 120 0E
65 Wilkie 52 27N 108 42W
73 Willcox 32 13N 109 53W
75 Willemstad 12 5N 69 0W
44 Willeroo 15 14S 131 37E
43 William Creek 28 58S 136 22E
45 Williams, Australia 33 0S 117 0E
73 Williams, U.S.A. 35 16N 112 11W
64 Williams Lake 52 20N 122 10W
68 Williamsburg 37 17N 76 44W
68 Williamson 37 46N 82 17W
68 Williamsport 41 18N 77 1W
46 Williamstown, Australia 37 46S 144 58E
56 Williston, S. Afr. 31 20S 20 53E
70 Williston, U.S.A. 48 10N 103 35W
72 Willits 39 28N 123 17W
70 Willmar 45 5N 95 0W
46 Willow Tree 31 40S 150 45E
56 Willowmore 33 15S 23 30E
42 Willows, Australia 23 45S 147 25E
72 Willows, U.S.A. 39 30N 122 10W
68 Wilmette 42 6N 87 44W
68 Wilmington, Del. 39 45N 75 32W
69 Wilmington, N.C. 34 14N 77 54W
68 Wilmington, Ohio 39 29N 83 46W
69 Wilson 35 44N 77 54W
73 Wilson, Mt. 37 55N 105 3W
46 Wilson's Promontory 39 5S 146 28E
7 Wilton 51 5N 1 52W
7 Wiltshire □ 51 20N 2 0W
45 Wiluna 26 40S 120 25E
56 Winburg 28 30S 27 2E
7 Winchester, U.K. 51 4N 1 19W
68 Winchester, Ind. 40 10N 84 56W
68 Winchester, Ky. 38 0N 84 8W
68 Winchester, Va. 39 14N 78 8W
68 Windber 40 14N 78 50W
6 Windermere, L. 54 20N 2 57W
56 Windhoek 22 35S 17 4E
42 Windorah 25 24S 142 36E
7 Windrush, R. 51 42N 1 25W
46 Windsor, Australia 33 34S 150 44E
63 Windsor, Nova Scotia 44 59N 64 5W
62 Windsor, Ont. 42 25N 83 0W
7 Windsor, U.K. 51 28N 0 36W
68 Windsor, U.S.A. 43 30N 72 25W
75 Windward Is. 13 0N 63 0W
64 Winfield, Canada 52 58N 114 26W
71 Winfield, U.S.A. 37 15N 97 0W
46 Wingen 31 50S 150 58E
62 Wingham 43 55N 81 25W
62 Winisk, R. 55 17N 85 5W
65 Winkler 49 15N 98 0W
53 Winneba 5 25N 0 36W
72 Winnemucca 41 0N 117 45W
65 Winnepegosis, L. 52 40N 100 0W
68 Winnetka 42 8N 87 46W
71 Winnfield 31 57N 92 38W
44 Winning 23 9S 114 32E
65 Winnipeg 49 50N 97 15W
65 Winnipeg, L. 52 30N 98 0W
65 Winnipegosis 52 40N 100 0W
70 Winona 44 2N 91 45W
68 Winooski 44 31N 73 11W
11 Winschoten 53 9N 7 3E
73 Winslow 35 2N 110 41W
69 Winston-Salem 36 7N 80 15W
69 Winter Haven 28 0N 81 42W
69 Winter Park 28 34N 81 19W
56 Winterhoek, Mt. 33 5S 19 35E
14 Winterthur 47 30N 8 44E
42 Winton 22 21S 143 0E
47 Winton 46 8S 168 20E
43 Wirrulla 32 24S 134 31E
6 Wisbech 52 39N 0 10E
70 Wisconsin □ 44 30N 90 0W
70 Wisconsin Rapids 44 25N 89 50W
8 Wishaw 55 46N 3 55W
15 Wisła, R. 54 22N 18 55E
14 Wismar 53 53N 11 23E
57 Witbank 25 51S 29 14E
6 Witham, R. 52 56N 0 4E
6 Withernsea 53 43N 0 2W
7 Witney 51 47N 1 29W
55 Witsand 34 24S 20 50E
14 Wittenberg 51 51N 12 39E
14 Wittenberge 53 0N 11 44E
44 Wittenoom 22 15S 118 20E
52 Witu 2 23S 40 26E
35 Wlingi 8 5S 112 25E
15 Włocławek 52 39 19 2E
15 Włodawa 51 34N 23 32E
46 Wodonga 36 5S 146 50E
35 Wokam, I. 5 45S 134 28E
62 Wolfe I. 44 7N 76 27E
14 Wolin, I. 53 55N 14 31E
80 Wollaston, Is. 55 40S 67 30W
65 Wollaston L. 58 20N 103 30W
60 Wollaston Pen. 69 30N 113 0W
46 Wollongong 34 25S 150 54E
56 Wolmaransstad 27 12S 26 13E
65 Wolseley, Canada 50 25N 103 15W
56 Wolseley, S. Afr. 33 26S 19 12E
58 Wolstenholme, C. 62 50N 78 0W
7 Wolverhampton 52 35N 2 6W
42 Wonarah P.O. 19 55S 136 20E
43 Wondai 26 20S 151 49E
45 Wongan Hills 30 53S 116 42E
38 Wŏnju 37 30N 127 59E
38 Wŏnsan 39 20N 127 25E
46 Wonthaggi 38 29S 145 31E
64 Wood Buffalo Nat. Park 59 30N 113 0W
45 Woodanilling 33 31S 117 24E
46 Woodend 37 20S 144 33E
72 Woodland 38 40N 121 50W
65 Woodridge 49 20N 96 20W
45 Woodroffe, Mt. 26 20S 131 45E
65 Woods, L. of the 49 30N 94 30W
42 Woodstock, Australia 19 22S 142 45E
62 Woodstock, Ont. 43 10N 80 45W
63 Woodstock, N.B. 46 11N 67 37W
7 Woodstock, U.K. 51 51N 1 20W
70 Woodstock, Ill. 42 17N 88 30W
47 Woodville 40 20S 175 53E
71 Woodward 36 24N 99 28W
45 Woolgangie 31 12S 120 35E
43 Woolgoolga 30 7S 153 12E
43 Woombye 26 40S 152 55E
46 Woomelang 35 37S 142 40E
43 Woomera 31 9S 136 56E
46 Woonona 34 32S 150 49E
68 Woonsocket 42 0N 71 30W
70 Woonsockett 44 5N 98 15W
45 Wooramel 25 45S 114 40E
45 Wooramel, R. 25 47S 114 10E
45 Wooroloo 31 45S 116 25E
68 Wooster 40 38N 81 55W
56 Worcester, S. Africa 33 39S 19 27E
7 Worcester, U.K. 52 12N 2 12W
68 Worcester, U.S.A. 42 14N 71 49W
6 Workington 54 39N 3 34W
6 Worksop 53 19N 1 9W
72 Worland 44 0N 107 59W
14 Worms 49 37N 8 21E
45 Worsley 33 15S 116 2E
7 Worthing 50 49N 0 21W
70 Worthington 43 35N 95 30W
35 Wosi 0 15S 128 0E
60 Wrangell 56 30N 132 25W
60 Wrangell Mts. 61 40N 143 30W
8 Wrath, C. 58 38N 5 0W
6 Wrekin, The, Mt. 52 41N 2 35W
6 Wrexham 53 5N 3 0W
64 Wright, Canada 51 45N 121 30W
35 Wright, Philippines 11 42N 125 2E
60 Wrigley 63 0N 123 30W
14 Wrocław 51 5N 17 5E
15 Września 52 21N 17 36E
45 Wubin 30 8S 116 30E
38 Wuchang, Heilungkiang 44 51N 127 10E
39 Wuchang, Hupei 30 34N 114 25E
39 Wuchow 23 26N 111 19E
38 Wuchung 38 4N 106 12E
39 Wuhan 30 32N 114 22E
39 Wuhsi=Wusih 31 30N 120 30E
39 Wuhu 31 21N 118 30E
53 Wukari 7 57N 9 42E
37 Wulumuchi 43 40N 87 50E
53 Wum 6 23N 10 4E
32 Wun 19 59N 78 52E
33 Wuntho 23 55N 95 45E

Wuppertal Zima

14 Wuppertal 51 15N 7 8E
45 Wurarga 28 15S 116 12E
14 Würzburg 49 46N 9 55E
39 Wusih 31 30N 120 30E
37 Wusu 44 10N 84 55E
38 Wutai Shan 39 4N 113 35E
37 Wutunghliao 29 25N 104 0E
37 Wuwei 38 0N 102 30E
39 Wuyi Shan, Mts. 26 40N 116 30E
38 Wuying 48 10N 129 20E
53 Wuyo 10 25N 11 50E
38 Wuyuan 41 45N 108 30E
45 Wyalkatchem 31 8S 117 22E
68 Wyandotte 42 14N 83 13W
43 Wyandra 27 12S 145 56E
46 Wycheproot 36 0N 143 17E
7 Wye, R. 51 37N 2 39W
7 Wymondham 52 34N 1 7E
56 Wynberg 34 0S 18 30E
44 Wyndham 15 33S 128 3E
43 Wynnum 27 29S 152 58E
43 Wynyard, Australia 40 59S 145 45E
65 Wynyard, Canada 51 45N 104 10W
72 Wyoming □ 42 48N 109 0W
46 Wyong 33 14S 151 24E
68 Wytheville 37 0N 81 3W

X

19 Xánthi 41 10N 24 58E
68 Xenia 39 42N 83 57W
39 Xi'an=Sian 34 2N 109 0E
37 Xieng Khouang 19 17N 103 25E
55 Xinavane 25 2S 32 47E
79 Xingu, R. 1 30S 51 53W
79 Xique-Xique 10 40S 42 40W

Y

42 Yaamba 23 8S 150 22E
37 Yaan 30 0N 102 59E
53 Yabassi 4 32N 10 2E
25 Yablonovy Khrebet 53 0N 114 0E
28 Ya'Bud 32 27N 35 10E
78 Yacuiba 22 0S 63 25W
32 Yadgir 16 45N 77 5E
28 Yagur 32 45N 35 4E
39 Yaicheng 18 14N 109 7E
53 Yajua 11 25N 12 50E
72 Yakima 46 42N 120 30W
53 Yako 13 2N 2 15W
38 Yakoshih 49 13N 120 35E
36 Yaku-Shima, I. 30 20N 130 30E
52 Yakuluku 4 22N 28 45E
25 Yakut A.S.S.R. □ 66 0N 125 0E
60 Yakutat 59 50N 139 44W
25 Yakutsk 62 5N 129 40E
34 Yala 6 45N 101 15E
42 Yalboroo 20 50S 148 30E
45 Yalgoo 23 16S 116 39E
74 Yalkubul, Pta. 21 32N 88 37W
46 Yallourn 38 10S 146 18E
23 Yalta 44 30N 34 10E
38 Yalu, R. 47 30N 123 30E
37 Yalung Kiang, R. 32 0N 100 0E
24 Yalutorovsk 56 30N 65 40E
36 Yamagata 37 55N 140 20E
36 Yamagata □ 38 30N 140 0E
36 Yamaguchi 34 10N 131 32E
36 Yamaguchi □ 34 20N 131 40E
24 Yamal Pol. 71 0N 70 0E
30 Yamama 24 5N 47 30E
36 Yamanashi □ 35 40N 138 40E
46 Yamba 29 30S 153 22E
35 Yamdena, I. 7 45S 131 20E
33 Yamethin 20 26N 96 9E
53 Yamil 12 55N 8 5E
44 Yampi, Sd. 15 15S 123 30E
39 Yamhsien 21 45N 108 31E
53 Yamrat 10 10N 9 55E
28 Yamun 32 29N 35 14E
32 Yamuna, R. 27 0N 78 30E
53 Yan 10 5N 12 15E
36 Yanai 33 58N 132 7E
22 Yanaul 56 25N 55 0E
53 Yanda Bayo 11 30N 10 55E
45 Yandanooka 29 18S 115 29E
33 Yandoon 17 2N 95 39E
54 Yangambi 0 47N 24 20E
39 Yangchow 32 25N 119 25E
38 Yangchuan 38 0N 113 29E
24 Yangi-Yer 40 17N 68 48E
39 Yangtze Kiang, R. 31 40N 122 0E
70 Yankton 42 55N 97 25W
43 Yanna 26 58S 146 0E
39 Yanping 22 25N 112 0E
39 Yao Shan, Mts. 24 0N 110 0E
53 Yaoundé 3 50N 1 35E
35 Yap Is. 9 30N 138 10E
35 Yapen, I. 1 50S 136 0E
35 Yapen, Teluk, G. 1 30S 136 0E
42 Yaraka 24 53S 144 3E
22 Yaransk 57 13N 47 56E
7 Yare, R. 52 40N 1 45E
22 Yarensk 61 10N 49 8E
37 Yarkand= Soche 38 24N 77 20E
32 Yarkhun, R. 36 30N 72 45E
63 Yarmouth 43 53N 65 45W
22 Yaroslavl 57 35N 39 55E
45 Yarra Yarra Lakes 29 12S 115 45E
44 Yarraloola 21 34S 115 52E
43 Yarraman 26 46S 152 1E
24 Yar-Sale 66 50N 70 50E
25 Yartsevo 60 20N 90 0E
78 Yarumal 6 58N 75 24W
47 Yasawa Is. 17 0S 177 23E
53 Yashi 12 25N 7 58E
46 Yass 34 50S 149 0E
28 Yas'ur 32 54N 35 10E
60 Yathkyed, L. 63 0N 98 0W
36 Yatsushiro 32 30N 130 40E
28 Yattah 31 27N 35 6E
28 Yavne 31 52N 34 45E
36 Yawatehama 33 27N 132 24E
31 Yazd 31 55N 54 27E
31 Yazdan 33 30N 60 50E
71 Yazoo City 32 48N 90 28W
33 Ye 15 15N 97 51E
45 Yealering 32 35S 117 30E
33 Yebyu 14 15N 98 13E
80 Yegros 26 20S 56 25W
38 Yehsien 37 12N 119 58E
25 Yelanskoye 61 25N 128 0E
43 Yelarbon 28 33S 150 49E
22 Yelets 52 40N 38 30E
8 Yell, I. 46 42N 2 20W
38 Yellow, R.= Hwang Ho, R. 37 32N 118 19E
26 Yellow Sea 35 0N 124 0E
45 Yellowdine 31 18S 119 39E
64 Yellowhead P. 53 0N 118 30W
64 Yellowknife 62 30N 114 10W
60 Yellowknife, R. 63 30N 113 30W
72 Yellowstone Nat. Park 44 35N 110 0W
72 Yellowtail Res. 45 6N 108 8W
42 Yelvertoft 20 13S 138 53E
53 Yelwa 10 50N 4 50E
29 Yemen ■ 15 0N 44 0E
33 Yenangyaung 20 30N 95 0E
39 Yencheng 36 44N 110 2E
53 Yendi 9 17N 0 22E
25 Yeniseysk 58 39N 92 4E
24 Yenisey, R. 68 0N 86 30E
24 Yeniseyskiy Zaliv 72 20N 81 0E
38 Yenki 43 12N 129 30E
38 Yentai 37 30N 121 22E
25 Yenyuka 58 20N 121 30E
7 Yeo, R. 51 1N 2 46W
32 Yeola 20 0N 74 30E
32 Yeotmal 20 20N 78 15E
7 Yeovil 50 57N 2 38W
42 Yeppoon 23 5S 150 47E
23 Yerevan 40 10N 44 20E
25 Yermakovo 52 35N 126 20E
25 Yerofey Pavlovich 54 0N 122 0E
28 Yeroham 30 59N 34 55E
23 Yershov 51 15N 48 27E
28 Yerushalayim= Jerusalem 31 47N 35 10E
7 Yes Tor 50 41N 3 59E
12 Yeu, Î.d' 46 42N 2 20W
39 Yeungchun 22 15N 111 40E
39 Yeungkong 21 55N 112 0E
23 Yeysk Stavo 46 40N 38 12E
19 Yiannitsa 40 46N 22 24E
31 Yibal 22 10N 56 8E
39 Yilan 24 47N 121 44E
38 Yin Shan, Mts. 41 0N 111 0E
38 Yinchwan 38 30N 106 20E
39 Yingcheng 31 0N 113 44E
38 Yingkow 40 38N 122 30E
39 Yingtan 28 12N 117 0E
54 Yirga Alem 6 34N 38 29E
19 Yíthion 36 46N 22 34E
38 Yitu 36 40N 118 24E
39 Yiyang 28 45N 112 16E
28 Yizre'el 32 34N 35 19E
20 Ylivieska 64 4N 24 28E
71 Yoakum 29 20N 97 10W
53 Yobe, R. 13 0N 13 45E
35 Yogyakarta 7 49S 110 22E
36 Yokkaichi 35 0N 136 30E
36 Yokohama 35 30N 139 32E
36 Yokosuka 35 20N 139 40E
53 Yola 9 10N 12 25E
34 Yom, R. 16 40N 100 14E
36 Yonago 35 25N 133 19E
38 Yongchon 35 55N 138 55E
68 Yonkers 40 57N 73 51W
12 Yonne □ 47 50N 3 40E
12 Yonne, R. 48 23N 2 58E
28 Yoqne'am 32 39N 35 7E
45 York, Australia 31 52S 116 47E
6 York, U.K. 53 38N 1 7W
70 York, Nebr. 40 55N 97 35W
68 York, Pa. 39 57N 76 43W
42 York, C. 75 55N 66 25W
44 York, Sd. 14 30S 125 0E
65 York Factory 57 0N 92 30W
6 York Wolds 54 0N 0 30W
43 Yorke, Pen. 34 40S 137 35E
65 Yorkton 51 11N 102 28W
45 Yornup 34 2S 116 10E
73 Yosemite Nat. Park 31 50N 119 30W
22 Yoshkar Ola 56 49N 47 10E
39 Yosu 34 47N 127 45E
28 Yotvata 29 53N 35 2E
9 Youghal 51 58N 7 51W
46 Young 34 19S 148 18E
43 Younghusband, Pen. 34 45S 139 15E
68 Youngstown 43 16N 79 2W
45 Yoweragabbie 28 10S 117 30E
39 Yoyang 29 27N 113 10E
68 Ypsilanti 42 18N 83 40W
72 Yreka 41 44N 122 40W
21 Ystad 55 26N 13 50E
8 Ythan, R. 57 26N 1 12W
25 Ytyk-kel 62 20N 133 28E
39 Yu Shan, Mt. 23 30N 121 0E
39 Yuan Kiang, R. 28 40N 110 30E
39 Yuanling 28 30N 110 5E
37 Yuanyang 23 10N 102 58E
72 Yuba City 39 12N 121 45W
74 Yucatán □ 21 30N 86 30W
75 Yucatán, Canal de 22 0N 86 30W
73 Yucca 34 56N 114 6W
24 Yudino 55 10N 67 55E
44 Yuendumu 22 16S 131 49E
19 Yugoslavia ■ 44 0N 20 0E
39 Yukikow 31 29N 118 17E
60 Yukon Territory □ 63 0N 135 0W
60 Yukon, R. 65 30N 150 0W
25 Yukti 63 20N 105 0E
39 Yülin, Hainan 18 10N 109 31E
39 Yülin Kwangsi-Chuang 22 30N 110 50E
73 Yuma, Ariz. 32 45N 114 45W
70 Yuma, Colo. 40 10N 102 43W
37 Yumen 41 13N 96 55E
45 Yuna 28 20S 115 0E
45 Yunndaga 29 45S 121 0E
39 Yungan 25 50N 117 25E
39 Yungchun 25 20N 118 15E
39 Yungfu 24 59N 109 59E
39 Yungshun 29 3N 109 50E
39 Yungtsi 34 50N 110 25E
39 Yunlin 23 45N 120 30E
37 Yunnan □ 25 0N 102 30E
39 Yunsiao 24 0N 117 20E
43 Yunta 32 35S 139 33E
24 Yurga 55 42N 84 51E
24 Yuribei 71 20N 76 30E
78 Yurimaguas 5 55S 76 0W
39 Yütu 5 0N 115 24E
38 Yutze 37 45N 112 45E
39 Yuyang 28 44N 108 46E
39 Yuyao 30 0N 121 20E
25 Yuzhno-Sakhalinsk 47 5N 142 5E
12 Yvelines □ 48 40N 1 45E
12 Yvetot 49 37N 0 44E

Z

11 Zaandam 52 26N 4 49E
25 Zabaykalskiy 49 40N 117 10E
29 Zabid 14 10N 43 17E
31 Zabol 31 0N 61 25E
31 Zāboli 27 10N 61 35E
15 Zabrzé 50 24N 18 50E
31 Zabul □ 32 0N 67 15E
74 Zacapa 14 59N 89 31W
74 Zacatecas 22 49N 102 34W
74 Zacatecas □ 23 30N 103 0W
74 Zacatecoluca 13 29N 88 51W
18 Zadar 44 8N 15 8E
53 Zadawa 11 30N 10 22E
34 Zadetkyi Kyun, I. 10 0N 98 25E
13 Zafra 38 26N 6 30W
14 Żagań 51 39N 15 22E
51 Zagazig 30 40N 31 12E
53 Zagnanado 7 15N 2 15E
18 Zagreb 45 50N 16 0E
30 Zagros, Kudhā-ye 33 45N 47 0E
28 Zahala 32 8N 34 49E
31 Zāhedān 29 30N 60 50E
30 Zahlah 33 52N 35 50E
54 Zaïre ■ 3 0S 23 0E
54 Zaïre, R. 6 4S 12 24E
25 Zakamensk 50 23N 103 17E
23 Zakavkazye 42 0N 44 0E
30 Zākhū 37 10N 42 50E
19 Zákinthos 37 47N 20 54E
19 Zákinthos, I. 37 45N 27 45E
51 Zalingei 13 5N 23 10E
57 Zambeze, R. 18 46S 36 16E
57 Zambézja □ 16 15S 37 30E
55 Zambia ■ 15 0S 28 0W
35 Zamboanga 6 59N 122 3E
74 Zamora, Mexico 20 0N 102 21W
13 Zamora, Sp. 41 30N 5 45W
15 Zamość 50 50N 23 22E
11 Zandvoort 52 22N 4 32E
68 Zanesville 39 56N 82 2W
30 Zanjan 36 40N 48 35E
19 Zante, I.= Zákinthos, I. 37 47N 20 54E
45 Zanthus 30 55S 123 29E
52 Zanzibar 6 12S 39 12E
52 Zanzibar, I. 6 12S 39 12E
50 Zaouiet Reggane 26 32N 0 3E
15 Západné Beskydy, Mts. 49 30N 19 0E
25 Zapadnyy Sayan 53 0N 94 0E
80 Zapala 39 0S 70 5W
22 Zapolyarnyy 69 26N 30 48E
23 Zaporozhye 47 50N 35 10E
13 Zaragoza 41 39N 0 53W
31 Zarand 30 46N 56 34E
78 Zaraza 9 21N 65 19W
53 Zari 13 5N 12 44E
53 Zaria 11 0N 7 40W
78 Zaruma 3 40S 79 30W
14 Żary 51 37N 15 10E
51 Zarzis 33 31N 11 2E
25 Zashiversk 67 25N 142 40E
32 Zaskar Mts. 33 15N 77 30E
56 Zastron 30 18S 27 7E
31 Zavareh 33 35N 52 28E
25 Zavitinsk 50 10N 129 20E
15 Zawiercie 50 30N 19 13E
25 Zayarsk 56 20N 102 55E
24 Zaysan, Oz. 48 0N 83 0E
15 Zduńska Wola 51 37N 18 59E
21 Zealand= Sjaelland 55 30N 11 30E
64 Zeballos 49 49N 126 50W
11 Zeebrugge 51 19N 3 12E
42 Zeehan 41 52S 145 25E
11 Zeeland □ 51 30N 3 50E
56 Zeerust 25 33S 26 6E
28 Zefat 32 58N 35 29E
29 Zeila 11 15N 43 30E
11 Zeist 52 5N 5 15E
28 Zeita 32 23N 35 2E
19 Zemun 44 51N 20 23E
14 Zerbst 51 59N 12 8E
25 Zeya 54 2N 127 20E
13 Zêzere, R. 40 0N 7 55W
24 Zhanatas 43 11N 81 18E
23 Zhdanov 47 5N 37 31E
25 Zheleznogorsk-Ilimskiy 56 34N 104 8E
25 Zhigansk 66 35N 124 10E
23 Zhitomir 50 20N 28 40E
22 Zhlobin 52 55N 30 0E
25 Zhupanovo 51 59N 15 9E
14 Zielona Góra 51 57N 15 31E
50 Ziguinchor 12 25N 16 20W
28 Zikhron Ya'aqov 32 34N 34 56E
30 Zile 40 15N 36 0E
15 Žilina 49 12N 18 42E
51 Zillah 28 40N 17 41E
37 Zilling Tso, L. 31 40N 89 0E
25 Zima 54 0N 102 5E

Climatic Statistics – 1

These four pages give temperature and precipitation statistics for over 80 stations, which are arranged by listing the continents and the places within each continent in alphabetical order. The elevation of each station, in metres above mean sea level, is stated beneath its name. The average monthly temperature, in degrees Celsius, and the average monthly precipitation, in millimetres, are given. To the right, the average yearly rainfall, the average yearly temperature, and the annual range of temperature (the difference between the warmest and the coldest months) are also stated.

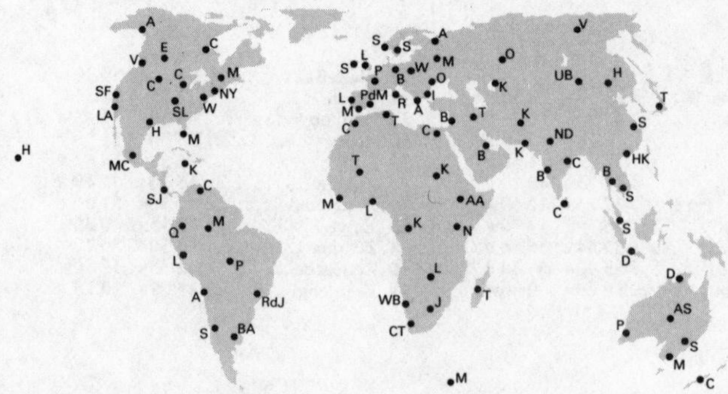

AFRICA		Jan.	Feb.	Mar.	Apr.	May	June	July	Aug.	Sept.	Oct.	Nov.	Dec.	Year	Annual Range
Addis Ababa, Ethiopia															
	Precipitation	201	206	239	102	28	<3	0	<3	3	25	135	213	1 151	
2 450 m	Temperature	19	20	20	20	19	18	18	19	21	22	21	20	20	4
Cairo, Egypt															
	Precipitation	5	5	5	3	3	<3	0	0	<3	<3	3	5	28	
116 m	Temperature	13	15	18	21	25	28	28	28	26	24	20	15	22	15
Cape Town, South Africa															
	Precipitation	15	8	18	48	79	84	89	66	43	31	18	10	508	
17 m	Temperature	21	21	20	17	14	13	12	13	14	16	18	19	17	9
Casablanca, Morocco															
	Precipitation	53	48	56	36	23	5	0	<3	8	38	66	71	404	
50 m	Temperature	13	13	14	16	18	20	22	23	22	19	16	13	18	10
Johannesburg, South Africa															
	Precipitation	114	109	89	38	25	8	8	8	23	56	107	125	709	
1 665 m	Temperature	20	20	18	16	13	10	11	13	16	18	19	20	16	10
Khartoum, Sudan															
	Precipitation	<3	<3	<3	<3	3	8	53	71	18	5	<3	0	158	
390 m	Temperature	24	25	28	31	33	34	32	31	32	32	28	25	29	9
Kinshasa, Zaire															
	Precipitation	135	145	196	196	158	8	3	3	31	119	221	142	1 354	
325 m	Temperature	26	26	27	27	26	24	23	24	25	26	26	26	25	4
Lagos, Nigeria															
	Precipitation	28	46	102	150	269	460	279	64	140	206	69	25	1 836	
3 m	Temperature	27	28	29	28	28	26	26	25	26	26	28	28	27	4
Lusaka, Zambia															
	Precipitation	231	191	142	18	3	<3	<3	0	<3	10	91	150	836	
1 277 m	Temperature	21	22	21	21	19	16	16	18	22	24	23	22	21	8
Monrovia, Liberia															
	Precipitation	31	56	97	216	516	973	996	373	744	772	236	130	5 138	
23 m	Temperature	26	26	27	27	26	25	24	25	25	25	26	26	26	3
Nairobi, Kenya															
	Precipitation	38	64	125	211	158	46	15	23	31	53	109	86	958	
1 820 m	Temperature	19	19	19	19	18	16	16	16	18	19	18	18	18	3
Tananarive, Madagascar															
	Precipitation	300	279	178	53	18	8	8	10	18	61	135	287	1 356	
1 372 m	Temperature	21	21	21	19	18	15	14	15	17	19	21	21	19	7
Timbuktu, Mali															
	Precipitation	<3	<3	3	<3	5	23	79	81	38	3	<3	<3	231	
301 m	Temperature	22	24	28	32	34	35	32	30	32	31	28	23	29	13
Tunis, Tunisia															
	Precipitation	64	51	41	36	18	8	3	8	33	51	48	61	419	
66 m	Temperature	10	11	13	16	19	23	26	27	25	20	16	11	18	17
Walvis Bay, South Africa															
	Precipitation	<3	5	8	3	3	<3	<3	3	<3	<3	<3	<3	23	
7 m	Temperature	19	19	19	18	17	16	15	14	14	15	17	18	18	5
AMERICA, NORTH															
Anchorage, Alaska, U.S.A.															
	Precipitation	20	18	15	10	13	18	41	66	66	56	25	23	371	
40 m	Temperature	−11	−8	−5	2	7	12	14	13	9	2	−5	−11	2	25
Cheyenne, Wyo., U.S.A.															
	Precipitation	10	15	25	48	61	41	53	41	31	25	13	13	376	
1 871 m	Temperature	−4	−3	1	5	10	16	19	19	14	7	1	−2	7	23
Chicago, Ill., U.S.A.															
	Precipitation	51	51	66	71	86	89	84	81	79	66	61	51	836	
251 m	Temperature	−4	−3	2	9	14	20	23	22	19	12	5	−1	10	27
Churchill, Man., Canada															
	Precipitation	13	15	23	23	23	48	56	69	58	36	28	18	406	
13 m	Temperature	−28	−27	−21	−10	−1	6	12	11	5	−3	−15	−24	−8	40

	Jan.	Feb.	Mar.	Apr.	May	June	July	Aug.	Sept.	Oct.	Nov.	Dec.	Year	Annual range
Edmonton, Alta., Canada														
Precipitation	23	15	20	23	46	78	84	58	33	18	18	20	439	
676 m Temperature	−15	−11	−5	4	11	14	16	15	10	5	−4	−11	3	31
Honolulu, Hawaii, U.S.A.														
Precipitation	104	66	79	48	25	18	23	28	36	48	64	104	643	
12 m Temperature	23	18	19	20	22	24	25	26	26	24	22	19	22	8
Houston, Tex., U.S.A.														
Precipitation	89	76	84	91	119	117	99	99	104	94	89	109	1 171	
12 m Temperature	12	13	17	21	24	27	28	29	26	22	16	12	21	17
Kingston, Jamaica														
Precipitation	23	15	23	31	102	89	38	91	99	180	74	36	800	
34 m Temperature	25	25	25	26	26	28	28	28	27	27	26	26	26	3
Los Angeles, Calif., U.S.A.														
Precipitation	79	76	71	25	10	3	<3	<3	5	15	31	66	381	
95 m Temperature	13	14	14	16	17	19	21	22	21	18	16	14	17	9
Mexico City, Mexico														
Precipitation	13	5	10	20	53	119	170	152	130	51	18	8	747	
2 309 m Temperature	12	13	16	18	19	19	17	18	18	16	14	13	16	7
Miami, Fla., U.S.A.														
Precipitation	71	53	64	81	173	178	155	160	203	234	71	51	1 516	
8 m Temperature	20	20	22	23	25	27	28	28	27	25	22	21	24	8
Montreal, Que., Canada														
Precipitation	97	76	89	66	79	86	94	89	94	86	89	91	1 036	
57 m Temperature	−10	−9	−3	5	13	19	21	19	15	8	1	−7	6	31
New York, N.Y., U.S.A.														
Precipitation	94	97	91	81	81	84	107	109	86	89	76	91	1 092	
96 m Temperature	−1	−1	3	10	16	20	23	23	21	15	7	2	8	24
St. Louis, Mo., U.S.A.														
Precipitation	58	64	89	97	114	114	89	86	81	74	71	64	1 001	
173 m Temperature	0	1	7	13	19	24	26	26	22	15	8	2	14	26
San Francisco, Calif., U.S.A.														
Precipitation	119	97	79	38	18	3	<3	<3	8	25	64	112	561	
16 m Temperature	10	12	13	13	14	15	15	15	17	16	14	11	14	7
San José, Costa Rica														
Precipitation	15	5	20	46	229	241	211	241	305	300	145	41	1 798	
1 146 m Temperature	19	19	21	21	22	21	21	21	21	20	20	19	20	2
Vancouver, B.C., Canada														
Precipitation	218	147	127	84	71	64	31	43	91	147	211	224	1 458	
14 m Temperature	3	4	6	9	13	16	18	18	14	10	6	4	10	15
Washington, D.C., U.S.A.														
Precipitation	86	76	91	84	94	99	112	109	94	74	66	79	1 064	
22 m Temperature	1	2	7	12	18	23	25	24	20	14	8	3	13	24

AMERICA, SOUTH

	Jan.	Feb.	Mar.	Apr.	May	June	July	Aug.	Sept.	Oct.	Nov.	Dec.	Year	Annual range
Antofagasta, Chile														
Precipitation	0	0	0	<3	<3	3	5	3	<3	3	<3	0	13	
94 m Temperature	21	21	20	18	16	15	14	14	15	16	18	19	17	7
Buenos Aires, Argentina														
Precipitation	79	71	109	89	76	61	56	61	79	86	84	99	950	
27 m Temperature	23	23	21	17	13	9	10	11	13	15	19	22	16	14
Caracas, Venezuela														
Precipitation	23	10	15	33	79	102	109	109	107	109	94	46	836	
1 042 m Temperature	19	19	20	21	22	21	21	21	21	21	20	20	21	3
Lima, Peru														
Precipitation	3	<3	<3	<3	5	5	8	8	8	3	3	<3	41	
120 m Temperature	23	24	24	22	19	17	17	16	17	18	19	21	20	8
Manaus, Brazil														
Precipitation	249	231	262	221	170	84	58	38	46	107	142	203	1 811	
44 m Temperature	28	28	28	27	28	28	28	28	29	29	29	28	28	2
Paraná, Brazil														
Precipitation	287	236	239	102	13	<3	3	5	28	127	231	310	1 582	
260 m Temperature	23	23	23	23	23	21	21	22	24	24	24	23	23	3
Quito, Ecuador														
Precipitation	99	112	142	175	137	43	20	31	69	112	97	79	1 115	
2 879 m Temperature	15	15	15	15	15	14	14	15	15	15	15	15	15	1
Rio de Janeiro, Brazil														
Precipitation	125	122	130	107	79	53	41	43	66	79	104	137	1 082	
61 m Temperature	26	26	25	24	22	21	21	21	21	22	23	25	23	5
Santiago, Chile														
Precipitation	3	3	5	13	64	84	76	56	31	15	8	5	358	
520 m Temperature	21	20	18	15	12	9	9	10	12	15	17	19	15	12

Climatic Statistics – 2

ASIA

		Jan.	Feb.	Mar.	Apr.	May	June	July	Aug.	Sept.	Oct.	Nov.	Dec.	Year	Annual range
Bahrain															
	Precipitation	8	18	13	8	<3	0	0	0	0	0	18	18	81	
5 m	Temperature	17	18	21	25	29	32	33	34	31	28	24	19	26	16
Bangkok, Thailand															
	Precipitation	8	20	36	58	198	160	160	175	305	206	66	5	1 397	
2 m	Temperature	26	28	29	30	29	29	28	28	28	28	26	25	28	5
Beirut, Lebanon															
	Precipitation	191	158	94	53	18	3	<3	<3	5	51	132	185	892	
34 m	Temperature	14	14	16	18	22	24	27	28	26	24	19	16	21	14
Bombay, India															
	Precipitation	3	3	3	<3	18	485	617	340	264	64	13	3	1 809	
11 m	Temperature	24	24	26	28	30	29	27	27	27	28	27	26	27	6
Calcutta, India															
	Precipitation	10	31	36	43	140	297	325	328	252	114	20	5	1 600	
6 m	Temperature	20	22	27	30	30	30	29	29	29	28	23	19	26	11
Colombo, Sri Lanka															
	Precipitation	89	69	147	231	371	224	135	109	160	348	315	147	2 365	
7 m	Temperature	26	26	27	28	28	27	27	27	27	27	26	26	27	2
Djakarta, Indonesia															
	Precipitation	300	300	211	147	114	97	64	43	66	112	142	203	1 798	
8 m	Temperature	26	26	27	27	27	27	27	27	27	27	27	26	27	1
Harbin, China															
	Precipitation	5	5	10	23	43	94	112	104	46	33	8	5	488	
160 m	Temperature	−18	−15	−5	6	13	19	22	21	14	4	−6	−16	3	40
Hong Kong															
	Precipitation	33	46	74	137	292	394	381	361	257	114	43	31	2 162	
33 m	Temperature	16	15	18	22	26	28	28	28	27	25	21	18	23	13
Kabul, Afghanistan															
	Precipitation	31	36	94	102	20	5	3	3	<3	15	20	10	338	
1 815 m	Temperature	−3	−1	6	13	18	22	25	24	20	14	7	3	12	28
Karachi, Pakistan															
	Precipitation	13	10	8	3	3	18	81	41	13	<3	3	5	196	
4 m	Temperature	19	20	24	28	30	31	30	29	28	28	24	20	26	12
New Delhi, India															
	Precipitation	23	18	13	8	13	74	180	172	117	10	3	10	640	
218 m	Temperature	14	17	23	28	33	34	31	30	29	26	20	15	25	20
Saigon, Vietnam															
	Precipitation	15	3	13	43	221	330	315	269	335	269	114	56	1 984	
9 m	Temperature	26	27	29	30	29	28	28	28	27	27	27	26	28	4
Shanghai, China															
	Precipitation	48	58	84	94	94	180	147	142	130	71	51	36	1 135	
7 m	Temperature	4	5	9	14	20	24	28	28	23	19	12	7	16	24
Singapore															
	Precipitation	252	173	193	188	173	173	170	196	178	208	254	257	2 413	
10 m	Temperature	26	27	28	28	28	28	28	27	27	27	27	27	27	2
Tehran, Iran															
	Precipitation	46	38	46	36	13	3	3	3	3	8	20	31	246	
1 220 m	Temperature	2	5	9	16	21	26	30	29	25	18	12	6	17	28
Tokyo, Japan															
	Precipitation	48	74	107	135	147	165	142	152	234	208	97	56	1 565	
6 m	Temperature	3	4	7	13	17	21	25	26	23	17	11	6	14	23
Ulan Bator, Mongolia															
	Precipitation	<3	<3	3	5	10	28	76	51	23	5	5	3	208	
1 325 m	Temperature	−26	−21	−13	−1	6	14	16	14	8	−1	−13	−22	−3	42

AUSTRALIA, NEW ZEALAND and ANTARCTICA

		Jan.	Feb.	Mar.	Apr.	May	June	July	Aug.	Sept.	Oct.	Nov.	Dec.	Year	Annual range
Alice Springs, Australia															
	Precipitation	43	33	28	10	15	13	8	8	8	18	31	38	252	
579 m	Temperature	29	28	25	20	15	12	12	14	18	23	26	28	21	17
Christchurch, New Zealand															
	Precipitation	56	43	48	48	66	66	69	48	46	43	48	56	638	
10 m	Temperature	16	16	14	12	9	6	6	7	9	12	14	16	11	10
Darwin, Australia															
	Precipitation	386	312	254	97	15	3	<3	3	13	51	119	239	1 491	
30 m	Temperature	29	29	29	29	28	26	25	26	28	29	30	29	28	5
Mawson, Antarctica															
	Precipitation	11	30	20	10	44	180	4	40	3	20	0	0	362	
14 m	Temperature	0	−5	−10	−14	−15	−16	−18	−18	−19	−13	−5	−1	−11	18

		Jan.	Feb.	Mar.	Apr.	May	June	July	Aug.	Sept.	Oct.	Nov.	Dec.	Year	Annual Range
Melbourne, Australia	Precipitation	48	46	56	58	53	53	48	48	58	66	58	58	653	
35 m	Temperature	20	20	18	15	13	10	9	11	13	14	16	18	15	11
Perth, Australia	Precipitation	8	10	20	43	130	180	170	149	86	56	20	13	881	
60 m	Temperature	23	23	22	19	16	14	13	13	15	16	19	22	18	10
Sydney, Australia	Precipitation	89	102	127	135	127	117	117	76	73	71	73	73	1 181	
42 m	Temperature	22	22	21	18	15	13	12	13	15	18	19	21	17	10

EUROPE and U.S.S.R.

		Jan.	Feb.	Mar.	Apr.	May	June	July	Aug.	Sept.	Oct.	Nov.	Dec.	Year	Annual Range
Archangel, U.S.S.R.	Precipitation	31	19	25	29	42	52	62	56	63	63	47	41	530	
13 m	Temperature	−16	−14	−9	0	7	12	15	14	8	2	−4	−11	0	31
Athens, Greece	Precipitation	62	37	37	23	23	14	6	7	15	51	56	71	402	
107 m	Temperature	10	10	12	16	20	25	28	28	24	20	15	11	18	18
Berlin, Germany	Precipitation	46	40	33	42	49	65	73	69	48	49	46	43	603	
55 m	Temperature	−1	0	4	9	14	17	19	18	15	9	5	1	9	20
Istanbul, Turkey	Precipitation	109	92	72	46	38	34	34	30	58	81	103	119	816	
114 m	Temperature	5	6	7	11	16	20	23	23	20	16	12	8	14	18
Kazalinsk, U.S.S.R.	Precipitation	10	10	13	13	15	5	5	8	8	10	13	15	125	
63 m	Temperature	−12	−11	−3	6	18	23	25	23	16	8	−1	−7	7	37
Lisbon, Portugal	Precipitation	111	76	109	54	44	16	3	4	33	62	93	103	708	
77 m	Temperature	11	12	14	16	17	20	22	23	21	18	14	12	17	12
London, U.K.	Precipitation	54	40	37	37	46	45	57	59	49	57	64	48	593	
5 m	Temperature	4	5	7	9	12	16	18	17	15	11	8	5	11	14
Málaga, Spain	Precipitation	61	51	62	46	26	5	1	3	29	64	64	62	474	
33 m	Temperature	12	13	15	17	19	29	25	26	23	20	16	13	18	17
Moscow, U.S.S.R.	Precipitation	39	38	36	37	53	58	88	71	58	45	47	54	624	
156 m	Temperature	−13	−10	−4	6	13	16	18	17	12	6	−1	−7	4	31
Odessa, U.S.S.R.	Precipitation	57	62	30	21	34	34	42	37	37	13	35	71	473	
64 m	Temperature	−3	−1	2	9	15	20	22	22	18	12	9	1	10	25
Omsk, U.S.S.R.	Precipitation	15	8	8	13	31	51	51	51	28	25	18	20	318	
85 m	Temperature	−22	−19	−12	−1	10	16	18	16	10	1	−11	−18	−1	40
Palma de Mallorca, Spain	Precipitation	39	34	51	32	29	17	3	25	55	77	47	40	449	
10 m	Temperature	10	11	12	15	17	21	24	25	23	18	14	11	17	15
Paris, France	Precipitation	56	46	35	42	57	54	59	64	55	50	51	50	619	
75 m	Temperature	3	4	8	11	15	18	20	19	17	12	7	4	12	17
Rome, Italy	Precipitation	71	62	57	51	46	37	15	21	63	99	129	93	744	
17 m	Temperature	8	9	11	14	18	22	25	25	22	17	13	10	16	17
Shannon, Irish Republic	Precipitation	94	67	56	53	61	57	77	79	86	86	96	117	929	
2 m	Temperature	5	5	7	9	12	14	16	16	14	11	8	6	10	11
Stavanger, Norway	Precipitation	93	56	45	70	49	84	93	118	142	129	125	126	1 130	
85 m	Temperature	1	1	3	6	10	13	15	15	13	9	6	3	8	14
Stockholm, Sweden	Precipitation	43	30	25	31	34	45	61	76	60	48	53	48	554	
44 m	Temperature	−3	−3	−1	5	10	15	18	17	12	7	3	0	7	21
Verkhoyansk, U.S.S.R.	Precipitation	5	5	3	5	8	23	28	25	13	8	8	5	134	
100 m	Temperature	−50	−45	−32	−15	0	12	14	9	2	−15	−38	−48	−17	64
Warsaw, Poland	Precipitation	27	32	27	37	46	69	96	65	43	38	31	44	555	
110 m	Temperature	−3	−3	2	7	14	17	19	18	14	9	3	0	8	22

Population of Cities

The population figures used are from censuses or more recent estimates and are given in thousands for towns and cities over 200 000 (over 500 000 in China). Where possible the population of the metropolitan areas is given e.g. Greater London, Greater New York, etc.

AFRICA

ALGERIA (1966)
Algiers ... 943
Oran ... 328
Constantine ... 254

ANGOLA (1970)
Luanda ... 475

CAMEROON (1970)
Douala ... 250

CANARY ISLANDS (1970)
Las Palmas ... 287

CONGO (1970)
Brazzaville ... 250

EGYPT (1970)
Cairo ... 4 961
Alexandria ... 2 032
El Giza ... 712
Suez ... 315
Port Said ... 313
El Mahalla el Kubra ... 256
Tanta ... 254
Subra el Khelma ... 253
El Mansura ... 212
Aswan ... 202

ETHIOPIA (1974)
Addis Abeba ... 1 083
Asmera ... 296

GHANA (1970)
Accra ... 738
Kumasi ... 345

IVORY COAST (1967)
Abidjan ... 420

KENYA (1973)
Nairobi ... 630
Mombasa ... 301

LIBYA (1969)
Tripoli ... 332

MALAGASY REP. (1971)
Tananarive ... 378

MOROCCO (1971)
Casablanca ... 1 561
Rabat-Salé ... 534
Marrakesh ... 390
Fès ... 380
Meknès ... 363
Oujda ... 317
Kénitra ... 302
Tétouan ... 273

MOZAMBIQUE (1970)
Maputo ... 384

NIGERIA (1971)
Lagos ... 1 477
Ibadan ... 1 000
Ogbomosho ... 387
Kano ... 357
Oshogbo ... 256
Ilorin ... 252
Abeokuta ... 226
Port Harcourt ... 217
Zaria ... 201
Ilesha ... 200

RHODESIA (1973)
Salisbury ... 502
Bulawayo ... 307

SENEGAL (1969)
Dakar ... 581

SIERRA LEONE (1974)
Freetown ... 214

SOMALI REP. (1972)
Mogadishu ... 230

SOUTH AFRICA (1970)
Johannesburg ... 1 434
Cape Town ... 1 096
Durban ... 721
Pretoria ... 562
Port Elizabeth ... 489
Germiston ... 281

SUDAN (1970)
Khartoum ... 648

TANZANIA (1970)
Dar-es-Salaam ... 344

TUNISIA (1966)
Tunis ... 648

UGANDA (1969)
Kampala ... 331

ZAÏRE (1972-4)
Kinshasa ... 2 008
Kananga ... 601
Lubumbashi ... 404
Mbuji Mayi ... 337
Kisangani ... 311

ZAMBIA (1972)
Lusaka ... 348
Kitwe ... 290
Ndola ... 201

ASIA

AFGHANISTAN (1973)
Kabul ... 534

BANGLADESH (1973)
Dacca ... 1 132
Chittagong ... 492
Khulna ... 468
Narayanganj ... 443

BURMA (1973)
Rangoon ... 3 189
Mandalay ... 401

CAMBODIA (1973)
Phnom Penh ... 2 000

CHINA (1970)
Shanghai ... 7 000
Peking ... 5 000
Tientsin ... 3 600
Shenyang ... 2 800
Wuhan ... 2 560
Canton ... 2 500
Chungking ... 2 400
Nanking ... 1 750
Harbin ... 1 670
Luta ... 1 650
Sian ... 1 600
Lanchow ... 1 450
Taiyuan ... 1 350
Tsingtao ... 1 300
Chengtu ... 1 250
Changchun ... 1 200
Kunming ... 1 100
Tsinan ... 1 100
Fushun ... 1 080
Anshan ... 1 050
Chengchow ... 1 050
Hangchow ... 960
Tangshan ... 950
Paotow ... 920
Tzepo ... 850
Changsha ... 825
Shihkiachwang ... 800
Tsitsihar ... 760
Soochow ... 730
Kirin ... 720
Suchow ... 700
Foochow ... 680
Nanchang ... 675
Kweiyang ... 660
Wusih ... 650
Hofei ... 630
Hwainan ... 600
Penki ... 600
Loyang ... 580
Nanning ... 550
Huhehot ... 530
Sining ... 500
Wulumchi ... 500

HONG KONG (1967)
Kowloon ... 2 195
Victoria ... 675

INDIA (1971)
Calcutta ... 7 005
Bombay ... 5 969
Delhi ... 3 630
Madras ... 2 470
Hyderabad ... 1 799
Bangalore ... 1 648
Ahmedabad ... 1 588
Kanpur ... 1 273
Nagpur ... 866
Poona ... 853
Lucknow ... 826
Agra ... 638
Jaipur ... 613
Varanasi ... 583
Indore ... 573
Madurai ... 548
Jabalpur ... 534
Allahabad ... 514
Patna ... 490
Surat ... 472
Baroda ... 467
Jamshedpur ... 465
Cochin ... 438
Dhanbad ... 433
Amritsar ... 433
Trivandrum ... 410
Gwalior ... 407
Srinagar ... 404
Ludhiana ... 401
Sholapur ... 398
Bhopal ... 392
Hubli-Dharwar ... 380
Meerut ... 268
Visakhapatnam ... 362
Mysore ... 356
Coimbatore ... 353
Vijaywada ... 344
Calicut ... 334
Bareilly ... 326
Jodhpur ... 319
Salem ... 308
Tiruchurapalli ... 306
Rajkot ... 300
Jullundur ... 296
Moradabad ... 272
Guntur ... 270
Ajmer ... 262
Kolhapur ... 259
Ranchi ... 256
Aligarh ... 254
Durg-Bhilainagar ... 245
Chandigarh ... 233
Gorakhpur ... 231
Bhavnagar ... 226
Saharanpur ... 226
Jamnagar ... 215
Mangalore ... 214
Belgaum ... 214
Kota ... 213
Ujjain ... 209
Durgapur ... 207
Warangul ... 207
Raipur ... 206

INDONESIA (1971)
Djakarta ... 4 576
Surabaja ... 1 556
Bandung ... 1 202
Semarang ... 647
Medan ... 636
Palembang ... 583
Ujung Pandang ... 435
Malang ... 422
Surakarta ... 414
Jogjakarta ... 342
Banjarmasin ... 282
Pontianak ... 218

IRAN (1972)
Tehran ... 3 774
Esfahan ... 575
Mashhad ... 562
Tabriz ... 493
Shiraz ... 356
Abadan ... 306
Ahvaz ... 286
Kermanshah ... 239

IRAQ (1970)
Baghdad ... 2 969
Basra ... 371
Mosul ... 293
Kirkuk ... 208

ISRAEL (1973)
Tel Aviv-Jaffa ... 1 146
Haifa ... 352
Jerusalem ... 326

JAPAN (1973)
Tokyo ... 11 612
Osaka ... 2 842
Yokohama ... 2 495
Nagoya ... 2 075
Kyoto ... 1 435
Kobe ... 1 339
Sapporo ... 1 131
Kitakyushu ... 1 051
Kawasaki ... 1 001
Fukuoka ... 915
Hiroshima ... 741
Chiba ... 574
Sendai ... 564
Amagasaki ... 538
Higashiosaka ... 497
Okayama ... 492
Hamamatsu ... 460
Kumamoto ... 460
Nagasaki ... 442
Kagoshima ... 442
Shizuoka ... 438
Himeji ... 427
Niigata ... 405
Gifu ... 403
Kurishiki ... 388
Funabashi ... 387
Wakayama ... 384
Nishinomiya ... 380
Toyonaka ... 375
Yokosuka ... 375
Kanazawa ... 371
Matsuyama ... 356
Sagamihara ... 344
Iwaki ... 332
Utsunomiya ... 326
Kawaguchi ... 325
Omiya ... 312
Asahikawa ... 311
Urawa ... 310
Naha ... 310
Matsudo ... 307
Takatsuki ... 304
Nagano ... 299
Oita ... 296
Takamatsu ... 288
Ichikawa ... 285
Hachioji ... 284
Toyama ... 283
Fukuyama ... 280
Suita ... 277
Toyohashi ... 274
Kochi ... 268
Hirakata ... 268
Shimonoseki ... 260
Aomori ... 259
Sasebo ... 258
Fujisawa ... 255
Koriyama ... 254
Akita ... 253
Maebashi ... 245
Tokushima ... 243
Neyagawa ... 243
Shimuzu ... 242
Kure ... 241
Yao ... 241
Fukushima ... 239
Yokkaichi ... 238
Machidla ... 238
Nara ... 238
Yatsuo ... 236
Hakodate ... 233
Ichinomiya ... 232
Toyota ... 228
Akashi ... 224
Fukui ... 224
Okazaki ... 222
Hachinohe ... 220
Miyazaki ... 217
Yamagata ... 212
Morioka ... 209
Takasaki ... 208
Kushiro ... 204
Hitachi ... 201
Numazu ... 200

JORDAN (1973)
Amman ... 583
Az Zarqa ... 220

KOREA, NORTH (1967-70)
Pyongyang ... 1 500
Chongjin ... 265

KOREA, SOUTH (1970)
Seoul ... 5 536
Pusan ... 1 881
Taegu ... 1 083
Inchon ... 646
Kwangju ... 503
Taejon ... 415
Chanju ... 263

LEBANON (1971)
Beirut ... 710

MACAU (1971)
Macau ... 248

MALAYSIA (1970)
Kuala Lumpur ... 452
Georgetown ... 270
Ipoh ... 248

MONGOLIA (1971)
Ulan Bator ... 282

PAKISTAN (1972)
Karachi ... 3 469
Lahore ... 2 148
Lyallpur ... 820
Hyderabad ... 624
Rawalpindi ... 615
Multan ... 544
Gujranwala ... 366
Peshawar ... 273
Sialkot ... 212
Sargodha ... 203

PHILIPPINES (1973)
Manila ... 1 436
Quezon City ... 896
Davao ... 464
Cebu ... 385
Caloocan ... 326
Iloilo ... 233
Pasay ... 231
Zamboanga ... 221
Bacolod ... 212

SAUDI ARABIA (1967)
Riyadh ... 300
Jedda ... 300
Mecca ... 250

SINGAPORE (1972)
Singapore ... 2 147

SRI LANKA (1973)
Colombo ... 618

SYRIA (1970)
Damascus ... 923
Aleppo ... 639
Homs ... 215

TAIWAN (1970-73)
Taipei ... 1 922
Kaohsiung ... 915
Tainan ... 495
Taichung ... 490
Chilung ... 334
Chiai ... 237
Shanchung ... 229
Hsinchu ... 205

THAILAND (1970)
Bangkok ... 1 867
Thonburi ... 628

TURKEY (1973)
Istanbul ... 3 135
Ankara ... 1 554
Izmir ... 819
Abana ... 454
Bursa ... 427
Gaziantep ... 353
Konya ... 324
Eskisehir ... 303
Kayseri ... 297
Diyarbakir ... 251
Samsun ... 242
Maras ... 237
Malatya ... 234
Izmit ... 233
Erzurum ... 226
Sivas ... 213
Siirt ... 211

VIETNAM, NORTH (1966)
Hanoi ... 920
Haiphong ... 390

VIETNAM, SOUTH (1971)
Saigon ... 1 825
Da-Nang ... 438

AUSTRALASIA

AUSTRALIA (1973)
Sydney ... 2 874
Melbourne ... 2 584
Brisbane ... 911
Adelaide ... 868
Perth ... 739
Newcastle ... 358
Wollongong ... 206

NEW ZEALAND (1973)
Auckland ... 290
Christchurch ... 285

EUROPE

ALBANIA (1971)
Tiranë ... 175

AUSTRIA (1971)
Vienna ... 1 859
Linz ... 357
Graz ... 314

BELGIUM (1971)
Brussels ... 1 075
Antwerp ... 673
Liège ... 440
Gent ... 225
Charleroi ... 214

BULGARIA (1973)
Sofia ... 937
Plovdiv ... 288
Varna ... 260

CZECHOSLOVAKIA (1974)
Prague ... 1 096
Brno ... 354
Bratislava ... 325
Ostrava ... 291

DENMARK (1970-73)
Copenhagen ... 1 378
Århus ... 245

FINLAND (1973-74)
Helsinki ... 845
Tampere ... 233
Turku ... 230

FRANCE (1975)
Paris ... 9 108
Lyon ... 1 167
Marseille ... 1 004
Lille ... 922
Bordeaux ... 589
Toulouse ... 495
Nantes ... 433
Nice ... 433
Rouen ... 389
Grenoble ... 389
Toulon ... 378
Strasbourg ... 356
St-Etienne ... 335
Lens ... 313
Nancy ... 278
Le Havre ... 265
Grasse-Cannes ... 254
Tours ... 246
Clermont-Ferrand ... 225
Valenciennes ... 224
Montpellier ... 223
Mulhouse ... 219
Rennes ... 213
Orléans ... 209
Dijon ... 208
Douai ... 203

GERMANY, EAST (1973)
East Berlin ... 1 089
Leipzig ... 574
Dresden ... 506
Karl-Marx-Stadt ... 302
Magdeburg ... 274
Halle ... 246
Rostock ... 207
Erfurt ... 202

GERMANY, WEST (1974)
West Berlin ... 2 048
Hamburg ... 1 752
München ... 1 337
Cologne ... 832
Essen ... 674
Frankfurt am Main ... 663
Dortmund ... 632
Düsseldorf ... 628
Stuttgart ... 625
Bremen ... 584
Nürnberg ... 515
Hannover ... 505
Duisburg ... 435
Wuppertal ... 410
Bochum ... 338
Gelsenkirchen ... 333

Mannheim 325
Bielefeld 321
Bonn 283
Kiel 266
Karlsruhe 261
Augsburg 257
Wiesbaden 252
Aachen 241
Oberhausen 241
Lübeck 236
Krefeld 221
Braunschweig 219
Kassel 213
Münster 200

GREECE (1971)
Athens 2 540
Thessaloniki 346

HUNGARY (1973)
Budapest 2 044

IRISH REPUBLIC (1971)
Dublin 650

ITALY (1973)
Rome 2 833
Milano 1 743
Napoli 1 222
Torino 1 199
Genova 813
Palermo 658
Bologna 494
Firenze 461
Catánia 397
Bari 367
Venézia 366
Trieste 272
Verona 270
Messina 256
Padova 237
Táranto 235
Cágliari 233
Bréscia 214

NETHERLANDS (1974)
Rotterdam 1 040
Amsterdam 1 002
s'Gravenhage 685
Utrecht 463
Eindhoven 350
Arnhem 277
Heerlen-Kerkrade ..265
Enschede-Hengelo ..238
Haarlem 235
Tilburg 211
Nijmegen 210
Groningen 203

NORWAY (1974)
Oslo 469
Bergen 215

POLAND (1973)
Warsaw 1 377
Lódz 788
Kraków 651
Wroclaw 557
Poznań 495
Gdańsk 394
Szczecin 356
Katowice 318
Bydgoszcz 306
Lublin 255
Gdynia 208
Zabrze 201

PORTUGAL (1972)
Lisbon 1 612
Oporto 1 315

RUMANIA (1973)
Bucharest 1 529
Cluj 213
Timisoara 205
Iasi 202

SPAIN (1970)
Madrid 3 146
Barcelona 1 745
Valencia 654
Sevilla 548
Zaragoza 480
Bilbao 410
Málaga 374
Las Palmas de Gran
Canaria 287
Murcia 244
Hospitalet 242
Valladolid 236
Córdoba 236
Palma de Mallorca ...234

SWEDEN (1973)
Stockholm 1 350
Göteborg 686
Malmö 451

SWITZERLAND (1974)
Zürich 719
Basel 381
Genève 321
Berne 285
Lausanne 227

U.S.S.R. (1975)
Moscow 7 528
Leningrad 4 243
Kiyev 1 887
Tashkent 1 552
Baku 1 359
Kharkov 1 330
Gorkiy 1 260
Novosibirsk 1 243
Kuybyshev 1 140
Sverdlovsk 1 122
Minsk 1 095
Tbilisi 984
Odessa 981
Chelyabinsk 947
Dnepropetrovsk ...941
Omsk 935
Donetsk 934
Kazan 931
Perm 920
Volgograd 885
Ufa 871
Yerevan 870
Rostov 867
Saratov 820
Alma-Ata 813
Riga 776
Zaporozhye 729
Voronezh 729
Krasnoyarsk 728
Krivoy Rog 620
Lvov 605
Karaganda 559
Yaroslavl 558
Novokuznetsk 519
Krasnodar 519
Irkutsk 497
Vladivostok 495
Tula 494
Izhevsk 489
Barnaul 488
Frunze 474
Zhdanov 451
Ivanovo 447
Astrakhan 445
Kishinev 432
Kemerovo 425
Voroshilovgrad ...423
Dushanbe 422
Vilnius 420
Penza 414
Nikolayev 412
Ulyanovsk 410
Ryazan 405
Orenburg 400
Tallinn 392
Nizhniy Tagil 390
Tomsk 386
Magnitogorsk 384
Kalinin 383
Groznyy 369
Arkhangelsk 369
Kirov 364
Bryansk 358
Murmansk 347
Gorlovka 341
Lipetsk 339
Kursk 338
Kaunas 337
Kaliningrad 331
Gomel 324
Tyumen 312
Kherson 299
Samarkand 293
Ulan Ude 287
Chimkent 284
Ashkhabad 280
Kurgan 278
Simferopol 275
Chita 275
Taganrog 272
Semipalatansk 265
Ordzhonikidze 265
Vitebsk 265
Orel 265
Vinnitsa 264
Vladimir 263
Sevastopol 259
Poltava 254
Ust-Kamenogorsk ..252
Tambov 252
Cheboksary 251
Sochi 244
Dneprodzerzhinsk .242
Smolensk 242
Kostroma 240
Kaluga 240
Orsk 237
Dzerzhinsk 235
Komsomólsk-na-
Amure 234
Mogilev 232
Rybinsk 230
Pavlodar 228
Dzhambul 228
Stavropol 226
Angarsk 224
Cherepovets 223
Saransk 223
Shakhty 217
Makhachkala 214
Kirovograd 211
Andizhan 210
Tselinograd 209
Zhitomir 209
Sterlitamak 205
Vologda 205
Cherkassy 205
Biysk 203
Kirovabad 203
Petrozavodsk 203

UNITED KINGDOM (1974)
London 7 168
Birmingham 1 003
Glasgow 816
Liverpool 561
Manchester 516
Sheffield 507
Leeds 499
Edinburgh 450
Bristol 419
Teesside 387
Belfast 374
Coventry 334
Bradford 290
Nottingham 288
Leicester 287
Hull 279
Cardiff 276
Wolverhampton 268
Stoke-on-Trent ...258
Plymouth 251
Derby 218
Sunderland 213
Southampton 213
Newcastle-upon-
Tyne 209
Portsmouth 200

YUGOSLAVIA (1971)
Belgrade 1 204
Zagreb 602
Skopje 388
Sarajevo 292
Ljubljana 258
Novi Sad 214

NORTH AMERICA

CANADA (1973)
Montréal 2 775
Toronto 2 692
Vancouver 1 116
Ottawa 619
Winnipeg 560
Edmonton 518
Hamilton 513
Québec 493
Calgary 431
St. Catharines ...308
London 293
Windsor 264
Kitchener 235
Halifax 222
Victoria 203

COSTA RICA (1973)
San Jose 395

CUBA (1970)
Havana 1 755
Santiago de Cuba ..292
Santa Clara 213

DOMINICAN REPUBLIC (1970)
Santo Domingo 671

EL SALVADOR (1971)
San Salvador 337

GUATEMALA (1973)
Guatemala City ...707

HAITI (1971)
Port-au-Prince 494

HONDURAS (1973)
Tegucigalpa 302

JAMAICA (1971)
Kingston 573

MEXICO (1974)
Mexico City 10 767
Guadalajara 1 857
Monterrey 1 543
Ciudad Juárez 497
León de los Aldamas ..469
Puebla de Zaragoza ..466
Tijuana 459
Torreón 356
Chihuahua 327
Mexicali 317
Acapulco de Juárez ..309
San Luis Potosí ..271
Veracruz Llave ...256
Cuernavaca 240
Mérida 234
Hermosillo 233
Culiacán 228
Aguascalientes ...213
Tampico 212
Salbillo 201

NICARAGUA (1971)
Managua 399

PANAMA (1974)
Panama 393

PUERTO RICO (1970)
San Juan 695

UNITED STATES (1970)
New York 11 571
Los Angeles 7 032
Chicago 6 979
Philadelphia 4 818
Detroit 4 200
San Francisco 3 109
Washington 2 861
Boston 2 754
Pittsburgh 2 401
St. Louis 2 363
Baltimore 2 071
Cleveland 2 064
Houston 1 985
Newark 1 957
Minneapolis-
St. Paul 1 814
Dallas 1 556
Seattle 1 422
Anaheim-Santa Ana 1 420
Milwaukee 1 404
Atlanta 1 390
Cincinnati 1 385
Paterson 1 359
San Diego 1 358
Buffalo 1 349
Miami 1 268
Kansas City 1 254
Denver 1 228
San Bernardino ...1 143
Indianapolis 1 110
San Jose 1 065
New Orleans 1 046
Tampa-
St. Petersburg ..1 013
Portland 1 009
Phoenix 968
Columbus 916
Providence 911
Rochester 883
San Antonio 864
Dayton 850
Louisville 827
Sacramento 801
Memphis 770
Fort Worth 762
Birmingham 739
Albany 722
Toledo 693
Norfolk 681
Akron 679
Hartford 664
Oklahoma City 641
Syracuse 636
Gary 633
Honolulu 629
Fort Lauderdale ..620
Jersey City 609
Greensboro 604
Salt Lake City ...558
Allentown 544
Nashville 541
Omaha 540
Grand Rapids 539
Youngstown 536
Springfield 530
Jacksonville 529
Richmond 518
Wilmington 499
Flint 497
Tulsa 477
Orlando 428
Fresno 413
Tacoma 411
Harrisburg 411
Charlotte 409
Knoxville 400
Wichita 389
Bridgeport 389
Lansing 378
Mobile 377
Oxnard 376
Canton 372
Davenport 363
El Paso 359
New Haven 356
Tucson 352
West Palm Beach ..349
Worcester 344
Wilkes-Barre 342
Peoria 342
Utica 341
York 330
Bakersfield 329
Little Rock 323
Columbia 323
Lancaster 320
Beaumont 316
Albuquerque 316
Chattanooga 305
Trenton 304
Charleston 304
Binghamton 303
Greenville 300
Reading 296
Austin 296
Shreveport 295
Newport News 292
Madison 290
Stockton 290
Spokane 287
Des Moines 286
Baton Rouge 285
Corpus Christi ...285
Fort Wayne 280
South Bend 280
Appleton 277
Las Vegas 273
Rockford 272
Duluth 265
Santa Barbara 264
Erie 264
Johnstown 263
Jackson 259
Lorain 257
Huntington 254
Augusta 253
Salinas 250
Vallejo 249
Pensacola 243
Columbus 239
Colorado Springs .236
Scranton 234
Ann Arbor 234
Evansville 233
Lawrence 232
Charleston 230
Raleigh 228
Huntsville 228
Hamilton 226
Saginaw 220
Eugene 213
Lowell 213
Fayetteville 212
Waterbury 209
New London 208
Stamford 206
Macon 206
Santa Rosa 205
Kalamazoo 202
Montgomery 201

SOUTH AMERICA

ARGENTINA (1970)
Buenos Aires 8 353
Rosario 811
Córdoba 799
La Plata 506
Mendoza 471
San Miguel de
Tucumán 366
Mar del Plata 300
Santa Fé 245
San Juan 224

BOLIVIA (1973)
La Paz 605

BRAZIL (1970)
São Paulo 5 241
Rio de Janeiro ...4 316
Belo Horizonte ...1 126
Recife 1 070
Salvador 1 018
Pôrto Alegre 887
Belém 572
Fortaleza 530
Brasília 517
Curitiba 498
Santo André 417
Goiania 371
Santos 345
Campinas 334
Nova Iguaçu 334
Niterói 298
Manaus 286
Osasco 285
Duque de Caxias ..259
Natal 256
Maceió 249
Juiz de Fora 224
Guarulhos 222
João Pessoa 204

CHILE (1971)
Santiago 3 069
Valparaíso 250

COLOMBIA (1972-73)
Bogotá 2 978
Medellin 1 270
Cali 1 077
Barranquilla 722
Bucaramanga 364
Cartagena 363
Manizales 319
Cucuta 259
Pereira 250
Ibagué 226

ECUADOR (1974)
Guayaquil 814
Quito 597

PARAGUAY (1972)
Asunción 388

PERU (1972)
Lima 3 158
Arequipa 305
Callao 296
Trujillo 242

URUGUAY (1969)
Montevideo 1 376

VENEZUELA (1971)
Caracas 2 175
Maracaibo 652
Barquisimeto 331

Population of Countries

Country	Area in thousands of square km	Population in thousands	Density of Population per sq. km	Capital Population in thousands
Afghanistan	647	18 796	29	Kabul (534)
Albania	29	2 416	84	Tiranë (175)
Algeria	2 382	16 275	7	Algiers (943)
Angola	1 247	5 812	5	Luanda (475)
Argentina	2 777	25 050	9	Buenos Aires (8 353)
Australia	7 687	13 339	2	Canberra (185)
Austria	84	7 528	90	Vienna (1 859)
Bangladesh	144	74 991	521	Dacca (1 132)
Belgium	31	9 804	321	Brussels (1 075)
Belize	23	136	6	Belmopan (3)
Benin	113	3 029	27	Porto-Novo (85)
Bhutan	47	1 146	24	Thimphu (10)
Bolivia	1 099	5 470	5	Sucre (107) La Paz (605)
Botswana	600	661	1	Gaborone (18)
Brazil	8 512	104 243	12	Brasilia (517)
Brunei	6	144	25	Bandar Seri Begawan (41)
Bulgaria	111	8 679	78	Sofia (937)
Burma	677	30 310	45	Rangoon (3 189)
Burundi	28	3 678	132	Bujumbura (107)
Cameroon	475	6 282	13	Yaoundé (178)
Cambodia	181	7 888	44	Phnom Penh (2 000)
Canada	9 976	22 479	2	Ottawa (619)
Central African Rep.	623	1 716	3	Bangui (187)
Chad	1 284	3 949	3	Ndjamena (193)
Chile	757	10 405	14	Santiago (3 069)
China	9 597	824 961	86	Peking (5 000)
Colombia	1 139	23 952	21	Bogotá (2 978)
Congo	342	1 313	4	Brazzaville (250)
Costa Rica	51	1 921	38	San José (395)
Cuba	115	9 090	79	Havana (1 755)
Cyprus	9	641	69	Nicosia (116)
Czechoslovakia	128	14 686	115	Prague (1 096)
Denmark	43	5 045	117	Copenhagen (1 378)
Dominican Republic	49	4 562	94	Santo Domingo (671)
Ecuador	284	6 951	25	Quito (597)
Egypt	1 001	36 417	36	Cairo (4 961)
El Salvador	21	3 980	186	San Salvador (337)
Equatorial Guinea	28	305	11	Rey Malabo (37) Bata (27)
Ethiopia	1 222	27 239	22	Addis Ababa (1 083)
Fiji	18	560	31	Suva (80)
Finland	337	4 682	14	Helsinki (845)
France	547	52 507	96	Paris (9 108)
French Guiana	91	58	1	Cayenne (25)
Fr. Terr. Afars & Issas	22	104	5	Djibouti (62)
Gabon	268	520	2	Libréville (57)
Gambia	11	510	45	Banjul (48)
Germany, East	108	17 166	159	East Berlin (1 089)
Germany, West	248	62 041	250	Bonn (283)
Ghana	239	9 607	40	Accra (738)
Greece	132	8 962	68	Athens (2 540)
Greenland	2 176	49	0·02	Godthaab (4)
Guatemala	109	5 540	51	Guatemala (707)
Guinea	246	4 312	18	Conakry (197)
Guyana	215	774	4	Georgetown (195)
Haiti	28	4 514	163	Port-au-Prince (494)
Honduras	112	2 933	26	Tegucigalpa (302)
Hong Kong	1	4 249	4 066	Victoria (675)
Hungary	93	10 458	112	Budapest (2 044)
Iceland	103	215	2	Reykjavik (98)
India	3 280	586 056	179	Delhi (3 630)
Indonesia	1 904	127 586	65	Djakarta (4 576)
Iran	1 648	31 955	19	Tehran (3 774)
Iraq	435	10 765	25	Baghdad (2 969)
Irish Republic	70	3 086	44	Dublin (650)
Israel	21	3 299	159	Jerusalem (326)
Italy	301	55 361	184	Rome (2 833)
Ivory Coast	322	4 765	15	Abidjan (420)
Jamaica	11	1 998	182	Kingston (573)
Japan	372	109 671	295	Tokyo (11 612)
Jordan	98	2 646	27	Amman (583)
Kenya	583	12 912	22	Nairobi (630)
Korea, North	121	15 439	128	Pyongyang (1 500)
Korea, South	98	33 459	340	Seoul (5 536)
Kuwait	16	929	52	Kuwait (295)
Laos	237	3 257	14	Vientiane (174)
Lebanon	10	2 784	268	Beirut (710)
Lesotho	30	1 016	33	Maseru (29)
Liberia	111	1 669	15	Monrovia (110)
Libya	1 760	2 346	1	Tripoli (332)
Luxembourg	3	342	132	Luxembourg (78)
Malagasy Republic	587	7 100	12	Tananarive (378)
Malawi	118	4 900	41	Zomba (20)
Malaysia	330	11 700	35	Kuala Lumpur (452)
Mali	1 240	5 561	4	Bamako (197)
Malta	0·3	323	1 024	Valletta (14)
Mauritania	1 031	1 290	1	Nouakchott (100)
Mauritius	2	872	426	Port Louis (137)
Mexico	1 973	58 118	29	Mexico (10 767)
Mongolia	1 565	1 403	1	Ulan Bator (282)
Morocco	447	16 880	38	Rabat (534)
Mozambique	783	9 029	12	Maputo (384)
Nepal	141	12 319	87	Katmandu (333)
Netherlands	41	13 541	332	Amsterdam (1 002)
New Zealand	269	3 027	11	Wellington (142)
Nicaragua	130	2 084	16	Managua (399)
Niger	1 267	4 476	4	Niamey (102)
Nigeria	924	61 270	66	Lagos (1 477)
Norway	324	3 987	12	Oslo (469)
Oman	212	743	3	Muscat (25)
Pakistan	804	68 214	85	Islamabad (77)
Panama	76	1 631	22	Panamá (393)
Papua New Guinea	462	2 652	6	Port Moresby (76)
Paraguay	407	2 572	6	Asunción (388)
Peru	1 285	15 383	12	Lima (3 158)
Philippines	300	41 457	138	Quezon City (896)
Poland	313	33 691	108	Warsaw (1 377)
Portugal	92	8 735	95	Lisbon (1 612)
Puerto Rico	9	3 031	341	San Juan (695)
Rhodesia	391	6 100	16	Salisbury (502)
Rumania	238	21 029	89	Bucharest (1 529)
Rwanda	26	4 123	157	Kigali (54)
Saudi Arabia	2 150	8 706	4	Riyadh (300)
Senegal	196	4 315	22	Dakar (581)
Sierra Leone	72	2 707	38	Freetown (214)
Singapore	0·6	2 219	3 819	Singapore (2 147)
Somali Republic	638	3 090	5	Mogadishu (230)
South Africa	1 221	24 920	20	Pretoria (562) Cape Town (1 096)
S. W. Africa	824	692	1	Windhoek (60)
Spain	505	35 225	70	Madrid (3 146)
Sri Lanka	66	13 679	208	Colombo (618)
Sudan	2 506	17 324	7	Khartoum (648)
Surinam	163	411	3	Paramaribo (182)
Swaziland	17	478	28	Mbabane (14)
Sweden	450	8 161	18	Stockholm (1 350)
Switzerland	41	6 481	157	Berne (285)
Syria	185	7 121	38	Damascus (923)
Taiwan	36	14 990	417	Taipei (1 922)
Tanzania	945	14 763	16	Dar-es-Salaam (344)
Thailand	514	41 023	80	Bangkok (1 867)
Togo	56	2 171	39	Lomé (193)
Trinidad and Tobago	5	1 064	207	Port of Spain (68)
Tunisia	164	5 641	34	Tunis (648)
Turkey	781	38 270	49	Ankara (1 554)
Uganda	236	11 172	47	Kampala (331)
United Arab Emirates	84	215	3	Dubai (70)
U.S.S.R.	22 402	252 064	11	Moscow (7 528)
United Kingdom	244	56 113	229	London (7 168)
United States	9 363	211 909	23	Washington (2 861)
Upper Volta	274	5 897	22	Ouagadougou (125)
Uruguay	178	3 028	17	Montevideo (1 376)
Venezuela	912	11 632	13	Caracas (2 175)
Vietnam, North	159	23 244	146	Hanoi (920)
Vietnam, South	174	19 367	111	Saigon (1 825)
Yemen (Sana)	195	6 477	33	Sana (120)
Yemen (South)	288	1 633	5	Aden (285)
Yugoslavia	256	21 151	83	Belgrade (1 204)
Zaïre	2 345	24 222	10	Kinshasa (2 008)
Zambia	753	4 751	6	Lusaka (348)